Study Guide to Accompan

Smith and Robers

BUSINESS LAW

Tenth Edition

RICHARD A. MANN
University of North Carolina – Chapel Hill

BARRY S. ROBERTS
University of North Carolina – Chapel Hill

Prepared by

NEELY S. INLOW
Lynchburg College

West Publishing Company
I(T)P An International Thomson Company

Pacific Grove • Albany • Belmont • Bonn • Boston • Cincinnati •
Detroit • Johannesburg • London • Madrid • Melbourne • Mexico City •
New York • Paris • Singapore • Tokyo • Toronto • Washington

WEST'S COMMITMENT TO THE ENVIRONMENT

In 1906, West Publishing Company began recycling materials left over from the production of books. This began a tradition of efficient and responsible use of resources. Today, 100% of our legal bound volumes are printed on acid-free, recycled paper consisting of 50% new fibers. West recycles nearly 27,700,000 pounds of scrap paper annually—the equivalent of 229,300 trees. Since the 1960s, West has devised ways to capture and recycle waste inks, solvents, oils, and vapors created in the printing process. We also recycle plastics of all kinds, wood, glass, corrugated cardboard, and batteries, and have eliminated the use of polystyrene book packaging. We at West are proud of the longevity and the scope of our commitment to the environment.

West pocket parts and advance sheets are printed on recyclable paper and can be collected and recycled with newspapers. Staples do not have to be removed. Bound volumes can be recycled after removing the cover.

Production, Prepress, Printing and Binding by West Publishing Company.

 TEXT IS PRINTED ON 10% POST CONSUMER RECYCLED PAPER

ISBN 0–314–22062–3

Table of Contents

Purpose and Use of the Study Guide

This Study Guide can be a valuable supplement to your textbook and classroom attendance. It was written to help you understand and recall the information presented in Smith, Mann, and Roberts' *Essentials of Business Law and the Legal Environment*, Fifth Edition. You should carefully read the appropriate chapter in your textbook before attempting to answer the questions in this guide.

The Study Guide supplements the cases and problems in the text. It contains the following components for each chapter.

1. A brief statement about the purpose of the chapter.

2. Chapter checkpoints to insure that you have learned the major points of the chapter.

3. A chapter outline.

4. A list of key terms from the chapter to which you are to supply definitions.

5. True/false review questions on major chapter concepts.

6. Multiple choice questions on major chapter concepts.

7. Short essay questions.

The Study Guide includes sample examinations containing cumulative questions and integrated questions at the end of each part.

The authors sincerely hope that you will find the study of business law to be interesting and challenging.

Study Tips for the Student

How to Study Law

The study of law is somewhat different from the study of other social sciences. Not only must you know a rule of law and the source of that law, but you must also know how to apply it. Sometimes students need to know more than one rule, because there may be a majority rule of law and a slightly different minority rule of law. This is because much of business law is based on state law. Sometimes that law is state common law; sometimes that law is state statutory law. In either case, there are many states, and the law differs from state to state. There are also general rules of law that are mentioned in the text. However, law is complex and for every general rule, there are frequently exceptions. Students must learn to be precise in applying the rule or the exception to the rule.

In studying each chapter, you should consider the following procedures:

1. Skim the chapter noting the main headings. Note the terms that are defined in the margins.

2. Read the chapter carefully before class.

3. After attending class and taking notes on the lecture, read the chapter again.

4. Underline, take notes, and outline the most important points in the chapter.

5. Write definitions to the terms listed in the study guide.

6. Answer the true/false, multiple choice, and essay questions.

7. Check your answers with those in the back of the study guide.

8. Review the questions, paying particular attention to the ones that were missed.

Law Exams

To prepare for law exams, you must learn both the rule (or rules) of law and the application of those rules. You should take an orderly, systematic approach to both your studying for and taking of the exam.

In taking law exams, issue identification is essential. The best way to recognize issues is by reading the text, including the cases, and then working through the case problems at the end of each chapter. In working problems on an exam, carefully consider all issues presented by the fact situation. There may be more than one issue that should be considered and analyzed, and there may be more than one rule of law that needs to be cited and applied. Frequently instructors will grade essay exams based upon the number of issues identified by a student and by the student's ability to recognize that more than one rule applies to a particular fact situation. Preciseness, specificity, and organization are the keys to doing well on a law exam. Finally, because there is not always a "correct" answer in law, the instructor may be looking for your analysis of the issues raised by the facts rather than a specific legal conclusion.

Chapter 1
Introduction to Law

PURPOSE

This chapter introduces the nature, classification and sources of law in the American legal system. The chapter discusses the concept of law in a general sense, and then examines the classifications and sources of American business law. Most of the chapter deals with the science of law, known as jurisprudence, and introduces the student to important basic terminology, concepts and principles that are essential to an understanding of later chapters.

CHAPTER CHECKPOINTS

After reading and studying this chapter, you should be able to:

1. Give a definition of law and distinguish between "law and justice" and "law and morality."

2. Define substantive law and procedural law and compare public law and private law.

3. Distinguish between civil law and criminal law and between law and equity.

4. Define the term "*stare decisis*" and discuss its importance to common law systems of law such as the one in the United States.

5. Identify and describe the sources of law in the American legal system.

CHAPTER OUTLINE

A. Nature of Law–Law is an instrument of social control whose function is to regulate within certain limitations, human conduct and human relations. It has evolved slowly and will continue to change, because it is not a pure science that is based upon unchanging and universal truths, but rather, it results from a continuous striving to develop a workable set of rules that balance the individual and group rights of a society.

1. Definition of Law–Numerous philosophers and jurists have attempted to define law. American jurists Oliver Wendell Holmes and Benjamin Cardozo defined law as predictions of the way that a court will decide specific legal questions. The English jurist Blackstone defined law as "a rule of civil conduct by the supreme power in a State, commanding what is right, and prohibiting what is wrong."

2. Functions of Law–The primary function of law is to maintain stability in the social, political and economic system while at the same time permitting change. This is accomplished by specific functions such as dispute resolution, protection of property, and preservation of the state.

3. Legal Sanctions–The means by which decisions of the courts are enforced. Without sanctions, laws would be ineffectual and unenforceable.

4. Law and Morals–The law is greatly affected by moral concepts, however, law and morality are not the same. There are ideas that are both moral and legal, yet many rules of law are completely unrelated to morals, and many moral precepts are not enforced by law.

5. Law and Justice–These are separate and distinct concepts, although without law, there can be no justice in the sense of fair, equitable and impartial treatment of competing interests and desires with due regard for the common good.

B. Classification of Law–There are a number of ways in which law can be classified. Basic to understanding these classifications are the terms *right* and *duty*. A *right* is the capacity of a person, with the aid of the law, to require another person or persons to perform, or refrain from performing, a certain act. A *duty* is the obligation imposed by law upon a person by which he is required to perform a certain act or to refrain from performing a certain act. There can be no right in one person without a corresponding duty resting upon some other person, or in some cases upon all other persons.

1. Substantive and Procedural Law–Substantive law creates, defines, and regulates legal rights and obligations. Procedural law sets forth the rules for enforcing the rights that exist because of substantive law.

2. Public and Private Law–Public law is that branch of substantive law that deals with the government's rights and powers and its relationship to individuals or groups. It consists of constitutional, administrative, and criminal law. Private law is that part of substantive law governing individuals and legal entities in their relationships with one another. Business law is primarily private law.

3. Civil and Criminal Law–Civil law is the law dealing with the rights and duties of individuals among themselves and is a part of private law. Criminal law is the law that involves offenses against the entire community and is a part of public law. In a civil action, the injured party (plaintiff) begins a lawsuit (sues) to recover compensation for the damages resulting from the

defendant's wrongful conduct. The plaintiff has the burden of proof which must be sustained by a preponderance (greater weight) of the evidence. The principal forms of relief under civil law are money damages and equitable remedies including specific performance and injunction. In a criminal action, the government brings a criminal proceeding against (prosecutes) a person accused of committing a crime. A crime is any act or omission prohibited by public law in the interest of protection of the public and made punishable by the government in a judicial proceeding brought by it. The government must prove criminal guilt beyond a reasonable doubt, a higher burden of proof than that required in a civil action. The principal sanctions under criminal law are capital punishment, imprisonment and fines.

C. Sources of Law—The sources of law in the American legal system are the federal and state constitutions, federal treaties, interstate compacts, federal and state statutes, the ordinances of countless local municipal governments, and executive orders, the rules and regulations of federal and state administrative agencies, and an ever-increasing volume of reported federal and state court decisions. The supreme law of the land is the United States Constitution. The Constitution provides that federal statutes and treaties shall be the supreme law of the land. Federal legislation and treaties are, therefore, paramount to state constitutions and statutes. The paramount law of each state is contained in its written constitution. Although a state constitution cannot deprive citizens of federal constitutional rights, it can guarantee rights beyond those provided in the United States Constitution.

1. Constitutional Law—A constitution is the fundamental law of a government establishing the governmental structure and allocating power among the levels of government, thereby defining political relationship. All other law in the United States is subordinate to the Federal Constitution. Incorporated into our Constitution is the principle of separation of powers, meaning that there are three distinct and independent branches of government—the federal judiciary, the Congress, and the executive branch. Courts have the authority to determine the constitutionality of legislative and executive acts under the principle of judicial review. The Constitution of the United States also specifies the rights and liberties of the people.

2. Judicial Law—The common law is a body of law that originated in England and is derived from judicial decisions. The American legal system is a common law system that relies heavily on the judiciary as a source of law and on the adversary system for settling disputes. The adversary system is one in which opposing parties initiate and present their case. In distinct contrast to common law systems are civil law systems, which are based on Roman law and depend upon comprehensive legislative enactments called codes and the inquisitorial system of determining disputes. In an inquisitorial system, the judiciary initiates, conducts and decides cases.

   a. Common Law—The courts in common law systems have developed a body of law that serves as precedent for determination of later controversies. This law is called case law, judge-made law, or common law. In order to evolve in a stable and predictable manner, the common law has developed by application of *stare decisis*. *Stare decisis* literally means "to stand by decisions" and is the principle that courts should apply rules decided in prior cases in deciding substantially similar cases.

   b. Equity—Equity is a body of law based upon principles distinct from common law and providing remedies not available at law. Equity developed because the common law in England became overly rigid and beset with technicalities and law courts could only provide limited remedies usually in the form of money damages. Individuals who could not obtain adequate relief from monetary awards began to petition the king directly for justice. He delegated these petitions to his chancellor who eventually developed a new second system of courts known as chancery or equity courts. An important difference between law and equity is that the chancellor could issue a decree ordering a party to perform a contractual duty (specific performance) or a decree ordering a party to do or refrain from doing a specified act (injunction). Reformation is an equitable remedy rewriting a contract to conform with the original intent of the contracting parties. Rescission is an equitable remedy invalidating a contract. Discretion was exercised by the courts of equity in providing remedies according to general legal principles developed over the years and known as maxims.

    c. Restatements of Law–The American Law Institute is composed of a distinguished group of lawyers, judges, and law teachers who have set out to prepare "an orderly restatement of the general common law of the United States." The Restatements they have developed cover many of the important areas of common law and are regarded as the authoritative statement of the common law of the United States, though not actually binding law.

3. Legislative Law–Since the end of the nineteenth century, legislation has become the primary source of new law and ordered social change in the United States. This emphasis on legislative or statutory law has occurred because common law is not well suited to making drastic or comprehensive changes. Some business law topics, such as contracts, agency, property and trusts, remain governed principally by the common law. However, most areas of commercial law have become largely statutory. In the second half of the twentieth century, there has been an increased need for uniformity and codification of business or commercial law. The most successful example of uniformity of legislative law is the Uniform Commercial Code (UCC) which has been adopted by all fifty states.

    a. Treaties–A treaty is an agreement between or among independent nations. The United States Constitution authorizes the president to enter into treaties with the advice and consent of the Senate "providing that two-thirds of the Senators present concur."

    b. Executive Orders–An executive order is a law issued by the president or the governor of a state.

4. Administrative Law–Administrative law is a branch of public law created by administrative agencies in the form of rules, regulations, orders, and decisions to carry out the regulatory powers and duties of those agencies. Because of the increasing complexity of the social, economic, and industrial life of the nation, the scope of administrative law has expanded enormously.

D. Legal Analysis–This refers to the method of analyzing and briefing federal and state judicial decisions. Decisions of state supreme courts and courts of appeal can be found in a regional reporter published by West Publishing Company. A citation that says 86 N.W.2d 689 (1957) means that the case cited can be found in volume 86 of the Northwestern Reporter, Second Series, on page 689 and that it was decided in 1957. The appellant is the party who appeals a decision. In appellate court decisions, the name of the appellant will sometimes appear first in the citation even though the appellant was the defendant in the trial court.

KEY TERMS

1. Substantive law

2. Procedural law

3. Public law

4. Private law

5. Civil law

6. Criminal law

7. Plaintiff

8. Defendant

9. Constitution

10. Common law system

11. Adversary system

12. Civil law system

13. Inquisitorial system

14. *Stare decisis*

15. Equity

16. Restatements

17. Legislative law

18. Treaty

19. Executive order

20. Administrative law

TRUE/FALSE

____   1. Although the law is greatly affected by moral concepts, morals and law are not the same.

_____ 2. In a criminal trial, the government must show that the defendant is guilty by a preponderance of the evidence.

_____ 3. A state statute may be valid even though it violates the federal constitution.

_____ 4. The courts of equity arose to provide relief to those who had no adequate remedy at common law.

_____ 5. Over the past century, the emphasis in law-making has shifted from legislatively-enacted (statutory) law to judge-made (common) law.

_____ 6. A constitution is a fundamental law of a particular level of government.

_____ 7. Because of the many statutes enacted by the legislatures of the states and by the federal government, the American legal system is considered to be a civil law system.

_____ 8. Under the principle of judicial review, the courts have the authority to determine the constitutionality of legislative and executive acts.

_____ 9. Restatements of law are a source of law written by legal scholars which are binding on the courts.

_____ 10. The law is constantly changing in an effort to meet the evolving needs of society.

_____ 11. In a civil action, the plaintiff must prove the case beyond a reasonable doubt.

_____ 12. The constitutionality of any law is ultimately decided by the Supreme Court of the United States.

_____ 13. Business law is primarily public law.

_____ 14. The Uniform Commercial Code is a federal statute that was adopted by Congress to make the law uniform among the states.

_____ 15. Legal sanctions are the means by which court decisions are enforced.

MULTIPLE CHOICE

_____ 1. Rules of substantive law:
   a. create, define, and regulate legal rights and obligations.
   b. determine when a binding contract is formed.
   c. define the essence of the law.
   d. all of the above.

_____ 2. Which of the following is not a category of private law?

    a. Tort law.

    b. Contract law.

    c. Criminal law.

    d. Property law.

_____ 3. Which of the following is not a category of public law?

    a. Constitutional law.

    b. Criminal law.

    c. Contract law.

    d. Administrative law.

_____ 4. While the principle of _stare decisis_ provides that courts will follow their precedents in making subsequent decisions, nevertheless a court may decline to follow its precedents:

    a. to correct an erroneous decision.

    b. to choose among conflicting precedents.

    c. in recognition of the fact that the needs of society change over time.

    d. all of the above.

_____ 5. Which of the following is NOT a characteristic of a court of equity?

    a. It may provide injunctive relief.

    b. It may reform or rescind a contract.

    c. It presides over jury trials.

    d. It may command a person to perform a contract.

_____ 6. A person who is injured by the wrongful act of another may bring a civil suit to:

    a. recover money damages.

    b. have the wrongdoer thrown in jail.

    c. order the wrongdoer to engage in or desist from certain conduct.

    d. (a) and (c), but not (b).

_____ 7. The appeals court decision in the case of State v. Dawson, 282 S.E.2d 284, may be found at:

    a. page 282 of volume 284 of the Southeastern Reporter, second series.

    b. page 284 of volume 282 of the Southeastern Reporter, second series.

    c. pages 282–284 of volume 2 of the Southeastern Reporter.

    d. none of the above.

_____ 8. Which of the following is NOT true of an action brought under criminal law?

    a. It involves a wrongful act.

    b. Criminal guilt must be proven beyond a reasonable doubt.

    c. It must be brought by the government.

    d. Conviction may result in payment of money damages to the victim.

_____   9. Sources of state law include:
   a. state judicial decisions.
   b. state constitutions and statutes.
   c. federal judicial decisions.
   d. a and b above.

_____ 10. In the criminal trial of State of West Virginia v. Dawson, the defendant in the action was:
   a. Dawson.
   b. the State of West Virginia.
   c. the victim of the crime.
   d. the federal government.

_____ 11. The highest source of law in the United States is:
   a. an executive order of the president.
   b. an interstate compact.
   c. the federal constitution.
   d. the state constitutions.

_____ 12. The most successful attempt by the National Conference of Commissioners on Uniform State Laws and the American Law Institute has been the:
   a. Uniform Commercial Code.
   b. Uniform Limited Partnership Act.
   c. Model Business Corporation Act.
   d. Uniform Probate Code.

_____ 13. A major difference between law and equity is that:
   a. today, in most states courts of law decide law cases and courts of equity decide equity cases.
   b. law originated in America and equity was developed in England.
   c. the plaintiff could seek money damages under law, while the plaintiff could seek specific performance under equity.
   d. equity was overly rigid, while law provided various remedies.

_____ 14. Which of the following is/are equitable remedies?
   a. Injunction.
   b. Reformation.
   c. Rescission.
   d. All of the above.

_____ 15. Bill Businessman files a lawsuit against Carl Contractor for breach of contract. This case is a/an:
   a. equitable action.
   b. criminal proceeding.
   c. civil lawsuit.
   d. public law case.

SHORT ESSAY

1. What are the major differences between common law systems and civil law systems?

    _____
    _____
    _____
    _____

2. Explain the concepts of "right" and "duty" as they relate to law.

    _____
    _____
    _____
    _____

3. Describe briefly the relationship between law and morals.

    _____
    _____
    _____
    _____

4. How are the Restatements of Law and the Uniform Commercial Code similar? How are they different?

    _____
    _____
    _____
    _____

5. George, who is driving while intoxicated, crashed into Alice. Alice was injured, and her car sustained damage. State the two types of actions that could be brought and list the differences between them.

    _____
    _____
    _____
    _____

Chapter 2
Business Ethics
and the Social Responsibility of Business

PURPOSE

Business ethics, as a branch of applied ethics, is the study and determination of right and good in business settings. Business ethics seeks to understand the moral issues that arise from business practices, institutions, and decision making and their relationship to generalized human values. Unlike the law, analyses of ethics have no central authority, such as court or legislatures, upon which to rely nor do they have well-defined universal standards. In this chapter, you study the most prominent ethical theories, then you examine ethical standards in business and conclude by exploring the ethical responsibilities of business.

CHAPTER CHECKPOINTS

After reading and studying this chapter, you should be able to:

1. Define business ethics.

2. Distinguish between law and ethics.

3. Identify and compare the various ethical theories.

4. Explain Kohlberg's stages of moral development.

5. Discuss the ethical responsibilities of business.

CHAPTER OUTLINE

    A. Law Versus Ethics–Law and morality are not the same. It is possible for acts that are legal to be immoral and equally possible for acts that are illegal to be considered morally preferable to following the law. Although legality is a reliable guide to moral behavior, it cannot be relied upon as an infallible standard for action. The individual must engage in independent determinations of both the legal requirements and the moral requirements of a course of action.

B. Ethical Theories–Philosophers have provided various ethical theories which help analyze issues of business ethics.

1. Ethical Fundamentalism–Under ethical fundamentalism or absolutism, individuals look to central authority or set of rules to guide them in ethical decision making.

2. Ethical Relativism–This is a doctrine asserting that actions must be judged by what individuals subjectively feel is right or wrong for themselves. It holds that when any two individuals or cultures differ regarding the morality of a particular issue or action, they are both correct because morality is relative. On the other hand, situational ethics holds that a person's actions must be judged by first putting oneself in the actor's situation.

3. Utilitarianism–This doctrine assesses good and evil in terms of the consequences of actions. It holds that moral actions are those that produce the greatest net pleasure compared to the net pain. Act utilitarianism assesses each separate act according to whether it maximizes pleasure over pain. Rule utilitarianism supports rules that on balance produce the greatest good. Utilitarian notions underlie cost-benefit analysis, an analytical tool used by many business and government managers.

4. Deontology–Deontology holds that actions must be judged by their motives and means as well as their results. The best-known deontological theory was proffered by Immanuel Kant. Under Kant's categorical imperative, for an action to be moral it must (1) be possible for it to be made a universal law to be applied consistently and (2) be respectful of the autonomy and rationality of all human beings and not treat them as an expedient.

5. Social Ethics Theories–Social ethics theories assert that special obligations arise from the social nature of human beings. These theories judge society in moral terms by its organization and by the way in which it distributes goods and services. Social egalitarians believe that society should provide all members with equal amounts of goods and services irrespective of their relative contributions. John Rawls proposed the theory of distributive justice which stresses equality of opportunity rather than results, while Robert Nozick proposed the libertarian theory which stresses market outcomes as the basis for distributing society's rewards.

6. Other Theories–Intuitionism holds that a rational person possesses inherent powers to assess the correctness of actions. The philosophy of good persons declares that if individuals wish to act morally, they should seek out and emulate the behavior of those individuals who always seem to know what the right choice is in any given situation and who always seem to do the right thing. The "Television Test" directs us to imagine that every ethical decision we make is being broadcast on nationwide television.

C. Ethical Standards in Business–Many ethical theories can be applied to the world of business.

1. Choosing an Ethical System–Lawrence Kohlberg observed that people progress through stages of moral development according to two major variables: age and education. During the first level–the preconventional level–a child's conduct is a reaction to the fear of punishment and, later, to the pleasure of reward. During adolescence–Kohlberg's conventional level–people conform their behavior to meet the expectations of groups. Some reach the third level–the

postconventional level–where they accept and conform to moral principles because they understand why the principles are right and binding.

2. Corporations as Moral Agents–Some insist that only people can engage in behavior that can be judged in moral terms. Opponents of this view insist that a sufficient number of attributes of responsibility inhere in corporations to permit judging corporate behavior from a moral perspective.

D. Ethical Responsibilities of Business–Our system has always recognized the need for some form of regulation of business, whether it be by competition, self-regulation, or government regulation.

1. Regulation of Business–Increased government intervention has occurred not only to preserve the competitive process in our economic system but also to achieve social goals extrinsic to the efficient allocation of resources. Such intervention attempts (1) to regulate both "legal" monopolies and "natural" monopolies; (2) to correct imperfections in the market system to preserve competition; (3) to protect specific groups from failures of the marketplace; and (4) to promote other social goals.

2. Corporate Governance–The five thousand largest U.S. firms currently produce over half of the nation's gross national product. Many observers insist that companies playing such an important role in economic life should have a responsibility to undertake projects that benefit society in ways that go beyond mere financial efficiency in producing goods and services.

3. Arguments against Social Responsibility–A number of arguments oppose business involvement in socially responsible activities.

   a. Profitability–Some argue that businesses are not organized to engage in social activities; they are structured to produce goods and services for which they receive money, and their social obligation is to return as much of this money to their direct stakeholders as possible.

   b. Unfairness–Whenever companies stray from their designated role of profitmaker, they take unfair advantage of company employees and shareholders.

   c. Accountability–Corporations are private institutions that are subject to a lower standard of accountability than are public bodies.

   d. Expertise–Even though a corporation has an expertise in producing and selling its product, it may not possess a talent for recognizing or managing socially useful activities.

4. Arguments in Favor of Social Responsibility–Critics contend that business must help to resolve societal problems and offer a number of arguments in support of their position.

   a. The Social Contract–Supporters of social roles for corporations assert that limited liability and other rights granted to companies carry a responsibility. Companies owe a moral debt to society to contribute to its overall well-being. A derivative of this is the stakeholder model which would impose on the corporation a fiduciary responsibility to all stakeholders, not just its stockholders.

   b. Less Government Regulation–Not only does anticipatory corporate action lessen the likelihood of government regulation, but social involvement by companies creates a climate of trust and respect that reduces the inclination of government to interfere in company business.

   c. Long-Run Profits–In the long run, enhanced goodwill created by involvement in social causes means stronger profits. Corporate actions to improve the well-being of their communities make these communities more attractive to citizens and more profitable for business.

KEY TERMS

1. Ethics

2. Business ethics

3. Ethical fundamentalism

4. Ethical relativism

5. Situation ethics

6. Utilitarianism

7. Act utilitarianism

8. Rule utilitarianism

9. Cost-benefit analysis

10. Deontology

11. Social egalitarians

12. Distributive justice

13. Libertarians

14. Intuitionism

TRUE/FALSE

_____   1. One definition of ethics is–the study of what is right or good for human beings.

_____   2. Under ethical fundamentalism, individuals look to a central authority or set of rules to guide them in ethical decision making.

_____   3. The best-known deontological theory was proffered by John Rawls.

_____   4. Lawrence Kohlberg felt that the two major variables in the stages of moral development were age and education.

_____ 5. The "Television Test" directs individuals to imagine that every ethical decision they make is being broadcast on nationwide television.

_____ 6. According to Kohlberg, most adults operate at the postconventional level where they accept and conform to moral principles because they understand why the principles are right and binding.

_____ 7. Enhanced goodwill due to corporate involvement in social causes often means stronger profits in the long run.

_____ 8. Intuitionism holds that rational persons possess inherent powers to assess the correctness of actions.

_____ 9. Libertarians stress market outcomes as the basis for distributing society's rewards.

_____ 10. Ethics, like laws, rely upon the courts and legislatures for well-defined universal standards.

_____ 11. Ethical relativism notions underlie cost-benefit analysis.

_____ 12. The chief criticism of utilitarianism is that it ignores justice.

_____ 13. Social egalitarians believe that society should provide all persons with equal amounts of goods and services irrespective of the contribution each makes to increase society's wealth.

_____ 14. Deontology holds that actions must be judged by their motives and means as well as by their results.

_____ 15. An argument in favor of corporate social responsibility is that the more responsibly companies act, the less the government must regulate them.

MULTIPLE CHOICE

_____ 1. Which of the following is/are a major form of Utilitarianism?
   a. Act utilitarianism.
   b. Rule utilitarianism.
   c. Distributive justice.
   d. Both a and b.

_____ 2. Dan religiously follows the teachings of the Bible. The approach Dan will take to ethical decision making is best described as:
   a. ethically fundamental.
   b. deontological.
   c. utilitarian.
   d. none of the above.

_____ 3. The relationship between a business and its owners results in ethical questions involving:
   a. corporate governance.
   b. shareholder voting.
   c. management's duties to shareholders.
   d. all of the above.

_____ 4. Which of the following statements is correct?
   a. Law and morality are the same.
   b. If something is legal, it is moral.
   c. The law is strongly affected by moral concepts.
   d. All of the above are correct.

_____ 5. The ethical theory which asserts that actions must be judged by what individuals feel is right or wrong for themselves is:
   a. ethical relativism.
   b. ethical fundamentalism.
   c. situational ethics.
   d. utilitarianism.

_____ 6. The approach to ethical decisionmaking where the person judging actually puts herself in the other person's shoes to understand what motivated him to make a particular decision is known as:
   a. act utilitarianism.
   b. situational ethics.
   c. ethical relativism.
   d. none of the above.

_____ 7. Ethical fundamentalism is also known as:
   a. situational ethics.
   b. utilitarianism.
   c. absolutism.
   d. none of the above.

_____ 8. The deontologist who proposed the categorical imperative similar to the Golden Rule was:
   a. John Rawls.
   b. Jeremy Bentham.
   c. Robert Nozick.
   d. Immanuel Kant.

_____ 9. The ethical theory that underlies the cost-benefit analysis is:
   a. utilitarianism.
   b. deontology.
   c. ethical fundamentalism.
   d. none of the above.

_____ 10. Aaron is a good student and citizen who conforms to the expectations of his family and peers as a result of loyalty, affection and trust. Aaron is in what stage of moral development according to Kohlberg's observations?
   a. Preconventional.
   b. Conventional.
   c. Postconventional.
   d. None of the above.

_____ 11. Arguments that have been used to support business involvement in socially responsible activities include:
   a. long-run profits.
   b. less government regulation.
   c. social contract.
   d. all of the above.

_____ 12. Arguments that have been used against business involvement in socially responsible activities include:
   a. profitability.
   b. unfairness.
   c. accountability.
   d. all of the above.

_____ 13. Martin is employed by a company to design aircraft. He chooses to work to design the safest aircraft possible, because he wants to save lives and feels a duty to provide the public with the safest possible aircraft. Martin is best described as a(an):
   a. utilitarian.
   b. ethical fundamentalist.
   c. deontologist.
   d. libertarian.

_____ 14. Martin is employed by a company to design aircraft. He uses a cost-benefit analysis and designs an aircraft that will have the most favorable cost-benefit ratio, ignoring safety devices that could significantly affect the safety of the aircraft. This decisionmaking approach is known as:
   a. utilitarianism.
   b. deontological.
   c. ethical fundamentalism.
   d. none of the above.

_____ 15. The ethical theory which asserts that society should provide all members with equal amounts of goods and services irrespective of their relative contributions is:
   a. distributive justice.
   b. ethical relativism.
   c. utilitarianism.
   d. social egalitarianism.

SHORT ESSAY

1. Compare the ethical theories of utilitarians and deontologists.

    _____

    _____

    _____

    _____

2. Explain the categorical imperative.

    _____

    _____

    _____

    _____

3. What are the arguments for and against corporate social responsibility?

    _____

    _____

    _____

    _____

4. Explain the three stages of moral development proposed by Lawrence Kohlberg.

    _____

    _____

    _____

    _____

5. You would like to propose to the board of directors of Big Bucks, Inc. that the corporation distribute three percent of its annual income to help the homeless. Discuss the ethical considerations of your proposal.

    _____

    _____

    _____

    _____

Chapter 3
Legal Process

PURPOSE

The purpose of this chapter is to introduce the student to procedural law and to the process of dispute resolution. The first part of the chapter discusses the structure and function of the federal and state court systems. The second part deals with jurisdiction, or the power of a court to hear and decide a case. The third part of the chapter discusses civil dispute resolution including the procedure in civil lawsuits.

CHAPTER CHECKPOINTS

After reading and studying the chapter, you should be able to:

1. Outline the courts in a state court system and in the federal court system.

2. Identify and define the various types of jurisdiction and compare the subject matter jurisdiction of the state courts to that of the federal courts.

3. Distinguish between "jurisdiction" and "venue".

4. Outline using correct terminology the process by which a civil lawsuit is begun and proceeds through the court system.

5. Discuss and compare the relative advantages and disadvantages of court adjudication and the methods of alternative dispute resolution.

CHAPTER OUTLINE

I.   The Court System–Courts are impartial tribunals established by government to settle disputes. A court may decide a case only when it has jurisdiction over both the dispute and the parties to that dispute. The United States has a dual court system in which the federal government as well as each of the fifty states has its own independent system.

A.   The Federal Courts–Article III of the U.S. Constitution says that judicial power of the United States shall be vested in one Supreme Court and such lower courts as Congress may establish. The federal court system consists of district courts, courts of appeals, a number of special courts, and the U.S. Supreme Court. Judges in the federal court system are appointed by the president for life, subject to confirmation by the Senate.

1.   District Courts–The district courts are general trial courts in the federal system. Most federal cases begin in the district court where the issues of fact are decided. Appeals go to the Circuit Court of Appeals of the appropriate circuit. In most cases, that decision is final. Congress has established judicial districts, and each state has at least one district, while certain states have more.

2.   Courts of Appeals–Congress has established eleven numbered circuits plus the D.C. circuit. Each circuit has a Court of Appeals which hears appeals from the district courts located within the circuit. They also review decisions of many administrative agencies, the Tax Court, and the Bankruptcy Court. The Courts of Appeals usually hear cases in panels of three judges, although they will sometimes hear cases *en banc* with all judges of the circuit. The function of appellate courts is to examine the record of a case on appeal and to determine whether the trial court committed prejudicial error. If so, the appellate court will reverse or modify the judgment of a lower court and if necessary remand or send it back to the lower court for further proceeding. If there is no error, the appellate court will affirm the decision of the lower court.

3.   The Supreme Court–The U.S. Supreme Court is the nation's highest tribunal. It consists of nine justices (Chief Justice and eight Associate Justices) who hear cases in Washington, D.C. The Court's principle function is to review decisions of the Federal Courts of Appeals and, sometimes those of the highest state courts or other tribunals, but the Supreme Court does have original jurisdiction in certain types of cases. Appeal by right is mandatory review by a higher court. Very few cases that come before the U.S. Supreme Court are appeals by right, because this method of appeal has virtually been eliminated by legislation enacted by Congress in 1988. Writ of certiorari refers to discretionary review by a higher court. Now almost all cases reaching the U.S. Supreme Court come to it by writ of certiorari. However, only a small percentage of the petitions for review are granted.

4.   Special Courts–Special courts in the federal judicial system include the U.S. Court of Federal Claims, the U.S. Bankruptcy Courts, the Tax Court, and the U.S. Court of Appeals for the Federal Circuit.

B.   State Courts–Each of the fifty states has its own independent court system where judges are usually elected for a stated term.

1. Inferior Trial Courts–These courts decide the least serious criminal and civil matters and usually do not keep a complete written record of their proceedings. Minor criminal cases such as traffic offenses are heard by inferior trial courts, which are referred to as municipal courts, justice of the peace courts, or traffic courts. Small claims courts are also inferior trial courts which hear civil cases involving a limited amount of money. Appeal from the decision of a small claims court is to a trial court of general jurisdiction where the appellant is entitled to a new trial (trial *de novo*).

2. Trial Courts–Each state has trial courts of general jurisdiction, which may be called county, district, superior, circuit, or common pleas court. These courts do not have a dollar limitation on their jurisdiction in civil cases and hear all criminal cases except minor offenses. These courts maintain formal records of their proceedings. Many states also have special trial courts such as probate courts and family courts.

3. Special Courts–Many states have special courts such as probate courts, with jurisdiction over will and estates, and family courts which have jurisdiction over divorce and child custody cases. Appeal is to the general state appellate courts.

4. Appellate Courts–The state's court of last resort is a reviewing court generally called the supreme court of the state. Except for those cases reviewed by the U.S. Supreme Court, the decision of this highest reviewing court is final. In addition, most states have intermediate appellate courts to handle the large volume of cases which are appealed.

II. Jurisdiction–Jurisdiction means the power or authority of a court to hear and decide a case. To resolve a lawsuit, a court must have both jurisdiction over the subject matter of the lawsuit and jurisdiction over the parties to a lawsuit.

A. Subject Matter Jurisdiction–Subject matter jurisdiction refers to the authority of a particular court to judge a controversy of a particular kind. Federal courts have limited subject matter jurisdiction, whereas state courts have jurisdiction over all matters that have not been given exclusively to the federal courts or expressly taken from them by Congress or the Constitution.

1. Federal Jurisdiction-The federal courts have exclusive jurisdiction over some areas that permit only federal courts to hear a case. They also have concurrent jurisdiction which is the authority of federal or state courts to hear the same case.

a. Exclusive Federal Jurisdiction–The federal courts have exclusive jurisdiction over federal criminal prosecution, admiralty, bankruptcy, antitrust, patent, trademark and copyright cases, suits against the United States, and cases arising under certain federal statutes.

b. Concurrent Federal Jurisdiction–There are two types of concurrent federal jurisdiction: federal question jurisdiction and diversity jurisdiction. Federal question jurisdiction allows a court to hear any case arising under the Constitution, statutes, or treaties of the United States, over which the federal courts do not have exclusive jurisdiction. Diversity of citizenship jurisdiction allows the federal courts to hear a case involving state law where there is diversity of citizenship and the amount in controversy exceeds $50,000. Diversity exists (1) when the plaintiffs are citizens of a state or states different from the state or states of which the defendants are citizens; (2) when a foreign country brings an action against citizens of the United States; or (3) when the controversy is between citizens of the United States and citizens of a foreign country. In any case involving concurrent jurisdiction, the plaintiff has the choice of bringing the action in either federal or state court.

2. Exclusive State Jurisdiction–State courts have exclusive jurisdiction over all other matters. All matters not granted to the federal courts in the Constitution or not exercised by Congress are solely within the jurisdiction of the states. These areas include but are not limited to property, torts, contracts, agency, commercial transaction and most crimes. Also included would be cases involving diversity of citizenship where the amount in controversy is $50,000 or less.

3. Choice of Law in State Courts–Even though some or all of the relavent events occur in state X, a court in state Y may be a proper forum. Conflict of laws rules vary from state to state.

4. *Stare Decisis* in the Dual Court System–The doctrine of *stare decisis* presents certain problems when there are two parallel court systems, but there are rules which determine which decisions are binding and those that are persuasive.

B. Jurisdiction over the Parties–Jurisdiction over the parties is the power of a court to bind the parties involved in the dispute. Its requirements may be met by (1) in personam jurisdiction; (2) in rem jurisdiction; or (3) attachment jurisdiction. The court's exercise of jurisdiction is valid under the due process clause of the Constitution if it satisfies the requirements of reasonable notification and reasonable opportunity to be heard and if the defendant has sufficient minimum contacts with the state.

1. *In Personam* Jurisdiction–*In personam* jurisdiction is personal jurisdiction of a court over the parties to a lawsuit in contrast to jurisdiction over their property. Personal jurisdiction may be obtained either (1) by serving process on the party within the state in which the court is located, or (2) by reasonable notification to a party outside the state in those instances where a "long-arm statute" applies. To serve process means to deliver a summons, which is an order to respond to a complaint lodged against a party. Most states have adopted long-arm statutes to expand their jurisdictional reach. These statutes allow courts to obtain jurisdiction over nonresident defendants under conditions that do not offend traditional notions of fair play and substantial justice. Personal jurisdiction may also arise from a party's consent such as when parties agree in a contract that any dispute will be subject to the jurisdiction of a specific court.

2. *In Rem* Jurisdiction–*In rem* jurisdiction is jurisdiction based on claims against property. Courts in a state have jurisdiction to adjudicate claims to property situated within the state if the plaintiff gives reasonable notice and an opportunity to be heard to those persons who have an interest in the property.

3. Attachment Jurisdiction–Attachment jurisdiction, or *quasi in rem* jurisdiction, is jurisdiction over property not based on claims against it. Like *in rem* jurisdiction, it is jurisdiction over property rather than over a person, but it is invoked by seizing the defendant's property located within the state to obtain payment of a claim against the defendant that is unrelated to the property seized. The basis of jurisdiction is the state's connection with the property; it does not depend on any connection between the state and the defendant.

4. Venue–Venue is the particular geographical place where a court with jurisdiction may hear a case. It is often confused with jurisdiction. Its purpose is to regulate the distribution of cases within a specific court system and to identify a convenient forum. Federal rules of venue determine the district or districts in a state in which the suit may be brought, while state rules of venue require that the suit be brought in a county where one of the defendants lives.

III. Civil Dispute Resolution–Our legal system has established an elaborate set of governmental mechanisms to settle disputes. The most prominent of these is judicial dispute resolution called litigation which is governed by the rules of civil procedure. In addition, there are several nongovernmental methods of dispute resolution referred to as alternative dispute resolution.

A. Civil Procedure–Civil disputes must follow the rules of civil procedure that are designed to resolve the dispute in a just, prompt, and inexpensive way.

1. The Pleadings–Pleadings are a series of responsive, formal, written statements in which each side to a lawsuit states its claims and defenses. The purpose of pleadings is to give notice and to establish the issues of fact and law presented and disputed. An "issue of fact" is a dispute between the parties regarding the events that gave rise to the lawsuit. An "issue of law" is a dispute between the parties as to what legal rule applies to these facts. The jury decides issues of fact, and the judge decides issues of law.

a. Complaint and Summons–The lawsuit begins when the complaint is filed by the plaintiff with the clerk of the trial court. The complaint is the initial pleading by the plaintiff stating his case. The county sheriff or deputy serves a summons and a copy of the complaint on the defendant commanding him to file an answer within a specific time. The summons is a written document that gives notice to the defendant that a suit has been brought against him. Proper service of the summons establishes the court's jurisdiction over the defendant.

b. Response to Complaint–If the defendant fails to respond at all to the summons and complaint, a default judgment will be entered against the defendant for the relief requested in the complaint. The defendant may make pretrial motions contesting the court's jurisdiction over him or asserting that the action is barred by the statute of limitations. A demurrer is a motion to dismiss for failure to state a claim. An answer is the defendant's pleading in response to the plaintiff's complaint. If the defendant does not make any pretrial motions, or if they are denied, the defendant must respond by filing an answer, which may contain denials, admissions, affirmative defenses and counterclaims. A reply is a pleading by the plaintiff in response to the defendant's answer. It may also contain admissions, denials, or affirmative defenses.

c. Judgment on the Pleadings–A judgment on the pleadings is a final binding determination on the merits of the case made by the judge after the pleadings. Either party may move for judgment on the pleadings which requests the judge to rule as a matter of law whether the facts as alleged in the pleadings of the nonmoving party are sufficient to grant the requested relief.

2. Pretrial Procedure

a. Discovery–Discovery is the pretrial exchange of information between opposing parties to a lawsuit. In preparation for trial, each party has the right to obtain relevant evidence, or facts that may lead to evidence from the other party. Pretrial discovery includes (1) pretrial depositions consisting of sworn testimony of the opposing party or other witnesses taken out of court; (2) sworn answers by the opposing party to written interrogatories or questions; (3) production of documents and physical objects in the possession of the opposing party; (4) examination by a physician of the physical and/or mental condition of the opposing party; and (5) admissions of facts set forth in a request for admissions submitted to the opposing party. A pretrial conference between the judge and the attorneys representing the parties may also be held (1) to simplify the issues in dispute; and (2) to encourage settlement of the dispute without a trial.

   b. Summary Judgment–If the evidence disclosed by discovery becomes so clear that a trial to determine the facts becomes unnecessary, one party may move for a summary judgment. A summary judgment is a final binding determination on the merits made by the judge before trial.

3. Trial–In all federal civil cases at common law involving more than twenty dollars, the U.S. Constitution guarantees the right to a jury trial. State constitutions often provide a similar right. Jury trials are not available in equity cases.

   a. Jury Selection–Assuming a timely demand for a jury has been made, the trial begins by selection of a jury. *Voir dire* is the preliminary examination of potential jurors. Each party has an unlimited number of challenges for cause, which allow a party to prevent a prospective juror from serving if the juror is biased or cannot be fair and impartial. Each party also has a limited number of peremptory challenges for which no cause is required to disqualify a prospective juror. By Supreme Court decision, the U.S. Constitution prohibits discrimination in jury selection based on race or gender.

   b. Conduct of Trial–After the jury has been selected, both attorneys make an opening statement about the facts that they expect to prove in the trial. The plaintiff and his witnesses then testify on direct examination by the plaintiff's attorney. Each is subject to cross-examination by the defendant's attorney. If the judge does not allow certain evidence to be introduced or certain testimony to be given, the attorney must make an offer of proof to preserve for review on appeal the question of its admissibility. After cross-examination, followed by redirect examination of witnesses, the plaintiff rests her case. At this time, the defendant may move for a directed verdict in his favor. A directed verdict is a final binding determination on the merits made by the judge after a trial has begun but before the jury renders a verdict. The judge may deny the motion for a directed verdict if there is any evidence on which the jury might possibly render a verdict for the plaintiff. If the judge denies the motion for a directed verdict, the defendant then has the opportunity to present evidence. After the defendant has presented his evidence and both parties have rested, then each party may move for a directed verdict. A directed verdict takes the case away from the jury and enters judgment for the party making the motion, because the evidence is so clear that reasonable persons could not differ about the outcome of the case. If these motions are denied, then the attorneys make closing statements to the jury.

   c. Jury Instructions–The attorneys have previously given written jury instructions on the applicable law to the trial judge, who gives those which he approves to the jury. These instructions are called charges in some states and advise the jury of the particular rules of law.

   d. Verdict–The jury then retires to the jury room to deliberate and to reach its verdict. A verdict is a formal decision by the jury on the questions submitted to it. In some jurisdictions, a special verdict is used, by which the jury makes specific written findings on each factual issue. The judge then applies the law to these findings and renders a judgment.

e. Motion Challenging Verdict–The unsuccessful party may then file a written motion for a new trial or for judgment notwithstanding the verdict. A motion for a new trial may be granted if (1) the judge committed prejudicial error; (2) the verdict is against the weight of the evidence; (3) the damages are excessive; or (4) the trial was not fair. A motion for judgment notwithstanding the verdict is similar to a motion for a directed verdict, except that it is made after the jury's verdict. A judgment notwithstanding the verdict is a final binding determination on the merits made by the judge after and contrary to the jury's verdict.

4. Appeal–To appeal a verdict, an attorney files a notice of appeal with the clerk of the trial court within the prescribed time. Where there is an intermediate court of appeals, it will usually be the reviewing court. In other states, the party appealing may appeal directly from the trial court to the state supreme court. The purpose of an appeal is to determine whether the trial court committed prejudicial error. Generally, only errors of law are reviewed by an appellate court. The appellate court does not hear any evidence. It decides the case on the records, abstracts, and briefs. After oral argument by the attorneys, the appellate court makes a decision and prepares a written opinion containing the reasons for its decision, the rules of law that apply, and its judgment.

5. Enforcement–If the judgment is in favor of the plaintiff and the defendant does not appeal, or the reviewing court affirms the judgment if he does appeal, the task of enforcement remains if the defendant does not pay the judgment. The plaintiff may proceed by execution or garnishment to collect the judgment.

B. Alternative Dispute Resolution–Because litigation is complex, time-consuming and expensive, several nonjudicial methods of dealing with disputes have developed. The most important of these alternatives to litigation is arbitration. Others include conciliation, mediation, and mini-trials. Alternative dispute resolution methods are especially suitable where privacy, speed, preservation of continuing relations, and control over the process are important to the parties.

1. Arbitration–Arbitration is a nonjudicial proceeding where a neutral third party selected by the disputants renders a binding decision. The parties in many cases are able to select an arbitrator with special expertise concerning the subject of the dispute. There are two basic types of arbitration–consensual and compulsory. Consensual arbitration occurs whenever parties to a dispute agree to submit the controversy to arbitration. They may do this in advance by agreeing in their contract that disputes will be resolved by arbitration or after the dispute by then agreeing to submit the dispute to arbitration. Consensual arbitration is the most common. Compulsory arbitration is required by statute for specific types of disputes such as those involving public employees like police officers or fire fighters. The decision of an arbitrator is called an award and is binding on the parties subject to limited judicial review.

2. Conciliation–Conciliation is a nonbinding process in which a third party (the conciliator) selected by the parties attempts to help them reach a mutually acceptable agreement.

3. Mediation–Mediation is a process in which a third party (the mediator) selected by the disputants helps them to reach a resolution of their disagreement. The mediator, unlike the conciliator, proposes possible solutions for the parties to consider, but like the conciliator he does not have the power to render a binding decision.

4. Mini-Trial–A mini-trial is a nonbinding process in which attorneys for the disputing parties present evidence to managers of the disputing parties and a neutral third party, and then the managers attempt to negotiate a settlement in consultation with the third party. A mini-trial typically occurs when both disputants are corporations.

5. Summary Jury Trial–A mock trial presented to a jury. The jury will return a nonbinding verdict which should, however, influence the parties in their negotiations.

KEY TERMS

1. Appeal by right

2. Writ of *certiorari*

3. Subject matter jurisdiction

4. Exclusive jurisdiction

5. Concurrent jurisdiction

6. Federal question

7. Diversity of citizenship

8. *In personam* jurisdiction

9. Service of process

10. Long-arm statute

11. *In rem* jurisdiction

12. Attachment jurisdiction

13. Venue

14. Pleadings

15. Complaint

16. Summons

17. Default judgment

18. Demurrer

19. Answer

20. Reply

21. Judgment on the pleadings

22. Discovery

23. Summary judgment

24. Voir dire

25. Directed verdict

26. Motion for new trial

27. Judgment notwithstanding the verdict

28. Execution

29. Garnishment

30. Appellant

31. Appellee

32. Arbitration

33. Conciliation

34. Mediation

35. Mini-trial

36. Summary Jury Trial

TRUE/FALSE

_____   1. A court may render a binding decision only when it has jurisdiction over the dispute and the parties to that dispute.

_____   2. A quorum of the U.S. Supreme Court consists of any five justices.

_____   3. The U.S. District Courts are the trial courts in the federal court system.

_____ 4. State court judges in most states receive lifetime appointments from the governor.

_____ 5. U.S. Supreme Court Justices are appointed for life by the President.

_____ 6. A corporation may be a citizen of more than one state for diversity of citizenship purposes.

_____ 7. A state court may have exclusive jurisdiction to hear a case involving diversity of citizenship.

_____ 8. There is no right to trial by jury in civil cases.

_____ 9. The decision of an arbitrator is binding on the parties.

_____ 10. Venue is the power of a court to hear and decide a case.

_____ 11. The U.S. Supreme Court normally exercises appellate jurisdiction although in certain instances it does exercise original jurisdiction.

_____ 12. A motion for a new trial may be granted if the trial court judge committed prejudicial error during the trial.

_____ 13. A deposition is a method of discovery consisting of sworn testimony of the opposing party or witness taken out of court.

_____ 14. The federal courts have exclusive jurisdiction of cases involving federal questions.

_____ 15. The Supreme Court has held that the U.S. Constitution prohibits discrimination in jury selection on the basis of race or gender.

MULTIPLE CHOICE

_____ 1. To render a binding decision, a court must have:
  a. subject matter jurisdiction.
  b. jurisdiction over the parties to the dispute.
  c. venue.
  d. a and b above

_____ 2. The main function of the appellate courts is to:
  a. keep criminals out of jail.
  b. review the decisions of the trial courts for prejudicial error.
  c. hear the testimony of witnesses.
  d. determine questions of fact.

_____ 3. The citizenship of an individual is:
   a. the state of his birth.
   b. the state where he is employed.
   c. the state where he is domiciled.
   d. any state where he has been domiciled.

_____ 4. Diversity of citizenship exists when:
   a. the plaintiff and defendant are citizens of different states.
   b. a foreign country brings an action against U.S. citizens.
   c. U.S. citizens bring an action against citizens of a foreign country.
   d. all of the above.

_____ 5. In a case where the appropriate state and federal courts have concurrent jurisdiction to hear the matter, the plaintiff may bring the action:
   a. in the state court only.
   b. in the federal court only.
   c. in the state court or the federal court.
   d. none of the above.

_____ 6. A party to a civil action who feels that there are no issues of fact to be determined by trial would most likely move for:
   a. a new trial.
   b. a summary judgment.
   c. a directed verdict.
   d. a judgment notwithstanding the verdict.

_____ 7. Which of the following is/are a part of the trial stage in civil procedure?
   a. answer.
   b. discovery.
   c. opening statement.
   d. garnishment.

_____ 8. Paul Plaintiff, a resident of Texas, and David Defendant, a resident of Colorado, are involved in a contract dispute amounting to eighty thousand dollars. The contract was executed in Texas. Paul may sue in:
   a. Colorado state court.
   b. Texas state court.
   c. Texas federal court.
   d. either Texas state court or Texas federal court.

_____ 9. In a civil action, the plaintiff is the party more likely to file:
    a. an answer.
    b. a reply.
    c. a counterclaim.
    d. a demurrer.

_____ 10. In a civil action, proper service of the summons establishes:
    a. the court's venue.
    b. the court's subject matter jurisdiction over the controversy.
    c. the court's jurisdiction over the defendant.
    d. all of the above.

_____ 11. Jurisdiction of a court over a party to a lawsuit is:
    a. _in personam._
    b. _in rem._
    c. attachment.
    d. venue.

_____ 12. Which of the following is a special court in the federal judicial system?
    a. U.S. Court of Federal Claims.
    b. U.S. Tax Court.
    c. U.S. Court of Appeals for the Federal Circuit.
    d. all of the above.

_____ 13. Most states have adopted long-arm statutes to expand their jurisdiction. Under such statutes nonresident defendants may be served if they:
    a. have committed a tort (civil wrong) within the state.
    b. own property within the state which is the subject of the lawsuit.
    c. have entered into a contract within the state.
    d. all of the above.

_____ 14. A motion to dismiss for failure to state a claim is also known as a/an:
    a. answer.
    b. demurrer.
    c. peremptory challenge.
    d. motion for a directed verdict.

_____ 15. Paul Plaintiff wants to be certain that a prospective juror is not selected. He may accomplish this through the use of:
    a. a challenge for cause.
    b. a peremptory challenge.
    c. voir dire examination.
    d. a demurrer.

SHORT ESSAY

1. Distinguish between "jurisdiction" and "venue."

_____

_____

_____

_____

2. In a civil trial, what procedure does the judge use in deciding whether to grant or deny a motion for a directed verdict?

_____

_____

_____

_____

3. Compare the relative advantages and disadvantages of court adjudication, arbitration and mediation.

_____

_____

_____

_____

4. Outline the major courts in the federal court system and in the state court system of the state where you live.

_____

_____

_____

_____

5. Outline using correct terminology the process by which a civil lawsuit is begun and proceeds through the court system.

_____

_____

_____

_____

Chapter 4
Constitutional Law

PURPOSE

The purpose of this chapter is to introduce the student to constitutional law as it relates to business and commerce. The first part of the chapter surveys some of the basic principles of constitutional law. The second part examines the allocation of power between the federal and state governments with respect to the regulation of business, with particular emphasis on the commerce clause. Finally, the third part discusses the constitutional restrictions imposed on the power of government to regulate business, with particular emphasis on the Bill of Rights.

CHAPTER CHECKPOINTS

After reading and studying this chapter, you should be able to:

1. Compare the principles of judicial review and preemption.

2. List the powers possessed by the federal government to regulate business and the Constitutional source of each power, as well as the powers possessed by the states.

3. List the limitations on government action to regulate business and identify the Constitutional source of each limitation.

4. Discuss the difference between substantive and procedural due process.

5. Identify the three tests used by courts in applying the Equal Protection Clause when deciding whether to uphold or to set aside a statute or administrative rule.

CHAPTER OUTLINE

A. Basic Principles–A number of concepts are basic to constitutional law in the United States.
   1. Federalism–Federalism means that governing power is divided between the federal government and the states. The U.S. Constitution enumerates the powers of the federal government and specifically reserves to the states or the people the powers not expressly delegated to the federal government.
   2. Federal Supremacy and Preemption–The supremacy clause of the U.S. Constitution provides that the federal constitution and federal laws are the supreme law of the land. Accordingly, any state constitutional provision or law that conflicts with the U.S. Constitution or valid federal laws or treaties is unconstitutional and may not be given effect. Federal preemption refers to the first right of the federal government to regulate matters within its powers to the possible exclusion of state regulation.
   3. Judicial Review–Judicial review describes the process by which the courts examine governmental actions to determine whether they conform to the U.S. Constitution. If governmental action violates the U.S. Constitution, under judicial review the courts will invalidate that action. It extends to legislation, acts of the executive branch, and the decisions of inferior courts. It includes the actions of both the federal and state governments and applies the same standards of constitutionality to both governments. The U.S. Supreme Court is the final authority as to the constitutionality of any federal or state law.
   4. Separation of Powers–Separation of powers is the allocation of powers among the legislative, executive and judicial branches of government. The purpose of this doctrine is to prevent any branch of government from gaining too much power. It also permits each branch to function without interference from any other branch.
   5. State Action–State action refers to actions taken by governments as opposed to actions taken by private individuals. Only the Thirteenth Amendment, which abolishes slavery or involuntary servitude, applies to the actions of private individuals. "State action" includes any actions of the federal and state governments and their subdivisions, such as city or county governments and agencies. It also may include action taken by private citizens if the state exercises coercive power over the challenged private action or has significantly encouraged the action.

B. Powers of Government–The U.S. Constitution created a federal government of enumerated powers. The Tenth Amendment declares that "the powers not delegated to the United States by the Constitution, nor prohibited by it to the States, are reserved to the States respectively, or to the people." Legislation enacted by Congress must, therefore, be based on a specific power granted to the federal government by the Constitution, or be reasonably necessary for carrying out an enumerated power. Some governmental powers may be exercised by the federal government while other governmental powers are concurrent.
   1. Federal Commerce Power–The U.S. Constitution provides that Congress has the power to regulate commerce with foreign nations and among the states. This commerce clause has two important effects: (1) it is a broad source of commerce power for the federal government to regulate the economy, and (2) it operates as a restriction on state regulations that obstruct or unduly burden interstate commerce. The U.S. Supreme Court interprets the commerce clause as

granting virtually complete power to Congress to regulate the economy and business. Legislation enacted under the commerce clause may only be invalidated (1) if it is clear that the activity regulated by the legislation does not affect interstate commerce, or (2) if it is clear that there is no reasonable connection between the regulatory means selected and the stated ends.

2. State Regulation of Commerce–In addition to acting as a broad source of federal power, the commerce clause also implicitly restricts the states' power to regulate activities if the result obstructs or unduly burdens interstate commerce.

    a. Regulations–In determining the extent of permissible state regulation affecting interstate commerce, the Court weighs and balances (1) the necessity and importance of the state regulation, (2) the burden it imposes on interstate commerce, and (3) the extent to which it discriminates against interstate commerce in favor of local concerns.

    b. Taxation–The commerce clause in conjunction with the import-export clause limits the power of the states to tax. The import-export clause provides: "No State shall, without the Consent of the Congress, lay any Imposts or Duties on Imports or Exports." Once goods enter the stream of interstate or foreign commerce, the power of the state to tax ceases and does not resume until the goods are delivered to the purchaser or the owner terminates the movement of the goods through interstate or foreign commerce. The due process clause of the Fourteenth Amendment also restricts the power of states to tax by requiring a sufficient nexus between the state and the person, thing, or activity to be taxed.

3. Federal Fiscal Powers–The federal government exerts a dominating influence over the national economy through its control of financial matters. In addition to the powers granted in the commerce clause, the sources of federal fiscal regulatory power include (1) the power to tax, (2) the power to spend, (3) the power to borrow and coin money, and (4) the power of eminent domain.

    a. Taxation–The federal government has broad power to tax limited by the following: (1) direct taxes other than income taxes must be apportioned among the states, (2) all custom duties and excise taxes must be uniform throughout the United States, and (3) no duties may be levied on exports from any state.

    b. Spending Power–The Constitution authorizes the federal government to pay debts and spend for the common defense and general welfare of the United States. The spending power of Congress is extremely broad and will be upheld so long as it does not violate a specific constitutional limitation on federal power.

    c. Borrowing and Coining Money–The U.S. Constitution also grants Congress the power to borrow money on the credit of the United States and to coin money. These two powers have enabled the federal government to establish a national banking system, the Federal Reserve System, and specialized federal lending programs such as the Federal Land Bank.

    d. Eminent Domain–Eminent domain is the power of government to take private property for public use upon payment of fair compensation. The power is recognized as one of the inherent powers of government in the federal Constitution and in the constitutions of the states. However, the Fifth Amendment carefully limits the power by providing: "nor shall private property be taken for public use without just compensation." The Supreme Court has held that the takings clause is incorporated through the Fourteenth Amendment and is therefore also applicable to the states.

C. Limitations on Government–The U.S. Constitution specifies certain powers that are granted to the federal government. Other unspecified powers have been reserved to the states. The limitations most applicable to business are: (1) the contract clause, (2) the First Amendment, (3) due process, and (4) equal protection. The first of these–the contract clause–applies only to the actions of state government whereas the other three apply to both the federal government and the states. None of these restrictions operates as an absolute limitation but instead triggers review to determine whether the governmental power exercised encroaches impermissibly upon the interest protected by the Constitution. Three levels of scrutiny are used. The least rigorous test is the rational relationship test, which requires that legislation bear a rational relationship to a legitimate governmental interest. The most exacting test is the strict scrutiny test, which requires that legislation be necessary to promote a compelling governmental interest. The intermediate test requires that legislation have a substantial relationship to an important governmental objective.

1. Contract Clause–The contract clause is a prohibition against the states' retroactively modifying public and private contracts. Article 1, Section 10 provides: "No State shall . . . pass any Law impairing the Obligation of Contracts . . . ." The Supreme Court has used the contract clause to restrict states from retroactively modifying public charters and private contracts. Although the contract clause does not apply to the Federal government, due process limits the Federal government's power to impair contracts.

2. First Amendment–The First Amendment contains a guarantee of free speech, but that protection is not absolute. Some forms of speech, such as obscenity, receive no protection.

   a. Corporate Political Speech–The First Amendment's guarantee of free speech applies not only to individuals but also to corporations, which may not be prohibited from speaking out on political issues. However, the U.S. Supreme Court has upheld a state statute prohibiting corporations from using general treasury funds to make independent expenditures in elections for public office.

   b. Commercial Speech–Commercial speech is expression related to the economic interests of the speaker and his audience, such as advertisements of products or services. The Court has established the principle that speech that does no more than propose a commercial transaction is entitled to a "lesser degree" of constitutional protection, but it is not wholly outside the protection of the First Amendment.

   c. Defamation–Defamation is a civil wrong or tort consisting of a false communication that injures a person's reputation by disgracing and diminishing the respect in which the person is held. Because defamation involves a communication, the protection extended to speech by the First Amendment applies. Public figures who pursue a cause of action for the tort of defamation or injury to their reputation by publication of false statements must prove actual malice or prove the defendant had knowledge of the falsity of the communication or acted in reckless disregard of its truth or falsity.

3. Due Process–The Fifth and Fourteenth Amendments respectively prohibit the federal and state governments from depriving any person of life, liberty, or property without due process of law. Due process has two different aspects: substantive due process and procedural due process.

   a. Substantive Due Process–Substantive due process requires that governmental action be compatible with individual liberties. Where fundamental rights of individuals under the Constitution are affected, the Court will carefully scrutinize the legislation to determine that it is necessary to promote a compelling state interest. Substantive due process addresses the constitutionality of the substance of a legal rule, not the fairness of the process by which the rule is applied.

   b. Procedural Due Process–Procedural due process requires that governmental action depriving a person of life, liberty or property be done through a fair procedure. Liberty for purposes of procedural due process generally includes the ability of individuals to engage in freedom of action and choice regarding their personal lives. Property, for the purpose of procedural due process, includes not only all forms of real and personal property but also certain benefits (entitlements) conferred by government, such as Social Security payments and food stamps.

4. Equal Protection–Equal protection requires that similarly situated persons be treated similarly by governmental action. The Fourteenth Amendment provides that "nor shall any State . . . deny to any person within its jurisdiction the equal protection of the laws." Although this amendment applies only to the actions of state governments, the Supreme Court has interpreted the due process clause of the Fifth Amendment to subject federal actions to the same standards of review. When governmental action involves classification of people, the equal protection guarantee applies. The Supreme Court will use one of three standards of review: (1) the rational relationship test, (2) the strict scrutiny test, or (3) the intermediate test.

   a. Rational Relationship Test–The rational relationship test applies to economic regulation and simply requires that it is conceivable that the classification bears some rational relationship to a legitimate governmental interest furthered by the classification. Courts will overturn the governmental action only if clear and convincing evidence shows that there is no reasonable basis justifying it.

   b. Strict Scrutiny Test–The strict scrutiny test is more exacting and allows the courts to independently determine whether the classification is constitutionally permissible. This test is applied when the governmental action affects fundamental rights or involves suspect classifications. Fundamental rights include most of the provisions of the Bill of Rights, the right to vote and some other rights such as interstate travel and access to criminal justice. Suspect classifications include those based on race or national origin.

   c. Intermediate Test–The intermediate test requires the governmental action to have a substantial relationship to an important governmental objective. This test has been applied to governmental action based on gender and legitimacy.

KEY TERMS

1. Supremacy clause

2. Federal preemption

3. Judicial review

4. Separation of powers

5. State action

6. Commerce clause

7. Federal fiscal powers

8. Eminent domain

9. Contract clause

10. Commercial speech

11. Procedural due process

12. Substantive due process

13. Equal protection

14. Rational relationship test

15. Strict scrutiny test

16. Intermediate test

TRUE/FALSE

_____   1. Judicial review describes the process by which the courts determine the constitutionality of government actions.

_____   2. The doctrine of federal preemption requires that a conflicting state regulation give way to the federal rule.

_____   3. State laws that burden interstate commerce will be invalidated pursuant to the Commerce Clause.

_____   4. Federalism is the division of governing power between the federal government and the states.

_____   5. The right of eminent domain permits the taking of private property for any purpose by government with fair compensation.

_____   6. Under the process of judicial review, the U.S. Supreme Court is the final authority as to the constitutionality of federal and state laws.

_____   7. Procedural due process refers to the decision-making process that results in depriving a person of life, liberty, or property.

_____ 8. Under the Fourteenth Amendment's rational relationship test, there is a strong presumption that the legislation is constitutional.

_____ 9. The contract clause of the U.S. Constitution applies only to the actions of state governments.

_____ 10. The Tenth Amendment reserves powers to the states that are not specifically delegated to the federal government.

_____ 11. While goods are in the stream of interstate commerce, they may be taxed by individual states.

_____ 12. If an activity is conducted solely in one state, it shall not be subject to regulation by federal government.

_____ 13. The strict scrutiny test requires that the legislature's classification be necessary to promote a compelling or overriding governmental interest.

_____ 14. The Fourteenth Amendment provides for equal protection to all persons.

_____ 15. The Supreme Court recently held that governmental restrictions of commercial speech must be absolutely the least severe necessary to achieve the governmental objective.

MULTIPLE CHOICE

_____ 1. Which of the following are considered to be fundamental principles which apply to both the powers of and the limitations on government?
   a. federal supremacy.
   b. judicial review.
   c. separation of powers.
   d. all of the above.

_____ 2. Exclusive federal powers include which of the following?
   a. to establish post offices.
   b. to coin currency.
   c. taxation.
   d. a and b above.

_____ 3. The equal protection clause is contained in the:
   a. Fifth Amendment.
   b. Fourteenth Amendment.
   c. First Amendment.
   d. Fourth Amendment.

_____ 4. Substantive due process rights would include all of the following except:
   a. right of privacy.
   b. right to interstate travel.
   c. right to have certain evidence excluded from a trial.
   d. right to vote.

_____ 5. For the purposes of procedural due process, the term "property" includes:
   a. real property and personal property only.
   b. real property and entitlements only.
   c. personal property and entitlements only.
   d. real property, personal property, and entitlements.

_____ 6. In equal protection cases involving fundamental rights or suspect classifications, which test would be used for review by the Supreme Court?
   a. Rational relationship test.
   b. Procedural due process test.
   c. Strict scrutiny test.
   d. Substantive relationship test.

_____ 7. Which of the following interests would require application of the strict scrutiny test?
   a. legitimacy.
   b. nonprotected speech.
   c. protected noncommercial speech.
   d. none of the above.

_____ 8. The main purpose of the Bill of Rights is to:
   a. provide restrictions on the powers of the states.
   b. provide the authority for federal government to regulate business.
   c. provide restrictions on the powers of the federal government.
   d. none of the above.

_____ 9. The Contract Clause restricts:
   a. the federal government from retroactively modifying contracts.
   b. the states from retroactively modifying contracts.
   c. the states from exercising the power of eminent domain.
   d. none of the above.

_____ 10. Which of the following federal "powers" stem from the Commerce Clause?
   a. The power to coin money.
   b. The power to tax.
   c. The power of eminent domain.
   d. None of the above are commerce clause powers.

_____ 11. The protection of the _____ Amendment applies to cases involving the tort of defamation.
   a. First
   b. Fourth
   c. Fifth
   d. Ninth

_____ 12. Which of the following would be considered property for purposes of procedural due process?
   a. Social security payments.
   b. Food stamps.
   c. Both social security and food stamps.
   d. Neither social security nor food stamps.

_____ 13. The _____ operates as a restriction on state regulations that obstruct or unduly burden interstate commerce.
   a. First Amendment
   b. Commerce Clause
   c. Contract Clause
   d. Due Process Clause

_____ 14. Which of the following is a true statement with regard to the Commerce Clause of the U.S. Constitution?
   a. It expressly excludes state regulation of interstate commerce.
   b. It expressly permits federal regulation of interstate commerce.
   c. It expressly excludes state regulation and expressly permits federal regulation.
   d. The U.S. Constitution makes no statement regarding regulation of commerce.

_____ 15. Which of the following constitutional limitations of power, most applicable to business, applies only to actions of state governments?
   a. The Contract Clause.
   b. The First Amendment.
   c. Due Process.
   d. Equal protection.

SHORT ESSAY

1. Briefly explain federal supremacy and preemption.

_____

_____

_____

_____

2. In equal protection cases, how does the rational relationship test compare with the strict scrutiny test?

3. Describe the factors used by the Supreme Court when deciding the extent to which state regulation may affect interstate commerce.

4. How does the Commerce Clause restrict the ability of states to regulate interstate commerce?

5. Explain the First Amendment's protection of free speech with respect to corporate political speech, commercial speech and defamation.

Chapter 5
Administrative Law

PURPOSE

The purpose of this chapter is to introduce the student to administrative agencies and examine the significant and necessary role of federal administrative agencies in our society. Administrative agencies are governmental entities (other than courts and legislatures) having authority to affect the rights of private parties. The chapter discusses the operation of administrative agencies and limits on administrative agencies.

CHAPTER CHECKPOINTS

After reading and studying this chapter, you should be able to:

1. List the three basic functions of administrative agencies.

2. Discuss pertinent provisions of the Administrative Procedure Act.

3. Compare the three types of rules promulgated by administrative agencies.

4. Explain formal and informal methods of adjudication.

5. Identify the limits placed upon administrative agencies.

CHAPTER OUTLINE

   A. Operation of Administrative Agencies–Most administrative agencies perform three basic functions: (1) to make rules, (2) to enforce the law, and (3) to adjudicate controversies. The term administrative process refers to the entire set of activities in which administrative agencies engage while carrying out their rulemaking, enforcement, and adjudicative functions. To address the issues raised by the concentration of these three functions in the same agency and to address questions raised regarding the propriety of having the same bodies which establish the rules also act as prosecutor and judge in determining whether the rules have been violated, Congress passed the Administrative Procedure Act (APA) in 1946.

1. Rulemaking–Rulemaking is the process by which an administrative agency enacts or promulgates rules of law. Under the APA, a rule is "the whole or a part of an agency statement of general or particular applicability and future effect designed to implement, interpret, or process law or policy. Three types of rules are promulgated by administrative agencies: legislative rules, interpretative rules, and procedural rules.

   a. Legislative Rules–Legislative rules, often called regulations, are substantive rules issued by an administrative agency under the authority delegated to it by the legislature. Legislative rules must be promulgated in accordance with the procedural requirements of the APA. Legislative rules have the force of law in contrast to interpretative and procedural rules.

   b. Interpretative Rules–Interpretative rules are statements issued by an administrative agency indicating its construction of its governing statute. Interpretative rules are exempt from the notice and comment requirement of the APA.

   c. Procedural Rules–Procedural rules are rules issued by an administrative agency establishing its organization, method of operation, and rules of conduct for practicing before it. Procedural rules are also exempt from the notice and comment requirements of the APA.

2. Enforcement–Agencies also investigate conduct to determine whether the statute or the agency's legislative rules have been violated. Agencies have traditionally been accorded great discretion to compel disclosure of information, subject to constitutional limitations.

3. Adjudication–After concluding an investigation, the agency may use formal or informal methods to resolve the matter. Most matters are informally adjudicated by procedures including advising, negotiating and settling. While not required to be used, the Administrative Dispute Resolution Act authorizes and encourages federal agencies to use alternative dispute resolutions. The formal procedure by which an agency resolves a matter (called adjudication) involves finding facts, applying legal rules to the facts, and formulating orders. An order is the final disposition made by an agency. Adjudication is in essence an administrative trial governed by certain standards set forth in the APA. The APA requires that notice be given of the hearing; that the agency give all interested parties the opportunity to submit "facts, arguments, offers of settlement, or proposals of adjustment"; and that a hearing be held if no settlement is reached. The hearing is presided over by an administrative law judge (ALJ) and is prosecuted by the agency. Juries are never used. Oral and documentary evidence may be introduced by either party. All decisions must include a statement of findings of fact and conclusions of law and the reasons or basis for them as well as a statement of the appropriate rule, order, sanction, or relief. In most instances orders are final unless appealed, and failure to comply with an order is subject to statutory penalty.

B. Limits on Administrative Agencies–An important and fundamental part of administrative law is the limits imposed by judicial review upon the activities of administrative agencies. Courts are not supposed to substitute their judgment on matters of policy for the agency's judgment, but the legislature and the executive branch may address the wisdom and correctness of an agency's action. Legally required public disclosure of agency actions provides further protection for the public.

1. Judicial Review–In exercising judicial review, the court may either compel agency action unlawfully withheld or set aside impermissible agency action if the error is prejudicial.

2. General Requirements–It is necessary for parties seeking to challenge agency action to (a) have standing and (b) have exhausted their administrative remedies. Judicial review is ordinarily available only for final agency action. In conducting a review, the court decides all relevant questions of law, interprets constitutional and statutory provisions, and determines the meaning or applicability of the terms of agency action.

3. Questions of Law–A review of questions of law includes determining whether the agency has: (1) exceeded its authority, (2) properly interpreted the applicable law, (3) violated any constitutional provision, or (4) acted contrary to the procedural requirements of the law.

4. Questions of Fact–One of three different standards will be used when reviewing factual determinations. The tests applied are: (a) the arbitrary and capricious test, (b) the substantial evidence test, or (c) the unwarranted by the facts standard.

5. Legislative Control–The legislature may exercise control through its budgetary power; by amending the agency's enabling statute; by establishing general guidelines such as the APA; by reversing or changing an agency rule through legislation; through review of agencies by Congressional oversight committees; and through the Congressional power to confirm high-level administrative appointments.

6. Control by Executive Branch–The president has the power to appoint and remove the chief administrator of an agency, but he has less control of independent agencies, because commissioners serve for a fixed term that is staggered with the president's term of office. The president also submits a budget to Congress and can impound moneys or restructure agencies unless disapproved by Congress.

C. Disclosure of Information–Congress has enacted disclosure statutes to enhance public and political oversight of agency activities. These statutes include:

1. Freedom of Information Act–The FOIA gives the public access to most records in the files of Federal administrative agencies.

2. Government in the Sunshine Act–The Government in the Sunshine Act applies to multimember bodies whose members are appointed by the President with the advice and consent of the Senate and requires such bodies to hold their meetings open to the public.

KEY TERMS

1. Administrative law

2. Administrative agency

3. Administrative process

4. Legislative rules

5. Interpretative rules

6. Procedural rules

7. Adjudication

8. Order

TRUE/FALSE

_____ 1. Interpretative rules establish an administrative agency's organization and method of operation.

_____ 2. Administrative law is a branch of private law.

_____ 3. Administrative agencies create more legal rules and adjudicate more controversies than all the legislatures and courts combined.

_____ 4. Rules issued by an administrative agency establishing its organization, method of operation, and rules of conduct are known as legislative rules.

_____ 5. Enabling statutes require that all administrative rules be made only after the opportunity for an agency hearing.

_____ 6. An individual who is involved in a hearing with an administrative agency has a right to a trial by jury.

_____ 7. Administrative agencies promulgate three types of rules: legislative, interpretative and procedural.

_____ 8. Most legislative rules are issued in accordance with the informal rulemaking procedures of the Administrative Procedure Act.

_____ 9. Courts formulate more policy by adjudicating than administrative agencies.

_____ 10. The order of an administrative law judge may be appealed to the governing body of the agency.

_____ 11. Judicial review acts as a check by a court on an order of an administrative agency.

_____ 12. Regulations which are proposed for adoption by a federal administrative agency are published in the Federal Register in order to provide notice before they become effective.

_____ 13. Most matters that come before administrative agencies are resolved by informal adjudication.

_____ 14. The substantial evidence test requires conclusions reached be supported by a rational basis.

_____ 15. The Negotiated Rulemaking Act requires agencies to use negotiated rulemaking.

MULTIPLE CHOICE

_____ 1. Federal administrative agencies are charged with which of the following?
  a. citizenship and naturalization.
  b. environmental protection.
  c. telecommunications.
  d. all of the above.

_____ 2. A decision by an administrative agency may be overturned if the agency:
  a. exceeded its authority.
  b. acted arbitrarily or capriciously.
  c. reached conclusions not supported by substantial evidence.
  d. all of the above.

_____ 3. Limits placed on administrative agencies include:
  a. judicial review of agency actions.
  b. appointment of administrators by the president.
  c. control of the budget by Congress.
  d. all of the above.

_____ 4. Rules issued by an administrative agency which are in effect "administrative statutes" are:
  a. interpretative rules.
  b. procedural rules.
  c. legislative rules.
  d. judicial rules.

_____ 5. In exercising judicial review, the court may:
  a. compel agency action unlawfully withheld.
  b. set aside impermissible agency action.
  c. both a and b.
  d. none of the above.

_____ 6. Which of the following are considered to be basic functions of most administrative agencies?
  a. to make rules.
  b. to enforce the law.
  c. adjudication.
  d. all of the above.

_____ 7. In conducting an investigation, the Securities and Exchange Commission could:
    a. issue subpoenas requiring production of documents.
    b. conduct searches without a warrant.
    c. compel disclosure of privileged information.
    d. none of the above.

_____ 8. In exercising its adjudicative power, an agency may:
    a. impose a fine.
    b. seize property.
    c. revoke a license.
    d. all of the above.

_____ 9. Which of the following is not an administrative agency?
    a. Food and Drug Administration.
    b. Equal Employment Opportunity Commission.
    c. U.S. Congress.
    d. Occupational Safety and Health Administration.

_____ 10. The decision of the administrative law judge:
    a. is not subject to review by the courts.
    b. can be set aside by the courts if the error is prejudicial.
    c. will automatically be reviewed by the agency.
    d. none of the above.

_____ 11. The legislature can exercise control over administrative agencies by:
    a. its budgetary power.
    b. by amending the enabling statute.
    c. changing an agency rule by specific legislation.
    d. all of the above.

_____ 12. Before OSHA can issue a regulation regarding safety in the workplace, it must:
    a. provide an opportunity for interested parties to participate in the rulemaking.
    b. determine that Congress supports the regulation.
    c. publish the regulation in the Code of Federal Regulations.
    d. all of the above.

_____ 13. In _____ rulemaking, the agency must base its rules upon consideration of the record of the agency hearing and include a statement of findings and conclusions on all material issues.
    a. informal
    b   formal
    c. hybrid
    d. none of the above

_____ 14. In exercising judicial review the court will inquire into whether the agency has:
   a. exceeded its authority.
   b. properly interpreted the applicable law.
   c. acted contrary to the procedural requirements of the law.
   d. all of the above.

_____ 15. Which of the following would have to be disclosed under the Freedom of Information Act?
   a. National defense secrets.
   b. Agency rules of practice.
   c. Trade secrets.
   d. Proposed regulations.

SHORT ESSAY

1. Discuss the three basic functions of administrative agencies.

_____

_____

_____

_____

2. Compare the formal, informal, and hybrid rulemaking processes.

_____

_____

_____

_____

3. Explain the process of judicial review upon the activities of administrative agencies.

_____

_____

_____

_____

4. Briefly discuss the Government in the Sunshine Act.

_____

_____

_____

_____

5. Define the three types of rules promulgated by administrative agencies.

_____

_____

_____

_____

Chapter 6
Criminal Law

PURPOSE

Whereas civil law defines duties, the violation of which constitutes a wrong against the injured party, the criminal law establishes duties, the violation of which is a wrong against the whole community. Civil law is a part of private law; criminal law is a part of public law. In a civil case, the injured party sues to recover compensation for the injury sustained. In a criminal case, the government brings a case against a person for a wrong against society. If the person accused is convicted, the wrongdoer will be punished by a fine or imprisonment or both. Some conduct may be both a crime and a civil wrong, or tort. The purpose of this chapter is to introduce the general principles of criminal law and criminal procedure as well as specific crimes and defenses relevant to business. Because of the increasing use of criminal sanctions to enforce governmental regulation of business, criminal law is an essential part of business law.

CHAPTER CHECKPOINTS

After reading and studying the chapter, you should be able to:

1. Distinguish between a tort and a crime and identify the essential elements of a crime.

2. Compare the procedure used in initiating and pursuing a civil case to the procedure used in initiating and pursuing a criminal case.

3. Identify and define the common property crimes and the common defenses to crimes.

4. Identify the protections for criminal defendants found in the U.S. Constitution and the source of each of these constitutional rights.

5. Outline the steps in a criminal prosecution using appropriate legal terminology.

CHAPTER OUTLINE

A. Nature of Crimes–A crime is any act or omission forbidden by public law in the interest of protecting society and made punishable by the government in a judicial proceeding brought by it. Crimes are prohibited and punished on grounds of public policy, which may include the protection of government, human life, or property. Other purposes of the criminal law include deterrence, rehabilitation, and retribution. Historically, criminal law was primarily common law, but today it is almost exclusively statutory.

1. Essential Elements–*Actus reus* is a wrongful or overt act. *Mens rea* is a criminal intent or mental fault. In general, both of these elements must be present to have a crime. *Actus reus* refers to all the nonmental elements of a crime, including the physical act that must be performed, the consequences of that act, and the circumstances under which it must be performed. *Mens rea,* or mental fault, refers to the mental element of a crime. Most common law and statutory crimes require subjective fault, which includes purposeful, knowing or reckless conduct. Other crimes require a lesser degree of mental fault, called objective fault. Objective fault involves gross deviation from the standard of care that a reasonable person would observe under the circumstances. Statutes usually refer to objective fault by such terms as "carelessness" or "negligence." Many regulatory statutes have totally dispensed with the mental element of a crime and impose liability without fault. Criminal liability without fault makes it a crime to do a specific act or to bring about a certain result without regard to the care exercised by that person.

2. Classification–Historically, crimes have been classified as *mala in se,* which are crimes such as murder that are morally wrong in themselves, or *mala prohibita,* which are crimes such as minor traffic offenses that are not morally wrong in themselves but that have been declared wrong by law. Today crimes are usually classified by their seriousness. A felony is a serious crime punishable by imprisonment in a penitentiary or by death. A misdemeanor is a less serious crime punishable by a fine or imprisonment in a local jail.

3. Vicarious Liability–Vicarious liability is liability imposed on one person for the acts of another person. Employers are vicariously liable for authorized criminal acts of their employees if the employer directed, participated in, or approved of the acts. Employers are ordinarily not liable for the unauthorized criminal acts of their employees. However, employers may be subject to a criminal penalty for the unauthorized act of an advisory or managerial person acting in the scope of employment. Moreover, employers may be criminally liable under liability without fault statutes for certain unauthorized acts of its employees, whether the employee is managerial or not.

4. Liability of a Corporation–Historically, corporations were not held criminally liable, because they did not possess the requisite criminal intent and, therefore, were incapable of committing a crime. Under the modern approach, a corporation may be liable for violation of statutes imposing liability without fault. In addition, a corporation may be liable where the offense is perpetrated by a high corporate officer or the board of directors. Punishment of a corporation is necessarily by fine and not imprisonment. Nonetheless, the individuals bearing responsibility for the criminal act face either/or both fines and imprisonment. The Federal Organizational Corporate Sentencing Guidelines became effective in 1991, with an overall purpose of imposing sanctions which will provide just punishment and adequate deterrence.

B. White-Collar Crime–The Justice Department defines white collar crime as nonviolent crime involving deceit, corruption, or breach of trust. It includes crimes committed by individuals–such as embezzlement and forgery–as well as crimes committed on behalf of a corporation–such as commercial bribery, product safety and health crimes, false advertising, and antitrust violations.

    1. Computer Crime–Computer crime is a special type of white-collar crime. Computer crime includes the use of a computer to steal money or services, to remove personal or business information, and to tamper with information. These crimes can be broken down into five general categories: (1) theft of computer hardware, software, or secrets; (2) unauthorized use of computer services; (3) theft of money by computer; (4) vandalism of computer hardware or software; and (5) theft of computer data.

    2. Racketeering Influenced and Corrupt Organizations Act–RICO was enacted in 1970 with the stated purpose of terminating the infiltration by organized crime into legitimate business. The act subjects enterprises that engage in a pattern of racketeering to severe civil and criminal penalties. A pattern of racketeering is defined as the commission of two or more predicate acts within a period of ten years. A predicate act is any of several criminal offenses listed in RICO. RICO is controversial, because businesses that are not involved in organized crime but that meet the "pattern of racketeering" test may be subjected to fines, forfeiture of property obtained due to a RICO violation, prison terms and treble damages in civil suits.

C. Crimes Against Business–Criminal offenses against property greatly affect businesses.

    1. Larceny–Larceny is the trespassory taking and carrying away of personal property of another with the intent to deprive the victim permanently of the goods.

    2. Embezzlement–Embezzlement is the fraudulent conversion of another's property by one who was in lawful possession of it. A conversion is any act that seriously interferes with the owner's rights in the property. In both larceny and embezzlement there is a misuse of the property of another, but in larceny the thief unlawfully possesses the property, whereas in embezzlement the thief lawfully possesses it.

    3. False Pretenses–False pretenses is the crime of obtaining title to property of another by means of materially false representations of an existing fact, with knowledge of its falsity, and made with the intent to defraud. Larceny does not cover this situation, because the victim voluntarily transfers the property to the thief. Other specialized crimes that are similar to false pretenses include mail fraud and securities fraud.

    4. Robbery–Robbery is larceny with the additional elements that the property is taken from the victim or in the immediate presence of the victim, and the taking is accomplished through either force or threat of force. Many statutes distinguish between simple robbery and aggravated robbery.

    5. Burglary–At common law, burglary was defined as breaking and entering the dwelling of another at night with the intent to commit a felony. Many modern statutes simply require that there be an entry into a building with the intent to commit a felony in the building.

    6. Extortion and Bribery–Extortion, or blackmail, is generally held to be the making of threats for the purpose of obtaining money or property. Bribery is the offer of money or property to a public official to influence the official's decision. Some jurisdictions make commercial bribery

illegal.   Commercial bribery is the use of bribery to acquire new business, obtain secret information or processes, or obtain kickbacks.

7. Forgery–Forgery is the intentional falsification or false making of a document with the intent to defraud.

8. Bad Checks–All jurisdictions have now enacted laws making it a crime to issue bad checks; that is, writing a check when there is not enough money in the account to cover the check.

D. Defenses to Crimes–The defenses most relevant to white-collar crimes and crimes against business include defense of property, duress, mistake of fact, and entrapment.

1. Defense of Person or Property–Individuals may use reasonable force to protect themselves, other individuals, and property. This defense enables a person to commit, without any criminal liability, what would otherwise be considered the crime of assault, battery, manslaughter, or murder. Under the majority rule, deadly force is never reasonable to protect property.

2. Duress–A person who is threatened with immediate, serious bodily harm to himself or another unless he engages in criminal conduct other than murder may raise the defense of duress.

3. Mistake of Fact–A person who reasonably believes the facts to be such that his conduct would not constitute a crime may use this defense to justify his conduct.

4. Entrapment–This defense arises when a law enforcement official induces a person to commit a crime when that person would not have done so otherwise.

E. Criminal Procedure–Each of the states and the federal government have procedures for initiating and coordinating criminal prosecutions. In addition, the first ten amendments to the U.S. Constitution (called the Bill of Rights) guarantee many defenses and rights of an accused. Most state constitutions have similar provisions. In addition, the Fourteenth Amendment prohibits state governments from denying any person of life, liberty, or property without due process of law.

1. Steps in Criminal Prosecution–Particulars of criminal procedure vary from state to state. In general, after arrest, the accused is booked and appears before a magistrate, commissioner, or justice of the peace, where formal notice of the charges is given, the accused is advised of his rights, and bail is set. Then a preliminary hearing is held to determine whether there is probable cause to believe the defendant is the one who committed the crime. The defendant is entitled to be represented by counsel. If there is probable cause, the case will be brought before a grand jury which issues an indictment or true bill if it finds sufficient evidence to justify a trial. The indictment is a grand jury charge that the defendant should stand trial. An information is used in misdemeanor cases rather than the indictment. An information is a formal accusation of a crime brought by a prosecuting officer and not a grand jury. The next step is an arraignment where the defendant is informed of the charge against him and he enters a plea. If his plea is "not guilty," he must stand trial and is entitled to a jury in most cases. In a criminal trial, (1) the defendant is presumed innocent, (2) the burden of proof on the prosecution is to prove guilt beyond a reasonable doubt, and (3) the defendant is not required to testify. If the jury's verdict is not guilty, the matter ends there. If the verdict is guilty, the judge will enter a judgment for conviction and set the case for the sentencing. The defendant may make a motion for a new trial or appeal to a reviewing court.

2. Fourth Amendment–The Fourth Amendment protects individuals against unreasonable searches and seizures. The amendment is designed to protect the privacy and security of individuals against arbitrary invasions by government officials. Although the Fourth Amendment by its terms applies only to the federal government, the Fourteenth Amendment makes it applicable to the states. When there is a violation of the Fourth Amendment, the exclusionary rule prohibits the introduction of the illegally seized evidence. The purpose of this rule is to discourage illegal police conduct and to protect individual liberty. To obtain a search warrant of a particular person, place or thing, the law enforcement official must demonstrate to a magistrate that he has probable cause to believe that the search will reveal evidence of criminal activity. Probable cause means that "the apparent facts set out in the affidavit of the requesting authority are such that a reasonably discreet and prudent man would be led to believe that there was a commission of the offense charged." A search without a warrant is permissible where: (1) there is hot pursuit of a fugitive, (2) voluntary consent is given, (3) an emergency requires such action, (4) there has been a lawful arrest, (5) evidence of a crime is in plain view of the law enforcement officer, or (6) delay would present a significant obstacle to the investigation.

3. Fifth Amendment–The Fifth Amendment protects persons against self-incrimination, double jeopardy, and being charged with a capital or infamous crime except by grand jury indictment. The prohibitions against self-incrimination and double jeopardy, but not the grand jury clause, also apply to the states through the due process clause of the Fourteenth Amendment. The privilege against self-incrimination extends only to testimonial evidence and not to physical evidence. Due process is basically the guarantee of a fair trial. In criminal cases, the defendant has the right to counsel, to confront and cross-examine adverse witnesses, to testify in his own behalf, to produce witnesses and offer other evidence, and to be free of any and all prejudicial conduct and statements.

4. Sixth Amendment–The Sixth Amendment provides that the federal government shall provide the accused with a speedy and public trial by an impartial jury, inform him of the nature and cause of the accusation, confront him with the witnesses against him, have compulsory process for obtaining witnesses in his favor, and have the assistance of counsel for his defense. The Fourteenth Amendment extends these guarantees to the states.

KEY TERMS

1. Crime

2. *Actus reus*

3. *Mens rea*

4. Subjective fault

5. Objective fault

6. Liability without fault

7. Felony

8. Misdemeanor

9. Vicarious liability

10. White-collar crime

11. Computer crime

12. RICO

13. Larceny

14. Embezzlement

15. False pretenses

16. Robbery

17. Burglary

18. Extortion

19. Bribery

20. Forgery

21. Bad checks

22. Defense of person or property

23. Duress

24. Mistake of fact

25. Entrapment

26. Preliminary hearing

27. Grand jury

28. Indictment

29. Information

30. Arraignment

31. Exclusionary rule

32. Probable cause

TRUE/FALSE

_____ 1. Criminal law establishes duties, the violation of which constitute a wrong against another individual.

_____ 2. To prove that a crime has been committed, it is necessary only to demonstrate that the defendant had the required criminal intent.

_____ 3. A corporation cannot be held criminally liable because a corporation cannot possess the requisite criminal intent.

_____ 4. A corporation may not be convicted of a criminal offense for the conduct of its employees.

_____ 5. A grand jury issues a decision called an indictment.

_____ 6. To establish the crime of larceny, it is not necessary to prove that there was an intent to deprive the victim permanently of her goods.

_____ 7. The Fifth Amendment protects individuals against unreasonable searches and seizures.

_____ 8. The exclusionary rule prohibits illegally seized evidence from being introduced into court.

_____ 9. The right to a jury trial is provided by the Sixth Amendment.

_____ 10. In a criminal trial, the prosecution must establish guilt beyond a reasonable doubt.

_____ 11. The right to counsel is found in the Fifth Amendment.

_____ 12. Duress can never be raised as a defense to the commission of a crime.

_____ 13. A woman may use deadly force to protect herself against an attack that threatens death or serious bodily harm.

_____ 14. A person who breaks into a vacant house and steals valuable household items has committed robbery.

_____ 15. The privilege against self-incrimination extends to both physical evidence and testimonial evidence alike.

MULTIPLE CHOICE

_____ 1. Which of the following would not be a defense available to a criminal defendant?
   a. mistake of fact.
   b. entrapment.
   c. duress.
   d. infancy.

_____ 2. Generally, a crime consists of which of the following?
   a. A wrongful or overt act.
   b. The requisite criminal intent.
   c. Both a and b.
   d. None of the above.

_____ 3. A crime punishable by a fine or imprisonment in local jail is called a:
   a. misdemeanor.
   b. felony.
   c. white collar crime
   d. _mala in se_.

_____ 4. Which of the following crimes involves an intentional misrepresentation of fact in order to defraud another?
   a. Extortion.
   b. Robbery.
   c. Burglary.
   d. False pretenses.

_____ 5. The stage of a criminal trial when the defendant is brought before the court, informed of the charge against him, and allowed to enter a plea, is the:
   a. preliminary hearing.
   b. arraignment.
   c. sentencing.
   d. indictment.

_____ 6. Taking property of another by one in lawful possession of that property is:
   a. extortion.
   b. robbery.
   c. false pretenses.
   d. embezzlement.

_____ 7. Which of the following is not an essential element of robbery?
   a. Non-trespassory taking.
   b. Carrying away of another's personal property.
   c. Directly from the victim.
   d. With the intent to deprive the victim permanently of the goods.

_____ 8. Individuals are protected against unreasonable searches and seizures by the:
   a. Fourth Amendment.
   b. Fifth Amendment.
   c. Sixth Amendment.
   d. Fourteenth Amendment.

_____ 9. The right to be represented by legal counsel is provided by:
   a. the Sixth Amendment.
   b. the Fourth Amendment.
   c. the Fourteenth Amendment.
   d. custom.

_____ 10. Computer crime involves the use of a computer:
   a. to steal money or services.
   b. to remove personal or business information.
   c. to tamper with information.
   d. all of the above.

_____ 11. A warrant is not required for a search by the police when:
   a. they have just witnessed a crime.
   b. they have a report from an informant that someone has stolen goods at her house.
   c. they would like to wiretap the phone of a suspected drug dealer.
   d. two of the above (a and b).

_____ 12. Violations of RICO could be considered:
   a. a civil wrong.
   b. a criminal wrong.
   c. a and b above.
   d. none of the above.

_____ 13. The rule which prohibits the introduction of illegally seized evidence is the:
   a. _mala in se_ rule.
   b. predicate act rule.
   c. due process rule.
   d. exclusionary rule.

_____ 14. How are crimes distinguished from other forms of unlawful conduct?
    a. They are prosecuted by the victims.
    b. They result in payment of damages to the victim.
    c. They are offenses against all of society and are punishable by a fine and/or imprisonment.
    d. All of the above.

_____ 15. If an employee of Risky Corporation dies because of unsafe conditions at the company plant which company officers were aware of and did nothing to alleviate, then:
    a. the officers only would be liable.
    b. the company only would be liable.
    c. both the officers and the company would be liable.
    d. neither the officers nor the company would be liable.

SHORT ESSAY

1. Indicate the various degrees of mental fault required for criminal conduct and give examples.

_____
_____
_____
_____

2. Discuss the four defenses most relevant to white-collar crimes and crimes against business.

_____
_____
_____
_____

3. State the purpose of the Racketeering Influenced and Corrupt Organizations Act (RICO).

_____
_____
_____
_____

4. Under the Fourth Amendment, a search warrant is not required in what situations?

_____
_____
_____
_____

5. Identify and discuss briefly the major constitutional protections for the accused in our criminal justice system.

_____

_____

_____

_____

Chapter 7
Intentional Torts

PURPOSE

The purpose of this chapter is to introduce the student to the law of intentional torts. The law of torts reallocates losses caused by human misconduct. A tort is defined as a civil wrong causing injury to persons, their property or their economic interests. In general, a tort is committed when a person owing a duty to another, breaches that duty and that breach proximately causes injury or damage to the owner of a legally protected interest. Torts may be inflicted intentionally, negligently, or without fault (strict liability). This chapter summarizes the general common law of intentional torts. All of the torts studied in this chapter require the element of intent. As defined in tort law, "intent" is not necessarily the desire to harm, but the desire to cause the consequences of an act or knowledge that the consequences are substantially certain to result from the act.

CHAPTER CHECKPOINTS

After reading and studying this chapter, you should be able to:

1. Define "intent" as used in the law of intentional torts and recognize fact situations where intent to commit a tort exists.

2. Identify and define the intentional torts that cause harm to the person and to the right of dignity.

3. Identify and define the business torts that cause harm to economic interests.

4. Identify and define the torts that involve interference with property.

5. Discuss the various privileges that protect a defendant from liability for defamation.

CHAPTER OUTLINE

A. Intent–Intent does not require a hostile or evil motive. It is enough that the actor desires to cause the consequences of his act or even that he believes those consequences are substantially certain to result.

B. Harm to the Person–The law provides protection against harm to the person.
    1. Battery–The intentional infliction of harmful or offensive bodily contact constitutes a battery.
    2. Assault–The intentional infliction of apprehension of immediate bodily harm or offensive contact is an assault.
    3. False Imprisonment–Intentional interference with a person's freedom of movement by unlawful confinement is false imprisonment.
    4. Infliction of Emotional Distress–Extreme and outrageous conduct intentionally or recklessly causing severe emotional distress is known as the intentional infliction of emotional distress.

C. Harm to Right of Dignity–The law also protects a person against interference with, or harm to, his right of dignity.
    1. Defamation–This tort consists of injury to a person's reputation by means of the publication of a false statement.
        a. Elements of Defamation–The burden of proof is on the plaintiff to prove the falsity of the defamatory statement. Slander is oral defamation. Libel is defamation that is communicated by writing, television, radio or the like. In either case, there must be a publication, which is communication to a person or persons other than the one who is defamed.
        b. Defenses to Defamation–Privilege is an immunity from tort liability. There are three kinds of privileges that apply to defamation: absolute, conditional, and constitutional. Absolute privilege protects the defendant regardless of his motive or intent and applies to statements made during a judicial proceeding, statements made by members of Congress on the floor of Congress, statements made by certain executive officers performing governmental duty, and statements made between spouses when they are alone. Qualified or conditional privilege depends on proper use of the privilege such as when a person publishes defamatory matter to protect his own legitimate interests or interests of others. It would also apply to letters of reference. Constitutional privilege applies to comments about public officials or public figures so long as the comments are made without malice. Malice is knowledge of the falsity or reckless disregard of the truth.
    2. Invasion of Privacy–Four distinct torts are included within invasion of privacy.
        a. Appropriation–The unauthorized use of another person's name or likeness for one's own benefit constitutes the tort of appropriation.
        b. Intrusion–Unreasonable and highly offensive interference with the seclusion of another is the tort of intrusion.

    c. Public Disclosure of Private Facts–Offensive publicity given to private information about another person is the public disclosure of private facts.

    d. False Light–Offensive publicity placing another in a false light constitutes the tort of false light.

    e. Defenses–Absolute, conditional and constitutional privilege are the allowable defenses.

3. Misuse of Legal Procedure–Three torts comprise the misuse of legal procedure: malicious prosecution, wrongful civil proceedings, and abuse of process. Each protects individuals from unjustifiable litigation. Malicious prosecution and wrongful civil proceedings impose liability for damages caused by improperly brought proceedings. Abuse of process consists of the use of a legal proceeding in order to accomplish a purpose for which it is not designed.

D. Harm to Property–The law also provides protection against invasions of a person's interests in property.

1. Real Property–Land and anything attached to it, such as buildings, trees, and minerals is real property.

    a. Trespass–Wrongful entry onto another's land is trespass to real property.

    b. Nuisance–Nontrespassory invasion of another's interest in the private use and enjoyment of his land constitutes the tort of nuisance.

2. Personal Property–Any type of property other than an interest in land is considered personal property.

    a. Trespass–An intentional dispossession or unauthorized use of the personal property of another is considered a trespass to personal property.

    b. Conversion–The intentional exercise of dominion or control over another's personal property is considered to be conversion.

E. Harm to Economic Interests–Economic or pecuniary interests include a person's existing and prospective contractual relations, a person's business reputation, a person's name and likeness, and a person's freedom from deception.

1. Interference with Contractual Relations–Intentionally causing one of the parties to a contract not to perform the contract is the tort of interference with contractual relations.

2. Disparagement–Publication of false statements resulting in harm to another's monetary interests constitutes disparagement.

3. Fraudulent Misrepresentation–A false statement made with knowledge of its falsity and intent to deceive constitutes the tort of fraudulent misrepresentation, which is also known as fraud in the inducement when associated with a contract.

F. Defenses to Intentional Torts–It is possible for the defendant to avoid liability if her conduct was privileged even though intentional. Conduct which furthers a significant social interest may protect the defendant.

1. Consent–Consent, which signifies that one is willing for an act to occur, negates the wrongfulness of the act. This is limited, however, only to conduct to which the plaintiff consented.

2. Consent to Criminal Act–Their is a split of authority with respect to criminal conduct as a valid defense. The underlying purpose of the statute making that conduct criminal is significant.

3. Privilege–Conditional or absolute privileges protect the defendant if applicable.

4. Self-Defense–The law permits a person to defend himself where time does not allow resort to the law.

5. Defense of Others–The privilege extends to the defense of third persons provided the third person possesses the privilege of self-defense under the circumstances.

6. Defense of Property–One may defend her property by the use of reasonable force, not intended or likely to cause death or serious bodily harm.

KEY TERMS

1. Tort

2. Exemplary or punitive damages

3. Intent

4. Battery

5. Assault

6. False imprisonment

7. Infliction of emotional distress

8. Defamation

9. Libel

10. Slander

11. Absolute privilege

12. Conditional privilege

13. Constitutional privilege

14. Appropriation

15. Intrusion

16. Public disclosure of private facts

17. False light

18. Misuse of legal procedure

19. Trespass to real property

20. Nuisance

21. Trespass to personal property

22. Conversion

23. Interference with contractual relations

24. Disparagement

25. Fraudulent misrepresentation

TRUE/FALSE

_____ 1. Infants are not held liable for their torts.

_____ 2. A person may be assaulted even though he is not afraid for his safety.

_____ 3. A person may be falsely imprisoned only if he is aware of the confinement.

_____ 4. Appropriation of a person's name or likeness must be unreasonable to constitute an invasion of privacy.

_____ 5. Truth is a complete defense to the tort of unreasonable publication of private facts.

_____ 6. A person may be liable for trespass to real property even though he causes no actual damage to the property itself.

_____ 7. A person may be liable for trespass to personal property even though he causes no actual damage to the property itself.

_____ 8. Truth is a complete defense to the tort of disparagement.

_____ 9. The same conduct may constitute both a crime and a tort.

_____ 10. Sexual harassment on the job is an example of intentional infliction of emotional distress.

_____ 11. Abuse of process consists of using a legal proceeding to accomplish a purpose for which the proceeding is not designed.

_____ 12. Arthur has a grudge against Bill. When Bill asks him to write a letter of reference to a prospective employer, Arthur readily agrees. He makes untrue statements in the letter, which prevent Bill from getting the job. Arthur is guilty of defamation.

_____ 13. Harold Homeowner signs a consent form to allow Dr. Bright to perform surgery on his left knee. Through a mix-up, Dr. Bright operates on Harold's right elbow. Dr. Bright has committed the tort of battery.

_____ 14. Conversion is an intentional exercise of dominion over another's real property.

_____ 15. Sarah Student is detained by a sales clerk and store manager at Marlin's Department Store and accused of shoplifting. The sales clerk is mistaken, having confused Sarah with someone else. Sarah is locked in a room and prevented from leaving. Marlin's is guilty of false imprisonment.

MULTIPLE CHOICE

_____ 1. Which of the following are principal objectives of the Law of Torts?
   a. To compensate persons who sustain loss or harm resulting from another's conduct.
   b. To place the cost of that compensation on society as a whole through a common fund.
   c. To prevent future harms and losses.
   d. a and c but not b.

_____ 2. A has committed an assault if he:
   a. aims an unloaded gun at B, tells her that he is going to shoot her, and she reasonably believes it.
   b. tells B that he is going to shoot her the next time he sees her with C.
   c. kisses B while she is sleeping.
   d. all of the above.

_____ 3. A is liable for defamation if she:
   a. tells B that C is an adulteress when C is an adulteress.
   b. tells D, her husband, that C is an adulteress when C actually is not an adulteress.
   c. tells E that C is an adulteress when C actually is not an adulteress.
   d. none of the above.

_____ 4. The unreasonable and highly offensive interference with the solitude or seclusion of another is an element of:
   a. defamation.
   b. intrusion.
   c. public disclosure of private facts.
   d. false light.

_____ 5. A is liable for trespass to real property if he:
   a. unknowingly crosses B's land while jogging.
   b. plays his stereo so loudly that C, his neighbor, can't sleep at night.
   c. tosses a gum wrapper and a cigarette butt onto D's front yard.
   d. (a) and (c) but not (b).

_____ 6. A is liable for interference with contractual relations if she:
   a. intends to interfere with the performance of another's contract.
   b. knows that her actions are substantially certain to interfere with the performance of another's contract.
   c. intends to interfere with another's prospective contractual relation.
   d. all of the above.

_____ 7. A is liable for fraudulent misrepresentation if she:
   a. induces B to rely justifiably on her false statements of fact.
   b. induces B to rely justifiably on her false statements of opinion.
   c. induces B to rely unjustifiably on her false statements of fact.
   d. induces B to rely unjustifiably on her true statements of fact.

_____ 8. Which of the following is not required in the commission of an intentional tort?
   a. A duty owed.
   b. A breach of the duty.
   c. Negligently causing.
   d. Injury or damage to another.

_____ 9. If Calvin offers Becky, an employee of Fran under a contract that has two years left, a yearly salary of $5,000 per year more than the contract between Becky and Fran, and Calvin is aware of the existing contract, he may be liable for:
   a. conversion.
   b. interference with contractual relations.
   c. disparagement.
   d. fraud.

_____ 10. The tort of conversion:
   a. includes the intentional destruction of personal property.
   b. includes the use of personal property in an unauthorized manner.
   c. entitles the possessor to recover the full value of the converted property.
   d. all of the above.

_____ 11. As used in tort law, _____ denotes that the actor desires to cause the consequences of his act.
   a. assault
   b. retaliation
   c. intent
   d. privilege

_____ 12. Arthur throws his garbage over the fence into Brian's yard. Arthur has committed the tort of:
    a. nuisance.
    b. trespass to real property.
    c. outrageous conduct.
    d. conversion.

_____ 13. In a defamation case, the defendant raises an issue involving the First Amendment to the U.S. Constitution. This is the defense of:
    a. consent.
    b. privilege.
    c. self-defense.
    d. defense of public property.

_____ 14. Which of the following is not a tort against the person?
    a. battery and assault.
    b. false imprisonment and trespass.
    c. defamation and invasion of privacy.
    d. nuisance and trespass to real property.

_____ 15. The unauthorized use of a person's name or likeness is:
    a. appropriation.
    b. intrusion.
    c. public disclosure of private facts.
    d. false light.

SHORT ESSAYS

1. What is the difference between trespass and nuisance?

_____
_____
_____
_____

2. Explain the meaning of "intent" as used in the law of torts.

_____
_____
_____
_____

3. Discuss business torts that cause harm to economic interests.

_____

_____

_____

_____

4. Arnold needs money to buy drugs, so he beats up Benjamin and steals his wallet. (a) What, if any, torts has Arnold committed? Explain. (b) What, if any, crimes has Arnold committed? Explain. (c) Discuss the differences between the civil tort action and the criminal action.

_____

_____

_____

_____

5. Discuss defenses to intentional torts.

_____

_____

_____

_____

Chapter 8
Negligence and Strict Liability

PURPOSE

This chapter introduces the student to the law of negligence and strict liability. Negligence involves conduct that creates an unreasonable risk of harm. Liability based upon negligence results from the failure to exercise reasonable care under the circumstances which failure proximately causes injury to another person or damage to his property. Negligence liability is based upon fault, but it is not based upon the intent to do something like the intentional torts. Liability based upon strict liability is liability without fault and without intent to commit an act which causes harm. Instead it is based upon the nature of the activity in which a person is engaging.

CHAPTER CHECKPOINTS

After reading and studying this chapter, you should be able to:

1. List and discuss the basic elements of negligence.

2. Define the reasonable person standard and how it is applied to various groups of people.

3. Explain and compare the duty of care which a property owner has to trespassers, licensees, and invitees.

4. Identify the defenses that are available in a tort action in negligence and those that are available in a tort action in strict liability.

5. List and discuss the activities which give rise to strict liability.

CHAPTER OUTLINE

I. Negligence–A person is negligent if he fails to exercise reasonable care under the circumstances. According to the Restatement, negligence is "conduct which falls below the standard established by law for the protection of others against unreasonable risk of harm." An action for negligence consists of three elements: (1) breach of duty of care, (2) proximate cause, and (3) injury.

   A. Breach of Duty of Care–A breach of duty of care occurs when the defendant fails to conform to the required standard of conduct established for the protection of others.
      1. Reasonable Person Standard–This is an objective and external standard which is the duty of care required to avoid being negligent. It is imposed by law and measured by the degree of carefulness that a reasonable person would exercise in a given situation. The reasonable person is a fictitious individual who is always careful and prudent and never negligent.
         a. Children–To avoid negligence, children must conform to the standard of a reasonable person of like age, intelligence and experience under like circumstances.
         b. Physical Disability–A person who is ill or physically disabled must conform to the standard of a reasonable person under like disability.
         c. Mental Deficiency–No allowance is made for insanity or other mental deficiency.
         d. Superior Skill or Knowledge–A person who is qualified to practice a profession or trade that requires special skill and expertise is required to use the same care and skill normally possessed by members of that profession or trade.
         e. Emergencies–In sudden, unexpected events that call for immediate action, the standard is that of a reasonable person under the circumstances–the emergency is considered part of the circumstances.
         f. Violation of Statute–If the statute is found to apply, the violation of it is negligence *per se*, that is, it is conclusive on the issue of negligent conduct.
      2. Duty to Act–Except in special circumstances, no one is required to aid another in peril. Exceptions include situations where special relations between the parties exist and where a person's conduct has injured another and left him helpless and in danger of further harm.
      3. Duties of Possessors of Land–The right of possessors of land to use that land for their own benefit and enjoyment is limited by their duty to do so in a reasonable manner. The possessor of land is required to exercise reasonable care in carrying on activities on his land in order to protect others who are not on the property. The duty to persons who come on the land depends on whether that person is a trespasser, a licensee or an invitee.
         a. Duty to Trespassers–A trespasser is a person who enters or remains on the land of another without permission or privilege to do so. Except for children there is no duty to maintain the land in a reasonably safe condition, but the owner is not free to inflict intentional injury on a trespasser.
         b. Duty to Licensees–A licensee is a person privileged to enter or remain on land by virtue of the consent of the lawful possessor; it includes members of the household, social guests, and salespersons calling at homes. The possessor must warn the licensee of dangerous activities and conditions of which the possessor has knowledge and which the licensee does not and is

not likely to discover. Some states have extended to licensees the same protection traditionally accorded invitees. A number of states have included social guests in the invitee category.

    c. Duty to Invitees–An invitee is a person invited upon land as a member of the public or for a business purpose. The duty of the possessor is to exercise reasonable care to protect them against dangerous conditions they are unlikely to discover.

  4. Res Ipsa Loquitur–This term means "the thing speaks for itself." It permits the jury to infer both negligent conduct and causation from the mere occurrence of certain types of events. It applies when the event is of a kind that ordinarily does not occur in the absence of negligence.

B. Proximate Cause–Proximate cause is judicially imposed limitations on a person's liability for the consequences of his negligence. In strict liability cases the courts impose a narrower rule of proximate cause.

  1. Causation in Fact–The defendant's negligence must be the actual cause of the plaintiff's injury. Under the "but for rule," the conduct is a cause of an event if the event would not have occurred in the absence of the person's negligent conduct. The "substantial factor test" states that the conduct is a cause of the event if the conduct is a substantial factor in bringing about the harm.

  2. Limitations on Causation in Fact–Unforeseeable consequences and superseding causes are taken into account in determining limitations on the causal connection between the defendant's negligence and the plaintiff's injury.

    a. Unforeseeable Consequences–The Restatement and a majority of the courts have adopted the position that even if the defendant's negligence is a cause in fact of the harm to the plaintiff, the conduct is not a proximate cause unless the defendant could have reasonably anticipated injuring the plaintiff or a class of persons of which the plaintiff is a member.

    b. Superseding Cause–A superseding cause is an intervening event or act that occurs after the defendant's negligent conduct and relieves him of liability for harm to the plaintiff caused in fact by both the defendant's negligence and the intervening event or act.

C. Injury–The plaintiff must prove that the defendant's negligence proximately caused harm to a legally protected interest.

D. Defenses to Negligence–As a general rule, any defense to an intentional tort is also available in an action in negligence, but there are additional defenses available in negligence cases.

  1. Contributory Negligence–Contributory negligence is conduct on the part of the plaintiff that falls below the standard to which he should conform for his own protection and that is a legal cause of the plaintiff's harm. In the few states where contributory negligence is still recognized, the plaintiff cannot recover any damages from the defendant. However, if the plaintiff was contributorily negligent, but the defendant had the last clear chance to avoid injury and did not do so, the contributory negligence of the plaintiff does not bar his recovery of damages.

  2. Comparative Negligence–The harshness of the contributory negligence doctrine has caused all but a few states to reject the all-or-nothing rule and to substitute the doctrine of comparative negligence. Under comparative negligence, damages are divided between parties in proportion to the degree of fault or negligence found against them.

3. Assumption of Risk—A plaintiff who has voluntarily and knowingly assumed the risk of harm arising from the negligent or reckless conduct of the defendant cannot recover from such harm. Assumption of risk is the plaintiff's express or implied consent to encounter a known danger.

II. Strict Liability—In some instances, a person may be held liable for injuries even though he has not acted intentionally or negligently. Such liability is called strict liability, absolute liability, or liability without fault. The doctrine of strict liability is not based on any particular fault of the defendant, but rather on the nature of the activity in which he is engaging.

A. Activities Giving Rise to Strict Liability—The activities that give rise to strict liability are: (1) maintaining abnormally dangerous conditions, (2) keeping animals, and (3) selling defective, unreasonably dangerous products.

1. Abnormally Dangerous Activities—Strict liability is imposed for extraordinary, unusual, abnormal, or exceptional activities, as determined in light of the place, time, and manner in which the activity is conducted. An abnormally dangerous activity is one which (1) necessarily involves a high degree of risk of serious harm to the person and/or chattels of others, which risk cannot be eliminated by the exercise of reasonable care, and (2) is not a matter of common usage. Activities to which the rule has been applied include storing explosives or flammable liquids in large quantities, blasting, crop dusting, drilling for or refining oil in populated areas, and emitting noxious gases or fumes into a settled community.

2. Keeping of Animals—Strict liability for harm caused by animals existed at common law and continues today. As a general rule, those who possess animals for their own purposes do so at their peril and must protect against harm to people and property.

   a. Trespassing Animals—Keepers of animals are generally held liable for any damages done if their animals trespass on the property of another. There are three exceptions to this rule: (1) keepers of cats and dogs are liable only for negligence; (2) keepers of animals are not strictly liable for animals straying from a highway on which they are being lawfully driven; and (3) in western states, keepers of farm animals are not strictly liable for harm caused by their trespassing animals that are allowed to graze freely.

   b. Nontrespassing Animals—Keepers of wild animals are strictly liable for harm caused by such animals, whether or not they are trespassing. Wild animals are defined as those that cannot be considered safe no matter how domesticated. This category includes bears, lions, elephants, monkeys, tigers, deer and raccoons. Domestic animals considered safe include dogs, cats, horses, cattle, and sheep.

3. Products Liability—A recent and important trend in the law is the imposition of a limited form of strict liability on the manufacturers and merchants who sell goods in a defective condition unreasonably dangerous to the user or consumer. Liability is imposed regardless of the seller's due care and applies to all merchant sellers.

B. Defenses to Strict Liability—Because the strict liability of one who carries on an abnormally dangerous activity, keeps animals, or sells defective products that are unreasonably dangerous is not based on his negligence, the ordinary contributory negligence of the plaintiff is not a defense. The full responsibility for preventing harm is on the defendant. Despite the rationale that disallows contributory negligence as a defense to strict liability, some states apply the doctrine of comparative negligence to products liability. Voluntary assumption of risk is a defense to an action based on strict liability.

KEY TERMS

1. Negligence

2. Reasonable person standard

3. Duty of care

4. Negligence *per se*

5. Trespasser

6. Licensee

7. Invitee

8. *Res ipsa loquitur*

9. Proximate cause

10. Causation in fact

11. But for rule

12. Substantial factor test

13. Superseding cause

14. Contributory negligence

15. Last clear chance

16. Comparative negligence

17. Assumption of risk

18. Strict liability

19. Abnormally dangerous activities

TRUE/FALSE

_____ 1. It is possible to be liable for injuries caused to another even though you have used reasonable care to prevent those injuries.

_____ 2. Negligence is defined as conduct which falls below the standard established by law for the protection of others against unreasonable risk of harm.

_____ 3. A possessor of land may inflict intentional injury upon a trespasser to eject him upon discovery of his presence on the land.

_____ 4. Negligent conduct is a legal cause of harm if the harm would not have occurred but for the negligent conduct.

_____ 5. A person will be liable for the foreseeable consequences of his negligence even though the actual harm results in an unforeseeable manner.

_____ 6. The law does not require one to come to the aid of another in peril.

_____ 7. A plaintiff who has proved all the required elements of a negligence action may nevertheless be denied recovery.

_____ 8. Whether an activity is considered abnormally dangerous or not usually depends on the circumstances under which the activity is conducted.

_____ 9. If a defendant's own negligence created an emergency situation, he is nevertheless liable for the consequences of this conduct even though he acted reasonably in the resulting situation.

_____ 10. A person who knowingly and voluntarily parks his car in a blasting zone has assumed the risk of harm and may not recover for damage to his car caused by the blasting.

_____ 11. The "but for" rule is a test for determining causation in fact.

_____ 12. A person with a mental deficiency will be held to the same reasonable person standard as a person of normal intelligence.

_____ 13. The possessor of land owes a higher duty of care to an invitee than to a licensee.

_____ 14. The Palsgraf case involved issues of contributory negligence.

_____ 15. The doctrine of strict liability is _not_ based on any particular fault of the defendant, but rather on the nature of the activity in which the defendant is engaging.

MULTIPLE CHOICE

_____ 1. P was injured when D drove his golfball into the back of P's head. If P wants to recover against D in negligence he must show which of the following?
   a. Breach of duty of care.
   b. Proximate cause.
   c. Injury.
   d. All of the above.

_____ 2. The standard of care applicable to a child is that of:
   a. the reasonable person.
   b. a reasonable person who is incapable of exercising the judgment of an adult.
   c. a reasonable person of like age, intelligence, and experience.
   d. a reasonable person who is mentally deficient.

_____ 3. Assume F violates a statute which is intended to protect restaurant patrons from food poisoning by requiring restaurant owners to install special refrigeration equipment. F may be sued under a standard of care based upon this statute if:
   a. A, a patron, falls down a poorly lit staircase on his way to the salad bar.
   b. B, a patron, becomes violently ill after eating tainted fruit salad.
   c. C, a patron, chokes on a chicken bone which was in his fruit salad.
   d. D, a waitress, dies after eating tainted fruit salad.

_____ 4. A is under an affirmative duty to come to the aid of B who is in danger if:
   a. A is B's best friend.
   b. A is responsible for B's predicament.
   c. A is a doctor.
   d. none of the above.

_____ 5. A possessor of land is liable for the injuries to his licensee if he fails to:
   a. warn her of a known defect which she is unlikely to discover.
   b. repair a known defect.
   c. warn her of a known defect which she is likely to discover.
   d. discover a defect.

_____ 6. A plaintiff who sues under _res ipsa loquitur_ must show that:
   a. the event which occurred would not normally occur in the absence of negligence.
   b. other possible causes have been eliminated by the evidence.
   c. both of the above.
   d. none of the above.

_____ 7. A may be relieved of liability for negligent harm to B if an intervening act:

    a. occurs after A's negligent conduct.

    b. is a cause in fact of B's injury.

    c. is a normal consequence of the situation created by A's negligent conduct.

    d. (a) and (b) but not (c).

_____ 8. In a state which does NOT recognize the doctrine of comparative negligence, A may recover from B for injuries proximately caused by B's negligence and A's contributory negligence if:

    a. B's fault was greater than A's fault.

    b. B's fault was less than A's fault.

    c. B had the last clear chance to avoid the injury.

    d. none of the above.

_____ 9. A, the owner of a dog, is strictly liable to B for harm caused by the dog if it:

    a. digs up B's flower bed.

    b. bites B when it has never attacked or bitten anyone before.

    c. bites B when it has bitten someone before.

    d. bites B when A knows that it frequently chases bicycle riders.

_____ 10. If A's abnormally dangerous activity injures B, B may not recover for her injuries if she:

    a. assumed the risk of harm.

    b. was more at fault than A.

    c. had the last clear chance to avoid the danger.

    d. was contributorily negligent.

_____ 11. Which of the following would not give rise to an action in strict liability?

    a. Storing explosives in large quantity.

    b. Crop dusting.

    c. Drilling for oil in an oil field.

    d. Blasting or pile driving.

_____ 12. The standard of care of a person who practices a profession is that of:

    a. the reasonable person.

    b. a reasonable person of like education and training.

    c. a reasonable person of the same age.

    d. none of the above.

_____ 13. Matthew negligently drives his automobile into Nancy who is crossing against the light. Nancy sustains damages in the amount of $10,000 and sues Matthew. The jury determines that Matthew's negligence contributed 75 percent to Nancy's injury and that Nancy's negligence contributed 25 percent to her injury. Under the doctrine of comparative negligence, Nancy can recover:

a. $0.
b. $2,500.
c. $7,500.
d. $10,000.

_____ 14. Zane Zookeeper is fleeing from an escaped tiger. You see his plight and wave for him to come into your house. He leaps up your front steps and slips on your skateboard which was left there from the night before. Your duty to Zane is:

a. not to intentionally injure him.
b. to warn him the skateboard is there.
c. to exercise reasonable care to protect him from falling on the skateboard.
d. you have no duty to Zane.

_____ 15. Sarah Student goes to Glamour department store to buy a dress. Sarah is a:

a. trespasser.
b. licensee.
c. public invitee.
d. business invitee.

SHORT ESSAY

1. Explain the reasonable person standard of care. When may the courts apply a statutory standard of care in determining negligence?

_____
_____
_____
_____

2. What are the elements which a plaintiff must prove in an action for negligence?

_____
_____
_____
_____

3. Discuss strict liability and indicate activities which give rise to the application thereof.

_____

_____

_____

_____

4. Distinguish between the duty of care a property owner has to trespassers, licensees, and invitees.

_____

_____

_____

_____

5. Compare the doctrine of contributory negligence and the doctrine of comparative negligence.

_____

_____

_____

_____

Part I
Sample Examination

MULTIPLE CHOICE

_____ 1. Harold Homeowner has a pet lion cub in a cage in his backyard. One of the neighbor children comes over to play. As the child is petting the animal, it nips him. The child is taken to the hospital emergency room where he receives two stitches. Harold is liable for this injury based on:
  a. negligence.
  b. intentional tort.
  c. strict liability.
  d. contributory negligence.

_____ 2. Harold Homeowner has a pet lion cub in a cage in his backyard. One of the neighbor children comes over to play. As the child is petting the animal, it nips him. Under this fact situation, the child is a:
  a. trespasser.
  b. business invitee.
  c. licensee.
  d. none of the above.

_____ 3. The federal courts have exclusive jurisdiction over _____ cases.
  a. bankruptcy
  b. federal question
  c. diversity of citizenship
  d. bankruptcy, federal question and diversity of citizenship

_____ 4. The ethical theory that holds moral actions must be judged by their motives and means as well as their results is:
  a. utilitarianism.
  b. ethical fundamentalism.
  c. deontology.
  d. ethical relativism.

_____ 5. A decree of an equity court ordering a party to refrain from certain conduct is:
  a. an injunction.
  b. reformation.
  c. specific performance.
  d. rescission.

_____ 6. The U.S. Supreme Court interprets the _____ as granting virtually complete power to Congress to regulate the economy and business.
   a. contract clause
   b. equal protection clause
   c. federal power to tax and spend
   d. commerce clause

_____ 7. Which of the following elements need not be proven in a negligence action?
   a. breach of duty of care.
   b. an unreasonably dangerous activity.
   c. proximate cause.
   d. injury.

_____ 8. The nonbinding process in which a third party is selected to help reach a mutually acceptable agreement is known as:
   a. mediation.
   b. arbitration.
   c. conciliation.
   d. consensual arbitration.

_____ 9. Authority of a particular court to adjudicate a controversy of a particular kind is known as:
   a. *in personam* jurisdiction.
   b. *in rem* jurisdiction.
   c. venue.
   d. subject matter jurisdiction.

_____ 10. The _____ protects all individuals against unreasonable searches and seizures and is intended to protect the privacy and security of individuals against arbitrary invasions by government officials.
   a. First Amendment
   b. Fourth Amendment
   c. Fifth Amendment
   d. Sixth Amendment

_____ 11. Sarah Student attends a professional basketball game with her boyfriend. When the forward passes the ball, the guard misses and the ball strikes Sarah, injuring her and permanently scarring her face. Sarah sues the team. A defense that the team is likely to raise is:
   a. contributory negligence.
   b. comparative negligence.
   c. proximate cause.
   d. assumption of risk.

_____ 12. Albert, a citizen of California, is injured in an auto accident, which occurs in Colorado and involves another car which is driven by Barbara, a citizen of Nebraska. Albert's medical expenses and property damage amount to $75,000. Albert sues in federal court based upon diversity jurisdiction.
   a. No diversity of citizenship exists, because both Albert and Barbara are U.S. citizens.
   b. Diversity exists because Albert is a citizen of California and the accident occurred in Colorado.
   c. Diversity exists because Albert is a citizen of California and Barbara is a citizen of Nebraska.
   d. The federal court will dismiss the suit, because the amount in controversy is less than the minimal jurisdiction amount.

_____ 13. For purposes of procedural due process, "property" includes:
   a. social security payments.
   b. food stamps.
   c. land.
   d. all of the above.

_____ 14. The intentional exercise of dominion or control over another's personal property that so seriously interferes with the other's right of control and which justly requires the payment of full value for the property is known as:
   a. theft.
   b. trespass to personal property.
   c. conversion.
   d. two of the above, (a) and (b).

_____ 15. Patricia Plaintiff has a case which can be brought in either the state or the federal court. Jurisdiction in the case is:
   a. _in rem._
   b. concurrent.
   c. exclusive.
   d. _quasi in rem._

_____ 16. The constitutional protection which guarantees the right to a speedy, public trial by jury is found in the:
   a. First Amendment.
   b. Fourth Amendment.
   c. Fifth Amendment.
   d. Sixth Amendment.

_____ 17. At the _____, the accused is informed of the charge against him and enters his plea.
   a. arraignment
   b. preliminary hearing
   c. information
   d. trial

_____ 18. At common law, _____ was defined as a breaking and entering of a dwelling house with the intent to commit a felony.
   a. theft
   b. robbery
   c. burglary
   d. stealing

_____ 19. The first right of the federal government to regulate matters within its powers to the possible exclusion of state regulation is known as:
   a. federal supremacy.
   b. federal preemption.
   c. judicial review.
   d. state action.

_____ 20. The Elmville City Council has passed an ordinance stating that no person of Iranian extraction shall be allowed to purchase property within the city limits. Mohammed Abou came to the U.S. as a student ten years ago from Iran. He has now graduated, works as an engineer in Elmville and would like to buy a house there. His attorney tells him the ordinance is unconstitutional and should be challenged. If Mohammed sues to challenge the ordinance, the court will apply the _____ standard.
   a. rational relationship
   b. strict scrutiny
   c. intermediate
   d. beyond a reasonable doubt

Chapter 9
Introduction to Contracts

PURPOSE

Knowledge of contract law is important to anyone involved in business, but is especially important for anyone in management. Virtually every business transaction and many of the everyday personal transactions into which we enter involve one or more contracts. Ordering something from a catalog, buying an item at a store, agreeing to work as an employee or hiring someone to work as an employee, opening a bank account, and signing a purchase agreement to buy real estate all involve contracts. This chapter summarizes the basic requisites of a binding contract and introduces the student to the sources of contract law and the basic terminology involved in contract law.

CHAPTER CHECKPOINTS

After reading and studying this chapter, you should be able to:

1. Define the term "contract."

2. List the sources of contract law and discuss their interrelationship.

3. List the essential elements of a contract.

4. Identify and define the various classifications of contracts.

5. Define the terms "quasi contract" and "promissory estoppel," and explain why certain promises are enforceable even though they do not meet all the requirements of a contract.

CHAPTER OUTLINE

A. Development of the Law of Contracts–In the nineteenth century, contract liability was imposed only when the parties complied strictly with the required formalities. Today contractual obligations are usually recognized whenever the parties clearly intend to be bound. In addition, promises are now enforced in certain circumstances even though they do not comply strictly with the basic requirements of a contract.
   1. Common Law–Contracts are primarily governed by state common law. An orderly presentation of this law is found in the Restatements of the Law of Contracts.
   2. The Uniform Commercial Code–Article 2 of the UCC governs sales of goods. A sale is a contract involving the transfer of title to goods from seller to buyer for a price. Goods are tangible personal property. Personal property is any property other than an interest in real property (land).
   3. Types of Contracts Outside the Code–The Code does not apply to employment contracts, service contracts, insurance contracts, contracts involving real property, and contracts involving patents and copyrights, all of which are governed by general common law. Real property is land and anything attached to it.

B. Definition of Contract–A contract is a binding agreement that the courts will enforce. The Restatement defines a contract as "a promise or a set of promises for the breach of which the law gives a remedy, or the performance of which the law in some way recognizes a duty." A breach is the failure to properly perform a contractual obligation.

C. Essentials of a Contract–The four basic requirements of a contract are: (1) manifestation of mutual assent, (2) consideration, (3) legality of object, and (4) capacity. In addition, in a limited number of instances, a contract must be in writing to be enforceable, although in most cases an oral contract is binding and enforceable.

D. Classification of Contracts–Contracts can be classified by their method of formation, their content, and their legal effect.
   1. Express and Implied Contracts–An express contract is an agreement of parties that is stated in words either in writing or orally; an implied in fact contract is one where agreement of the parties is inferred from their conduct.
   2. Bilateral and Unilateral Contracts–A bilateral contract is one in which both parties exchange promises; a unilateral contract is one in which only one party makes a promise.
   3. Valid, Void, Voidable and Unenforceable Contracts–A valid contract is one that meets all of the requirements of a binding contract and is, therefore, an enforceable agreement. A void agreement is no contract at all and is without legal effect. A voidable contract is not wholly lacking in legal effect; it is a contract, but because of the manner in which it was formed or a lack of capacity of a party to it, the law permits one or more of the parties to avoid the legal duties created by the contract. An unenforceable contract is one for the breach of which the law does not provide a remedy.
   4. Executed and Executory–An executed contract is one that has been fully performed by all of the parties. An executory one has not been fully performed.

5. Formal and Informal Contracts–A formal contract is an agreement which is legally binding because of its particular form or mode of expression; informal contracts are all oral or written contracts other than formal contracts.

E. Promissory Estoppel–Promissory estoppel is a doctrine enforcing noncontractual promises where there has been justifiable reliance on the promise and justice requires the enforcement of the promise. A noncontractual promise is enforceable when it is made under circumstances that should lead the promisor reasonably to expect that the promisee will be induced by the promise to take definite and substantial action or forbearance in reliance on the promise, and the promisee does take such action or forbearance.

F. Quasi Contract–This is an obligation not based upon contract that is imposed by law to avoid injustice; also called an implied in law contract. The elements of such a recovery are: (1) a benefit conferred upon the defendant by the plaintiff; (2) an appreciation or knowledge by the defendant of the benefit; and (3) acceptance or retention by the defendant of the benefit under circumstances making it inequitable for the defendant to retain the benefit without payment of its value.

KEY TERMS

1. Sale

2. Goods

3. Consideration

4. Capacity

5. Breach

6. Express contract

7. Implied in fact contract

8. Bilateral contract

9. Unilateral contract

10. Promisor

11. Promisee

12. Valid contract

13. Void contract

14. Voidable contract

15. Unenforceable contract

16. Executed contract

17. Executory contract

18. Formal contract

19. Informal contract

20. Promissory estoppel

21. Quasi contract

TRUE/FALSE

_____ 1. The law of contracts arises primarily from social necessity.

_____ 2. As defined by the UCC, a sale is a contract involving the transfer of title to goods from seller to buyer for a price.

_____ 3. A contract to provide legal services for a fee is governed by Article 2 of the UCC.

_____ 4. As defined by the UCC, goods are movable, tangible and intangible personal property.

_____ 5. Where general contract law has not been specifically modified by the Code, the common law of contracts continues to apply.

_____ 6. An informal contract is any contract, whether oral or written, that does not depend upon formality for its legal validity.

_____ 7. A contract may be formed orally or by a writing, but it may not be inferred merely from the conduct of the parties.

_____ 8. The courts will presume that the parties intended to form a unilateral contract when it is unclear whether a unilateral or a bilateral contract has been formed.

_____ 9. A bilateral contract results from the exchange of a promise for an act, whereas a unilateral contract results from the exchange of a promise for a return promise.

_____ 10. An executory contract is one in which there are one or more unperformed promises by any party to the contract.

_____ 11. A quasi contract is not a contract, but rather is an obligation imposed regardless of the intention of the parties in order to assure a just and equitable result.

_____ 12. A negotiable instrument is an example of an informal contract.

_____ 13. In certain circumstances, noncontractual promises are enforced under the doctrine of promissory estoppel in order to avoid injustice.

_____ 14. Thomas says to Steve, "If you will paint my garage, I will pay you $75," Steve replies, "It's a deal." Under these facts, Thomas and Steve are both promisors and promisees.

_____ 15. In a "quasi-contract" situation, the remedy granted will be similar to a breach of contract remedy.

MULTIPLE CHOICE

_____ 1. All of the following are relevant to defining the principles of contract law EXCEPT:
   a. federal common law.
   b. state common law.
   c. Restatements of the Law of Contracts.
   d. Uniform Commercial Code.

_____ 2. The Uniform Commercial Code defines goods as:
   a. tangible and intangible personal property.
   b. tangible personal property.
   c. land and anything attached to it.
   d. none of the above.

_____ 3. The Uniform Commercial Code governs sales in all states except:
   a. Alabama.
   b. North Carolina.
   c. Virginia.
   d. Louisiana.

_____ 4. The remedies provided for breach of contract include:
   a. compensatory damages.
   b. punitive damages.
   c. reliance damages.
   d. a and c but not b.

_____ 5. An executed contract is one in which:
   a. all duties under it have been performed by all parties to the contract.
   b. at least one party has performed all of its duties under the contract.
   c. there are one or more unperformed promises by any party to the contract.
   d. the contract is wholly unperformed by one or more of the parties.

_____ 6. Each of the following is an essential element of a binding promise EXCEPT:
   a. mutual assent.
   b. consideration.
   c. capacity.
   d. a writing signed by the parties.

_____ 7. A promise or a set of promises for the breach of which the law gives a remedy, or the performance of which the law in some way recognizes a duty, is best described as:
   a. a promise.
   b. an agreement.
   c. a contract.
   d. none of the above.

_____ 8. A manifestation of the intention to act or refrain from acting in a specified way is best described as:
   a. a promise.
   b. an agreement.
   c. a contract.
   d. none of the above.

_____ 9. A contract that is neither express nor implied in fact, but rather is implied in law is called:
   a. a formal contract.
   b. a unilateral contract.
   c. a quasi contract.
   d. an executed contract.

_____ 10. UCC Article 2 applies to contracts involving which of the following?
   a. the services of an accountant.
   b. an employment relationship.
   c. the sale of a television set.
   d. the sale of a private residence.

_____ 11. A contract in which both parties exchange promises is a/an:
   a. formal contract.
   b. quasi contract.
   c. implied in fact contract.
   d. bilateral contract.

_____ 12. A contract in which one party seeks an act in exchange for a promise is a/an:
   a. quasi contract.
   b. bilateral contract.
   c. implied in fact contract.
   d. unilateral contract.

_____ 13. A contract which fails to satisfy the requirements of the statute of frauds is:
   a. valid.
   b. void.
   c. voidable.
   d. unenforceable.

_____ 14. Bill Businessman places an ad in the local newspaper saying, "Reward: $50 for return of my golden retriever named Fido." The ad lists his address and telephone number. If Tim Teenager finds Fido and returns him to Bill, there will be:
   a. a formal contract requiring that Bill pay Tim $50.
   b. a bilateral contract, because two people are involved.
   c. an implied in fact contract requiring that Bill pay Tim $50.
   d. a unilateral contract, because Bill has promised to pay $50 but Tim hasn't promised anything.

_____ 15. The test to determine whether the parties intended to enter into a contract is:
   a. an objective test.
   b. a subjective test.
   c. an implied in law test.
   d. the reasonable man test.

SHORT ESSAY

1. Discuss how state common law, the Restatements of the Law of Contracts, and Article 2 of the UCC combine to form the law of contracts.

_____

_____

_____

_____

2. Arthur Accountant orally agrees to serve as an accountant for Clem Client in exchange for Clem's promise to pay Arthur an annual salary of $15,000. Describe this contract in terms of the following classifications: formal/informal; express/implied; unilateral/bilateral; valid/void/voidable/unenforceable; executory/executed.

_____

_____

_____

_____

3. Explain why and how certain promises are enforceable even though they do not meet all the requirements of a contract.

_____

_____

_____

_____

4. Distinguish between a contract and a gift and explain why one is enforceable and the other is not.

_____

_____

_____

_____

5. What is a quasi contract? Explain your answer.

_____

_____

_____

_____

Chapter 10
Mutual Assent

PURPOSE

For a contract to exist, the parties must have an agreement. This agreement can be either oral or written. In a bilateral contract, the agreement involves a promise for a promise; in a unilateral contract, the agreement involves a promise for either an act or a forbearance to act. In determining whether there is an agreement, it is necessary to analyze whether there has been an offer and whether there has been an acceptance of that offer by someone to whom it was made. The test for making this determination is the objective standard based upon intent as determined from the words and actions of the parties. This chapter examines the essentials of an offer, the duration of offers, and acceptance of offers. In this chapter, students must learn both the common law contract rules and the rules that are found in Article 2 of the UCC, because both rules are essential to a complete understanding of contract law.

CHAPTER CHECKPOINTS

After reading and studying the chapter, you should be able to:

1. List the essentials of an offer, identify the offeror and the offeree, and recognize when an offer comes to an end.

2. Compare the traditional common law approach to the requirement of definiteness to that found in Article 2 of the UCC and the Restatement.

3. Define the common law "mirror image rule" and explain how this rule has been modified by the Code's Battle of the Forms provision.

4. Recognize the effective moment of acceptance of an offer and discuss the effect of the means of acceptance.

5. Identify a firm offer and explain how the Code's firm offer provision differs from the rule at common law.

CHAPTER OUTLINE

I. Offer–An offer is defined as an indication of willingness to enter into a contract. An offeror is the person making the offer. An offeree is the person to whom the offer is made.

    A. Essentials of an Offer–An offer must be communicated to the offeree, must manifest an intent to enter into a contract, and must be sufficiently definite and certain.

        1. Communication–To have the mutual assent required to form a contract, the offeree must know about the offer. The offeror must communicate the offer in an intended manner. The communication must be made or authorized by the offeror. An offer need not be stated or communicated by words. Conduct from which a reasonable person may infer a proposal in return for either an act or a promise amounts to an offer. An offer may be made to the general public, but no person can accept such an offer unless he knows that the offer exists.

        2. Intent–To have legal effect, an offer must manifest an intent to enter into a contract.

            a. Preliminary Negotiations–Initial communications between the potential parties to a contract in many cases take the form of preliminary negotiations rather than an offer. A statement that may indicate a willingness to make an offer is not itself an offer.

            b. Advertisements–Advertisements are generally considered to be invitations seeking offers, because they are not sufficiently definite and certain. However, if the advertisement or announcement contains a definite promise of something in exchange for something else and confers a power of acceptance, it may constitute an offer.

            c. Auction Sales–The auctioneer at an auction sale does not make offers to sell the property being auctioned but invites offers to buy. The bid is an offer, and if it is accepted, a contract results. A bidder is free to withdraw his bid at any time prior to its acceptance, and the auctioneer is free to withdraw the goods unless the sale is advertised to be without reserve.

        3. Definiteness–The terms must be clear enough to provide a court with a basis for determining the existence of a breach and for giving an appropriate remedy.

            a. Open Terms–Under the UCC, an offer for the purchase or sale of goods may leave open particulars of performance. The Code provides standards to determine open terms and requires such specification be made in good faith and within limits set by commercial reasonableness. Good faith is defined as honesty in fact in the conduct or transaction concerned. Commercial reasonableness is a standard measured by the judgment of reasonable persons familiar with the customary practices in the type of transaction involved and with regard to the facts and circumstances of the case.

            b. Output and Requirements Contracts–Output and requirements contracts are valid under the Code so long as there is an objective standard for their application and the parties act in good faith. An output contract is an agreement of a buyer to purchase the entire output of a seller's factory. A requirements contract is an agreement of a seller to supply a buyer with all his requirements for certain goods.

B. Duration of Offers–An offeree's power to accept an offer continues until the offer terminates.
  1. Lapse of Time–An offer remains open for the specified time period. If no time is stated, the offer will terminate after a reasonable period of time.
  2. Revocation–Cancellation of an offer by an offeror brings an offer to an end. The offeror may revoke the offer by giving notice to the offeree. The notice effectively terminates the offer when it is received by the offeree. An offer made to the general public is revoked only by giving equivalent publicity to the revocation as was given to the offer. Certain limitations have been imposed on the offeror's power to revoke.
    a. Option Contracts–Contracts which provide that an offer will stay open for a specified period of time are enforceable if they comply with all of the requirements of a contract, including the payment of consideration by the offeree to the offeror, and such offers cannot be revoked.
    b. Firm Offers Under the Code–A merchant is bound to hold open an offer to buy or sell goods for a stated period not over three months, if the merchant gives assurance in a signed writing that it will be held open. The firm offer is enforceable even though no consideration is given.
    c. Statutory Irrevocability–Some offers such as bids for the construction of a building or public work made to a governmental body are irrevocable by statute.
    d. Irrevocable Offers of Unilateral Contracts–The offeror is obligated not to revoke the offer for a reasonable time where the requested act necessarily requires time and effort on the part of the offeree. This obligation arises when the offeree begins the invited performance, and the offeror's duty of performance is conditional on completion of the invited performance according to the terms of the offer.
    e. Promissory Estoppel–An offeror may be prevented from revoking an offer prior to its acceptance if the offer was made under circumstances that should lead the offeror reasonably to expect that the offeree will be induced by the offer to take action in reliance on the offer.
  3. Rejection–The refusal to accept an offer is effective when received by the offeror and terminates the power of acceptance.
  4. Counteroffer–A counteroffer is a counterproposal from the offeree to the offeror and indicates a willingness to contract but on terms different from the original offer. It operates as a rejection and terminates the original offer upon receipt by the offeror. It also operates as a new offer. A conditional acceptance is an acceptance of an offer contingent upon the acceptance of an additional or different term.
  5. Death or Incompetency–Death or incompetency of either the offeror or the offeree terminates the offer.
  6. Destruction of Subject Matter–If the subject matter of the offer is destroyed, the offer is terminated.
  7. Subsequent Illegality–If the purpose or subject matter of the offer becomes illegal, the offer is terminated.

II. Acceptance of Offer–Acceptance is a manifestation of a willingness to enter into a contract on the terms of the offer.

    A. Communication of Acceptance
        1. General Rule–In the case of a bilateral offer, acceptance must be communicated to the offeror. In the case of a unilateral offer, however, notice of acceptance is usually not required.
        2. Silence as Acceptance–Silence is usually not an acceptance unless it becomes one by custom, usage, or course of dealing. There is no legal duty to reply to an offer.
        3. Effective Moment of Acceptance–An offer, revocation, rejection and counteroffer are effective when received. An acceptance is generally effective upon dispatch unless the offer specifically provides otherwise, the offeree uses an unauthorized means of communication, or the acceptance follows a prior rejection.
            a. Stipulated Provisions in the Offer–If the offer specifically stipulates the means of communication to be used by the offeree, the acceptance must conform to that specification. Moreover, the rule that an acceptance is effective when dispatched or sent does not apply where the offer provides that the acceptance must be received by the offeror.
            b. Authorized Means–Historically, an authorized means of communication was the means expressly authorized by the offeror, or if none was authorized, it was the means used by the offeror. The Restatement and the Code both now provide that where the language in the offer or the circumstances do not otherwise indicate, an offer to make a contract shall be construed to authorize acceptance in any reasonable manner. Under this rule, an authorized means is any reasonable means of communication.
            c. Unauthorized Means–When the means used by the offeree is unauthorized, the traditional rule is that acceptance is effective when and if received by the offeror, provided it is received within the time the authorized means would have arrived. Under the Restatement, if these conditions are met, then the effective time for the acceptance is the moment of dispatch.
            d. Acceptance Following a Prior Rejection–When an acceptance follows a prior rejection the first communication received by the offeror is the effective one.
        4. Defective Acceptances–A late or defective acceptance does not create a contract.

    B. Variant Acceptances–A variant acceptance is one that contains terms different from or additional to those in the offer. It receives different treatment by the common law and the Code.
        1. Common Law–An acceptance must be positive and unequivocal. It must be a mirror image of the offer. The mirror image rule provides that an acceptance cannot deviate from the terms of the offer. Any communication by the offeree that attempts to modify the offer is not an acceptance but a counteroffer.
        2. Code–The mirror image rule is modified by the Code. The Code focuses on the intent of the parties and attempts to alleviate the battle of the forms where the buyer uses a standardized form which favors the buyer and the seller uses a standardized form which favors the seller. If the offeree does not expressly make acceptance conditional upon the offeror's assent to the additional or different terms, a contract is formed.

KEY TERMS

1. Objective standard of contracts

2. Offer

3. Offeror

4. Offeree

5. Auction sale

6. Without reserve

7. Open terms

8. Good Faith

9. Commercial reasonableness

10. Output contract

11. Requirements contract

12. Revocation

13. Option contract

14. Firm offer

15. Rejection

16. Counteroffer

17. Conditional acceptance

18. Acceptance

19. Authorized means

20. Mirror image rule

21. Intent

TRUE/FALSE

_____ 1. An offer is a proposal, expressed either in words or by conduct, by one person to another indicating a willingness to enter into a contract.

_____ 2. In order to have the mutual assent requisite to the formation of a contract, the offeror must have communicated the offer and the offeree must have knowledge of the offer.

_____ 3. A contract exists if both parties' actions manifest recognition by each of a contract's existence.

_____ 4. An offeror's manifestation of intent to enter into a contract is judged by an objective standard.

_____ 5. The UCC imposes an obligation of good faith in the performance or enforcement of every contract within its scope.

_____ 6. A contract for the sale of goods must specify the price or be defective.

_____ 7. If an offer does not state the time within which the offeree may accept, the offer will terminate upon the expiration of a reasonable time.

_____ 8. In order for an offeror's revocation of his offer to be effective, notice of the revocation must be directly communicated to the offeree before acceptance.

_____ 9. A rejection is effective at the moment of its dispatch by the offeree.

_____ 10. Under the common law mirror image rule, an offeree's acceptance will not be effective if it deviates from the exact terms of the offer.

_____ 11. Under the UCC, if both parties are merchants, additional terms contained in the offeree's unconditional acceptance will become part of the contract provided they do not materially alter the agreement and are not objected to either in the offer itself or within a reasonable period of time.

_____ 12. Under the Restatements of Contracts and the Code, unless language in the offer, or the circumstances under which it is made indicate otherwise, an offer shall be construed as inviting acceptance in any reasonable manner.

_____ 13. William, who just purchased a new computer which won't work properly, screams, "I'll sell this thing for $10", and thereby makes an offer.

_____ 14. Although an offeree is generally under no duty to reply to an offer, by custom, usage, or course of dealing, silence or inaction by the offeree may operate as an acceptance.

_____ 15. At an auction announced to be "without reserve," the auctioneer is free to withdraw the goods from sale at any time prior to a bid's acceptance.

MULTIPLE CHOICE

_____ 1. In order for an offer to have legal effect, it must:
  a. be communicated to the offeree.
  b. manifest an intent to enter into a contract.
  c. be sufficiently definite and certain in its terms.
  d. all of the above.

_____ 2. An offer can be effectively communicated to an offeree by:
  a. a writing only.
  b. spoken words only.
  c. a writing or by spoken words only.
  d. a writing, by spoken words, or by conduct from which a reasonable person could infer a promise.

_____ 3. Which of the following would be an offer?
  a. Will you buy my computer for $1000?
  b. I sure would like to sell this computer for $1000.
  c. I'll sell you this computer for $1000.
  d. None of the above are offers.

_____ 4. Advertisements, circulars, quotation sheets and other similar business communications usually do not constitute offers because:
  a. they do not contain a promise.
  b. they leave unexpressed many terms which would be necessary to the making of a contract.
  c. both (a) and (b).
  d. none of the above.

_____ 5. Whether or not a person's words or conduct constitutes an offer is determined according to:
  a. the subjective intent of the offeror.
  b. the subjective intent of the offeree.
  c. the objective, reasonable person standard.
  d. none of the above.

_____ 6. With respect to agreements for the sale of goods, the Code provides standards by which omitted terms may be ascertained, provided:
   a. the parties actually agreed upon the open term but negligently failed to include it in the written contract.
   b. the parties actually discussed the open term but intentionally failed to include it in the written contract.
   c. the parties intended to enter into a binding contract regardless of whether they actually discussed the open term or not.
   d. the parties did not intend to enter into a binding contract regardless of whether they actually discussed the open term or not.

_____ 7. Which of the following will terminate an offer?
   a. Lapse of a reasonable time.
   b. A counteroffer.
   c. Rejection.
   d. All of the above.

_____ 8. An offeree generally may cancel or revoke his offer at any time prior to its acceptance unless the offer:
   a. is an option contract.
   b. is a merchant's firm offer under the Code.
   c. contemplates a unilateral contract and the offeree has begun the invited performance.
   d. all of the above.

_____ 9. A rejection of an offer by the offeree is effective:
   a. at the moment that the offeree signs the notice of rejection.
   b. at the moment that the offeree dispatches the notice of rejection.
   c. at the moment that the offeror receives the notice of rejection.
   d. none of the above.

_____ 10. Under the Code, if two parties, at least one of whom is not a merchant, intend to enter into a binding contract but the offeree in his acceptance includes additional terms for the contract, those terms are construed as:
   a. mere surplus and are ignored.
   b. proposals for addition to the contract.
   c. terms of the contract provided they do not materially alter the agreement.
   d. terms of the contract provided they are not material and are not objected to by the offeror within a reasonable time.

_____ 11. Pat mails Trish an offer to buy Blackacre. Trish receives the offer on May 1. On May 2, Trish delivers a letter of acceptance to National Express, but due to their error the letter is not sent by the company until May 3. Pat receives the acceptance on May 4. A contract was formed on

_____.
   a. May 1
   b. May 2
   c. May 3
   d. May 4

_____ 12. Which of the following would be subject to Article 2 of the UCC?
   a. An agreement to clean someone's yard for $25.
   b. An option to buy a vacant lot.
   c. An agreement to perform at a charity fund-raiser.
   d. None of the above is subject to the UCC.

_____ 13. A leading manufacturer of electronic equipment writes a letter to its wholesale distributors offering to sell its most popular VCR for $100 and stating that it will accept orders at that price for 30 days. This is a/an:
   a. option to sell.
   b. auction without reserve.
   c. firm offer.
   d. requirements contract.

_____ 14. A merchant is one who:
   a. by his occupation holds himself out as having knowledge or skill peculiar to the goods or practices involved.
   b. deals in goods of the type in question.
   c. employs an agent or broker whom he holds out as having special knowledge or skill peculiar to the goods or practices involved.
   d. all of the above.

_____ 15. Carol Customer sees an ad in a newspaper for a clock radio at $8. She goes to the store and wants to buy the item advertised in the newspaper at the price quoted. Carol is:
   a. making a counteroffer.
   b. making an offer to buy.
   c. making an acceptance of the store's offer to sell.
   d. making an acceptance of the store's firm offer.

SHORT ESSAY

1. Distinguish between an offer and a preliminary negotiation by indicating the necessary elements of a valid offer.

   _____

   _____

   _____

   _____

2. An offer confers upon the offeree a power of acceptance that continues until the offer terminates. Identify and discuss briefly seven ways in which an offer may be terminated other than by acceptance.

   _____

   _____

   _____

   _____

3. Compare briefly the traditional and modern theories of variant acceptance of an offer as shown by the common law "mirror image rule" and by the rules of the UCC.

   _____

   _____

   _____

   _____

4. Discuss the effective moment of acceptance, explaining the means of acceptance.

   _____

   _____

   _____

   _____

5. List two situations where the Code rule differs from the common law. Give both the Code rule and the common law rule.

   _____

   _____

   _____

   _____

Chapter 11
Conduct Invalidating Assent

PURPOSE

This chapter deals with situations when an apparent acceptance of an offer and consent to a contract will be legally ineffective. In general, the law says in certain situations the manifested consent by one of the parties is not effective, because it was not knowingly and voluntarily given. In some situations what seems to be a contract will be considered to be a void agreement, or one that is totally lacking in legal effect and cannot be enforced by either party. In other situations, a contract will be merely voidable. If a contract is voidable, it can either be enforced or avoided by one party, or in some cases, either party. Some of these situations include duress, undue influence, fraud, nonfraudulent misrepresentation, and mistake.

CHAPTER CHECKPOINTS

After reading and studying this chapter, you should be able to:

1. Distinguish between duress by threats of physical force and duress by improper threats and discuss the legal effect of each type of duress.

2. Distinguish between a fraudulent misrepresentation and a nonfraudulent misrepresentation.

3. List the elements of fraud in the inducement and distinguish between fraud in the inducement and fraud in the execution.

4. Distinguish between unilateral mistake of fact and mutual mistake of fact and discuss the legal effect of each type of mistake.

5. Identify fact situations involving duress, undue influence, fraud, nonfraudulent misrepresentation, and mistake.

CHAPTER OUTLINE

A. Duress–Duress is the wrongful act or threat that overcomes the free will of a party. There are two basic types of duress.
   1. Physical Compulsion–Physical duress or coercion involving physical force or the threat of physical force renders the agreement void.
   2. Improper Threats–Duress by means of improper threats or acts, including economic and social coercion, makes the contract voidable at the option of the coerced party. This second type of duress is more common. The test for duress is subjective.

B. Undue Influence–The unfair persuasion of a person by a party in a dominant position based on a relationship of trust or confidence renders a contract voidable. The law very carefully scrutinizes contracts between those in a relationship of trust and confidence that is likely to permit one party to take unfair advantage of the other, such as a guardian and ward.

C. Fraud–There are two distinct types of fraud: fraud in the execution and fraud in the inducement.
   1. Fraud in the Execution–This type of fraud is extremely rare and renders a contract void. It consists of a misrepresentation that deceives the other party as to the nature of the document evidencing the contract.
   2. Fraud in the Inducement–Fraud in the inducement, generally referred to as fraud or deceit, is an intentional misrepresentation of a material fact by one party to the other, who consents to enter into a contract in justifiable reliance on the misrepresentation. When this type of fraud exists, there is a contract, but it is voidable at the option of the defrauded party. There are five requisite elements to fraud in the inducement.
      a. False Representation–A false representation or misrepresentation is a positive statement or conduct that misleads. Concealment which is action taken to keep another from learning a fact can form the basis for fraud. Silence ordinarily will not constitute a misrepresentation except in the case of a fiduciary who owes a duty of trust, loyalty and confidence to another.
      b. Fact–There must be a misrepresentation of a material fact; only on rare occasions will the misrepresentation of an opinion form a basis for fraud, such as an expression of opinion by someone holding himself out as an expert. Statements of value by a salesperson are generally considered to be puffing or sales talk. A statement of fact should also be distinguished from a prediction of the future. Misrepresentations of law are generally not considered to be misrepresentations of fact, but rather of opinion.
      c. Materiality–A misrepresentation is material if (1) it would be likely to induce a reasonable person to manifest his assent or (2) the maker knows that it would be likely to induce the recipient to do so.
      d. Knowledge of Falsity and Intention to Deceive–The misrepresentation must have been known by the one making it to be false and made with intent to deceive, or scienter, which can consist of actual knowledge, lack of belief in the statement's truthfulness, or reckless indifference to its truthfulness.
      e. Justifiable Reliance–A person is not entitled to relief unless he has justifiably relied on the misrepresentation. There is no fraud if the complaining party's decision was in no way influenced by the misrepresentation.

D. Nonfraudulent Misrepresentation–Nonfraudulent misrepresentation is a material, false statement that induces another to rely justifiably but is made without scienter. Negligent misrepresentation is a false representation made without due care in ascertaining its truthfulness; innocent misrepresentation is a false representation made without knowledge of its falsity but with due care. To obtain relief for nonfraudulent misrepresentation, all other elements of fraud must be present and the misrepresentation must be material.

E. Mistake–A mistake is an understanding that is not in accord with existing fact.
1. Mutual Mistake–A mutual mistake is one where both parties have a common but erroneous belief forming the basis of a contract. If the mistake relates to a basic assumption on which the contract is made and has a material effect on the agreed exchange, then it is voidable by the adversely affected party unless he bears the risk of mistake.
2. Unilateral Mistake–A unilateral mistake is an erroneous belief of only one of the parties to a contract. Relief will be granted only where the nonmistaken party knows, or reasonably should know, that such a mistake has been made or where the mistake was caused by the fault of the nonmistaken party.
3. Assumption of Risk of Mistake–If a party has undertaken to bear the risk of mistake, then he will not be able to avoid the contract even though the mutual or unilateral mistake would have otherwise permitted the party to do so.
4. Effect of Fault upon Mistake–The Restatement provides that a mistaken party's fault in not knowing or discovering a fact before making a contract does not prevent him from avoiding the contract "unless his fault amounts to a failure to act in good faith and in accordance with reasonable standards of fair dealing." This rule does not, however, apply to failure to read a contract.
5. Mistake in Meaning of Terms–There is no manifestation of mutual assent where the parties attach materially different meanings to their manifestations and neither party knows or has reason to know the meaning attached by the other.

KEY TERMS

1. Duress

2. Undue influence

3. Fraud in the execution

4. Fraud in the inducement

5. Misrepresentation

6. Concealment

7. Fiduciary

8. Puffing

9. Scienter

10. Negligent misrepresentation

11. Innocent misrepresentation

12. Mutual mistake

13. Unilateral mistake

TRUE/FALSE

_____ 1. Duress in the form of physical force renders the resulting agreement voidable.

_____ 2. Duress in the form of improper threats must be explicit in order to render the resulting contract voidable.

_____ 3. In deciding whether a threat is sufficient to constitute duress, the fact that the act or threat would not affect a person of average strength and intelligence is determinative.

_____ 4. It has generally been held that contracts induced by threats of criminal prosecution are voidable, regardless of whether the coerced party had committed an unlawful act.

_____ 5. Before one can avoid a contractual obligation based upon undue influence, there must exist a confidential relationship between the parties involved.

_____ 6. Fraud in the inducement consists of a misrepresentation that deceives the defrauded person as to the very nature of the contract being entered into.

_____ 7. Fraud in the inducement will result in the contract being void.

_____ 8. Actionable fraud can usually be based on a statement of opinion as well as a statement of fact.

_____ 9. A misrepresentation of law is usually not grounds for actionable fraud because one is presumed to know the law.

_____ 10. When parties are dealing at arm's length, silence or nondisclosure almost always amounts to fraud.

_____ 11. Justifiable reliance does not require that the misrepresentation contribute substantially to the misled party's decision to enter into the contract.

_____ 12. A contract induced by an innocent misrepresentation is actionable provided all of the remaining elements of fraud are present.

_____ 13. In a legally challenged contract between a guardian and his ward, the law presumes that the guardian took advantage of the ward.

_____ 14. Harold Homeowner went to Al's Auto Dealership to look at cars. Harold found a 1980 Plymouth Horizon that he thought would be a good car for his teenagers to drive to school. Al said, "This is the best car in town." Harold buys it for $1,000. Two weeks later, the car breaks down. Al is guilty of fraud in the inducement.

_____ 15. Bill Businessman has decided to buy a copying machine on an installment contract from the Business Supply Store. After looking at machines, Bill is in a hurry, so he signs the agreement without reading it. Later, he discovers that the interest rate is 22% and that there are no guarantees on the machine. Bill can avoid the contract based on mistake.

MULTIPLE CHOICE

_____ 1. A contract assented to by a party acting under improper physical coercion is:
   a. void.
   b. voidable at the election of the coerced party.
   c. binding on both parties.
   d. none of the above.

_____ 2. In determining whether an improper threat constitutes duress, it must be shown that:
   a. the threat would have induced a reasonable person to assent to the contract.
   b. the threat was intended by the coercing party to coerce assent on the part of the person claiming to be the victim of duress.
   c. the threat actually coerced assent on the part of the person claiming to be the victim of duress.
   d. none of the above.

_____ 3. In which of the following situations would silence or nondisclosure constitute a misrepresentation?
   a. A person fails to disclose a fact known to her.
   b. She knows that the disclosure of the fact would correct a mistake upon which the other party is relying.
   c. Nondisclosure of the fact amounts to a failure to act in good faith.
   d. All of the above.

_____ 4. The requisite elements of fraud in the inducement include:
   a. a false representation of material fact.
   b. a representation made with knowledge of its falsity and the intention to deceive.
   c. a false representation justifiably relied upon.
   d. all of the elements above are required to be shown.

_____ 5. A misrepresentation is material in which of the following:
  a. Seller believes goods are of less value than buyer believes them to be, but seller remains silent.
  b. Seller represents a fact knowing it would be likely to induce a reasonable buyer to manifest his assent.
  c. Seller knows the misrepresentation would be likely to induce the buyer to act.
  d. b or c but not a.

_____ 6. Knowledge of falsity and intention to deceive under fraud in the inducement may be shown by:
  a. actual knowledge of its falsity.
  b. lack of belief of the statement's truthfulness.
  c. reckless indifference as to its truthfulness.
  d. all of the above.

_____ 7. A package is delivered to your door and the deliveryman asks you to sign a receipt for the package. You actually sign a promissory note promising to pay the deliveryman $5,000! The note is:
  a. void due to fraud in the execution.
  b. voidable due to fraud in the execution.
  c. void due to fraud in the inducement.
  d. voidable due to fraud in the inducement.

_____ 8. The law grants relief in a situation involving mistake only where there has been:
  a. a unilateral mistake by one party as to the nature of the subject matter of the contract.
  b. a mutual mistake of material fact.
  c. a unilateral mistake by one party to the contract occasioned by his failure to read the document before assenting to it.
  d. a unilateral mistake by one party to the contract as to its legal effect.

_____ 9. In order for an act or threat to constitute duress, it needs to be at least:
  a. contrary to public policy.
  b. tortious but not necessarily criminal.
  c. a criminal act or threat.
  d. none of the above.

_____ 10. A contract entered into or induced by undue influence on the part of the dominant party is:
  a. valid.
  b. void.
  c. voidable.
  d. unenforceable.

_____ 11. Carl Contractor submits a bid that contains an error in addition.
   a. This is a unilateral mistake. Carl is bound by the error.
   b. Carl is guilty of fraud in the inducement.
   c. If the error is an obvious one that the other party knew of when it accepted the contract, Carl can avoid the contract.
   d. Carl can avoid the contract based upon duress.

_____ 12. Which of the following would be a statement of fact?
   a. This is the best typewriter for the price available.
   b. This is the one that I would recommend.
   c. This furniture was refinished last year.
   d. With a few more lessons, you should be able to compete in the regional dance competition.

_____ 13. A fiduciary owes which of the following duties?
   a. trust.
   b. loyalty.
   c. confidence.
   d. all of the above.

_____ 14. When both parties are mistaken as to a material fact regarding the subject matter of the contract, the contract:
   a. must still be enforced.
   b. is voidable based on unilateral mistake.
   c. can only be avoided if both parties agree.
   d. can be avoided by either party.

_____ 15. Which of the following would be unable to raise the defense of duress?
   a. A cowardly person who is easily threatened.
   b. A person threatened with a civil lawsuit unless he pays an agreed sum of money.
   c. A person threatened with a criminal prosecution unless he signs an agreement to pay some missing money.
   d. A person threatened with economic coercion.

SHORT ESSAY

1. Identify the types of duress and discuss the legal effect of each.

_____

_____

_____

_____

2. a. List the elements necessary to establish *fraud in the inducement*.
    b. Can the statement of an opinion constitute fraud in the inducement? Explain.
    c. What is the difference between a false statement of fact and "puffing?" Explain.

    _____

    _____

    _____

    _____

3. The Main Street Gazette and Ned of Ned's Newsstand have entered into a contract under the terms of which the Gazette has agreed to ship its newspaper, the *Morning Disturber*, to Ned, a newspaper distributor in Elmville, U.S.A. In order to sell a morning newspaper, Ned must receive the papers and have them on the newsstand by 12 midnight. Accordingly, the parties agreed that the Gazette would ship the papers from its plant in Metro City to Elmville on the Silver Streak, a train that arrives in Elmville at 10:00 p.m. Unbeknownst to either party, however, the Silver Streak's schedule has been changed effective the first date of their contract so that the newspaper will not arrive in Elmville until 2:00 a.m., which is too late for distribution. No other trains pass through Elmville and the shipment of the newspapers by truck or airplane is impractical. Ned sues the Main Street Gazette for breach of contract when the first shipment arrives too late for him to sell. Discuss the enforceability of the contract.

    _____

    _____

    _____

    _____

4. Discuss nonfraudulent misrepresentation.

    _____

    _____

    _____

    _____

5. Define *undue influence* and describe the circumstances under which it generally occurs.

    _____

    _____

    _____

    _____

Chapter 12
Consideration

PURPOSE

For an agreement to be a binding contract, there must be legally sufficient consideration. Consideration is the "price" paid to make a promise enforceable; it is the bargained for element of exchange that is necessary to make a contract binding on the parties. Generally, a promise made without consideration, which is known as a gratuitous promise, is not enforceable. This chapter discusses the two basic elements of consideration: (1) legal sufficiency (something of value) and (2) bargained-for exchange. It also discusses certain contracts that are enforceable without consideration.

CHAPTER CHECKPOINTS

After reading and studying this chapter, you should be able to:

1. Distinguish between legal sufficiency of consideration and adequacy of consideration and recognize when there is legally sufficient consideration to enter into a bilateral or a unilateral contract.

2. Distinguish between an illusory promise and a promise that constitutes legally sufficient consideration in fact situations involving output and requirements contracts, exclusive dealing contracts, and conditional promises.

3. Discuss why a contractual agreement to perform a preexisting obligation lacks consideration, why the settlement of a disputed debt for a lesser amount discharges the debt, and why the settlement of an undisputed debt for a lesser amount lacks consideration.

4. Explain the concept of bargained-for exchange and discuss whether it is present in fact situations involving past consideration and third parties.

5. Identify and discuss contracts that are enforceable even though they are not supported by consideration.

CHAPTER OUTLINE

A. Legal Sufficiency–As a general rule, a contract cannot be enforced without legally sufficient consideration. A gratuitous promise is one made without consideration and therefore is not legally enforceable. To be legally sufficient, the consideration for the promise must be either a legal detriment to the promisee or a legal benefit to the promisor. Legal detriment means (1) the doing (or undertaking to do) that which the promisee was under no prior legal obligation to do, or (2) the refraining from doing (or undertaking to refrain from doing) that which he was previously under no legal obligation to refrain from doing. Legal benefit means obtaining something that one had no prior legal right to obtain. Usually, where there is a legal detriment to the promisee, there is also a legal benefit to the promisor. The promisor is the person making the promise. The promisee is the person receiving a promise.

1. Adequacy–The requirement of legal sufficiency is not at all concerned with whether the bargain was good or bad. Adequacy is not required where the parties have freely agreed to the exchange.

2. Unilateral Contracts–In a unilateral contract a promise is exchanged for an act or forbearance to act. Since only one promise exists, the promisor gives consideration in the form of the promise while the promisee gives consideration in the form of either an act or a forbearance to act.

3. Bilateral Contracts–In a bilateral contract there is an exchange of promises. Thus, each party is both a promisor and a promisee. The promises are binding provided there is either a legal benefit to the promisor or a legal detriment to the promisee. Each promise is the consideration for the other, which is referred to as mutuality of obligation.

4. Illusory Promises–A promise that imposes no obligation on the promisor is illusory, and it cannot serve as consideration. An illusory promise can be distinguished from other promises that do impose obligations of performance upon the promisor and thus can be legally sufficient consideration.

   a. Output and Requirements Contracts–An output contract is an agreement to sell all of one's production. A requirements contract is an agreement to buy all of one's needs. These contracts are not illusory.

   b. Exclusive Dealing Contracts–An exclusive dealing contract is one where a manufacturer grants the sole right to sell goods in a defined market to a distributor. There is an implied obligation imposed on the manufacturer to use his best efforts to supply the goods and on the distributor to use her best efforts to promote their sale. With these implied obligations there is legally sufficient consideration.

      c. Conditional Promises–A conditional promise is one where the obligations are contingent upon the occurrence of a stated event. It is sufficient consideration unless the promisor knows at the time of making the promise that the condition cannot occur.

  5. Preexisting Obligations–The law does not regard the performance of or promise to perform a preexisting legal duty, public or private, as either a legal detriment or a legal benefit. A public duty is one that does not arise out of contract but is imposed by tort law or criminal law. Public officials are under a preexisting obligation to perform their duties by virtue of their public office. Performance of or promise to perform a preexisting contractual duty which is neither doubtful nor the subject of an honest dispute is also legally insufficient consideration, because the doing of what one is legally bound to do is neither a detriment to a promisee nor a benefit to a promisor.

      a. Modification of a Preexisting Contract–Under the common law, a modification of an existing contract must be supported by mutual consideration to be enforceable. The Code has modified the common law rule by providing that a contract for the sale of goods can be modified without new consideration, if the parties act in good faith.

      b. Substituted Contracts–In a substituted contract the parties agree to rescind their original contract and to enter into a new one. Substituted contracts are perfectly valid and effective to discharge the original contract and to impose the obligations under the new contract.

      c. Settlement of a Liquidated Debt–An undisputed debt is an obligation whose existence and amount is not contested. Under the common law, payment of a lesser sum of money than is owed in consideration of a promise to discharge such a liquidated debt is legally insufficient to support the promise of discharge. An early payment or a payment in a different manner than originally agreed can constitute legally sufficient consideration.

      d. Settlement of an Unliquidated Debt–A disputed debt is an obligation whose existence or amount is contested. A promise to settle a validly disputed claim in exchange for an agreed payment or other performance is supported by consideration.

B. Bargained-For Exchange–A bargained-exchange is a mutually agreed upon exchange.

  1. Past Consideration–The element of exchange is absent where a promise is given for an act already done. Therefore, unbargained-for past events are not consideration, despite their designation as past consideration.

  2. Third Parties–Consideration to support a promise may be given to a person other than the promisor if the promisor bargains for that exchange. Also, consideration may be given by some person other than the promisee.

C. Contracts Without Consideration–Certain transactions are enforceable without consideration.

  1. Promises to Perform Prior Unenforceable Obligations–In certain circumstances the courts will enforce new promises to perform an obligation that originally was not enforceable or has become unenforceable by operation of law.

    a. Promise to Pay Debt Barred by the Statute of Limitations–Every state has a statute of limitations which provides a time period in which a lawsuit must be initiated. A new promise by the debtor to pay the debt is binding without consideration and renews the running of the statute for a second statutory period.

    b. Promise to Pay Debt Discharged in Bankruptcy–Such a promise is enforceable without consideration. However, the Bankruptcy Code imposes a number of requirements before the promise may be enforced.

    c. Voidable Promises–A new promise to perform a voidable obligation that has not previously been avoided is enforceable without new consideration.

    d. Moral Obligation–A promise made to satisfy a preexisting moral obligation is unenforceable for lack of consideration. The Restatement, however, provides that a promise made for "a benefit previously received by the promisor from the promisee is binding to the extent necessary to prevent injustice."

2. Promissory Estoppel–This is a doctrine that makes gratuitous promises enforceable to avoid injustice and applies when a promise that the promisor should reasonably expect to induce detrimental reliance does induce such action or forbearance by the promisee. A common application of the doctrine is to charitable subscriptions. The Restatement has relaxed the reliance requirement for charitable subscriptions so that actual reliance need not be shown; probability of reliance is sufficient.

3. Contracts Under Seal–Under the common law, no consideration for a promise under seal was necessary. Some states still follow this rule.

4. Promises Made Enforceable by Statute–Some gratuitous promises that would otherwise be unenforceable have been made binding by statute.

    a. Contract Modifications–The UCC provides that a contract for the sale of goods can be effectively modified without new consideration, provided the modification is made in good faith.

    b. Renunciation–Under the Code, any claim or right arising out of an alleged breach of contract can be discharged without consideration by a written waiver or renunciation signed and delivered by the aggrieved party.

    c. Irrevocable Offers–Under the Code, a written offer signed by a merchant offeror to buy or sell goods is not revocable for lack of consideration during the time stated but not to exceed three months.

KEY TERMS

1. Consideration

2. Gratuitous promise

3. Legal sufficiency

4. Legal detriment

5. Legal benefit

6. Adequacy of consideration

7. Promisor

8. Promisee

9. Mutuality of obligation

10. Illusory promise

11. Output contract

12. Requirements contract

13. Exclusive dealing contract

14. Conditional promise

15. Substituted contract

16. Undisputed debt

17. Disputed debt

18. Bargained-exchange

19. Past consideration

20. Statute of limitations

21. Promissory estoppel

TRUE/FALSE

_____ 1. The doctrine of consideration requires only that the promise or performance of one party be legally sufficient.

_____ 2. To be legally sufficient, the consideration for the promise must be either a legal detriment to the promisee or a legal benefit to the promisor.

_____ 3. The adequacy of consideration is the same as the legal sufficiency of consideration.

_____ 4. A contract under which the parties' obligation to perform arises only on the happening of a stated event lacks the requisite mutuality of obligation if the specified event may never occur.

_____ 5. The performance of a preexisting contractual obligation that is neither doubtful nor the subject of honest dispute is not legally sufficient consideration, because the doing of what one is legally bound to do is neither a detriment to the promisee nor a benefit to the promisor.

_____ 6. At common law, a modification of an existing contract does not need to be supported by new consideration.

_____ 7. In a unilateral contract, each promise is the consideration for the other, a relationship that has been referred to as mutuality of obligation.

_____ 8. Words of promise that make the performance of the purported promisor entirely optional nevertheless are sufficient to make the promise binding.

_____ 9. The agreement of a seller to sell her entire production to a particular purchaser is an illusory agreement because the purchaser doesn't know the quantity being purchased.

_____ 10. In the absence of legal consideration, a promise may nevertheless be enforceable under the doctrine of promissory estoppel if the promisee has relied on the promise to his detriment.

_____ 11. Under the Code, a merchant's offer to buy or sell goods is not revocable for lack of consideration, during the time stated that it is open or if no time is stated, for a reasonable time, but in either event for a period not to exceed three months.

_____ 12. Under the Code, the modification of a contract for the sale of goods requires the furnishing of additional consideration just as required under the common law.

_____ 13. Bill Businessman agrees to buy 2,000 widgets from the Widget Corporation of America next year for $60 a widget if he wants to for his business. This is an illusory contract.

_____ 14. Bill Buyer purchased 500 pairs of shoes from Sam Seller at a contract price of $1,000. Fifty of the shoes were defective and a dispute arose as to the amount due and owing under the contract. Finally, Bill sent a check for $800, marked it paid in full, and sent a letter to Sam explaining his reasons for thinking $800 was fair. Sam didn't respond, but he did cash the check. The debt is discharged.

_____ 15. Bill Businessman has a bad day one Monday morning and signs a contract to buy a piece of real property for $250,000. Later he realizes he has been had, because the property is only worth $100,000. Bill can avoid the contract based on inadequacy of consideration.

MULTIPLE CHOICE

_____ 1. The requirement of consideration is satisfied by:
- a. a promise exchanged for a promise.
- b. a promise exchanged for an act.
- c. both a and b.
- d. neither a nor b.

_____ 2. To be legally sufficient, the consideration for a promise must be:
- a. a legal detriment to the promisee.
- b. a legal benefit to the promisor.
- c. both a and b.
- d. neither a nor b.

_____ 3. Debbie promises to pay Bill $2,000 if Bill paints Debbie's house. Bill doesn't say a word but goes and paints Debbie's house. This is an example of:
- a. a unilateral contract.
- b. a bilateral contract.
- c. a gratuitous contract.
- d. none of the above.

_____ 4. Which of the following would be an illusory promise?
- a. Sara agrees to sell her total production to Bill.
- b. Bill agrees to buy his total widget requirement from Sara.
- c. Bill agrees to buy all the widgets he wants from Sara.
- d. Bill agrees to buy Sara's total production of widgets if he inherits enough money from Uncle John to do so.

_____ 5. Which of the following is legally sufficient consideration?
- a. The performance of a preexisting public obligation.
- b. The performance of a preexisting contractual obligation.
- c. The settlement of an undisputed matured debt of $10,000 arising out of the purchase of land for $8,500.
- d. The settlement of a debt subject to honest dispute as to its amount.

_____ 6. Which of the following is necessary in order to satisfy the consideration requirement?
- a. legal sufficiency.
- b. bargained-for exchange.
- c. both a and b.
- d. neither a nor b.

_____ 7. Which of the following promises must be supported by consideration to be enforceable?
   a. A promise to pay a debt barred by the statute of limitations.
   b. A promise to pay a debt discharged in bankruptcy.
   c. A promise that has been justifiably relied on by the promisee to his detriment.
   d. A modification of an existing contract under common law.

_____ 8. A promise by Andrew to pay Barry $1,000 if he refrains from suing Andrew, which is accepted by Barry not suing is:
   a. supported by consideration.
   b. enforceable because Barry has incurred a legal detriment by refraining from bringing suit.
   c. enforceable because Andrew has received a legal benefit.
   d. all of the above.

_____ 9. A promise made under circumstances that should lead the promisor reasonably to expect that the promisee will be induced by the promise to act or forbear from acting in reliance on the promise may be enforceable under the doctrine of:
   a. gratuitous promises.
   b. promissory estoppel.
   c. waiver.
   d. *res ipsa loquitur*.

_____ 10. Under the Code, which of the following promises requires consideration to be binding?
   a. A promise under seal.
   b. A written and signed renunciation of a right arising out of a contractual breach.
   c. A good faith modification of an existing contract.
   d. A merchant's firm offer.

_____ 11. Widget Manufacturing Corporation of America contracts with the Poly Plastic Company of Wisconsin to buy from Poly all of the plastic it will need next year in its manufacturing process. This is an example of a/an:
   a. illusory contract.
   b. requirements contract.
   c. output contract.
   d. exclusive dealing contract.

_____ 12. Crime Stoppers offers a reward of $500 for information leading to the arrest and conviction of a criminal who has committed several recent burglaries. Paul Police Officer has been working on the case and applies for the reward based upon information he has gathered while on duty. Paul cannot collect the reward under the:
   a. legal detriment rule.
   b. inadequacy of consideration rule.
   c. preexisting duty rule.
   d. promissory estoppel rule.

_____ 13. Slick owes Gullible $50. Slick offers to let Gullible have Slick's pocket knife if he will accept $25 and forgive the rest of the debt. Later Gullible sues for the balance of the debt.
   a. Gullible will win because there was no consideration.
   b. Gullible will lose because he should have sued as soon as he got the knife.
   c. Slick will win because the knife constituted legally sufficient consideration.
   d. Slick will lose because he still owes $25.

_____ 14. Carl Contractor pledges to contribute $500 to the local United Fund for charity.
   a. This promise lacks consideration and will not be enforced.
   b. This promise is a firm offer under the Code and will be enforced.
   c. There is the probability of reliance by the United Fund and the promise will be enforced under the doctrine of promissory estoppel.
   d. This promise is a preexisting public obligation and will be enforced.

_____ 15. Colleen agrees to pay $10 for David's computer which is worth $300. Colleen's consideration:
   a. is not legally sufficient.
   b. appears to be inadequate but is probably legally sufficient.
   c. is a forbearance.
   d. is inadequate but the contract will be enforced based on moral obligation.

SHORT ESSAY

1. Discuss briefly what is meant by "mutuality of consideration". Define the terms "legal detriment" and "legal benefit."

_____
_____
_____
_____

2. What are the essential elements of consideration? Is the adequacy of consideration a concern in determining legal sufficiency? Explain.

_____
_____
_____
_____

3. What is an illusory contract?

_____
_____
_____
_____

4. Sam Student has just graduated from Ivory Towers University and has been offered a graduate assistantship if he wants to pursue an MBA. Big Bucks, Inc., offers him a $35,000 management position if he will move to California and begin work in three weeks. Based on this promise of a job, Sam turns down the graduate assistantship and moves to California. When he contacts Big Bucks, they say they have changed their mind and no longer need him. What recourse does Sam have? Explain.

_____

_____

_____

_____

5. Give some examples of transactions which are enforceable even though they are not supported by consideration.

_____

_____

_____

_____

Chapter 13
Illegal Bargains

PURPOSE

This chapter discusses the requirement that a promise or agreement have a lawful objective in order to be binding. Such a promise or agreement is illegal and unenforceable if the formation or performance of it is criminal, tortious, or otherwise contrary to public policy. Such agreements are properly termed "illegal bargains" or "illegal agreements," because by definition the term "contract" denotes an agreement which is legally enforceable. The chapter divides the topic into agreements that are (1) violations of statutes and (2) violations of public policy. It then discusses the effect of illegality including some exceptions to the general rule that illegal agreements are not enforceable.

CHAPTER CHECKPOINTS

After reading and studying the chapter, you should be able to:

1. Identify the statutes that frequently raise issues regarding enforceability of an agreement.

2. Distinguish between a regulatory license and a revenue raising license and explain the effect of an unlicensed person's agreement to perform services in situations involving both types of licenses.

3. Identify the two types of situations where restraints of trade typically arise and give an example of enforceable and unenforceable restraints in each type of situation.

4. Define the term "exculpatory clause" and give an example of an enforceable and an unenforceable exculpatory clause.

5. Explain why illegal bargains are generally unenforceable; then list five situations where such an agreement will be enforced despite its illegality.

CHAPTER OUTLINE

A. Violations of Statutes—Generally, agreements declared illegal by statute will not be enforced by the courts.
1. Licensing Statutes—A license is a formal authorization to engage in certain practices. A regulatory license is a measure designed to protect the public against unqualified persons. Examples are statutes prescribing standards for the practice of law or medicine. A revenue license is a measure to raise money. If the statute is regulatory, a person cannot recover for professional services unless he has the required license. However, if the law is for revenue purposes only, agreements for unlicensed services are enforceable.
2. Gambling Statutes—A wager is an agreement that one party will win or lose depending upon the outcome of an event in which the only interest is the gain or loss. Courts generally refuse to recognize the enforceability of a gambling agreement, although some states permit certain regulated gambling such as state-operated lotteries.
3. Usury Statutes—Such laws establish a maximum rate of interest; rates and application vary greatly from state to state. For a transaction to be usurious, courts require evidence of the following factors: (a) a loan (b) of money (c) that is repayable absolutely and in all events, and (d) for which an interest charge is exacted in excess of the interest rate allowed by law.
4. Sunday Statutes—Although common law does not prohibit Sunday contracts, some states have by statute prohibited certain types of commercial activities on Sunday. Referred to as Blue Laws, they usually do not restrict activities involving "necessity" or "charity".

B. Violations of Public Policy—Certain agreements have a tendency to be injurious to the public or public good and are contrary to public policy.
1. Common Law Restraint of Trade—A restraint of trade is any agreement that eliminates or tends to eliminate competition or otherwise obstructs trade or commerce. One type of restraint of trade is a covenant not to compete, which is an agreement to refrain from entering into a competing trade, profession or business. Today, covenants not to compete are enforceable if: (1) the purpose of the restraint is to protect a property interest of the promisee, and (2) the restraint is no more extensive than is reasonably necessary to protect that interest. Restraints typically arise in two situations: (a) the sale of a business, and (b) employment contracts.
   a. Sale of a Business—As part of an agreement to sell a business, the seller frequently promises not to compete in a particular business in a defined area for a stated period of time. Courts will enforce these if they are reasonable as to time period, geographic area, and hardship imposed upon the promisor and the public.
   b. Employment Contracts—Employees are frequently required to sign employment contracts prohibiting them from competing with their employers during the time of employment and for a stated period after termination. Such agreements are readily enforced during employment; after termination, the employer must demonstrate the restriction is necessary to protect legitimate interests such as trade secrets.
2. Exculpatory Clauses—An exculpatory clause excuses one party from liability for his own tortious conduct. Generally, exculpatory clauses relieving a person from tort liability for harm caused intentionally or recklessly are unenforceable as violating public policy. Ones that excuse a party

from liability for harm caused by negligent conduct are scrutinized carefully by the courts and have also been held unenforceable in certain cases.

3. Unconscionable Contracts–An unconscionable contract is unfair or unduly harsh. The Code and Restatement both limit the enforcement of unconscionable contracts. Procedural unconscionability refers to unfair or irregular bargaining, while substantive unconscionability refers to oppressive or grossly unfair contractual terms. These concepts are applied to determine the enforceability of certain contracts, such as adhesion contracts which is a standard-form contract where the preparer offers the other party the contract on a "take-it-or-leave-it" basis.

4. Tortious Conduct–A promise to commit a tort is unenforceable as contrary to public policy.

5. Corrupting Public Officials–Agreements that may adversely affect the public interest through the corruption of public officials or the impairment of the legislative process are unenforceable.

C. Effect of Illegality–In most cases, neither party can recover under an illegal agreement, because both parties are *in pari delicto* (in equal fault). Exceptions are as follows:

1. Party Withdrawing Before Performance–A party to an illegal agreement may, before performance, withdraw from the transaction and recover whatever has been contributed, if the party has not engaged in serious misconduct.

2. Party Protected by Statute–If a statute makes an agreement illegal in order to protect one of the parties, the protected party usually has the right to withdraw from the illegal agreement and to recover the money paid. For example, an investor protected by a law prohibiting the sale of unregistered securities may have the right to recover the money paid.

3. Party Not Equally at Fault–A party who entered into an illegal agreement based upon fraud, duress or undue influence is not equally at fault and will be allowed to recover payments made or property transferred.

4. Excusable Ignorance–An agreement that appears to be entirely permissible may be illegal by reason of facts and circumstances of which one of the parties is unaware. The courts permit the party who is ignorant of the illegality to maintain a lawsuit against the other party for damages.

5. Partial Illegality–A contract may be partly unlawful and partly lawful. It may be possible to separate the illegal from the legal part, and the legal part will be enforced.

KEY TERMS

1. Licensing statute

2. Regulatory license

3. Revenue license

4. Wager

5. Usury statute

6. Restraint of trade

7. Covenant not to compete

8. Exculpatory clause

9. Unconscionable contracts

10. Procedural unconscionability

11. Substantive unconscionability

TRUE/FALSE

_____ 1. The law does not provide a remedy for the breach of an unenforceable agreement.

_____ 2. In the absence of a specific statutory provision, an unlicensed person engaged in a business or profession for which a license is required cannot recover for services rendered if the licensing statute was enacted in order to raise revenue.

_____ 3. A regulatory licensing statute is one designed to protect the public against unqualified persons.

_____ 4. Sara bets Bill that Hilltop High will win the big game. This is an enforceable agreement.

_____ 5. Usury statutes establish the minimum rate of permissible interest that may be contracted for between a lender and a borrower of money.

_____ 6. An exculpatory clause is a contractual clause that exempts a party from liability for his own poor business judgment in entering into a contract.

_____ 7. If a court finds that a part of a contract is unconscionable, it must deny enforcement of the entire contract.

_____ 8. Courts, in their effort to support and uphold public policy favoring the employer's right to protect his business, uphold employment restrictions which operate against the public policy favoring full opportunity for individuals to gain employment.

_____ 9. Subject to a few exceptions, neither party to an illegal contract can sue the other for breach nor recover for any performance rendered.

_____ 10. First Bank issues a consumer loan to Happy Homemaker at an annual rate of interest of 16%. This is an illegal contract, because First Bank is in violation of state usury law.

_____ 11. Big Bucks, Inc. pays Andrew Attorney to lobby for a law that would increase its annual income. This is an illegal contract.

_____ 12. Donna is in her last semester of dental school. On weekends she cleans the teeth of her friends and relatives and then sends them a bill for $25. This is an illegal contract, because Donna is not a licensed dentist.

_____ 13. A covenant not compete is enforceable if it is reasonable.

_____ 14. The president of Big Bucks, Inc. pays a state official $500 to give the corporation's application for a government contract special consideration. This is an illegal contract.

_____ 15. Carol Customer signs a consumer purchase agreement for a VCR in which she agrees to make monthly payments. The contract also provides that if she misses a payment, she will confess judgment and pay all costs necessary in enforcing the contract without raising any defenses against the lender. This is an unconscionable contract.

MULTIPLE CHOICE

_____ 1. An agreement is illegal and unenforceable if its formation or performance is:
   a. criminal.
   b. tortious.
   c. contrary to public policy.
   d. all of the above.

_____ 2. A regulatory licensing statute is one intended to:
   a. raise revenue.
   b. protect the public against unqualified persons.
   c. prevent gambling.
   d. prevent excessive rates of interest.

_____ 3. Which of the following is not required in order to have a usurious transaction?
   a. Evidence of a loan.
   b. Evidence of money.
   c. Evidence of repayability in all events.
   d. Interest within allowable legal limits.

_____ 4. In general, an agreement not to compete with one's employer during one's employment is enforceable if:
   a. the purpose of the restraint is to protect the employer's business.
   b. the restraint is no more extensive than is reasonably necessary to protect the employer's business.
   c. both (a) and (b).
   d. neither (a) nor (b).

_____ 5. An agreement in a contract that attempts to excuse one party from liability for her own negligence is called:
   a. a clause obstructing the administration of justice.
   b. an exculpatory clause.
   c. a restraint of trade.
   d. an illusory promise.

_____ 6. An agreement to refrain from a particular trade, profession, or business is enforceable if:
   a. the purpose of the restraint is to protect a property interest of the promisee.
   b. the restraint is no more extensive than is reasonably necessary to protect the interest.
   c. the secretary of state has approved the agreement.
   d. (a) and (b) but not (c).

_____ 7. In considering whether a covenant not to compete included in the sale of a business is reasonable, courts will consider all of the following factors except:
   a. the geographic area covered.
   b. the time period for which the restraint is to be in effect.
   c. the hardship imposed on the promisor.
   d. the price that the promisee paid for the business.

_____ 8. In general, if a promise is illegal:
   a. only the promisor can sue the promisee for breach and recover any performance rendered.
   b. only the promisee can sue the promisor for breach and recover any performance rendered.
   c. neither the promisor nor the promisee can sue the other for breach and recover any performance rendered.
   d. both the promisor and the promisee can sue the other for breach and recover any performance rendered.

_____ 9. All of the following situations represent exceptions to the strict rule of unenforceability of illegal agreements except:
   a. where a party to the illegal agreement withdraws from the transaction prior to the performance.
   b. where one of the parties to the agreement is a party protected by the statute violated.
   c. where the parties are not equally at fault.
   d. where the parties are *in pari delicto*.

_____ 10. Where one party to an illegal contract is less at fault than the other, she may:
   a. enforce the entire contract.
   b. receive no assistance from the court at all.
   c. recover out-of-pocket expenses only.
   d. recover payments made or property transferred.

_____ 11. Which of the following would most likely be considered a regulatory licensing law?
    a. A state statute requiring a license to practice medicine.
    b. A state statute requiring that beauticians pass an examination and pay a yearly licensing fee.
    c. A state statute requiring that public school teachers complete a required course of study and pay a yearly licensing fee.
    d. All of the above.

_____ 12. Lucky Larson runs an illegal gambling business. Every month he pays a local judge $500 for protection. If Lucky is arrested and convicted in a trial before the same judge, and then sues the judge for breach of contract, what will be the likely result?
    a. The contract will be unenforceable because it is a violation of public policy.
    b. The contract will be enforced, because both parties are _in pari delicto_.
    c. Lucky will be able to have the contract rescinded and get back the payments he made to the judge.
    d. The judge will be ordered to pay the money to the government as a fine.

_____ 13. A man and a woman make mutual promises to marry. Unknown to the woman, the man is already married.
    a. This is an agreement to commit a crime which renders the agreement void.
    b. Both parties are _in pari delicto_.
    c. If the woman is unaware of the man's other marriage, she could pursue an action for money damages against him.
    d. Two of the above are correct, (a) and (c).

_____ 14. Ron Realtor owns an apartment complex, which he rents to low income tenants. A clause in the lease agreement states that the tenants will hold Ron harmless from any claim against him by anyone injured in the entryway or common areas of the building.
    a. This is a valid exculpatory clause.
    b. This is an invalid restrictive covenant in restraint of trade.
    c. This is an invalid exculpatory clause.
    d. This is a valid restrictive covenant in restraint of trade.

_____ 15. Exculpatory clauses excusing negligent conduct are enforceable if they:
    a. exempt an employer from liability to an employee.
    b. exempt a public service business to a customer.
    c. both a and b.
    d. neither a nor b.

SHORT ESSAY

1. Explain the "restatement" approach to illegal bargains.

   _____
   _____
   _____
   _____

2. What are the two types of licensing statutes? How do they differ in their legal effect if violated?

   _____
   _____
   _____
   _____

3. Distinguish between "unconscionable contracts" and "contracts of adhesion."

   _____
   _____
   _____
   _____

4. Briefly discuss the effect of illegality and the exceptions to the general rule.

   _____
   _____
   _____
   _____

5. Briefly discuss "Restraint of Trade."

   _____
   _____
   _____
   _____

Chapter 14
Contractual Capacity

PURPOSE

Everyone is regarded as having the capacity to enter into a binding promise or agreement unless the law for public policy reasons holds that an individual lacks such capacity. In this chapter, you learn the classes of persons who lack contractual capacity and the effect on the agreement when one of the parties to it is a member of a protected class. The classes who lack contractual capacity include minors, incompetent persons, and intoxicated persons. Most of this chapter focuses on how a protected party can successfully avoid a contract and the situations when a protected party will be held responsible for a contractual obligation despite having membership in a protected class.

CHAPTER CHECKPOINTS

After reading and studying this chapter, you should be able to:

1. List the classes of persons who lack contractual capacity and discuss the effect of lack of capacity on the contracts of each class.

2. Recognize necessary items for a minor and discuss a minor's liability for necessary items.

3. Recognize when a minor has disaffirmed a contract in contrast to when a minor has ratified a contract, and discuss the effect of a minor's misrepresentation of age on the power to disaffirm.

4. Discuss the liability of minors for torts connected with a contract.

5. Compare the liability of minors to that of incompetent persons and to that of intoxicated persons.

CHAPTER OUTLINE

A. Minors–A minor is a person who is under the age of legal majority, which is 18 in most jurisdictions today.

1. Liability of Contracts–A minor's contracts are voidable at the minor's option.

a. Disaffirmance–The exercise of a minor's power to avoid a contract is known as disaffirmance. A minor may disaffirm a contract at any time before reaching the age of majority and within a reasonable time after she becomes of age as long as she has not already ratified the contract. Disaffirmance may be either express or implied; no particular form is necessary so long as it shows an intention not to be bound. Some contracts, such as those for student loans or medical care may not be avoided. The majority hold that the minor's duty upon disaffirmance is to return any property he has received from the other party, provided he has it in his possession at the time of disaffirmance. Under the UCC, a person who buys goods from a minor and therefore has voidable title has the power to transfer valid title to a good faith purchaser for value.

b. Ratification–A minor has the option of ratifying a contract after reaching majority; it makes the contract binding from the beginning. Ratification must validate the whole contract, both as to burdens and benefits. Ratification can occur in three ways: (1) express, (2) implied from conduct, and (3) failure to make a timely disaffirmance.

2. Liability for Necessaries–Necessaries are items that reasonably supply a person's needs. Minors are liable for the reasonable value of necessary items, which may be different from the contract or selling price. Necessaries include those things that the minor needs to maintain himself in a particular station in life.

3. Liability for Misrepresentation of Age–The states do not agree whether a minor who fraudulently misrepresents her age when entering into a contract has the power to disaffirm. The prevailing view is that a minor may nevertheless disaffirm. Other states either require the minor to restore the other party to the position she had before the contract or allow the defrauded party to recover damages against the minor in tort.

4. Liability for Tort Connected with Contract–Generally minors are liable for their torts. However, if a tort and a contract are so connected that to enforce the tort action the court must enforce the contract, the minor is not liable in tort.

B. Incompetent Persons

1. Person Under Guardianship–A guardianship is the relationship under which a person (the guardian) is appointed to preserve and control the property of another (the ward). Contracts made by a person under guardianship by court order are void. However, the person dealing with the ward may be able to recover the fair value of any necessaries provided to the incompetent. The contracts of the ward may be ratified by the guardian during the period of guardianship or by her on termination of the guardianship.

2. Mental Illness or Defect–A mentally incompetent person is one who is unable to understand the nature and effect of his acts. If a person is mentally incompetent, their agreement is voidable. Under the traditional test, a person is mentally incompetent if he is unable to comprehend the subject of the contract, its nature, and its probable consequences. Such a person is liable for the

reasonable value of necessaries on the principle of quasi contract. An incompetent person may ratify or disaffirm contracts when he becomes competent or during a lucid period.

C. Intoxicated Persons–The effect of intoxication is similar to that given to contracts that are voidable because of incompetency. A person may avoid any contract that he enters into if the other party has reason to know that, because of intoxication, he is unable to understand the nature and consequences of his actions. The options of ratification or disaffirmance remain, although the courts are more strict with the requirement of restitution on disaffirmance than they are with the agreements of an incompetent person. Intoxicated persons are liable in quasi contract for necessaries furnished during their incapacity.

KEY TERMS

1. Contractual capacity

2. Minor

3. Disaffirmance

4. Ratification

5. Necessaries

6. Guardianship

7. Mentally incompetent

TRUE/FALSE

_____ 1. As a general rule, a contract entered into by a minor is voidable at the minor's option.

_____ 2. Recovery for necessaries furnished to a minor is based upon the reasonable value of the item furnished and not the contract price.

_____ 3. If a minor ratifies a contract he cannot thereafter disaffirm it.

_____ 4. Except in the case of a contract to transfer land, a minor can disaffirm a contract before attaining his majority or within a reasonable time thereafter.

_____ 5. A disaffirmance must be express and cannot be implied from the conduct.

_____ 6. Under the Code, a person buying goods from a minor has the power to transfer valid title to the goods to a good faith purchaser for value.

_____ 7. In most states, a minor who fraudulently misrepresented his age at the time the contract was entered into may nevertheless disaffirm the contract.

_____ 8. If a tort and a contract are so connected that to enforce the tort action the court must enforce the minor's contract, the court will enforce the contract and the minor will be liable in tort.

_____ 9. In order to prove that a person with a mental defect lacks the necessary capacity to enter into a contract, it must be shown that the person is permanently insane.

_____ 10. It may be possible to avoid a contractual agreement even though a person understands what she is doing but cannot control her behavior thereby failing to act in a reasonable or rational way.

_____ 11. To avoid a contract, an intoxicated person must act promptly, on regaining his capacity, to disaffirm.

_____ 12. If a minor contracts for a necessary, she will be liable for the full contract price.

_____ 13. Seventeen year old Tim Teenager has just completed a course in business law. He now wants to disaffirm his student loan agreements. Most states allow a minor to avoid contracts for student loans.

_____ 14. Under the traditional cognitive ability test, a person is mentally incompetent if he or she is unable to comprehend the subject of the contract, its nature, and its probable consequences.

_____ 15. In determining contractual capacity under the cognitive ability test, individuals who are taking prescribed medication are treated the same as those who are incompetent.

MULTIPLE CHOICE

_____ 1. Which of the following would lack contractual capacity?
   a. Bill, who is 16, wants to buy a speedboat.
   b. Sara, who has been adjudicated mentally incompetent, buys a fur coat.
   c. Richard, who is seriously intoxicated, agrees to sell his car.
   d. all of the above.

_____ 2. Which of the following would be required of a minor who disaffirms her contract?
   a. She must return any property she has received from the other party, provided it is in her possession.
   b. She must pay a reasonable amount for the use of the property.
   c. She must make restitution.
   d. All of the above are possible depending on the jurisdiction.

_____ 3. A contract entered into by a minor is:
   a. voidable at the election of the minor only.
   b. voidable at the election of the other party only.
   c. voidable at the election of either.
   d. only a above is correct.

_____ 4. In a contract for necessaries, a minor is liable for:
   a. the list price of the items furnished.
   b. the agreed price of the items furnished.
   c. the reasonable value of the items furnished.
   d. the wholesale cost of the items furnished.

_____ 5. If a minor purchases a car and then continues to use it for one year after obtaining his majority, his action constitutes:
   a. a disaffirmance of the contract.
   b. a ratification of the contract.
   c. a breach of the contract.
   d. none of the above.

_____ 6. A minor may disaffirm a contract for personal property:
   a. before attaining majority.
   b. on the day he attains majority.
   c. within a reasonable time after reaching majority.
   d. all of the above.

_____ 7. A person who lacks sufficient mental capacity to enter into a contract is one who is:
   a. adjudicated incompetent by a court decree.
   b. incompetent, although not adjudicated as such by a court decree.
   c. unable to understand the nature and effect of his act.
   d. all of the above.

_____ 8. One does not possess sufficient contractual capacity to enter into a contract if it is shown that he is:
   a. slightly intoxicated.
   b. intoxicated and unable to understand the nature and consequences of his acts.
   c. both of the above.
   d. none of the above.

_____ 9. Which of the following is (are) liable in quasi-contract for necessaries furnished to them during their incapacity?
   a. Emancipated minors.
   b. Persons incompetent but not so adjudicated.
   c. Intoxicated persons.
   d. All of the above.

_____ 10. Which of the following would constitute an effective ratification?
  a. Ratification through express language.
  b. Ratification through conduct.
  c. Ratification through failure to make a timely disaffirmance.
  d. Any of the above.

_____ 11. Which of the following is NOT true with regard to necessary items?
  a. A car can be a necessary item.
  b. A contract for medical care can be avoided.
  c. What is necessary will vary from person to person.
  d. The liability for necessary items will be the reasonable value of the items, which may differ from the contract amount.

_____ 12. When can a minor disaffirm a contract?
  a. Only before reaching the age of majority.
  b. At any time after reaching the age of majority.
  c. At any time either prior to or immediately after reaching the age of majority.
  d. None of the above.

_____ 13. Martha, who is a minor, contracts with Alice, who is an adult.
  a. Alice may disaffirm the contract at any time.
  b. Alice may disaffirm the contract when Martha becomes an adult.
  c. Alice may ratify the contract when Martha reaches the age of 18.
  d. Alice may not disaffirm the contract.

_____ 14. Hester is 95 years old and under the legal guardianship of his daughter. One day he receives a telephone call from a magazine salesman and orders 10 magazines, so he will have something to read during the day while his daughter works.
  a. This contract is valid.
  b. This contract is voidable.
  c. This contract is void.
  d. None of the above.

_____ 15. Tim Teenager agrees to fix Harold Homeowner's computer for $50. Unfortunately, Tim hasn't had a lot of experience and damages the computer beyond repair. Harold wants to sue.
  a. Harold cannot successfully sue, because the tort is not clearly separate from the contract.
  b. Harold can successfully sue under Article 2 of the Code.
  c. Harold can successfully sue, because the tort was intentional.
  d. Harold cannot successfully sue, because he was contributorily negligent in selecting Tim to do the work.

SHORT ESSAY

1. Indicate the classes of persons lacking contractual capacity and the effect of that incapacity.

    _____
    _____
    _____
    _____

2. Explain a minor's liability for necessaries.

    _____
    _____
    _____
    _____

3. Discuss ratification and how it may be accomplished.

    _____
    _____
    _____
    _____

4. Tim Teenager, who is 17 years old, shows a false ID to the loan officer at First Bank. Based upon the mistaken belief that Tim is of legal age, the bank officer gives Tim a $10,000 loan to buy a used sports car. Tim defaults on the loan two months later after the car has been destroyed in a collision. Tim, who is still 17, informs the bank that he has decided to avoid the contract. What are Tim's rights? What are the bank's rights?

    _____
    _____
    _____
    _____

5. Don, who is mentally incompetent, enters into a contract with Lucy Landowner to purchase some land. Discuss the enforceability of the contract. If Don has been adjudicated incompetent by a court and enters such a contract, what would the result be?

    _____
    _____
    _____
    _____

Chapter 15
Contracts in Writing

PURPOSE

In general, oral contracts are just as enforceable as written contracts. However, there are some exceptions to this general rule. In this chapter, you will study (1) the types of contracts that must be in writing to be enforceable, (2) the parol evidence rule, and (3) the rules of contractual interpretation. The statute of frauds specifies those contracts that must be in writing to be enforceable. If a given contract is within the statute of frauds, it must comply with the requirements of the statute to be enforceable.

In this chapter, you also study the parol evidence rule. When the parties have reduced their agreement to a complete and final written expression, the parol evidence rule honors this written document by not allowing the parties to introduce any evidence in a lawsuit that would vary or contradict the terms of the written document. There are some situations or exceptions when this rule does not apply and parol evidence is admissible. Further, the Restatement and the Code permit supplemental consistent evidence to be introduced into a court proceeding.

The chapter ends with the rules for interpretation of contracts that are found in the Restatement. These rules are a useful aid in determining the meaning of a contract. These rules permit the parties to introduce evidence if the meaning of the written words is not clear.

CHAPTER CHECKPOINTS

After reading and studying the chapter, you should be able to:

1. List and discuss the situations that fall within the general statute of frauds.

2. Summarize and discuss the provisions of the UCC Article 2 statute of frauds.

3. Define the parol evidence rule, and identify six general types of situations when the rule does not apply and parol evidence can be used even though there is a written contract.

4. Define the terms "course of performance," "course of dealing" and "usage of trade," and discuss their relevance to contractual interpretation and the UCC parol evidence rule.

5. Summarize the rules for interpretation of contracts that are found in the Restatement.

CHAPTER OUTLINE

I. Statute of Frauds–The statute of frauds requires that in order to be enforceable, certain contracts must either be in writing or must be evidenced by a written memorandum signed by the party to be charged (the one you want to sue). The statute of frauds does not relate to any kind of fraud practiced in the making of a contract but rather relates to proof or evidence of a contract.

   A. Contracts within the Statute of Frauds–If a contract is "within" the statute, it must comply with the requirements of the statute, i.e., a writing is necessary.
      1. Suretyship Provision–A suretyship is a promise to pay the debts of another. The surety is the person who promises to pay the debts of another. The principal debtor is the person whose debt is being supported. The suretyship provision applies to a contractual promise by a surety (the promisor) to a creditor (the promisee) to perform the duties or obligations of a third person (the principal debtor) if the principal debtor does not perform.
         a. Original Promise–If the promisor makes an original promise by undertaking to become primarily liable, then the statute of frauds does not apply. This provision of the statute only applies to a collateral promise. A collateral promise is an undertaking to be secondarily liable, that is, liable if the principle debtor does not perform. "If X doesn't pay, I will," is collateral, because the promisor is not the one who is primarily liable. An original promise (one to become primarily liable) is not collateral.
         b. Main Purpose Doctrine–This is an exception that the courts have developed to the suretyship provision. It is also known as the leading object rule. If the main purpose or object of the promisor/surety is to provide an economic benefit to herself, then the promise comes within the exception and is outside the statute, i.e., no writing is necessary to enforce the promise against the promisor.
         c. Promise Made to Debtor–Courts have interpreted the suretyship provision NOT to include promises made to the debtor. A promise made to a debtor is enforceable without writing.
      2. Executor–Administrator Provision–An executor or administrator is a person appointed to settle a decedent's estate. If an executor or administrator promises to answer personally for a duty of the decedent, the promise is unenforceable unless in writing. This provision is a specific application of the suretyship provision.
      3. Marriage Provision–The marriage provision does NOT apply to mutual promises to marry. It applies if a promise to marry is made in consideration of some other promise, such as where a man or his parents promise a woman to convey title to property if she marries him.

4. Land Contract Provision–An interest in land is any right, privilege, power or immunity in real property. It includes ownership interests in land, leases, mortgages, options and easements. Under this provision, a promise to transfer an interest in land must be in writing. However, under the part performance exception, if the transferee has paid a portion or all of the purchase price and either taken possession of the real estate or started to make valuable improvements on the land in reasonable reliance on the contract, an oral contract may be enforced.

5. One Year Provision–The statute of frauds requires that all contracts that cannot be fully performed within one year of the making of the contract must be in writing.
    a. The Possibility Test–The test for whether a contract is within the one-year provision is whether it is possible, under the terms of the contract, for the agreement to be performed within one year; the test is not whether it is likely to be performed within one year from its formation.
    b. Computation of Time–The year runs from the time the agreement is made, not from when the performance is to begin.
    c. Full Performance by One Party–When one party has fully performed, most courts hold that the promise of the other party is enforceable even if performance was not possible within one year.

6. Sales of Goods–The UCC provides that a contract for the sale of goods for the price of $500 or more is not enforceable without a writing.
    a. Admission–The Code permits an oral contract for the sale of goods to be enforced against a party who in his pleading, testimony, or otherwise in court admits that a contract was made, but limits enforcement to the quantity of goods he admits.
    b. Specially Manufactured Goods–The Code permits enforcement of an oral contract for goods specially manufactured for a buyer which cannot be readily resold in the ordinary course of the seller's business.
    c. Delivery or Payment and Acceptance–Under the Code, delivery and acceptance of part of the goods or payment and acceptance of part of the price validates the oral contract.

7. Modification or Rescission of Contracts within the Statute of Frauds–Oral contracts modifying existing contracts are unenforceable if the resulting contract is within the statute of frauds.

B. Compliance with the Statute of Frauds–Even though a contract is within the statute of frauds, it will be enforced if there is a sufficient writing or memorandum which complies with the requirements of the statute.

1. General Contract Provisions–The general statutes require that the writing (1) specify the parties to the contract; (2) specify the subject matter and essential terms of the unperformed promises; and (3) be signed by the party to be charged or her agent. The note or memorandum may be formal or informal. The signature may be by initials, printed, or typewritten, and need not be at the bottom of the page. A personal letter or handwritten note would suffice. It may consist of several papers, none of which would be sufficient by itself.

2. Sale of Goods–The Article 2 statute of frauds provision is more liberal. It requires merely a writing (a) sufficient to indicate that a contract has been made between the parties; (b) signed by the party against whom enforcement is sought or by her authorized agent or broker; and (c) specifying the quantity of goods to be sold.

C. Effects of Noncompliance–The oral contract is unenforceable.
   1. Full Performance–After all the promises of an oral contract have been performed by all parties, the statute of frauds no longer applies.
   2. Restitution–If a party to a contract that is unenforceable because of the statute of frauds has acted in reliance upon the contract, the party may recover in restitution the benefits conferred upon the other.
   3. Promissory Estoppel–Oral contracts within the statute of frauds have been enforced where the party seeking enforcement has reasonably and foreseeably relied upon a promise, and injustice can only be avoided by enforcement of the promise.

II. Parol Evidence Rule–Neither party to a written contract is later permitted to show that the contract they made is different from the terms and provisions that appear in the written agreement.

A. The Rule–When a contract is expressed in a writing that is intended to be the complete and final expression of the rights and duties of the parties, the parol evidence rule, which also applies to wills and deeds, excludes prior oral or written negotiations or agreements of the parties or their contemporaneous oral agreements that vary or change the integrated written contract.

B. Situations to Which the Rule Does Not Apply–The rule is considered to be a substantive rule of law that defines the limits of a contract. It does not apply to the following situations: (1) a contract that is partly written and partly oral; (2) a clerical or typographical error that obviously does not represent the agreement of the parties; (3) the lack of contractual capacity of one of the parties, such as proof of minority, intoxication, or mental incompetency; (4) a defense of fraud, misrepresentation, duress, undue influence, mistake, illegality, lack of consideration, or other invalidating cause; (5) a condition precedent that was orally agreed upon at the time of the contract's execution and to which the entire agreement was made subject; and (6) a subsequent mutual rescission or modification of the contract.

C. Supplemental Evidence–Under the Restatement and the Code, a written contract may be explained or supplemented by course of dealing, usage of trade, course of performance or evidence of consistent additional terms. A course of dealing is a sequence of previous conduct between the parties that establishes a common basis for understanding. A usage of trade is a practice or method of dealing regularly observed and followed in a place, vocation or trade. Course of performance is the manner and extent to which the respective parties have accepted successive tenders of performance by the other party without objection. Supplemental consistent evidence is admissible if it does not contradict the terms of the original agreement and would probably not have been included in the original contract.

III. Interpretation of Contracts–The Restatement defines interpretation as the ascertainment of the meaning of a promise or agreement or a term of the promise or agreement. Rules for interpretation include: (1) all the circumstances are considered and the principal purpose of the parties is given great weight; (2) a writing is interpreted as a whole; (3) commonly accepted meanings are used unless a different intention is manifested; (4) technical terms are given their technical meaning; (5) wherever possible, the intentions of the parties are interpreted as consistent with each other and with course of performance, course of dealing or usage of trade; (6) an interpretation that gives a reasonable, lawful, and effective meaning to all terms is preferred; (7) specific terms are given greater weight than general language; (8) separately negotiated terms are given greater weight than standardized terms or those not separately negotiated; (9) the order for interpretation is express terms, course of performance, course of dealing and usage of trade; and (10) where a term has several possible meanings, the term will be interpreted against the party who supplied the contract or term; (11) written provisions prevail over typed or printed provisions, and typed provisions prevail over printed; (12) if an amount payable is set forth in conflicting words and figures, the words control the figures.

KEY TERMS

1. Statute of frauds

2. Suretyship

3. Surety

4. Collateral promise

5. Main purpose doctrine

6. Parol evidence rule

7. Integrated contract

8. Course of dealing

9. Usage of trade

10. Course of performance

TRUE/FALSE

_____ 1. It is optional with the parties, under the statute of frauds, whether to reduce their agreement to writing.

_____ 2. The statute of frauds does not relate to the circumstances surrounding the making of a contract or to the validity of a contract.

_____ 3. A promise to a creditor to perform the duties and obligations of a third party is "collateral" and therefore subject to the statute of frauds when the promise is to pay only upon the default of the one primarily obligated.

_____ 4. Where the "main purpose" of the promisor is to obtain an economic benefit for herself that she did not previously have, the promise is outside the statute, and need not be in writing to be enforceable.

_____ 5. The most important aspect of the "marriage provision" pertains to mutual promises to marry.

_____ 6. The UCC provides that a contract for the sale of goods for the price of $500 or more must satisfy the requirements of the statute of frauds.

_____ 7. In order to comply with the requirements of most statute of frauds, the writing or memorandum must be signed by both parties to the agreement.

_____ 8. The parol evidence rule applies to all integrated written contracts and deals with what terms are part of the contract.

_____ 9. The parol evidence rule is a rule of evidence that prohibits the parties from subsequently orally modifying their written contract.

_____ 10. Rules of contractual interpretation are incorporated within the statute of frauds.

_____ 11. A writing must be signed by both parties in order to meet the memorandum requirement of the statute of frauds.

_____ 12. A course of dealing is a practice or method of dealing regularly observed and followed in a place, vocation or trade.

_____ 13. Under the parol evidence rule, words can be introduced in court which vary or contradict the terms of an integrated contract.

_____ 14. Under the "main purpose rule," an oral contract which would ordinarily require a writing can be enforced.

_____ 15. The parol evidence rule does not apply to parol evidence which is used to show a subsequent mutual rescission of a contract.

MULTIPLE CHOICE

_____ 1. The following promises or contracts are within the statute of frauds EXCEPT:
   a. the promise of an executor or administrator that he personally will pay all of the decedent's creditors in full.
   b. a promise to marry made in consideration for some promise other than a reciprocal promise to marry.
   c. a promise made by a father to his son by which the father will pay the son's debt in the event of his son's default.
   d. a promise made by a father to his son's creditor to pay the son's debt in the event of his son's default.

_____ 2. Which of the following contracts are within the statute of frauds and therefore must meet its requirements in order to be enforceable:
   a. a contract to sell one-half acre lots of land in a 60 acre lot subdivision.
   b. a six month lease of an apartment.
   c. a deed granting an easement.
   d. a and c above.

_____ 3. In a contract for the sale of goods costing more than $500, the statute of frauds provisions apply except:
   a. where an admission has been made.
   b. where the goods have been specially manufactured.
   c. where there has been a delivery of and payment for the goods.
   d. all the above are exceptions to statute of frauds provisions.

_____ 4. All of the following are required of a writing to satisfy the requirements of the general statute of frauds EXCEPT:
   a. it must be signed by the party to be charged or his agent.
   b. it must be signed by the party seeking to enforce the contract or his agent.
   c. it must specify the parties to the contract.
   d. it must specify with reasonable certainty the subject matter of the unperformed promises as well as their essential terms.

_____ 5. Under the statute of frauds provision of the UCC, if a writing that is otherwise sufficient incorrectly states the quantity term agreed upon by the parties, the contract is:
   a. unenforceable.
   b. enforceable, but only to the extent of the quantity of goods stated in the writing.
   c. enforceable to the extent of the quantity term orally agreed upon by the parties.
   d. enforceable to the extent determined by the court to be fair and reasonable at the time of enforcement of the contract.

_____ 6. By an oral agreement entered into on January 1, 1995, A hires B to work for eleven months starting on February 1, 1995. This contract is:
   a. enforceable because B is to work for only eleven months.
   b. enforceable because this contract is outside the statute of frauds.
   c. unenforceable because it cannot be performed within one year.
   d. a and b above.

_____ 7. If a contract is expressed in a writing that is intended by the parties to be the complete and final expression of their rights and duties under the contract, the parol evidence rule precludes the admission into evidence of all of the following EXCEPT:
   a. prior oral negotiations or agreements of the parties.
   b. prior written negotiations of the parties.
   c. a subsequent oral agreement between the parties to modify the terms of the contract.
   d. a contemporaneous oral agreement between the parties that varies or changes the written contract.

_____ 8. The parol evidence will bar the introduction of:
   a. evidence that one of the parties to the contract was a minor.
   b. evidence of fraud in the formation of the contract.
   c. evidence of usage and custom that is not inconsistent with the terms of the written agreement.
   d. evidence of a letter written prior to the execution of the final contract stating that the price to be charged for the goods was $2.00 each rather than $2.10 as provided in the final contract.

_____ 9. A party seeking to introduce evidence of a subsequent oral agreement modifying a written employment contract from 2 to 3 years would be:
   a. admissible under both the statute of frauds and the parol evidence rule.
   b. inadmissible because of the statute of frauds.
   c. inadmissible because of the parol evidence rule.
   d. inadmissible because of both the parol evidence rule and the statute of frauds.

_____ 10. Which of the following is not a rule of contract interpretation?
   a. Words and other conduct are interpreted in light of all the circumstances, and if the principal purpose is ascertainable, it is given greater weight.
   b. Unless a different intention is manifested, technical terms and words of art are given their technical meaning.
   c. Express terms, usage of trade, course of dealing and course of performance are weighed in that order.
   d. Separately negotiated or added terms are given greater weight than standardized terms or other terms not separately negotiated.

_____ 11. Arthur writes a letter to Bob in which he promises to pay Clark's debts if Clark doesn't pay.
   a. Arthur's promise is a primary promise.
   b. Arthur's promise is an original promise.
   c. Arthur's promise is a collateral promise.
   d. Arthur's promise falls within the main purpose doctrine.

_____ 12. Which of the following contracts need not be in writing to be enforced?
   a. Arthur agrees to buy Bob's house for $60,000.
   b. Clara's Aunt Amanda promises Clara $1,000 if she will marry Brad.
   c. Bill Buyer agrees to buy $450 in goods from Sam Seller.
   d. Oscar agrees to work for Big Bucks, Inc., for 2 years beginning June 1.

_____ 13. Which of the following would constitute an exception to the statute of frauds?
   a. Oral evidence of fraud is offered.
   b. The contract has been partially performed.
   c. The contract was completed within one year.
   d. The contract is partly oral and partly written.

_____ 14. Which of the following would meet the signature requirement of the statute of frauds?
   a. Big Bucks, Inc., signs a contract with a signature stamp.
   b. Bill Buyer has a printed acceptance of an order form which contains the name of Sam Seller showing receipt of an order for 200 widgets at a price of $600.
   c. Arthur types his initials at the bottom of a written memorandum.
   d. All of the above meet the signature requirement.

_____ 15. In order for a note or memorandum to satisfy the requirements of the statute of frauds it must:
   a. be in existence at the time of litigation.
   b. be signed by the party to be charged or by her agent.
   c. specify the parties to the contract.
   d. b and c but not a.

SHORT ESSAY

1. Identify five situations which fall within the statute of frauds.

_____

_____

_____

_____

2. Identify two instances in which a contract to transfer an interest in land need not be in writing, and give an example of each.

_____

_____

_____

_____

3. Compare the requirements for a writing to comply with the general statute of frauds and the UCC version. Which is easier to satisfy? Why? List three alternative methods of compliance with the UCC version.

_____

_____

_____

_____

4. Identify six situations to which the parol evidence rule does not apply.

_____

_____

_____

_____

5. Big Bucks, Inc. hires Betty as director of personnel under a two-year employment contract. After six months, the president of Big Bucks and Betty orally agree to modify her existing contract including a change in salary and job description. Discuss the enforceability of the oral contract modifying the existing contract.

_____

_____

_____

_____

Chapter 16
Third Parties to Contracts

PURPOSE

In prior chapters, you studied contracts that involved only two parties. In this chapter, you study the rights and duties of third parties who are not parties to the contract, but who have rights or duties under the contract. These rights or duties arise by (1) an assignment of the rights of a party to the contract, (2) a delegation of the duties of a party to the contract, or (3) the express terms of a contract entered into for the benefit of a third person.

The early common law placed a great deal of emphasis on privity of contract. Because of this principle, under ordinary circumstances, only the original parties to a contract may bring an action to enforce it in the event of a breach. However, today third party beneficiaries and assignees are frequently allowed to enforce a contract against the original parties. With some exceptions, a party to a contract today can assign her rights or delegate her duties to a third party.

CHAPTER CHECKPOINTS

After reading and studying the chapter, you should be able to:

1. Distinguish between an assignment of rights and a delegation of duties, and identify situations when assignments and delegations are not permitted by the law.

2. Recognize the assignor, the assignee, the delegator, the delegatee, the obligor and the obligee in various fact situations.

3. Discuss the majority rule, the minority rule and the Restatement rule for situations involving successive assignments of the same right and the priorities of assignee claimants.

4. Distinguish third-party beneficiary contracts and novations from assignments and delegations.

5. Identify intended donee beneficiaries, intended creditor beneficiaries, and incidental beneficiaries, and discuss the relative rights of each in enforcing a contract.

CHAPTER OUTLINE

A. Assignment of Rights–An assignment is the voluntary transfer to a third party of the rights arising from a contract. The assignor is the party making an assignment. The assignee is the party to whom the contract rights are assigned. An obligor is a party who owes a duty under a contract, while an obligee is a party to whom a duty is owed under a contract. The delegation of a duty is the transfer to a third party of a contractual obligation. The delegator is the party who delegates his duty to a third party. The delegatee is a third party to whom the delegator's duty is delegated. The obligee is the party to whom a duty of performance is owed under a contract.

1. Law Governing Assignments–The law governing assignments arises primarily from the common law of contracts and U.C.C. articles 2 and 9.

2. Requirements of an Assignment–The Restatement defines an assignment as a manifestation of the assignor's intention to transfer a contract right such that the assignor's right to performance is extinguished. Although no special form or words are needed to create an assignment, the UCC imposes a writing requirement on all assignments beyond $5000.00. No consideration is necessary to make an assignment effective.

    a. Revocability of Assignments–If the assignee gives consideration in exchange for the assignment, then there is a contract. The assignor may not revoke the assignment without the assent of the assignee. If the assignment is gratuitous, it is revocable by the assignor and is terminated by the assignor's death, incapacity, or subsequent assignment, unless effective delivery has been made.

    b. Partial Assignments–A partial assignment is a transfer of a portion of the contractual rights to one or more assignees.

3. Rights that are Assignable–Most contract rights are assignable. The right to the payment of money is the most common contractual right that may be assigned.

4. Rights that are Not Assignable–Some contract rights are not assignable.

    a. Assignments that Materially Increase the Duty, Risk or Burden–An assignment is ineffective where performance by the obligor to the assignee would be materially different from performance to the assignor, such as an automobile liability insurance policy.

    b. Assignments of Personal Rights–Where the rights under a contract are of a highly personal nature they cannot be assigned. An example would be an agreement of two persons to marry one another.

    c. Express Prohibition against Assignment–The Restatement and Article 2 of the Code say that unless circumstances indicate the contrary, a prohibition of assignment will be construed as barring only the delegation to the assignee of the assignor's duty of performance and not the assignment of rights.

      d. Assignments Prohibited by Law–Federal and state statutes prohibit or regulate certain assignments such as those of the right to future wages.

  5. Rights of the Assignee

      a. Obtains Rights of Assignor–The assignee stands in the shoes of the assignor, but acquires no new rights. He takes the assigned right with all of the defenses, defects, and infirmities that the obligor would have against the assignor. The obligor may assert rights of setoff or counterclaim. Waivers of rights against assignees are valid under the Code, but the FTC has invalidated them in consumer credit transactions.

      b. Notice–A valid assignment does not require that notice be given to the obligor, however, such notice is advisable because an assignee will lose his rights against the obligor if the obligor pays the assignor without notice of the assignment.

  6. Implied Warranties of Assignor–Four implied warranties are imposed by law upon the transferor of contract rights. The four warranties are (1) that he will do nothing to defeat or impair the assignment; (2) that the assigned right actually exists and is subject to no limitations or defenses other than those stated; (3) that any writing evidencing the right is genuine; and (4) that he has no knowledge of any fact that would impair the value of the assignment.

  7. Express Warranties of Assignor–The assignor is further bound by any explicitly made contractual promises regarding the contract rights transferred.

  8. Successive Assignments of the Same Right–The majority rule in the U.S. is that the first assignee in point of time prevails over later assignees. In England and a minority of states, the first assignee to notify the obligor prevails.

B. Delegation of Duties–Duties are not assignable, but their performance may be delegated to a third person. A delegation of duties is a transfer to a third party of a contractual obligation. It does not extinguish the delegator's obligation to perform. When the delegatee accepts the delegated duty, both the delegator and the delegatee are liable for performance of the duty to the obligee.

  1. Delegable Duties–Contractual duties are generally delegable, however, a delegation will not be permitted if (1) the nature of the duties are personal; (2) the performance is expressly made non-delegable; or (3) the delegation is prohibited by statute or public policy.

  2. Duties of the Parties–When there has been a delegation of duties and an assumption of the delegated duties, both the delegator and the delegatee are liable to the obligee for proper performance of the original contractual duty. If the delegator desires to be discharged of the duty, he may enter into a novation which is an agreement obtaining the consent of the obligee to substitute a third person in his place. The delegator is then discharged and the third party is bound to the obligee.

C. Third-Party Beneficiary Contracts–Third-party beneficiary contracts are contracts in which one party promises to render performance to a third person.

  1. Intended Beneficiary–An intended beneficiary is a third party intended by the two contracting parties to receive a benefit from their contract.

      a. Donee Beneficiary–A third party is an intended donee beneficiary if the promisee's purpose in bargaining for and obtaining the agreement was to make a gift to the beneficiary. An example is the beneficiary of a life insurance policy.

b. Creditor Beneficiary–A third person is an intended creditor beneficiary if the promisee intends the performance of the promise to satisfy a legal duty owed to the beneficiary, who is a creditor of the promisee.

c. Rights of Intended Beneficiary–An intended donee beneficiary may enforce the contract against the promisor only. An intended creditor beneficiary may sue either or both parties.

d. Vesting of Rights–A contract for the benefit of an intended beneficiary confers rights that the beneficiary may enforce. Until the rights vest, however, the promisor and promisee may vary or completely discharge these rights. There is considerable variation among the states as to when vesting takes place. These views include: (1) immediately upon making the contract, (2) when the third party learns of the contract and assents to it, and (3) when the third party changes his position in reliance upon the promise made for his benefit.

2. Incidental Beneficiaries–An incidental beneficiary is one whom the parties to a contract did not intend to benefit, but who nevertheless would derive some benefit from its performance. Incidental beneficiaries have no rights under a contract.

KEY TERMS

1. Obligor

2. Obligee

3. Assignment of rights

4. Assignor

5. Assignee

6. Delegation of duties

7. Delegator

8. Delegatee

9. Partial assignment

10. Implied warranty

11. Express warranty

12. Novation

13. Third-party beneficiary contract

14. Intended beneficiary

15. Incidental beneficiary

16. Donee beneficiary

17. Creditor beneficiary

TRUE/FALSE

_____ 1. A person who owes a duty under a contract is an obligee.

_____ 2. After an effective assignment of rights, both the assignor and the assignee have a right to the obligor's performance.

_____ 3. After an effective delegation of duties, both the delegator and the delegatee are liable to the obligee for performance of the contractual duty.

_____ 4. Although no special words or particular form are necessary to create an assignment, an assignment must be supported by consideration to be effective.

_____ 5. Where the assignee gives consideration in exchange for an assignment, a contract exists between the assignor and the assignee and the assignor may not revoke the assignment.

_____ 6. In a novation, the delegator will be discharged and the third party will become directly bound on her promise to the obligee.

_____ 7. Under the Restatement and the Code, unless the language or circumstances indicate otherwise, an assignment of "all my rights under the contract" is both an assignment of rights and a delegation of the assignor's duties under the contract.

_____ 8. If successive assignments have taken place, the majority rule is that the first assignee to notify the obligor will prevail in a dispute among the successive assignees.

_____ 9. A third party is an intended beneficiary if the promisee's purpose in bargaining for and obtaining the promisor's promise was to make a gift to the beneficiary.

_____ 10. The rights of an intended beneficiary vest at the time of the making of the contract or at the time he learns of its making, whichever is later.

_____ 11. In an action by the intended beneficiary of a third-party beneficiary contract, the promisor may assert any defense that would have been available to him had the action been brought by the promisee.

_____ 12. Most contract rights, including rights under an option contract, are assignable.

_____ 13. Harold Homeowner sells his used car to Tim Teenager and assigns his rights in his auto liability insurance policy to Tim. This is a valid assignment.

_____ 14. Sarah orders a microwave oven from Marlin's Department Store and requests that it be delivered to her sister Theresa. Theresa is a third-party intended beneficiary.

_____ 15. Under Art. 2 of the UCC a right to damages for breach of contract can be assigned despite a contractual provision to the contrary.

MULTIPLE CHOICE

_____ 1. A gratuitous assignment is:
   a. valid even though not supported by consideration.
   b. not revocable by the assignor.
   c. not terminated by the assignor's death.
   d. all of the above.

_____ 2. In the case of a gratuitous assignment, which of the following would not be revocable?
   a. The donee-assignee receives payment of a claim from the obligor.
   b. The donee-assignee obtains a judgment against the obligor.
   c. The donee-assignee obtains a new contract with the obligor.
   d. None of the above would be revocable.

_____ 3. Which of the following assignments of contract rights are not assignable?
   a. Assignments that would materially increase the risk or burden on the obligor.
   b. Assignments which would transfer a personal contract right.
   c. Assignments which are prohibited by law.
   d. All of the above.

_____ 4. An assignee of a contract right:
   a. acquires all of the rights of the assignor.
   b. acquires new, additional rights by virtue of the assignment.
   c. takes the assigned rights free of all of the defenses to which the rights would be subject in an action by the assignor against the obligor.
   d. all of the above.

_____ 5. Which of the following would not be assignable?
   a. A owes B $50. B assigns his right to collect to C.
   b. A contract right to land or other goods.
   c. Teacher assigns to her best friend her contract right to teach.
   d. All of the above.

_____ 6. In the absence of an expressed intention to the contrary, an assignor who receives value makes all of the following implied warranties to the assignee with respect to the assigned right EXCEPT:
    a. that he will do nothing to defeat or impair the assignment.
    b. that the obligor will pay the assigned debt.
    c. that the assigned right actually exists.
    d. that he has no knowledge of any fact that would impair the value of the assignment.

_____ 7. A delegation of contractual duties will not be permitted if:
    a. the duties are of a personal nature.
    b. the contract is silent with respect to the assignment.
    c. the delegation is for payment of monies.
    d. None of the above will be permitted.

_____ 8. The delegator remains bound to perform his contractual duties even after a delegation unless the delegation is:
    a. a gratuitous delegation.
    b. a delegation for value.
    c. a novation.
    d. none of the above.

_____ 9. A contract in which the promisor agrees to render a certain performance to a third person is called:
    a. a third-party beneficiary contract.
    b. an assignment of rights.
    c. a delegation of duties.
    d. a novation.

_____ 10. An intended creditor beneficiary of a third-party beneficiary contract has rights against:
    a. the promisee/debtor only.
    b. the promisor only.
    c. both the promisee and the promisor.
    d. neither the promisee nor the promisor.

_____ 11. A life insurance policy naming a spouse as a beneficiary is a common example of a/an:
    a. assignment.
    b. delegation of duties.
    c. third-party donee beneficiary contract.
    d. third-party incidental beneficiary contract.

_____ 12. Clara sells her house to Donald. The house has a mortgage which is held by First Bank. As part of the transaction, First Bank agrees to discharge Clara from the mortgage and to allow Donald to assume the obligation. This is a/an:
   a. assignment of rights.
   b. delegation of duties.
   c. novation.
   d. third-party creditor beneficiary contract.

_____ 13. Arthur and Bob enter into a contract. Bob later delegates his duty of performance to Clark. Which of the following is true?
   a. If Clark fails to perform, Bob has a duty to perform.
   b. Arthur will always have to accept Clark's performance.
   c. The delegation is valid only if all three parties agree.
   d. Bob must compensate Clark for accepting the delegation.

_____ 14. The law does not recognize the rights of a/an:
   a. assignee.
   b. incidental beneficiary.
   c. intended beneficiary.
   d. donee beneficiary.

_____ 15. Ace Wrecking Service, Inc. contracts to demolish Al's old warehouse and build a new office building in its place. Ace fails to perform and Charlie, Al's neighbor, wants to enforce the agreement as a third party beneficiary. Charlie is a/an:
   a. intended beneficiary.
   b. donee beneficiary.
   c. incidental beneficiary.
   d. creditor beneficiary.

SHORT ESSAY

1. Identify the parties involved in an assignment/delegation and briefly discuss each with respect to rights and duties.

_____
_____
_____
_____

2. Distinguish between an assignment of rights and a delegation of duties. How does an assignor's rights after an assignment differ from a delegator's duties after a delegation?

_____

_____

_____

_____

3. Identify rights which are not assignable and briefly discuss each.

_____

_____

_____

_____

4. The Student Center at ABC University contracts with Rocky Nelson, a famous rock singer, to perform at the university. Can Rocky assign his rights and delegate his duties under this contract? Explain.

_____

_____

_____

_____

5. Identify the classes of third party beneficiaries and discuss the relative enforcement rights of each.

_____

_____

_____

_____

Chapter 17
Performance, Breach and Discharge

PURPOSE

In this chapter, you study the termination of contractual duties and the methods by which a party who has been bound by contractual duties is discharged from those duties. Most contracts are discharged by performance when each party does what she has promised to do. However, performance may be defective in which case there is a breach. In such a case, the defaulting party is not discharged. The consequences to the breaching party depend upon the seriousness of the breach. The contract may also be discharged by the agreement of the parties to a rescission, substituted agreement, novation, or an accord and satisfaction. In some situations, the contract may be discharged by operation of law. Such is the case when a party is discharged by impossibility, bankruptcy, or the statute of limitations. Also, many contractual promises are not absolute promises to perform but rather are conditional promises that depend on the happening or nonhappening of a specific event.

CHAPTER CHECKPOINTS

After reading and studying the chapter, you should be able to:

1. Recognize express conditions, implied-in-fact conditions, implied-in-law conditions, concurrent conditions, conditions precedent and conditions subsequent, and discuss the effect of each type of condition upon a contract.

2. Identify fact situations in which discharge by agreement of the parties occurs and distinguish a mutual rescission, a substituted contract, an accord and satisfaction and a novation.

3. Identify and discuss the ways in which discharge may be brought about by operation of law.

4. Compare the common law concept of material breach to the perfect tender rule of the UCC.

5. Distinguish full performance, tender of performance and substantial performance.

CHAPTER OUTLINE

A. Conditions–A condition is an event whose happening or nonhappening affects a duty of performance.
   1. Express Conditions–An express condition is explicitly set forth in language. It exists where performance is explicitly made contingent on the happening or nonhappening of a stated event.
      a. Satisfaction of a Contracting Party–The parties to a contract may agree that performance by one of them shall be to the satisfaction of the other, who will not be obligated to perform unless he is satisfied. This is an express condition to the duty to perform. If the contract does not clearly indicate that satisfaction is subjective, the law assumes an objective satisfaction standard.
      b. Satisfaction of a Third Party–A contract may condition the performance of a party, subject to the condition that the performance be approved by a third party.
   2. Implied-in-Fact Conditions–These are conditions that are contingencies understood but not expressed by the parties.
   3. Implied-in-Law Conditions–These are not contained in the language of the contract but are imposed by law in order to accomplish a just and fair result.
   4. Concurrent Conditions–These occur when the mutual duties of performance are to take place at the same time.
   5. Condition Precedent–This is an event which must occur or not occur before performance is due.
   6. Condition Subsequent–This is an event which terminates a duty of performance.

B. Discharge by Performance–A discharge is a termination of a contractual duty. Performance is the fulfillment of a contractual obligation. Discharge by performance is the most frequent method of discharging a contractual duty. A tender is an offer of performance. In a bilateral contract, the refusal of a tender is a repudiation that discharges the tendering party from further duty to perform the contract.

C. Discharge by Breach–A breach is a wrongful failure to perform the terms of a contract. A breach is always a basis for an action for damages by the injured party.
   1. Material Breach–Nonperformance which significantly impairs the aggrieved party's rights under the contract is a material breach. An uncured material breach by one party discharges the aggrieved party from any further duty under the contract.
      a. Prevention of Performance–One party's substantial interference with or prevention of performance by the other constitutes a material breach and discharges the other party to the contract.
      b. Perfect Tender Rule–The Code alters the common law doctrine of material breach by adopting what is known as the perfect tender rule. This rule says that performance must

strictly comply with contractual duties.

2. Substantial Performance–This is performance that is incomplete but that does not defeat the purpose of the contract. If a party substantially performs, the common law will generally allow that party to obtain the other party's performance less any damages caused by the partial performance.

3. Anticipatory Repudiation–This is a breach of contract before performance is due by announcing that one will not perform or by committing an act which makes it impossible to perform. It is treated as a breach, discharging the nonrepudiating party and permitting her to bring suit immediately as if it were a breach.

4. Material Alteration of Written Contract–A material fraudulent alteration of a written contract discharges the entire contract.

D. Discharge by Agreement of the Parties–The parties may by agreement discharge each other from performance by rescission, substituted contract, accord and satisfaction, or novation.

1. Mutual Rescission–A rescission is a new contract accepted by both parties in satisfaction of the parties' duties under the original contract.

2. Substituted Contracts–A substituted contract is an agreement between the parties to rescind their old contract and replace it with a new contract.

3. Accord and Satisfaction–An accord and satisfaction is substituted performance under a contract (the accord) and the discharge of the prior contractual obligation by performance of the new duty (the satisfaction).

4. Novation–A novation is a substituted contract involving a new third-party promisor or promisee.

E. Discharge by Operation of Law–Discharge can be brought about by operation of law.

1. Impossibility–Impossibility means that the performance cannot be done. There are two types of impossibility–subjective and objective. Subjective impossibility refers to the situation where it is impossible for the promisor to perform due to financial inability or because he personally lacks the capability to do so. Subjective impossibility does not excuse the promisor from liability for breach of contract. Objective impossibility means that no one is able to perform. It will generally be held to excuse the promisor or to discharge his duty of performance.

a. Destruction of the Subject Matter–Destruction of the subject matter without the fault of the promisor is an excusable impossibility.

b. Subsequent Illegality–If performance becomes illegal or impractical as a result of a change in the law, the duty of performance is discharged.

c. Frustration of Purpose–Where the purpose of a contract has been frustrated by unexpected circumstances that deprive the performance of the value attached to it by the parties, the courts generally regard the frustration as a discharge.

d. Commercial Impracticability–Commercial impracticability means that performance can only be accomplished under unforeseen and unjust hardship. The Restatement and the Code take the view that commercial impracticability will excuse performance, even though the performance is not literally impossible.

2. Bankruptcy–This is a method of discharge which is available to a debtor who obtains an order of discharge by the bankruptcy court.

3. Statute of Limitations–All states have statutes providing time limitations within which to bring an action. When the statute of limitations has run, the debt is not discharged, but the creditor cannot maintain an action against the debtor.

KEY TERMS

1. Condition

2. Express condition

3. Implied-in-fact condition

4. Implied-in-law condition

5. Concurrent conditions

6. Condition precedent

7. Condition subsequent

8. Discharge

9. Performance

10. Tender

11. Breach

12. Material breach

13. Perfect tender rule

14. Substantial performance

15. Anticipatory repudiation

16. Rescission

17. Substituted contract

18. Accord and satisfaction

19. Novation

20. Frustration of purpose

21. Commercial impracticability

TRUE/FALSE

_____ 1. The happening or nonhappening of an event subjects neither party to liability, even though it may prevent a party from acquiring a right or deprive her of a right.

_____ 2. Even if a contract is expressly made subject to a subjective condition of satisfaction, courts generally will apply an objective, reasonable person standard to evaluate its performance.

_____ 3. In the absence of an agreement to the contrary, the law assumes that the respective performances under a contract are concurrent conditions.

_____ 4. A condition is an event whose happening or nonhappening affects a duty of performance under a contract.

_____ 5. Under the Code, failure to perform any aspect required by the conditions expressed in the contract will be considered a material breach.

_____ 6. Under the Perfect Tender Rule the Code provides that _any_ deviation in a sales contract constitutes a material breach.

_____ 7. A rescission must satisfy all of the essentials of an ordinary contract to be effective.

_____ 8. A promisor's good faith personal belief that she lacks the necessary capability or competence to perform her contractual duties will excuse her from liability for nonperformance.

_____ 9. Under the Restatement and Code view of impossibility, commercial impracticability will excuse liability of nonperformance.

_____ 10. In most states, the running of the period of the statute of limitations bars the creditor's right to bring an action.

_____ 11. Harold Homeowner has a household insurance policy which requires that he notify the company within two weeks of any loss before he is eligible to receive payment for his loss. The notification requirement is a condition precedent.

_____ 12. Carl Contractor builds a house for Harold and Happy Homemaker. The contract calls for extragrade stain resistant carpet. The pattern selected by the Homemakers is not available when the carpeting is supposed to be installed, so Carl substitutes a comparable grade similar carpet. Carl has substantially performed the contract. Substantial performance plus a small amount of damages will discharge Carl's contractual obligations, even if the Homemakers think the substituted carpet ruins the house.

_____ 13. An unauthorized change in the terms of a written contract by a person who is not a party to the contract will discharge the contract.

_____ 14. Carl Contractor has a contract with Big Bucks, Inc., to build a new office complex. The contract provides that Carl must furnish a certificate of occupancy and conformity with the fire code before Big Bucks has an obligation to pay. The furnishing of the certificate is an implied-in-fact condition subsequent to the construction of the building.

_____ 15. Brian owes Albert $500. Brian, Albert and Clarence agree that Brian will be discharged from the obligation and that Clarence will pay the debt. This is a novation.

MULTIPLE CHOICE

_____ 1. A condition that is understood by the parties to be part of their agreement, but is not included in their express contract, is called:
   a. an implied-in-law condition.
   b. an implied-in-fact condition.
   c. a concurrent condition.
   d. a condition precedent.

_____ 2. Which of the following would constitute a discharge of the contract?
   a. Where all parties have fully performed.
   b. Where either or both parties have breached the contract.
   c. Where the parties agree to rescind.
   d. All of the above.

_____ 3. An uncured material breach of contract:
   a. gives rise to a cause of action for damages by the aggrieved party.
   b. operates as an excuse for nonperformance by the aggrieved party.
   c. discharges the aggrieved party from any further duty under the contract.
   d. all of the above.

_____ 4. The happening or nonhappening of a condition:
   a. prevents a party for acquiring a right.
   b. deprives a party of a right.
   c. subjects both parties to liability.
   d. a or b above but not c.

_____ 5. Which one of the following statements is NOT a correct principle to be applied in determining what constitutes a material breach?
   a. A failure to timely perform a promise is a material breach even if time is not of the essence.
   b. Partial performance is a material breach if an essential part of the contract is not performed.
   c. If quantitatively significant, a breach will be considered material.
   d. An intentional breach of a contract is generally held to be material.

_____ 6. Which of the following has occurred if, prior to the date that performance is due, a party announces that he will not perform or commits an act that renders him unable to perform?
a. an anticipatory novation.
b. an anticipatory repudiation.
c. a prevention of performance.
d. a material alteration of a written contract.

_____ 7. An agreement between three parties to substitute a new promisee or promisor in place of an existing promisee or promisor is called:
a. a condition subsequent.
b. a mutual rescission.
c. an accord and satisfaction.
d. a novation.

_____ 8. Which of the following would not be considered a discharge by agreement?
a. A novation.
b. A mutual rescission.
c. An accord and satisfaction.
d. An anticipatory repudiation.

_____ 9. A promisor will be excused from liability for failure to perform under a contract on grounds of impossibility when:
a. she is financially unable to perform.
b. she personally lacks the capability or competency to perform.
c. no one, including the promisor, is able to perform.
d. all of the above.

_____ 10. The effect of a party's failure to bring an action before expiration of the period of the statute of limitations is:
a. to discharge the promisor from liability.
b. to act as a mutual rescission.
c. to bar the right to bring an action.
d. to act as an accord and satisfaction.

_____ 11. A contract in which the promisee agrees to accept and the promisor agrees to render a substituted performance in satisfaction of an existing contractual duty is called:
a. a material alteration of a written contract.
b. an accord.
c. a substantial performance.
d. a novation.

_____ 12. Edward has agreed to buy Donna's C.D. player. Edward agrees to pay Donna when the C.D. player is delivered. This transaction involves:
   a.   implied-in-fact conditions subsequent.
   b.   implied-in-law conditions subsequent.
   c.   express concurrent conditions.
   d.   express conditions precedent.

_____ 13. David and Edward entered into a written contract involving the performance of some marketing services. A week later, they both changed their minds and agreed in writing to cancel the contract. This is an example of:
   a.   accord and satisfaction.
   b.   novation.
   c.   substituted contract.
   d.   mutual rescission.

_____ 14. Clarence owes David $50 for a used television which he bought last year at David's garage sale. The two agree that the debt can be paid by Clarence mowing David's lawn for six weeks. The new contract is a/an:
   a.   satisfaction.
   b.   novation.
   c.   accord.
   d.   rescission.

_____ 15. An offer to perform one's obligation under a contract is a:
   a.   novation.
   b.   tender.
   c.   condition precedent.
   d.   condition subsequent.

SHORT ESSAY

1. Discuss "satisfaction" and the role it plays in conditional contracts.

_____
_____
_____
_____

2. At common law, when is a party excused from liability for nonperformance of a contractual duty on grounds of impossibility? How have the Restatement and the Code altered this rule?

   _____

   _____

   _____

   _____

3. Explain the "perfect tender rule" and how it differs from the common law approach.

   _____

   _____

   _____

   _____

4. Identify and briefly discuss the ways a contract might be discharged by operation of law.

   _____

   _____

   _____

   _____

5. Give an example of a condition precedent, condition subsequent and concurrent conditions.

   _____

   _____

   _____

   _____

Chapter 18
Remedies

PURPOSE

This chapter discusses the remedies that are available to the injured party when the other party breaches the contract by failing to perform his contractual duties. The primary objective of contract remedies is to compensate the injured party for the loss resulting from the breach. The relief the court can give an injured party is what it regards as an equivalent of the promised performance. In this chapter, you study the most common remedies available for breach of contract. These include the legal remedy of money damages and the equitable remedies of specific performance, injunction, and reformation. You also study the remedy of restitution, which is available as an alternative remedy for a party injured by breach and to a party who has avoided a contract for reasons such as lack of capacity, duress, undue influence or fraud. Sometimes an injured party will have more than one remedy available to him, and the injured party must elect a remedy and then cannot pursue another inconsistent remedy. Remedies under Article 2 of the Code differ from those available at common law and are discussed in Chapter 23.

CHAPTER CHECKPOINTS

After reading and studying the chapter, you should be able to:

1. List and discuss the various types of money damages.

2. Identify and discuss the two ways to measure damages for misrepresentation.

3. Identify the equitable remedies that are available for breach of contract and discuss the circumstances under which these remedies are available.

4. Define restitution and list the situations when restitution is available to the injured party.

5. List and discuss situations where the remedies of the injured party will be limited.

CHAPTER OUTLINE

A. Interests Protected by Contract Remedies–One or more of the following interests are protected:
1. Expectation Interest–A benefit of the bargain interest.
2. Reliance Interest–Reimbursed for loss caused by reliances on the contract.
3. Restitution Interest–Conferred benefit restored.

B. Monetary Damages–A judgment awarding monetary damages is the most frequently granted judicial remedy for breach of contract.
1. Compensatory Damages–These are contract damages placing the injured party in as good a position as if the other party had performed. The amount of damages is generally the loss of value to the injured party caused by the other party's failure to perform or by his deficient performance minus the loss or cost avoided by the injured party plus incidental damages plus consequential damages.
   a. Loss of Value–In general, this is the difference between the value of the promised performance of the breaching party and the value of the actual performance rendered by the breaching party.
   b. Incidental Damages–These are damages arising directly out of a breach of contract, such as costs incurred to acquire the nondelivered performance from another source. Incidental damages are added to the loss of value.
   c. Consequential Damages–These are damages not arising directly out of a breach but that are a foreseeable result of the breach, such as lost profits and injury to persons or property resulting from defective performance.
   d. Expenses Saved–The recovery by the injured party is reduced by any cost or loss she has avoided by not having to perform.
2. Nominal Damages–These are a small sum of money awarded where a contract has been breached but the loss is either negligible or unproved.
3. Reliance Damages–Instead of seeking compensatory damages, the injured party may seek reimbursement for foreseeable loss caused by his reliance on the contract. This results in placing the injured party in as good a position as he would have been in had the contract not been made. These might be preferred when an injured party is unable to establish his lost profits with reasonable certainty or when the contract itself is unprofitable.
4. Damages for Misrepresentation–The basic remedy for misrepresentation is rescission of the contract, but an alternative remedy under common law and an additional remedy under the Code is a suit for damages. The measure of damages generally depends upon whether the misrepresentation is fraudulent or nonfraudulent.
   a. Fraud–A minority of states allow the injured party to recover out-of-pocket damages, which is the difference between the value received and the value given. The majority of states permit the defrauded party to recover damages based upon the benefit-of-the-bargain rule,

which is the difference between the value received and the value of the fraudulent party's performance as represented.

    b. Nonfraudulent Misrepresentation–The Restatement permits out-of-pocket damages but not benefit-of-the-bargain damages where the misrepresentation is not fraudulent.

5. Punitive Damages–Punitive damages are monetary damages in addition to compensatory damages awarded to a plaintiff in certain situations involving willful, wanton, or malicious conduct. Their purpose is to punish the defendant and thus to discourage him and others from similar wrongful conduct. The Restatement provides that punitive damages are not recoverable for a breach of contract unless the conduct constituting the breach is also a tort for which punitive damages are recoverable.

6. Liquidated Damages–These are reasonable damages agreed to in advance by the parties to a contract. If the liquidated damages clause is a reasonable forecast of the loss that may result from the breach, the provision will be enforced. If the sum bears no reasonable relationship to the amount of probable loss, it is unenforceable as a penalty. If the clause is invalid, a party is entitled to ordinary breach of contract remedies.

7. Limitations on Damages–Certain limitations are imposed upon monetary damages to ensure that damages can be taken into account at the time of contracting, that damages are compensatory and not speculative, and that damages do not include loss that could have been avoided by reasonable efforts.

    a. Foreseeability of Damages–Compensatory or reliance damages are recoverable only for loss that the party in breach had reason to foresee as a probable result of the breach when the contract was made. The test of foreseeable damages is objective based on what the breaching party had reason to foresee.

    b. Certainty of Damages–Damages are not recoverable for loss beyond an amount that the injured party can establish with reasonable certainty.

    c. Mitigation of Damages–When a breach of contract occurs, the injured party may not recover damages for loss that he could have avoided by reasonable effort and without undue risk, burden, or humiliation.

C. Remedies in Equity–If damages will not adequately compensate an injured party, the court may in its discretion grant a remedy in equity.

1. Specific Performance–This is a court decree ordering the breaching party to render the promised performance. It is not ordinarily available for breach of contract, because the usual remedy for breach is an action at law for money damages. It is available only in the case of breach of contract for the sale of personal property where the goods are rare or unique, such as for a famous painting or statue, an original manuscript, a patent or copyright, shares of stock in a closely held corporation, or an heirloom. Courts will always grant specific performance in case of breach of contract for the sale of real property. Specific performance is not available in contracts for personal services.

2. Injunctions–An injunction is a court order prohibiting a party from doing a specific act. Where damages for breach would be inadequate, a court may grant an injunction against breach of a contractual duty. An employee's promise of exclusive personal services may be enforced by an

injunction against serving another employer as long as the employee would have other reasonable means of making a living and the services are unusual in character.

D. Restitution–This is the restoration of the injured party to the position he was in before the contract was made. It is available (1) as an alternative remedy for a party injured by breach, (2) for a party in default, (3) for a party who may not enforce the contract because of the statute of frauds, and (4) on rescission of a voidable contract.

1. Party Injured by Breach–It is available if the other party totally breaches the contract by nonperformance or repudiation.

2. Party in Default–The party who has partly performed but is in default such that the other party's duty to perform is discharged is entitled to restitution for any benefit she has conferred in excess of the loss she has caused by her breach.

3. Statute of Frauds–Where a contract is unenforceable because of the statute of frauds, but the party has nevertheless acted in reliance on the contract, the party may recover in restitution the benefits conferred on the other in reliance on the contract.

4. Voidable Contracts–A party who has avoided a contract for lack of capacity, duress, undue influence, fraud, misrepresentation, or mistake is entitled to restitution for any benefit he has conferred on the party.

E. Limitations on Remedies

1. Election of Remedies–If a party is injured by a breach of contract and has more than one remedy available to him, he may pursue more than one remedy unless the remedies are inconsistent or the other party materially changes his position in reliance on the choice of one of them.

2. Loss of Power of Avoidance–A party with a power of avoidance may lose that power under certain circumstances.

   a. Affirmance–A party who has the power to avoid a contract for lack of capacity, duress, undue influence, fraud, misrepresentation, or mistake will lose that power by affirming the contract.

   b. Delay–If a party has the power to rescind a contract but does not do so within a reasonable time, then the power of avoidance may be lost.

   c. Rights of Third Parties–The power of avoidance is limited by the intervening rights of third parties. For example, the right to rescind may be lost where a third party good faith purchaser acquires an interest in the subject matter of the contract before the right to rescind has been exercised.

KEY TERMS

1. Compensatory damages

2. Incidental damages

3. Consequential damages

4. Reliance damages

5. Nominal damages

6. Out-of-pocket damages

7. Benefit-of-the-bargain damages

8. Punitive damages

9. Liquidated damages

10. Foreseeable damages

11. Mitigation of damages

12. Reformation

13. Specific performance

14. Injunction

15. Restitution

TRUE/FALSE

_____   1. The primary objective of contract remedies is to compensate the injured party for the loss resulting from the contract breach by attempting to provide an equivalent of the promised performance.

_____   2. Loss of value is the difference between the value of the promised performance of the breaching party and the value of the expected performance to the non-breaching party.

_____   3. Damages are recoverable for losses beyond those that the party in breach had reason to foresee as being a probable result of its breach when it entered into the contract.

_____   4. Consequential damages would include lost profits and injury to property resulting from defective performance.

_____   5. Even if an unforeseeable, extraordinary loss results from a breach of contract, the injured party may still recover for any ordinary loss resulting from the breach.

_____   6. In most states, the measure of damages for misrepresentation would be the same regardless of whether or not the misrepresentation was fraudulent or nonfraudulent.

_____ 7. Punitive damages are not recoverable for a breach of contract unless the breach also gives rise to a tort for which punitive damages are recoverable.

_____ 8. A contract provision by which the parties agree in advance to the damages to be paid in event of breach is enforceable even if it is NOT a reasonable forecast of the loss that would result from the breach.

_____ 9. When a breach of contract occurs, the injured party has a duty to take steps to minimize the damages that he may sustain.

_____ 10. Specific performance may be ordered in a contract situation calling for personal services.

_____ 11. A court may grant an equitable remedy even though the terms of the agreement prohibit such relief, if the court feels an injustice would otherwise occur.

_____ 12. Under the doctrine of election of remedies, the injured party's choice of one available remedy will bar his choice of an additional, consistent remedy.

_____ 13. The power of avoidance may be lost if the party having the power does not rescind within a reasonable time.

_____ 14. Compensatory damages are only recoverable for damages that were foreseeable when the contract was made.

_____ 15. An action to recover damages for breach of contract may be maintained even though the plaintiff has not sustained any loss from the breach.

MULTIPLE CHOICE

_____ 1. Contract remedies are available to protect one or more of the following interests of the injured party:
   a. expectation interest.
   b. reliance interest.
   c. restitution interest.
   d. all of the above.

_____ 2. Which of the following would not be an appropriate measure of monetary damages?
   a. Compensatory damages.
   b. Consequential damages.
   c. Unforeseeable damages.
   d. Incidental damages.

_____ 3. Money damages are only recoverable for losses that the party in breach had reason to foresee as a probable result of such breach at the time that:
   a. the parties began negotiations.
   b. the parties entered into the contract.
   c. the breach occurred.
   d. none of the above.

_____ 4. Acting in reliance on X's intentional misrepresentation as to a drill press's capabilities, Y purchases the press from X for $17,000. Although the value of the press, if it had performed as promised, would be $10,000, its actual delivered value is $4,000. Under the benefit-of-the-bargain rule, Y could recover:
   a. nothing.
   b. $3,000.
   c. $6,000.
   d. $7,000.

_____ 5. Through a clerical error, an annuity policy which should be paying $500 per month is actually paying $50 per month. Upon proper proof of the error, a court of equity might elect which of the following remedies?
   a. Specific performance.
   b. An injunction.
   c. Reformation.
   d. Restitution.

_____ 6. An equitable remedy would be granted in which of the following?
   a. Where the remedy at law is inadequate.
   b. Where the contract is without consideration.
   c. Where relief would cause the defendant unreasonable hardship.
   d. Where the contract involves undue influence.

_____ 7. In which of the following instances is restitution available as a remedy for breach of contract?
   a. When one party totally fails to perform its obligations.
   b. When a party may not enforce the contract because of the statute of frauds.
   c. Upon the avoidance of a voidable contract.
   d. All of the above.

_____ 8. A party with a power of avoidance may lose that power if:
   a. he affirms the contract.
   b. he delays unreasonably in exercising the power of disaffirmance.
   c. the rights of third parties intervene.
   d. all of the above.

_____ 9. An action to recover damages even though the plaintiff cannot prove any injury or loss would result in an award of:
  a. reliance damages.
  b. expectation damages.
  c. nominal damages.
  d. all of the above.

_____ 10. A liquidated damages provision will be enforced only if it is:
  a. a reasonable estimate of the loss that may result from the breach of contract.
  b. designed to punish a party if he breaches a contract.
  c. a substitute for a penalty.
  d. none of the above.

_____ 11. Sam Seller contracts to sell 200 tables to Bill Buyer at a price of $50 a table. Bill repudiates the contract, whereupon Sam sells the tables to Paula Purchaser at a price of $45 a table. Sam's action in selling the chairs to another buyer is known as:
  a. liquidated damages.
  b. specific performance.
  c. mitigation of damages.
  d. restitution.

_____ 12. Carl Contractor has a contract to build an office complex for Big Bucks, Inc. A clause in the contract calls for Carl to pay $2,000 a day for each day's delay after the date the contract is scheduled for completion.
  a. This is a compensatory damages clause.
  b. This is a liquidated damages clause that may be an unenforceable penalty clause.
  c. Big Bucks will be given the benefit-of-the-bargain in calculating damages.
  d. Big Bucks will only be allowed to recover nominal damages in the case of a breach.

_____ 13. Arthur, a world-famous rock star, has a contract to perform at the Superdome on New Year's Eve. However, he decides he would rather spend the night with his family and friends so he informs the owners of the Superdome.
  a. The owners of the Superdome are entitled to specific performances, because Arthur's services are unique.
  b. The owners of the Superdome will have to wait until after January 1 to sue for breach of contract.
  c. The owners of the Superdome are entitled to damages, but they are not entitled to specific performance.
  d. Because an adequate remedy at law is available here, a court would be unable to issue an injunction prohibiting Arthur from performing at Madison Square Garden on New Year's Eve if they gave him a better offer.

_____ 14. Sam Seller has a contract to provide 100 widgets to Bill Buyer at a price of $10 a widget. Delivery is due on October 1. Due to unanticipated delays, Sam is unable to get the widgets to Bill until October 2. Bill is not harmed by the delay but sues anyway, because he is angry at Sam.
   a. Sam's failure to deliver the goods on October 1 is a violation of the Code's perfect tender rule, even if it is not a material breach.
   b. Bill cannot sue, because this is not a material breach.
   c. If Bill cannot establish any incidental or consequential damages as a result of the breach, he will only be able to recover nominal damages.
   d. Two of the above are correct, (a) and (c).

_____ 15. Bill Businessman pays $500 down on a new computer to be used in the office. The salesman has told him the computer has a 100,000 megabyte memory. Bill learns from other sources that this is blatantly untrue and realizes now that the salesman induced him to enter into the contract based upon fraud in the inducement, but the company refuses to return the down payment. If Bill sues, an appropriate remedy would be:
   a. injunction.
   b. punitive damages.
   c. nominal damages.
   d. rescission and restitution.

SHORT ESSAY

1. Discuss monetary damages and identify by type.

   _____

   _____

   _____

   _____

2. What is the doctrine of mitigation of damages? What will the effect be of the injured party's failure to take the appropriate steps?

   _____

   _____

   _____

   _____

3. What are the two major types of equitable remedies? Discuss each type, including an explanation of when each is available.

_____

_____

_____

_____

4. What is restitution? Explain when it might be appropriate.

_____

_____

_____

_____

5. Big Bucks Inc. hires Jill for one year for $20,000 as an administrative assistant. Big Bucks fires Jill without cause after one month, and she incurs $300 in fees to find comparable employment which will pay her $18,000 annually. How much and what types of damages, if any, may Jill recover from Big Bucks?

_____

_____

_____

_____

Part II
Sample Examination

MULTIPLE CHOICE

_____ 1. Damages that are calculated by taking the difference between the value received and the value given are _____ damages.
- a. reliance
- b. nominal
- c. out-of-pocket
- d. benefit-of-the-bargain

_____ 2. A contract involving the exchange of a promise for an act is a/an _____ contract.
- a. unilateral
- b. bilateral
- c. formal
- d. informal

_____ 3. Article 9 of the UCC applies to sales of:
- a. real property.
- b. secured transactions.
- c. goods.
- d. services.

_____ 4. A negotiable instrument such as a check is an example of a/an _____ contract.
- a. formal
- b. unilateral
- c. implied
- d. informal

_____ 5. In consideration of $500 being paid to Amanda by Barbara, Amanda gives Barbara the right to purchase her house for a price of $85,000 any time within thirty days. This is an example of a/an:
- a. firm offer.
- b. option.
- c. implied condition subsequent.
- d. revocation.

_____ 6. David owes Charles an undisputed debt of $500. David writes a check for $400, and then puts "paid in full" in the notation section of the check. Charles cashes the check.
   a. This is a valid accord and satisfaction.
   b. This is a valid novation.
   c. Charles can still collect the $100, because there was no consideration given for accepting less than the full amount of the debt.
   d. None of the above.

_____ 7. Which of the following will invalidate a contract?
   a. Unilateral mistake.
   b. A material misstatement of opinion.
   c. Undue influence.
   d. Failure to read a document.

_____ 8. Which of the following will terminate an offer?
   a. Rejection.
   b. Counteroffer.
   c. Death of the offeree.
   d. All of the above.

_____ 9. Words such as "provided that," "on condition that," and "as soon as" usually precede a/an:
   a. express condition.
   b. implied-in-fact condition.
   c. implied-in-law condition.
   d. condition subsequent.

_____ 10. Which of the following is untrue regarding an enforceable restraint on trade?
   a. The purpose must be to protect a property interest of the promisee.
   b. The restraint can be no more extensive than is reasonably necessary to protect the interest.
   c. The restraints frequently involve the sale of a business.
   d. The reasonableness of the restraint has no relationship to the geographic area covered.

_____ 11. Barbara owes Anita $1,000. On June 1, Anita for value assigns the debt to Carol. Thereafter, on June 15, Anita assigns the same right to Darla.
   a. Under the majority rule in the United States, Carol will prevail over Darla.
   b. Under the English rule which is followed in a minority of states, the first assignee to notify Barbara will prevail.
   c. Under the Restatement, the first assignee to notify Barbara will prevail.
   d. Two of the above are correct, (a) and (b).

_____ 12. A/an _____ does have a right to enforce a contract.
   a. creditor beneficiary
   b. donee beneficiary
   c. incidental beneficiary
   d. a and b, but not c

_____ 13. Ron Roadbuilder has a contract to build a highway for the state of Wisconsin. The contract requires that the highway be completed by September 15. If the highway is not completed by that date, the contract requires that Ron be assessed $200 per day in damages. The $200 per day is:
   a. punitive damages.
   b. liquidated damages.
   c. nominal damages.
   d. an illegal penalty.

_____ 14. Carl Contractor has a contract to build a house. He delegates the plumbing to Paul's Plumbing Company. Paul's Plumbing improperly performs the job.
   a. Carl remains responsible, even though he delegated the duty.
   b. Paul alone has responsibility for the improperly performed plumbing.
   c. Carl can assign his rights under the contract, but he cannot delegate his duties.
   d. Two of the above are correct, (a) and (c).

_____ 15. Damages that arise directly out of the breach, such as the costs incurred to acquire the nondelivered performance from another source are known as _____ damages.
   a. consequential
   b. incidental
   c. nominal
   d. reliance

_____ 16. Sarah Student agrees to go to work for Big Bucks, Inc. upon her graduation from Ivory Towers University on June 12. The contract is for one year, beginning on September 1. She agrees to the contract in a telephone conversation on May 1.
   a. Sarah needs a writing signed by Big Bucks in order to enforce the contract, because the contract cannot by its terms be performed within one year from her graduation on June 12.
   b. Sarah needs a writing signed by Big Bucks in order to enforce the contract, because the contract cannot by its terms be performed within one year from its making on May 1.
   c. Sarah does not need a writing to enforce this contract, because it can be performed within one year of September 1.
   d. This is a contract between merchants, which requires no writing under the UCC statute of frauds.

_____ 17. Which of the following are assignable?
    a. Money due.
    b. Contract to buy a car.
    c. Contract to paint a house.
    d. All the above are assignable.

_____ 18. Ron Roadbuilder pledges $150,000 to the building fund of the First Missionary Church. Based upon Ron's pledge, the church enters into a contract for the construction of a new building. Now Ron's company has missed getting three new jobs he had counted on getting for the year. Ron tells the church he has changed his mind and has no intention of paying his pledge.
    a. There is no consideration for Ron's pledge, and it is not enforceable.
    b. There is no consideration for Ron's pledge, but it is enforceable based upon promissory estoppel.
    c. Under the Restatement, the church's probable reliance upon Ron's pledge is sufficient to make it enforceable.
    d. Two of the above are correct, (b) and (c).

_____ 19. Which of the following is/are enforceable without consideration?
    a. Mel Merchant sends a letter to Ralph Retailer offering to sell him widgets at $5 per widget and stating that the offer will continue for two weeks.
    b. Mel Merchant makes a promise to sell widgets to Ralph Retailer at $5 per widget, but then modifies the contract in good faith to a price of $6 per widget due to an increase in the cost of supplies.
    c. Arthur promises to pay a $100 debt which has been discharged in a bankruptcy proceeding. The promise is approved by the bankruptcy judge.
    d. All of the above.

_____ 20. Which of the following is an equitable remedy?
    a. Injunction.
    b. Specific performance.
    c. Consequential damages.
    d. A and B above.

Chapter 19
Relationship of Principal and Agent

PURPOSE

The law of agency is essential to business, because almost every type of contract or business transaction can be conducted through an agent. Agency is especially important in the case of partnerships and corporations. Partnership is founded on the agency of the partners; each partner is an agent of the partnership. Each partner has the authority to bind the partnership in transactions pertaining to partnership business. Sole proprietors may, and often do, employ agents to work for them. Because a corporation is an artificial entity, it can only act through the agency of its officers and employees. There are two main parts of agency law: (1) the internal part or the relationship between the principal and the agent, and (2) the external part or the relationship between the agent and the principal with third parties. In this chapter, you study the nature and function of agency and other topics involving the internal part of agency law. Agency is primarily governed by state common law, which is presented in an orderly fashion in the Restatements of the Law of Agency.

CHAPTER CHECKPOINTS

After reading and studying this chapter, you should be able to:

1. Distinguish among (a) an agency relationship, (b) an employment relationship, and (c) an independent contractor relationship.

2. Discuss how an agency relationship comes into existence.

3. List and discuss the duties owed by an agent to her principal.

4. List and discuss the duties owed by a principal to his agent.

5. Identify the ways in which an agency relationship is terminated.

CHAPTER OUTLINE

A. Nature of Agency–Agency is the relationship existing between two persons known as principal and agent through which the agent is authorized to act for and on behalf of the principal. An agent is one who represents a principal in business dealings with third persons. The parties to the contract are the principal and the third person; the agent is simply an intermediary. The agent may negotiate the terms of a contract with others and bind the principal to such contracts.

   1. Scope of Agency Purposes–As a general rule, whatever business activity a person may accomplish personally, he may do through an agent.

   2. Other Legal Relations–Two other legal relationships overlap with agency: employer-employee and principal-independent contractor. The employment relationship is one in which the employer has the right to control the physical conduct of the employee. An independent contractor is a person who contracts with another to do a particular job and is not subject to the control of the other. Although all employees are agents, not all agents are employees. Agents who are not employees are independent contractors.

B. Creation of Agency–Agency is a consensual relationship that may be formed by contract or agreement between the principal and agent. An agency created without consideration is a gratuitous agency.

   1. Formalities–No particular formality is required in a contract of agency. The contract may be express or inferred from the conduct of the principal. If the agency is for more than one year or involves sale of land, it must be in writing according to the statute of frauds. A power of attorney is a written, formal appointment of an agent.

   2. Capacity–The capacity to be a principal and act through an agent depends on the capacity of the principal to do the act herself. The appointment of an agent by a minor or an incompetent not under a guardianship and any resulting contracts are voidable. However, minors and incompetents not under guardianship can act as agents. The contract of agency may be voidable, but the contract between the principal and the third party is valid.

C. Duties of Agent to Principal–Because the relationship of principal and agent is ordinarily created by contract, the duties of the agent to the principal are primarily determined by the provisions of the contract. In addition, the agent is subject to various other duties imposed by law. An agent is liable for any loss caused to the principal for breach of any of these duties.

   1. Duty of Obedience–The duty of obedience requires the agent to act in the principal's affairs only as authorized by the principal and to obey all reasonable instructions and directions of the principal. However an agent is not under a duty to follow orders to perform illegal or unethical acts.

   2. Duty of Diligence–An agent must act with reasonable care and skill in performing the work for which he is employed.

   3. Duty to Inform–An agent must use reasonable efforts to give the principal information that is relevant to the affairs entrusted to her and that, as the agent knows or should know, the principal would desire to have. Notice to an agent is notice to her principal.

   4. Duty to Account–The agent is under a duty to maintain and provide the principal with a true and

complete account of money or other property that the agent has received or expended on behalf of the principal. An agent must also keep the principal's property separate from his own.

5. Fiduciary Duty–A fiduciary duty is one of utmost loyalty and good faith owed by agent to principal.

   a. Conflicts of Interest–An agent must act solely in the interest of his principal and not in his own interest or in the interest of another. An agent may not represent his principal in any transaction in which he has a personal interest, nor act on behalf of adverse parties to a transaction, unless the principal consents.

   b. Duty Not to Compete–An agent cannot compete with his principal or act on behalf of a competitor.

   c. Confidential Information–An agent may not use or disclose confidential information obtained in the course of the agency for her own benefit or contrary to the interest of her principal. Confidential information includes unique business methods, trade secrets, business plans, and customer lists. However, an agent may reveal confidential information that the principal is committing or is about to commit a crime.

   d. Duty to Account for Financial Benefits–An agent is under a duty to account to the principal for any financial benefit received by her as a direct result of transactions conducted on behalf of the principal, including bribes, kickbacks, and gifts. Also, an agent is not permitted to make a secret profit out of any transaction subject to the agency.

   e. Principal's Remedies–Principal may discharge the agent, avoid the transaction, recover against the agent in tort and contract actions as well as in restitution. The agent also loses the right to compensation.

D. Duties of Principal to Agent–The agent has certain rights against the principal which result in certain duties that the principal owes to the agent.

1. Contractual Duties–The contractual duties owed by a principal to an agent are the duties of compensation, reimbursement, and indemnification.

   a. Compensation–A principal has a duty to compensate her agent unless the agent has agreed to serve gratuitously. If the agreement does not specify a definite compensation, a principal is under a duty to pay the reasonable value of authorized services performed by her agent. An agent loses the right to compensation by (1) breaching the duty of obedience, (2) breaching the duty of loyalty or (3) willfully breaching the agency contract.

   b. Reimbursement–A principal is under a duty to pay back authorized payments agent has made on principal's behalf.

   c. Indemnification–A principal is under a duty to pay agent for losses incurred while acting, as directed by principal.

2. Tort Duties–A principal is under a duty to disclose to an agent those risks involved in the agency, of which the principal knows or should know. If the agent is an employee, the principal owes the duty to provide an employee with reasonably safe conditions of employment and to warn the employee of any unreasonable risk involved in the employment.

E. Termination of Agency–The agency is terminated when the consent of the principal is withdrawn or otherwise ceases to exist. On termination of the agency, the agent's actual authority ends, and she is not entitled to compensation for services subsequently rendered. Termination may take place by the acts of the parties or by operation of law.

1. Acts of the Parties–Termination by the acts of the parties may occur by the provisions of the original agreement, by the subsequent acts of both principal and agent, or by the subsequent act of either one of them.

    a. Lapse of Time–Authority conferred upon an agent for a specified time terminates at the expiration of that period. If no time is specified, authority terminates at the end of a reasonable period.

    b. Fulfillment of Purpose–The authority of an agent to perform a specific act or to accomplish a particular result is terminated when the act is performed or the result is accomplished by the agent.

    c. Mutual Agreement of the Parties–The agency relationship is created by agreement and may be terminated at any time by mutual agreement of the principal and the agent.

    d. Revocation of Authority–A principal may revoke an agent's authority at any time. But if such revocation constitutes a breach of contract by the principal, the agent may recover damages from the principal.

    e. Renunciation by the Agent–The agent has the power to put an end to the agency by notice to the principal that she renounces the authority given her by the principal. If the parties have contracted that the agency continue for a specified time, an unjustified renunciation prior to the expiration of the time is a breach of contract.

2. Operation of Law–As a matter of law, an agency relationship is terminated by the following events.

    a. Bankruptcy–Bankruptcy is a proceeding in a federal court affording relief to financially troubled debtors. The filing of the petition in bankruptcy usually terminates all the debtor's existing agency relationships.

    b. Death–The death of the principal terminates the authority of the agent. The authority given to an agent by a principal is strictly personal, therefore the agent's death also terminates the agency.

    c. Incapacity–Incapacity of the principal that occurs after the formation of the agency terminates the agent's authority. Also, subsequent incapacity of an agent to perform the acts authorized by the principal terminates the agent's authority.

    d. Change in Business Conditions–The authority of an agent is terminated by notice or knowledge of a change in the value of the subject matter or of a change in business conditions from which the agent should reasonably infer that the principal would not consent to an exercise of the authority given to him.

    e. Loss or Destruction of the Subject Matter–Where the authority of the agent relates to a specific subject matter that becomes lost or destroyed, her authority is thereby terminated.

    f. Loss of Qualification of Principal or Agent–Failure to acquire or loss of a regulatory license will terminate the agency.

    g. Disloyalty of Agent–If an agent, without the knowledge of her principal, acquires interests adverse to those of the principal or otherwise breaches her duty of loyalty to the principal, her authority to act on behalf of the principal is terminated.

    g. Change of Law–A change in the law that takes effect after the employment of the agent may cause the performance of the authorized act to be illegal, or criminal. Such a change in the law terminates the agency relationship.

    h. Outbreak of War–Where the outbreak of war places the principal and agent in the position of alien enemies, the authority of the agent is terminated because its exercise is illegal.

3. Irrevocable Agencies–When the agency is coupled with an interest of the agent, it is an irrevocable agency. This occurs where the agent has a security interest in the subject matter of the agency. The authority of the agent may not be revoked by the principal. In addition, incapacity or bankruptcy of the principal will not terminate the authority of the agent. The death of the principal also will not terminate the agency unless the duty for which the security was given terminates with the death of the principal.

KEY TERMS

1. Agency *a consensual relationship that may be formed by contract or agreement between the principal and agent where agent is authorized to act on the behalf of the principal*

2. Principal

3. Agent

4. Employment relationship *employer has the right to control the conduct of employee*

5. Independent contractor *contracts to do a particular job & is not subject to the control of the other*

6. Power of attorney *—written formal appt of an agent*

7. Fiduciary duty *utmost loyalty & good faith owed by agent to principal*

8. Reimbursement *principal is under a duty to pay agent for authorized pymts agent had made on principals behalf*

9. Indemnification *principal is under a duty to pay agent for losses incurred while acting in agent capacity*

10. Agency coupled with an interest *— is irrevocable — when an agent has a security interest in the subject matter of the agency*

TRUE/FALSE

T 1. Most contracts or business transactions can be created or conducted through an agent.

F 2. An agent who is incompetent to bind himself by contract may not make a contract which is binding on his principal.

T 3. An agent is under a duty to keep her principal's property separate from her own.

_T_ 4. A principal is under no duty to reimburse his agent for unauthorized expenses the agent incurs.

_T_ 5. Generally, any person has the capacity to be an agent.

_F_ 6. A person who engages an independent contractor to do a specific job has a right to control the conduct and activities of the independent contractor in the performance of his contract.

_T_ 7. Although all employees are agents, not all agents have to be employees.

_T_ 8. A power of attorney is a formal appointment of an agent.

_F_ 9. An agent has no duty to account for property or gifts received.

_F_ 10. An agency contract must be in writing.

_T_ 11. The principal-agent relationship is a fiduciary relationship.

_T_ 12. A principal may revoke an agent's authority at any time, but if he does, he may be in breach of his contract with the agent.

_T_ 13. Brian is appointed an agent for Independent Investors, Inc. Two months later, Brian files for bankruptcy because of personal debts arising prior to beginning work for III. Brian's agency is terminated by the bankruptcy.

_F_ 14. An agency coupled with an interest can be revoked at any time.

_T_ 15. While an agent may not use or disclose confidential information, she may reveal confidential information that the principal is about to commit a crime.

MULTIPLE CHOICE

_b_ 1. An agent may be appointed to perform all of the following except:
   a. perform a contract for personal services.
   b. commit an illegal act.
   c. negotiate the terms of a contract for personal services.
   d. buy or sell goods.

_b_ 2. Any contracts resulting from the appointment of an agent by a minor are:
   a. void.
   b. voidable.
   c. unenforceable.
   d. none of the above.

3. An agent who violates his fiduciary duty is liable to his principal:
   a. for breach of contract.
   b. in tort for losses caused.
   c. in restitution for profits made.
   d. all of the above.

 4. Assume that S wants to sell his house and B is interested in buying it. If A is an agent who normally handles such transactions, A may represent:
   a. S or B, but not both.
   b. S and B, but only with the informed consent of S.
   c. S and B, but only with the informed consent of B.
   d. S and B, but only with the informed consent of S and B.

 5. Where the agent has an interest in the subject matter of the agency, the agent's authority is terminated by:
   a. the death of the principal.
   b. the bankruptcy of the principal.
   c. a revocation of authority.
   d. the mutual agreement of the parties.

 6. Mel Merchant owns a retail store. Sarah Salesclerk works for Mel in the store. The relationship between Sarah and Mel is an example of:
   a. employer and independent contractor only.
   b. employer and employee only.
   c. principal and agent only.
   d. both employer and employee, as well as principal and agent.

7. Bill Businessman hires Andrew Attorney to represent him in a lawsuit. The relationship between Bill and Andrew is an example of:
   a. employer and independent contractor only.
   b. employer and employee only.
   c. principal and agent only.
   d. both employer and independent contractor, as well as principal and agent.

 8. Which of the following is not a duty owed by an agent to her principal?
   a. Obedience.
   b. Accounting.
   c. To inform.
   d. All of the above are duties of the agent.

_d_ 9. Peter Principal listed a parcel of real estate with Ron Realtor pursuant to a listing agreement which was good for 90 days. Two months later, Peter decides not to sell the property and revokes Ron's authority.
   a. Peter cannot revoke Ron's authority.
   b. Peter has the power to revoke Ron's authority, but does not have the right to revoke it.
   c. Peter may be liable to Ron for damages for breach of contract.
   d. Two of the above are correct, (b) and (c).

_d_ 10. A principal owes an agent a duty of:
   a. reimbursement.
   b. indemnification.
   c. compensation.
   d. all of the above.

_b_ 11. An agency will terminate by operation of law upon the happening of all but which one of the following?
   a. Bankruptcy.
   b. Fulfillment of purpose.
   c. Death of the principal.
   d. Disloyalty of agent.

_b_ 12. If an agent, authorized to sell certain property of her principal for $10,000, sells it for $11,000, then:
   a. she may pocket the additional $1,000.
   b. she has a duty to account to the principal for the additional $1,000.
   c. she must give the $1,000 back to the third party.
   d. none of the above.

_d_ 13. Which of the following acts will not terminate an agency?
   a. Lapse of time.
   b. Revocation of authority.
   c. Renunciation by the agent.
   d. All of the above will terminate the agency.

_d_ 14. The agency relationship is important in the operation of:
   a. partnerships.
   b. corporations.
   c. sole proprietorships.
   d. all of the above.

_____ *o*   15. The principal is under a duty to _____ the agent for losses incurred or suffered while
acting as directed by the principal.
a. indemnify
b. compensate
c. reimburse
d. none of the above

SHORT ESSAY

1. How may an agency relationship be terminated?

    Acts of parties → lapse of time / fullfilment of purpose / mutual agreement / revocation of authority / renunciation of the agent
    Operation of law → Bankruptcy / Death of principal / Incapacity of principal / Changes in business conditions / loss or destruction of subject matter / Disloyalty of agent

2. What are the practical consequences of an agent's fiduciary duty?

    Conflict of interest   principal may discharge the agent /
    Duty not to compete   ⎞ avoid the transaction / Recover against
    Confidential info   ⎬ the agent in tort & contract actions
    Duty to acct for financial benefits ⎠ as well as restitution / agent also
                                    loses right to compensation

3. What are the remedies available to the principal for violation of duties by an agent?

    _____
    _____
    _____
    _____
    _____

4. What is an irrevocable agency? Explain.

    An irrevocable agency is when the agent has a security interest in the subject matter of the agency
    Authority of agent may not be revoked by principal
    Incapacity / bankruptcy will not terminate / death will not terminate unless the subject matter terminates w/ the death of principal

5. P appoints A as her agent to sell goods in markets where the highest price can be obtained. A sells the
    goods in a market that is glutted and obtains a low price, although a higher price could have been
    obtained in another market. If P sues A, what would be the result?

    P would win   Duty of Care
                       Duty of obedience
    Restitution for difference
          Breach of duty of diligence

Chapter 20
Relationship With Third Parties

PURPOSE

In this chapter, you study the external part of agency involving the relationship between the agent and third parties with reference to the liability of the agent and of the principal to those third parties. In general with regard to contracts, the principal and the third party are bound to those contracts the principal actually authorizes plus those the principal has apparently authorized. In addition to studying the contractual liability of the principal and agent, you also study the liability of the principal and agent for torts and crimes committed by the agent.

CHAPTER CHECKPOINTS

After reading and studying this chapter, you should be able to:

1. Distinguish between and identify actual authority and apparent authority.

2. Discuss the liability of principal and the agent to third parties upon termination of the agency relationship.

3. Distinguish between a disclosed principal, an undisclosed principal and a partially disclosed principal and discuss the contract liability of each with respect to third parties.

4. Define the doctrine of respondeat superior and discuss when a principal will be liable for the torts of his agent under the doctrine.

5. Discuss the contract liability and the tort liability of an agent to third parties.

CHAPTER OUTLINE

I. Relationship of Principal and Third Persons–The purpose of an agency relationship is to allow the principal to extend his business activities by authorizing agents to enter into contracts with third persons on the principal's behalf. Pursuant to the agency relationship, the principal has contract liability and potential tort liability.

    A. Contract Liability of the Principal–The power of an agent is his ability to change the legal status of his principal. An agent has the power to bind his principal whenever he has actual or apparent authority. This power of an agent to act for his principal in business transactions is the basis of agency. The contract liability of a principal also depends upon whether the principal is disclosed, partially disclosed, or undisclosed. A disclosed principal is one whose existence and identity are known. A partially disclosed principal is one whose existence is known but whose identity is not known. An undisclosed principal is one whose existence and identity are not known.

        1. Types of Authority–There are two basic types of authority: actual and apparent. Actual authority is the power conferred upon agent by actual consent given by principal. Apparent authority is power conferred upon agent by acts or conducts of principal that reasonably lead a third party to believe that agent has such power.

            a. Actual Express Authority–The express authority of an agent is found in the words of the principal, spoken or written, and communicated to the agent.

            b. Actual Implied Authority–Implied authority is inferred from words or conduct manifested to the agent by the principal. It may arise from custom and usages of the business. Also general authority to manage a business for a principal confers certain implied authority on the agent.

            c. Apparent Authority–Apparent authority is power that arises out of words or conduct of a disclosed or partially disclosed principal manifested to third persons which they are reasonably induced to rely upon the assumption that actual authority exists. When there is apparent authority but not actual authority the principal is bound by the act of the agent. However, the agent has violated the duty of obedience and is liable to the principal.

        2. Delegation of Authority–If an agent is authorized to appoint or select other persons, called subagents, to perform or assist in the performance of the agent's duties, the acts of the subagent are binding on the principal to the same extent as if they had been done by the agent.

        3. Effect of Termination of Agency Upon Authority–On the termination of an agency, the agent's actual authority ceases. Notice of such termination to third persons is not required if termination is by death, incapacity or impossibility of performance. The bankruptcy of the principal terminates, without notice, the power of an agent to affect the principal's property, which passes to the trustee in bankruptcy. In other cases, apparent authority continues until the third party has actual knowledge or receives actual notice, if the party is one (1) with whom the agent had previously dealt on credit, (2) to whom the agent has been specially accredited, or (3) with whom the agent has begun to deal where the principal has knowledge of such dealing. Actual notice is the

knowledge actually and expressly communicated. All other third parties must have actual knowledge or constructive notice. Constructive notice is knowledge imputed by law. It includes publication in a newspaper of general circulation in the area where the agency is regularly carried on.

4. Ratification–Ratification is the affirmance by one person of a prior unauthorized act that another has done as his agent. The ratification of such act or contract binds the principal and the third party as if the agent had been initially authorized.

   a. Requirements of Ratification–The principal must show an intent to ratify the entire act or contract with knowledge of all material facts concerning the transaction. It may be manifested by express language or implied from conduct of the principal.

   b. Effect of Ratification–Ratification is equivalent to prior authority. Therefore, the respective rights, duties, and remedies of the principal and the third party are the same as if the agent had originally possessed due authority.

5. Fundamental Rules of Contractual Liability–The following rules summarize the contractual relations between the principal and the third party: (1) a disclosed principal and the third party are contractually bound if the agent acts within her actual or apparent authority in making the contract; (2) a partially disclosed principal and the third party are contractually bound if the agent acts within her actual or apparent authority in making the contract; (3) an undisclosed principal and the third party are contractually bound if the agent acts within her actual authority in making the contract unless the principal is excluded by the terms of the contract or his existence is fraudulently concealed; and (4) no principal is contractually bound to a third party if the agent acts without any authority unless a disclosed or partially disclosed principal ratifies the contract.

B. Tort Liability of the Principal–Tort liability may arise directly or indirectly (vicariously) from authorized or unauthorized acts of the agent.

1. Direct Liability of Principal–A principal is directly liable in damages resulting from directing an agent to commit a tort and failing to exercise care in employing competent agents.

   a. Authorized Acts of Agent–A principal who authorizes his agent to commit a tortious act concerning the property or person of another is liable for the injury or loss sustained by that person.

   b. Unauthorized Acts of Agent–A principal who conducts activities through an employee or other agent is liable for harm resulting from the principal's negligent or reckless conduct in hiring, instructing, supervising, or controlling the employee or other agent.

2. Vicarious Liability of Principal for Unauthorized Acts of Agent–Vicarious liability is indirect legal responsibility for the act of another. The liability of a principal for unauthorized torts by an agent depends primarily on whether the agent is an employee or not. An employee is an agent employed to perform services for a principal-employer and whose physical conduct in the performance of the service is controlled or subject to the right to control by the principal. A principal is liable for an unauthorized tort committed by an employee in the course of his employment. If the agent's physical conduct is not controlled by the principal, then the agent is an independent contractor and the principal is not liable for tortious conduct.

   a. *Respondeat Superior*–This means "let the superior respond." This is a form of liability without fault and is based on the rationale that a person who carries out his business activities through the use of employees should be liable for their tortious conduct in carrying out those business purposes.

    b. Torts of Independent Contractor–The doctrine of *respondeat superior* does not apply to torts committed by an independent contractor because he is not an employee.

C. Criminal Liability of the Principal–A principal is liable for the authorized criminal acts of his agents only if the principal directed, participated in, or approved of the acts.

II. Relationship of Agent and Third Persons–The function of an agent is to assist in the conduct of the principal's business by carrying out his orders. Generally, the agent acquires rights against third parties and incurs no liabilities to them. However, there are several exceptions.

A. Contract Liability of Agent–The agent is not normally a party to the contract he makes with a third person on behalf of a disclosed principal.

    1. Disclosed Principals–When the agent is acting on behalf of a disclosed principal, the agent ordinarily incurs no liability on the contract to either party.

        a. Unauthorized Contracts–If an agent exceeds his actual and apparent authority, the principal is not bound. If the agent does not have authority to bind the principal, the agent is liable to the third party for damages if the agent has expressly or impliedly warranted that he has authority, unless the principal ratifies the contract or the third party knew that the agent was unauthorized.

        b. Agent Assumes Liability–An agent may agree to become liable on a contract between the principal and the third party by making the contract in her own name, by co-making the contract with the principal, or by a guarantee of the contract.

    2. Partially Disclosed Principal–Whether the particular transaction is authorized or not, an agent for a partially disclosed principal is liable on the contract to the third party. If the agent is authorized to make the contract, then both the agent and the partially disclosed principal are liable.

    3. Undisclosed Principal–The agent is personally liable upon a contract she enters into with a third person on behalf of an undisclosed principal, unless the third person, after discovering the existence and identity of the principal, elects to hold the principal to the contract.

    4. Nonexistent or Incompetent Principal–A person who purports to act as agent for a principal, whom both the agent and the third party know to be nonexistent or incompetent, is personally liable on a contract entered into with a third person on behalf of such a principal.

B. Tort Liability of Agent–An agent is personally liable for his tortious acts that injure third persons, whether or not such acts are authorized by the principal and whether or not the principal may also be liable.

C. Rights of Agent Against Third Person–An agent who makes a contract with a third person on behalf of a disclosed principal usually has no right of action against the third person for breach of contract, because the agent is not a party to the contract.

KEY TERMS

1. Disclosed principal *a principal whose identity & existence are known*

2. Partially disclosed principal *existence is known but not identity*

3. Undisclosed principal *existence & identity are not known*

4. Actual authority *power conferred upon agent by actual consent given by principal*

5. Apparent authority *power conferred upon agent by acts or conducts of principal that reasonably lead a 3rd party to believe agent has such power*

6. Express authority *found in the words of the principal - spoken/written & communicated to agent*

7. Implied authority *authority is inferred from words or conduct manifested to the agent by principal it may arise from customs or usages of business*

8. Subagent

9. Actual notice

10. Constructive notice

11. Ratification *the affirmance by one person of a prior unauthorized act that another has done as his agent - binds principal & 3rd party as if the agent had been initially authorized*

12. Vicarious liability *indirect legal responsibility for the act of another*

13. *Respondeat superior*
   does not apply to independent contractors

TRUE/FALSE

__T__ 1. The power of an agent is her ability to change the legal status of her principal.

____ 2. Unless the principal is disclosed, an agent has no apparent authority. *disclosed/partially disclosed*

__F__ 3. An agent may not ordinarily appoint a subagent to perform the agent's duties.

__T__ 4. An agent's actual authority is terminated by a revocation of authority. *principal*

____ 5. An agent's apparent authority is terminated by a renunciation of authority. *agent*

__X__ 6. A principal may not be held liable for the wrongful acts of his agent if the agent acted in flagrant disobedience of the principal's instructions.

__T__ 7. Under the doctrine of *respondeat superior*, a principal may be held liable for the torts of her agent even though the agent is sufficiently solvent to pay for the damage himself. *employee - employer*

_T_ 8. An employer may be subject to criminal penalty for acts of an employee who is acting within the scope of her employment.

_____ 9. The bankruptcy of the principal does not affect the agent's power with respect to property passing to a bankruptcy trustee.

_____ 10. An agent who is personally liable on a contract has no right of action against the third person for breach of the contract.

_F_ 11. An undisclosed principal is one whose existence is known but whose identity is not known.

_____ 12. An agent who enters into a contract on behalf of an incompetent principal may be personally liable on that contract.

_____ 13 A principal-employer is vicariously liable for the unauthorized acts of an agent-employee.

_F_ 14. Implied authority is actual authority derived from the written or spoken words of the principal.

_T_ 15. A principal may be liable to a third party based upon an agent's apparent authority even though the agent had no actual authority.

MULTIPLE CHOICE

_d_ 1. Sara tells Bill that he may sell her stereo for her. Bill's authority is:
   a. express authority.
   b. actual authority.
   c. implied authority.
   d. a and b, but not c.

_c_ 2. An agent may be liable to his principal for exceeding his actual authority even though his acts are within the scope of his:
   a. express authority.
   b. implied authority.
   c. apparent authority.
   d. none of the above.

_c_ 3. An agent has apparent authority to bind her principal in any transaction in which:
   a. third persons have no knowledge of the agency relationship.
   b. the existence and identity of the principal are undisclosed.
   c. third persons reasonably rely upon the existence of actual authority as indicated by the principal's conduct.
   d. none of the above.

principal

  A 4. When an agency is terminated by revocation of authority, the agent's apparent authority continues with respect to third parties with whom the agent had previously dealt until they:

    a. receive actual notice of the termination.

    b. receive constructive notice of the termination.

    c. read of the termination in a newspaper of general circulation.

    d. none of the above.

5. Apparent authority continues until the third party has actual knowledge or notice of termination in which of the following situations?

    a. The agent has previously dealt with the third party on credit.

    b. The agent has been specially accredited.

    c. The principal should know that the agent has begun to deal with the third party.

    d. All of the above.

 6. Ratification of an unauthorized contract is effective to bind the principal and a third person to the contract even though:

    a. the principal does not ratify the entire contract.

    b. the principal does not notify the third person of his intent to ratify the contract.

    c. the third person has already notified the principal of his withdrawal from the contract.

    d. the agent failed to indicate to the third person that his acts were on behalf of the principal.

 _d_ 7. Assume that P and P's agent A, conspire to injure C so that she can't run in the big race. Which of the following is true?

    a. P has committed both a crime and a tort.

    b. P has committed a tort but not a crime.

    c. A has committed a tort and a crime.

    d. Two of the above.

_a_ 8. The doctrine of _respondeat superior_ imposes liability upon:

    a. an employer.

    b. an employee.

    c. an independent contractor.

    d. a fellow servant.

 A 9. Assume that A enters into a contract with T on behalf of A's undisclosed principal, P. If T fails to discover the existence of P, whom may T hold to performance of the contract?

    a. A only.

    b. P only.

    c. A or P but not both.

    d. Neither A nor P.

C   10. Assume that A enters into a contract with T on behalf of A's undisclosed principal, P. If T discovers the existence and identity of P, whom may T hold to performance of the contract?
   a.   A only.
   b.   P only.
   c.   A or P but not both.
   d.   Neither A nor P.

d   11. General authority to manage or operate a business for a principal confers implied authority on the agent to do all except which one of the following:
   a.   hire employees.
   b.   purchase equipment and supplies.
   c.   make repairs.
   d.   agent may do all of the above.

b   12. P writes a letter to A authorizing her to sell his car. A tries to sell the car to C, telling him that although it isn't her car she has authority to sell it. In this case P would be a:
   a.   disclosed principal.
   b.   partially disclosed principal.
   c.   undisclosed principal.
   d.   none of the above.

b   13. P writes a letter to A authorizing her to sell his car and sends a copy of the letter to T, a prospective buyer. The next day P writes a letter to A revoking the authority to sell the car but does not send a copy of this letter to T. If A contracts to sell the car to T:
   a.   P will be liable on the contract based upon A's implied authority.
   b.   P will be liable on the contract based upon A's apparent authority.
   c.   P will not be liable because A did not have actual authority.
   d.   none of the above.

A   14. Page and Company hires Ed to deliver merchandise to Page's customers. While driving the company's truck on his way to make a delivery, Ed negligently causes the truck to hit Tim's car and injure Tim.
   a.   Page is liable to Tim because Ed was acting within the scope of employment.
   b.   Page is not liable to Tim because Ed was not acting within the scope of employment.
   c.   Page is not liable to Tim because Ed is an independent contractor.
   d.   None of the above.

C   15. Page and Company hires Ed to deliver merchandise to Page's customers. After making the scheduled deliveries, Ed drives the company's truck to a nearby city to visit his girlfriend. While in the city, Ed negligently causes the truck to hit Tony's car and injure Tony.
   a.   Page is not liable to Tony because Ed is an independent contractor.
   b.   Page is liable to Tony because Ed was acting within the scope of employment.
   c.   Page is not liable to Tony because Ed was not acting within the scope of employment.
   d.   None of the above.

SHORT ESSAY

1. What is the difference between actual authority and apparent authority?

    Actual authority is spoken/written words by principal communicated to agent. app
    apparent authority is arises out of words or conduct of a disclosed or partially disclosed principal manifested to 3rd persons which they a reasonably induced to believe agent has authority

2. What is the difference between having the power to bind one's principal and having the right to bind him?

    An agent has the power to bind principal when the principal is legally bound by the act of the agent. Agent has right to bind principal whenever he may do so w/out violating the duty of obedience by exceeding his actual authority

3. Discuss the negligent hiring doctrine.

    _____
    _____
    _____
    _____

4. Discuss termination of agency authority and its effect on liability.

    _____
    _____
    _____
    _____

5. Dan entered into a contract to remodel the Majestic Restaurant owned by Riverside Restaurant, Inc. Rob, part owner and president of Riverside, signed the contract, "Rob Swanton." When a dispute arose over the contract, Dan brought suit against Rob for breach of contract. Rob contends that he has no personal liability for the contract and that only Riverside is liable. What is the result?

    _____
    _____
    _____
    _____

Part III
Sample Examination

TRUE/FALSE

_T_ 1. If an agent is acting on behalf of a disclosed principal and is acting with *actual* authority, then the principal and the third party will be bound by a contract that the agent negotiates with the third party on behalf of the principal.

_T_ 2. A principal can generally accomplish through an agent whatever business activity she could accomplish personally.

_T_ 3. The principal generally retains the power to revoke the agent's authority, even though he may be liable for resulting damage to the agent.

_T_ 4. An employer has a duty to provide an employee with reasonably safe conditions of employment and to warn the employee of any unreasonable risk involved in the employment.

_T_ 5. Should a principal become bankrupt, the agent's authority will terminate without notice.

_F_ 6. Independent contractors are not subject to liability because they are not truly agents.

_T_ 7. Carl Contractor hires Andrew Attorney to negotiate a contract on his behalf. Andrew is both an independent contractor and an agent acting on behalf of Carl.

_F_ 8. An employer is never liable for intentional torts committed by his employees. ?

_F_ 9. Although the agent has duties to the principal, the principal has no duties to the agent.

_F_ 10. Ron Realtor is hired by Lyle Landowner to find a purchaser for a 10 acre hobby farm he owns in the country. Two days later, Paula Purchaser comes to Ron and asks him whether he would be willing to be her agent in finding a small acreage in the country for her to buy. Ron agrees. Ron can serve as agent to both Lyle and Paula in arranging a deal between them without violating any of his duties as an agent.

MULTIPLE CHOICE

_____ 11. The Individual Indemnity Insurance company hires Audrey Agent to sell insurance for it. Audrey makes her own hours and drives her own automobile to see prospects. While hurrying to see a customer, Audrey drives a little too fast for the weather conditions and negligently injures a pedestrian. The pedestrian sues Individual Indemnity for his injuries.
a. The pedestrian can recover from Individual Indemnity.
b. Audrey was an independent contractor for whose physical acts Individual Indemnity was not liable.
c. Audrey's authority to sell insurance policies means that Individual Indemnity will be liable for policies which Audrey sells on its behalf.
d. Two of the above are correct, (b) and (c).

_d_ 12. Ratification by a principal of an unauthorized act may occur by:
a. silence that indicates consent.
b. express statements.
c. acceptance of the benefits of the contract.
d. all of the above.

_b_ 13. When a principal terminates an agent who has dealt with third parties and has collected accounts on the principal's behalf, the principal must give the third parties _____ notice of the termination of the agent's authority.
a. constructive
b. actual
c. no
d. written

_b_ 14. Power conferred upon an agent by acts or conduct of the principal that reasonably lead a third party to believe that the agent has such power is known as:
a. actual authority.
b. apparent authority.
c. implied authority.
d. constructive authority.

_c_ 15. Sam is a salesman at the Paymart Discount Store. He inadvertently misrepresents the capabilities of a computer which he sells to Thomas. Thomas is upset and sues the Paymart Store.
a. Paymart has no liability, because it did not authorize the misrepresentation.
b. Paymart has no liability, because Sam's misrepresentation was not a tort.
c. Paymart is responsible for Sam's unauthorized misrepresentations.
d. None of the above.

C   16. One who contracts with another to do a job but who is not subject to the control of the other is known as:
- a. agent.
- b. principal.
- c. independent contractor.
- d. employee.

C   17. Apparent authority continues beyond termination, requiring actual notice if a third party is one:
- a. with whom the agent had previously dealt.
- b. to whom the agent has been specially accredited.
- c. both a and b.
- d. neither a nor b. Apparent authority never continues beyond termination.

b   18. A principal is generally liable for the torts committed by an _____ within the scope of his employment but not for the torts of an _____ .
- a. employee, agent
- b. employee, independent contractor
- c. independent contractor, employee
- d. independent contractor, agent

b   19. The requirement that an agent act with reasonable care and skill in his employment is:
- a. duty of obedience.
- b. duty of diligence.
- c. duty to account.
- d. fiduciary duty.

C   20. Arthur authorizes Bob to sell his eighty acres of farm land for $800 per acre. Subsequently, oil is discovered on the neighboring land and Arthur's land greatly increases in value. Bob is aware of this, but Arthur is not.
- a. Bob can sell the land to his brother for $800 per acre.
- b. Bob can sell the land to a stranger for $800 per acre, but not to his brother.
- c. Bob's authority to sell the land is terminated by operation of law.
- d. Bob's authority to sell the land is terminated by the acts of the parties.

Chapter 21
Introduction to Sales

PURPOSE

The sale of goods is the most common and important of all commercial transactions. The law of sales was originally part of the Law Merchant. It was eventually absorbed into the common law and then codified in Article 2 of the Uniform Commercial Code. Article 2 has been adopted in all states, except Louisiana, as well as in the District of Columbia and the Virgin Islands. The critical role of the law of sales is to establish a framework in which present and future exchanges may take place in a predictable, certain, and orderly fashion with a minimum of transaction costs. In this chapter, you begin your study of Article 2 of the UCC, which governs contracts involving the sale of goods and is a specialized branch of both the law of contracts and the law of personal property. Chapter 19 covers the basic definitions and the fundamental principles of Article 2 of the Code.

CHAPTER CHECKPOINTS

After reading and studying the chapter, you should be able to:

1. Define the terms "sale" and "goods" and distinguish a sale of goods from a lease of goods.

2. List and discuss the fundamental principles of Article 2.

3. List and discuss the selected rules found in Article 2 that apply to merchants.

4. Summarize the UCC battle of the forms provision and discuss how it varies from the common law mirror image rule.

5. Compare the Article 2 parol evidence rule and statute of frauds provisions to the common law parol evidence rule and the general statute of frauds provisions discussed earlier in this text.

CHAPTER OUTLINE

I. Nature of Sales Contracts–The law of sales found in Article 2 of the Code is a specialized branch of both the law of contracts and the law of personal property.

    A. Definitions–The Code defines a sale as the transfer of title to goods from seller to buyer for a price. Goods are movable, tangible, personal property and include the unborn young of animals, growing crops, and other items attached to real property but removed by the seller.

        1. Governing Law–Sales transactions are governed by Article 2 of the Code, but where general contract law has not been specifically modified by the Code, general contract law continues to apply. Transactions not within the scope of Article 2 include employment contracts, service contracts, insurance contracts, contracts involving real property, and contracts for the sale of intangibles such as stocks, bonds, patents, and copyrights.

        2. Nonsales Transactions in Goods–Bailments, leases, and gifts are not sales, but can significantly affect goods nonetheless. Courts have begun to apply Code provisions by analogy to these transactions as well as to secured transactions.

    B. Fundamental Principles of Article 2–The purpose of Article 2 is to modernize, clarify, simplify, and make uniform the law of sales. The Code's open-ended drafting includes the following fundamental concepts.

        1. Good Faith–All parties to contracts under the Code must perform their obligations in good faith. The Code defines good faith as honesty in fact in the conduct or transaction concerned. In the case of a merchant, it also includes the observance of reasonable commercial standards of fair dealing in the trade.

        2. Unconscionability–Every contract of sale may be scrutinized by the courts to determine whether in its commercial setting, purpose, and effect, it is unconscionable. The court may refuse to enforce an unconscionable contract or any part of it found to be unconscionable or may limit its application to prevent an unconscionable result. Procedural unconscionability involves scrutiny for the presence of "bargaining naughtiness." In other words, it involves an analysis of the fairness of the bargaining process or the presence of procedural irregularities such as burying terms in the fine print of a contract. Substantive unconscionability deals with the actual terms of the contract and looks for oppressive or grossly unfair provisions such as an exorbitant price or an unfair exclusion or limitation of contractual remedies.

        3. Expansion of Commercial Practices–The Code places great emphasis on course of dealings and usage of trade in interpreting agreements. A course of dealing is a sequence of previous conduct between the parties that may fairly be regarded as establishing a common basis of understanding for interpreting their expressions and agreement. A usage of trade is a practice or method of dealing regularly observed and followed in a place, vocation or trade.

        4. Sales By and Between Merchants–The Code establishes separate rules that apply to transactions between merchants or involving a merchant as a party. A merchant is a dealer in goods or a person who by his occupation holds himself out as having knowledge or skill peculiar to the goods or practices involved, or who employs an agent or broker whom he holds out as having such knowledge or skill. These rules exact a higher standard of conduct from merchants because of

their knowledge of trade and commerce and because merchants as a class generally set the standards.

5. Liberal Administration of Remedies–The Code provides that its remedies shall be liberally administered in order to place the aggrieved party in as good a position as if the defaulting party had fully performed. It also provides that where no specific remedy is expressly provided, the courts should provide an appropriate remedy.

6. Freedom of Contract–Most Code provisions are not mandatory, but instead permit the parties by agreement to vary or displace them altogether, except that the obligations of good faith, diligence, reasonableness, and care may not be disclaimed by agreement.

7. Validation and Preservation of Sales Contracts–The Code reduces formal requisites to the bare minimum and attempts to preserve agreements whenever the parties manifest an intention to enter into a contract

II. Formation of a Sales Contract–The Code's approach to validation is to recognize contracts whenever the parties manifest an intent to contract.

   A. Manifestation of Mutual Assent–In order for a contract to exist there must be an objective manifestation of mutual assent: an offer and an acceptance.
      1. Definiteness of an Offer–At common law, the terms of a contract were required to be definite and certain. The Code provides that a contract does not fail for indefiniteness even though one or more terms may have been omitted. The Code provides standards by which omitted essential terms may be ascertained and supplied, provided the parties intended to enter into a binding agreement.
         a. Open Price–The parties may enter into a contract for the sale of goods even though they have no agreement on the price. The Code provides that the price is a reasonable one at the time for delivery where the agreement (1) says nothing as to price, (2) provides that the parties shall agree later as to the price and they fail to so agree, or (3) fixes the price in terms of some agreed market or other standard or as set by a third person or agency and the price is not so set.
         b. Open Delivery–Absent specific instructions, delivery must be made within a reasonable time, in a single delivery at the seller's place of business.
         c. Open Quantity: Output and Requirements Contracts–Output contracts which are agreements for the entire output of a seller for a stated period and requirements contracts which are agreements for the seller to supply the buyer with all her requirements of certain goods are enforceable by the application of an objective standard based on the good faith of both parties. The quantities may not be disproportionate to any stated estimate or the prior output or requirements.
         d. Code Provisions–Code provisions also govern terms of payment, duration of contracts, and particulars of performance should the parties fail to agree on these matters in their agreement.
      2. Irrevocable Offers–A firm offer is a signed writing by a merchant to hold open an offer for the sale or purchase of goods. Such an offer is irrevocable for the stated period up to a maximum of

three months even if no consideration is given to the merchant offeror for the promise. An option is a contract to hold open an offer; it is binding on the offeror.

3. Variant Acceptances–The Code modifies the common law mirror image rule under which an acceptance cannot vary from the terms of the offer. Under the common law rule where two businesses exchange preprinted forms with varying terms, no contract exists, even if the parties intend that there be a contract. The Code addresses this battle of the forms problem by focusing on the intent of the parties. The issue then becomes whether the offeree's different terms become part of the contract. If both parties are merchants, the additional terms will be part of the contract if they do not materially alter the agreement; if neither of the parties are merchants or if the additional terms do materially alter the offer, they are merely construed as proposals for addition to the contract. Different terms proposed by the offeree will not become part of the contract unless specifically accepted by the offeror. If the offeree expressly makes his acceptance conditioned upon assent to the additional or different terms, no contract is formed.

4. Manner of Acceptance–An offer to make a contract invites acceptance in any manner and by any medium reasonable under the circumstances unless clearly indicated otherwise. An offer to buy goods for prompt or current shipment may be accepted either by a prompt promise to ship or by prompt shipment.

5. Auctions –Under the Code, if an auction is announced to be *without reserve*, the auctioneer may not withdraw articles for sale. Unless the auction is announced to be without reserve it is *with reserve* and the auctioneer may withdraw items at any time until completion of the sale.

B. Consideration–The Code has relaxed the common law rule in several respects. A contract for the sale of goods can be modified without new consideration. In addition, a written waiver or renunciation signed and delivered by the aggrieved party discharges a claim of right arising out of a breach, even if there is no consideration. A firm offer is not revocable for lack of consideration.

C. Form of the Contract
1. Statute of Frauds–The Code provides that a contract for the sale of goods costing $500 or more is not enforceable unless there is some writing sufficient to evidence the existence of a contract between the parties.
   a. Modification of Contracts–An agreement modifying a contract must be in writing if the resulting contract is within the statute of frauds. Conversely, a modification that takes a contract outside of the statute of frauds may be oral.
   b. Written Compliance–The statute of frauds compliance provisions under the Code are more liberal than the rules under general contract law. The Code requires some writing (1) sufficient to indicate that a contract has been made between the parties, (2) signed by the party against whom enforcement is sought or by her authorized agent or broker, and (3) including a term specifying the quantity of goods. Under the Code a writing may be sufficient even if it omits or incorrectly states a term agreed upon.
   c. Exceptions–An oral contract for the sale of goods is enforceable against a party who admits in his pleading, testimony or otherwise in court that a contract was made. Enforcement is limited to the quantity of goods admitted. An oral contract for specially manufactured goods is also enforceable against the buyer. Finally, delivery and acceptance of part of the goods or

payment of part of the price and acceptance of the payment validates the contract but only for the goods that have been delivered and accepted or for which payment has been accepted.

2. Parol Evidence–Contractual terms that are set forth in a writing intended by the parties as a final expression of their agreement may not be contradicted by evidence of any prior agreement or of a contemporaneous oral agreement, but under the Code they may be explained or supplemented by: (a) course of dealing, usage of trade or course of performance, and (b) evidence of consistent additional terms.

3. Seal–Seals are inoperative under the Code with respect to contracts for the sale of goods.

D. Fundamentals of Article 2A-Leases–Article 2A-Leases was approved for adoption by the drafters of the Code in 1987 and subsequently amended in 1990. It is an attempt to codify in one statute all the rules governing the leasing of personal property. A few states have enacted the 1987 version while a greater number have adopted the 1990 version of Article 2A.

1. Definition of a Lease–A lease of goods is a transfer of the right to possession and use of goods for a term in return for consideration.

2. Warranties–Article 2A carries over the warranty provisions of Article 2 with minor revisions.

3. Default and Remedies–Article 2A provides for both lessor's remedies upon the lessee's default and for lessee's remedies upon the lessor's default. It also emphasizes freedom of the parties to contract among themselves and permits the lease agreement to include rights and remedies for default in addition to, or in substitution for those provided in Article 2A.

4. Consumer Leases–The definition of a consumer lease requires that (1) the transaction meet the definition of a lease under Article 2A; (2) the lessor be regularly engaged in the business of leasing or selling goods; (3) the lessee be an individual, not an organization; (4) the lessee take the lease interest primarily for a personal, family, or household purpose; and (5) the total payments under the lease do not exceed $25,000. Article 2A contains a number of provisions that apply to consumer leases and may not be varied by agreement of the parties.

5. Finance Leases–Whereas in the typical lease situation the lessor is also the supplier of the goods, in a finance lease arrangement the lessor is a separate party from the supplier. The lessor's primary function in a finance lease is to provide financing to the lessee for a lease of goods provided by the supplier.

KEY TERMS

1. Sale   *The transfer of title to goods from seller to buyer for a price*

2. Goods   *Movable, tangible, personal property*

3. Good faith   *honesty in fact in the conduct or transaction concerned*

4. Procedural unconscionability   *analysis for the fairness of the bargaining process*

5. Substantive unconscionability   *deals w/ the actual terms of the contract looks for unfair provisions*

6. Course of dealing   *a sequence of previous conduct between the parties that may be regarded as establishing a common basis of understanding*

7. Usage of trade *a practice or method of dealing*

8. Merchant *a dealer in goods or a person who by his occupation holds himself out as having knowledge or skill peculiar to the goods involved*

9. Lease *a lease of goods is a transfer of the right to possession and use of goods for a term in return for consideration*

10. Firm offer *signed writing by a merchant to hold open an offer for the sale or purchase of goods*

TRUE/FALSE

___T___ 1. A sale is defined as the transfer of title of goods from seller to buyer for a price.

___T___ 2. Where general contract law has not been specifically modified by Article 2 of the Code, principles of general contract law govern.

___F___ 3. A transfer, for a term, of the right to possession and use of goods is a lease. *for consideration*

___T___ 4. The doctrine of unconscionability permits the courts to resolve issues of unfairness explicitly on that basis without recourse to formalistic rules or legal fictions.

___F___ 5. Most of the Code's provisions restrict the parties from varying or displacing them by agreement.

___T___ 6. A merchant's firm offer is irrevocable for the stated period, not to exceed 3 months, even though no consideration is given to the merchant-offeror for that promise.

___F___ 7. The Code has adopted the common law mirror image rule stating that an acceptance cannot deviate from the terms of the offer.

___F___ 8. Under the Code, a unilateral offer must be accepted by a prompt shipment of the goods accompanied by notice to the buyer within a reasonable time.

___F___ 9. Under the Code, a modification of an existing contract must be supported by consideration to be binding.

___F___ 10. Under the Code, if a contract that was previously within the statute of frauds is modified so as to no longer fall within it, the modified contract must be in writing.

___T___ 11. A farmer who grows corn is a merchant with respect to corn.

___T___ 12. If an auction is not announced as being "without reserve" it is, under the Code, "with reserve".

___T___ 13. Firm offers are not revocable for lack of consideration.

___T___ 14. When the Article 2 parol evidence rule applies, parol evidence may be used to establish a course of dealing.

_____ 15.   In order for a contract for the sale of goods to be enforceable under the Code, it must specify the price.

MULTIPLE CHOICE

_____ 1.   Which of the following transactions would be governed by Article 2 of the UCC?
   a.   The sale of a house.
   b.   The sale of a typewriter.
   c.   The lease of a typewriter.
   d.   A contract of employment.

_____ 2.   Which of the following would not be governed by Article 2 of the UCC?
   a.   Employment contracts.
   b.   Service contracts.
   c.   Sales of goods contracts.
   d.   none of the above would be covered.

_____ 3.   For a merchant, "good faith" requires:
   a.   "honesty in fact in the conduct or transaction concerned."
   b.   "reasonable commercial standards of fair dealing in the trade."
   c.   neither (a) nor (b).
   d.   both (a) and (b).

_____ 4.   A "merchant" is defined by the Code as a person:
   a.   who is a dealer in the goods involved.
   b.   who by his occupation holds himself out as having knowledge or skill peculiar to the goods or practices involved.
   c.   who employs an agent or broker whom he holds out as having knowledge or skill peculiar to the goods or practices involved.
   d.   all of the above.

_____ 5.   Which of the following is not a requirement for a commercial lease?
   a.   The lessor be regularly engaged in the business of leasing or selling goods.
   b.   The lessee be an organization.
   c.   The total of the payments not exceed an amount specified by each state.
   d.   The transaction meet the definition of a lease under Article 2A.

_____ 6.   Under the Code, if a nonmerchant seller's acceptance contains a term in addition to those contained in the nonmerchant buyer's offer, the additional term is:
   a.   ignored.
   b.   construed as a proposal for an addition to the contract.
   c.   construed as part of the contract even if it materially alters the agreement.
   d.   construed as part of the contract unless the buyer expressly objects to its inclusion.

7. Under the Code, which of the following requires consideration to be binding?
   a. A modification of an existing contract.
   b. A contract to sell goods.
   c. A written discharge of a claim after a breach of contract.
   d. A merchant's firm offer.

8. In order to comply with the Code's version of the statute of frauds, the party seeking to enforce the contract must have a writing that:
   a. is sufficient to indicate a contract has been made.
   b. is signed by the party sought to be charged.
   c. indicates the quantity of goods to be exchanged.
   d. all of the above.

9. Under the Code, seals are effective with respect to:
   a. contracts for the sale of goods.
   b. offers to buy goods.
   c. offers to sell goods.
   d. none of the above.

10. A practice or method of dealing regularly observed and followed in a place, vocation, or trade describes:
   a. a "usage of trade."
   b. a "course of performance."
   c. a "course of dealing."
   d. an express term in a contract.

11. A signed writing by a merchant to hold open an offer is:
   a. an option.
   b. a firm offer.
   c. parol evidence of an agreement.
   d. none of the above.

12. Under the UCC statute of frauds, which of the following must be included in the required memoranda?
   a. The signatures of both parties.
   b. The shipment terms.
   c. The quantity of goods sold.
   d. The time for delivery.

_____ *c* 13. The UCC statute of frauds applies to contracts for the sale of goods of a price of _____ or more.
   a. $100
   b. $300
   c. $500
   d. $5,000

_____ *d* 14. Bill Buyer writes to Sam Seller and orders 100 tables.
   a. Sam can accept this offer by sending a confirmation of the order.
   b. Sam can accept this offer by shipping the tables.
   c. Sam must both send a confirmation and ship the tables to accept the offer.
   d. Sam can accept either by sending a confirmation of the order or by shipping the tables.

_____ *d* 15. Under the Code, the price is a reasonable one at the time for delivery where the agreement:
   a. says nothing as to price.
   b. provides that the parties shall agree later and they fail to so agree.
   c. fixes the price in terms of some agreed market standard and the price is not so set.
   d. all of the above.

SHORT ESSAY

1. When is Article 2 of the UCC applicable? When is it inapplicable?
   Sales transactions are governed by article 2 of the code. Article 2 is inapplicable involving employment contracts, service contracts, insurance contracts, contracts involving real property & contracts for the sale of intangibles

2. Define the terms "sale" and "goods."
   Sale — the transfer of title to goods from seller to buyer for a price
   goods are movable, tangible, personal property

3. Explain the concept of "Freedom of Contract."
   most code provisions are not mandatory, but instead permit the parties by agreement to vary or displace them altogether. obligations of good faith, diligence, reasonableness and care may not be disclaimed

4. What is a "firm offer?" What are its characteristics?

    a firm offer is a signed writing by a merchant to hold open an offer for the sale or purchase of goods irrevocable for a stated period up to 3 months – even if there is no consideration given to the merchant for the promise

5. If the parties have an oral contract for the sale of 100 bushels of wheat at a price of $4.50 per bushel and later orally agree to increase the quantity to 150 bushels at the same price per bushel, is the agreement, as modified, enforceable? Why or why not?

    the increase to 150 bushels caused the contract to fall w/in the statute of frauds & therefore the modification must be in writing to be enforceable

    $$
    \begin{array}{r}
    100 \\
    4.5 \\
    \hline
    500 \\
    4000 \\
    \hline
    450.0
    \end{array}
    $$

    $$
    \begin{array}{r}
    ^2 2150 \\
    4.5 \\
    \hline
    750 \\
    6000 \\
    \hline
    675.0
    \end{array}
    $$

    over $500 limit for
    Statute of frauds

Chapter 22
Performance

PURPOSE

In a sales contract as in other contracts, the obligations of the parties are determined by their contractual agreement. The contract may expressly state whether the seller must deliver the goods prior to the buyer's payment of the price, or whether the buyer must pay the price before the seller must deliver the goods. However, if there is no specific agreement of the parties, these terms will be supplied by the Code, common law, course of dealing, usage of trade, and course of performance. Performance is the carrying out of contractual obligations according to the terms of the contract so that the obligations are discharged. The basic obligation of the seller is to transfer and deliver the goods. The basic obligation of the buyer is to accept and pay for the goods in accordance with the contract. Unless the parties have agreed otherwise, tender of performance by one party is a condition to performance by the other party. In this chapter, you study the Code provisions that apply to the performance by the buyer and by the seller in a sales contract. These provisions vary depending upon the shipment terms of the contract and whether there has been a breach by one of the parties. You also study the circumstances under which the buyer or the seller may be excused from contractual obligations.

CHAPTER CHECKPOINTS

After reading and studying the chapter, you should be able to:

1. Distinguish a shipment contract from a destination contract and discuss the Code provisions regarding tender in each type of contract.

2. Explain the perfect tender rule and the three limitations upon it.

3. Distinguish between rejection and revocation of acceptance by the buyer and discuss the circumstances under which the buyer may exercise each of these rights.

4. Identify and discuss the excuses for nonperformance.

5. Discuss how a breach by one of the parties affects the obligations of performance by the other in various fact situations.

CHAPTER OUTLINE

A. Performance by the Seller–Unless the parties have agreed otherwise, tender of performance by one party is a condition to performance by the other party. Tender of delivery requires that the seller put and hold goods that conform to the contract at the buyer's disposition and that he give the buyer reasonable notification to enable him to take delivery. Tender must be made at a reasonable time and kept open for a reasonable period of time.

   1. Time and Manner of Tender–Tender must be made at a reasonable time, and the goods tendered must be kept available for the period reasonably necessary to enable the buyer to take possession of them. If no definite time for delivery is fixed by the terms of the contract, the seller is allowed a reasonable time after entering into the contract within which to tender the goods to the buyer. The buyer has a reasonable time within which to accept delivery. A contract may not be performed piecemeal or in installments unless the parties so agree.

   2. Place of Tender–If no place is specified in the contract, the place for delivery is the seller's place of business, or if he has none, his residence. If the contract is for the sale of identified goods that the parties know at the time of making the contract are located elsewhere than the seller's place of business or residence, the location of the goods is the place for delivery. Any agreements by the parties by use of delivery terms determines the place where the seller must tender delivery of the goods.

      a. Shipment Contracts–The delivery terms "F.O.B. place of shipment," "F.A.S. seller's port," "C.I.F.," and "C. & F." are all shipment contracts. In these cases the seller's tender of performance occurs at the point of shipment, provided the seller meets certain specified conditions designed to protect the interests of the absent buyer. The seller is required to: (1) deliver the goods to a carrier; (2) make a contract for their transportation that is reasonable according to the nature of the goods and the other circumstances; (3) obtain and promptly deliver or tender to the buyer any document necessary to enable the buyer to obtain possession of the goods from the carrier; and (4) promptly notify the buyer of the shipment.

      b. Destination Contracts–The terms "F.O.B. city of buyer," "ex-ship," and "no arrival, no sale" indicate a destination contract. A destination contract requires the seller to tender delivery of conforming goods at a specified destination. The seller must place the goods at the buyer's disposition and give the buyer reasonable notice to enable him to take delivery. He must also tender any necessary documents of title.

  c. Goods Held by Bailee–The seller may either tender a document of title or obtain an acknowledgment by the bailee of the buyer's right to possess the goods where they are in the possession of a bailee.

3. Perfect Tender Rule–Under this rule, the seller's tender of performance must conform exactly to the contract. If the goods or the tender fail in any respect to conform to the contract, the buyer may (1) reject the whole lot, (2) accept the whole lot, or (3) accept any commercial unit or units and reject the rest. There are three qualifications of the buyer's right to reject the goods upon the seller's failure to comply with the perfect tender rule.

  a. Agreement by the Parties–The parties may limit the operation of the perfect tender rule.

  b. Cure by the Seller–When the time for performance under the contract has not expired or when the seller has shipped nonconforming goods in the belief that the nonconforming tender would be acceptable, the Code recognizes that a seller may cure or correct his nonconforming tender.

  c. Installment Contracts–The buyer generally does not have to pay any part of the price of the goods until the entire quantity specified in the contract has been delivered or tendered to her. However, an installment contract expressly provides for delivery of the goods in separate lots or installment and usually for payment of the price in installments. If the contract is silent as to payment, the seller may demand payment for each lot if the price can be apportioned. The buyer may reject a nonconforming installment if it substantially impairs the value of that installment and cannot be cured. When the nonconformity or default of one or more of the installments substantially impairs the value of the whole contract, the buyer can treat the breach as a breach of the whole contract.

B. Performance by the Buyer–A buyer is obligated to accept conforming goods and to pay for them according to the contract terms. Unless otherwise agreed, payment or tender of payment by the buyer is a condition to the seller's duty to tender and to complete any delivery.

1. Inspection–Unless otherwise agreed, the buyer has a right to inspect the goods before payment or acceptance to determine whether they conform to the contract. In a C.O.D. contract, payment must be made prior to inspection, but payment in such cases is not acceptance of the goods. The buyer is allowed a reasonable time to inspect the goods and may lose his right to reject them or to revoke his acceptance if he fails to inspect the goods within a reasonable time.

2. Rejection–This is a manifestation by the buyer of his unwillingness to become the owner of the goods. It must be made within a reasonable time after the goods have been tendered or delivered. It is not effective unless the buyer reasonably notifies the seller. A merchant buyer who has rightfully rejected goods is obligated to follow reasonable instructions from the seller about disposing of the goods, when the seller has no agent at the place of rejection. If the rejected goods are perishable or threaten to decline in value speedily, the buyer is obligated to make reasonable efforts to sell them for the seller's account.

3. Acceptance–This means the buyer is willing to become the owner of the goods tendered or delivered to him by the seller. Acceptance precludes any rejection of the goods accepted.

Acceptance may be express or implied. It occurs when the buyer (1) signifies to the seller that the goods conform to the contract, (2) signifies to the seller that he will take the goods in spite of their nonconformity, or (3) fails to make an effective rejection of the goods. Acceptance of any part of a commercial unit is acceptance of the entire unit.

4. Revocation of Acceptance–The buyer may rescind his acceptance of the goods based upon their nonconformity if the nonconformity substantially impairs their value. Revocation is not effective until notice is given to the seller. Notice must be given within a reasonable time after the buyer discovers or should have discovered the grounds for revocation and before the goods have undergone any substantial change not caused by their own defects. Revocation of acceptance gives the buyer the same rights and duties with respect to the goods as if he had rejected them.

5. Obligation of Payment–In the absence of an agreement, payment is due at the time and place where the buyer is to receive the goods even though the place of shipment is the place of delivery.

C. Obligations of Both Parties–If parties to a sales contract fail to allocate risks that future events may or may not occur, the Code contains provisions which relieve the parties from obligation of full performance under the contract.

1. Casualty to Identified Goods–If the contract is for goods that are identified when the contract was made, and those goods are totally lost or damaged without fault of either party and before the risk of loss has passed to the buyer, the contract is avoided. Each party is excused from his performance obligation under the contract. Where the goods are partially destroyed, the buyer has the option to avoid the contract or to accept the goods with due allowance for the deterioration or deficiency in quantity.

2. Nonhappening of Presupposed Condition–The seller is excused from her duty of performance on the nonoccurrence of presupposed conditions that were a basic assumption of the contract, unless the seller has expressly assumed the risk. The Code excuses performance when performance may not be literally impossible, but where it is commercially impracticable. This requires more than mere hardship. The impracticability must be a result of an unforeseen supervening event not within the contemplation of the parties at the time of contracting.

3. Substituted Performance–Where neither party is at fault and the agreed manner of delivery of goods becomes commercially impracticable, a substituted manner of performance must be tendered and accepted.

4. Right to Adequate Assurance of Performance–When reasonable grounds for insecurity arise regarding either party's performance, the other party may demand a written assurance and suspend his own performance until he receives that assurance. If the assurance is not received within a reasonable time not exceeding thirty days, the contract is repudiated.

5. Right to Cooperation–Where performance is dependent upon one party's cooperation and that is not forthcoming, the other party is excused regarding delay in her own performance and may either proceed to perform in any reasonable manner or may treat the failure to cooperate as a breach.

6. Anticipatory Repudiation–This is a clear indication by either party to a contract that he is unwilling or unable to perform his obligations under the contract before performance is due. If the anticipatory repudiation substantially impairs the value of the contract, the aggrieved party may (1) await performance for a commercially reasonable time or (2) resort to any remedy for breach.

KEY TERMS

1. Tender of delivery _requires that the seller put & hold goods that conform to the contract at the buyer's disposition & the give buyer reasonable notification to enable him to take delivery_

2. Shipment contract

3. F.O.B. _Free on Board_

4. F.A.S.

5. C.I.F.

6. C. & F.

7. Destination contract

8. Ex-ship

9. No arrival, no sale

10. Perfect tender rule _sellers tender of performance must conform exactly to the contract_

11. Cure _a seller may cure or correct his nonconforming tender_

12. Installment contract

13. Inspection _the buyer has the right to inspect the goods before pymt or acceptance to determine conformity_

14. Rejection _unwillingness of buyer to become owner of goods_

15. Acceptance _acceptance may be express or implied — failure to make an effective rejection is considered acceptance_

16. Revocation of acceptance _buyer may rescind acceptance based upon their nonconformity_

17. Identified goods

18. Commercial impracticability

19. Anticipatory repudiation

212   Chapter 22

TRUE/FALSE

_____ 1. Tender of performance by one party is a condition to performance by the other party.

_____ 2. Tender of conforming goods by the seller entitles him to acceptance of them by the buyer.

_____ 3. Under the Code, the seller must tender all of the goods purchased under the contract in a single delivery and payment by the buyer is due on such tender, unless the parties specify otherwise in the contract.

_____ 4. Unless the parties agree otherwise, the buyer has a right to inspect the goods before payment or acceptance.

_____ 5. Under a shipment contract, the seller need only deliver the goods to a carrier and make a reasonable contract for their shipment.

_____ 6. Under the Code, the operation of the perfect tender rule may not be limited by agreement of the parties to the contract.

_____ 7. If a buyer refuses a tender of nonconforming goods without informing the seller of the nature of the defect, he cannot then assert that defect as a breach of contract by the seller if the defect was curable.

_____ 8. If a nonconforming installment of goods substantially impairs the value of the whole contract, then the buyer can treat the breach of the installment as a breach of the whole contract.

_____ 9. The buyer may lose the right to revoke acceptance in a C.O.D. shipment by failing to inspect the goods within a reasonable time.

_____ 10. If goods that were identified when the contract was made are totally lost or damaged without fault of either party and before risk of loss passes to the buyer, the contract is avoided.

_____ 11. A party is not excused from his duty of performance under a contract upon the nonoccurrence of a presupposed condition unless that condition was a basic assumption underlying the contract.

_____ 12. A buyer's basic obligation under a sales contract is to accept and pay for the goods.

_____ 13. Under a shipment contract, a seller is required to tender delivery of the goods to a carrier for delivery to the buyer.

_____ 14. The delivery terms "F.O.B. city of buyer," "ex-ship," and "no arrival, no sale" indicate that the contract is a shipment contract.

_____ 15. Where a practical alternative exists, neither seller nor buyer is excused on the grounds that delivery in the express manner provided in the contract is impossible.

MULTIPLE CHOICE

1. A party may fulfill her contractual duty of performance and place the other party in default by all of the following except by:
   a. performing according to the contract.
   b. tendering her performance according to the contract.
   c. assuming that the other party will not perform according to the contract.
   d. being excused from tender of performance under the contract.

2. Tender of conforming goods by the seller entitles him to:
   a. acceptance of the goods by the buyer.
   b. payment of the contract price by the buyer.
   c. both acceptance of the goods and payment of the contract price by the buyer.
   d. neither acceptance of the goods nor payment of the contract price by the buyer.

3. Which of the following is not correct?
   a. The seller has a duty to keep goods tendered for a period reasonably necessary for the buyer to take possession of them.
   b. A destination contract requires a seller to tender delivery of conforming goods at a specified destination.
   c. Unless otherwise agreed, a contract is performable in installments.
   d. None of the above is correct.

4. If either the tender of delivery or the goods fail in any respect to conform to the contract, the buyer may:
   a. reject the whole lot.
   b. accept the whole lot.
   c. accept any commercial unit or units and reject the rest.
   d. all of the above.

5. Under a destination contract, the seller must do all of the following except:
   a. place the goods at the buyer's disposition at the specified destination.
   b. give the buyer reasonable notice to enable him to take delivery.
   c. tender the necessary documents of title if such documents are involved in the transaction.
   d. inspect the goods upon arrival at the specified destination to ensure that they are conforming.

6. Under a shipment contract the seller is required to do which of the following?
   a. deliver the goods to a carrier.
   b. promptly notify the buyer of the shipment.
   c. provide the buyer with any necessary documents to obtain possession of the goods.
   d. all of the above.

_a_   7. The buyer must reject nonconforming goods under the perfect tender rule except where:
   a.   the parties agree to limit the buyer's right to reject nonconforming goods.
   b.   the seller refuses to cure a nonconforming tender of delivery.
   c.   the nonconformity of an installment does not substantially impair the value of the whole contract.
   d.   all of the above.

_b_   8. Which of the following is an incorrect statement concerning a buyer's right to inspect goods upon delivery?
   a.   Unless the parties agree otherwise, the buyer has the right to inspect the goods before payment or acceptance.
   b.   If the contract requires payment for the goods before acceptance, payment is required before inspection and operates as an acceptance of the goods.
   c.   The buyer may lose his right to reject or revoke acceptance of nonconforming goods if he fails to inspect them within a reasonable time.
   d.   The buyer must bear the expenses of inspection, but he may recover those costs from the seller if the goods prove to be nonconforming and are rejected.

_b_   9. After rejection of nonperishable goods, a merchant buyer who has received no instructions from the seller within a reasonable time after notice of rejection may:
   a.   store the goods for the seller's account.
   b.   reship the goods to the seller.
   c.   resell the goods for the seller's account.
   d.   all of the above.

_d_   10. An effective acceptance occurs when the buyer:
   a.   signifies to the seller that the goods conform to the contract.
   b.   signifies to the seller that he will keep the goods.
   c.   fails to make an effective rejection of the goods.
   d.   all of the above.

_a_   11. Acceptance of the goods precludes a buyer from:
   a.   rejecting the goods.
   b.   revoking his acceptance.
   c.   suing the seller for breach for any nonconformity that could not be reasonably discovered by inspection.
   d.   all of the above.

_b_   12. If the goods contracted for are partially destroyed before risk of loss has passed to the buyer:
   a.   the contract is avoided.
   b.   the contract is voidable at the buyer's option.
   c.   the contract is voidable at the seller's option.
   d.   the contract is neither void nor voidable at either party's election.

_C_ 13. Which of the following would indicate a shipment contract?
  a. Ex-ship.
  b. No arrival, no sale.
  c. C.I.F.
  d. All of the above.

_d_ 14. If the contract does not designate the proper place of delivery of the goods the seller must:
  a. deliver to buyers place of business.
  b. deliver to buyers residence.
  c. call buyer and deliver according to instructions.
  d. none of the above.

_d_ 15. Which of the following is a reason shipping terms in a contract for sale of goods are important?
  a. They determine who must bear the risk of loss.
  b. They determine who must pay the shipping costs.
  c. They determine whether the buyer may inspect before payment.
  d. All of the above are affected by the shipping terms of a contract.

SHORT ESSAY

1. What constitutes "tender"?
   tender of performance by one party is a condition of performance by the other party

2. What must a seller do to discharge her obligation to tender delivery of goods under a shipment contract?
   tender of delivery occurs at the shipping point - the seller must deliver goods to carrier for delivery to buyer

3. What is meant by the "perfect tender rule?"
   The sellers tender of performance must conform exactly to the terms of the contract

4. What is the difference between rejection and revocation of acceptance? What are the buyer's rights under each?

rejection – manifestion of buyer's unwillingness to become owner of goods
revocation of acceptance → the buyer may rescind his acceptance of the
goods based upon their non conformity if the noncomformity
substantially impairs their value. Revocation is not effective until notice is
given to seller within reasonable time

5. Under what conditions can the parties to a contract be relieved of their obligations of full performance?

_____
_____
_____
_____

Chapter 23
Transfer of Title and Risk of Loss

PURPOSE

The common law historically determined the rights and duties of the buyer and seller arising out of a sales contract based upon the principle of title. Under the Code, title has some significance, but the Code approaches each legal issue arising in a sales contract on its own merits. It provides separate and specific rules to control various transactional situations. In this chapter, you study the Code rules governing transfer of title and other property rights, the passage of risk of loss, and the transfer of goods sold in bulk.

CHAPTER CHECKPOINTS

After reading and studying this chapter, you should be able to:

1. Distinguish between a shipment contract and a destination contract and discuss the Code rules for risk of loss for each type of contract.

2. Explain the rules for passage of title and risk of loss in situations where there is no movement of the goods and (a) the seller is a merchant, (b) the seller is not a merchant, (c) there is a document of title, and (d) there is no document of title.

3. Distinguish between a void title and a voidable title and discuss the Code rule that applies when the owner of goods entrusts them to a merchant who then sells them to a good faith purchaser in the ordinary course of business.

4. Distinguish between a sale on approval and a sale or return and give the Code rule for risk of loss in each situation.

5. Define the term "bulk transfer" and summarize the Code provisions regarding such a transfer of assets.

CHAPTER OUTLINE

A. Transfer of Title–Transfer of title is fundamental to the existence of a sale of goods. Title cannot pass under a sales contract until existing goods have been identified to the contract.

    1. Identification–This is the designation of specific goods as goods to which the contract of sale refers. Identification may be made at any time and in any manner agreed upon by the parties. In the absence of explicit agreement, identification takes place (1) for goods already existing and identified, upon the making of the contract; (2) for future goods, when the seller ships, marks or otherwise designates goods to the contract; or (3) for crops to be grown and animal offspring to be born within twelve months, when the crops are planted or the offspring conceived. If the goods are fungible, identification of a share of undivided goods occurs when the contract is entered into.

        a. Insurable Interest–For a contract or policy of insurance to be valid, the insured must have an insurable interest in the subject matter. The Code extends an insurable interest to a buyer's interest in goods that have been identified to the contract, enabling the buyer to purchase insurance on the goods. The seller also has an insurable interest in the goods.

        b. Security Interest–The Code defines "security interest" as an interest in personal property or fixtures that ensures payment or performance of an obligation. Security interests are governed by Article 9 of the Code.

    2. Passage of Title–Title passes when the parties intend it to pass, provided the goods are in existence and have been identified. Where there is no specific agreement of the parties, the Code provides rules to determine when title passes to the buyer.

        a. Physical Movement of the Goods–When delivery is to be made by moving the goods, title passes at the time and place where the seller completes his performance with reference to delivery. When and where delivery occurs depends upon whether the contract is a shipment contract or a destination contract. In a shipment contract, the seller is required to tender delivery of the goods to a carrier for delivery to the buyer. Title passes to the buyer at the time and place that the seller delivers the goods to the carrier for shipment to the buyer. In a destination contract, the seller is required to tender delivery of the goods at a particular destination. Title passes to the buyer on tender of the goods at the destination. Tender means that the seller offers conforming goods to the buyer and gives the buyer notice that the goods are available.

        b. No Movement of the Goods–When delivery is to be made without moving the goods, title passes either (a) on delivery of a document of title where the contract calls for delivery of such a document; or (b) at the time and place of contracting where the goods at that time have been identified either by the seller or the buyer as the goods to which the contract refers and no documents are to be delivered. Where the goods are not identified at the time of contracting, title passes when the goods are identified.

    3. Power to Transfer Title–If the seller is the rightful owner or is authorized to sell the goods, then he has the right to transfer title. In some situations unauthorized sellers may have the power to transfer good title to certain buyers. In general, the purchaser of goods obtains such title as his transferor either has or had the power to transfer. A purported sale by a thief or finder or ordinary bailee of goods does not transfer title to the purchaser. However, to encourage and make

secure good faith acquisitions of goods, it is necessary that bona fide (good faith) purchasers for value be protected under certain circumstances. A good faith purchaser is defined as one who acts honestly, gives value, and takes the goods without notice or knowledge of any defect in the title of his transferor.

    a. Void and Voidable Title to Goods–A void title is no title. A thief or finder of goods has no title and can transfer none. A voidable title is one acquired under circumstances that permit the former owner to rescind the transfer and revest herself with title, as in the case of mistake, common duress, undue influence, fraud in the inducement, misrepresentation, or sale by a person without contractual capacity. If a buyer who has voidable title should resell the goods to a good faith purchaser for value, the good faith purchaser acquires good title, and the original seller's right of rescission is cut off.

    b. Entrusting of Goods to a Merchant–The Code protects buyers of goods in the ordinary course of business from merchants who deal in goods of that kind, where the owner has entrusted possession of the goods to the merchant. A buyer in the ordinary course of business is defined as a person who buys in ordinary course, in good faith, and without knowledge that the sale to him is in violation of anyone's ownership rights. When a merchant wrongfully sells an item that has been entrusted to him, as between the good faith purchaser in the ordinary course of business and the owner who has entrusted the goods to the merchant, the good faith purchaser from the merchant is preferred. The original owner's recourse is against the merchant for money damages; he cannot get back the goods. However, the Code does not protect the bona fide purchaser from a merchant when the goods have been entrusted to the merchant by a thief or finder or by someone who is completely unauthorized to entrust the goods.

B. Risk of Loss–This term addresses the allocation of loss between seller and buyer where the goods have been damaged, destroyed or lost without the fault of either the seller or the buyer.

    1. Risk of Loss Where There is a Breach–Where one party breaches the contract, the Code places the risk of loss on that party.

        a. Breach by the Seller–If the seller ships goods to the buyer that do not conform to the contract, the risk of loss remains on the seller until the buyer has accepted the goods or the seller has remedied the defect.

        b. Breach by the Buyer–Where conforming goods have been identified to the contract that the buyer repudiates or breaches before risk of loss has passed to him, the seller may treat the risk of loss as resting on the buyer "for a commercially reasonable time" to the extent of any deficiency in the seller's effective insurance coverage.

    2. Risk of Loss in Absence of a Breach–Where there is no breach, risk of loss may be allocated by agreement of the parties.

        a. Agreement of the Parties–The parties may by agreement shift the allocation of risk of loss or divide the risk between them.

        b. Trial Sales–Under the Code there are two types of trial sales: a sale on approval and a sale or return. Unless otherwise agreed, if the goods are delivered primarily for the buyer's use, the transaction is a sale on approval; if they are delivered primarily for resale by the buyer, it is a sale or return. In a sale on approval, possession, but not title to the goods, is transferred to the buyer for a stated period of time or, if none is stated, for a reasonable time. Both title and risk of loss remain with the seller until "approval" or acceptance of the goods by the buyer. In a sale or return, the goods are sold and delivered to the buyer with an option to return them to the seller. The risk of loss is on the buyer, who also has title until she revests it in the seller by a return of the goods. A consignment is a delivery of possession of personal property to an agent for sale by the agent and, under the Code, is regarded as a sale or return.

   c. Contracts Involving Carriers–If the contract does not require the seller to deliver the goods at a particular destination but merely to the carrier (a shipment contract), risk of loss passes to the buyer when the goods are delivered to the common carrier. If the seller is required to deliver them to a particular destination (a destination contract), risk of loss passes to the buyer at the destination when the goods are tendered to the buyer.

   d. Goods in Possession of Bailee–When goods are held by a bailee, the risk of loss passes to the buyer (1) if a negotiable document of title is involved, when the buyer receives the document; (2) if a nonnegotiable document of title is involved, when the document is tendered to the buyer; and (3) if no documents of title are used, either (a) when the seller tenders to the buyer written directions to the bailee to deliver the goods to the buyer or (b) when the bailee acknowledges the buyer's right to possession of the goods.

   e. All Other Sales–If the seller is a merchant, risk of loss passes to the buyer on the buyer's receipt of the goods. If the seller is not a merchant, it passes on tender of the goods from the seller to the buyer.

C. Bulk Sales–Article 6 of the Code applies to such sales and defines a bulk transfer as a transfer not in the ordinary course of the transferor's business of a major part of his inventory. Bulk sales law is designed to prevent a debtor from secretly liquidating all or a major part of his assets by bulk sale and conceal or divert the proceeds of the sale without paying his creditors. In 1988, drafters of the Code recommended that Article 6 be repealed by the states because the changes in the business and legal contexts in which sales are conducted have made regulation of bulk sales unnecessary. For states that desire to continue bulk sales regulation there is a revised Article 6 designed to afford better protection to creditors and minimize obstacles to good faith transactions.

KEY TERMS

1. Identification

2. Fungible

3. Insurable interest

4. Shipment contract

5. Destination contract

6. Good faith purchaser

7. Buyer in ordinary course of business   *a person who buys in ordinary course in good faith & w/out knowledge of violating anyone's rights*

8. Entrustment

9. Risk of loss

10. Sale on approval

11. Sale or return

12. Consignment

13. Bulk transfer

TRUE/FALSE

___T___ 1. In a sale of fungible goods, identification occurs when a contract is entered into.

___T___ 2. A security interest in personal property is an interest which ensures payment or performance of an obligation.

___F___ 3. Under the Code, only those persons with title to or a lien on goods have an insurable interest in those goods.

___T___ 4. When goods are to be moved to be delivered, title passes whenever the seller completes his performance with reference to delivery of the goods.

___T___ 5. A seller may have the power but not the right to sell goods in his possession to certain buyers.

___T___ 6. *F* If a minor sells goods to a good faith purchaser for value, the Code, as the common law, allows the minor to disaffirm and retake the goods.

___T___ 7. *good faith purchaser* A buyer in the ordinary course of business is defined by the Code as one who acts honestly, gives value, and takes without notice or knowledge of any defect in the title of his transferor.

___T___ 8. If risk of loss is placed on the seller, then he has no right to recover the purchase price for lost or damaged goods from the buyer.

___T___ 9. *F* Under both the common law and the Code, risk of loss is determined by ownership of the goods and whether title has been transferred.

___F___ 10. Under the Code, risk of loss is allocated by the Code and an agreement by the parties to shift or divide the risk is not controlling.

_____ 11. Where possession of, but not title to, goods is transferred to a buyer, risk of loss passes with possession.

__T__ 12. Under the Code, a sale on consignment is regarded as a sale or return.

__T__ 13. In a shipment contract, risk of loss passes to the buyer upon delivery of the goods to the carrier.

__F__ 14. If a seller breaches a contract by shipping nonconforming goods to the buyer, risk of loss remains on the buyer until the buyer properly returns the goods to the seller.

__T__ 15. In the case of a nonmerchant seller, risk of loss passes to the buyer upon tender of the goods.

MULTIPLE CHOICE

_b_ 1. A destination contract requires the seller to deliver the goods to a particular destination and title passes to the buyer:
   - a. at the time and place that the seller delivers the goods to the carrier for shipment to the buyer's place of business.
   - b. upon tender of the goods to the buyer at that destination.
   - c. upon delivery of a document of title.
   - d. at the time and place that the contract is entered into.

_d_ 2. A seller has an insurable interest in goods if:
   - a. the goods have been identified as the goods to which the contract of sale refers.
   - b. the seller has title to the goods.
   - c. the seller has a security interest in the goods.
   - d. all of the above.

_C_ 3. Tender requires the seller to do all of the following except:
   - a. put and hold conforming goods at buyer's disposition.
   - b. notify buyer goods are available.
   - c. supply buyer with a bill of exchange.
   - d. keep good available for a reasonable time.

_b_ 4. If goods are to be delivered without movement and are represented by a document of title, title passes:
   - a. at time and place of contract.
   - b. upon delivery of document of title.
   - c. upon tender of delivery.
   - d. none of the above.

_b_   5. Under the Code, a merchant entrusted with the possession of goods has the power to transfer good title to a buyer in the ordinary course of business if the entruster is:
   a.   a thief.
   b.   the owner of the goods.
   c.   one who found the goods.
   d.   all of the above.

_b_   6. Unless otherwise agreed, if the goods are delivered primarily for the buyer's use the transaction is a:
   a.   bulk sale.
   b.   sale on approval.
   c.   sale or return.
   d.   consignment.

_d_   7. In a sale on approval, risk of loss passes to the buyer when:
   a.   the contract is entered into by the parties.
   b.   the goods are sent by the seller.
   c.   the goods are received by the buyer.
   d.   the goods are accepted by the buyer.

_c_   8. In a shipment contract, risk of loss passes to the buyer when:
   a.   the parties enter into the contract.
   b.   the goods leave the seller's business.
   c.   the goods are delivered to a carrier.
   d.   the goods are received by the buyer.

destination contract   _FOB California would be shipment contract_

_b_   9. Lisa operates a boutique in New York City. She orders ten gowns from Ferre, a designer in California. They are sent "F.O.B. New York City," but they do not arrive at the boutique. Which statement is true?
   a.   Lisa bears the risk of loss because this is a shipment contract.
   b.   Ferre bears the risk of loss because this is a destination contract.
   c.   In this type of contract, risk of loss passes to the buyer when the goods are delivered to the common carrier.
   d.   None of the above.

_c_   10. In an ordinary contract in which the merchant-seller is required to tender or deliver the goods to a nonmerchant buyer, risk of loss passes to the buyer:
   a.   when the parties enter into the contract.
   b.   upon the seller's tender of the goods to the buyer.
   c.   when the buyer receives the goods.
   d.   none of the above.

_C_   11. If the seller ships nonconforming goods to the buyer, the risk of loss remains on the seller until:
   a.   the buyer accepts the goods.
   b.   the seller remedies the defect in the goods.
   c.   (a) or (b).
   d.   both (a) and (b).

_A_   12. Margaret goes to Jack's furniture store, selects a dining table, and pays Jack $500 for it. Jack agrees to stain the table a darker color and deliver it. Jack stains the table and notifies Margaret that it is ready for delivery. Prior to delivery the table is accidentally destroyed by fire. Which statement is true?   *risk of loss absence of breach*
   a.   Margaret can recover the $500 payment from Jack.
   b.   Margaret cannot recover the $500 payment from Jack.
   c.   The risk of loss is on the buyer, Margaret.
   d.   None of the above.

_C_   13. Goods which are not existing or identified are classified as:
   a.   inventory goods.
   b.   consumer goods.
   c.   future goods.
   d.   none of the above.

_?_   14. Which of the following is true regarding a consignment?
   a.   Title is in the buyer.
   b.   The buyer's creditors can obtain possession of the goods.
   c.   The buyer bears the expense of return of the goods.
   d.   All of the above.

_d_   15. A sale of a major part of the inventory other than in the ordinary course of the transferor's business would be called a:
   a.   C.I.F. sale.
   b.   sale on approval.
   c.   sale or return.
   d.   bulk transfer.

SHORT ESSAY

1.   Compare the significance of the concept of title under the common law with its role under the Code in allocating risk of loss.

_____
_____
_____
_____

2. Identify and discuss the various types of trial sales.

    Sale on approval

    Sale on return

    Consignment

3. Explain the significance of entrusting goods to a merchant and what effect that has on title to those goods.

4. Sterling Seller delivers nonconforming goods to Brenda Buyer which she accepts.   Later, Brenda discovers a hidden defect in the goods and revokes her acceptance.   If the goods are subsequently destroyed by an accidental fire and Brenda has insured the goods for 80% of their fair market value of $10,000, who will bear the risk of loss?

    Seller will be responsible for the 20% insufficiency in insurance coverage

5. Discuss briefly when one obtains an insurable interest.

    The code extends the insurable interest rights to a buyer who has an interest in goods that have been identified to a contract

Chapter 24
Products Liability:
Warranties and Strict Liability in Tort

PURPOSE

In this chapter you study the liability of manufacturers and sellers of goods to buyers, users, consumers, and bystanders for damages caused by defective products. The buyer of goods expects that his purchase will meet certain standards. If these standards are not met, then the manufacturer or seller may be liable for damages. The liability of manufacturers and sellers has expanded so much in recent years that product liability is now considered to be a separate and distinct field of law that combines and enforces rules and principles of contracts, sales, negligence, strict liability and statutory law. In this chapter, you study warranty and strict liability in tort.

CHAPTER CHECKPOINTS

After reading and studying this chapter, you should be able to:

1. Identify and describe the warranties found in Article 2 of the Code.

2. Compare the provisions of the Code's implied warranty of merchantability to the implied warranty of fitness for a particular purpose.

3. Discuss the defenses that may be raised by the seller in an action based on warranty and compare the defenses to an action based on warranty of merchantability to those in an action based on section 402A of the Restatement of Torts.

4. Discuss the concept of privity of contract and how the Code approaches the issue of horizontal privity.

5. List and discuss the elements of an action based upon strict liability in tort under Section 402A of the Restatement of Torts.

CHAPTER OUTLINE

I. Warranties–A warranty is an obligation of the seller to the buyer concerning title, quality, characteristics, or condition of goods. A seller is not required to warrant goods, but when the warranties are prescribed by the Code, he must act affirmatively in the manner prescribed by the Code to effectively disclaim liability for these implied warranties.

    A. Types of Warranties–A warranty may arise out of the mere existence of a sale (warranty of title), any affirmation of fact or promise made by the seller to the buyer (express warranty), or the circumstances under which the sale is made (implied warranty).

        1. Warranty of Title–The warranty of title is the obligation of the seller to convey the right of ownership without any lien. Under the Code, the seller implicitly warrants that (1) the title conveyed is good and its transfer rightful and (2) the goods have no security interest or other lien of which the buyer had no knowledge at the time of contracting.

        2. Express Warranties–An express warranty is an affirmation of fact or promise about the goods, a description of the goods, or a sample model of the goods, which becomes part of the basis of the bargain. The seller does not need to use formal words such as "warrant" or "guarantee" nor have knowledge of the falsity of a statement in order to be liable for breach of an express warranty.

            a. Creation–An express warranty can be created by the seller either orally or in writing by an affirmation of fact or promise that relates to the goods, a description of the goods, or a sample model of the goods, which becomes part of the basis of the bargain. It can be in regard to quality, condition, capacity, performability, or safety of the goods. As a general rule, statements of value or opinion do not create a warranty.

            b. Basis of Bargain–Affirmation, promises, descriptions, samples, or models made or used by the seller constitute a part of the basis of the bargain if they are part of the buyer's assumption underlying the sale.

        3. Implied Warranties–An implied warranty is a contractual obligation arising out of certain circumstances of the sale. It exists by operation of law and is not found in the language of the sales contract.

    a. Merchantability–Under the Code a merchant seller makes an implied warranty of the merchantability of goods that are of the kind in which he deals. This is a warranty of the merchant seller that the goods are reasonably fit for the ordinary purposes for which they are manufactured and sold, and that they are of fair, average quality.

    b. Fitness for Particular Purpose–Any seller, whether or not he is a merchant, makes an implied warranty that the goods are fit for a stated purpose, provided the seller selects the product knowing the buyer's intended use and that the buyer is relying on the seller's judgment. This warranty pertains to the specific purpose, rather than the ordinary purpose, of the goods. A seller's conduct may involve both the implied warranty of merchantability and the implied warranty of fitness for a particular purpose.

B. Obstacles to Warranty Actions–A number of obstacles can limit the effectiveness of warranty as a basis for recovery.

  1. Disclaimer of Warranties–A disclaimer is a negation of a warranty. The Code calls for a reasonable construction of words or conduct to disclaim or limit warranties.

    a. Express Exclusions–A warranty of title may be excluded only by specific language or by certain circumstances, including judicial sale or a sale by a sheriff, executor, or foreclosing lienor. In such cases the seller is clearly offering to sell only such title as he or a third person has in the goods. The language of a disclaimer or modification of an implied warranty of merchantability must mention "merchantability" and, in the case of a writing, it must be conspicuous. A disclaimer of an implied warranty of fitness for the particular purpose of the buyer must be in writing and conspicuous. Unless the circumstances indicate otherwise, all implied warranties are excluded by expressions like "as is," "with all faults," or other language calling the buyer's attention to the exclusion of warranties. Implied warranties may also be excluded by course of dealing, course of performance or usage of trade.

    b. Buyer's Examination or Refusal to Examine–If the buyer inspects the goods before entering the contract, implied warranties do not apply to defects that are apparent on examination. There are no implied warranties as to defects that an examination ought to have revealed where the buyer has examined as fully as she desires, or where the buyer has refused to examine the goods.

    c. Federal Legislation Relating to Warranties of Consumer Goods–The Federal Trade Commission administers and enforces the Magnuson–Moss Warranty Act. The act is designed to protect purchasers of consumer goods by providing that warranty information be clear and useful. The act defines consumer goods as those which are normally used for personal, family, or household purposes. It provides that a seller who makes a written warranty cannot disclaim any implied warranty.

  2. Limitation or Modification of Warranties–The Code permits a seller to limit or modify the buyer's remedies for breach of warranty, such as time limits within which the warranty is effective. One exception is the prohibition against unconscionable limitations or exclusions of consequential damages.

3. Privity of Contract–During the nineteenth century, the law became established that a plaintiff could not recover for breach of warranty unless he was in a contractual relationship with the defendant. This relationship is known as privity of contract. <u>Horizontal privity determines</u> who <u>benefits from a warranty and therefore may bring a cause of action</u>. It pertains to noncontracting parties who are injured by the defective goods, including users, consumers, and bystanders who are not the contracting purchaser. The Code provides three alternatives which state different limits for horizontal privity. The least comprehensive and most widely adopted alternative provides that a seller's warranty, whether express or implied, extends to any natural person who is in the family or household of the buyer or who is a guest in his home if it is reasonable to expect that such a person may use, consume, or be affected by the goods and who is injured in person by breach of the warranty. A seller may not exclude or limit the operation of this section for injury to a person. Alternative B extends Alternative A to "any natural person who may reasonably be expected to use, consume or be affected by the goods." Alternative C further expands the coverage of the section to any person, not just natural persons, and to property damage as well as personal injury. <u>Vertical privity determines who is liable for breach of warranty</u>. It pertains to remote sellers within the chain of distribution, such as manufacturers and wholesalers, with whom the consumer purchaser has not entered into a contract. Most states have eliminated the requirement of vertical privity in warranty actions.

4. Notice of Breach of Warranty–If the buyer fails to notify the seller of any breach within a reasonable time, she is barred from any remedy against the seller.

5. Plaintiff's Conduct–Contributory negligence of the buyer is no defense to an action against the seller for breach of warranty. However, if a buyer discovers a defect in the goods that may cause an injury and nevertheless proceeds to make use of them, he will not be permitted to recover damages from the seller. This is the voluntary assumption of a known risk.

II. Strict Liability in Tort–Section 402A of the Restatement, Second, Torts, imposes strict liability in tort on merchant sellers for both personal injuries and property damage resulting from selling a product in a defective condition, unreasonably dangerous to the user or consumer. The essential distinction between strict liability in tort and negligence is that actions in strict liability do not require the plaintiff to prove that the injury-producing defect resulted from any specific act of negligence of the seller. It applies even though the seller has exercised all possible care in the preparation and sale of his product.

A. Requirements of Strict Liability–Section 402A imposes strict liability in tort if: (1) the defendant was engaged in the business of selling such a product; (2) the defendant sold the product in a defective condition; (3) the defective condition made the product unreasonably dangerous to the user or consumer or to his property; (4) the defect in the product existed at the time it left the hands of the defendant; (5) the defective condition was attributable to the defendant; (6) the plaintiff sustained physical harm or property damage by use or consumption of the product; and (7) the defective condition was the proximate cause of the injury or the damage. Liability based on Section 402A is tort liability and arises out of the common law, not out of the UCC.

1. Merchant Sellers–Section 402A imposes liability only upon a person who is in the business of selling the product involved.

2. Defective Condition–In an action to recover damages under the rule of strict liability in tort, the plaintiff must prove a defective condition in the product, but she need not prove how or why the product became defective. Defects may arise through faulty manufacture, faulty product design, or inadequate warning, labeling, packaging, or instructions.

   a. Manufacturing Defect–A defect of this kind occurs when the product is not properly made. Thus, it fails to meet its own manufacturing specifications. A chair that was missing screws would constitute a manufacturing defect.

   b. Design Defect–A defect of this kind occurs when the product is made as specified but is dangerous or hazardous because the design is inadequate. Design defects result from poor engineering, poor choice of materials, and poor packaging. The Ford Pinto contained a design defect, because the fuel tank was placed too close to its rear axle, causing fuel tank explosions when the car was hit from the rear.

   c. Failure to Warn–A seller has a duty to provide adequate warning of possible danger, to provide appropriate directions for safe use, and to package the product in a safe manner.

3. Unreasonably Dangerous–Section 402A liability applies only if the defective product is unreasonably dangerous. An unreasonably dangerous product is one that contains a danger beyond that which would be contemplated by the ordinary consumer who purchases it with the common knowledge of its characteristics. Most courts let the jury decide what a consumer would reasonably expect.

B. Obstacles to Recovery–Obstacles to recovery in warranty cases generally do not present problems in strict liability actions under Section 402A.

   1. Disclaimers and Notice–Strict liability is based on tort law and therefore is not subject to contractual defenses. It is not governed by the Code, not affected by contractual limitations or disclaimers, and not subject to any requirement that notice be given to the seller by the injured party within a reasonable time. However, in commercial transactions, most courts have allowed enforcement of clear and specific disclaimers of Section 402A liability between merchants of relatively equal economic power.

   2. Privity–With respect to horizontal privity, strict liability in tort of manufacturers and other sellers extends not only to buyers, users, and consumers, but also to injured bystanders. In terms of vertical privity, strict liability extends to any seller who is in the business of selling the product, including a wholesaler or distributor as well as the manufacturer and the retailer. The rule of strict liability in tort also applies to the manufacturer of a defective component part.

   3. Plaintiff's Conduct–The element common to all products liability defenses is that the plaintiff's improper conduct played such a contributing role in the injury that it would be unfair to blame the product or its seller.

      a. Contributory Negligence–Contributory negligence is conduct on the part of the plaintiff that falls below the standard to which he should conform for his own protection and that is the legal cause of the plaintiff's harm. Section 402A rejects contributory negligence as a defense.

      b. Comparative Negligence–Under comparative negligence, damages are apportioned between the parties in proportion to the degree of fault or negligence found against the parties. Most courts apply comparative negligence to strict liability cases.

c. Voluntary Assumption of the Risk–Assumption of risk is the plaintiff's express or implied consent to encounter a known danger. This is a defense in an action based on strict liability in tort. The burden of proof of this defense is on the defendant.

d. Misuse or Abuse of the Product–Misuse or abuse occurs when the injured party knows, or should know, that he is using the product in a manner not contemplated by the seller. This is a defense to a strict liability case. A manufacturer will not avoid liability using this defense if the misuse of the product was foreseeable.

4. Subsequent Alteration–Section 402A provides that liability only exists if the product reaches "the user or consumer without substantial change in the condition in which it is sold."

5. Statute of Repose–Lawsuits have frequently been brought against manufacturers many years after the product has been sold. In response, many states have adopted statutes of repose. These laws limit the time period for which a manufacturer is liable for injury caused by its product. After a statutory time period has elapsed, a manufacturer ceases to be liable for harm caused by its defective products.

KEY TERMS

1. Warranty _an obligation of the seller to the buyer concerning title, quality, characteristics or condition of goods_

2. Warranty of title _obligation of seller to convey the right of ownership & title w/out lien_

3. Express warranty _affirmation of fact or promise about the goods, description of the goods which becomes the basis of the bargain_

4. Basis of the bargain _Affirmation, promise, description used by seller which constitute the basis of the bargain if they are underlying the sale_

5. Implied warranty

6. Implied warranty of merchantability

7. Implied warranty of fitness for particular purpose

8. Disclaimer of warranties

9. Consumer goods

10. Privity

11. Horizontal privity _Who can sue_

12. Vertical privity _who can be sued_

13. Strict liability in tort

14. Manufacturing defect

15. Design defect

16. State of the art

17. Statute of repose

TRUE/FALSE

_T_ 1. A warranty creates a duty on the part of the seller to ensure that the good she sells will conform to certain qualities, characteristics or conditions.

_F_ 2. The Code requires that a seller make certain warranties which cannot be disclaimed.

_F_ 3. The Code's implied warranty of fitness is a warranty by a merchant seller that the goods are reasonably fit for the ordinary purposes for which they are manufactured and sold.

_T_ 4. Application of the implied warranty of fitness for a particular purpose does not depend on whether the seller is a merchant.

_F_ 5. The expression "as is" will only disclaim the implied warranty of merchantability if it is in writing and conspicuous.

_F_ 6. Most states have eliminated the requirements of horizontal privity but have retained vertical privity requirements in warranty actions.

_T_ 7. Strict liability in tort generally is not subject to disclaimer, exclusion, or modifications by contractual agreement.

_F_ 8. Strict liability in tort may arise from a manufacturing defect in the product but not from a mere defective design.

_F_ 9. The strict liability in tort of manufacturers and other sellers extends only to buyers and their families.

_F_ 10. The doctrine of strict liability in tort may be held to be applicable to merchant sellers for personal injuries but not property damage.

_T_ 11. The Code permits a seller to limit or modify the buyer's remedies for breach.

_F_ 12. Under the Magnuson-Moss Act, no seller providing a written warranty can effectively disclaim any implied warranty.

_F_ 13. Contributory negligence by the user of a defective product that is unreasonably dangerous will prevent the user from pursuing a claim based on Section 402A.

_T_ 14. Any seller can make an implied warranty of fitness for a particular purpose, but only a merchant can make an implied warranty of merchantability.

_F_ 15. Harold Homeowner buys a defective toaster at a neighborhood garage sale and is injured slightly when it explodes. Harold can sue his neighbor for breach of implied warranty of merchantability.

MULTIPLE CHOICE

_b_ 1. A promise made by the seller constitutes an express warranty provided:
   a. the buyer relied upon the promise.
   b. the promise constitutes a part of the basis of the bargain.
   c. either (a) or (b).
   d. both (a) and (b).

_d_ 2. A warranty is an obligation of the seller to the buyer concerning which of the following:
   a. Title.
   b. Quality.
   c. Condition of the goods.
   d. All of the above.

_a_ 3. In order for the implied warranty of fitness for a particular purpose to apply:
   a. the seller must, at the time of contracting, have reason to know of the particular purpose.
   b. the buyer must actually rely on the seller's skill and judgment to furnish suitable goods.
   c. (a) or (b).
   d. both (a) and (b).

_b_ 4. Which of the following will NOT bar an injured buyer from recovering in an action against the seller for breach of warranty?
   a. The buyer's failure to notify the seller of any breach of warranty within a reasonable time after he discovered it or should have discovered it.
   b. The buyer's contributory negligence.
   c. The buyer's voluntary assumption of the known risk.
   d. An explicit, conspicuous disclaimer.

_d_ 5. The doctrine of strict liability in tort applies only if:
   a. the seller is engaged in the business of selling the product that caused the harm.
   b. The product was sold in a defective condition unreasonably dangerous to the user or consumer.
   c. the plaintiff sustained physical harm or property damage by use or consumption of the product.
   d. all of the above.

6. A party injured by a defective product can establish that it was defective by showing that the product had which of the following:
   a. a manufacturing defect.
   b. a design defect.
   c. inadequate instructions enclosed.
   d. all of the above.

7. Strict liability in tort is applicable only if the product is:
   a. defective.
   b. somewhat dangerous to the user or consumer.
   c. (a) or (b).
   d. either (a) or (b).

8. An injured party's recovery under the doctrine of strict liability in tort will be barred by:
   a. a valid disclaimer of liability included in the contract of sale.
   b. the failure of the injured party to give notice to the seller within a reasonable time.
   c. subsequent alteration of the product.
   d. the lack of privity between the injured party and the seller.

9. A party injured by a product that is defective because of a defective component can bring an action under the doctrine of strict liability in tort against all of the following EXCEPT:
   a. the seller of the finished product.
   b. the assembler of the finished product.
   c. the manufacturer of a nondefective chassis to which the assembler attached the defective component.
   d. the manufacturer of the defective component used without essential change in the final product.

10. Which of the following, even if properly shown, is NOT a complete defense to a claim of strict liability in tort?
    a. Comparative negligence.
    b. Voluntary assumption of the risk.
    c. Product misuse.
    d. Subsequent alteration.

11. Mel Merchant sells lawn mowers at his retail store. Mel impliedly warrants:
    a. that the mowers are the best available.
    b. that the mowers are fit for lawn mowing and are of fair, average quality.
    c. that all possible safety devices have been incorporated into the design.
    d. that the mowers will last at least two years.

_____ 12. In order to establish the defense of voluntary assumption of the risk, the defendant must show which of the following?
   a.   that the plaintiff was aware of the particular risk involved.
   b.   that the plaintiff voluntarily and unreasonably decided to encounter the known risk.
   c.   (a) or (b).
   d.   both (a) and (b).

_____ 13. Which of the following would constitute an express warranty?
   a.   Sam Seller shows a sample to Bill Buyer and says the product in the box is just like it.
   b.   Sam Seller says the VCR Bill Buyer wants to buy is "the best around." opinion?
   c.   Sam Seller says the VCR Bill Buyer wants to buy will give him many hours of enjoyment.
   d.   Sam Seller tells Bill Buyer that he really likes the RCA VCR better than the Sharpe one. opinion

_____ 14. Which of the following defenses can be used against the plaintiff in a strict liability case?
   a.   Voluntary assumption of the risk.
   b.   Misuse of the product.
   c.   Subsequent alteration of the product.
   d.   All of the above.

_____ 15. Liability of manufacturers and sellers for injury caused by products may be based on which of the following:
   a.   Negligence.
   b.   Misrepresentation.
   c.   Violation of statutory duty.
   d.   All the above.

SHORT ESSAY

1. List and describe several types of warranties found in Article 2 of the Code.

     Warranty of title
     express warranties
     implied warranty of merchantability
     implied warranty of fitness to a particular purpose

2. Compare and contrast the implied warranties of merchantability and fitness for a particular purpose. Can either be disclaimed? How?

     Implied warranty of merchantability pertains to merchants to
     be disclaimed it must be in writing & be conspicuous
     and mention merchantability

3. What must an injured party show to recover under a theory of strict liability in tort? What obstacles, if any, will bar his recovery and what traditional defenses will not?

_____

_____

_____

_____

4. List and discuss the kinds of defects which can give rise to a defective condition in a product.

_____Design defect_____

_____Mfg defect_____

_____

_____

5. What is a statute of repose? Explain.

_____limits the time period for which a manufacturer is liable

___for injury caused by its product_____

_____

_____

Chapter 25
Remedies

PURPOSE

Breach is the failure of a party to perform his obligations under the contract. In a sales contract, breach may consist of the seller's delivery of defective goods, too few goods, the wrong goods, or no goods. The buyer may breach by failing to accept conforming goods or by failing to pay for conforming goods which he has accepted. In this chapter, you study the remedies that are available to the buyer and the seller in the case of a breach by the other party. The Code provides separate and distinct remedies for the seller and for the buyer. Each of the remedies available is specifically keyed to the type of breach and the situation of the goods. The purpose of the remedies provided by the Code is to put the aggrieved party in as good a position as if the other party had fully performed. The Code provides that its remedies should be liberally administered to accomplish this purpose. In providing its various remedies, the Code has rejected the doctrine of election of remedies by providing that the remedies for breach are cumulative. Whether one remedy bars another depends entirely on the facts of the individual case.

CHAPTER CHECKPOINTS

After reading and studying this chapter, you should be able to:

1. List and describe the remedies available to the seller under the Code.

2. List and describe the remedies available to the buyer under the Code.

3. Identify and discuss the various kinds of money damages available to the seller and the buyer.

4. Distinguish between specific performance and replevin and discuss under what circumstances each is available.

5. Identify and describe the basic types of contractual provisions that affect the remedies available in the event of a breach and the limitations that the Code imposes upon these provisions.

CHAPTER OUTLINE

A. Remedies of the Seller–When the buyer defaults, the seller has been deprived of the rights for which he bargained. The buyer's default may consist of (1) wrongfully rejecting the goods; (2) wrongfully revoking acceptance; (3) failing to make a payment due on or before delivery; or (4) repudiating the contract in whole or in part. The seller's goods oriented remedies for these defaults are withholding delivery of the goods, stopping delivery of the goods by a carrier, identifying conforming goods to the contract not already identified, and reclaiming the goods on the buyer's insolvency. The seller's money oriented remedies include reselling the goods and recovering damages, recovering damages for nonacceptance of the goods or repudiation of the contract, recovering the price, and recovering incidental damages. The seller can also cancel the contract which is an obligation oriented remedy. The Code's remedies are cumulative; more than one may be used by an aggrieved seller.

1. To Withhold Delivery of the Goods–A seller may withhold delivery of the goods to a buyer who has wrongfully rejected or revoked acceptance of the goods, who has failed to make a payment due on or before delivery, or who has repudiated the contract. Where the contract calls for installments, any breach of an installment that impairs the value of the whole contract will permit the seller to withhold the entire undelivered balance of the goods. If the seller discovers that the buyer is insolvent, the seller may refuse to deliver the goods except for cash.

2. To Stop Delivery of the Goods–If the buyer is insolvent, the seller may stop any delivery; if the buyer repudiates or otherwise breaches, the seller may stop carload, truckload, planeload or larger shipments. The seller must timely notify the carrier or other bailee to stop delivery of the goods. After this notification, the carrier or bailee who holds the goods must deliver them in accordance with the directions of the seller. The seller must pay any charges or damages incurred by the carrier or bailee.

3. To Identify Goods to the Contract–On breach by the buyer, the seller may identify to the contract conforming goods in her possession or control that were not so identified at the time she learned of the breach. The seller may either complete the manufacture of unfinished goods and identify them to the contract or cease the manufacture and resell the unfinished goods for scrap or salvage value. The seller must exercise reasonable judgment to minimize her loss.

4. To Resell the Goods and Recover Damages–In the case of wrongful rejection or revocation, repudiation, or failure to make timely payment, the seller may resell the goods concerned or the undelivered balance of the goods. If the resale is made in good faith and in a commercially

reasonable manner, the seller may recover the difference between the contract price and the resale price, together with any incidental damages, less expenses saved because of the buyer's breach. The seller is not accountable to the buyer for any profit made on any resale of the goods. A good faith purchaser at a resale takes the goods free of any rights of the original buyer.

5. To Recover Damages for Nonacceptance or Repudiation–In the event of the buyer's wrongful rejection or revocation, repudiation, or failure to make timely payment, the seller may recover damages from the buyer measured by the difference between the unpaid contract price and the market price at the time and place of tender of the goods, plus incidental damages, less expenses saved in consequence of the buyer's breach.

6. To Recover the Price–The Code permits the seller to recover the price in three situations: (1) where the buyer has accepted the goods; (2) where the goods have been lost or damaged after the risk of loss has passed to the buyer; and (3) where the goods have been identified to the contract and there is no ready market available for their resale at a reasonable price.

7. To Recover Incidental Damages–In the same action in which the seller seeks damages for the difference between the contract price and the resale price or in cases to recover the price, the seller may recover incidental damages. Incidental damages include any commercially reasonable charges, expenses, or commissions resulting from the breach.

8. To Cancel the Contract–Where the buyer wrongfully rejects or revokes acceptance of the goods, or fails to make a payment due on or before delivery, or repudiates the contract in whole or in part, the seller may cancel the part of the contract that concerns the goods directly affected. If the breach is of an installment contract and it substantially impairs the whole contract, the seller may cancel the entire contract. The Code defines cancellation as putting an end to the contract by one party by reason of a breach by the other.

9. To Reclaim the Goods upon the Buyer's Insolvency–The unpaid seller may reclaim goods from an insolvent buyer by demand made to the buyer within ten days after the buyer has received the goods. If the buyer has committed fraud by a misrepresentation of her solvency made to the seller in writing within three months prior to delivery of the goods, the ten-day limitation does not apply. This right is subject to the rights of a buyer in the ordinary course of business or other good faith purchaser. Use of this remedy precludes the use of all other remedies.

B. Remedies of the Buyer–The seller's default may consist of repudiating the contract, failing to deliver the goods without repudiation, or delivering goods that do not conform to the contract. The buyer's obligation oriented remedy for these defaults is cancellation of the contract. The money oriented remedies include recovery of payments made, cover and recovery of damages, recovery of damages for nondelivery, recovery of damages for breach of warranty, recovery of incidental damages and recovery of consequential damages. The goods oriented remedies of the buyer are to recover identified goods if the seller is insolvent, replevy the goods, obtain specific performance or obtain a security interest in the goods. The buyer, upon proper notice to the seller, may deduct damages from the price due for any breach by the seller.

1. To Cancel the Contract–Where the seller fails to make delivery or repudiates the contract, or where the buyer rightfully rejects or justifiably revokes acceptance of goods tendered or delivered, the buyer may cancel the contract with respect to any goods involved. If the breach concerns the whole contract, the buyer may cancel the entire contract. The buyer must give notice of cancellation and is excused from further performance or tender on his part.
2. To Recover Payments Made–On the seller's breach, the buyer may recover as much of the price as he has paid.
3. To Cover–On the seller's breach, the buyer may obtain "cover." This means that the buyer may in good faith and without unreasonable delay proceed to purchase goods or make a contract to purchase goods in substitution for those due under the contract of the seller. The buyer may also recover the difference between the cost of cover and the contract price, plus any incidental and consequential damages, less expenses saved in consequence of the seller's breach. The buyer is not required to obtain cover, and his failure to do so does not bar him from any other remedy provided in the Code. However, the buyer may not recover consequential damages that could have been prevented by cover.
4. To Recover Damages for Nondelivery or Repudiation–If the seller repudiates the contract or fails to deliver the goods, or if the buyer rightfully rejects or justifiably revokes acceptance, the buyer is entitled to recover damages measured by the difference between the market price at the time when the buyer learned of the breach and the contract price, together with incidental and consequential damages, less expenses saved in consequence of the seller's breach. This remedy is an alternative to cover and is available only to the extent the buyer has not covered. The buyer who elects this remedy may not recover those consequential damages that could have been avoided by cover.
5. To Recover Identified Goods on the Seller's Insolvency–Where existing goods are identified to the contract of sale, the buyer acquires a special property interest in the goods. This interest exists even though the goods are nonconforming, and the buyer has the right to return or reject them. Identification may be made by either the buyer or the seller. Under the Code the buyer has the right to recover from an insolvent seller goods in which he has a special property interest. This right exists where the seller, who is in possession or control of the goods, becomes insolvent within ten days after receipt of the first installment of the price. To exercise the right, the buyer must tender to the seller any unpaid portion of the price. If the buyer has identified the goods, he may recover the goods only if they conform to the contract.
6. To Sue for Replevin–Replevin is an action at law to recover specific goods in the possession of a defendant that are being unlawfully withheld from the plaintiff. The buyer may replevy goods where the seller has repudiated or breached the contract if (1) the buyer is unable to obtain cover or (2) the goods have been shipped under reservation of a security interest in the seller and satisfaction of this security interest has been made or tendered.

7. To Sue for Specific Performance–This is an equitable remedy compelling the party in breach to perform the contract according to its terms. At common law specific performance is available only if the legal remedies are inadequate. The Code continues the availability of specific performance and has sought to further a more liberal attitude towards its use.

8. To Enforce a Security Interest in the Goods–A buyer who has rightfully rejected or justifiably revoked acceptance of goods that remain in her possession or control has a security interest in these goods to the extent of any payment of the price that she has made and for any expenses reasonably incurred in their inspection, receipt, transportation, care and custody. The buyer may hold such goods and resell them in the same manner as an aggrieved seller may resell goods. The buyer must account to the seller for any excess of net proceeds of the resale over the amount of the security interest.

9. To Recover Damages for Breach in Regard to Accepted Goods–Where the buyer has accepted nonconforming goods and has given timely notification to the seller of the breach of contract, the buyer is entitled to recover from the seller the damages resulting in the ordinary course of events from the seller's breach. In the event of breach of warranty, the measure of damages is the difference between the value of the goods that have been accepted and the value that the goods would have had if they had been as warranted. Incidental and consequential damages may also be recovered.

10. To Recover Incidental Damages–The buyer may recover incidental damages in addition to covering, damages for nondelivery or repudiation, and breach of warranty. Incidental damages include expenses reasonably incurred in inspection, receipt, transportation, care and custody of goods rightfully rejected and any commercially reasonable expense connected to obtaining cover or to the delay or other breach.

11. To Recover Consequential Damages–In many cases the above remedies will not fully compensate the aggrieved buyer for her losses. Under the Code, the buyer has the opportunity to recover consequential damages resulting from the seller's breach, including (1) any loss resulting from the buyer's requirements and needs of which the seller at the time of contracting had reason to know and which could not reasonably be prevented by cover or otherwise, and (2) injury to person or property proximately resulting from any breach of warranty.

C. Contractual Provisions Affecting Remedies–The parties to a sales contract may modify, exclude, or limit by agreement the remedies or damages available for breach of that contract.

1. Liquidation or Limitation of Damages–The parties may specify the amount or measure of damages that either party may recover in the event of a breach by the other party. The amount of such damages must be reasonable in light of the anticipated or actual loss resulting from a breach, the difficulties of proof of loss, and the inconvenience or lack of feasibility of otherwise obtaining an adequate remedy. A provision fixing unreasonably large liquidated damages is void as a penalty, while an unreasonably small amount might be stricken on the grounds of unconscionability.

2. Modification or Limitation of Remedy by Agreement–The contract between the parties may expressly provide for remedies in addition to those in the Code. It may also limit or change the measure of damages recoverable for breach. A remedy in a contract is optional unless it is expressly agreed to be exclusive of other remedies. Where an exclusive remedy fails in its essential purpose, resort may be had to the remedies provided by the Code. The contract may limit or exclude consequential damages unless such limitation or exclusion would be unconscionable. Limitation of consequential damages for personal injury from breach of warranty in the sale of consumer goods is always unconscionable, whereas limitation of such damages where the loss is commercial is not.

3. Statute of Limitations–The parties may reduce the period of limitation to not less than one year but not extend this statutory four-year period. Upon the occurrence of a breach, a cause of action accrues, without regard to the injured parties' knowledge of the breach.

KEY TERMS

1. Insolvency

2. Incidental damages

3. Cancellation

4. Cover

5. Replevin

6. Specific performance

7. Consequential damages

8. Liquidated damages

TRUE/FALSE

__T__   1. The purpose of the Code's remedial provisions is to place the aggrieved party in as good a position as if the other party had fully performed.

__F__   2. An obligation oriented remedy is one that provides the aggrieved party with the opportunity to recover monetary damages.

_T_   3. The Code has rejected the doctrine of election of remedies, providing that remedies for breach are cumulative in nature.

   4. The aggrieved seller's right to stop delivery of goods by a carrier or other bailee upon learning of the buyer's insolvency ceases when a negotiable document of title covering the goods is negotiated to the buyer.

_T_   5. If a seller in good faith and in a commercially reasonable manner resells goods which were wrongfully rejected by the buyer, the seller may recover from the buyer the difference between the contract price and the resale price, plus any incidental damages incurred.

   6. Goods resold by an aggrieved seller must be sold at a public sale.

_T_   7. The Code permits an aggrieved seller to bring an action to recover the price where the goods have been identified to the contract and there is no ready market available for their resale.

_T_   8. If a buyer breaches an installment contract in a manner that substantially impairs the whole contract, the seller may cancel the entire contract.

_F_   9. An aggrieved buyer may make a reasonable contract of cover and then seek to recover from the seller the difference between the cost of cover and the market price, plus any incidental and consequential damages. _contract price_

   10. In the event of a breach of warranty, the measure of damages is the difference at the time and place of the acceptance between the value of the accepted goods and the value of the goods as warranted.

_T_   11. Under the Code the parties may, by agreement, limit, modify or exclude remedies or damages available for breach.

_T_   12. The Code allows parties to a contract to specify the extent of damages in the event of a breach.

_F_   13. The Code has rejected the common law remedy of replevin.

_T_   14. The Code gives the buyer the right to demand perfect tender of performance.

_T_   15. Upon discovering the seller is insolvent, a buyer may recover goods from the seller in which she has as special property interest and for which she had paid part or all of the price.

MULTIPLE CHOICE

_C_   1. Which of the following is not a money oriented remedy?
   a. Cover and obtain damages.
   b. An action to recover market price damages.
   c. Cancellation.
   d. An action to recover damages for nonconformity.

_b_   2. Under the Code, the equity meaning of insolvency is:
   a. that a person has no assets.
   b. that a person is unable to pay her debts as they become due.
   c. that a person's total liabilities exceed the value of all her assets.
   d. none of the above.

_b_   3. Which of the following is not a sellers' remedy?
   a. Withhold delivery.
   b. Cover.
   c. Resell the goods.
   d. Cancel the contract.

_C_   4. Sam Seller in Seattle agrees to sell goods to Bill Buyer in Buffalo for $20,000 F.O.B. Buffalo, delivery on June 15. Bill wrongfully rejects the goods. The market price of the goods on June 15 in Buffalo is $15,000. Sam incurred $1,000 in incidental expenses while saving $500 in expenses. How much would Sam be allowed to recover from Bill?
   a. $20,000.
   b. $15,000.
   c. $5,500.
   d. $5,000.

_d_   5. A seller's right to stop delivery ceases when:
   a. the buyer receives the goods.
   b. the bailee of goods acknowledges to the buyer that he holds them for the buyer..
   c. a negotiable document of title is negotiated to the buyer.
   d. any of the above.

_b_   6. The Code permits the seller to bring an action to recover the price in all of the following cases except:
   a. where the buyer has accepted the goods but has failed to make a payment.
   b. where the goods have been identified to the contract and a ready market is available for their resale at a reasonable price.
   c. where conforming goods have been lost or damaged after risk of loss has passed to the buyer.
   d. all of the above.

d

7. If an aggrieved party rightfully cancels a contract:
   a. he discharges any obligation of future performance that he might have under the contract.
   b. he retains any remedy for breach of the whole contract or of any unperformed balance.
   c. neither (a) nor (b).
   d. both (a) and (b).

8. Which of the following is not a correct statement concerning an unpaid seller's attempt to reclaim goods from an insolvent buyer?
   a. The seller must demand that the goods be returned within twenty days after the buyer has received them unless the buyer has fraudulently misrepresented his solvency to the seller.
   b. The seller, if successful in reclaiming the goods from an insolvent buyer, may not seek other remedies with respect to the goods.
   c. The seller's right to reclaim the goods is subject to the rights of a buyer in the ordinary course of business or other good faith purchaser.
   d. All of the above.

9. Of the following remedies, which is not available to the buyer?
   a. To sue for replevin.
   b. To resell the goods.
   c. To cover.
   d. To cancel the contract.

10. Where a seller fails to make deliver, or repudiates, the buyer may:
    a. cover and recover damages.
    b. recover payments made.
    c. recover market price damages.
    d. all of the above.

11. If the seller repudiates the contract, the buyer is entitled to recover damages from the seller in an amount equal to the difference between the contract price and the market price of goods when:
    a. the parties entered into the contract.
    b. the breach occurred.
    c. the buyer learned of the breach.
    d. none of the above.

12. Bill Buyer contracted to buy 1000 widgets from Sam Seller for $5,000. Sam shipped defective widgets, but Bill accepted them and properly notified Sam of the breach. As warranted, the widgets were valued at $7,000, but as received they were worth $4,000. If Bill is successful in his suit for breach of warranty against Sam, he will be allowed to recover:
    a. $1,000.
    b. $2,000.
    c. $3,000.
    d. $7,000.

_a_ 13. Sam Seller has shipped 100 widgets to Bill Buyer pursuant to a contract. The next day Sam discovers that Bill is insolvent. On learning this:
   a. Sam may stop delivery.
   b. Sam must cancel the contract.
   c. Sam has no recourse available under the Code.
   d. Sam may cover and sue for damages.

_____ 14. Which of the following would be recoverable as consequential damages?
   a. Expenses reasonably incurred in inspection, receipt, transportation, and care and custody of goods rightfully rejected.
   b. Expenses for injury to person or property proximately resulting from breach of warranty.
   c. Damages of $100 per day in accordance with a negotiated contractual provision.
   d. All of the above are recoverable as consequential damages.

_c_ 15. Bill Businessman ordered 10 office chairs for his office. Two of the chairs delivered were defective.
   a. Bill must either send all of the chairs back or pay for all of them.
   b. Bill is entitled to ten new chairs.
   c. Bill can reject the two defective chairs and accept the others.
   d. Since Bill has already received the chairs, his only remedy is revocation of acceptance.

SHORT ESSAY

1. What remedies are available to a buyer who rightfully rejects a seller's tender of nonconforming goods?
   recover damages diff between the mkt price & contract price at the time buyer learned of breach   incidental, consequential damages less expenses saved
   _____
   _____

2. What remedies are available to a buyer after the seller repudiates their contract?
   _____
   _____
   _____
   _____

3. What remedies are available to the seller after the buyer has wrongfully rejected a conforming tender of goods?
   _____
   _____
   _____
   _____

4. Explain the remedy of cover.

_____

_____

_____

_____

5. Under what conditions may the parties to a contract limit or modify remedies available for its breach?

_____

_____

_____

_____

Part IV
Sample Examination

MULTIPLE CHOICE

_____ 1. A contract involving the rendition of a service is governed primarily by the:
   a. federal law.
   b. state common law.
   c. UCC.
   d. none of the above.

_____ 2. Mike Mechanic has a used car that he would like to sell. He puts an ad in the local newspaper. Bill Buyer comes to his house to look at the car and asks what kind of condition it is in. Mike says, "As a mechanic, I think the car is in good running order and should give you no problems for at least 60 days." Based on that statement, Bill purchases the car.
   a. Mike's statement is an express warranty.
   b. The sale by Mike gives rise to a warranty of merchantability.
   c. Mike's statement does not constitute an express warranty.
   d. None of the above.

_____ 3. Sam Seller agrees to sell 100 widgets to Bill Buyer at a price of $600. No mention is made of the time for delivery.
   a. The goods must be delivered within two weeks.
   b. The goods must be delivered within a reasonable time.
   c. The goods must be delivered within thirty days.
   d. There is no contract, because an essential term has been omitted.

_____ 4. Catherine telephoned Al's Office Supply and ordered ten boxes of pens at $30 a box. Later that day, she decided that since the pens were on sale she would order twenty boxes. She called the store back to modify her order. What result?
   a. There is no consideration so the contract is unenforceable.
   b. The modified contract is unenforceable because a writing was required.
   c. The modified contract is enforceable.
   d. None of the above.

_____ 5. Which of the following doctrines would a court apply where the seller's price was exorbitant?
    a. validation.
    b. substantive unconscionability.
    c. procedural unconscionability.
    d. none of the above.

_____ 6. Sam Seller learns of Bill Buyer's insolvency while the goods are in transit.
    a. Sam is out of luck and can't do much.
    b. Sam can stop delivery.
    c. If Sam stops delivery, he will be in breach of contract.
    d. Sam will have to deliver the goods and then file a claim with the bankruptcy court.

_____ 7. A form of action at law that a party may use to recover specific goods that are in possession of the defendant is known as:
    a. specific performance.
    b. replevin.
    c. stopping goods in transit.
    d. reclaiming of the goods.

_____ 8. Happy Homemaker brings her VCR to Al's Quick Fix Repair Shop to have the head cleaned. While the VCR is in the shop, Carol Customer comes to the store and asks Al its price. Al says $50, so Carol pays him $50 cash and takes the VCR home. When Happy comes to the shop to pick up her VCR, it isn't there.
    a. Happy has entrusted the VCR to Al's Repair Shop.
    b. Al can transfer good title to the VCR to Carol.
    c. If Happy brings a replevin action against Carol, she will recover the goods.
    d. Two of the above are correct, (a) and (b).

_____ 9. If a buyer may in good faith purchase needed goods for those due under a contract, he avails himself of the remedy of:
    a. replevin.
    b. cover.
    c. tender of delivery.
    d. specific performance.

_____ 10. To protect purchasers of consumer goods, Congress enacted the:
    a. Statute of Frauds.
    b. Magnuson-Moss Warranty Act.
    c. UCC.
    d. All of the above.

_____ 11. In an action based upon Section 402A of the Restatement, the defendant manufacturer can raise the defense(s) of:
   a. misuse or abuse of the product.
   b. voluntary assumption of the risk.
   c. comparative negligence.
   d. all of the above.

_____ 12. Bill Buyer accepts 1,000 widgets from Sam Seller, and then discovers a latent defect in them that could not have been found earlier by a reasonable inspection.
   a. Bill must keep the goods, because he has already accepted them.
   b. Bill may revoke his acceptance.
   c. Bill is entitled to the difference between the value of the goods which have been accepted and the value that the goods would have had if they had been as warranted.
   d. Two of the above are correct, (b) and (c).

_____ 13. Harold Homeowner used his lawn mower to trim his hedges. In the process he severely injured his hand. In a lawsuit against the manufacturer, the manufacturer is likely to raise the defense of:
   a. comparative negligence.
   b. assumption of the risk.
   c. misuse of the product.
   d. subsequent alteration.

_____ 14. Unless otherwise agreed by the parties, transfer of title in a shipment contract occurs when:
   a. the documents of title are delivered.
   b. payment is received.
   c. the seller delivers the goods to the carrier for shipment to the buyer.
   d. the goods are delivered to the buyer.

_____ 15. Sam Seller, who is located in New York, has a contract to sell 1,000 widgets to Bill Buyer, who is located in San Francisco. The contract is a shipment contract. Sam delivers the goods to Downs Transport for delivery. En route to San Francisco, the goods are destroyed.
   a. Bill bears the risk of loss.
   b. Sam bears the risk of loss.
   c. Bill and Sam will each share half of the loss.
   d. Bill has no interest in the goods, because he has not yet accepted them.

_____ 16. Sam Seller ships nonconforming goods to Bill Buyer. The risk of loss remains on Sam until:
   a. the goods are delivered to the carrier.
   b. Bill has had an opportunity to inspect the goods.
   c. Sam corrects the defect in the goods.
   d. Bill pays for the goods.

_____ 17. A merchant is defined as a person:
  a. who is a dealer in the goods.
  b. who by his occupation holds himself out as having knowledge or skill peculiar to the goods or practices involved.
  c. who employs an agent or broker whom he holds out as having such knowledge or skill.
  d. all of the above.

_____ 18. Which of the following need not be proved by the buyer in bringing a warranty action?
  a. A warrant has been breached.
  b. The breach proximately caused the loss suffered.
  c. The buyer purchased the subject item.
  d. Notice of the breach was given to the seller.

_____ 19. Under a _____ contract, the buyer must pay for the goods before he can exercise his right to inspect.
  a. C.I.F.
  b. C.O.D.
  c. F.O.B.
  d. F.O.S.

_____ 20. In which of the following situations does the Code permit the seller to recover the price plus incidental damages?
  a. Where the buyer has accepted the goods.
  b. Where conforming goods have been lost and risk of loss has passed to the buyer.
  c. Where the goods have been identified and no ready market exists for resale.
  d. All of the above.

Chapter 26
Negotiable Instruments

PURPOSE

Modern business could not be conducted without the use of checks, drafts, promissory notes, and certificates of deposit, all of which are commercial paper. The way rights and obligations are acquired in commercial paper is important because of the huge volume of daily transactions in these instruments. In this chapter, you study the concept of negotiability and the form necessary for an instrument to qualify as a "negotiable instrument." Negotiability invests commercial paper with a high degree of marketability and commercial utility. It allows commercial paper to be freely transferable and enforceable by a person with the rights of a holder in due course against any person obligated on the paper, subject only to a limited number of defenses.

CHAPTER CHECKPOINTS

After reading and studying this chapter, you should be able to:

1. Discuss the concept and importance of negotiability.

2. Identify the payee, drawee, maker, drawer and holder of a check, draft, note and certificate of deposit.

3. Identify and discuss the types of commercial paper that are promises to pay and those that are orders to pay.

4. List and discuss the formal requirements that an instrument must meet in order to qualify as a negotiable instrument.

5. Discuss the effect of the following on negotiability: (1) omissions of a statement of consideration or of a place where the instrument is drawn or payable; (2) the presence or absence of a seal; (3) postdating, antedating or not dating an instrument; (4) an incomplete instrument; and (5) an ambiguity within an instrument.

CHAPTER OUTLINE

A. Negotiability–This is a legal concept that makes written instruments a readily accepted form of payment in substitution for money.

   1. Development of the Law of Negotiable Instruments–Originally, a contract right to the payment of money could not be assigned because a contractual promise ran to the specific promisee. This rule prevented the owner of the right from selling or disposing of it. Eventually, the law permitted an assignment of contractual rights and allowed the assignee to recover against the obligor. However, an innocent assignee bringing an action against the obligor was subject to all defenses available to the obligor, and the obligor has the same liability to the assignee as to the assignor. Since the promise to pay was subject to all of the defenses available against the assignor, transferees were reluctant to acquire the promise and to pay for it. Accordingly, the law of negotiable instruments developed the concept of the holder in due course, whereby certain good faith transferees who gave value acquired the right to be paid, free of most of the defenses to which an assignee would be subject. In July 1990, the American Law Institute and the National Conference of Commissioners on Uniform Laws approved a Revised Article 3. The new Article maintains the basic scope and content of Article 3.

   2. Assignment Compared with Negotiation–The concept of negotiability applies to commercial paper, which is governed by Article 3 of the Code, to documents of title, which are governed by Article 7, and to investment securities, which are governed by Article 8. Negotiability invests commercial paper with a high degree of marketability and commercial utility. It allows commercial paper to be freely transferable and enforceable by a person with the rights of a holder in due course against any person obligated on the paper, subject only to a limited number of defenses. To have the full benefit of negotiability, commercial paper must not only meet the requirements of negotiability, but it must also be acquired by a "holder in due course."

B. Types of Negotiable Instruments–There are four types of commercial paper. Drafts and checks are orders or directions to pay money. Notes and certificates of deposit are promises to pay money.

   1. Drafts–A draft involves three parties. The drawer orders the drawee to pay a sum certain in money to the payee. The same party may appear in more than one capacity; for instance, the drawer may also be the payee. A time draft is one payable at a specified future date. A sight draft is payable on presentation to the drawee. A trade acceptance, which is a form of time draft, is frequently used as a credit device in commercial transactions.

   2. Checks–A check is a specialized form of draft, namely an order to pay money drawn on a bank

and payable on demand. There are three parties also involved in a check: the drawer, who orders the drawee, a bank, to pay the payee on demand. A cashier's check is a check drawn by a bank on itself to the order of a named payee.

3. Notes–A promissory note involves two parties. One party, the maker, promises to pay to the order of a second party, the payee, a stated sum of money, either on demand or at a stated future date.

4. Certificates of Deposit–A certificate of deposit is a specialized form of promise to pay money that is given by a bank. The bank is the maker and promises to pay the payee, who is named in the C.D.

C. Formal Requirements of Negotiable Instruments–Negotiability is wholly a matter of form. All of the information required to determine whether an instrument is negotiable must be found within the four corners of the instrument. No reference to any other source is required or permitted. To be negotiable an instrument must (1) be in writing, (2) be signed, (3) contain a promise or order to pay, (4) be unconditional, (5) be for a sum certain in money, (6) contain no other promise or order, (7) be payable on demand or at a definite time, and (8) be payable to order or to bearer.

1. Writing–The writing requirement is broadly construed. Any tangible expression is sufficient to satisfy the requirement. Most negotiable instruments are written on paper, but this is not required.

2. Signed–A note or certificate of deposit must be signed by the maker; a draft or check must be signed by the drawer. A signature is any symbol executed or adopted by a party with the intention to validate a writing. An X, a thumb print, initials, trade name, or assumed name will suffice. Normally, a maker or drawer signs in the lower right-hand corner of the instrument, but this is not required.

3. Promise or Order to Pay–A negotiable instrument must contain a promise or order to pay money in the case of a note or certificate of deposit, or an order to pay in the case of a draft or check. A promise must be more than a mere acknowledgment of indebtedness. An "I.O.U." is not a promise to pay. An order is a direction or command to pay. It must be more than an authorization or request. The usual way to express an order is by the use of the word "pay" or the phrases "Pay to the order of," or "Pay bearer."

4. Unconditional–This requirement is to prevent the inclusion of any term that could reduce the promised obligation. A promise or order to pay is unconditional if it is absolute and not subject to any contingencies or qualifications. A promise or order is conditional if (a) the instrument states that it is subject to or governed by any other agreement, or (b) the instrument states that it is to be paid only out of a particular fund or source.

a. Reference to Other Agreements–The restriction against reference to another agreement is to enable any person to determine the right to payment provided by the instrument without having to look beyond its four corners. If such right is made subject to the terms of another agreement, the instrument is nonnegotiable.

b. The Particular Fund Doctrine–Revised Article 3 eliminates the particular fund doctrine by providing that a promise or order is not made conditional because payment is to be made only out of a particular fund. An order or promise to pay only out of a particular fund is conditional and destroys negotiability, because payment depends on the existence and sufficiency of the particular fund. However, a promise or order to pay, coupled with a mere indication of a particular fund out of which reimbursement is to be made or a particular account to be debited with the amount, does not impair negotiability, because the drawer's or the maker's general credit is relied on and charging a particular account is merely a bookkeeping entry to be followed after payment.

5. Money–The purpose of this requirement is to enable the holder to determine from the instrument the amount that she is entitled to receive. This term means a legal tender authorized or adopted by a sovereign government as part of its currency. A fixed amount in French francs, German marks, Italian lira, Japanese yen, or other foreign currency is negotiable.

  a. Fixed Amount–This requirement must be considered from the point of view of the holder, not the maker or drawer. The holder must be assured of a determinable minimum payment. A frequent provision that is permissible is a provision in a note that the maker will pay, in addition to the face amount and specified interest, costs of collection and attorney's fees on default in payment. Rates may be different before and after default, or before and after a specified date. A sum payable is a fixed amount even though it is payable in installments, or with a fixed discount if paid before maturity, or a fixed addition if paid after maturity.

6. No Other Undertaking or Instruction–An instrument that contains an undertaking or instruction promise or order to do an act in addition to the payment of money, is not negotiable, however the Code sets out a list of terms and provisions that may be included without adversely effecting negotiability.

7. Payable on Demand or at a Definite Time–This requirement is intended to promote certainty in determining the present value of a negotiable instrument.

  a. Demand Paper–Demand paper has always been considered sufficiently certain as to time of payment, because it is the holder who makes the demand and thus sets the time for payment. An instrument qualifies as being payable on demand if it is payable "at sight" or "on presentation." Instruments payable at a definite time are called time paper. An instrument that by its terms is payable only on an act or event whose time of occurrence is uncertain is not payable at a definite time, even though the act or event has occurred.

  b. At a Fixed Period after Sight–This clause is frequently used in drafts. Such an instrument is negotiable, because the clause means a fixed period after acceptance. A simple mathematical calculation makes the maturity date certain. If the instrument is payable at a fixed time subject to acceleration by the holder, it satisfies the requirement of being payable at a definite time. Acceleration may be upon the happening of an event without impairing negotiability. Finally, a provision in an instrument granting the holder an option to extend the maturity of the instrument for an indefinite period nor a provision permitting the obligor of an instrument to extend the maturity date to a further definite time will affect negotiability.

  c. At a Definite Time and on Demand–If demand is not made prior to the specified date, the instrument becomes payable at a definite time on the fixed date.

8. Payable to Order or to Bearer–A negotiable instrument must contain words indicating that the maker or drawer intends that it pass into the hands of someone other than the payee. The magic words of negotiability are "to the order of" or "to bearer."

    a. Payable to Order–The following are correct forms for order instruments: "Pay to the order of Jane Jones," "Pay to Jane Jones or her order," and "Pay to Jane Jones or her assigns." The person to whose order the instrument is payable must be designated with reasonable certainty. The payee may be an individual, the maker or drawer, the drawee, two or more payees, an office, an estate, a trust, a partnership or unincorporated association, or a corporation.

    b. Payable to Bearer–A bearer instrument is payable (1) to bearer or the order of bearer, (2) to a specified person or bearer, or (3) to "cash" or to the order of "cash."

9. Terms and Omissions and Their Effect on Negotiability

    a. Dating of the Instrument–In general, the negotiability of an instrument is not affected by the fact that it is undated, antedated, or postdated. A postdated instrument is a time instrument. If a check is issued on January 2, 1992, and postdated to January 21, 1992, then the drawer's bank is not authorized to pay the instrument until January 21, 1992.

    b. Incomplete Instruments–If an essential term such as a promise or order, the designation of the payee, the amount payable, or the time for payment is omitted, the instrument is not negotiable until it is completed.

    c. Ambiguous Instruments–The Code establishes rules to resolve common ambiguities. This promotes negotiability by providing a degree of certainty to the holder. If it is unclear whether an instrument is a draft or a note, the holder may treat it as either and present it for payment to the drawee or the person signing it. Handwritten words control typewritten words, and typewritten words control printed words. If the amount payable is set forth on the face of instrument in both figures and words, and the amounts differ, the words control the figures.

KEY TERMS

1. Commercial paper

2. Negotiability *legal concept that makes written instruments a readily accepted form of pymt or substitution for money*

3. Instrument

4. Draft

5. Drawer

6. Drawee

7. Payee

8. Check

9. Demand

10. Promissory note

11. Maker

12. Certificate of deposit

13. Negotiable instrument

14. Signature

15. Promise to pay

16. Order to pay

17. Money

18. Demand paper

19. Time paper

20. Order paper

21. Bearer paper

TRUE/FALSE

__T__ 1. Negotiability is a legal concept that makes written instruments an accepted form of payment in substitution for money.

__F__ 2. A draft involves only two parties, the drawer and the drawee. 3 parties payee drawer drawee

__F__ 3. A sight draft is one payable at a specified future date.

__F__ 4. An instrument is nonnegotiable if the obligor may extend the maturity of the instrument for a definite period of time.

__T__ 5. An instrument is nonnegotiable if the holder may extend the maturity of the instrument for an indefinite period of time.

_____ 6. A trade acceptance is a sight draft. F

__T__ 7. An instrument, otherwise negotiable, is negotiable bearer paper if by its terms it is payable to "cash."

__F__ 8. An instrument is negotiable even though it is incomplete as to the amount payable.

_____ 9. An instrument may be payable to the maker or drawer.

__F__ 10. In resolving ambiguities, printed words control typewritten and handwritten words, and typewritten words control handwritten words.

__T__ 11. A cashier's check is a check drawn by a bank on itself to the order of a named payee.

__F__ 12. A note must be signed by the drawer while a draft must be signed by the maker.

note must be signed by maker   draft must be signed by drawer

__T__ 13. An order or promise to pay only out of a particular fund is negotiable.

_____ 14. An instrument payable with a stated rate of interest is an obligation for a sum certain.

__T__ 15. The treasurer of Big Bucks Inc. uses a stamp to sign checks drawn on the corporate account. This meets the signature requirement of negotiability.

MULTIPLE CHOICE

__d__ 1. Which of the following are negotiable instruments?
   a. A draft.
   b. A check.
   c. A promissory note.
   d. All of the above.

__c__ 2. A check drawn by a bank upon itself to the order of a named payee is a:
   a. promissory note.
   b. certificate of deposit.
   c. cashier's check.
   d. none of the above.

__c__ 3. The legal concept of negotiability makes written instruments:
   a. acceptable as a substitute for money.
   b. acceptable as a credit device.
   c. both (a) and (b).
   d. none of the above.

__d__ 4. A signature on an instrument may:
   a. appear in the upper right hand corner.
   b. be a thumbprint.
   c. be an assumed name.
   d. all of the above.

b 5. An instrument is nonnegotiable if it:

- a. refers to the existence of a separate agreement.
- b. states that it is subject to the terms of a separate agreement.
- c. is attached to a separate agreement.
- d. is made payable to the "assigns of Richard Roe."

d 6. An instrument is nonnegotiable if it:

- a. relies upon the general credit of the drawer or maker.
- b. directs that a particular account be debited after payment.
- c. directs that payment be made out of a particular fund.
- d. states that it is given in consideration for the purchase of a blue suit.

c 7. An instrument is nonnegotiable if it:

- a. is payable with interest "at current rate."
- b. provides for the recovery of costs and attorney's fees upon default.
- c. is payable with a fixed addition if paid after maturity.
- d. is payable at a stated rate of interest which will increase by 2% upon default.

b 8. An instrument is nonnegotiable if it:

- a. contains a promise or order to pay 800 French francs.
- b. provides that the payee, by cashing it, acknowledges full satisfaction of an obligation of the drawer.
- c. contains a promise to deliver goods.
- d. is payable on or before January 1, 1993.

d 9. An instrument is nonnegotiable if:

- a. it is payable upon an event uncertain as to time of occurrence.
- b. it is undated and payable 90 days after date.
- c. the obligor may extend the maturity of the instrument for an indefinite period of time.
- d. all of the above.

d 10. A certificate of deposit is a written acknowledgment by a bank of the receipt of money wherein the bank promises which of the following? To repay:

- a. on demand.
- b. at a stated future date.
- c. with a stated rate of interest.
- d. all of the above.

_____ 11. If an instrument is postdated it is considered to be a :

- a. sight draft.
- b. time draft.
- c. certificate of deposit.
- d. none of the above.

_____ 12. First Bank is the holder of a note which states that it is secured by a mortgage.
    a. The note is nonnegotiable, because it refers to another agreement.
    b. The note is nonnegotiable, because it is subject to another agreement.
    c. The note is nonnegotiable, because it violates the particular fund doctrine.
    (d.) The note is negotiable.

_b_ 13. Carol Customer deposits $10,000 at First Bank and gets a certificate of deposit from the bank.
    a. Carol is the maker of the certificate.
    b. First Bank is the maker of the certificate.
    c. Carol is the drawer of the certificate.
    d. First Bank is the drawer of the certificate.

_d_ 14. Which of the following would create a bearer instrument?
    a. "Pay to the order of cash."
    b. "Pay to the order of Jane Smith or bearer."
    c. "Pay to the order of bearer."
    d. All of the above would create bearer paper.

_____ 15. A promise or order is unconditional unless it states which of the following:
    a. An express condition to payment.
    b. That the promise or order is subject to or governed by another writing.
    c. That rights or obligations are stated in another writing.
    (d.) All of the above.

SHORT ESSAY

1. Explain the concept of negotiability and discuss its importance.

_____
_____
_____
_____

2. Is the following instrument, "I.O.U., Adam Brown $100, /s/ Joe Green," negotiable? Explain.

_____
_____
_____
_____

3. Distinguish between "order" paper and "bearer" paper.

_____

_____

_____

_____

4. Carol Contractor is the holder of an otherwise negotiable draft that contains the following notation: "Charge this against Construction Account 7890." What effect does this notation have upon the negotiability of the instrument? Explain.

_____

_____

_____

_____

5. Is the following instrument, "ABC Corp. promises to pay $100,000 to Johnson provided the helicopter sold meets all contractual specifications," negotiable? Explain.

_____

_____

_____

_____

Chapter 27
Transfer

PURPOSE

The primary advantage of commercial paper is the ease with which it can be transferred. Negotiation is the transfer of a negotiable instrument in such a manner that the transferee becomes a holder. This concept is important, because only a holder of an instrument can become a holder in due course and thus be entitled to greater rights than the transferor may have possessed. The rights of a holder in due course are the reason why negotiable instruments move easily in the marketplace. In this chapter you study the methods by which commercial paper may be transferred. In particular, you study the requirements of negotiation and the methods by which bearer paper and order paper may be negotiated.

CHAPTER CHECKPOINTS

After reading and studying this chapter, you should be able to:

1. Distinguish a transfer by negotiation from a transfer by assignment and discuss the ramifications of the distinction.

2. Define the term "holder" and discuss how a person becomes a holder of bearer paper in contrast to how a person becomes the holder of order paper.

3. Distinguish between a blank indorsement and a special indorsement and give an example of each.

4. Distinguish between a qualified indorsement and an unqualified indorsement and give an example of each.

5. List the various types of restrictive indorsements and give an example of each.

CHAPTER OUTLINE

A. Negotiation–Negotiation is the transfer of a negotiable instrument in such a manner that the transferee becomes a holder. A holder is defined as "a person who is in possession of an instrument drawn, issued or indorsed to him or to his order or to bearer or in blank". The transfer of a nonnegotiable instrument operates as an assignment. An assignment is the voluntary transfer to a third party of the rights arising from a contract. Whether a transfer is by "assignment" or "negotiation," the transferee acquires the rights that his transferor had. If a transfer is by negotiation and the person to whom it is negotiated is a holder in due course, then the transferee may acquire more rights than his transferor had. The requirements for negotiation depend upon whether the instrument is bearer paper or order paper.

1. Negotiation of Bearer Paper–A bearer instrument is transferred by mere possession and is therefore comparable to cash. Because bearer paper (an instrument payable to bearer) runs to whoever is in possession of it, a finder or a thief of bearer paper would be a holder even though he did not receive possession by voluntary transfer.

2. Negotiation of Order Paper–If the instrument is order paper (an instrument payable to order), both possession and indorsement (signatures) by the appropriate parties are necessary for the transferee to become a holder. Any transfer for value of an instrument not payable to bearer gives the transferee the specifically enforceable right to have the unqualified indorsement of the transferor, unless the parties otherwise agreed. Negotiation takes effect only when a proper indorsement is made, at which time the transferee of order paper becomes a holder of the instrument. Otherwise, the transferee has nothing more than the contract rights of an assignee.

   a. The Impostor Rule–This rule is an exception to the general rule that negotiation of an order instrument requires a valid indorsement by the person to whose order the instrument is payable. It involves a situation where a confidence man impersonates another and deceives a third party into delivering a negotiable instrument to the impostor in the name of the other person. The Code provides that the indorsement of the impostor or of any other person in the name of the named payee is effective if the impostor has induced the maker or drawer to issue the instrument to him using the name of the payee.

   b. The Fictitious Payee Rule–Under this rule an indorsement by any person in the name of a named payee is effective if an agent or employee of the maker or drawer has supplied her with the name of the payee for fraudulent purposes. The rule also applies where a person signs as or on behalf of a maker or drawer and does not intend the payee to have an interest in the instrument.

3. Partial Transfer–An indorsement conveying less than the entire instrument or any unpaid balance is not a negotiation, but is considered to be a partial assignment.

4. Negotiations Subject to Rescission–If a negotiation conforms to the appropriate requirements, it is effective to transfer the instrument though the transaction in which it occurs is voidable or even void.

B. Indorsements–An indorsement is a signature other than that of a maker, drawer, or acceptor that alone or accompanied by other words is made on an instrument for the purpose of (i) negotiating the instrument, (ii) restricting payment of the instrument, or (iii) incurring liability on the instrument. The type of indorsement used affects its subsequent negotiation. Every indorsement is either (1) blank or special, (2) restrictive or nonrestrictive, and (3) qualified or unqualified, but these indorsements are not mutually exclusive. An indorser who merely signs her name on the back of an instrument makes a blank, nonrestrictive, unqualified indorsement.

1. Blank Indorsements–A blank indorsement specifies no indorsee and may consist of merely the signature of the indorser or her authorized agent. A blank indorsement converts order paper into bearer paper and therefore may be negotiated by delivery alone without further indorsement.

2. Special Indorsements–A special indorsement specifically designates the person to whom or to whose order the instrument is to be payable (order paper). An indorsement reading "Pay Edward" is interpreted as meaning "Pay to the order of Edward." Any further negotiation would require Edward's indorsement. A holder of an instrument with a blank indorsement may protect himself by converting the blank indorsement to a special indorsement by writing over the signature of the indorser any contract consistent with the character of the indorsement.

3. Restrictive Indorsements–A restrictive indorsement attempts to restrict the rights of the indorsee in some fashion. The UCC defines four kinds of restrictive indorsements: conditional indorsements, indorsements prohibiting further transfer, indorsements for deposit or collection, and indorsements in trust. Only the last two are effective.

    a. Indorsements for Deposit or Collection–These are the most frequently used restrictive indorsements. They are designed to place the instrument in the banking system for deposit or collection. Examples include: "for collection," "for deposit," and "pay any bank." Such indorsements effectively limit further negotiation to those consistent with the limitation and put all nonbanking persons on notice as to who has a valid interest in the paper.

    b. Indorsements in Trust–In this type of indorsement the indorser creates a trust for the benefit of himself or others. Examples are: "Pay Trish in trust for Boris," "Pay Trish for Boris," "Pay Trish for the account of Boris," and "Pay Trish as agent for Boris." In these indorsements, Trish is a fiduciary subject to liability for any breach of her obligation.

    c. Indorsements with Ineffective Restrictions–In a conditional indorsement, the indorser makes the rights of the indorsee subject to the happening or nonhappening of a specified event. Example: "Pay Adam, but only if the good ship Jolly Jack arrives in Chicago harbor by November 15, 1992." In the instrument itself this language would make it nonnegotiable. But indorsers are permitted to condition the rights of their indorsees without destroying negotiability. Revised Article 3 nullifies the effect of conditional indorsements by providing that an indorsement that states a condition to the right of a holder to receive payment is ineffective to condition payment.

    An indorsement may by its express terms attempt to prohibit further transfer, such as an indorsement stating "Pay only Tom Thomas." The Code provides that no restrictive indorsement prevents further transfer or negotiation of the instrument. In effect, an indorsement that purports to prohibit further transfer of the instrument operates the same as an unrestricted indorsement.

4. Qualified and Unqualified Indorsements–Unqualified indorsers guarantee payment of the instrument if certain conditions are met. An indorser may disclaim liability on the contract of indorsement, but only if the indorsement so declares and the disclaimer is written on the instrument. The customary manner of disclaiming an indorser's liability is to add the words "without recourse," either before or after his signature. A "without recourse" indorsement is called a qualified indorsement. A qualified indorsement does not eliminate all liability of an indorser. It disclaims contract liability, but it does not remove the warranty liability of the indorser.

5. Formal Requirements of Indorsements
    a. Place of Indorsement–An indorsement must be written on the instrument or on a paper, called an allonge, affixed to the instrument. An allonge may be used even if the instrument contains sufficient space for the indorsement. Customarily, indorsements are made on the back or reverse side of the instrument, starting at the top and continuing down.
    b. Incorrect or Misspelled Indorsement–If the name of the payee or indorsee is misspelled, or is a name different from the holder, the holder may require the indorsement in the name stated or in the holder's correct name or both. The person paying or taking the instrument for value may require the indorser to sign both names.

KEY TERMS

1. Negotiation _transfer of a negotiable instrument in such a manner that the transferee becomes a holder_
2. Assignment _– the transfer of a nonnegotiable instrument – a voluntary transfer to a 3rd party of the rights arising from a contract_
3. Holder
4. Indorsement _a signature other than that of a maker, drawer for purposes of negotiating instrument; restricting pmt_
5. Blank indorsement _specifies no indorsee — converts order paper into bearer paper_
6. Special indorsement _specifically designates the person to whom the instrument is to be payable_
7. Restrictive indorsement _attempts to restrict the rights of the indorsee_
8. Qualified indorsement _"without recourse" indorsement_ } _does not eliminate all liability of an indorser — disclaims contract liability but not warranty liability of indorser_
9. Allonge _paper affixed to the instrument_

TRUE/FALSE

_F_ 1. A nonnegotiable instrument is not transferable. *becomes an assignment*

_F_ 2. An indorsement written on a piece of paper clipped to the instrument is not valid. *allonge*

_T_ 3. The indorsement of an impostor or of any other person in the name of the named payee is effective if the impostor has induced the maker or drawer to issue the instrument to him.

_T_ 4. The transfer of an instrument operates as an assignment.

_____ 5. Negotiation of an order instrument requires a valid indorsement by the person to whose order the instrument is payable.

_____ 6. Assignment is the transfer of a negotiable instrument in such a manner that the transferee becomes a holder.

_____ 7. Forging the signature of an indorsee breaks the chain of title to the instrument.

_F_ 8. A qualified indorsement destroys the instrument's negotiability.

_T_ 9. An indorsement conveying less than the entire instrument operates as a partial assignment and not as a negotiation.

_____ 10. A restrictive indorsement prevents further negotiation of the instrument.

_F_ 11. A check which is "payable to cash" requires an appropriate indorsement for further negotiation.

_____ 12. A thief or finder of order paper which has been indorsed in blank can transfer good title to a subsequent holder who may qualify as a holder in due course.

_F_ 13. An indorser who has indorsed a negotiable instrument with a qualified indorsement stating that it is "without recourse" has no liability of any kind to subsequent holders. *warranty liability*

_T_ 14. A blank indorsement can be converted into a special indorsement.

_____ 15. An allonge may be used only if the instrument does not contain sufficient space for an indorsement.

MULTIPLE CHOICE

___C___ 1. Indorsement by the appropriate parties is necessary to:
    a. transfer an instrument by assignment.
    b. negotiate a bearer instrument.
    c. negotiate an order instrument.
    d. (a) and (c) but not (b).

___d___ 2. Which of the following is not needed to be a holder of a bearer instrument?
    a. a transfer for value.
    b. possession of the instrument.
    c. the indorsement of the transferor.
    d. an allonge.

___b___ 3. The Code provision which holds that a transferee acquires the rights of a holder in due course if the transferor has such right is known as:
    a. an allonge.
    b. shelter rule.
    c. impostor rule.
    d. none of the above.

___d___ 4. Negotiability is destroyed if an instrument is indorsed with the words:
    a. "pay to A only."
    b. "pay to the order of A."
    c. "pay to A or his order."
    d. none of the above.

_____ 5. An indorsement is ineffective as a negotiation if it:
    a. is not dated.
    b. conveys only the unpaid balance on the instrument.
    c. is forged.
    d. (b) and (c) but not (a).

_____ 6. Bearer paper may be converted into order paper by:
    a. a blank indorsement.
    b. a special indorsement.
    c. a restrictive indorsement.
    d. a qualified indorsement.

d   7. If H, the holder of a note, indorses it, "Pay A, but only if P is elected President in November," the indorsement is:
   a.   blank, restrictive, qualified.
   b.   special, nonrestrictive, qualified.
   c.   blank, nonrestrictive, unqualified.
   d.   special, restrictive, unqualified.

c   8. An indorsement which reads "Pay only if the goods are delivered by December 1, without recourse, Jane Jones" is:
   a.   blank, nonrestrictive, qualified.
   b.   blank, restrictive, unqualified.
   c.   blank, restrictive, qualified.
   d.   special, restrictive, unqualified.

   9. Which of the following is an example of an effective restrictive indorsement?
   a.   "Pay A only."
   b.   "Pay any bank."
   c.   "Pay A, without recourse."
   d.   All of the above.

   10. With respect to negotiation, which of the following is true?
   a.   The transferee becomes a holder.
   b.   An impostor may never transfer a negotiable instrument.
   c.   The transferor has no liability with respect to the transferred instrument.
   d.   None of the above are true.

c   11. First Bank issued a certificate of deposit to Harold Homeowner. At Harold's request, the instrument was made payable to bearer.
   a.   A thief could never redeem the certificate.
   b.   The instrument needs a blank indorsement to be redeemed.
   c.   Harold places a special, qualified indorsement on the instrument, he will avoid making a guarantee of its payment.
   d.   None of the above.

d   12. Sarah Salesclerk indorsed her paycheck with her signature and the words "for deposit only." This indorsement is a:
   a.   blank indorsement.
   b.   special indorsement.
   c.   restrictive indorsement.
   d.   blank, restrictive indorsement.

_____ 13. An indorsement made by a person that is not the holder of the instrument is a/an:
    a. blank indorsement.
    b. restrictive indorsement.
    c. anomalous indorsement.
    d. none of the above.

_b_ 14. The customary manner of disclaiming an indorser's liability is to add the words:
    a. "pay any bank."
    b. "without recourse."
    c. "for deposit only."
    d. "pay to the order of."

_C_ 15. If there is no more room on an instrument, further indorsements can be written on a separate piece of paper firmly affixed to the instrument. This piece of paper is known as a/an:
    a. amendment.
    b. fixture.
    c. allonge.
    d. attachment.

SHORT ESSAY

1. Distinguish between order paper and bearer paper. Explain how each are negotiated.

2. Explain the difference between a transfer by negotiation and a transfer by assignment.

3. Identify and discuss restrictive indorsements.

4. Can a negotiation be set aside if the underlying transaction is void or voidable? Explain.

_____

_____

_____

_____

5. Explain an indorsement "without recourse."

_____

_____

_____

_____

Chapter 28
Holder in Due Course

PURPOSE

The concept of holder in due course is the most significant aspect of negotiability; it is a concept that is unique to negotiable instruments. A mere holder of an instrument acquires it subject to all claims and defenses against it. However, a holder in due course in a nonconsumer credit transaction takes the instrument free of all claims of other parties and free of all defenses to the instrument except for a very limited number of claims that are specifically set forth in the Code. The holder in due course has a preferred position in the law, because such a position encourages the free negotiability of commercial paper by minimizing the risks that are assumed by an innocent purchaser of the instrument. A holder is a person in possession of an instrument that contains all necessary indorsements. However, not every holder is a holder in due course. In addition to being a holder, a holder in due course must have taken the instrument for value, in good faith, without notice that it is overdue or dishonored, and without notice of any defense or claim to it on the part of any person. In this chapter, you study how a transferee becomes a holder in due course and the advantages of being a holder in due course.

CHAPTER CHECKPOINTS

After reading and studying this chapter, you should be able to:

1. List and discuss the requirements for becoming a holder in due course.

2. Discuss the preferred position of a holder in due course and determine whether a holder is a holder in due course.

3. Explain the shelter rule and the limitations of the rule.

4. Distinguish between a real defense and a personal defense and identify the most common examples of each.

5. Discuss the effect of the Federal Trade Commission rule upon the status of a holder in due course.

CHAPTER OUTLINE

A. Requirements of a Holder in Due Course–To acquire the preferential rights of a holder in due course, a person must meet the requirements of the Code or must "inherit" these rights under the shelter rule.

   1. Holder–A holder is a person who has both possession of an instrument and all necessary indorsements. A holder is a person who is in possession of a negotiable that is payable to bearer or to an identified person if the identified person is in possession.

   2. Value–A holder in due course must have given value. A holder who was given an instrument as a gift cannot be a holder in due course, because she has not given value. Value in the law of commercial paper is not the same as consideration under the law of contracts. Value, for purposes of negotiable instruments, is defined as: (1) the actual performing of the agreed promise; (2) the acquiring of a security interest or other lien on the instrument; (3) the taking of the instrument in payment of or as security for an antecedent debt; (4) the giving of a negotiable instrument; or (5) the giving of an irrevocable commitment to a third party.

      a. Executory Promise–An executory promise, an unperformed obligation, is not the giving of value to support holder-in-due-course status because it has not been performed. A holder takes an instrument for value to the extent that the agreed consideration has been given. The Code provides two exceptions to this rule: (1) the giving of a negotiable instrument, and (2) the making of an irrevocable commitment to a third party.

      b. Security Interest–Where an instrument is given as security for an obligation, the lender is regarded as having given value to the extent of his security interest.

      c. Antecedent Debt–Under the Code, a holder gives value when she takes an instrument in payment of or as security for an antecedent debt.

   3. Good Faith–The Code defines good faith as "honesty in fact and the observance of reasonable commercial standards of fair dealing." The observance of reasonable commercial standards of fair dealing is comparable to the definition of good faith applicable to merchants under the Code.

   4. Lack of Notice–To become a holder in due course, a holder must take the instrument without notice that it is: (1) overdue, (2) dishonored, or (3) subject to any claim or defense. A person has notice of a fact when (a) he has actual knowledge of it; or (b) he has received a notice or notification of it; or (c) from all the facts and circumstances known to him at the time in question he has reason to know that it exists. Since the applicable standard is "actual notice," "notice received," or "reason to know," constructive notice through public filing or recording is not of itself sufficient notice to prevent a person from becoming a holder in due course. To be effective, notice must be received at such a time and way that will give the recipient a reasonable opportunity to act on it.

      a. Notice an Instrument is Overdue–To be a holder in due course, the purchaser must take the instrument without notice that it is overdue. Time paper is due on its stated due date if the stated day is a business day or, if not, on the next business day. Demand paper is not overdue for purposes of holder in due course status unless the purchaser has notice that she is taking it after demand has been made, or until it has been outstanding for a reasonable length of time. In the case of a demand note, a reasonable period of time is sixty days. For checks, a reasonable period of time is presumed to be thirty days.

  b. Notice an Instrument Has Been Dishonored–Dishonor is the refusal to pay or accept an instrument when it becomes due. If a transferee has notice that an instrument has been dishonored, he cannot become a holder in due course.

  c. Notice of a Claim or Defense–A purchaser of an instrument cannot become a holder in due course if he purchases it with notice of a defense or claim to it. A defense to the instrument is a justification or shield protecting a person from liability on it, whereas a claim to the instrument is an assertion of ownership of it.

  d. Without Reason to Question its Authenticity–A party may become a holder in due course only if the instrument "does not bear such apparent evidence of forgery or alteration or is not otherwise so irregular or incomplete as to call into question its authenticity." It makes no difference if the holder does not have notice of such irregularity or incompleteness, it depends only upon whether the instrument's defect is apparent and whether the taker should have reason to know of the problem.

B. Holder in Due Course Status–A payee may become a holder in due course. Also, any transferee of a holder in due course acquires this status.

  1. A Payee May Be a Holder in Due Course–The Code provides that a payee may be a holder in due course if he satisfies the holder in due course requirements. Where the payee is not an immediate party to the transaction, he will not be subject to any claims and most defenses if he meets the requirements of a holder in due course.

  2. The Shelter Rule–The transferee of an instrument acquires the same rights in the instrument that the transferor had. Therefore, even if a holder does not qualify to be a holder in due course, he acquires all the rights of one if some previous holder of the instrument has been a holder in due course. However, a transferee (1) who has himself been a party to any fraud or illegality affecting the instrument, or (2) who as a prior holder had notice of a claim or defense, may not obtain the rights of a holder in due course by reacquiring the instrument from a subsequent holder who is either a holder in due course or who has the rights of one. In other words, he cannot improve his position by reacquiring the instrument.

  3. Special Circumstances Denying Holder in Due Course Status–When an instrument is acquired in a way other than the ordinary flow of commerce, the transferee does not acquire HDC status.

C. The Preferred Position of a Holder in Due Course–In a nonconsumer transaction, a holder in due course takes the instrument (1) free from all claims on the part of any person and (2) free from all defenses of any party with whom he has not dealt except for a limited number of defenses that are available against anyone, including a holder in due course.

  1. Real Defenses–Real defenses are available against all holders, including holders in due course. The real defenses are as follows:

a. Infancy–The Code does not state when infancy is available as a defense or the conditions under which it may be asserted. Rather, it provides that infancy is a defense available against a holder in due course to the extent that it is a defense to a simple contract under the laws of the state involved.

b. Void Obligations–When the obligation on an instrument originates in such a way that under the law of the state involved it is void, the Code authorizes the use of this defense against a holder in due course. Incapacity, duress, and illegality of the transaction are defenses that may render the obligation of a party voidable or void. To the extent that the underlying transaction is voidable only, the defense is not effective against a holder in due course.

c. Fraud in the Execution–Fraud in the execution of an instrument renders the instrument void and therefore is a valid defense against a holder in due course. The Code describes fraud in the execution as misrepresentation that induced the party to sign the instrument with neither knowledge nor a reasonable opportunity to obtain knowledge of its character or its essential terms.

d. Discharge in Insolvency Proceedings–If a party's obligation on an instrument is discharged in a bankruptcy or any other insolvency proceeding, he has a valid defense in any action brought against him on the instrument, including one by a holder in due course.

e. Discharge of Which the Holder Has Notice–Any holder, including a holder in due course, takes the instrument subject to any discharge of which he has notice. If a holder acquires an instrument with notice that all prior parties have been discharged, he cannot become a holder in due course.

f. Unauthorized Signature–A person's signature on an instrument is unauthorized when it is made without authority. A person whose signature is unauthorized or forged cannot be held liable on the instrument in the absence of estoppel or ratification, even if the instrument is negotiated to a holder in due course. Any unauthorized signature is totally invalid as that of the person whose name is signed unless he ratifies it or is precluded from denying it. The signature operates only as the signature of the unauthorized signer. A person may, however, be estopped from asserting this defense because her conduct caused reliance by a third party.

g. Alteration–An alteration is any unauthorized change that modifies the obligation of any party to the instrument or an unauthorized addition or change to an incomplete instrument concerning the obligation of a party. An alteration that is fraudulently made discharges a party whose obligation is affected, except where that party assents or is precluded by their own negligence from raising the defense.

2. Personal Defenses–These are contractual defenses that are good against assignees and holders but not holders in due course. Among the personal defenses are (1) lack of consideration; (2) failure of consideration; (3) breach of contract; (4) fraud in the inducement; (5) illegality that does not render the transaction void; (6) duress, undue influence, mistake, misrepresentation, or incapacity that does not render the transaction void; (7) setoff or counterclaim; (8) discharge of which the holder in due course does not have notice; (9) nondelivery of an instrument; (10) unauthorized completion of an incomplete instrument; (11) payment without obtaining surrender

of the instrument; (12) theft of a bearer instrument or an instrument payable to him; and (13) lack of authority of a corporate officer or an agent or partner as to the particular instrument.

D. Limitations on Rights of Holder in Due Course–The preferential position of a holder in due course has been severely limited by a Federal Trade Commission rule that applies to consumer credit contracts. The rule applies to sellers and lessors of consumer goods, which are defined to include goods for personal, family or household use. It also applies to lenders who advance money to finance the consumer's purchase of consumer goods or services. The rule is intended to prevent situations in which a consumer is required to make payments to a holder in due course when the product or services purchased are defective or when the transaction involves fraud in the inducement. This occurs when the purchaser executes and delivers to the seller a negotiable instrument which the seller then negotiates to a holder in due course. The buyer's defense that the goods were defective or that the seller committed fraud in the inducement, even if valid against the seller, cannot be raised against a holder in due course of the instrument. The FTC rule preserves the claims and defenses of consumers by requiring that a conspicuous notice be included in the consumer credit contract. The purpose of this notice is to inform a subsequent holder that he takes the instrument subject to all claims and defenses which the buyer could assert against the seller. In effect, when the rule applies, it places the holder in due course in the position of an assignee.

KEY TERMS

1. Holder

2. Holder in due course

3. Value

4. Executory promise

5. Antecedent debt

6. Good faith

7. Dishonor

8. Shelter rule

9. Real defense

10. Personal defense

11. Material alteration

TRUE/FALSE

_____ 1. A transferee need not be a holder in order to become a holder in due course.

_____ 2. A person may acquire the rights of a holder in due course even though he does not take the instrument for value.

_____ 3. The concept of value in the law of negotiable instruments is the same as that of consideration under the law of contracts.

_____ 4. A check is presumed overdue if it has been outstanding more than 30 days.

_____ 5. A payee may be a holder in due course.

_____ 6. Personal defenses may not be asserted against a holder in due course.

_____ 7. A person may be a holder in due course even if he takes the instrument after all of the parties to the instrument have been discharged regardless of whether or not he has notice of the discharge.

_____ 8. The Federal Trade Commission rule places a holder in due course of an instrument in the position of an assignee if the instrument concerns a debt arising out of a consumer credit contract.

_____ 9. When an incomplete instrument has been completed in an authorized manner, a subsequent holder in due course may enforce the instrument as completed.

_____ 10. Under the Code, a person has notice of a fact if he has reason to know that it exists from all of the facts and circumstances known to him at the time in question.

_____ 11. When an instrument is acquired in a way other than the ordinary flow of commerce, holder in due course status is not available.

_____ 12. Bill Buyer issued a note to Sam Seller in return for goods to be used as inventory. Bill's customers later complained that the goods were defective, so Bill dishonored the note. Sam can assert holder in due course status to enforce the note against Bill.

_____ 13. Under the shelter rule a transferee will acquire the rights of a holder in due course regardless of the rights held by the transferor.

_____ 14. Happy Homemaker issues a $25 check to her niece for graduation. The niece is a holder in due course.

_____ 15. Hal Hoodlum holds a gun to Bill Buyer's head and forces him to sign a note for $5,000. Hal then transfers the note to First Bank who now wants to collect $5,000 from Bill. Bill can assert the defense of duress against First Bank in order to avoid payment.

MULTIPLE CHOICE

_____ 1. A person is a holder if he possesses an instrument:
   a. issued to his order or to bearer.
   b. indorsed to him.
   c. (a) or (b).
   d. (a) and (b).

_____ 2. A person may acquire the rights of a holder in due course if he takes the instrument:
   a. for value.
   b. in bad faith.
   c. with notice that it has been dishonored.
   d. all of the above.

_____ 3. A holder takes an instrument for value when he:
   a. makes an irrevocable commitment to his transferor.
   b. promises to pay the agreed consideration.
   c. takes the instrument as security for an antecedent debt.
   d. (a) and (c) but not (b).

_____ 4. A purchaser takes an instrument in good faith if:
   a. he believes there is nothing wrong with it.
   b. he knows there is something wrong with it.
   c. a prudent man under the circumstances would not have known that something was wrong with it, but the purchaser in fact knows something is wrong with it.
   d. (a) and (c) but not (b).

_____ 5. The shelter rule does not apply in which of the following situations?
   a. Where the holder has been party to a fraud affecting the instrument.
   b. Where the holder has been party to an illegal act affecting the instrument.
   c. Where the holder was a prior holder with notice of a claim.
   d. None of the above.

_____ 6. Assume M issues a note to P which is successively negotiated to A, B, C, and H. If H is a holder in due course with respect to all the parties to the instrument, then H is subject to the personal defenses of:
   a. A only.
   b. B only.
   c. C only.
   d. none of the above.

_____ 7. Assume M issues a note to P which is successively negotiated to A, B, C, and H. If H is a holder in due course with respect to all the parties to the instrument, then H is subject to the real defenses of:
a. A only.
b. B only.
c. C only.
d. all of the above.

_____ 8. A party to an instrument has a real defense if his obligation on the instrument:
a. is void.
b. is voidable.
c. has been discharged.
d. is the result of fraud in the inducement.

_____ 9. A forged signature operates as the signature of:
a. the person whose name is forged.
b. the forger.
c. any person who takes the instrument with notice that the signature has been forged.
d. none of the above.

_____ 10. Under the FTC's holder in due course rule, the consumer may successfully assert:
a. real defenses.
b. personal defenses.
c. real and personal defenses.
d. none of the above.

_____ 11. Which of the following constitutes value for purposes of holder in due course status?
a. The taking of an instrument in payment of an antecedent debt.
b. An executory promise to pay money.
c. The acquiring of a security interest in the instrument.
d. (a) and (c) only.

_____ 12. A holder may become a holder in due course if she takes the instrument without notice that it is:
a. overdue.
b. dishonored.
c. given for value.
d. (a) and (b) only.

_____ 13. Which of the following is NOT a real defense?
a. Minority.
b. Unauthorized signature.
c. Duress.
d. Lack of consideration.

_____ 14. Paula Payee by means of fraud in the inducement induces Michael Maker to sign an instrument payable to her. Paula subsequently negotiates the instrument to Harry Holder, a holder in due course. Paula later reacquires the note from Harry.
   a. Paula can invoke the shelter rule.
   b. Paula is a holder in due course if she gave value to Harry.
   c. Paula remains subject to the defense of fraud and cannot invoke the shelter rule.
   d. Paula can invoke the shelter rule and may be a holder in due course if she gave value to Harry.

_____ 15. Carol Customer has a checking account with First Bank. She deposits a $300 check in her account and then writes a check to Marlin's Department Store in the amount of $100 which First Bank then pays from her account.
   a. First Bank is a holder in due course in the amount of $300.
   b. First Bank is a holder in due course in the amount of $100.
   c. First Bank is not a holder in due course, because it has not given value.
   d. First Bank is not a holder in due course, because it has a customer relationship with Carol.

SHORT ESSAY

1. What is meant by "good faith"?

   _____
   _____
   _____
   _____

2. Explain the difference between a holder and a holder in due course.

   _____
   _____
   _____
   _____

3. Explain the shelter rule and limitations thereon.

   _____
   _____
   _____
   _____

4. P induces M, by fraud in the inducement, to make a note payable to her order and then negotiates it to H, a holder in due course. After the note is overdue, H gives it to B, who has notice of the fraud. What are the rights of B?

_____

_____

_____

_____

5. Bill Buyer makes a note payable to the order of Sam Seller for $2,000. Sam negotiates it to Hal Hoodlum, who changes the amount to $20,000 and negotiates it to Harry Holder, who qualifies as a holder in due course. What rights does Harry have in the instrument? Explain.

_____

_____

_____

_____

Chapter 29
Liability of Parties

PURPOSE

In this chapter, you study the liability of parties arising out of negotiable instruments and the ways in which liability may be terminated. There are two types of liability associated with commercial paper: (1) contractual liability, which may be either primary liability on the instrument or secondary liability on the instrument; and (2) warranty liability, which applies to persons who transfer an instrument and to persons who receive payment or acceptance of an instrument. Contractual liability on the instrument is only imposed upon persons who have signed the instrument. However, warranty liability is not based upon having signed the instrument; it is imposed upon both signers and nonsigners of an instrument.

CHAPTER CHECKPOINTS

After reading and studying this chapter, you should be able to:

1. Distinguish among and discuss contractual liability and warranty liability.

2. Discuss the liability for authorized signatures and for unauthorized signatures.

3. Summarize the liability of makers, acceptors, drawees, drawers, indorsers and accommodation parties.

4. Compare the warranties on transfer with those on presentment.

5. Discuss the ways that liability of the parties to an instrument may be discharged.

CHAPTER OUTLINE

I. Contractual Liability–All parties whose signatures appear on a negotiable instrument incur certain contractual liabilities, unless they disclaim liability. The maker of a promissory note and the acceptor of a draft assume primary or unconditional liability. Primary liability is an absolute obligation to pay a negotiable instrument. Drawers of drafts and checks and indorsers of all instruments incur secondary or conditional liability if the instrument is not paid. Secondary liability is an obligation to pay a negotiable instrument subject to conditions of presentment, dishonor, notice of dishonor, and sometimes protest. Accommodation parties sign a negotiable instrument for the purpose of lending their credit to another party. Accommodation parties have liability based upon the manner in which they sign. If they sign as makers, they have primary liability; if they sign as indorsers, they have secondary liability.

A. Signature–Signature is broadly defined to include any name, word, or mark, whether handwritten, typed, or printed so long as it is made with the intention of authenticating the instrument. It may be made by the individual or the individual's agent.

1. Authorized Signatures–An agent who executes a negotiable instrument on behalf of his principal is not liable if the instrument is executed properly and the agent is authorized. The correct form to avoid liability is "P, principal, by A, agent." If an agent signs only his name to an instrument and does not indicate that he is signing in a representative capacity and does not state the name of the principal, then only the agent is liable on the instrument. If an agent indicates that he is signing in a representative capacity but does not disclose the name of his principal, then the principal is liable if the payee knows that the agent represents the principal. As to any subsequent party, and as to the payee if he does not know that the agent represents the principal, the principal is not liable and the agent alone is liable. If the agent reveals both her name and her principal's name, but does not indicate her representative capacity, both are liable. However, the agent may prove the agency relationship by parol evidence and avoid liability. Under revised Article 3, if an agent signs as a drawer without indicating his status and the check is payable from an account of the represented and identified party, the representative is not liable provided he is an authorized agent.

2. Unauthorized Signatures–This includes both forgeries and signatures made by an agent without proper power to do so. An unauthorized signature is generally not binding on the person whose name appears on the instrument, but it is binding on the unauthorized signer whether or not her own name appears on the instrument. However, an unauthorized signature does bind the person whose name is signed if that person by his negligence substantially contributes to the making of the unauthorized signature. A subsequent holder in due course will not be subject to the defense of unauthorized signature. Also, an unauthorized signature may be ratified by the person whose name appears on the instrument.

3. Ratification of Unauthorized Signature–The person whose name appears on the instrument may ratify an unauthorized signature relieving the actual signer from liability on the instrument. This does not of itself affect any rights the person ratifying the signature may have against the actual signer.

4. Negligence Contributing to Unauthorized Signature–Any person who by his negligence substantially contributes to the making of an unauthorized signature will be estopped from asserting the lack of authority as a defense against a holder in due course or one who has paid the instrument in good faith.

B. Liability of Primary Parties–The makers and acceptors are primarily liable.
   1. Makers–The maker of a note is obligated to pay the instrument according to its terms at the time of issuance, or in the case of an incomplete instrument, according to its terms when completed. Primary liability also applies to issuers of cashier's checks and to issuers of drafts drawn on the drawer.
   2. Acceptors–A drawee has no liability on the instrument until she accepts it, at which time she becomes an acceptor and primarily liable. Certification is a special type of acceptance consisting of the drawee bank's promise to pay the check when presented for payment.

C. Liability of Secondary Parties–The drawers and indorsers (including a payee who indorses) are secondarily liable.
   1. Indorsers and Drawers–If the instrument is not paid by a primary party and the conditions precedent to the liability of secondary parties are satisfied, then a secondary party is liable unless he has disclaimed his liability.
   2. Disclaimer of Liability by Secondary Parties–Both drawers and indorsers may disclaim secondary liability by drawing or indorsing instruments "without recourse." Drawers of checks may not disclaim contractual liability. Such a person does not incur the normal contractual liability, but he may be liable for breach of warranty.
   3. Conditions Precedent to Liability–A condition precedent is an event, or events, that must occur before liability arises. The condition precedent to the liability of the drawer of an unaccepted draft is dishonor. Condition precedent to the liability of any indorser or the drawer of an accepted draft are dishonor and notice of dishonor. If these conditions are not met, a party's conditional obligation on the instrument is discharged unless the conditions are excused.
      a. Dishonor–Dishonor generally involves the refusal to pay an instrument when demand is made by or on behalf of a person entitled to enforce the instrument. What constitutes dishonor varies depending upon the type of instrument and whether presentment is required.
         (1) Note–A demand note is dishonored if the maker does not pay it on the day of presentment. A note payable at a definite time is dishonored if it is not paid on the date it is presented or its due date, whichever is later if (i) the terms of the note require presentment or (ii) the note is payable at or through a bank. All other time notes need not be presented and are dishonored if they are not paid on their due date.
         (2) Drafts–An unaccepted draft payable on demand is dishonored if not paid upon presentment. An accepted demand draft is dishonored if the acceptor does not pay it on the day presented.
         (3) Checks–A check is dishonored where it is presented for payment directly to the payor/drawee bank for immediate payment and there is a refusal to pay. More

commonly, a check being presented through the normal collection process is dishonored if the payor bank makes timely return of the check, sends timely notice of dishonor or nonpayment, or becomes accountable for the amount of the check.

b. Notice of Dishonor–The obligation of an indorser of any instrument and of a drawer of a draft accepted by a nonbank is not enforceable unless the indorser or drawer are given notice of dishonor or the notice is otherwise excused.

c. Presentment and Notice of Dishonor Excused–Presentment will be excused if (i) the person entitled to enforce the instrument cannot reasonably present the instrument, (ii) the maker or acceptor has repudiated the obligation to pay, is dead, or is in insolvency proceedings, (iii) the terms of the instrument do not require presentment in order to hold the indorser or drawer liable, (iv) the drawer of indorser has waived the right of presentment, (v) the drawer instructed the drawee not to pay or accept the draft, or (vi) the drawee was not obligated to the drawer to pay the draft.

4. Liability for Conversion–Conversion is a tort whereby a person becomes liable in damages because of her wrongful control over the personal property of another. The law applicable to conversion of personal property applies to instruments.

II. Termination of Liability–The Code specifies the methods by and extent to which the liability of any party, primary or secondary, is discharged. It also specifies when the liability of all parties is discharged.

A. Payment–Payment to a party entitled to enforce the instrument will discharge liability.

B. Tender of Payment–Any party liable on an instrument who makes tender of full payment to a person entitled to enforce the instrument when or after payment is due is discharged from all subsequent proper liability for interest, but does not relieve her of liability for the face amount of the instrument or any interest, should her tender be refused.

C. Cancellation and Renunciation–Intentional cancellation of the instrument by the person entitled to enforce the instrument results in a discharge of all parties. Accidental destruction or cancellation by someone other than the holder does not have such an effect.

III. Liability Based on Warranty–There are two types of warranties: transferor's warranties and presenter's warranties. The warranties may be disclaimed by agreement between the immediate parties, but they are effective otherwise whether or not the transferor or presenter signs the instrument.

A. Warranties on Transfer–These warranties are given by any person who transfers an instrument and receives consideration. If the transfer is by delivery, the warranties run only to the immediate transferee. If the transfer is by indorsement, whether qualified or unqualified, the warranties run to "any subsequent holder who takes the instrument in good faith." The warranties of the transferor are as follows:

1. Entitlement to Enforce–The transferor warrants that he has the entitlement to enforce the instrument to obtain payment or acceptance on behalf of one who has good title and the transfer is otherwise rightful.

2. Signatures Authentic and Authorized–The transferor warrants that all signatures are authentic or authorized.

3. No Alteration–The transferor warrants that the instrument has not been materially altered.

4. No Defenses–The transferor warrants that the instrument is not subject to defense or claim in recoupment of any party.

5. No Knowledge of Insolvency–The transferor warrants that he has no knowledge of any insolvency proceedings instituted by the maker, acceptor, or drawer of an unaccepted instrument.

B. Warranties on Presentment–Any party who pays or accepts an instrument must do so in strict compliance with the orders contained in that instrument. In the case of a note, a maker who pays the wrong person will not be discharged from his obligation to pay the correct person. If a drawee pays the wrong person he generally cannot charge the drawer's account. The presenter's warranty of entitlement to is essentially the same as the transferor's warranty. She warrants that she has or is a person entitled to enforce the instrument.

1. Genuineness of Drawer's Signature–Presenters warrant that they have no knowledge that the signature of drawer is unauthorized.

2. No Alteration–The presenter, except for a holder in due course acting in good faith to a maker or drawer, warrants against material alteration.

3. All other Payors–The only warranty given is that the warrantor is a person entitled to enforce the instrument.

D. Impairment of Recourse or Collateral–A holder discharges any party to the instrument to the extent any of the party's rights are adversely affected by any of several acts listed in the Code.

E. Reacquisition–When an instrument is returned to or reacquired by a prior party to the instrument, any intervening party is discharged from liability as against the reacquiring party and against any subsequent parties who are not holders in due course without notice of the discharge.

F. Other Methods of Discharge–Other methods by which a party's liability may be discharged include: (1) fraudulent and material alteration; (2) discharge of the drawer and prior indorsers by certification of a check procured by the holder; and (3) unexcused delay in presentment, notice of dishonor, or protest. A party may also be discharged by agreeing to pay money in exchange for discharge.

KEY TERMS

1. Contractual liability

2. Warranty liability

3. Primary liability

4. Secondary liability

5. Accommodation party

6. Acceptance

7. Acceptor

8. Certification

9. Presentment

10. Dishonor

11. Protest

12. Transferor's warranty

13. Presenter's warranty

14. Discharge

TRUE/FALSE

_____ 1. A person may be liable on a negotiable instrument even if he doesn't sign it.

_____ 2. A forger will be liable on an instrument even though he signs someone else's name and not his own.

_____ 3. The liability of an accommodation party is determined by the capacity in which she signs.

_____ 4. The acceptor of a draft or check assumes primary liability on the instrument.

_____ 5. An unauthorized signature may not be ratified even by the person whose name appears on the instrument.

_____ 6. A bank that pays an instrument on a forged indorsement will not be liable for conversion if it acted in good faith.

_____ 7. If an agent makes a note on behalf of a principal but just signs his own name and not the principal's name, then both the agent and the principal are liable on the instrument.

_____ 8. An indorser may disclaim contractual liability by using the notation "without recourse."

_____ 9. If an instrument is transferred by delivery alone (without indorsement) warranties in transfer run to the immediate transferee only.

_____ 10. An indorser is completely discharged from liability on an instrument if due presentment for payment has not been made.

_____ 11. Noncompliance with conditions precedent has a different effect on the liability of an indorser than on a drawers' liability.

_____ 12. Andrew is the indorser of a note for $1,000 on which Michael is the maker. Andrew becomes immediately liable for the face amount when the note becomes due.

_____ 13. The discharge of a party is not effective against a subsequent holder in due course unless she has notice of the discharge when she takes the instrument.

_____ 14. David Drawer wrote a check for $1,000 payable to Paul Payee. Paul altered the check to read $11,000 and negotiated the check to Harold, a holder in due course. Paul is liable to Harold under the transferor's warranties.

_____ 15. Any necessary notice of dishonor must be given by a bank before midnight on the first banking day after the banking day when it receives notice of dishonor.

MULTIPLE CHOICE

_____ 1. A signature may be:
   a. printed.
   b. made by an authorized agent.
   c. typed.
   d. all of the above.

_____ 2. A drawee bank becomes liable on a check when:
   a. the check is written.
   b. the drawer issues the check.
   c. the payee indorses the check.
   d. the bank accepts the check.

_____ 3. An indorser may disclaim contractual liability on an instrument if his indorsement contains the words:
   a. "time is of the essence."
   b. "Caveat Emptor."
   c. "without recourse."
   d. "notice of dishonor."

_____ 4. Presentment may be made by which of the following?
   a. Mail.
   b. At a place specified in the instrument.
   c. Through a clearinghouse.
   d. All of the above.

_____ 5. Presentment may be made by which of the following?
  a. Mail.
  b. At a place specified in the instrument.
  c. Through a clearinghouse.
  d. All of the above.

_____ 6. If the completion of an incomplete instrument is unauthorized:
  a. a holder of an incomplete instrument that has been fraudulently completed may recover as completed.
  b. a holder in due course may recover from the maker as completed.
  c. (a) and (b).
  d. none of the above.

_____ 7. Which of the following is not a warranty of transfer?
  a. No material alteration.
  b. Maker is solvent.
  c. Entitlement to enforce.
  d. Signatures genuine.

_____ 8. The parties that are secondarily liable for payment of an instrument include:
  a. makers and acceptors.
  b. makers and drawers.
  c. drawers and indorsers.
  d. drawers and acceptors.

_____ 9. Which of the following is not an example of conversion?
  a. A drawee to whom a draft is delivered for acceptance refuses to return it on demand.
  b. An instrument is paid on a forged indorsement.
  c. A holder unjustifiably impairs any collateral given on an instrument by a party to that instrument.
  d. A drawee to whom an instrument is delivered for payment refuses on demand either to pay or to return it.

_____ 10. A holder who strikes out an indorser's signature:
  a. has discharged that indorser.
  b. is liable for conversion.
  c. has broken the chain of title.
  d. is not entitled to payment.

_____ 11. An indorser who is required to pay an instrument has no right of recourse against:
  a. subsequent indorsers.
  b. prior indorsers.
  c. makers and acceptors.
  d. any party.

_____ 12. Susan Kalinowsky owns a business and is known for business purposes as Susan Monroe. She signs her business checks and notes as Susan Monroe.
   a. Susan is liable on these checks and notes, because her signature is valid.
   b. Susan has no liability, because her signature is under an assumed name.
   c. Susan is a fictitious payee.
   d. Susan has secondary liability because the business has primary liability.

_____ 13. A presenter warrants:
   a. that all signatures are genuine and authorized.
   b. that there are no defenses against the instrument.
   c. that he has entitlement to enforce.
   d. that no defenses are good against him.

_____ 14. Harold is the holder of a check that has been dishonored by First Bank. Harold may seek payment:
   a. from the drawee.
   b. from the drawer.
   c. from the indorsers.
   d. from either the drawer or the indorsers.

_____ 15. Which of the following will terminate a commercial transaction?
   a. Tender of payment.
   b. Reacquisition.
   c. Renunciation.
   d. All of the above.

SHORT ESSAY

1. Explain the difference between contractual liability and warranty liability.

   _____
   _____
   _____
   _____

2. Your roommate writes a check to you and you indorse it "Pay to Cathy" and your signature, and give it to Cathy to pay a debt you owe her. Cathy writes "Without recourse, Cathy" and gives it to Ben. Ben quickly presents it to the bank for payment, but payment is refused. What can Ben do?

   _____
   _____
   _____
   _____

3. What are the differences between primary and secondary liability?

    _____
    _____
    _____
    _____

4. How may liability of the parties to an instrument be discharged?

    _____
    _____
    _____
    _____

5. You are the president of Big Bucks, Inc. You have authority to sign instruments on behalf of the company. If you sign a note with your name and indicate that you are president but do not name the company, who is liable on the note?

    _____
    _____
    _____
    _____

Chapter 30
Bank Deposits, Collections, and Funds Transfers

PURPOSE

Today most goods and services are bought and sold without a physical transfer of cash. Credit cards, charge accounts, and various deferred payment plans have made cash sales increasingly rare. The credit sales are usually settled by check rather than cash. Generally, the buyer's check must journey from the seller-payee's bank (depositary bank), where the check is deposited by the seller for credit to his account, to the buyer-drawer's bank (payor bank) for payment. In the collection process, checks can also pass through one or more banks (intermediary banks) so that it may be collected and the appropriate entries recorded. In recent years, the amount of payment made by electronic funds transfers has also increased. The dollar volume of commercial payments made by wire transfer far exceeds the dollar amount made by checks and credit cards. In this chapter you study the bank deposit-collection system and electronic funds transfers.

CHAPTER CHECKPOINTS

After reading and studying this chapter, you should be able to:

1. Define and distinguish among the depositary, payor, intermediary and collecting banks.

2. Define provisional credit, and discuss how and when credit becomes final.

3. Discuss the obligations imposed on the customer and on the payor bank as part of their relationship.

4. Define electronic fund transfer, compare it to the check collection process of Article 4 and outline the major provisions of the Electronic Fund Transfer Act.

5. Discuss the scope of Article 4A of the UCC which covers wholesale funds transfers.

CHAPTER OUTLINE

I. Bank Deposits and Collections–Article 4 of the UCC provides the principal rules governing the bank collection process.

    A. Collection of Items–The depositary bank is the bank in which the payee or holder deposits a check for credit. Provisional credit is tentative credit for the deposit of an instrument until final credit is given. If the bank permits a customer to draw funds against provisional credit, the bank has given value and is a holder in due course. When the amount of the check has been collected from the payor bank, which is also the drawee bank, the credit becomes final. The Competitive Equality Banking Act of 1987 expedited the availability of funds by establishing maximum time periods for a bank to hold various types of instruments. A bank may be both the depositary bank and the payor bank; however, in most cases they are different banks. When the two are different banks, a check must pass from one bank to the other, either directly through a clearinghouse or through one or more intermediary banks. An intermediary bank is a bank involved in the collection process other than the depositary or payor bank. A clearinghouse is an association of banks for the purpose of settling accounts on a daily basis.

        1. Collecting Banks–A collecting bank is any bank handling the item for payment except the payor bank. In the usual situation where the depositary and payor banks are different, the depositary bank gives a provisional credit to its customer, transfers the item to the next bank in the chain, receiving a provisional credit or "settlement" from it, and so on to the payor bank, which then debits the drawer's account. When the check is paid, the provisional settlements become final. If the payor bank does not pay the item, the process must be reversed so that ultimately the depositary bank charges the account of the customer who deposited the check. He must then seek recovery from the drawer or indorsers. A collecting bank is an agent of the owner of the check until settlement becomes final. Any credit given is provisional until settlement becomes final at which time the depositary collecting bank changes from an agent of the depositor to a debtor of the depositor. The effect of this agency rule is that the risk of loss remains with the owner and any chargebacks go to her, not to the collecting bank.

            a. Duty of Care–A collecting bank must use ordinary care in handling an item transferred to it for collection. It must act within a reasonable time after receipt of the item and must choose a reasonable method of forwarding the item for presentment.

            b. Duty to Act Timely–A collecting bank acts timely if it acts within the midnight deadline. The midnight deadline means midnight of the banking day following the banking day on which the bank receives the item or notice of its dishonor. If a bank receives a check on Monday, it must take proper action by midnight on Tuesday. The Code allows banks to fix an afternoon hour of 2:00 P.M. or later as a cutoff hour for bookkeeping purposes in order to meet the midnight deadline.

    c. Indorsements–When an item is restrictively indorsed with words such as "pay any bank," it is locked into the bank collection system. When a bank forwards an item for collection, it normally indorses it "pay any bank." This protects the bank by making it impossible for the item to stray from regular collection channels. If there was no indorsement, the bank becomes a holder when it takes possession if the customer was a holder and if the bank meets the other requirements of a holder in due course.

    d. Warranties–Customers and collecting banks give basically the same warranties as those given by parties under Article 3 of the Code on presentment and transfer.

    e. Final Payment–Under the Code, final payment occurs when the payor bank does any of the following: (1) pays an item in cash; (2) settles and does not have the right to revoke the settlement through agreement, statute, or clearinghouse rule; (3) makes a provisional settlement and does not revoke it in the time and manner permitted by statute, clearinghouse rule, or agreement.

  2. Payor Banks–Under its contract with the drawer, the payor or drawee bank agrees to pay to the payee or his order checks that are issued by the drawer, provided the order is not countermanded by a stop payment order and provided there are sufficient funds in the drawer's account. When a payor bank that is not also a depositary bank receives a demand item other than for immediate payment over the counter, it must either return the item or give its transferor a provisional settlement before midnight of the banking day on which the item is received.

B. Relationship Between Payor Bank and Its Customer–The relationship between a payor bank and its checking account customer is primarily the product of their contractual arrangement. A bank may not (1) disclaim responsibility for its lack of good faith; (2) disclaim responsibility for its failure to exercise ordinary care; or (3) limit its damages for breach of such lack or failure.

  1. Payment of an Item–A payor bank owes a duty to its customer, the drawer, to pay checks properly drawn by her on an account that has sufficient funds to cover the items. The drawee is not liable on a check until it accepts the item. However, if a bank improperly refuses payment, it will incur liability to its customer from whose account the item should have been paid. If the customer has enough money in his account, the bank is liable to the customer for any dishonor, because there is no basis for it to refuse payment. If a wrongful dishonor occurs through mistake, the bank's liability is limited to actual damages proved, including damages for arrest or other consequential damages. A bank is under no obligation to pay an uncertified check that is over six months old. However, a bank is not obligated to dishonor such a check. When a payor receives an item for which there are insufficient funds in the account, but which is otherwise properly payable, the bank may either (1) dishonor the item and return it; or (2) pay the item and charge the customer's account even though an overdraft is created as a result. The customer may be liable to pay a service charge and interest on the overdraft.

  2. Stop Payment Orders–The drawer of a check may issue a stop payment order. To be effective, a stop payment order must be received by the bank in time to give it a reasonable opportunity to act on it. An oral stop payment order is binding on the bank for fourteen calendar days. The

normal practice is for a customer to confirm an oral stop payment order in writing. The written order is effective for six months and may be renewed in writing. It is possible that when the check is dishonored by the bank, the drawer may incur liability to the holder, particularly if the holder is a holder in due course against whom personal defenses are not effective.

3. Bank's Right to Subrogation on Improper Payment–If a payor bank pays an item over a stop payment order or otherwise in violation of its contract with the drawer or maker, the payor bank is subrogated to the rights of (a) any holder in due course on the item against the drawer or maker; (b) the payee or any other holder against the drawer or maker; and (c) the drawer or maker against the payee or any other holder. This allows a bank to pay a holder in due course when the drawer's defense is a personal one notwithstanding the fact that the drawer has issued a valid stop payment order.

4. Disclosure Requirements–In 1992, Congress enacted the Truth in Savings Act, which provides that disclosures must be made in clear and conspicuous writing and must be given to consumers when an account is opened or service is provided and must include the following: (a) the annual percentage yield and the percentage rate; (b) how variable rates are calculated and when the rates may be changed; (c) balance information; (d) when and how interest is calculated and credited; (e) the amount of fees that may be charged and how calculated; and (f) any limitation on the number or amount of withdrawals or deposits.

5. Customer's Death or Incompetence–If either a payor or collecting bank does not know that a customer has been adjudicated incompetent, the bank's authority to accept, pay, or collect the item is not impaired. Neither death nor adjudication of incompetence of a customer revokes a payor or collecting bank's authority to accept, pay, or collect an item until the bank knows of the condition and has a reasonable opportunity to act on this knowledge. Even though the bank knows of the death of its customer, it may for ten days after the date of death act on the instrument unless a person claiming an interest in the account orders the bank to stop making payments.

6. Customer's Duties–The Code imposes affirmative duties on bank customers and fixes time limits within which they must assert their rights. The customer is required to exercise reasonable care and promptness to examine the bank statement and items to discover an unauthorized signature or an alteration; he must notify the bank promptly. The customer must examine the statement and items within a reasonable time, which in no event may exceed fourteen days and must notify the bank of unauthorized signatures and alterations. Any alterations or unauthorized signatures on instruments by the same wrongdoer and paid by the bank during that period will still be the responsibility of the bank, but any paid thereafter but before the customer notifies the bank may not be asserted against it. The customer must always report an alteration or unauthorized signature within one year from the time the statement or items were made available to him or be barred from asserting them against the bank. Any unauthorized indorsement must be asserted within three years from the time the bank statements and items containing such indorsements are made available to the customer.

II. Electronic Fund Transfers–Financial institutions seek to substitute EFTs for checks to eliminate the paperwork involved in processing checks and to eliminate the "float" that a drawer of a check enjoys as a result of having the use of his funds during the check processing period between issuing the check and final payment. An electronic fund transfer has been defined as "any transfer of funds, other than a transaction originated by check, draft, or similar paper instrument, which is initiated through an electronic terminal, telephonic instrument, or computer or magnetic tape so as to order, instruct, or authorize a financial institution to debit or credit an account." EFTs have brought about considerable confusion concerning the legal rights of customers and financial institutions. A partial solution has been the enactment of the Electronic Fund Transfer Act, but important legal problems remain.

A. Types of Electronic Fund Transfers–Currently there are several EFTs in use.
  1. Automated Teller Machines–ATMs permit customers to conduct various transactions with their bank through the use of electronic terminals. After activating an ATM with a plastic identification card and a secret number, customers can deposit and withdraw funds from their accounts, transfer funds between accounts, obtain cash advances from bank credit card accounts, and make payments on loans.
  2. Point-of-Sale Systems–Point-of-sale (POS) systems permit consumers to transfer funds from their bank account to a merchant automatically. The POS machines are located within the merchant's store and are activated by the consumer's identification card and code.
  3. Direct Deposits and Withdrawals–Direct deposits of payroll, Social Security and other payments can be made through an electronic terminal when the deposit has been authorized in advance by the consumer. Automatic withdrawals to pay insurance premiums, utility bills, or automobile loan payments are common examples of this type of EFT.
  4. Pay-by-Phone Systems–These permit customers to pay bills by telephoning the bank's computer system and directing a transfer of funds to a designated third party or between accounts.
  5. Wholesale Electronic Funds Transfers–These are commonly called wholesale wire transfers and involve the movement of funds between financial institutions, between financial institutions and businesses, and between businesses.

B. Consumer Funds Transfers–Because of the unique characteristics of electronic systems and inadequate legislation, Congress enacted the Electronic Fund Transfer Act (EFTA). This act "provides a basic framework establishing the rights, liabilities, and responsibilities of participants in electronic fund transfers" with primary emphasis on "the provision of individual consumer rights." The act does not govern electronic transfers between financial institutions, between financial institutions and businesses, and between businesses. The act is administered by the Board of Governors of the Federal Reserve System.
  1. Disclosure–The terms and conditions of electronic fund transfers involving a consumer's account must be disclosed in readily understandable language at the time the consumer contracts for such services.
  2. Documentation and Periodic Statements–The financial institution must provide the consumer with written documentation of each transfer made from an electronic terminal at the time of the transfer–a receipt. The receipt must clearly state the amount involved, the date, the type of transfer, the identity of the consumer's accounts involved, the identity of any third party

involved, and the location of the terminal involved. The institution must also provide periodic statements for each account of the consumer.

3. Preauthorized Transfers–A preauthorized transfer from a consumer's account must be authorized in advance by the consumer in writing, and a copy of the authorization must be provided to the consumer when made. A consumer may stop payment of any preauthorized EFT by notifying the financial institution orally or in writing at any time up to three business days before the scheduled transfer.

4. Error Resolution–The consumer has sixty days after the financial institution sends a periodic statement in which to notify the financial institution of any errors that appear on the statement. The financial institution is required to investigate and report the results within ten business days. If it determines that an error did occur, it must properly correct it. Failure to investigate in good faith makes the financial institution liable for treble damages.

5. Consumer Liability–A consumer's liability is limited to a maximum of $50 if the consumer notifies the financial institution within two days after he learns of the loss or theft. If the consumer does not report the unauthorized use within two days, he is liable for losses up to $500. If the consumer fails to report the unauthorized use within sixty days, he is liable for losses resulting from any unauthorized EFT that would not have occurred but for the failure of the consumer to report the loss within sixty days.

6. Liability of Financial Institution–A financial institution is liable to a consumer for all damages proximately caused by its failure to make an EFT according to the terms and conditions of an account. However, it will not be liable if (1) the consumer's account has insufficient funds through no fault of the financial institution, (2) the funds are subject to legal process, (3) the transfer would exceed an established credit limit, (4) an electronic terminal has insufficient cash, or (5) circumstances beyond the institution's control prevent the transfer. The institution is also liable for failure to stop payment of a preauthorized transfer when instructed to do so in accordance with the terms and conditions of the account.

C. Wholesale Funds Transfers–Article 4A, Funds Transfers, is designed to provide a statutory framework for a payment system that is not covered by existing Articles of the UCC or the EFTA. It provides that the rights and obligations of the parties to a funds transfer covered by the article are subject to contrary agreement of the parties.

1. Scope of Article–It covers wholesale funds transfers and defines a funds transfer as a "series of transactions, beginning with the originator's payment order, made for the purpose of making payment to the beneficiary of the order. The term includes any payment order issued by the originator's bank or an intermediary bank intended to carry out the originator's payment order. A funds transfer is completed by acceptance by the beneficiary of the originator's payment order."

   a. Payment Order–This is an instruction of a sender to a receiving bank to pay, or to cause another bank to pay, a fixed or determinable amount of money to a beneficiary.

   b. Parties–The originator is the sender of the payment order or, in a series of payment orders, it is the sender of the first payment order. A sender is the party who gives an instruction to the receiving bank. The bank to which the sender's instruction is addressed is the receiving bank. The originator's bank is either the bank that receives the original payment order or the originator if the originator is a bank. The beneficiary's bank is the bank identified in a payment order to credit the beneficiary's account and is the last bank in the chain of a funds transfer. The beneficiary is the person to be paid by the beneficiary bank. An intermediary bank is any receiving bank, other than an originator's bank or a beneficiary's bank, that receives a payment order.

   c. Excluded Transactions–If any part of a funds transfer is governed by the EFTA such coverage is excluded from Article 4A coverage. Article 4A also excludes debit transactions but covers credit transactions.

2. Acceptance–If a receiving bank is not the beneficiary's bank, it does not subject itself to any liability until it accepts the instrument. Acceptance by a receiving bank other than the beneficiary's bank occurs when the receiving bank executes the order. If a beneficiary's bank accepts a payment order, the bank is obliged to pay the beneficiary the amount of the order.

3. Erroneous Execution of Payment Orders–If a receiving bank mistakenly executes a payment order for an amount greater than the authorized amount, the bank is only entitled to payment of the amount of the sender's correct order. The receiving bank is entitled to recover from the beneficiary of the erroneous order the amount in excess of the authorized amount.

4. Unauthorized Payment Orders–If a bank establishes commercially reasonable security measures agreed to by the customer for preventing unauthorized transmissions and properly follows its process, the customer must pay the order even if it was unauthorized.

KEY TERMS

1. Depositary bank

2. Payor bank

3. Intermediary bank

4. Collecting bank

5. Provisional credit

6. Final Credit

7. Clearinghouse

8. Midnight deadline

9. Stop payment order

10. Electronic fund transfer

TRUE/FALSE

_____ 1. When Bill deposits a check in his bank, the bank credits his account and receives a final credit in the amount of the check.

_____ 2. A collecting bank is strictly liable for mishandling an item transferred to it for collection.

_____ 3. Once a check is restrictively indorsed with words such as "pay any bank", only a bank may acquire the rights of a holder.

_____ 4. A payor bank which dishonors an item must either return the item or send written notice of dishonor before midnight of the banking day on which the item is received.

_____ 5. A bank may not pay its customer's check and charge her account for the full amount if there are insufficient funds in her account to cover the check.

_____ 6. Where there are insufficient funds in a customer account, the bank may charge items received on that account on any given day, in any order it deems convenient..

_____ 7. A bank is required to dishonor its customer's check if the check is over six months old.

_____ 8. An oral stop payment order is binding on the bank for fourteen days.

_____ 9. A consumer's liability for unauthorized electronic fund transfer is limited to $100 if the consumer notifies the financial institution within two days after she learns of the loss.

_____ 10. Point-of-sale systems enable a consumer automatically to transfer funds from his bank account to a merchant seller.

_____ 11. The payor bank and the drawee bank are the same bank.

_____ 12. The first bank to receive a check for payment is the payee bank.

_____ 13. Under Article 4A of the UCC, a funds transfer is completed by acceptance by the beneficiary's bank of a payment order for the benefit of the beneficiary of the originator's payment order.

_____ 14. Consumers are now able to transfer funds automatically from their own bank accounts to a merchant by means of point-of-sale (POS) systems.

_____ 15. Pending final payment, various banks in the collection process make a series of provisional settlements.

MULTIPLE CHOICE

_____ 1. If a check is not paid for any reason, the payor bank should:
a. return it to the drawer.
b. return it to the drawee.
c. return it to its transferor.
d. throw it away.

_____ 2. A depositary bank may treat a check as having been received on Monday if the check was actually received late in the afternoon on:
a. Tuesday.
b. Wednesday.
c. Thursday.
d. Friday.

_____ 3. In presenting an item for payment, a collecting bank may delay presentment for up to:
a. one calendar day.
b. one banking day.
c. three banking days.
d. one week.

_____ 4. Which of the following is responsible for examining a check for prior restrictive indorsements?
a. The depositary bank.
b. The intermediary bank.
c. The payor bank.
d. All of the above must examine it for restrictive indorsements.

_____ 5. Final payment of an item occurs during the processing of the item by:
a. the depositary bank.
b. the intermediary bank.
c. the payor bank.
d. none of the above.

_____ 6. Which is not true under the Competitive Equality Banking Act of 1987?
a. Wire transfers must clear by the next business day.
b. Local checks must clear within one business day.
c. Nonlocal checks must clear in seven intervening business days.
d. Government checks must clear by the next business day.

_____ 7. A collecting bank that transfers an item and receives a settlement gives which of the following warranties to its transferee?
   a. He is a person entitled to enforce the instrument.
   b. All signatures are authentic and authorized.
   c. Both a and b.
   d. Neither a nor b.

_____ 8. Banks may not do which of the following?
   a. Disclaim responsibility for lack of good faith.
   b. Disclaim responsibility for failure to exercise ordinary care.
   c. Limit its damages for breach.
   d. It may not do any of the above.

_____ 9. A written stop payment order:
   a. is valid for 60 days.
   b. is valid for 90 days.
   c. may be renewed in writing.
   d. (a) and (c) but not (b).

_____ 10. If a consumer does not report the loss or theft of his electronic fund transfer card within two days he is liable for losses up to:
   a. $500.
   b. $250.
   c. $50.
   d. any unauthorized use.

_____ 11. The Electronic Fund Transfer Act imposes liability on a customer for unauthorized transfers in the maximum amount of:
   a. $50 in most circumstances.
   b. $100 in most circumstances.
   c. $500 if the consumer fails to notify the financial institution within two days after learning of the loss or theft.
   d. (a) and (c) only.

_____ 12. Any bank to which an item is transferred in the course of collection, other than the depositary or payor banks, is a/an _____ bank.
   a. drawee
   b. intermediary
   c. clearinghouse
   d. federal

_____ 13. First Bank pays a check over a stop payment order of its customer.
   a. First Bank is subrogated to the rights of any holder in due course on the item against the drawer or maker.
   b. First Bank is subrogated to the rights of the payee or any other holder against the drawer or maker.
   c. First Bank is subrogated to the rights of the drawer or maker against the payee or any other holder.
   d. All of the above are correct.

_____ 14. A/an _____ permits a consumer to transfer funds from his bank account to a merchant automatically. With this system, machines are located within the merchant's store and are activated by the consumer's identification card and code.
   a. automated teller machine
   b. point-of-sale system
   c. direct deposit and withdrawal
   d. pay-by-phone system

_____ 15. Which of the following is not a type of electronic funds transfer?
   a. An ATM transaction.
   b. A point of sale transaction.
   c. A money order transaction.
   d. All of the above are ETFs.

SHORT ESSAY

1. Explain the effect of a restrictive indorsement with words such as "pay any bank."

   _____
   _____
   _____
   _____

2. What is provisional credit? When does it become final?

   _____
   _____
   _____
   _____

3. Arthur issued a check to Brad. Carl stole the check, forged Brad's indorsement, and cashed the check at Arthur's bank. What are the rights of Arthur and of the bank?

_____

_____

_____

_____

4. David had a bank card that he used for EFT transactions with First Bank. On Tuesday, a thief stole David's wallet, including the bank card. David immediately notified the bank. Nevertheless, the thief withdrew $1,000 from David's account on Wednesday using the card. Discuss David's liability under this fact situation.

_____

_____

_____

_____

5. East Company instructs its bank, First National Bank, to pay $1,000,000 to West Company, also a customer of First National Bank. First National executes the payment order by crediting West's account with $1,000,000 and notifying West that the credit has been made and is available. Identify the parties to this funds transfer under Article 4A of the UCC.

_____

_____

_____

_____

Part V
Sample Examination

MULTIPLE CHOICE

_____ 1. Carl Criminal breaks into Brenda's apartment, steals her checkbook, then makes a check for $100 payable to "cash" and signs Brenda's name in the lower right hand corner of the check. Which of the following is correct regarding this instrument?
   a. Carl is the drawer of the check.
   b. Brenda is the drawer of the check.
   c. The instrument is nonnegotiable.
   d. Carl is a fictitious payee.

_____ 2. Bill Businessman has a bearer instrument for $200. He transfers it to Acme Corporation, but does not indorse it. Which of the following is correct regarding this transaction?
   a. Bill incurs contract liability, but not warranty liability by transferring this bearer instrument.
   b. Bill incurs warranty liability, but not contract liability by transferring this bearer instrument.
   c. Bill incurs both contract and warranty liability by transferring this bearer instrument.
   d. Bill incurs neither contract nor warranty liability by transferring this bearer instrument.

_____ 3. First Bank pays an instrument with a forged indorsement which is drawn on the account of Big Bucks, Inc.
   a. First Bank may charge the account of Big Bucks.
   b. First Bank has no recourse against the person from whom it received the check.
   c. First Bank is liable to the named payee for conversion.
   d. None of the above is correct.

_____ 4. First Bank receives a check drawn on one of its accounts from American Bank, an intermediary collecting bank, at 10:00 a.m. Monday during banking hours. When must First Bank either pay or dishonor the item?
   a. Immediately.
   b. By midnight on Monday.
   c. By midnight on Tuesday.
   d. By 3:00 p.m. on Tuesday.

_____ 5. Harold Homeowner calls First Bank to issue a stop payment order on a check he has issued to a door to door salesman selling magazines.
   a. The stop payment order is binding on the bank for 10 days.
   b. The stop payment order is binding on the bank for 14 days.
   c. The stop payment order is binding on the bank for six months.
   d. Oral stop payment orders have no validity under the Code.

_____ 6. Which of the following is a type of commercial paper?
   a. Check.
   b. Note.
   c. Certificate of deposit.
   d. All the above.

_____ 7. Which of the following is not a valid purpose of an indorsement?
   a. To negotiate the instrument.
   b. To restrict payment of the instrument.
   c. To validate the instrument.
   d. To incur liability on the instrument.

_____ 8. After a busy day of running errands, Happy Homemaker stops at the grocery store, writes a check for groceries, but fails to insert the date. The instrument as issued by Happy is:
   a. a negotiable demand instrument.
   b. a negotiable time instrument.
   c. nonnegotiable.
   d. an assignment of funds to the grocery store.

_____ 9. Sarah Student indorses a check "For deposit only." This is a _____ indorsement.
   a. qualified
   b. restrictive
   c. special
   d. blank

_____ 10. Sarah Student has a check that is payable to her order. She indorses it in blank. The instrument is now:
   a. nonnegotiable.
   b. bearer paper.
   c. an incomplete instrument.
   d. order paper.

_____ 11. Bill Businessman signs a blank check and then leaves it on his desk. His son Junior picks it up, and then uses it to buy a $500 VCR from the local electronic store by completing the instrument and making it payable to the store. As the drawer of the check, Bill:
   a. has no liability on the instrument because it was an incomplete instrument when he signed it.
   b. has no liability, because it was not completed according to his authorization.
   c. will be liable since his negligence in leaving the blank check on his desk contributed to the unauthorized completion of the check.
   d. can sue the bank if they pay the check from Bill's account.

_____ 12. Which is required to become a holder in due course?
   a. Take the instrument for value.
   b. Take the instrument in good faith.
   c. Take the instrument without notice.
   d. All of the above are required.

_____ 13. Harold is a holder in due course of a negotiable instrument. He takes it:
   a. free from all defenses.
   b. subject to real defenses.
   c. subject to personal defenses.
   d. subject to all defenses.

_____ 14. Bill Buyer issues a check for $500 payable to the order of Sam Seller and drawn on First Bank.
   a. First Bank is the drawer; Sam is the drawee; and Bill is the payee.
   b. Bill is the drawer; Sam is the payee; and First Bank is the drawee.
   c. Bill is the drawer; Sam is the drawee; and First Bank is the payee.
   d. First Bank is the holder; Sam is the payor; and Bill is the drawee.

_____ 15. Sam Seller accepted a $400 negotiable demand note from Bill Buyer for goods he sold to him. Sam then negotiated the note to Carl Contractor who qualified as a holder in due course. Carl later indorsed the note to his son Junior as a gift. Unfortunately, Sam had misrepresented the goods to Bill and Bill now wants to dishonor the note based upon fraud in the inducement. Junior, of course, knew nothing about the dealings between Sam and Bill when he accepted the $400 note as a gift from his father.
   a. Junior is a holder in due course.
   b. The defense of fraud in the inducement can be asserted against Junior, because he is not a holder in due course.
   c. Junior is not a holder in due course, but under the shelter rule he has the rights of one. The defense of fraud in the inducement cannot be asserted against him.
   d. Junior is a mere assignee and has no right to collect the note.

_____ 16. In order for a transferee of a negotiable instrument to become a holder, the transfer must be made by:
   a. negotiation.
   b. indorsement.
   c. assignment.
   d. delivery.

_____ 17. An indorsement which includes a signature and the words "without recourse" is a _____ indorsement.
   a. blank
   b. special
   c. qualified
   d. restrictive

_____ 18. In what way is a note distinguishable from a draft?
   a. A note contains an order to pay.
   b. A draft contains an order to pay.
   c. A draft is a two party instrument.
   d. A note is a three party instrument.

_____ 19. Which of the following is "money" for purposes of negotiability?
   a. American dollars.
   b. French francs.
   c. Mexican pesos.
   d. All of the above.

_____ 20. Under the revised Article 3 the period during which a nonbank must give notice of dishonor is:
   a. 3 days.
   b. 10 days.
   c. 15 days.
   d. 30 days.

Chapter 31
Formation of General Partnerships

PURPOSE

A business enterprise may be operated or conducted by a sole proprietor, a joint venture, a general partnership, a limited partnership, a limited liability company, a corporation, or by some other form of business organization. Partnerships are an important form of business organization in that they allow individuals with different expertise, backgrounds, resources and interests to bring their various skills together to form a more competitive enterprise. The law of partnerships is uniform throughout the United States, because most states have adopted the Uniform Partnership Act with only a few variations. In Chapters 31 through 33 you study general partnerships, and in Chapter 34 you study limited partnerships and other types of unincorporated business associations.

CHAPTER CHECKPOINTS

After reading and studying this chapter, you should be able to:

1. Identify and discuss the situations when a partnership is treated as a legal entity and those situations for which it is treated as a legal aggregate.

2. List the main provisions which should be included in a partnership agreement.

3. Give the UPA definition of a partnership, discuss the tests for the existence of a partnership, and define the different types of partners.

4. Distinguish between partnership capital and partnership property.

5. Discuss the rights that a partner has in partnership property in contrast to the rights that a partner has in the partnership itself.

CHAPTER OUTLINE

A. Nature of Partnership–Partnerships allow individuals with different expertise, backgrounds, resources, and interests to bring their various skills together to form a more competitive enterprise. Today the law governing partnerships is the Uniform Partnership Act, which has been adopted in all states except Louisiana. Areas not provided for by the act are governed by the rules of law and equity.

   1. Definition of Partnership–The UPA defines a partnership as "an association of two or more persons to carry on as co-owners a business for profit."

   2. Entity Theory–A legal entity is an organization having a separate legal existence from its members. It is a unit with the capacity of possessing legal rights and being subject to legal duties. A legal entity may acquire, own, and dispose of property. It may also enter into contracts, commit wrongs, sue and be sued. At common law, a partnership was regarded as a legal aggregate, a group of individuals not having a legal existence separate from its members. The UPA treats a partnership as a legal entity for some purposes.

      a. Partnership as a Legal Entity–The UPA recognizes a partnership as a legal entity distinct from its members in that (1) assets of the firm are treated as those of the business and are considered separate and distinct from the individual assets of its members; (2) title to real estate may be acquired by a partnership in the partnership name; (3) a partner is accountable as a fiduciary to the partnership; (4) every partner is considered an agent of the partnership; and (5) under the doctrine of marshaling of assets, partnership creditors have a prior right to partnership assets while creditors of the individual members have a prior right to the separate assets of their individual debtors.

      b. Partnership as a Legal Aggregate–Because a partnership is considered an aggregate for some purposes, it can neither sue nor be sued in the firm name unless a statute specifically allows it. The debts of the partnership are ultimately the debts of the individual partners. In addition, a partnership generally lacks continuity of existence. The Internal Revenue Code treats a partnership as an aggregate. The partnership must file an information return, but the individual partners and not the partnership pay the taxes. Partnership income is taxed to the individual partners regardless of whether the income is actually distributed.

   3. Types of Partners–A general partner is a member of either a general or limited partnership with unlimited liability for its debts, full management powers, and a right to share in the profits. A limited partner is a member of a limited partnership with liability for its debts only to the extent of his capital contribution. A silent partner is a partner who takes no part in the partnership business. A secret partner is one whose membership in the firm is not disclosed to the public. A dormant partner is one who is both a silent and secret partner.

B. Formation of a Partnership–Partnership formation is simple and may be done consciously or unconsciously. A partnership may result from an oral or written agreement, an informal arrangement, or from the conduct of the parties. If two or more individuals share the control and profits of a business, the law may deem them partners regardless of how they characterize their relationship.

   1. Articles of Partnership–It is preferable but not required that the partners put their agreement in writing. A written agreement creating a partnership is referred to as the partnership agreement or

the articles of partnership. Unless the agreement provides otherwise, the partners may amend it only by unanimous consent. It should include: (1) the firm name and the identity of the partners; (2) the nature and scope of the partnership business; (3) the duration of the partnership; (4) the capital contributions of each partner; (5) the division of profits and sharing of losses; (6) the duties of each partner in the management; (7) a provision for salaries, if desired; (8) restrictions on the authority of partners to bind the firm; (9) provisions on the withdrawal of a partner; and (10) a provision for continuation of the business by the remaining partners. A writing is not required for the formation of a partnership. However, a contract to form a partnership to continue for a period longer than one year is within the statute of frauds and requires a writing to be enforceable. A partnership should have a firm name but may not use a name that would be likely to indicate to the public that it is a corporation.

2. Tests of Partnership Existence–Partnerships can be formed without the slightest formality. There are three components to the UPA definition, all of which have to be met to have a partnership: (1) an association of two or more persons, (2) conducting a business for profit, (3) which they co-own.

   a. Association–A partnership must have two or more persons who agree to become partners. Any natural person having full capacity may enter into a partnership. A minor may become a partner, but he has the right to disaffirm the partnership agreement at any time in order to avoid personal liability. A nonadjudicated incompetent may become a partner, although incompetency affords the copartners a ground for seeking dissolution by court decree. A partnership agreement entered into by an adjudicated incompetent is void. A corporation is a "person" within the meaning of the UPA and may enter into a partnership; a partnership may also be a member of another partnership.

   b. Business for Profit–Co-ownership does not of itself establish a partnership, even though the co-owners share the profits derived from use of the property. There must be a business in addition to the co-ownership of property. Social clubs, fraternal orders, civic societies, and charitable organizations cannot be partnerships. Co-ownership of the means or instrumentality of accomplishing a single business transaction or a limited series of transactions may result in a joint venture but not a general partnership.

   c. Co-ownership–Although co-ownership of property used in business is not sufficient for the existence of a partnership, the co-ownership of a business is essential. In determining whether co-ownership of a business exists, the two most important factors are sharing of profits and the right to manage and control the business. The receipt of profits of a business is prima facie evidence that he is a partner in a business unless the profits are received in payment (1) of a debt; (2) of wages of an employee or rent to a landlord; (3) of an annuity to a widow or representative of a deceased partner; (4) of interest on a loan; or (5) as consideration for the sale of the good will of a business. The sharing of gross returns, in contrast to profits, does not of itself establish a partnership. Nor does participation in the management or control of a business furnish conclusive proof of a partnership relation. However, an agreement to share losses furnishes strong evidence of an ownership interest.

3. Partnership Capital and Property–The total money and property contributed by the partners and dedicated to the permanent use in the enterprise is the partnership capital. Partnership property is the sum of all of the partnership assets. It may vary in amount, whereas partnership capital is

a fixed amount, changed only by an amendment to the articles of partnership. Where there is no express agreement, an intention that property is partnership property may be inferred from any of the following: (1) the property was improved with partnership funds; (2) the property was carried on the books of the partnership as an asset; (3) taxes, liens, or expenses were paid by the partnership; (4) income or proceeds of the property were treated as partnership funds; or (5) admissions or declarations by the partners.

4. Rights in Specific Partnership Property–A partner's ownership interest in any specific item of partnership property is that of a tenant in partnership. Tenancy in partnership is equal among the co-partners, but gives no right to possess the property for any other purpose; a partner may not make an assignment of his right in specific partnership property; a partner's interest in specific property is not subject to attachment or execution by his individual creditors; and upon the death of a partner, his right in specific partnership property vests in the surviving partner or partners.

5. Partner's Interest in the Partnership–In addition to owning an interest in every specific item of partnership property, each partner has an interest in the partnership that is defined as his share of the profits and surplus and is stated to be personal property.

   a. Assignability–A partner may sell or assign his interest in the partnership. The new owner does not become a partner, does not succeed to the right to participate in management, and does not have access to the information available to a partner as a matter of right. He is merely entitled to receive the share of profits and rights on liquidation to which the assigning partner would be entitled.

   b. Creditors' Rights–A partner's interest is subject to the claims of creditors who may obtain a charging order against the partner's interest. A creditor who has charged the interest of a partner with a judgment debt may apply for the appointment of a receiver who will receive and hold for the creditor the share of profits that would ordinarily be paid to the partner, but who does not become a partner himself.

KEY TERMS

1. Partnership *association of 2 or more persons to carry on as co-owners of a business for profit*
2. Legal entity *organization having a separate legal existence from its members*
3. Legal aggregate *a group of individuals not having a legal existence separate from its members*
4. General partner *unlimited liability for partnership debts / full mgmt powers / right to share in profits*
5. Limited partner *liability to partnership debts only to the extent of its capital contribution*
6. Silent partner *takes no part in the partnership business*
7. Secret partner *membership in the firm is not disclosed to the public*
8. Dormant partner *both silent & secret*

9. Articles of partnership *written agreement*

10. Joint venture *1 time deal*

11. Partnership capital *all money & property contributed by partners and dedicated to*

12. Partnership property *permanent use of partnership*

13. Tenancy in partnership *Sum of all partnership assets*

14. Interest in partnership *equal among the partners*

15. Charging order *judicial lien against a partner's interest in the partnership*

TRUE/FALSE

T 1. A partnership is an association of two or more persons to carry on as co-owners a business for profit.

T 2. Any one partner may be held liable for the entire indebtedness of the partnership.

F 3. A partnership is required to pay federal income tax on its income. *partners individual income taxed as personal not business*

T 4. The Internal Revenue Code treats a partnership as an aggregate. *True*

T 5. A limited partner is one who is liable for the partnership debt only to the extent of her capital contribution.

T 6. A person may be a partner even though he has no authority to conduct the ordinary activities of the business.

F 7. Although dormant partners elect to take no part in the partnership business, they are, nevertheless, known to the public as partners.

T 8. A partner may not ordinarily withdraw his capital contribution without the consent of all the partners.

F 9. Upon the death of a partner, his right in specific partnership property vests in his heirs.

T 10. Partners may agree to share the profits and losses of the business unequally.

T 11. The UPA is a "gap-filler" in that the partners can agree to provisions in their partnership agreement that are different from those in the UPA.

T 12. Areas not covered by the UPA are governed by the rules of law and equity.

_____ 13. The sharing of losses has no relevance as to the existence of a partnership.

__F__ 14. When a partner sells his interest in the partnership the buyer becomes a new partner.

__F__ 15. Should a creditor obtain a charging order, she thereby becomes a partner in the partnership.

MULTIPLE CHOICE

__a__ 1. Under the UPA, a partnership may be formed by two or more:
   a. individuals.
   b. partnerships.
   c. corporations.
   d. all of the above.

__b__ 2. A general partner is one:
   a. who is liable for partnership indebtedness only to the extent of the capital which he has contributed.
   b. who has full management power.
   c. whose membership in the firm is not disclosed to the public.
   d. none of the above.

_____ 3. No person may become the member of a partnership without the consent of:
   a. at least one partner.
   b. two or more partners.
   c. a majority of the partners.
   d. all of the partners.

__C__ 4. An organization having a legal existence separate from that of its members is known as a:
   a. legal aggregate.
   b. joint venture.
   c. legal entity.
   d. none of the above.

__b__ 5. Which of the following is not characteristic of the legal entity theory of partnerships?
   a. Assets of the firm are treated as those of the business.
   b. Title to real estate must be acquired by individual partners.
   c. Every partner is considered an agent of the partnership.
   d. Partnership creditors have prior right to partnership assets.

_c_ 6. No writing is required in order to enforce:
  a. a contract for the transfer of interest in land to or by a partnership.
  b. a contract to form a partnership for a period longer than one year.
  c. the promise of an incoming partner to assume existing debts incurred in the prior operations of the business.
  d. all of the above.

_c_ 7. One who has a contractual arrangement with a partner which entitles him to a share of that partner's profit is a:
  a. general partner.
  b. limited partner.
  c. subpartner.
  d. serviant partner.

____ 8. Able and Baker are engaged in continuous transactions of buying and selling real estate over a period of time and are carrying on a business of trading in real estate. What are they?
  a. Partnership.
  b. Corporation.
  c. Joint venture.
  d. None of the above.

_d_ 9. A person who is entitled to receive a share of the profits of a partnership is prima facie a partner unless the payment is of:
  a. a debt to a creditor.
  b. rent to a landlord.
  c. wages to an employee.
  d. all of the above.

_d_ 10. Title to real estate which is purchased with partnership funds may stand in the name of:
  a. the partnership.
  b. an individual partner.
  c. a third party.
  d. all of the above.

____ 11. One who has consented to be held as a partner whether he is a real partner or not is a/an:
  a. silent partner.
  b. ostensible partner.
  c. dormant partner.
  d. limited partner.

d 12. Which of the following is necessary to establish the existence of a partnership?
   a. The partners must have a formal written agreement.
   b. The partners must all be above the age of majority.
   c. The partners must follow all rules set forth in the UPA.
   d. The partners must carry on as co-owners a business for profit.

b 13. Arthur, Betty and Christopher are partners in a business that owns an apartment building in the firm's name. Upon Arthur's death, Arthur's ownership interest in the specific partnership property:
   a. vests in the remaining partners.
   b. vests in the remaining partners and Arthur's estate.
   c. must be divided among the two remaining partners and Arthur's heirs.
   d. vests in Arthur's estate.

b 14. A partner that is both silent and secret is a:
   a. limited partner.
   b. dormant partner.
   c. general partner.
   d. special partner.

a 15. A partner who is liable for firm indebtedness only to the extent of the capital she has contributed or has agreed to contribute is a:
   a. limited partner.
   b. dormant partner.
   c. general partner.
   d. silent partner.

SHORT ESSAY

1. What are the factors considered by a court in determining whether a partnership exists?
   (1) Association of 2 or more persons
   (2) conducting a business for profit
   (3) co-ownership

2. What are the main provisions which should be included in a partnership agreement?
   firm name & identity of partners
   nature & scope of partnership business
   duration of partnership
   capital contributions of each partner
   division of profits / losses

3. Distinguish between the legal entity theory and the legal aggregate theory.

legal entity — seperate existence from members — possess legal rights & subject to legal duties — may acquire own & dispose of property. Enter into contracts

legal aggregate → a group of individuals not having a legal existence seperate from its members

4. List and identify the various types of partners.

general   dormant
limited
silent
secret

5. You and your best friend have decided to form a partnership and buy an apartment complex to be rented to college students. Based upon what you learned in your business law course, you have decided to enter into a written partnership agreement. What terms should you include?

Chapter 32
Operation of General Partnerships

PURPOSE

In this chapter, you study the interactions among the partners as well as with third persons in the operation and management of a partnership. The first part of the chapter focuses on the rights and duties of the partners among themselves, which are determined by the partnership agreement, the common law, and the Uniform Partnership Act. The second part of the chapter focuses on the relations of partners to third persons dealing with the partnership, which are governed by the laws of agency, contracts, and torts as well as by the UPA.

CHAPTER CHECKPOINTS

After reading and studying this chapter, you should be able to:

1. List and discuss the three principal duties owed by a partner to her copartners.

2. List and discuss the principal rights of a partner.

3. Discuss the contract liability of a partner and of the partnership.

4. Discuss under what circumstances the partnership and the partners will have tort liability.

5. Discuss the effect of an admission by a partner and notice or knowledge of a partner.

CHAPTER OUTLINE

I. Relationships Among Partners–The law imposes certain obligations on the parties to a partnership and also gives them specific rights. The parties may by agreement vary these rights and obligations so long as standards of fairness are met and so long as the rights of third parties are not affected.

    A. Duties Among Partners–The principal legal duties imposed upon partners in their relationship are (1) the fiduciary duty (duty of loyalty), (2) the duty of obedience, and (3) the duty of care. Each partner also has a duty to inform his copartners and a duty to account to the partnership.

        1. Fiduciary Duty–Each partner owes a duty of absolute and utmost good faith, fairness and loyalty to his partners. The fiduciary duty requires that a partner not make a profit other than his agreed compensation, not compete with the partnership, and not otherwise profit from the relationship at the expense of the partnership. Every partner must account to the partnership for any benefit and hold as trustee for it any profits he made without the consent of the other partners from any transaction connected with the formation, conduct, or liquidation of the partnership or from use by him of its property. He may not prefer himself over the firm, nor may he even deal at arm's length with his partners. His duty is one of undivided and continuous loyalty to his partners. A partner cannot acquire for herself a partnership asset or opportunity without the consent of all the partners. Partners must disclose fully and accurately all material facts to the other partners.

        2. Duty of Obedience–A partner must act in obedience to the partnership agreement and to any business decisions properly made by the partnership. A partner who violates this duty is individually liable to his partners for any resulting loss.

        3. Duty of Care–A partner must manage the partnership affairs without culpable negligence. Culpable negligence is something more than ordinary negligence, yet short of gross negligence. Honest errors of judgment or the failure to use ordinary skill in transacting business are not culpable negligence.

    B. Rights Among Partners–Partners have certain rights which include: (1) rights in specific partnership property; (2) an interest in the partnership; (3) the right to share in distributions; (4) the right to participate in management; (5) the right to choose associates; and (6) the right of enforcement. The first two were covered in the last chapter; the remaining ones are covered in this chapter.

        1. Right to Share in Distributions–A distribution is a transfer of partnership property from the partnership to a partner. Distributions include a division of profits, a return of capital contributions, a repayment of a loan or advance made by a partner to the partnership, and a payment made to compensate a partner for services rendered to the partnership.

            a. Right to Share in Profits–Each partner is entitled, unless otherwise agreed, to a share of the profits. Conversely, unless otherwise agreed, each partner must contribute toward any losses sustained by the partnership. If there is no agreement about dividing the profits, the partners share profits equally, regardless of the ratio of their financial contributions. Unless otherwise agreed, the partners bear losses in the same proportion in which they share profits.

   b. Right to Return of Capital–After all partnership creditors have been paid, each partner is entitled to be repaid his capital contribution when the firm is terminated. Unless otherwise agreed, a partner is not entitled to interest on his capital contribution, unless there is a delay in the return of it. In such case, he is entitled to the legal rate of interest.

   c. Right to Return of Advances–If a partner makes advances (loans) over and above his capital contribution, he is entitled to repayment of the advances plus interest. His position as a creditor of the firm, however, is subordinate to nonpartner creditors but is superior to the partners' right to return of capital. A partner who has incurred personal liability on behalf of the partnership is entitled to indemnification or repayment.

   d. Right to Compensation–The UPA provides that, unless otherwise agreed, no partner is entitled to remuneration for acting in the partnership business. Even if one partner performs a disproportionate share of the work of conducting the business, he is not entitled to a salary. He is only entitled to a share of the profits, unless the partnership agreement provides otherwise. A surviving partner is entitled to reasonable compensation for services in winding up the partnership affairs.

2. Right to Participate in Management–Unless otherwise agreed, each partner has an equal voice in management of the business. The majority generally governs the actions and decisions of the partnership, except that all partners must consent to any actions that are contrary to the partnership agreement. Accounting and law firms frequently have two classes of partners (junior and senior partners) or three classes of partners (junior, senior, and managing partners) and concentrate most or all management authority in a committee of a few partners or even in just one partner.

3. Right to Choose Associates–Because of the fiduciary relationship between partners and because each partner has a right to participate in management and to act as an agent of the partnership, no partner may be forced to accept any person as a partner whom he does not choose. *Delectus personae* is the term which refers to a partner's right to choose who may become a member of the partnership; it is a term which literally means "choice of the person." The UPA provides that "No person can become a member of a partnership without the consent of all the partners." That is why the purchaser of a partner's interest in the partnership does not become a partner.

4. Enforcement Rights–Partnership law provides the partners with the means to enforce rights and duties created by the partnership relationship.

   a. Right to Information and Inspection of the Books–Each partner may demand full information about all partnership matters, and each partner has a duty to supply other partners with full and accurate information of all things affecting the partnership. Unless otherwise agreed, the books of the partnership are to be kept at the principal place of business, and each partner has the right to inspect them and to copy any of them.

   b. Right to an Account–A formal account is a complete review of all financial transactions of the partnership. The UPA grants to each partner the right to an account whenever (1) he is wrongfully excluded from the partnership business or possession of its property by his copartners, (2) the partnership agreement provides, (3) a partner makes a profit in violation of his fiduciary duty, or (4) other circumstances render it just and reasonable. If a partner does not get a requested account or is dissatisfied with it, she may bring an accounting which is an equitable proceeding for a comprehensive and effective settlement of all partnership affairs.

II. Relationship Between Partners and Third Parties–Under agency law a principal is liable on contracts made on his behalf by his duly authorized agents and is liable in tort for the wrongful acts his employees commit in the course of their employment. Most problems between partners and third persons require the application of principles of agency law.

A. Contracts of Partnership–The act of every partner binds the partnership on transactions within the scope of partnership business unless the partner does not have actual or apparent authority to so act. If the partnership is bound, each general partner has unlimited personal liability. The UPA provides that partners are jointly liable on all debts and contract obligations of the partnership. Joint liability means that a creditor must sue all of the partners as a group.

   1. Authority to Bind Partnership–A partner may bind the partnership by her act if (a) she has actual authority, express or implied, to perform the act, or (b) she has apparent authority to perform the act. Where there is no actual or apparent authority, the partnership is bound only if it ratifies the act.

      a. Actual Express Authority–The actual express authority of the partners may be set forth in the partnership agreement or in additional oral or written agreements between the partners. The UPA provides that the partnership is not bound by the following acts unless authorized by all of the partners: (1) assignment of partnership property for the benefit of its creditors; (2) disposal of the good will of the business; (3) any act that would make it impossible to carry on the ordinary business of the partnership; (4) confession of a judgment; or (5) submission of a partnership claim or liability to arbitration. A confession of judgment is a written agreement by a debtor authorizing a creditor to obtain a court judgment in the event the debtor defaults. A partner who does not have actual authority may not bind the partnership by any act which does not appear to be for the carrying on of the business in the usual way. This includes: (1) execution of contracts of guaranty or suretyship in the firm name, (2) sale of partnership property not held for sale in the usual course of business, and (3) payment of individual debts out of partnership assets.

      b. Actual Implied Authority–This is authority that is neither expressly granted nor expressly denied but is reasonably deduced from the nature of the partnership, the terms of the partnership agreement, or the relations of the partners. Examples include hiring and firing employees and purchasing property necessary for the business.

      c. Apparent Authority–It is authority that in view of the circumstances and the conduct of the parties, may be reasonably considered to exist by a third person who has no knowledge or notice of the lack of actual authority. A partner has apparent authority to indorse checks and notes, make warranties in selling goods, and enter into contracts for advertising.

   2. Partnership by Estoppel–Partnership by estoppel imposes partnership duties and liabilities on a nonpartner who has either represented himself or consented to be represented as a partner.

B. Torts and Crimes of Partnership–The UPA provides that a partnership is liable for loss or injury caused by any wrongful act or omission of any partner while acting within the ordinary course of the business of the partnership or with the authority of his copartners. If the partnership is liable, then each partner has unlimited personal liability for the partnership obligation. Partners are jointly and severally liable for a tort or breach of trust committed by any partner or by an employee of the firm in the course of partnership business. Joint and several liability is liability where a creditor may sue the partners jointly as a group or separately as individuals. If more than one judgment is received, payment of any one of the judgments satisfies all of them. The partner committing the tort is directly liable to the third party and must also indemnify the partnership for damages it pays to the third party.

A partner is not criminally liable for the crimes of her partners unless she authorized or participated in them. Neither is the partnership liable for crimes of individual partners or employees unless a statue imposes vicarious liability.

C. Admissions of and Notice to a Partner–An admission by any partner may be used against the partnership. A partnership is bound by (1) notice to any partner of any matter relating to partnership affairs, (2) the knowledge of the partner acting in a particular matter acquired while he was a partner, and (3) the knowledge of any other partner who reasonably could and should have communicated it to the acting partner. A demand on one partner as a representative of the firm is a demand on the partnership.

D. Liability of Incoming Partner–A person admitted as a partner into an existing partnership is liable for all of the obligations of the partnership arising before his admission as though he had been a partner when such obligations were incurred, although this liability may be satisfied only out of partnership property. Liability of an incoming partner for preexisting debts and obligations of the firm is limited to his capital contribution. His liability for obligations that arise after his admission into the partnership is unlimited.

KEY TERMS

1. Distribution *Transfer of partnership property from the partnership to a partner / division of profit / return of capital contribution / repymt of loan or advance*

2. *Delectus personae*
choice of the person

3. Formal account

4. Accounting
— creditors sue all must sue partners as a group — contracts

5. Joint liability
joint & several liability — a creditor may sue the partners jointly as a group or seperately as individuals

Torts

6. Partnership by estoppel   *imposes partnership duties & liabilities on a nonpartner who has either represented himself or consented as a partner*

7. Joint and several liability

TRUE/FALSE

_T_ 1. Every partner owes a duty of good faith, fairness, and loyalty to the other partners.

_T_ 2. A partner who fails to use ordinary care and skill in discharging his assigned duties will be personally liable to his partners for any resulting loss.

_F_ 3. A partner may engage in one or more competing businesses.

_T_ 4. Partnership by estoppel imposes partnership duties and liabilities on a nonpartner who has represented himself as a partner.

_T_ 5. A partner who sells goods on credit to an insolvent party is personally liable to the partnership for the unpaid debt.

_T_ 6. Unless otherwise agreed, partners bear losses in the same proportion in which they share profits.

_F_ 7. A partner who performs a disproportionate share of the partnership duties is entitled to a salary in addition to his share of the profits.

_F_ 8. A partner may not ordinarily inspect the books of the partnership after business hours.

____ 9. It is permissible, in a partnership agreement, to provide for admission of a new partner by a less-than-unanimous vote.

_T_ 10. A partner who commits a tort in the ordinary course of the business of the partnership must indemnify the partnership for any damages it pays to the third party.

_F_ 11. A partner's right to participate in the management of the partnership depends upon the size of his capital contribution.

_T_ 12. Partners have joint liability on contracts and joint and several liability on torts.

_F_ 13. Partners are entitled to repayment of capital contributions upon termination ahead of all other partnership obligations.

_F_ 14. A majority vote of the partners is sufficient to admit a new partner into the partnership.

_T_ 15. A partnership is bound by notice to any partner of a matter relating to partnership affairs.

MULTIPLE CHOICE

___ 1. Which of the following is a legal duty imposed upon partners in their relationship with one another?
   a. Fiduciary duty.
   b. Duty of obedience.
   c. Duty of care.
   d. All of the above.

___ 2. The rights and duties of the partners with respect to the third persons with whom the partnership deals are determined by:
   a. the partnership agreement.
   b. the Uniform Third Persons Act.
   c. the Uniform Partnership Act.
   d. none of the above.

___ 3. A partner has which of the following rights?
   a. Right to share in profits.
   b. Right to return of capital when the firm is terminated.
   c. Right to return of advances before nonpartner creditors are paid.
   d. (a) and (b) but not (c).

___ 4. A person who is entitled to participate in the management of a partnership is generally:
   a. an individual partner's assignee.
   b. an individual partner's judgment creditor.
   c. a receiver for an individual partner's interest.
   d. none of the above.

___ 5. The fiduciary duty imposed upon partners requires which of the following:
   a. That a partner not make a profit other than her agreed compensation.
   b. That a partner not compete with the partnership.
   c. That a partner not profit at the expense of the partnership.
   d. All of the above.

___ 6. A partner may bind the partnership by an act which is not apparently within the scope of the partnership business if he has:
   a. express authority to perform the act.
   b. implied authority to perform the act.
   c. either (a) or (b).
   d. neither (a) nor (b).

_____ 7. A partner who has actual authority from a majority of his copartners may bind the partnership to:

    a. an assignment of partnership property for the benefit of its creditors.

    b. a sale of partnership property held for sale in the usual course of business.

    c. a sale of partnership property not held for sale in the usual course of business.

    d. a contract of suretyship in the firm name.

_____ 8. The liability of an incoming partner upon antecedent debts and obligations of the firm is:

    a. unlimited.

    b. limited to his capital contribution.

    c. limited to his accrued and unpaid share of the profits.

    d. none of the above.

_____ 9. The books of the partnership may be:

    a. kept at the home of one of the partners.

    b. inspected with permission from all partners.

    c. inspected by any certified accountant on behalf of a creditor.

    d. none of the above.

_____ 10. An action for an accounting may be brought:

    a. at law.

    b. in equity.

    c. at law or in equity.

    d. none of the above.

_____ 11. When a partner commits a tort in the course of partnership business:

    a. only the tortfeasor is liable.

    b. the partnership has no liability.

    c. the rules of agency apply.

    d. the partnership will only have liability for intentional torts.

_____ 12. Ann and Betty were partners in a business. They represented to First Bank that Carl was a partner with them. When contacted by First Bank, Carl did not deny the representation, because he was seriously considering the possibility of joining the business. First Bank loaned the money, but Ann and Betty defaulted. First Bank is entitled to collect from:

    a. Carl only.

    b. Ann, Betty and Carl jointly.

    c. Ann, Betty or Carl severally.

    d. Ann and Betty jointly but not from Carl.

_a_ 13. A partner has the right to an account whenever:
   a. the partnership agreement allows one.
   b. he is wrongfully excluded from the partnership business.
   c. circumstances render it just and reasonable.
   d. all of the above.

_c_ 14. Arthur breaches his fiduciary duty to the Main Street Partnership by usurping a partnership opportunity. As a result of his breach of this duty, the partnership suffered a loss of $10,000 and Arthur made a secret profit of $20,000.
   a. Arthur must pay the firm triple damages.
   b. Arthur must pay the firm $10,000.
   c. Arthur must pay the firm the $20,000 secret profit and the $10,000 loss.
   d. Arthur need not pay the firm anything.

_d_ 15. For which of the following acts would a partner not need the approval of all other partners?
   a. Execution of contracts of guaranty.
   b. Sale of partnership property not held for sale in the usual course of business.
   c. Payment of individual debts from partnership assets.
   d. Sale of partnership property held for sale in the usual course of business.

SHORT ESSAY

1. What are the principal rights of a partner?
   Right to share in distributions / right to share in profits
   right to return in capital (termination of partnership)
   Right to participate in mgmt / right to choose associates

2. What are the principal duties of a partner?

3. Discuss the liability of partners for the torts and crimes of partnerships.

4. Arthur, Bob and Clark have a partnership, but their agreement is silent as to the sharing of profits and losses.   Arthur's capital contribution is $12,000; Bob's capital contribution is $6,000; Clark's contribution is a computer and other equipment valued at $3,400. How would the partners divide a $36,000 profit?

_____

_____

_____

_____

5. Fred, a partner in Fastime, an express mail delivery partnership, negligently drove the delivery truck and caused a wreck with Sue. Sue was injured, so she files a lawsuit. Discuss who is liable to Sue for her damages.

_____

_____

_____

_____

Chapter 33
Dissolution of General Partnerships

PURPOSE

In this chapter you study the three stages that lead to the extinguishment of a partnership: (1) dissolution, (2) winding up or liquidation, and (3) termination. Dissolution occurs when the partners cease to carry on the business together. The partnership is not terminated by dissolution but continues until the winding up of the partnership affairs is completed. During the winding up stage, receivables are collected, payments are made to creditors, and the remaining assets are distributed to the partners. When the winding up has been completed, the partnership is terminated.

CHAPTER CHECKPOINTS

After reading and studying this chapter, you should be able to:

1. Identify when dissolution occurs by act of the partners, by operation of law and by court order.

2. Explain the effect of dissolution upon the authority and liability of the partners.

3. List the order in which the assets of a partnership are distributed to creditors and partners as set forth in the UPA.

4. Compare and distinguish the rights of partnership creditors and creditors of the partners under the UPA and the Bankruptcy Code.

5. Identify and discuss the situations in which a partnership may continue to do business after dissolution.

CHAPTER OUTLINE

A. Dissolution–The Uniform Partnership Act defines dissolution as the change in the relation of the partners caused by any partner's ceasing to be associated in the carrying on of the business.

   1. Causes of Dissolution–Dissolution may be brought about by (1) an act of the partners, (2) operation of law, or (3) court order. Under the UPA, the assignment of a partner's interest, a creditor's charging order on a partner's interest, and an accounting are not cause for dissolution, although they were at common law.

      a. Dissolution by Act of the Partners–A partner always has the power to dissolve a partnership, but whether he has the right to do so is determined by the partnership agreement. A partner who wrongfully dissolves a partnership may be liable to the remaining partners. A partnership is rightfully dissolved by act of the partners when (1) they expressly agree to dissolve the partnership; (2) the period of time provided in the agreement has ended or the purpose for which the partnership was formed has been accomplished; (3) a partner withdraws from a partnership at will (one with no definite term or specific undertaking); or (4) a partner is expelled in accordance with a power to expel conferred by the partnership agreement.

      b. Dissolution by Operation of Law–A partnership is dissolved by operation of law upon (1) the death of a partner, (2) the bankruptcy of a partner or of the partnership, or (3) the subsequent illegality of the partnership. A partnership of lawyers would be dissolved if one of its members were disbarred from the practice of law.

      c. Dissolution by Court Order–A court will order a dissolution if it finds that: (1) a partner has been adjudicated mentally incompetent or suffers some other incapacity that prevents him from functioning as a partner; (2) a partner is guilty of conduct prejudicial to the business or has willfully and persistently breached the partnership agreement or has conducted himself so that it is impracticable to carry on business; (3) the partnership business can be carried on only at a loss; or (4) other circumstances render a dissolution equitable. An assignee of a partner's interest or a partner's personal creditor who has obtained a charging order against the partner's interest is entitled to a dissolution by court decree.

   2. Effects of Dissolution–A partnership is not terminated, but continues until the winding up is completed. Dissolution brings about restrictions on the authority of partners to act for the partnership.

      a. Authority–A partner's actual authority to act for the partnership terminates, except so far as may be necessary to wind up partnership affairs. Actual authority includes completing existing contracts, collecting debts owed the partnership, selling partnership assets, and paying partnership obligations. Apparent authority persists and binds the partnership for acts within the scope of the partnership business unless notice of the dissolution is given to the third party. A third party who extends credit to the partnership before dissolution may hold the partnership liable for any transaction that would bind the partnership before dissolution, unless the third party has knowledge or actual notice (knowledge expressly communicated) of the dissolution. A third party who knew of or had dealt with the partnership, but had not extended credit to it before dissolution can hold the partnership liable unless he has knowledge, actual notice, or constructive notice (knowledge imputed by law) of dissolution. An ad in a newspaper is constructive notice. No notice need be given to third parties who had no knowledge of the partnership before its dissolution.

b. Existing Liability–Dissolution of the partnership does not of itself discharge the existing liability of any partner, however, the cause of dissolution may discharge an executory contract.

B. Winding Up–The process of liquidation is called winding up and involves completing unfinished business, collecting debts, reducing assets to cash, taking inventory, auditing the partnership books, paying creditors, and distributing the remaining assets to the partners. Fiduciary duties of the partners continue during winding up.

1. The Right to Wind Up–On dissolution any partner has the right to insist on the winding up of the partnership unless the partnership agreement provides otherwise. A partner who has wrongfully dissolved the partnership or who has been expelled according to the terms of the partnership agreement, however, cannot force the liquidation of the partnership. All nonbankrupt partners who have not wrongfully dissolved the partnership have the right to wind up the partnership affairs. On petition of a partner, his legal representative, or his assignee, a court may appoint a receiver who has authority to wind up the business under the court's direction.

2. Distribution of Assets–After all of the partnership assets have been collected and reduced to cash, they are then distributed to the creditors and partners. Under the UPA, the liabilities of a partnership are to be paid out of partnership assets in the following order: (1) amounts owing to creditors other than partners; (2) amounts owing to partners other than for capital and profits; (3) amounts owing to partners for capital contributions; and (4) amounts owing to partners for profits. The partners may by agreement change the internal priorities (2, 3 and 4), but not the preferred position of third parties (1). The UPA also provides, in the absence of any contrary agreement, each partner shall share equally in the profits and surplus remaining after all liabilities are satisfied and must contribute towards the losses, whether capital or otherwise, sustained by the partnership according to his share in the profits. If the partnership is insolvent, the partners individually must contribute their respective share of the losses in order to pay the creditors. If one partner is insolvent or bankrupt, the other partners must contribute the additional amount necessary to pay the firm's liabilities. Any partner who pays more than his proper share of the losses has the right of contribution against the other partners who have not paid their share.

a. Solvent Partnership–A, B, and C form the ABC Company partnership. A contributes $6,000 capital, B contributes $4,000 capital, and C contributes services but no capital. A loans the partnership $3,000. There is no agreement as to the proportions for sharing profits and losses. At liquidation the assets are $54,000, and liabilities to creditors are $26,000. The partnership is solvent and has a profit of $15,000 ($54,000 - $39,000 = $15,000). The partners share the profits equally, with each receiving $5,000. After the outside creditors have been paid, A will receive $14,000 ($3,000 for repayment of the loan, $6,000 for capital and $5,000 for share of profits); B will receive $9,000 ($4,000 for capital and $5,000 for share of profits); and C will receive $5,000 (for share of profits).

b. Insolvent Partnership–If the same partnership still owed creditors $26,000, but had assets of only $12,000, the partnership would have sustained a loss of $27,000. This is calculated by subtracting the total liabilities ($39,000) from the total assets ($12,000). Each partner's share of the loss will be $9,000. A will receive nothing ($3,000 for the loan plus $6,000 for capital minus $9,000 for his share of losses); B must make an additional contribution of $5,000 to make good his share of the loss ($4,000 for capital minus $9,000 for his share of losses); and C must contribute $9,000 (his share of losses).

    c. Contribution of Partner on Insolvency–In the insolvent partnership example above, if A were individually insolvent the result would be the same because A was not required to contribute any additional monies. If A and B were solvent and C was insolvent C would be unable to pay. Therefore A and B would have to contribute equally. As C's share of the loss is $9,000, A and B must each contribute $4,500. Thus in total A will have to contribute $4,500 and B $9,500 to satisfy unpaid claims of partnership creditors. If A and C were individually insolvent and B was solvent, B would be required to pay the entire $14,000 which represents his unpaid share plus a contribution of the full amount of C's unpaid share.

3. Marshaling of Assets–This doctrine only applies when the assets of a partnership and of its members are administered by a court of equity. Marshaling of assets means segregating and considering the assets and liabilities of the partnership separately from the respective assets and liabilities of the individual partners. Partnership creditors are entitled to be satisfied first out of partnership assets. They have a right to recover any deficiency out of the individually owned assets of the partners, subordinate, however, to the rights of the nonpartnership creditors to those assets. Nonpartnership creditors have first claim to the individually owned assets of their respective debtors, and their claims to partnership assets are subordinate to claims of partnership creditors. If the partnership is a debtor under the Bankruptcy Code, a trustee is appointed to administer the estate of the debtor. If the partnership property is insufficient to pay all the claims against the partnership, then the trustee is directed to seek recovery of the deficiency first from the general partners who are not bankrupt, then against the estates of bankrupt partners on the same basis as other creditors of the bankrupt partner.

C. Continuation after Dissolution–After dissolution, the partnership must either be liquidated or the remaining partners must continue the partnership. The UPA gives each partner the right to have the partnership liquidated except in a limited number of instances where the partners have the right to continue the partnership.

1. Right to Continue Partnership–The remaining partners have the right to continue the partnership when (1) the partnership has been dissolved in violation of the partnership agreement, (2) a partner has been expelled in accordance with the partnership agreement, or (3) all the partners agree to continue the business.

    a. Continuation after Wrongful Dissolution–A partner who wrongfully withdraws cannot force the liquidation of the firm. The aggrieved partners can either liquidate the firm and recover damages for the breach of the partnership agreement or continue the firm by buying out the withdrawing partner. The withdrawing partner is entitled to realize his interest less the amount of damages the other partners have sustained as a result of the breach. The interest of the withdrawing partner is calculated without considering the goodwill of the business; the remaining partners may use the capital contribution of the wrongdoing partner for the unexpired period of the agreement. They must, however, indemnify him against present and future partnership liabilities.

b. Continuation after Expulsion–A partner expelled according to the partnership agreement cannot force liquidation of the partnership. He is entitled to be discharged from all partnership liabilities by either payment or a novation and to receive in cash the net amount due him from the partnership.

c. Continuation Agreement of the Partners–The most reliable way of assuring the preservation of a partnership business after dissolution is a continuation agreement. Such an agreement permits the remaining partners to keep partnership property, carry on its business, and provide a specified settlement with the outgoing partners.

2. Rights of Creditors–Whenever a partnership is continued after dissolution, a new partnership is formed even though a majority of the old partners are present in the new combination. The creditors of the old partnership have claims against the new partnership and may also proceed to hold all the members of the dissolved partnership personally liable. If a withdrawing partner has made arrangements with the remaining partners to have them assume obligations, creditors whose claims arose prior to dissolution may still proceed against the withdrawing partner. A withdrawing partner may protect herself by giving notice to creditors that she is no longer a member of the firm. Actual notice must be given to creditors who extended credit to the partnership prior to its dissolution. Constructive notice may be given to those who knew of the partnership but had not extended credit to it before its dissolution.

KEY TERMS

1. Dissolution

2. Partnership at will

3. Actual notice

4. Constructive notice

5. Winding up

6. Liquidation

7. Marshaling of assets

8. Termination

9. Continuation agreement

TRUE/FALSE

_____ 1. A partnership is dissolved whenever it undergoes any change in membership.

_____ 2. A partner always has the power to dissolve the partnership, but he may not have the right to do so unless it is expressed in the partnership agreement.

_____ 3. A partnership is rightfully dissolved when a partner withdraws from a partnership at will.

_____ 4. Following dissolution only a court official may complete an existing partnership contract.

_____ 5. Except where the partnership is a debtor under the Bankruptcy Code, the doctrine of marshaling of assets applies only when the assets are administered by a court of equity.

_____ 6. A retiring partner will not be discharged from his existing liabilities even though he enters into a novation with the continuing partners.

_____ 7. Partners bear losses equally even though profits may be shared according to some other plan or arrangement.

_____ 8. The UPA provides that amounts owing to partners for capital contributions are to be paid first upon dissolution of a partnership.

_____ 9. A partner who wrongfully withdraws from the partnership is liable to the remaining partners for damages resulting from the breach of the partnership agreement.

_____ 10. A partner's personal creditor who has obtained a charging order against the partner's interest is entitled to a dissolution by court decree.

_____ 11. A retiring partner may be liable upon contracts which are entered into by the partnership subsequent to his withdrawal.

_____ 12. A partner expelled according to the partnership agreement can force liquidation of the partnership.

_____ 13. Partnership creditors are entitled to be first satisfied out of partnership assets.

_____ 14. The doctrine of marshaling of assets applies in every dissolution of a partnership.

_____ 15. In order to avoid liability for firm debts incurred after her withdrawal from the firm, a withdrawing partner must give actual notice to persons who extended credit to the partnership prior to its dissolution.

MULTIPLE CHOICE

_____ 1. Dissolution is brought about by:
   a. the assignment of a partner's interest.
   b. the bankruptcy of a partner.
   c. a creditor's charging order on a partner's interest.
   d. all of the above.

_____ 2. Which of the following will not bring about a dissolution?
   a. The death of a partner.
   b. The bankruptcy of a partner.
   c. An action for an accounting.
   d. A withdrawal in violation of the partnership agreement.

_____ 3. A court will order a dissolution if it finds that:
   a. a partner is insane.
   b. a partner has willfully breached the partnership agreement.
   c. the business can be carried on only at a loss.
   d. all of the above.

_____ 4. Ashley, Barbara, and Clarence form a partnership to erect an office building. If Ashley assigns her interest to Terrance, Terrance may petition the court to dissolve the partnership:
   a. at any time.
   b. as soon as partnership liabilities exceed partnership assets.
   c. as soon as the building is completed.
   d. none of the above.

_____ 5. Apparent authority is not sufficient to bind the partnership after dissolution if:
   a. the third party extended credit to the partnership prior to dissolution.
   b. the third party never extended credit to the partnership prior to dissolution but nevertheless knew of the partnership.
   c. the third party never extended credit to the partnership prior to dissolution nor knew of the partnership.
   d. (b) and (c) but not (a).

_____ 6. A partner can force the liquidation of the partnership if:
   a. he has wrongfully dissolved the partnership.
   b. he has been expelled pursuant to the partnership agreement.
   c. the partnership agreement provides for the continuation of the partnership.
   d. none of the above.

_____ 7. Dissolution comes about when any partner ceases to be associated with the carrying on of the business. In which of the following situations may the remaining partners continue the partnership?
   a. In the case of a wrongful dissolution.
   b. In the case of expulsion.
   c. In the case of agreement of the partners.
   d. All of the above.

_____ 8. Ashley, Barbara, and Clarence form a partnership with Ashley contributing $1,000 capital, Barbara contributing $5,000 capital, and Clarence contributing $10,000 capital. Each partner has also loaned the partnership $2,000 which has not been repaid. When the partnership is liquidated, its assets are $50,000 and its liabilities to creditors are $25,000. How much will Ashley receive?
   a. $1,000.
   b. $2,000.
   c. $4,000.
   d. None of the above.

_____ 9. Ashley, Barbara, and Clarence form a partnership with Ashley contributing $2,000 capital, Barbara contributing $10,000 capital, and Clarence contributing $16,000 capital. Each partner has also loaned the partnership $2,000 which has not been repaid. When the partnership is liquidated, its assets are $50,000 and its liabilities to creditors are $25,000. How much will Barbara receive?
   a. $4,000.
   b. $8,000.
   c. $12,000.
   d. None of the above.

_____ 10. Ashley, Barbara, and Clarence form a partnership with Ashley contributing $6,000 capital, Barbara contributing $10,000 capital, and Clarence contributing $14,000 capital. Each partner has also loaned the partnership $5,000 which has not been repaid. When the partnership is liquidated, its assets are $50,000, its liabilities to creditors are $50,000, and Ashley is insolvent. How much will Clarence receive?
   a. $1,000.
   b. $2,000.
   c. $4,000.
   d. None of the above.

_____ 11. Ashley and Barbara are partners in a partnership in which no fixed duration has been specified.
   a. This is a partnership at will.
   b. This is a partnership by estoppel.
   c. This is a partnership in perpetuity.
   d. This is a limited partnership.

_____ 12. David, Elvis and Fred are partners in the DEF Company. David causes a dissolution of the partnership in breach of the partnership agreement and is expelled in accordance with the agreement.
   a. David can compel the liquidation of the partnership.
   b. David is liable to Elvis and Fred for damages caused by the breach.
   c. Elvis and Fred can continue in business, but they must pay David for his interest in the firm less damages sustained as the result of his breach.
   d. Two of the above are correct, (b) and (c).

_____ 13. David, Elvis and Fred are partners in the DEF Company. David retires from the partnership.
   a. David has no further liability to partnership creditors.
   b. David has liability to creditors whose claims arose prior to dissolution.
   c. To protect himself, David should give actual notice of his leaving the firm to creditors who extended credit to the firm while he was a member.
   d. Two of the above are correct, (b) and (c).

_____ 14. The process of segregating and considering separately the assets and liabilities of the partnership and the respective assets and liabilities of the individual partners is known as:
   a. marshaling of assets.
   b. dissolution.
   c. winding up.
   d. termination.

_____ 15. If one partner is _____, the other partners must contribute the additional amount necessary to pay the firm's liabilities.
   a. incompetent
   b. insolvent
   c. in violation of the partnership agreement
   d. planning to retire

SHORT ESSAY

1. What steps are usually taken in winding up the affairs of a partnership?

_____

_____

_____

_____

2. Explain how a partnership may continue to do business after dissolution.

_____

_____

_____

_____

3. What is the order of distribution of assets in the winding up process?

_____

_____

_____

_____

4. In 1988, David, Elvis and Fred formed a partnership to practice tax accounting. Each contributed $15,000 in capital. In 1989, David loaned the partnership $5,000. In 1990, Elvis loaned the firm $10,000. In early 1991, the partnership was dissolved and Fred agreed to do the winding up with the agreement that he be paid $2,000 for his services. The firm has assets of $123,000 and debts to outside creditors of $40,000. How will the $123,000 be distributed?

_____

_____

_____

_____

5. Explain the effect of dissolution on the authority of a partner to act for the partnership.

_____

_____

_____

_____

Chapter 34
Limited Partnerships
And Limited Liability Companies

PURPOSE

In this chapter, you study limited partnerships and other types of unincorporated business associations, such as joint ventures and business trusts. Although these forms of business associations are not as common as general partnerships, sole proprietorships and corporations, they do meet special business and investment purposes that make each appropriate in certain circumstances. In recent years, limited partnerships have become more common as investment vehicles similar to owning stock in a corporation. The limited partnership has limited liability for limited partners and has certain tax advantages that make it an attractive vehicle for a variety of investments.

CHAPTER CHECKPOINTS

After reading and studying this chapter, you should be able to:

1. Compare a limited partnership to a general partnership with respect to formation, liability of the partners, management, and dissolution.

2. Compare the liability of the general partner to that of the limited partner.

3. List and discuss the activities in which a limited partner may engage without forfeiting limited liability under the RULPA.

4. List the order in which the assets of a limited partnership are distributed to creditors, limited partners, and general partners.

5. List the main characteristics of and distinguish among limited partnerships, joint ventures, and business trusts.

CHAPTER OUTLINE

A. Limited Partnerships–Limited partnerships are statutory creations. Before 1976 the governing statute in all states except Louisiana was the Uniform Limited Partnership Act (ULPA). In 1976 the National Conference of Commissioners on Uniform State Laws developed the Revised Uniform Limited Partnership Act (RULPA). More than forty states have adopted the 1976 RULPA. In 1985 the National Conference revised the RULPA. The 1985 Act makes almost no change in the basic structure of the 1976 RULPA and does not alter the underlying philosophy of the Act. The ULPA, RULPA and the 1985 Act are supplemented by the Uniform Partnership Act, which applies to limited partnerships in any case not provided for in the Limited Partnership Act.

   1. Definition–A limited partnership is a partnership formed by two or more persons under the laws of a state and has one or more general partners and one or more limited partners. A person includes a natural person, partnership, limited partnership, trust, estate, association, or corporation. It differs from a general partnership in that (1) there must be a statute in effect providing for the formation of limited partnerships; (2) the limited partnership must substantially comply with the requirements of that statute; and (3) the liability of a limited partner for partnership debts or obligations is limited to the extent of the capital he has contributed or agreed to contribute.

   2. Formation–Although a general partnership may be formed without special procedures, a limited partnership requires substantial compliance with the limited partnership statute. Failure to do so may result in the limited partners not obtaining limited liability.

      a. Filing of Certificate–To form a limited partnership under the RULPA, two or more persons must file a signed certificate in the office of the secretary of state of the state in which the limited partnership has its principal office. The certificate must include the following information: (1) the name of the limited partnership; (2) the address of the office and the name and address of the agent for service of process; (3) the name and the business address of each general partner; (4) the latest date upon which the limited partnership is to dissolve; and (5) any other matters the general partners decide to include. The certificate of limited partnership must be amended if a new general partner is admitted, a partner withdraws, or a general partner becomes aware that any statement in the certificate was or has become false.

      b. Name–The surname of a limited partner may not be included in the partnership name unless it is also the surname of a general partner or unless the business had been carried on under that name before the admission of that limited partner. A limited partner who knowingly permits his name to be used in violation of this provision is liable to any creditor who did not know that he was a limited partner. The name may not be the same as or deceptively similar to any corporation or other limited partnership. The name must also contain without abbreviation the words "limited partnership."

      c. Contributions–The contribution of a partner may be cash, property, services rendered, a promissory note, or an obligation to contribute cash, property or to perform services. A promise by a limited partner to contribute to the limited partnership is not enforceable unless it is in a signed writing. Should a partner fail to make a required capital contribution described in a signed writing, she may be held liable to contribute the cash value of the stated contribution.

d. Defective Formation–The limited partnership is formed when the certificate is filed if it substantially complies with the requirements of the statute. If there is no certificate filed or if one is filed but does not substantially meet the statutory requirements, the formation is defective. Where formation is defective, the limited liability of the limited partners is jeopardized. The 1985 Act greatly reduces the risk that a limited partner will be exposed to liability because of an inadvertent omission from the certificate.

e. Foreign Limited Partnerships–A limited partnership is considered "foreign" in any state in which it has not been formed. The laws of the state under which a foreign limited partnership is organized govern its organization, internal affairs, and the liability of its limited partners. However, all foreign limited partnerships must register with the secretary of state before transacting any business in the state. A partnership that fails to register may not bring enforcement actions in the state's courts, although it may defend itself in the state's courts.

3. Rights–The rights of the parties are usually set forth in the articles of limited partnership and the limited partnership agreement. Unless otherwise agreed or provided in the act, a general partner in a limited partnership has all the rights and powers of a partner in a general partnership. A general partner may also be a limited partner.

a. Control–The general partners have almost exclusive control and management of the limited partnership. If a limited partner shares in the management or control of the association, he may forfeit his limited liability. Under the 1976 act, a limited partner who exercises the powers of a general partner has the liability of a general partner to all third parties who transact business with the partnership. If the limited partner's participation in control of the business is not substantially the same as the exercise of the powers of a general partner, he is liable as a general partner only to those persons who transact business with the limited partnership with actual knowledge of his participation in control. Under the 1985 Act, a limited partner who participates in the control of the business is liable only to those persons who transact business with the limited partnership reasonably believing, based upon the limited partner's conduct, that the limited partner is a general partner. The RULPA enumerates certain activities in which a limited partner may engage without being deemed to have taken part in control of the business. They include but are not limited to: (1) being a contractor for, or an agent or employee of the limited partnership or of a general partner; (2) consulting with and advising a general partner with respect to the business of the limited partnership; (3) acting as surety for the limited partnership; (4) approving or disapproving an amendment to the partnership agreement; and (5) voting on various fundamental changes in the limited partnership.

b. Voting Rights–The partnership agreement may grant to all or a specified group of general or limited partners the right to vote on any matter. If, however, the agreement grants limited partners voting powers beyond the act's safe harbor provisions, a court may hold that the limited partners have participated in control of the business. The RULPA does not require that limited partners have the right to vote on matters as a class separate from the general partners, although the partnership agreement may provide for such a right.

c. Choice of Associates–After the formation of a limited partnership, the admission of additional limited partners requires the written consent of all partners unless the partnership agreement provides otherwise, and new general partners may be admitted only with the specific written consent of all partners. Under the 1985 Act, the written partnership agreement determines the procedure for authorizing the admission of additional general partners. The written consent of all partners is required only if the partnership agreement fails to deal with this issue.

d. Withdrawal–A general partner may withdraw from a limited partnership at any time by giving written notice to the other partners. If the withdrawal violates the partnership agreement, the limited partnership may recover damages from the withdrawing general partner. A limited partner may withdraw as provided in the limited partnership certificate or, under the 1985 Act, the written partnership agreement. Upon withdrawal, a withdrawing partner is entitled to receive any distribution to which she is entitled under the partnership agreement, subject to the restrictions discussed below. If the partnership agreement makes no provision, the partner is entitled to receive the fair value of her interest in the limited partnership as of the date of withdrawal based upon her right to share in distributions from the limited partnership.

e. Assignment of Partnership Interest–A partnership interest is a partner's share of the profits and losses of a limited partnership and the right to receive distributions of partnership assets. It is considered to be personal property. Unless otherwise provided in the partnership agreement, a partner may assign his partnership interest without dissolving the limited partnership, although the assignee does not become a partner and may not exercise the rights of a partner. An assignee may become a limited partner if all other partners consent.

f. Profit and Loss Sharing–The profits and losses are allocated among the partners as provided in the partnership agreement. If the partnership agreement has no such written provision, then the profits and losses are allocated on the basis of the value of contributions actually made by each partner. Limited partners are not liable for losses beyond their capital contribution. Under the 1985 Act, the agreement sharing profits and losses must be in writing.

g. Distributions–The partners share distributions of cash or other assets of a limited partnership as provided in writing in the partnership agreement. The 1985 Act requires such an agreement to be written. The RULPA allows partners to share in distributions in a different proportion than they share in profits. In the absence of an agreement in writing, the distributions are made on the basis of the value of contributions actually made by each partner. A partner who is entitled to a distribution has the status of a creditor, but a partner may not receive a distribution unless there are sufficient assets after the distribution to pay all liabilities other than those owing to partners on account of their partnership interests.

h. Loans–Both general and limited partners may be secured or unsecured creditors of the partnership, subject to applicable state and federal bankruptcy and fraudulent conveyance statutes.

    i.   Information–The partnership must maintain within the state an office at which basic organizational and financial records are kept. Each partner has the right to inspect and copy any of the partnership records.

    j.   Derivative Actions–A limited partner has the right to bring an action on behalf of a limited partnership to recover a judgment in its favor if the general partners have refused to bring the action.

4.   Duties and Liabilities–The duties and liabilities of general partners are quite different from those of limited partners.

    a.   Duties–A general partner has a fiduciary relationship to the general and limited partners. It remains unclear whether a limited partner is a fiduciary to the general partners or to the partnership. The RULPA does not distinguish between the duty of care owed by a general partner to a general partnership and that owed by a general partner to a limited partnership. A limited partner owes no duty of care to a limited partnership as long as he remains a limited partner.

    b.   Liabilities–The limited personal liability offered to limited partners is one of the most appealing features of a limited partnership. Limited liability means that once a limited partner has paid her contribution she has no further liability to the limited partnership or its creditors. The general partners have unlimited external liability. Any general partner who knew or should have known that the limited partnership certificate contained a false statement is liable to anyone who suffers loss by reliance on that false statement.

5.   Dissolution–As with a general partnership, the three steps are (1) dissolution, (2) winding up or liquidation, and (3) termination. The causes of dissolution and the priorities in the distribution of assets are different from those in a general partnership.

    a.   Causes–The limited partners do not have the right or the power to dissolve the partnership, except by decree of the court. Under the RULPA the following events trigger a dissolution after which the partnership must be liquidated: (1) the expiration of the time period specified in the certificate; (2) the happening of events specified in writing in the partnership agreement; (3) the unanimous written consent of all the partners; (4) the withdrawal of a general partner, unless either (a) the written provisions of the partnership agreement permit the remaining general partners to continue the business or (b) all partners agree in writing to continue the business; or (5) a decree of judicial dissolution, which may be granted whenever it is not reasonably practicable to carry on the business in conformity with the partnership agreement.

    b.   Winding Up–Unless otherwise provided in the partnership agreement, the general partners who have not wrongfully dissolved the partnership may wind up its affairs. Under certain circumstances, the limited partner may wind up the affairs.

    c.   Distribution of Assets–The priorities for distribution are as follows: (1) creditors including partners who are creditors except with respect to liabilities for distributions; (2) partners and ex-partners in satisfaction of liabilities for unpaid distributions; (3) partners for the return of contributions except as otherwise agreed; and (4) partners for their partnership interests in the proportions in which they share in distributions, except as otherwise agreed.

B. Limited Liability Companies

As of May 1996, all states have enacted LLC statutes except Hawaii and Vermont. A limited liability company is a noncorporate business organization that provides limited liability to all owners, permits all of its members to participate in management of the business, and, if properly structured, is taxed as a partnership.

1. Formation–Formation requires substantial compliance with a state's limited liability company statute. Many states require at least two members in order to be recognized as a separate legal entity. Individual members then are not liable for the debts and obligations of the LLC. The LLC can then contract in its own name and carry on any lawful business activity. Some states restrict the permissible activities of LLCs.

    a. Filing–LLC statutes generally require the central filing of articles of organization in a designated state office.

    b. Name–The words "limited liability company" or the abbreviation "LLC" are generally required to be a part of the name.

    c. Contribution–Contributions by a member to an LLC may be cash, property, services rendered, a promissory note, or other obligation to contribute cash, property, or perform services.

    d. Operating Agreement–A required operating agreement is the basic contract governing the affairs of the company and the source of rights and duties of its members.

    e. Foreign Limited Liability Companies–An LLC is "foreign" in any state other than that in which it was formed and must register with the secretary of state before transacting any business in the state. Failure to register deprives the company of filing enforcement actions until it does register, although it may defend itself in the state's courts.

2. Rights of Members–A member's interest in the LLC includes two components: (i) the financial interest, which is the right to distributions and (ii) the management interest, which typically includes the right to manage, vote, obtain information, and bring enforcement actions.

    a. Profit and Loss Sharing–The operating agreement determines how the partners allocate the profits and losses which, in the absence of agreement, are typically allocated on the basis of the value of the member's contribution.

    b. Distribution–Distribution of cash or other assets is provided for in the operating agreement but, in the absence of agreement, is typically made on the basis of the contributions each member has made.

    c. Withdrawal–Most statutes allow a member to withdraw upon giving notice as specified in the operating agreement and demand payment of her interest. Some states permit the operating agreement to deny members the right to withdraw.

    d. Management–in the absence of a contrary agreement, each member typically has equal rights in the management of an LLC. A manager may but does not have to be a member of the LLC.

    e. Voting–Voting rights are often expressed by statute, subject to a contrary provision in an LLC's operating agreement. Typically members have the right to vote to (i) adopt or amend the operating agreement, (ii) admit any person as a member, (iii) sell all or substantially all of the LLC's assets prior to dissolution, and (iv) merge the LLC with another LLC.

      f.   Bringing an Action–A member has the right to bring an action on behalf of a limited liability company to recover a judgment in its favor if the managers or members with authority to bring the action have refused to do so.

      g.   Assignment of LLC Interest–A member's financial interest may be assigned without affecting the LLC. The assignee does not become a member and may not exercise any rights of a member.

  3. Duties–As with general and limited partnerships, the duties of care and loyalty apply to LLCs. Who has these duties depends upon whether the LLC is a manager-managed or member-managed LLC.

      a.   Manager-Managed LLCs–Managers generally have by statute a duty of care to refrain from grossly negligent, reckless, or intentional conduct; however, in some states, this duty is to act as a prudent person would in similar circumstances.

      b.   Member-Managed LLCs–Members of member-managed LLCs have the same duties of care and loyalty that managers have in manager-managed LLCs.

  4. Liabilities–Limited personal liability is extended to all members and managers within and LLC. A member who fails to make an agreed contribution is liable to the LLC for the deficiency. A member receiving a return of her contribution in violation of the LLC's operating agreement is liable to the LLC for the amount of the contribution wrongfully returned.

  5. Dissolution–Dissolution occurs upon (a) the dissociation of a member, (b) the expiration of the LLC's agreed duration or the happening of any of the events specified in the articles, (c) the unanimous written consent of all the members, or (d) a decree of judicial dissolution.

      a.   Dissociation–Voluntary withdrawal, death, incompetence, expulsion, or bankruptcy all would constitute a member's dissociation with the LLC. Most statutes permit the non-dissociating members to continue the LLC by unanimous consent or by majority vote.

      b.   Distribution of Assets–Most statutes provide default rules for distributing the assets of a limited liability company.

C. Other Unincorporated Business Associations

  1. Joint Ventures–A joint venture is a form of business association organized to carry out a particular business enterprise for profit. It is an association of persons who combine their property, money, efforts, skill, and knowledge for the purpose of carrying out a single business operation for profit. Examples include a securities underwriting syndicate, a syndicate formed to acquire a certain tract of land for subdivision and resale, joint research by corporations, and the manufacturing and sale of goods in a foreign country.

  2. Limited Liability Partnerships–Since 1991, about forty states have enacted limited liability partnership statutes authorizing a general partnership that limits the liability of its partners. Filing with the secretary of state is required and all LLPs must designate themselves as such. While the earlier statutes did not provide limited liability of all partners from all obligations, a more recent trend is to provide limited liability for all debts and obligations except where (a) a partner committed the wrongful act giving rise to the liability or where (b) a partner supervised the partner, employee, or agent who committed the wrongful act.

  3. Limited Liability Limited Partnerships–A LLLP is a limited partnership in which the liability of the general partners has been limited to the same extent as in an LLP. Where authorized, the

general partners in a LLLP obtain the same degree of liability limitation that general partners can achieve.

4. Mining Partnership–A mining partnership is an association formed by owners of mineral rights in land for the purpose of operating a mine and extracting minerals for mutual profit. A mining partnership differs from a general partnership in that a mining partner has the right to sell his interest, the death of a partner does not dissolve a mining partnership, and members have limited power to bind other members of the mining partnership.

5. Limited Partnership Associations–Limited partnership associations closely resemble a corporation. Its legal existence is distinct from that of its members. Members' liabilities are limited to capital contributions and members may participate in management. While shares are freely transferable, the transferee does not become a member in the association unless elected by the other members.

6. Business Trusts–A trust is a transfer of the legal title to certain specific property to one person for the use and benefit of another. A business trust is managed by a trustee for the benefit of a beneficiary; it is established to conduct a business for profit. Like an ordinary trust between natural persons, a business trust may be created by a voluntary agreement without authorization or consent of the state. It has three distinguishing characteristics: (1) the trust estate is devoted to the conduct of a business; (2) each beneficiary is entitled to a certificate evidencing his ownership of a beneficial interest in the trust that he is free to sell or transfer; and (3) the trustees must have the exclusive right to manage and control the business free from control of the beneficiaries.

KEY TERMS

1. Limited partnership
2. Limited liability
3. Joint venture
4. Business trust
5. Limited Liability Company

TRUE/FALSE

_____ 1. The liability of a limited partner for partnership debts or obligations is usually limited to his capital contribution.

_____ 2. As in general partnerships, limited partnerships are governed primarily by state common law.

_____ 3. A limited partner is liable to the partnership for the difference between what he has actually contributed and that which is stated on the certificate.

_____ 4. A limited partnership is considered "foreign" if any of its business activities take place outside the United States.

_____ 5. It is possible for a general partner to also be a limited partner and share in profits, losses and distributions as such.

_____ 6. A limited partner may not assign his interest without the consent of all of the partners.

_____ 7. Unless otherwise agreed, under the RULPA the profits of a limited partnership are allocated on the basis of the value of contributions actually made by each partner.

_____ 8. A joint venture is an association of two or more persons to engage in a single business transaction for a profit.

_____ 9. The RULPA draws a distinction between the duty of care owed by a general partner to a general partnership and that owed to a limited partnership.

_____ 10. The liability of a general partner in a limited partnership for partnership debts or obligations is limited to his capital contribution.

_____ 11. A limited partner has the same power to dissolve the partnership that a general partner has.

_____ 12. Statutory compliance is required in the formation of a limited liability company.

_____ 13. A limited liability company permits all of its members to participate in management of the business.

_____ 14. A limited liability company is a noncorporate business organization that provides limited liability to all of its members.

_____ 15. Under the 1985 RULPA, a limited partner is less likely to incur the liability of a general partner by participating in certain activities of the partnership.

MULTIPLE CHOICE

_____ 1. A limited partnership may be composed of:
   a. one general partner and one limited partner.
   b. two limited partners.
   c. one general partner and two limited partners.
   d. (a) and (c) but not (b).

_____ 2. The names of all limited partners should be included in:
  a. the certificate of limited partnership.
  b. the name of the partnership.
  c. each partner's income tax return.
  d. all of the above.

_____ 3. The capital contribution of a limited partner may be made in:
  a. cash.
  b. services.
  c. property.
  d. all of the above.

_____ 4. Under the RULPA, if a limited partnership transacts business in a foreign state without first registering to transact business in that state:
  a. its limited partners will be liable as general partners in the foreign state's courts.
  b. it may not defend itself in the foreign state's courts.
  c. it may not bring enforcement actions in the foreign state's courts.
  d. (b) and (c) but not (a).

_____ 5. Under the RULPA, a limited partner forfeits his limited liability if he:
  a. becomes an agent of the limited partnership.
  b. advises a general partner with respect to the business of the limited partnership.
  c. votes on a change in the nature of the business.
  d. participates in the daily management of the business.

_____ 6. If a limited partner makes a loan to the partnership, he is entitled to repayment of the loan:
  a. before general creditors of the partnership are repaid.
  b. on a pro rata basis with general creditors of the partnership.
  c. after general creditors of the partnership are repaid.
  d. none of the above.

_____ 7. A limited partnership is dissolved upon:
  a. the death of a limited partner.
  b. the bankruptcy of a limited partner.
  c. the withdrawal of a general partner.
  d. all of the above.

_____ 8. Under the RULPA, unless otherwise agreed, a limited partner is entitled to repayment of his capital contribution:
  a. before general partners are repaid their capital contributions.
  b. on a pro rata basis with general partners.
  c. after general partners are repaid their capital contributions.
  d. none of the above.

_____ 9. The first priority in distributing the assets of a limited partnership is:
   a. partners for their partnership interests.
   b. partners for the return of their contributions.
   c. partners in satisfaction of liabilities for unpaid distributions.
   d. creditors, including partners who are creditors.

_____ 10. Which of the following is not a condition necessary to protect the limited liability status of limited partners?
   a. A certificate of limited partnership must be filed.
   b. The surname of a limited partner must be used in the partnership name.
   c. A limited partner must not take part in control of the business.
   d. the certificate of limited partnership contains no false statements.

_____ 11. Under the 1985 Act which of the following need not be included in the certificate of limited partnership?
   a. The name of the limited partnership.
   b. The address of its office.
   c. The name and business address of each general partner.
   d. The name and business address of each limited partner.

_____ 12. Which of the following is a characteristic of a business trust?
   a. The trust estate is devoted to the conduct of a business.
   b. Each beneficiary is entitled to a certificate evidencing his ownership of a beneficial interest in the trust that he is free to sell.
   c. The trustees must have the exclusive right to manage and control the business free from control of the beneficiaries.
   d. All of the above.

_____ 13. In a limited liability company, each member has:
   a. unlimited liability.
   b. liability to $500.
   c. liability to $5,000.
   d. limited liability to all debts and obligations of the company.

_____ 14. Bill Businessman is a limited partner in the Hickory Street Limited Partnership. With regard to liability for the debts and obligations of the Hickory Street Limited Partnership, Bill will generally have:
   a. no liability.
   b. unlimited personal liability.
   c. limited personal liability.
   d. absolute liability.

_____ 15. Which of the following is characteristic of a Limited Liability Company?
- a. Provides limited liability to *all* of its owners.
- b. Permits *all* of its owners to participate in management.
- c. Is taxed as a partnership.
- d. All of the above.

SHORT ESSAY

1. When may a limited partner rightfully withdraw from a limited partnership?

_____

_____

_____

_____

2. When may a limited partner be subject to unlimited personal liability for the debts and obligations of the partnership?

_____

_____

_____

_____

3. Explain what activities a limited partner may participate in without losing liability protection.

_____

_____

_____

_____

4. Describe a limited liability company and indicate its advantages.

_____

_____

_____

_____

5. Describe a limited liability partnership.

_____

_____

_____

_____

Part VI
Sample Examination

MULTIPLE CHOICE

_____ 1. A general partner may do which of the following without the consent or ratification of the limited partners?
   a. Admit a general partner.
   b. Act as an agent for the partnership.
   c. Dissolve the partnership and wind up the business.
   d. (b) and (c) but not (a).

_____ 2. A limited partner has limited liability provided which of the following conditions is met?
   a. There is substantial good faith compliance with the requirement that a certificate of limited partnership be filed.
   b. The surname of the limited partner does not appear in the partnership name.
   c. The limited partner does not take part in control of the business.
   d. All of the above.

_____ 3. One who elects to be a partner but whose membership in the firm is not disclosed to the public is a:
   a. dormant partner.
   b. secret partner.
   c. silent partner.
   d. general partner.

_____ 4. Arthur and Byron agree to form a partnership. Arthur contributes $3,000 in assets and agrees to devote full time to the partnership. Byron contributes $1,000 and agrees to devote full time to the partnership. How will Arthur and Byron share their profits and losses?
   a. Arthur will get 3/4 and Byron 1/4.
   b. Arthur will get 2/3 and Byron 1/3.
   c. Arthur and Byron will share profits and losses equally.
   d. Arthur will get 1/3 and Byron will get 2/3.

_____ 5. Unless a partnership can both sue and be sued in the firm name, it would likely be considered to be which of the following?
   a. A legal entity.
   b. A legal aggregate.
   c. A partnership by estoppel.
   d. A business association.

_____ 6. Which of the following is correct regarding a limited partnership?
   a. Limited partners cannot have voting rights.
   b. All partners have limited liability.
   c. It can only be created pursuant to statutory provisions.
   d. A general partner cannot be named in the partnership name.

_____ 7. The death of a partner will dissolve a:
   a. limited partnership.
   b. general partnership.
   c. both (a) and (b).
   d. neither (a) nor (b).

_____ 8. In order to _____ a foreign limited partnership must register with the office of the secretary of state.
   a. do business in Canada
   b. defend the partnership in a lawsuit
   c. bring an enforcement action in the state's courts
   d. solicit capital contributions from new limited partners

_____ 9. The _____ manage(s) a business trust.
   a. general partner
   b. trustee
   c. managing partner
   d. beneficiaries

_____ 10. Paul Partner is a partner in the Elm Street Partnership which owns the office building where its headquarters are located. Paul's interest in the building is that of a:
   a. joint tenant.
   b. tenant in the entirety.
   c. tenant in common.
   d. tenant in partnership.

_____ 11. Anita and Melva form an organization to collect donations and establish a food shelf for needy people. They raise money through a series of activities and jointly manage the enterprise. Are they a partnership?
   a. Yes, because each has a voice in management.
   b. Yes, because they both contribute to the project.
   c. No, because they have no written partnership agreement.
   d. No, because they are not running a business for profit.

_____ 12. The UPA provides that partners are _____ liable on all debts and contract obligations of the partnership.
   a. jointly
   b. strictly
   c. partially
   d. not

_____ 13. Under the UPA, the principal test to determine the existence of a partnership is:
   a. whether there is a written partnership agreement.
   b. whether the partners share equally in management.
   c. whether there is a sharing of profits and losses among the partners.
   d. whether each of the partners contributes capital.

_____ 14. In which of the following situations may a partner invoke the power of a court of equity to decree an accounting of partnership affairs?
   a. A partner is wrongfully excluded from the partnership business.
   b. The partnership agreement provides for one.
   c. A partner makes a profit in violation of his fiduciary duty.
   d. A partner may seek an accounting in all of the above situations.

_____ 15. Which of the following is correct regarding the distribution of assets upon the termination of a partnership?
   a. A partner's capital is returned before partner creditors are paid.
   b. Profits are returned before capital contributions.
   c. Outside creditors are paid before partner creditors.
   d. Capital contributions are returned before outside creditors are paid.

_____ 16. Which of the following require a unanimous vote of the partners to a general partnership?
   a. Disposal of the goodwill of the business.
   b. Relocating the partnership office across the street.
   c. Submission of a partnership claim or liability to arbitration.
   d. Both disposal of the goodwill of the business and submission of a partnership claim or liability to arbitration.

_____ 17. Upon the winding up of a limited partnership, assets must be distributed to: (1) creditors, (2) partners for return of contributions, (3) partners in satisfaction of liabilities for unpaid distributions, and (4) partners for their partnership interests. The priorities in distributing these are:
   a. 1, 2, 3, 4.
   b. 1, 3, 2, 4.
   c. 2, 3, 4, 1.
   d. 4, 3, 2, 1.

_____ 18. Which of the following are considered to be interests of members of a limited liability company?
   a. Financial interest..
   b. Management interest.
   c. Both (a) and (b).
   d. Neither (a) nor (b).

_____ 19. Which of the following is/are required to form a limited liability company?
   a. File articles of organization in a designated state office.
   b. Must have at least three members.
   c. Must have a minimum of $500,000 capital.
   d. All of the above.

_____ 20. Under RULPA which of the following are "safe harbor" provisions?
   a. Consulting with a general partner.
   b. Approving an amendment to the partnership agreement.
   c. Voting on fundamental changes in the limited partnership.
   d. All of the above.

Chapter 35
Nature, Formation, and Powers

PURPOSE

A corporation is a separate entity from its shareholders that is created by law and is distinct from the individuals who create it. The corporation is the dominant form of business organization in the United States, accounting for 90 percent of the gross revenues of all business entities. Corporations have achieved this dominance because their attributes of limited liability, free transferability of shares, and continuity enable them to attract great numbers of widespread investors. The use of the corporation as a means of doing business has allowed vast concentrations of wealth and capital that have transformed this country from an agrarian to an industrial economy. Corporate law differs slightly from state to state, because each state has its own business corporation statute. However, most statutes contain many of the provisions found in the Model Business Corporation Act. The MBCA sets a standard for the statutory law of business corporations.

CHAPTER CHECKPOINTS

After reading and studying this chapter, you should be able to:

1. List the principal attributes of a corporation and compare the corporate form of organization to the partnership and limited partnership.

2. Discuss the liability of the promoter of a corporation and the fiduciary duty of a promoter.

3. Define a corporation *de jure* and a corporation *de facto* and compare the approach of the MBCA with regard to defective incorporation to that of the common law.

4. Define "piercing the corporate veil" and discuss the circumstances under which courts are likely to pierce a corporate veil.

5. Define the term *ultra vires* and discuss the common law and modern approaches to acts of a corporation that are *ultra vires*.

CHAPTER OUTLINE

I. Nature of Corporations–A corporation may be formed only by substantial compliance with a state incorporation statute.

   A. Corporate Attributes–The principal attributes of a corporation are that (1) it is a legal entity; (2) it provides limited liability to its shareholders; (3) its shares of stock are freely transferable; (4) it may have perpetual existence; (5) its management is centralized; and it is considered, for some purposes, (6) a person, and (7) a citizen.
      1. Legal Entity–A corporation is a legal entity separate and apart from its shareholders with rights and liabilities entirely distinct from theirs.
      2. Creature of the State–A corporation may be formed only by substantial compliance with a state incorporation statute.
      3. Limited Liability–A corporation is a legal entity and is therefore liable out of its own assets for its debts. Generally, the shareholders have limited liability for the corporation's debts that does not extend beyond the amount of their investment.
      4. Free Transferability of Corporate Shares–In the absence of contractual restrictions, shares in a corporation may be freely transferred by sale, gift or pledge. Transfers of shares of stock are governed by Article 8 of the UCC.
      5. Perpetual Existence–Unless otherwise stated in its articles of incorporation, a corporation has perpetual existence and does not terminate upon the death, withdrawal, or addition of a shareholder, director, or officer.
      6. Centralized Management–The shareholders of a corporation elect the board of directors which manages the business affairs of the corporation. The board must then appoint officers to run the day-to-day operations of the business.
      7. As a Person–A corporation is considered a person within the meaning of the due process clause of the Fifth and Fourteenth Amendments to the U.S. Constitution and of the equal protection clause of the Fourteenth Amendment. A corporation also enjoys the right of a person to be secure against unreasonable searches and seizures, as provided for in the Fourth Amendment. However, a corporation is not a person within the meaning of the clause in the Fifth Amendment that protects a "person" against self-incrimination.
      8. As a Citizen–A corporation is regarded as a citizen of the state of its incorporation and of the state in which it has its principal office for the purpose of determining whether diversity of citizenship exists for jurisdiction in the federal courts. It is not a citizen as the term is used in the Fourteenth Amendment privileges and immunities of citizenship clause.

   B. Classification of Corporations–Corporations may be classified as public or private, profit or non-profit, domestic or foreign, publicly held or closely held, and professional. These classifications are not mutually exclusive.

1. Public or Private–A public corporation is one that is created to administer a unit of local civil government or one created by the United States to conduct public business. A private corporation is founded by and composed of private persons for private purposes and has no governmental duties.

2. Profit or Nonprofit–A profit corporation is one founded for the purpose of operating a business for profit. A nonprofit corporation is one whose profits must be used exclusively for the charitable, educational, or scientific purpose for which it was formed.

3. Domestic or Foreign–A corporation is a domestic corporation in the state in which it is incorporated. It is a foreign corporation in every other state or jurisdiction. In states other than the state of incorporation, a corporation must obtain a certificate of authority to do business. This involves filing certain information with the secretary of state, the payment of prescribed fees, and the designation of a resident agent. In most states, an unlicensed foreign corporation is not entitled to maintain a suit in the state courts until it has obtained a certificate of authority, but it may defend against an action brought against it. Many states impose fines on the corporation's officers and directors and hold them personally liable on contracts made within the state.

4. Publicly Held or Closely Held–A publicly held corporation is one whose shares are owned by a large number of people and are widely traded. A corporation is closely held when its outstanding shares of stock are held by a small number of persons, who frequently are relatives or friends. Shareholders are usually active in the management and control of the business. Generally, closely held corporations are subject to the general incorporation statute that governs all corporations. Some states have enacted special legislation to accommodate the needs of closely held corporations. A Statutory Close Corporation Supplement to the Model and Revised Acts has been promulgated.

5. Subchapter S Corporation–The Internal Revenue Code permits a corporation meeting specified requirements to elect to be taxed essentially as though it were a partnership.

6. Professional Corporations–All states have statutes that permit the practice of professions by duly licensed individuals in the corporate form. There is a Model Professional Corporation Supplement to the MBCA.

II. Formation of a Corporation–Under a general incorporation statute, the formation of a corporation requires the performance of several acts by various groups, individuals, and state officials.

A. Organizing the Corporation–Promoters of a corporation procure offers by subscribers to buy stock and prepare the incorporation papers.
   1. Promoters–A promoter is a person who takes the necessary steps to organize a corporation. This person arranges for the capital and financing of the corporation, assembles the necessary assets, equipment, licenses, personnel, leases and services.
      a. Promoters' Contracts–Promoters enter into contracts in anticipation of the creation of the corporation. If these contracts are executed by the promoter in her own name and there is no further action, the promoter is liable on such contracts and the corporation, when it is created, is not automatically liable. The corporation is liable only if it adopts the contract.
      b. Promoters' Fiduciary Duty–The promoters have a fiduciary relationship among themselves, and with the corporation, its subscribers, and its initial shareholders. This duty requires good

faith, fair dealing and full disclosure. Promoters must account for any secret profit; failure to do so may violate federal or state securities laws.

2. Subscribers–A subscriber is a person who agrees to purchase initial stock in a corporation. A preincorporation subscription is an offer to purchase capital stock in a corporation yet to be formed. The majority of courts regards a subscription as a continuing offer to purchase stock from a nonexisting entity which is incapable of accepting the offer until created. Under this view, a subscription may be revoked at any time prior to its acceptance. A minority of jurisdictions treat a subscription as a contract among the various subscribers which is irrevocable except with the consent of all of them. The Revised Act provides that a subscription is irrevocable for a period of six months, unless otherwise provided in the subscription agreement or unless all of the subscribers consent to the revocation of the subscription. If the corporation accepts during the period of irrevocability, a binding contract exists.

3. Selection of State for Incorporation–Incorporation is normally in the state where the corporation is located and performs the principal part of its business. Statutory provisions may, however, make some states more attractive than others, and incorporation may be obtained in any state by duly qualifying and complying with statutory requirements.

B. Formalities of Incorporation–Typically, the incorporators execute and deliver to the secretary of state the articles of incorporation. Under the Revised Act, once the certificate of incorporation (charter) is issued, the board of directors holds an organizational meeting for the purpose of adopting bylaws, appointing officers, and carrying on any other business.

1. Selection of Name–Most incorporation laws require that the name contain a word or words that clearly indicate it is a corporation. A name must be distinguishable from that of another domestic corporation or of a foreign corporation authorized to do business within the state.

2. Incorporators–The incorporators are the persons who sign the articles of incorporation filed with the secretary of state of the state of incorporation.

3. Articles of Incorporation–Under the Revised Act, the articles of incorporation (charter) must include the name of the corporation, the number of authorized shares, the street address of the registered office and the name of the registered agent, and the name and address of each incorporator.

4. Organizational Meeting–The Revised Act requires that an organizational meeting be held to adopt bylaws, appoint officers, and carry on any other business brought before the meeting.

5. Bylaws–The bylaws of a corporation are the rules and regulations that govern its internal management. The bylaws may contain any provision for managing the business and regulating the affairs of the corporation that is not inconsistent with law or the articles of incorporation. The bylaws do not have to be publicly filed. Under the Revised Act, the board of directors may amend or repeal the bylaws unless the articles of incorporation or other sections of the Revised Act reserve that power exclusively to the shareholders. Under the Statutory Close Corporation Supplement, a close corporation may elect not to adopt any bylaws if necessary information is included either in a shareholder agreement or in the articles of incorporation.

III. Recognition or Disregard of Corporateness–Because a corporation is a creature of the state, corporate attributes such as limited liability and perpetual existence are recognized when the enterprise complies with the state's requirements for incorporation. The consequences of noncompliance with the statutory incorporation procedure depend on the seriousness of the error.

A. Defective Incorporation–Simplified incorporation procedures have greatly reduced the frequency of defective incorporation. Possible consequences of defective incorporation include: (1) the state brings an action for involuntary dissolution; (2) associates are held personally liable to a third party; (3) the association asserts that it is not liable on an obligation; or (4) a third party asserts that it is not liable to the association.

   1. Common Law Approach–Under the common law, a defectively formed corporation was sometimes accorded corporate attributes.

      a. Corporation *de Jure*–A corporation *de jure* is one that has been formed in substantial compliance with the incorporation statute and the organizational procedure. Such a corporation may not be challenged by anyone.

      b. Corporation *de Facto*–A corporation *de facto* is one that is not *de jure,* because of a failure to comply substantially with the incorporation statute. Nevertheless, it is recognized for most purposes as a corporation. There must be a *bona fide* attempt to comply with the law organizing a corporation under a general incorporation statute, and there must be the actual exercise of corporate power by conducting business in the belief that a corporation has been formed. The state can challenge the existence of a *de facto* corporation in a *quo warranto* ("by what right") action.

      c. Corporation by Estoppel–Estoppel does not create a corporation. It operates only to prevent a person from raising the question of a corporation's existence where the necessary elements of holding out and reliance are present.

      d. Defective Corporation–If the associates who purported to form a corporation have not formed either a *de jure* or a *de facto* corporation and the doctrine of estoppel does not apply, then some or all of the associates will be held unlimitedly liable for the obligations of the business.

   2. Statutory Approach–Under the Revised Act, the filing of the articles of incorporation by the secretary of state is conclusive proof that the incorporators have satisfied all conditions precedent to incorporation. The Revised Act imposes liability only on persons who purport to act as or on behalf of a corporation, knowing that there was no incorporation. The Model Act and many states provide that a "certificate of incorporation shall be conclusive evidence that all conditions precedent required to be performed by the incorporators have been complied with and that the corporation has been incorporated under this Act, except as against this state."

B. Piercing the Corporate Veil–Courts will pierce the corporate veil of a properly formed corporation when it is used to defeat public convenience, commit wrongdoing, protect fraud, or circumvent the law. Courts have done so most frequently with closely held corporations in parent-subsidiary relationships.

   1. Closely Held Corporations–Courts will pierce the corporate veil where shareholders have: (1) not conducted the business on a corporate basis, (2) not provided an adequate financial basis for the business, or (3) used the corporation to defraud. Under the Statutory Close Corporation Supplement, a court may pierce the corporate veil of a close corporation if the same

circumstances would justify imposing personal liability on the shareholders of a general business corporation, but a court may not pierce the corporate veil just because the corporation is a statutory close corporation.

2. Parent-Subsidiary–A subsidiary corporation is one in which one corporation, the parent corporation, owns at least a majority of the subsidiary's shares and therefore has control over it. Courts will pierce the corporate veil and hold the parent liable for the debts of the subsidiary if (1) both corporations are not adequately capitalized, or (2) the formalities of separate corporate procedures are not observed, or (3) each corporation is not held out to the public as separate enterprises, or (4) the funds of the two corporations are commingled, or (5) the parent corporation completely dominates the operation of the subsidiary to advance only the parent's own interests.

IV. Corporate Powers–A corporation has only those powers that the state has conferred on it. These powers are those expressly set forth in the statute and articles of incorporation and powers reasonably implied from them.

A. Sources of Corporate Powers

1. Statutory Powers–The general powers of a corporation are typically set forth in the incorporation statute and include: (1) to have perpetual succession; (2) to sue and be sued; (3) to acquire and dispose of property; (4) to make contracts, borrow money, and secure any of its obligations; (5) to lend money; (6) to be a promoter, partner, member, associate, or manager of any partnership or other entity; (7) to conduct its business within or without this state; (8) to establish pension plans and other employee benefit plans; and (9) to make charitable donations.

2. Express Charter Powers–The objects or purposes for which a corporation is formed are stated in its articles of incorporation. These powers must relate to a legitimate business activity or industry within the purview of the general statute.

3. Implied Powers–A corporation has authority to take any action that is necessary or convenient to and consistent with the execution of any of its express powers and the operation of the business that it was formed to conduct.

B. *Ultra Vires* Acts–Any action taken or contract made by a corporation that goes beyond the express and implied powers is *ultra vires*. This term means that the act is not within the scope and type of acts that the corporation is legally empowered to perform.

1. Effect of *Ultra Vires* Acts–Traditionally, *ultra vires* contracts were unenforceable as null and void. Under the modern approach, courts allow the *ultra vires* defense where the contract is wholly executory on both sides. Almost all statutes including the Revised Act have abolished the defense of *ultra vires* in an action by or against a corporation.

2. Remedies for *Ultra Vires* Acts–Although under modern statutes *ultra vires* may no longer be used defensively against liability, the following ways to redress *ultra vires* acts are provided by the Revised Act: (1) a shareholder may bring an action against the corporation to enjoin the act; (2) the corporation, or a shareholder derivatively, may bring an action against the incumbent or former directors or officers for exceeding their authority; or (3) the attorney general of the state of incorporation may bring an action to dissolve the corporation or to enjoin it from transacting unauthorized business.

C. Liability for Torts and Crimes–A corporation is liable for the torts and crimes committed by its agents in the course of their employment. The doctrine of *respondeat superior* imposes full liability on a corporation for torts committed by its agents and employees during the course of their employment. A corporation may be liable for violation of statutes imposing liability without fault. A corporation may also be liable where the offense is perpetuated by a high corporate officer or the board of directors. Punishment of a corporation for crimes is by fine and not imprisonment.

KEY TERMS

1. Legal entity

2. Limited liability

3. Corporation

4. Public corporation

5. Private corporation

6. Profit corporation

7. Nonprofit corporation

8. Domestic corporation

9. Foreign corporation

10. Publicly held corporation

11. Closely held corporation

12. Professional corporation

13. Promoter

14. Subscriber

15. Articles of incorporation

16. Incorporators

17. Charter

18. Bylaws

19. Corporation *de jure*

20. Corporation *de facto*

21. Corporation by estoppel

22. Piercing the corporate veil

23. Subsidiary corporation

24. Parent corporation

25. *Ultra vires*

TRUE/FALSE

_____ 1. A corporation may be formed only by substantial compliance with a state incorporation statute.

_____ 2. A corporation may sue or be sued by any other party, as well as contract with any other party, including its own shareholders.

_____ 3. A shareholder is neither a principal nor an agent of the corporation.

_____ 4. A nonprofit corporation may make a profit.

_____ 5. A promoter who enters into a preincorporation contract in the name of the corporation is ordinarily personally liable on that contract.

_____ 6. A corporation is a legal entity separate and apart from its shareholders.

_____ 7. Under the Internal Revenue Code, Subchapter S, a corporation's *income*, if qualifying, is taxed only at the shareholder level.

_____ 8. The bylaws of a corporation may not be changed without shareholder approval.

_____ 9. A corporation de Facto is a corporation in fact because it has been formed in substantial compliance with the applicable statutes.

_____ 10. Under the MBCA, persons who assume to act as a corporation without authority to do so are subject to unlimited personal liability for the debts of the enterprise.

_____ 11. A general statement of corporate purpose is sufficient to give rise to all of the powers necessary to accomplish that purpose.

_____ 12. A corporation is liable for the torts and crimes committed by its agents in the course of their employment.

_____ 13. A corporation may be liable for torts committed by its employees within the scope of their employment.

_____ 14. The Model Business Corporation Act is the federal statute governing corporations in the United States.

_____ 15. A public corporation, such as General Motors Corporation, is one that is created to do business with the general public.

MULTIPLE CHOICE

_____ 1. A corporation:
- a. may sue or be sued by one of its shareholders.
- b. is dissolved by a transfer of its stock from one individual to another.
- c. may not own or deal in real property.
- d. all of the above.

_____ 2. A corporation is dissolved by:
- a. the death of a director.
- b. the withdrawal of an officer.
- c. the bankruptcy of a shareholder.
- d. none of the above.

_____ 3. The officers of a corporation:
- a. must be shareholders of the corporation.
- b. are elected by the shareholders of the corporation.
- c. are appointed by the board of directors of the corporation.
- d. (a) and (c) but not (b).

_____ 4. A corporation recognized for most purposes as a corporation but not formed in compliance with statutory requirements is a:
- a. corporation _de jure_.
- b. corporation _de facto_.
- c. corporation by estoppel.
- d. defective corporation.

_____ 5. A corporation becomes liable on a preincorporation contract made by promoters in the name of the corporation and in its behalf when:
- a. the contract is executed.
- b. the corporation is formed.
- c. the corporation adopts or ratifies the contract.
- d. none of the above.

_____ 6. The promoters of a corporation owe a fiduciary duty to:
   a. each other.
   b. subscribers.
   c. initial shareholders.
   d. all of the above.

_____ 7. The existence of a *de facto* corporation can be challenged by:
   a. the state.
   b. creditors of the corporation.
   c. debtors of the corporation.
   d. none of the above.

_____ 8. Piercing the corporate veil:
   a. invalidates the contracts of the corporation.
   b. imposes personal liability upon the shareholders for the obligations of the corporation.
   c. denies the corporation access to the state's courts.
   d. (b) and (c) but not (a).

_____ 9. Under the MBCA, a corporation may:
   a. lend money to its employees.
   b. be a shareholder in other corporations.
   c. make charitable contributions.
   d. all of the above.

_____ 10. Under the MBCA, the defense of *ultra vires* in an action for breach of contract by or against a corporation:
   a. is unavailable.
   b. is available where the contract is wholly executory on both sides.
   c. is available where the corporation has received full performance from the other party.
   d. is available where the other party has received full performance from the corporation.

_____ 11. Possible consequences of a defective incorporation would include:
   a. state action for involuntary dissolution.
   b. associates are personally liable to third parties.
   c. third parties may assert that they are not liable to the association.
   d. all of the above.

_____ 12. The city of San Francisco would best be described as which of the following?
   a. A public corporation.
   b. A corporation formed pursuant to the Model Business Corporation Act.
   c. A close corporation.
   d. A domestic corporation.

_____ 13. Albert invested $500 in the stock of the Ajax Corporation. Six months later, Ajax filed for bankruptcy with debts of $50,000. What is the amount of Albert's liability?
   a. $500.
   b. $50,000.
   c. Albert is liable for a portion of the debt based upon the ratio of the number of shares he held to the total number of shares outstanding and can be liable for more than his initial investment.
   d. Albert has no liability, because he is a creditor of the corporation.

_____ 14. Which of the following would be considered to be corporate assets?
   a. Perpetual existence.
   b. Transferability of shares.
   c. Centralized management.
   d. All of the above.

_____ 15. The authority for a corporation to act comes from which of the following?
   a. Incorporation statutes.
   b. Express charter powers.
   c. Implied powers.
   d. All of the above.

SHORT ESSAY

1. Identify the attributes of a corporation.

_____
_____
_____
_____

2. Define "ultra vires" and explain ultra vires acts.

_____
_____
_____
_____

3. When is a court likely to pierce the corporate veil?

_____
_____
_____
_____

4. Albert, a truck driver employed by the Carryall Corporation, while on a business errand, negligently runs over Brenda, a pedestrian. Brenda sues Albert and Carryall Corporation to recover damages for her injuries. What is the result?

_____

_____

_____

_____

5. What are the sources of corporate power?

_____

_____

_____

_____

Chapter 36
Financial Structure

PURPOSE

In this chapter, you study debt and equity investment securities which are the two principal sources for financing corporations. Equity securities represent an ownership interest in the corporation and include both common and preferred stock. Bonds are debt securities and do not represent an ownership interest in the corporation. Instead, they create a debtor-creditor relationship between the corporation and the bondholder. Retained earnings are also essential to the financial structure of a corporation. This chapter discusses debt and equity securities as well as payment of dividends and other distributions to shareholders. It also examines the transfer of debt and equity securities.

CHAPTER CHECKPOINTS

After reading and studying this chapter, you should be able to:

1. Define the characteristics of and distinguish between debt and equity securities.

2. Identify and describe the principal types of debt and equity securities.

3. Give the MBCA definition of the term "distribution" and then list and summarize the various types of distributions.

4. List and discuss the legal restrictions upon the payment of dividends and other distributions. Compare the various tests for the legality of distributions that are commonly found in state corporate statutes.

5. Summarize the provisions of Article 8 of the UCC with respect to the transfer of investment securities.

CHAPTER OUTLINE

I. Debt Securities–Debt securities (also called bonds) are a source of capital creating no ownership interest and involving the corporation's promise to repay funds lent to it.

    A. Authority to Issue Debt Securities–The Revised Act provides that every corporation has the power to borrow money and issue its notes, bonds, and other obligations. The board may issue bonds without the consent of the shareholders.

    B. Types of Debt Securities–Debt securities are usually issued under an indenture, which is a debt agreement that specifies the terms of the loan in great detail.

        1. Unsecured Bonds–These are usually called debentures; the holders of them are only unsecured creditors who rank equally with other general creditors. Debenture agreements frequently impose limitations on corporate borrowing, payment of dividends, and redemption and reacquisition of shares. They may also require the maintenance of specified minimum reserves.

        2. Secured Bonds–Secured bonds are enforceable as liens on specific corporate property. These bonds provide the security of specific corporate property in addition to the general obligation of the corporation. After resorting to the specified security, the holder of the bond becomes a general creditor for the unsatisfied amount of the debt.

        3. Income Bonds–Income bonds condition the payment of interest on corporate earnings. Participating bonds call for a stated percentage of return regardless of earnings, with additional payments dependent on earnings.

        4. Convertible Bonds–Convertible bonds may be exchanged, usually at the option of the holder, for other securities of the corporation at a specified ratio.

        5. Callable Bonds–Callable bonds are subject to a redemption provision that permits the corporation to redeem or call (pay off) all or part of the issue before maturity at a specified redemption price.

II. Equity Securities–An equity security is a source of capital creating an ownership interest in the corporation. The shareholders of a corporation are owners of it who occupy a position of greater financial risk than creditors. Shares confer on their owner a threefold interest in the corporation: (1) the right to participate in control, (2) the right to participate in the earnings of the corporation, and (3) the right to participate in the residual assets of the corporation on dissolution.

    A. Issuance of Shares–The state of incorporation regulates the issuance of shares.

        1. Authority to Issue–The initial amount of shares to be issued is determined by the promoters or incorporators. A corporation may only sell the number of shares authorized in the articles of incorporation. Any unauthorized shares that are purportedly issued by the corporation are void. Article 8 of the UCC provides remedies for the holders of unauthorized shares. The number of shares authorized can be increased or decreased only by amending the corporate charter. Thus, it is common for the articles of incorporation to authorize more shares than the board intends to immediately issue.

        2. Preemptive Rights–A shareholder's proportionate interest in the corporation can be changed by either a nonproportionate issuance of additional shares or a nonproportionate reacquisition of

outstanding shares. When additional shares are issued, a shareholder may have the preemptive right to purchase a proportionate part of the new issue. Preemptive rights are frequently used in closely held corporations, because without them a shareholder may be unable to prevent a dilution of his ownership interest in the corporation. At common law, shareholders have preemptive rights to the issuance of additionally authorized shares. Modern statutes allow the articles of incorporation to deny or limit preemptive rights.

3. Amount of Consideration for Shares–Shares are deemed fully paid and nonassessable when a corporation receives the consideration for which the board of directors, or the shareholders if the charter so directs, authorized the issuance of the shares.

   a. Par Value Stock–Par value shares may be issued for any amount, not less than par, set by the board of directors or shareholders. The par value must be stated in the articles of incorporation. The par value consideration constitutes the stated capital of the corporation; any consideration in excess of par value constitutes capital surplus. The Revised Act, the 1980 amendments to the MBCA and about twenty states have eliminated the concepts of par value, stated capital, and capital surplus. Under these acts, all shares may be issued for such consideration as authorized by the board of directors or, if the charter so provides, the shareholders.

   b. No Par Value Stock–Shares without par value may be issued for any amount set by the board of directors or shareholders. The entire consideration received constitutes stated capital unless the board of directors allocates a portion of the consideration to capital surplus. If there is a liquidation preference, only consideration in excess of that preference may be allocated to capital surplus.

   c. Treasury Stock–Treasury stock is shares that a corporation buys back after it has issued them; they are issued but not outstanding in contrast to shares owned by shareholders, which are issued and outstanding. Treasury stock may be resold by the corporation for any amount set by the board of directors, even if that amount is less than par value. Treasury shares have neither voting rights nor preemptive rights; no dividend is paid on treasury stock.

4. Payment for Shares–The two major issues regarding payment for shares are (1) what type of consideration may validly be accepted in payment, and (2) who determines the value placed upon consideration received in payment.

   a. Type of Consideration–In some states, cash, property, and services actually rendered are acceptable as valid consideration, but promissory notes and future services are not. The Revised Act has liberalized these rules by specifically validating for the issuance of shares consideration consisting of any tangible or intangible property or benefit to the corporation, including cash, services performed, contracts for future services, and promissory notes.

   b. Valuation of Consideration–The directors are responsible for determining the value to be placed upon consideration exchanged for shares. In the majority of jurisdictions, the judgment of the board of directors as to the value of the consideration is conclusive so long as it is made without fraud and in good faith.

5. Liability for Shares–A purchaser of shares has no liability to the corporation or to its creditors with respect to shares except to pay the corporation the consideration for which the shares were authorized.

B. Classes of Shares–Corporations are generally authorized to issue more than one class of stock. The usual classifications are common and preferred shares. The Revised Act has eliminated the terms common and preferred, but it permits the issuance of classes of shares with different preferences, limitations, and relative rights.

  1. Common Stock–Common stock does not have any special contract rights or preferences. It generally represents the greatest proportion of the corporation's capital structure and bears the greatest risk of loss in the event the enterprise fails.

  2. Preferred Stock–Preferred stock has contractual rights superior to common stock with regard to dividends, assets on liquidation, or both. The contractual rights and preferences of preferred stock must be stated in the articles of incorporation.

     a. Dividend Preferences–No dividend is payable on any class of stock unless it has been declared by the board of directors. Preferred stock with a dividend preference receives full dividends before any dividend may be paid to holders of common stock. Preferred stock may provide that dividends are cumulative, noncumulative, or cumulative to the extent earned. If the board does not declare regular dividends on preferred stock with cumulative dividends, the omitted dividends cumulate. No dividend may be declared on the common stock until all dividend arrearages are declared and paid. If noncumulative, dividends do not cumulate. Cumulative-to-the-extent earned shares cumulate unpaid dividends only to the extent funds were legally available to pay such dividends in that period. Preferred stock may be participating. With participating preferred stock, the stockholder can share to some extent in additional dividends that are paid by the firm.

     b. Liquidation Preferences–After a corporation is dissolved, its assets liquidated, and the claims of its creditors satisfied, the remaining assets are distributed *pro rata* among the shareholders according to their priority as provided in the articles of incorporation. When a liquidation preference is provided, preferred stock has priority over common to the extent stated in the articles of incorporation. In addition, if specified, preferred shares may participate beyond the liquidation preference in a stated ratio with other classes of shares.

     c. Additional Rights and Limitations–Preferred stock may have additional rights and limitations. It may be denied voting rights, for example, or it may be redeemable or convertible.

  3. Stock Rights–A corporation may issue stock rights or stock options entitling the holders of them to purchase from the corporation shares of a specified class. A stock warrant is a type of stock option that typically has a longer term and is freely transferable. Stock options and warrants are used for incentive compensation plans and for raising capital by making one class of securities more attractive by including rights to purchase shares in another class.

III. Dividends and Other Distributions–In its discretion, the board of directors determines when to declare distributions and dividends and in what amount. In determining its distribution policy, the board will be influenced by the corporation's working capital requirements, the expectations of shareholders and the tax consequences of such distributions.

A. Types of Dividends and Other Distributions–The Revised Act defines a distribution as "a direct or indirect transfer of money or other property (except its own shares) or incurrence of indebtedness, by a corporation to or for the benefit of its shareholders in respect of any of its shares, whether by dividend or by purchase, redemption or other acquisition of its shares. A distribution may be in the form of a declaration or payment of a dividend; a purchase, redemption, or other acquisition of shares; a distribution of indebtedness; or otherwise."

1. Cash Dividends–The most customary dividend is the cash dividend, declared and paid at regular intervals from legally available funds.

2. Property Dividends–Distributions to shareholders may be made in the form of property.

3. Stock Dividends–A ratable distribution of additional shares of capital stock to the corporation shareholders.

4. Stock Split–The corporation breaks the issued and outstanding shares into a greater number of shares, each representing a proportionally smaller interest in the corporation.

5. Liquidating Dividends–A distribution of capital assets to shareholders is referred to as a liquidating dividend. Most incorporation statutes require that the shareholder be informed if a distribution is a liquidating dividend.

6. Redemption of Shares–Redemption is the repurchase by the corporation of its own shares, usually at its own option. The Model Act and the statutes of many states permit preferred shares to be redeemed but do not allow common stock to be redeemed. The power of redemption must be expressly mentioned in the articles of incorporation.

7. Acquisition of Shares–A corporation may acquire its own shares which are referred to as treasury shares. Under the Revised Act, such shares are authorized but unissued. As with redemptions, the acquisition of shares is a distribution to shareholders and has an effect similar to a dividend.

B. Legal Restrictions on Dividends and Other Distributions–All states have statutes restricting the funds that 5 are legally available for dividends and other distributions of corporate assets in order to protect creditors. Lenders impose restrictions that are even more stringent than the statutory restrictions on the declaration of dividends and distributions. The equity insolvency test prohibits the payment of any dividend or other distribution when the corporation is insolvent or when payment of the dividend would make the corporation insolvent. Insolvency means that the corporation is unable to pay its debts as they become due in the usual course of business. Additional restrictions are based upon the corporation's assets, whereas the equity insolvency test is based upon the corporation's cash flow.

1. Definitions–Asset-based restrictions involve the concepts of earned surplus, surplus, net assets, stated capital, and capital surplus. Earned surplus consists of the undistributed net profits, income, gains, and losses from the date of incorporation. Surplus means the excess of the net assets of the corporation over its stated capital. Net assets are the amount by which the total assets of a corporation exceed the total debts of the corporation. Stated capital is the sum of the consideration received for issued stock, except that part of the consideration properly allocated to capital surplus, and including any amount transferred to stated capital when stock dividends are declared. For par value shares, the amount of stated capital is the total par value of all of the issued shares. For no par shares, the stated capital is the consideration received for all the no par shares, except for that amount allocated to an account designated as capital surplus or paid-in surplus. Capital surplus means the entire surplus of a corporation other than its earned surplus. Capital surplus may result from the allocation of part of the consideration received for no par

shares, or from any consideration in excess of par value received for par shares, or from a higher appraisal of certain corporate assets.

2. Legal Restrictions on Cash Dividends
   a. Earned Surplus Test–Many states permit dividends to be paid only from earned surplus. Dividends may not be paid if the corporation is or would be rendered insolvent in the equity sense by the payment. The MBCA used this test until 1980.
   b. Surplus Test–A number of states are less restrictive and permit dividends to be paid out of any surplus–earned or capital. Some states express this test by prohibiting dividends that impair stated capital. Dividends may not be paid if the corporation is or would be rendered insolvent in the equity sense by the payment.
   c. Net Asset Test–The MBCA as amended in 1980 and the Revised Act have adopted a net asset test. Under this test, dividends may be paid unless the corporation's total assets after payment of the dividend would be less than the sum of its total liabilities and the maximum amount that then would be payable for all outstanding shares having preferential rights in liquidation.

3. Legal Restrictions on Liquidating Distributions–Even those states that do not permit cash dividends to be paid from capital surplus will usually permit distributions in partial liquidation from that source. Prior to 1980 the MBCA followed the earned surplus test for the payment of cash dividends, but it nevertheless allowed dividends in partial liquidation to be paid from capital surplus. No such distribution may be made when the corporation is insolvent or would become insolvent by the distribution.

4. Legal Restrictions on Redemption and Acquisition of Shares–Most states have statutory restrictions on redemption in order to protect creditors and the holders of other classes of stock. A corporation may not redeem or purchase its redeemable shares when insolvent or when such redemption or purchase would render it insolvent or reduce its net assets below the aggregate amount payable on shares having prior or equal rights to the assets of the corporation on involuntary dissolution. A corporation may purchase its own shares only out of earned surplus or if the articles of incorporation permit or if the shareholders approve, out of capital surplus.

C. Declaration and Payment of Distributions–The board declares dividends and other distributions; this power may not be delegated. If the charter provides for mandatory dividends, the board must comply with the provision. There can be no discrimination among shareholders of the same class in the declaration of dividends.
   1. Shareholders' Right to Compel a Dividend–Where the directors have failed to declare a dividend, a shareholder may bring a suit in equity to require the directors to declare a dividend. However, courts are reluctant to issue such an injunction, because it involves substituting the court's business judgment for that of the directors elected by the shareholders.
   2. Effect of Declaration–A debtor-creditor relationship exists between a corporation and its shareholders once a dividend has been declared but has not yet been paid.

D. Liability for Improper Dividends and Distributions–The Revised Act imposes personal liability on the directors of a corporation who vote for or assent to the declaration of a dividend or other distribution contrary to the state statute or the articles of incorporation. The damages are the amount of the dividend or distribution that exceeds the amount that could lawfully have been paid. A director is not liable if she acted in good faith, with due care, and in a manner she reasonably believed to be in the best interests of the corporation. A director is entitled to rely in good faith on financial statements presented by the corporation's officers, public accountants, or finance committee. The existence of statutory liability on the part of the directors does not relieve shareholders from the duty to make repayment. A shareholder who receives an illegal dividend with knowledge of their unlawful character has a duty to refund it to the corporation.

IV. Transfer of Investment Securities–The statutory rules applicable to the transfer of securities are contained in Article 8 of the UCC, which is entitled "Investment Securities." Article 8 applies not only to stocks, but also to bonds, debentures, voting trust certificates, certificates of beneficial interest in a business trust, and to any other "interest in property of or an enterprise of the issuer or an obligation of the issuer" that is of a "class or series" and "issued or dealt in as a medium for investment."

A. Ownership of Securities
   1. Record Ownership–A security is intangible personal property; it exists independently of a certificate. Article 8 permits the issuance and transfer of certificated and uncertificated securities. A certificated security is one represented by a certificate; an uncertificated security is one not represented by a certificate. The transfer of uncertificated securities is registered on books maintained for that purpose by the issuer.
   2. Duty of Issuer to Register Transfer of Certificated Security–The issuing corporation is under a duty to register the transfer of its certificated securities and issue new certificates to the new owner. The only way to sell, pledge, or dispose of certificated securities is by transfer of the certificate. Registration is necessary to receive dividends, notices and periodic reports of the corporation.
   3. Lost, Destroyed, or Stolen Certificated Securities–If a certificated security has been lost, destroyed, or stolen, the owner is entitled to a new certificate provided she (1) requests it before the issuer has notice that the "missing" certificate has been acquired by a *bona fide* purchaser; (2) files a sufficient indemnity bond with the issuer; and (3) satisfies other reasonable requirements of the issuer, such as furnishing a sworn statement regarding the loss.

B. Transfer of Securities
   1. Restrictions on Transfer–In the absence of a specific agreement, shares of stock are freely transferable. Most incorporation statutes have no provisions governing transfer restrictions. The common law allows such restrictions if they are for a lawful purpose and do not unreasonably restrain or prohibit transferability. The UCC provides that an otherwise valid share transfer is ineffective against a person with actual knowledge of it unless the restriction is conspicuously noted on the share certificate or in the initial transaction statement for an uncertificated security. The Revised Act and some state statutes permit transfer restrictions for any reasonable purpose but require that such restrictions be noted on the certificate or contained in the information statement of uncertificated securities.
   2. Statute of Frauds–Under the Code, a contract for the sale of securities is not enforceable unless one of the following conditions is satisfied: (1) a writing signed by the party against whom enforcement is sought stating the quantity of the described securities and the price; (2)

performance by acceptance of delivery or acceptance of payment; (3) failure to object in writing within ten days to a written confirmation binding on the sender; or (4) an admission in pleading, testimony or otherwise in court that a contract was made.

3. Manner of Transfer–Under the Code, a certificated security is transferred by delivery of the certificate alone, if it is in bearer form or indorsed in blank. If in registered form, transfer is made by delivery of the certificate with either (1) the indorsement of "an appropriate person" on it; or (2) a separate document of assignment and transfer signed by "an appropriate person." The transfer of an uncertificated security occurs at the time the transfer is registered. The holder of an unindorsed certificate can compel indorsement, but he becomes a *bona fide* purchaser only when the indorsement is supplied.

4. Bona Fide Purchasers–A "*bona fide* purchaser" is one who for value in good faith and without notice of any adverse claim takes delivery of a certificated security in bearer form or in registered form issued to her or indorsed to her in blank. A *bona fide* purchaser by negotiation takes title free of all adverse claims not conspicuously noted on the certificate. A *bona fide* purchaser from a thief, finder, or other unauthorized person is thus protected.

5. Transfer Warranties–A person who transfers a certificated security to a purchaser for value warrants that (1) the transfer is effective and rightful; (2) the security is genuine and has not been materially altered; and (3) he knows of no fact that might impair the validity of the security.

6. Forged or Unauthorized Indorsement–The owner of a security is not deprived of his title by a transfer of the certificate bearing a forged or unauthorized indorsement. If the purchaser of a security that bears a forged or unauthorized indorsement resells and transfers it to a *bona fide* purchaser, the seller is liable for the value of the security at the time of the sale, because he has breached the warranty that the transfer is effective and rightful. Title cannot be transferred through a forged or unauthorized indorsement.

KEY TERMS

1. Debt security

2. Indenture

3. Debenture

4. Secured bond

5. Income bond

6. Participating bond

7. Convertible bond

8. Callable bond

9. Equity security

10. Share

11. Blue Sky Laws

12. Preemptive right

13. Par value stock

14. Stated capital

15. Capital surplus

16. No par value stock

17. Treasury stock

18. Common stock

19. Preferred stock

20. Cumulative dividend

21. Noncumulative dividend

22. Stock option

23. Distribution

24. Insolvent

25. Earned surplus

26. Surplus

27. Net assets

28. Earned surplus test

29. Surplus test

30. Net asset test

31. Certificated security

32. Uncertificated security

TRUE/FALSE

_____ 1. Equity securities create a debtor-creditor relationship between the corporation and the shareholder.

_____ 2. It is legal for a board of directors to issue bonds or other obligations in the corporate name without shareholder approval.

_____ 3. In order to change the amount of authorized shares, the charter must be amended.

_____ 4. Shares without par value may be issued for any amount set by the board of directors.

_____ 5. The rights of preferred shareholders are subordinate to the rights of all of the creditors of the corporation.

_____ 6. The declaration of distributions is a function of the shareholders to be determined at a called meeting for that purpose.

_____ 7. Shares of common stock are frequently redeemable by the corporation at a call price stated in the stock certificate.

_____ 8. A secured creditor is one whose claim is not only enforceable against the general assets of the corporation, but also against individual shareholders within the same class.

_____ 9. Under the MBCA, a corporation may purchase its own shares only out of earned surplus.

_____ 10. Once properly declared, a cash dividend is considered a debt owing by the corporation to the shareholders.

_____ 11. In most states, an unsuspecting shareholder who receives an illegal dividend from an insolvent corporation cannot be compelled to make a refund.

_____ 12. Any director who assents to an improper dividend would be liable for the amount of the dividend under the Revised Act.

_____ 13. Under the earned surplus test, capital surplus may be used for the payment of dividends.

_____ 14. In most states, a corporation may not redeem shares when it is insolvent.

_____ 15. The MBCA requires that a par value be set for the stock of a corporation.

MULTIPLE CHOICE

_____ 1. Big Bucks Corporation issued bonds that provided the bondholder could exchange the bond for twenty shares of common stock. This bond is referred to as a:
  a. callable bond.
  b. secured bond.
  c. convertible bond.
  d. none of the above.

_____ 2. Which of the following does not represent a shareholder interest in a corporation?
  a. The right to participate in control.
  b. The right to participate in earnings.
  c. The right to participate in residual assets upon dissolution.
  d. The right to participate in daily management.

_____ 3. The par value of a share of stock must:
  a. be stated in the articles of incorporation.
  b. reflect the actual value of the share.
  c. reflect the actual price paid to the corporation.
  d. (b) and (c) but not (a).

_____ 4. Treasury shares may be:
  a. voted.
  b. paid dividends.
  c. sold at less than par value.
  d. none of the above.

_____ 5. Under the Revised Act, valid consideration for the issuance of capital stock includes:
  a. promissory notes.
  b. real property.
  c. future services.
  d. all of the above.

_____ 6. A corporation's repurchase of its own shares is known as:
  a. a liquidating dividend.
  b. a redemption of shares.
  c. an acquisition of shares.
  d. none of the above.

_____ 7. Capital surplus may result from:
  a. an allocation of part of the consideration received for no par shares.
  b. any consideration in excess of par value received for par shares.
  c. a reappraisal upward of certain corporate assets.
  d. all of the above.

_____ 8. A shareholder may maintain an action at law against the corporation to recover a dividend whenever:
  a. unreserved and unrestricted earned surplus is available for payment of the dividend.
  b. the dividend may be paid out of capital surplus without impairing stated capital.
  c. the dividend has been formally declared by resolution of the board of directors.
  d. all of the above.

_____ 9. A declared and proper cash dividend:
  a. may be revoked unless actually distributed.
  b. cannot be rescinded as against nonassenting shareholders.
  c. is considered a debt owing by the corporation to the shareholders.
  d. (b) and (c) but not (a).

_____ 10. The corporate board of a distillery declared and paid a dividend in bonded whiskey. Such a dividend would be classified as a:
  a. cash dividend.
  b. property dividend.
  c. liquid dividend.
  d. none of the above.

_____ 11. If 1000 shares of stock are issued at a price of $100 a share and the par value is $75 per share, how much of the consideration constitutes stated capital?
  a. $25,000.
  b. $100,000.
  c. $75,000.
  d. None of the above.

_____ 12. Which of the following tests for the payment of dividends is the most restrictive?
  a. The surplus test.
  b. The earned surplus test.
  c. The net assets test.
  d. The insolvency test.

_____ 13. Which of the following tests for the payment of dividends is the least restrictive?
  a. The surplus test.
  b. The earned surplus test.
  c. The net assets test.
  d. The insolvency test.

_____ 14. Bonds that are subject to a redemption provision which permit the corporation to redeem or pay off all or a part of the issue before maturity at a specified redemption price are known as _____ bonds.
   a. secured
   b. income
   c. callable
   d. convertible

_____ 15. A bond which calls for a stated percentage of return regardless of earnings is known as:
   a. secured bond.
   b. income bond.
   c. callable bond.
   d. convertible bond.

SHORT ESSAY

1. What are the rights of a shareholder?

   _____
   _____
   _____
   _____

2. Discuss the difference between debt securities and equity securities.

   _____
   _____
   _____
   _____

3. Explain the difference between cumulative, noncumulative and cumulative to the extent earned dividends on preferred stock.

   _____
   _____
   _____
   _____

4. Discuss the liability of directors and shareholders for improper dividends and distributions.

   _____
   _____
   _____
   _____

5. Julie owns 100 shares of Big Bucks, Inc. The total number of shares outstanding is 1000, and Big Bucks plans to issue 500 new shares. If Julie has preemptive rights, explain what she is entitled to do in this situation.

_____

_____

_____

_____

Chapter 37
Management Structure

PURPOSE

In this chapter, you study the pyramidal corporate structure that is required by state incorporation statutes. Shareholders are the base of the pyramid as the residual owners of the corporation. Their role is to elect the board of directors who manage the ordinary business matters of the corporation. Directors have broad authority to delegate power to the officers and agents of the corporation. The directors appoint the officers who in turn hire and fire the personnel necessary to operate and run the day-to-day affairs of the corporation. In this chapter, you study the statutory provisions regarding the management structure of corporations.

CHAPTER CHECKPOINTS

After reading and studying this chapter, you should be able to:

1. Compare the statutory model of corporate governance to the actual governance of closely held corporations and publicly held corporations.

2. Compare straight and cumulative voting and discuss who benefits from cumulative voting.

3. Summarize the role of the board of directors in corporate governance and discuss the liability of directors under the business judgment rule.

4. Summarize the enforcement rights of shareholders.

5. List and discuss the duties of directors and officers.

CHAPTER OUTLINE

I. Corporate Governance–The statutory model of corporate management accurately describes the actual governance of only a few corporations. The great majority of corporations are closely held by a small number of shareholders who take an active part in the management of the business. In most states, closely held corporations must adhere to the general corporate statutory model. The rigid formalities imposed by general corporation statutes impose a burden on the closely held corporation where the owners are usually the managers. These formalities may be necessary and desirable in publicly held corporations where management and ownership are separated, but in a closely held corporation they are unnecessary and meaningless. The 1969 amendments to the MBCA included several liberalizing provisions for closely held corporations, which have been carried over to the Revised Act. Some states have enacted special legislation to accommodate the needs of closely held corporations. A Statutory Close Corporations Supplement to the Model Acts was promulgated.

II. Role of Shareholders–The role of the shareholders is generally restricted to electing directors, approving certain extraordinary matters, approving corporate transactions that are void or voidable unless ratified, and bringing suits to enforce these rights.

    A. Voting Rights of Shareholders–In most states, a shareholder is entitled to one vote for each share of stock that she owns, unless the articles of incorporation provide otherwise. Statutes generally permit the issuance of one or more classes of nonvoting stock so long as one class of shares has voting rights.

        1. Shareholder Meetings–Shareholders may exercise their voting rights at both annual and special shareholder meetings. Annual meetings are required and must be held at a time fixed by the by-laws. If the annual meeting is not held within the earlier of six months after the end of the corporation's fiscal year or fifteen months after its last annual meeting, any shareholder may petition and obtain a court order requiring that a meeting be held. The Close Corporation Supplement states that no annual meeting need be held unless a written request is made by a shareholder at least thirty days in advance of the date specified for the meeting. Special meetings may be called by the board of directors, holders of at least 10% of the shares, or such other persons authorized in the articles of incorporation. Written notice must be given in advance, but may be waived in writing by any shareholder entitled to notice.

        2. Quorum and Voting–A quorum of shares must be represented, either in person or by proxy, and once a quorum is present, it is present for the rest of the meeting. A quorum is usually a majority of shares entitled to vote.

        3. Election of Directors–Directors are elected each year at the annual meeting of the shareholders. Where a board consists of nine or more directors, the charter or bylaws may provide for a classification or division of directors into two or three classes. If directors are divided into two classes, they are elected once a year in alternate years for a two-year term; if into three classes, for three-year terms in order to provide continuity in the membership of the board. Where there

are two or more classes of stock, each class may elect a specified number of directors.

    a. Straight Voting–Normally, each shareholder has one vote for each share owned, and directors are elected by a plurality of votes.

    b. Cumulative Voting–In most states and under the Revised Act, cumulative voting is permitted. Cumulative voting entitles the shareholders to multiply the number of votes they are entitled to cast by the number of directors for whom they are entitled to vote and cast the product for a single candidate or distribute the product among two or more candidates. It permits a minority shareholder, or group of shareholders to obtain representation on the board. The formula for determining how many shares a minority shareholder with cumulative voting rights must have in order to secure representation on the board is as follows:

$$X = \frac{ac}{b + 1} + 1$$

a = the number of shares voting

b = the number of directors to be elected

c = the number of directors desired to be elected

X = the number of shares necessary to elect the number of directors desired

4. Removal of Directors–Directors may be removed with or without cause by a majority vote of the shareholders. If a corporation has cumulative voting, removal of a director requires sufficient votes to prevent his election.

5. Approval of Fundamental Changes–The board manages the ordinary affairs of the corporation. Extraordinary matters involving fundamental changes require shareholder approval.

6. Concentrations of Voting Power–Devices are available to enable shareholders to combine their voting power to obtain or maintain control or maximize the impact of cumulative voting.

    a. Proxies–A proxy is the authorization by a shareholder to an agent to vote his shares at a particular meeting or on a particular question. Generally, proxies must be in writing to be effective and the duration is limited by statute to no more than eleven months. A proxy is revocable unless conspicuously stated to be irrevocable and coupled with an interest, such as when shares are held as collateral. The solicitation of proxies by publicly held corporations is regulated by the Securities Exchange Act of 1934.

    b. Voting Trusts–A voting trust is a device by which one or more shareholders separate the voting rights of their shares from the ownership of them. The shareholders confer on a trustee the right to vote or act for them by signing an agreement and transferring their shares to the trustee. Most states limit the duration of these to ten years.

    c. Shareholder Voting Agreements–Shareholders may agree in writing to vote in a specified manner for the election or removal of directors or on any matter subject to shareholder approval. These are not limited in duration as are voting trusts. Such agreements are frequently used in closely held corporations in order to provide each shareholder with greater control over who becomes a shareholder, which is sometimes referred to as *delectus personae*.

B. Enforcement Rights of Shareholders–The law provides shareholders with certain enforcement rights to protect their interests in the corporation.

1. Right to Inspect Books and Records–In most states shareholders have the right to inspect books and records for a proper purpose and to copy parts of them. The Revised Act provides that every shareholder is entitled to examine specified corporate records upon prior written request if the demand is made in good faith, for a proper purpose, and during regular business hours at the corporation's principal office. Many states limit this right to shareholders who own a minimum number of shares or have been shareholders for a minimum period of time. The MBCA requires that a shareholder either must own 5% of the outstanding shares or must have owned his shares for at least six months but a court may order an inspection when neither condition is met. Proper purpose for inspection means a purpose that is reasonably relevant to that shareholder's interest in the corporation; it includes determining its financial condition, the value of its shares, the existence of mismanagement, or the names of other shareholders for communication on corporate affairs.

2. Shareholder Suits–The ultimate recourse of a shareholder is to bring suit against or on behalf of the corporation. Shareholder suits are either direct suits or derivative suits.

   a. Direct Suits–A direct suit may be brought by a shareholder to enforce a claim that the shareholder has against the corporation based on his ownership of shares. Any recovery goes to the shareholder plaintiff. A class suit is a direct suit in which one or more shareholders purport to act as a representative of a class of shareholders to recover for injuries to the entire class.

   b. Derivative Suits–A derivative suit is a cause of action brought by one or more shareholders on behalf of the corporation to enforce a right belonging to the corporation. Recovery usually goes to the corporation's treasury so that all of the shareholders can benefit proportionately. In most states, a shareholder must have owned shares at the time the complained of transaction occurred and made a demand on the board of directors to enforce the corporate right before bringing suit.

3. Shareholder's Right to Dissent–A shareholder has the right to dissent from certain corporate actions that require shareholder approval. These actions include most mergers, consolidations, compulsory share exchanges and a sale or exchange of all or substantially all of the assets of the corporation not in the usual and regular course of business.

III. Role of Directors and Officers–Management of a corporation is vested by statute in its board of directors, which determines general corporate policy and appoints officers to execute that policy and to administer the day-to-day operations of the corporation. Both the directors and the officers owe certain duties to the corporation as well as to the shareholders and are liable for breaching these duties. Shareholders who own a sufficient number of shares to have effective control over the corporation are called "controlling shareholders." Controlling shareholders are in some instances held to the same duties as directors and officers. All shareholders in a close corporation are sometimes held to a fiduciary duty similar to that imposed upon partners.

A. Function of the Board of Directors–The directors are neither trustees nor agents of the shareholders or of the corporation. However, they are fiduciaries who must perform their duties in good faith, in the best interests of the corporation, and with due care. The Revised Act states that "all corporate powers shall be exercised by or under authority of, and the business and affairs of the corporation managed under the direction of, its board of directors," subject to any limitation set forth in the articles of incorporation. In some corporations, the corporate powers are exercised by the board of directors; on the other hand, in publicly held corporations, the corporate powers are exercised under the authority of the board, which formulates major management policy but does not involve itself in the day-to-day management. Under the Revised Act, a corporation having fifty or fewer shareholders may dispense with or limit the authority of a board by describing in its articles of incorporation who will perform some or all of the duties of a board.

1. Selection and Removal of Officers–In most states, the board of directors has the responsibility to choose the corporate officers and may remove any officer at any time. Officers are agents of the corporation and are delegated their responsibilities by the board of directors.

2. Capital Structure–The board of directors determines the capital structure and financial policy of the corporation. The board has the power to (1) fix the selling price of newly issued shares unless the power to do so is reserved to the shareholders by the articles of incorporation; (2) determine the value of the consideration received by the corporation in payment for shares issued; (3) borrow money, issue notes, bonds, and other obligations, and secure any of the corporation's obligations; and (4) sell, lease, or exchange assets of the corporation in the usual and regular course of business.

3. Fundamental Changes–The board of directors has the power to amend or repeal the bylaws, unless this power is reserved to the shareholders by the articles of incorporation. The board also initiates actions such as proceedings to amend the articles of incorporation or to effect a merger, which require shareholder approval.

4. Dividends–The board declares the amount and type of dividends, subject to restrictions in the state statute, the articles of incorporation, and any corporate loan and preferred stock agreements. It also may purchase, redeem, or acquire shares of the corporation's equity securities.

5. Management Compensation–The board usually determines the compensation of officers and in a number of states, fixes the compensation of board members.

B. Election and Tenure of Directors–The incorporation statute, articles of incorporation and the bylaws determine the qualifications that individuals must possess in order to serve as directors; they also determine the election, number, tenure, and compensation of directors.

1. Election, Number and Tenure of Directors–The initial board of directors is generally named in the articles of incorporation and serves until the first meeting of the shareholders at which directors are elected. Thereafter, directors are elected at annual meetings and hold office for one year unless their terms are staggered. If the shares represented at a meeting do not constitute a quorum, or the shareholders are deadlocked and unable to elect a new board, the incumbent directors continue as "holdover" directors until their successors are duly elected and qualified. Some states require three or more directors but the trend is to permit one or more directors. The number of directors may be increased or decreased, within statutory limits, by amendment to the bylaws or charter.

2. Vacancies and Removal of Directors–The Revised Act provides that a vacancy in the board may be filled by the shareholders or by the affirmative vote of a majority of the remaining directors. The term of a director elected to fill a vacancy expires at the next shareholders' meeting when directors are elected. The common law rule permits removal of a director for cause by action of the shareholders. The Revised Act permits removal of one or more of the directors or of the entire board by the shareholders. Such a removal can be with or without cause and would be at a special meeting called for that purpose. The Revised Act permits the articles to provide for removal of directors only for cause.

3. Compensation of Directors–Traditionally directors were paid a fee or honorarium for attendance at meetings, but they did not receive salaries for their services. The Revised Act now specifically authorizes the board to fix the compensation of directors unless there is a contrary provision in the articles or bylaws.

C. Exercise of Directors' Functions–Directors only have the power to bind the corporation when acting as a board. The board may act only at a meeting or by the written consent signed by all of the directors, if written consent without a meeting is authorized and not contrary to the charter or bylaws.

1. Quorum and Voting–A majority constitutes a quorum. Although most states do not permit a quorum to be set at less than a majority, the Revised Act allows the articles or bylaws to authorize a quorum to consist of as few as one-third. The articles or bylaws may require a greater number than a simple majority. If a quorum is present, the act of the majority in attendance is the act of the board, unless the articles or bylaws state otherwise. Closely held corporations sometimes require either a supermajority or unanimous quorum for all meetings or for votes on some matters. The Revised Act requires a quorum when "a vote is taken." Thus, a board may act only when a quorum is present.

2. Action Taken without a Meeting–The Revised Act and most states provide that any action required or permitted by the statute to be taken at a meeting of the board may be taken without a meeting if a consent in writing is signed by all of the directors.

3. Delegation of Board Powers–If allowed by the articles of incorporation or bylaws, the board of directors may appoint one or more committees by majority vote of the full board. All committee members must be directors. Committees may exercise all of the authority of the board except for certain matters specified in the statute.

4. Directors' Inspection Rights–Directors have the right to inspect corporate books and records so they can competently perform their duties.

D. Officers–The officers are appointed by the board of directors to hold the offices provided in the bylaws. Statutes generally require that the officers consist of a president, one or more vice presidents, a secretary and a treasurer. A person may hold more than one office at one time, except for the offices of president and secretary. The Revised Act permits a corporation to designate whatever officers it wants. No number is specified, but one officer must be delegated the responsibility for preparing the minutes and authenticating the records of the corporation. Under the Revised Act, the same individual may hold all of the offices of a corporation.

1. Selection and Removal of Officers–Under most state statutes, officers are appointed by the board and serve at its pleasure. They may be removed by the board either with or without cause.

2. Role of Officers–Officers are fiduciaries of the corporation. Unlike directors, however, they are agents of the corporation. The roles of the various officers are set forth in the corporate bylaws.

3. Authority of Officers–Under the Model Act, officers have such authority as may be provided in the bylaws or prescribed by the board to the extent consistent with the bylaws. The authority of an officer to bind the corporation may be (1) actual express, (2) actual implied, or (3) apparent.

    a. Actual Express Authority–Actual express authority results from the manifestation of assent by the corporation to the officer to act on behalf of the corporation. This authority arises from the incorporation statute, the articles of incorporation, the bylaws, and resolutions of the board of directors.

    b. Actual Implied Authority–As agents of the corporation, officers have implied authority to do what is reasonably necessary to perform their actual, delegated authority.

    c. Apparent Authority–Apparent authority arises from acts of the principal that lead third parties to reasonably and in good faith believe that an officer has the required authority. It might arise when a third party relies upon the fact that an officer has exercised the same authority in the past with board consent.

    d. Ratification–A corporation may ratify the unauthorized acts of its officers. Ratification relates back to the original transaction; it may be express or implied from the corporation's acceptance of the benefits of the contract.

E. Duties of Directors and Officers–Directors and officers are not insurers of business success. Thus, a corporation may not recover damages from directors and officers for losses resulting from poor business judgment. Generally, directors and officers owe the duties of obedience, diligence, and loyalty to the corporation.

1. Duty of Obedience–Directors and officers must act within their respective authority. In some jurisdictions they are held absolutely liable for unauthorized acts; in others, they are liable only for intentionally or negligently exceeding their authority.

2. Duty of Diligence–Directors and officers must exercise ordinary care and prudence. The Revised Act and most states require that a director or officer discharge his duties (1) in good faith; (2) with the care an ordinarily prudent person in a like position would exercise under similar circumstances; and (3) in a manner he reasonably believes to be in the best interests of the corporation. So long as they act in good faith and with due care, courts under the "business judgment rule" will not substitute their judgment for the board's or its officer's. Directors and officers are liable for bad faith, negligent conduct and sometimes for failing to act.

    a. Reliance on Others–Directors and officers are permitted to entrust work to others. If they have carefully selected employees, they are not personally liable for the negligent or willful wrongs of employees. An officer or director will be held liable for losses resulting from an employee's carelessness, theft, or embezzlement if he knew or ought to have known about the losses. Directors may rely upon information provided them by officers or employees of the corporation, committees of the board, or legal counsel or public accountants.

    b. Business Judgment Rule–The business judgment rule protects directors from liability for honest mistakes of judgment. To benefit from the business judgment rule, a director or officer must make an informed decision without any conflict of interest, have a rational basis for making it, and reasonably believe it is in the best interests of the corporation.

3. Duty of Loyalty–The officers and directors owe a fiduciary duty of loyalty to the corporation and to its shareholders. The essence of a fiduciary duty is the subordination of self-interest to the interest of the person or persons to whom the duty is owing. The remedy for breach of this duty is a suit by the corporation, or a derivative suit by a shareholder, to require the fiduciary to pay the profits he obtained through the breach.

    a. Conflict of Interests–A contract between an officer or director and the corporation will be upheld if it is honest and fair. The Revised Act and most states provide that such transactions are neither void nor voidable if they are approved after full disclosure by either the disinterested directors or by the shareholders or if they are fair and reasonable to the corporation.

    b. Loans to Directors–The Model Act and some states prohibit loans to directors without authorization from the shareholders for each loan. Most states permit loans either on a general or limited basis. The Revised Act permits such loans if the loan is approved (1) by a majority of disinterested shareholders, or (2) by the board after determining that the loan benefits the corporation.

    c. Corporate Opportunity–Directors and officers may not usurp any corporate opportunity that in fairness belongs to the corporation. A corporate opportunity is an opportunity in which the corporation has a right, property interest, or expectancy.

    d. Transactions in Shares–The issuance of shares at a favorable price to management to the exclusion of other shareholders violates the fiduciary duty. The duty is also violated by issuing shares to a director at a fair price if the purpose of the issuance is to perpetuate corporate control rather than to raise capital or serve some other interest of the corporation. Officers and directors who have access to inside advance information not available to the public that may affect the market value of shares of the corporation are covered by federal statutes, which require disclosure of material facts that may affect the value of stock.

    e. Duty Not to Compete–Directors and officers may not compete with the corporation. A director or officer who breaches his fiduciary duty by competing with the corporation is liable for damages caused to the corporation. Officers and directors may not use corporate personnel, facilities, or funds for their own benefit or disclose the trade secrets of the corporation to others.

4. Indemnification of Directors and Officers–Directors and officers incur personal liability for breaching any of the duties they owe to the corporation and shareholders. Many modern incorporation statutes allow the corporation to indemnify an officer or director for liability if he acted in good faith and in a manner reasonably believed to be in the best interests of the corporation, so long as he has not been adjudged negligent or liable for misconduct. The Revised Act provides for mandatory indemnification of directors and officers for reasonable expenses incurred by them in the wholly successful defense of any proceeding brought against them as directors or officers.

5. Liability Limitation Statutes–At least forty states have enacted a statute limiting the liability of directors. Most of these states, including Delaware, authorize corporations–with shareholder approval–to limit or eliminate the liability of directors for some breaches of duty. A few states permit limiting the liability of officers.

KEY TERMS

1. Proxy

2. Quorum

3. Cumulative voting

4. Voting trust

5. Shareholder agreement

6. Direct suit

7. Class suit

8. Derivative suit

9. Business judgment rule

10. Corporate opportunity

TRUE/FALSE

_____ 1. Special meetings of a corporation may be called by any shareholder who holds at least 10 percent of the shares.

_____ 2. Cumulative voting means a shareholder normally has one vote for each share owned.

_____ 3. Shareholders may exercise their right to vote only at annual meetings and may not vote at special meetings.

_____ 4. Any recovery in a shareholder's direct suit usually goes to the corporate treasury so that all shareholders can benefit proportionately.

_____ 5. A shareholder may not bring a derivative suit without first making demand upon the board of directors to enforce the corporate right.

_____ 6. Shareholders may agree in writing to vote in a specified manner for the election or removal of directors.

_____ 7. Once established, the number of directors may not be increased or decreased.

_____ 8. A majority of the members of the board of directors constitutes a quorum.

_____ 9. A shareholder has the right to dissent from certain corporate actions that require shareholder approval.

_____ 10. Generally, proxies need not be in writing to be effective.

_____ 11. Officers may be removed by the board with or without cause.

_____ 12. Whenever an officer breaches his fiduciary duty, he forfeits his right to compensation during the period he engaged in the breach.

_____ 13. Cumulative voting permits a minority shareholder to obtain minority representation on the board of directors if she owns a certain minimum number of shares.

_____ 14. In some states the liability of directors and officers may be limited by shareholder action.

_____ 15. A voting trust is the written authorization by a shareholder to an agent to vote his shares at a particular meeting.

MULTIPLE CHOICE

_____ 1. Special shareholder meetings may be called by:
   a. any member of the board of directors.
   b. any shareholder.
   c. any person so authorized in the articles of incorporation.
   d. all of the above.

_____ 2. The board of directors may be classified into:
   a. three groups.
   b. six groups.
   c. nine groups.
   d. none of the above.

_____ 3. Big Bucks, Inc. has two shareholders, Arthur and Brad, and 100 shares of voting stock. If Big Bucks, Inc. uses cumulative voting, how many shares would Arthur need to elect three of the five directors?
   a. 50.
   b. 51.
   c. 60.
   d. 61.

_____ 4. In general, a proxy:
a. must be in writing to be effective.
b. is not revocable unless coupled with an interest.
c. transfers legal title to the stock.
d. (a) and (b) but not (c).

_____ 5. A suit brought by a shareholder to enforce a right belonging to the corporation is a:
a. direct suit.
b. derivative suit.
c. suit to pierce the corporate vail.
d. none of the above.

_____ 6. In classifying directors with regard to their relationship to the corporation, they would probably best be classified as:
a. trustees.
b. agents.
c. fiduciaries.
d. none of the above.

_____ 7. Assume that Big Bucks, Inc. has nine directors. What is the minimum number of directors that may bind the corporation?
a. One.
b. Three.
c. Five.
d. Nine.

_____ 8. Which of the following could an executive committee appointed by the board properly do?
a. Amend the bylaws.
b. Set management compensation.
c. Declare dividends.
d. All of the above.

_____ 9. Under the MBCA, the same person may not simultaneously hold the office of:
a. president and vice-president.
b. president and secretary.
c. president and treasurer.
d. secretary and treasurer.

_____ 10. A contract between a director and the corporation is neither void nor voidable, if:
a. it is approved after full disclosure by the board of disinterested directors.
b. it is fair and reasonable to the corporation.
c. either (a) or (b).
d. neither (a) nor (b).

_____ 11. In order for a director to effectively dissent from a board action she must do which of the following in addition to dissenting?
   a. Have her dissent entered in the minutes of the meeting.
   b. File a written dissent with the presiding officer before adjournment.
   c. Deliver a written dissent to the corporation immediately after adjournment.
   d. Any of the above is effective.

_____ 12. Which of the following is correct regarding the role of the shareholders of a corporation?
   a. They have no voice in policy matters.
   b. They exercise control over policy by electing directors.
   c. They are consulted regularly by management when decisions must be made on broad policy matters.
   d. Contracts which they make on behalf of the corporation are binding on it.

_____ 13. Which of the following is not a function of the board of directors?
   a. Selecting and removing officers.
   b. Determining fundamental changes.
   c. Declaring dividends.
   d. Setting management compensation.

_____ 14. The Ajax Corporation has two shareholders–Albert with 75 shares and Brad with 25 shares. The board of directors consists of four directors. Under cumulative voting, how many shares must Brad own in order to be assured of electing one director if all four directors come up for election at the same time?
   a. 20.
   b. 21.
   c. 24.
   d. 25.

_____ 15. Which of the following rights do shareholders normally have?
   a. They may by a majority vote remove a director or the entire board of directors in a meeting called for that purpose.
   b. They have an unqualified right to inspect the corporate books and records of the corporation.
   c. They have the right to approve fundamental changes in the corporation.
   d. Two of the above are correct, (a) and (c).

SHORT ESSAY

1. When may a shareholder be denied his right to inspect the books and records of the corporation?

   _____

   _____

   _____

   _____

2. List five actions that may be initiated by the board of directors but require shareholder approval.

   _____

   _____

   _____

   _____

3. List four actions that may be taken by the board of directors without shareholder approval.

   _____

   _____

   _____

   _____

4. List and explain the enforcement rights of shareholders.

   _____

   _____

   _____

   _____

5. Explain the "Business Judgment Rule".

   _____

   _____

   _____

   _____

Chapter 38
Fundamental Changes

PURPOSE

Certain fundamental changes in a corporation require shareholder approval because they are outside the authority of the board of directors of the corporation. These include charter amendments, the sale or lease of all or substantially all of the corporation's assets, compulsory share exchanges, dissolution, mergers, and consolidations. Each of these is a fundamental change, because it alters the basic structure of the corporation. The approval of the shareholders does not need to be unanimous. This means that a minority of shareholders may oppose the change. In such cases, the minority shareholders have the right to recover the fair value of their shares if they follow the appraisal remedy procedure found in the state statute. In this chapter, you study the legal aspects of the various fundamental changes in a corporation.

CHAPTER CHECKPOINTS

After reading and studying this chapter, you should be able to:

1. List and discuss the charter amendments which do not require shareholder approval and those which give dissenting shareholders an appraisal remedy.

2. List and discuss the corporate combinations which do not require shareholder approval and those which give dissenting shareholders an appraisal remedy.

3. Discuss the relative rights of the shareholders and the board of directors in tender offers, going private transactions and compulsory share exchanges.

4. Define a cash-out combination and a management buyout and discuss the fairness of each to shareholders.

5. List and discuss the ways in which voluntary and involuntary dissolutions may occur.

CHAPTER OUTLINE

A. Charter Amendments–Shareholders do not have a vested property right resulting from any provision in the articles of incorporation; therefore corporate charters may be amended.
    1. Approval by Directors and Shareholders–The typical procedure for amending the articles of incorporation requires the board of directors to adopt a resolution setting forth the proposed amendment, which then must be approved by a majority vote of the shareholders. After approval, articles of amendment are filed with the secretary of state. Under the Model Act, dissenting shareholders are given an appraisal remedy only if an amendment materially and adversely affects the shareholder's rights. Under the Revised Act, the required shareholder approval must be by majority of all votes entitled to be cast on the amendment if the amendment would give rise to dissenters' rights. All other amendments must only be approved by a majority of the votes cast unless the act or the charter requires a greater vote.
    2. Approval by Directors–The Revised Act permits the board to adopt certain amendments without shareholder action unless the articles of incorporation provide otherwise.

B. Combinations–It may be desirable and profitable for a corporation to acquire all or substantially all of the assets of another corporation or corporations. This may be accomplished by (1) purchase or lease of the assets, (2) purchase of a controlling stock interest in other corporations, (3) merger with other corporations, or (4) consolidation with other corporations.
    1. Purchase or Lease of All or Substantially All of the Assets–In this transaction, there is no change in the legal personality of either corporation. Each corporation continues its separate existence with only the form or extent of the assets altered. Generally, the purchaser does not assume the other's liabilities.
        a. Regular Course of Business–If the sale or lease of all or substantially all of its assets is in the usual and regular course of business of the selling or lessor corporation, approval by its board of directors is required, but shareholder authorization is not.
        b. Other Than in Regular Course of Business–Shareholder approval is necessary if such a sale or lease is not in the usual and regular course of business. In most states, dissenting shareholders of the selling corporation are given an appraisal remedy.
    2. Purchase of Shares–The purchase of a corporation's stock is an alternative to the purchase of its assets. When one corporation acquires all or a controlling interest of the stock of another corporation, there is no change in the legal existence of either corporation. The acquiring corporation acts through its board of directors. The capital structure of the subsidiary remains unchanged. No formal shareholder approval of either corporation is required.
        a. Sale of Control–A privately negotiated transaction is possible when a controlling interest is owned by one or a few shareholders. The sale must be made with due care. The controlling shareholders must make a reasonable investigation to establish that the transfer is not being made to purchasers who plan to act contrary to the best interests of the corporation.

b. Tender Offer–A tender offer is a general invitation to all of the shareholders of a target company to tender their shares for sale at a specified price. Tender offers for publicly held companies are frequently subject to federal securities regulation.

3. Compulsory Share Exchange–A compulsory share exchange is a transaction by which a corporation becomes the owner of all the outstanding shares of one or more classes of another corporation by an exchange that is compulsory on all owners of the acquired shares. Although they produce results similar to a merger, compulsory share exchanges are used instead of mergers where it is desirable that the acquired corporation does not go out of existence as in the formation of holding company systems for insurance companies and banks. The board of directors of each corporation and the shareholders of the corporation whose shares are being acquired must approve the compulsory share exchange. Dissenting shareholders are given an appraisal remedy.

4. Merger–A merger is the combination of the assets of two or more corporations into one of the corporations. One corporation, known as the surviving corporation, receives title to all of the assets. The other corporation, known as the merged corporation, ceases to exist as a separate entity. All debts and other liabilities of the merged corporation are assumed by the surviving corporation. The board of directors and the shareholders of each corporation must approve the merger by a majority vote of the shares entitled to vote. In a short-form merger, a corporation that owns at least 90% of the outstanding shares of a subsidiary may merge the subsidiary into itself without approval by the shareholders of either corporation. Dissenting shareholders of the subsidiary have the right to obtain payment from the parent for their shares, but the shareholders of the parent do not have an appraisal remedy.

5. Consolidation–A consolidation is the combination of two or more corporations into a new corporation which is known as the consolidated corporation. Each of the constituents ceases to exist, all of their debts and liabilities are assumed by the new corporation. A consolidation requires the approval of the boards of each constituent corporation and the affirmative vote of the holders of a majority of the shares entitled to vote. Dissenting shareholders have an appraisal remedy.

6. Going Private Transactions–Corporate combinations are sometimes used to take a publicly held corporation private in order to eliminate minority interests, to reduce the burdens of the federal securities laws, or both. One method of going private is for a majority shareholder to acquire the corporation's shares through purchases on the open market or through a tender offer. Cash-out combinations are also possible.

   a. Cash-out Combinations–These are used to eliminate minority shareholders by forcing them to accept cash or property for their shares. A cash-out combination is often used after a person or company has acquired a large interest in a target company through a tender offer. The tender offeror then seeks to eliminate all other shareholders, thereby achieving complete control of the target company. Some states require that such cash-out combinations have a valid business purpose and that they are fair to all concerned.

   b. Management Buyout–A management buyout is a transaction by which existing management increases its ownership of a corporation and eliminates its public shareholders. Because of the extensive use of borrowed funds, management buyouts are commonly called leveraged buyouts. A critical issue raised by a management buyout is its fairness to the shareholders of the existing corporation that is purchased by the new corporation created by management and then issues bonds to institutional investors to raise cash to purchase the existing corporation.

7. Dissenting Shareholders–A dissenting shareholder is one who opposes a fundamental change and has the right to receive the fair value of her shares.

   a. Transactions Giving Rise to Dissenters' Rights–Most states grant dissenters' rights to dissenting shareholders (1) of a corporation selling or leasing all or substantially all of its property or assets not made in the usual or regular course of business; (2) of each corporation that is a party to a merger, except in a short-form merger; and (3) of each corporation that is a party to a consolidation.

   b. Procedure–If a shareholder dissents and strictly complies with the provisions of the statute, he is entitled to receive the fair value of his shares.

   c. Appraisal Remedy–A dissenting shareholder is entitled to payment of the fair value of his shares plus accrued interest; fair value means the value immediately before the action to which the dissenter objects takes place.

C. Dissolution–Although a corporation may have perpetual existence, it may be terminated in a number of ways. Dissolution does not terminate the corporation's existence, but it does require that the corporation wind up its affairs and liquidate its assets.

   1. Voluntary Dissolution–Voluntary dissolution may be brought about by a resolution of the board of directors approved by the affirmative vote of the holders of a majority of the shares of the corporation entitled to vote at a meeting of the shareholders duly called for that purpose.

   2. Involuntary Dissolution–A corporation may be involuntarily dissolved by administrative dissolution or by judicial dissolution.

      a. Administrative Dissolution–The secretary of state may commence a proceeding to dissolve a corporation if (1) it does not pay within sixty days after they are due any franchise taxes or penalties; (2) it does not deliver its annual report to the secretary of state within sixty days after it is due; (3) it is without a registered agent or registered office for sixty days or more; (4) it does not notify the secretary of state within sixty days that its registered agent or registered office has been changed, that its registered agent has resigned, or that its registered office has been discontinued; or (5) its period of duration stated in its articles of incorporation expires.

      b. Judicial Dissolution–Judicial dissolution may occur by: (a) court action brought by the attorney general of the state of incorporation; (b) court action brought by shareholders when it is established that the directors are deadlocked in the management, that the acts of directors are illegal or fraudulent, that assets are being misapplied or wasted, or that the shareholders are deadlocked; and (c) court action instituted by a creditor on a showing that the corporation has become unable to pay its debts and obligations as they mature in the regular course of its business.

   3. Liquidation–A corporation must cease carrying on its business except as is necessary to wind up once dissolution has occurred. When a corporation is dissolved, its assets are liquidated and used first to pay the expenses of liquidation and its creditors according to their respective contract or lien rights. Any remainder is distributed to shareholders proportionately according to their contract rights. Stock with liquidation preference has a priority over common stock.

4. Protection of Creditors–The statutory procedures usually prescribe procedures to safeguard the interests of creditors of the corporation. Typically, notice must be mailed to known creditors, general publication of notice, and preservation of claims against the corporation.

KEY TERMS

1. Fundamental change

2. Tender offer

3. Compulsory share exchange

4. Merger

5. Short-form merger

6. Consolidation

7. Cash-out combination

8. Management buyout

9. Dissenting shareholder

10. Appraisal remedy

11. Fair value

12. Voluntary dissolution

13. Involuntary administrative dissolution

14. Involuntary judicial dissolution

15. Liquidation

TRUE/FALSE

_____ 1. Changes which alter the basic structure of the corporation require only board approval.

_____ 2. Shareholder approval for fundamental changes requires a majority of all votes entitled to be cast.

_____ 3. A sale of substantially all of a corporation's assets within the usual course of business requires shareholder authorization.

_____ 4. Charter amendments do not affect the existing rights of nonshareholders.

_____ 5. Debts and other liabilities of a merged corporation are not assumed by the surviving corporation.

_____ 6. In a consolidation of two or more corporations, each of the constituent corporations ceases to exist.

_____ 7. Voluntary dissolution may be brought about by action on the part of the holders of a majority of the outstanding shares of stock.

_____ 8. Involuntary dissolution by judicial proceeding may be instituted by the creditors of the corporation.

_____ 9. In a merger the surviving corporation assumes all debts of the merged corporation.

_____ 10. When liquidation is involuntary, it is carried out by a court-appointed receiver.

_____ 11. When a corporation is dissolved, its assets are liquidated and used first to pay the expenses of liquidation and the shareholders according to their respective contract rights.

_____ 12. Under a compulsory share exchange, approval of the shareholders of the acquiring corporation is required.

_____ 13. A shareholder, who dissents and strictly complies with the provisions of the incorporating statute, is entitled to receive the fair value of her shares.

_____ 14. All amendments to the articles of incorporation require shareholder approval.

_____ 15. There are no statutory provisions to protect creditors upon the dissolution of a corporation.

MULTIPLE CHOICE

_____ 1. Under the MBCA, a corporation may amend its charter to:
   a. change its corporate name.
   b. change the preferential rights of shares.
   c. deny preemptive rights.
   d. all of the above.

_____ 2. Charter amendments become effective upon:
   a. adoption of a resolution by the board setting forth the proposed amendment.
   b. approval by a majority vote of the shareholders.
   c. execution and filing of articles of amendment with the secretary of state.
   d. issuance of the certificate of amendment by the secretary of state.

_____ 3. A corporation ceases to exist as a separate entity when:
   a. all or substantially all of its assets are purchased by another corporation.
   b. a controlling interest in its stock is purchased by another corporation.
   c. it is merged into another corporation.
   d. all of the above.

_____ 4. The sale or lease of all or substantially all of a corporation's assets in the usual course of its business requires approval by its:
   a. board of directors.
   b. shareholders.
   c. board of directors and shareholders.
   d. none of the above.

_____ 5. Under the revised Act, which of the following amendments would directors _not_ be allowed to make without shareholder action?
   a. Extend the duration of a corporation that was incorporated when limited duration was required by law.
   b. Making minor name changes.
   c. Altering a preferential right of the shares.
   d. Changing each issued and unissued authorized share of an outstanding class into a greater number of whole shares if the corporation has only one class of shares.

_____ 6. A corporation which purchases the assets of another corporation does not assume the other's liability unless:
   a. the purchaser agrees to assume the seller's liability.
   b. the transaction amounts to a merger.
   c. the purchaser is a mere continuation of the seller.
   d. all of the above.

_____ 7. A merger requires the approval of:
   a. the board of directors of the merged corporation.
   b. the board of directors of the surviving corporation.
   c. the shareholders of the surviving corporation.
   d. all of the above.

_____ 8. The merger of a wholly-owned subsidiary into its parent requires the approval of:
   a. the board of directors of the parent corporation.
   b. the board of directors and shareholders of the subsidiary corporation.
   c. the board of directors and shareholders of each corporation.
   d. the shareholders of the subsidiary corporation.

_____ 9. If a wholly-owned subsidiary is merged into its parent, an appraisal remedy is available to the shareholders of:
   a. the parent corporation.
   b. the subsidiary corporation.
   c. both the parent and the subsidiary.
   d. none of the above.

_____ 10. A consolidation requires the approval of:
   a. the board of directors of each constituent corporation.
   b. the shareholders of each constituent corporation.
   c. the board of directors and shareholders of each constituent corporation.
   d. none of the above.

_____ 11. A general invitation to all of the shareholders of a target company to tender their shares for sale at a specified price is referred to as a:
   a. consolidation.
   b. merger.
   c. compulsory share exchange.
   d. tender offer.

_____ 12. A _____ is a transaction by which existing management increases its ownership of a corporation and eliminates its public shareholders.
   a. short-form merger
   b. consolidation
   c. leveraged buyout
   d. compulsory share exchange

_____ 13. Involuntary dissolution may occur by administrative action taken by:
   a. the attorney general.
   b. shareholders under certain circumstances.
   c. both a and b.
   d. neither a nor b.

_____ 14. Common amendments to capital structure provisions include which of the following?
   a. Increasing or decreasing authorized shares.
   b. Reclassifying shares.
   c. Eliminating preemptive rights.
   d. All of the above.

_____ 15. Which of the following is correct regarding shareholder approval of charter amendments?
   a. The Revised Act permits the board to adopt certain amendments without shareholder approval.
   b. Under the Model Act, a dissenting shareholder is given an appraisal remedy only if an amendment materially and adversely affects his rights.
   c. Under the Revised Act, if the amendment would give rise to dissenters' rights, it must be approved by a majority of all votes entitled to be cast on the amendment.
   d. All of the above are correct.

SHORT ESSAY

1. List five examples of fundamental changes.

   _____
   _____
   _____
   _____

2. Outline the procedure for amending the articles of incorporation.

   _____
   _____
   _____
   _____

3. By what methods may a corporation acquire all or substantially all of the assets of another corporation?

   _____
   _____
   _____
   _____

4. What transactions give rise to dissenters' rights in most states?

_____

_____

_____

_____

5. Discuss mergers, explaining how they occur and the effects thereof.

_____

_____

_____

_____

Part VII
Sample Examination

MULTIPLE CHOICE

_____ 1. The legal document that the incorporators of a corporation prepare and submit to the state in order to establish a corporation is known as the:
a. summons.
b. articles of incorporation.
c. certificate of registration.
d. corporate bylaws.

_____ 2. Which of the following is/are correct regarding the bylaws of a corporation?
a. They are rules and regulations which govern internal management and are adopted by the shareholders.
b. They are adopted and amended by the shareholders.
c. Both a and b are correct.
d. Neither a nor b is correct.

_____ 3. A corporation that acts within the authority granted to it in its charter is known as _____ acts.
a. proxy
b. _de jure_ corporation
c. _de facto_ corporation
d. none of the above

_____ 4. In which of the following situations will the directors of a corporation be liable?
a. The directors refuse to declare dividends even though the corporation has retained earnings.
b. Two directors miss a meeting because they are ill and don't notify the others.
c. The directors violate the business judgment rule in their corporate dealings.
d. The directors make an honest mistake in judgment when they decide to move the corporate headquarters to a new location.

_____ 5. The amount by which the total assets of a corporation exceed the total debts of the corporation is referred to as the corporation's:
a. earned surplus.
b. surplus.
c. net assets.
d. stated capital.

6. The test which the MBCA now uses to determine whether a corporation can legally pay a dividend is known as the _____ test.
   a. surplus
   b. earned surplus
   c. net asset
   d. none of the above

7. Under the Revised Act, if a charter simply states that the corporation has preemptive rights, the shareholder has preemptive rights to which of the following:
   a. shares issued as compensation to employees.
   b. shares issued within six months of incorporation.
   c. shares issued for consideration other than money.
   d. none of the above.

8. A lawsuit brought by a shareholder on behalf of the corporation to enforce a right belonging to the corporation is known as:
   a. a direct suit.
   b. a class suit.
   c. a derivative suit.
   d. none of the above.

9. Under the Revised Act, directors who vote for or assent to the payment of an illegal dividend have liability to the:
   a. shareholders.
   b. corporation.
   c. creditors of the corporation.
   d. all of the above.

10. Tel-Ko Corporation has two shareholders. Arthur has 64 shares and Bill has 36 shares. The board of directors consists of three directors. How many shares does Bill need to elect one director under cumulative voting?
    a. 26.
    b. 36.
    c. 40.
    d. 51.

11. In which of the following is shareholder approval required?
    a. A corporation sells substantially all of its assets outside of the regular course of business.
    b. There are amendments to the articles of incorporation.
    c. The board of directors has approved a merger of a corporation with another.
    d. All of the above situations require shareholder approval.

_____ 12. Bill Businessman sues the Tel-Ko Corporation in a stockholder derivative suit and wins the case. The judgment will be paid to:
   a. Bill personally.
   b. all of the shareholders as a dividend.
   c. the corporate treasury.
   d. the board of directors.

_____ 13. Which of the following would not be a shareholder right?
   a. The right to elect the corporate directors.
   b. The right to elect the corporate officers.
   c. The right to approve the sale of any real estate owned by the corporation.
   d. b and c are not shareholder rights.

_____ 14. A corporation is considered to be a "person" for purposes of:
   a. the Fifth Amendment due process clause.
   b. the Fourteenth Amendment due process clause.
   c. the Fifth Amendment right against self-incrimination.
   d. the Fifth and Fourteenth Amendments due process clauses.

_____ 15. A corporation that is owned by a few shareholders and whose shares are not actively traded is known as a _____ corporation.
   a. closely held
   b. Subchapter S
   c. public
   d. nonprofit

_____ 16. The rules and regulations that govern the internal management of a corporation are normally found in the:
   a. articles of incorporation.
   b. corporate charter.
   c. corporate bylaws.
   d. state statute.

_____ 17. Which of the following are normally not included in the articles of incorporation of a corporation?
   a. The address of the registered office of a corporation.
   b. The number of authorized shares.
   c. The name and address of each incorporator.
   d. The term of office to be served by the corporate officers.

_____ 18. A combination of the assets of two or more corporations into one of the corporations is a :
   a. merger.
   b. consolidation.
   c. tender offer.
   d. cash-out combination.

_____ 19. A _____ is a transaction by which existing management increases its ownership of a corporation and eliminates its public shareholders.
   a. management buyout
   b. leveraged buyout
   c. tender offer
   d. consolidation

_____ 20. Bradley signed a five year lease for office space on behalf of the Ajax Corporation, which has not yet been formed, but which Bradley is promoting.
   a. Bradley is personally liable on the lease.
   b. Bradley is not liable, because he is an agent of the Ajax Corporation.
   c. The Ajax Corporation is liable on the lease.
   d. . Two of the above are correct, (b) and (c).

Chapter 39
Secured Transactions in Personal Property

PURPOSE

Today our economy runs on borrowed funds. A lender typically incurs certain collection risks; therefore the law has developed several devices to maximize the likelihood that the loan will be repaid. The most important of these is the secured transaction which is an agreement by the borrower granting the lender the right to reach specified property of the borrower to pay off the debt if the borrower fails to do so. A secured transaction includes two elements: (1) a debt or obligation to pay money, and (2) an interest of the creditor in specific property of the debtor that secures performance of the obligation. Financing transactions involving security in personal property where the debtor consents to provide a security interest are governed by Article 9 of the Uniform Commercial Code. In this chapter, you study secured transactions in personal property including the rules of attachment, perfection, and priorities of secured parties.

CHAPTER CHECKPOINTS

After reading and studying this chapter, you should be able to:

1. Define the terms "attachment" and "perfection" and identify when a security interest attaches and when it becomes perfected.

2. List the three classifications of collateral according to the nature of the collateral and explain how a security interest in each is perfected.

3. Distinguish between a purchase money security interest and a nonpurchase money security interest and explain the legal effect of each.

4. Explain what rights the creditor in a secured transaction has in the event of a default by the debtor.

5. Discuss the priorities among parties with competing interests in collateral.

CHAPTER OUTLINE

A. Essentials of Secured Transactions–Secured transactions in personal property are governed by Article 9 if the debtor consents to provide a security interest in personal property to secure the payment of a debt. A secured transaction is an agreement by which one party obtains a security interest in the personal property of another to secure the payment of a debt. A common type of consensual secured transaction covered by Article 9 occurs when a person who wants to buy goods does not have either the cash or sufficient credit standing to obtain the goods on open credit. The seller obtains a security interest in the goods to secure payment of all or part of the price. If the buyer borrows the purchase price from a third party and pays the seller in cash, the third-party lender may take a security interest in the goods. In every secured transaction there is a debtor, a secured party, collateral, a security agreement, and a security interest. A debtor is a person who owes payment or performance of an obligation. A secured party is the creditor-lender, seller, or other person who possesses the security interest in the collateral. Collateral is the property subject to the security interest. A security agreement is the agreement that creates or provides for a security interest, which in its broadest sense is an interest in personal property or fixtures that secures payment or performance of an obligation. A purchase money security interest is a security interest in goods purchased, which interest is retained either by the seller of the goods or by a lender who advances the purchase price.

B. Classification of Collateral–Some provisions of Article 9 state special rules that apply only to particular kinds of collateral. Collateral is classified according to its nature and its use. Classifications according to nature include the following categories.
1. Goods–Goods are tangible personal property that can be moved when the security interest in them becomes enforceable. Goods are subdivided into (1) consumer goods, (2) farm products, (3) inventory, and (4) equipment. An item may fall into different classifications depending on its use or purpose.
   a. Consumer Goods–Goods are consumer goods if they are used or bought for use primarily for personal, family or household purposes.
   b. Farm Products–The Code defines farm products as "crops or livestock or supplies used or produced in farming operations or if they are products of crops or livestock in their unmanufactured states."
   c. Inventory–Inventory includes goods held for sale or lease and raw materials, work in process, or materials used or consumed in a business. A retailer or wholesaler's merchandise would be classified as inventory.
   d. Equipment–Goods are classified as equipment if they are used or purchased for use primarily in business. If goods used in a business are not categorized as inventory, farm products, or consumer goods, they are classified as equipment.
   e. Fixtures–Fixtures are goods that are so firmly attached to real property that they are considered part of the real estate. State law other than the Code determines whether and when

goods become fixtures. A security interest under Article 9 may be created in goods that become fixtures. Under certain circumstances, a perfected security interest in fixtures has priority over a conflicting security interest or mortgage in the real property to which the goods have been attached.

2. Indispensable Paper–Three kinds of collateral involve rights evidenced by indispensable paper. These are (1) chattel paper, (2) instruments, and (3) documents.

   a. Chattel Paper–Chattel paper is a writing or writings that evidence both a monetary obligation and a security interest in or a lease of specific goods. A secured party may borrow against or sell the security agreement of his debtor along with his interest in the collateral.

   b. Instruments–Instruments include negotiable instruments, stocks, bonds, and other investment securities. An instrument is any writing that evidences a right to payment of money, that is transferable by delivery with any necessary indorsement or assignment, and that is not of itself a security agreement or lease.

   c. Documents–Documents include documents of title, such as bills of lading and warehouse receipts, that may be either negotiable or nonnegotiable.

3. Intangibles–The Code also recognizes two other kinds of collateral. These are accounts and general intangibles.

   a. Accounts–An account or account receivable is the right to payment for goods sold or leased, or for services rendered. It is not evidenced by an instrument or chattel paper.

   b. General Intangibles–General intangibles are any personal property other than goods, accounts, chattel paper, documents, instruments, and money. It is a catchall category of collateral not otherwise covered. It includes goodwill, literary rights, and interests in patents, trademarks, and copyrights to the extent they are not regulated by federal statute.

C. Attachment–Attachment describes the creation of a security interest that is enforceable against the debtor. It is a prerequisite to a security interest's enforceability against parties other than the debtor. Until a security interest "attaches," it is ineffective against the debtor. A security interest attaches to the described collateral when: (1) the secured party gives value; (2) the debtor acquires rights in the collateral; and (3) the security agreement is signed by the debtor.

1. Value–Value is broadly defined to include consideration under contract law, a binding commitment to extend credit, and an antecedent debt.

2. Debtor's Rights in Collateral–As a general rule, the debtor is deemed to have rights in collateral if he owns the collateral, possesses it, or if he is in the process of acquiring it from the seller.

3. Security Agreement–A security agreement cannot attach unless there is an agreement between the debtor and creditor granting, creating, or providing the creditor a security interest in the debtor's collateral. With the exceptions of pledges, the agreement must (1) be in writing, (2) be signed by the debtor, and (3) contain a reasonable description of the collateral. No written security agreement is required when the collateral is pledged or is in the possession of the secured party pursuant to an agreement. A pledge is the delivery of personal property to a creditor as security for the payment of a debt.

   a. Consumer Goods–Federal regulation prohibits a credit seller or lender from obtaining a consumer's grant of a security interest in household goods. This rule does not apply to purchase money security interests or to pledges.

b. After-Acquired Property–A security agreement may provide a secured party with a security interest in after-acquired property, which is property the debtor does not own or have rights to but may acquire at some time in the future. The Code limits the operation of an after-acquired property clause against consumers. No such interest can be claimed in consumer goods acquired more than ten days after the secured party gives value.

c. Proceeds–Proceeds are the consideration received for the sale, exchange, or other disposition of the collateral. Unless otherwise agreed, a security agreement gives the secured party rights to proceeds.

d. Future Advances–The obligations covered by a security agreement may include future advances. A debtor may obtain a line of credit from a creditor for advances to be made at some later time.

D. Perfection–Perfection refers to the enforceability of a security agreement against third parties. It occurs when the security interest has attached and when all applicable steps required for perfection have been taken. If these steps are taken before the security agreement attaches, it is perfected at the time it attaches. Depending upon the type of collateral, a security interest may be perfected in the following ways.

1. Filing a Financing Statement–A general method of perfecting a security interest under Article 9 is by filing a financing statement. A financing statement is a document filed by the secured party to provide notice of the security interest. It must contain the names and addresses of the secured party and the debtor, a reasonable description of the type or items of collateral, and the signature of the debtor. Where no maturity date is stated on a financing statement, the statement is effective for five years from the date of filing. This period may be extended for an additional five-year period by the filing of a continuation statement within six months prior to the expiration. In most states, a security interest in motor vehicles must be perfected by a notation on the certificate of title rather than by filing a financing statement. A certificate of title is an official representation of ownership.

a. Where to File–The Code provides three alternative provisions regarding where to file a financing statement. These differ as to which types of collateral are to be filed locally or centrally. The first alternative provides that where the collateral is fixtures, timber to be cut, or minerals to be extracted, the filing should be local in the office where a real estate mortgage would be filed. All other filings are to be made centrally with the secretary of state or other designated state official. The second alternative stipulates local filing for fixtures, farm products, consumer goods, timber, minerals, and farming equipment. All other filings are central. This is the most widely adopted alternative. The third alternative is the same as the second except that where central filing is required, the secured party must also file locally in some situations.

b. Improper Filing–If a secured party fails to file the financing statement in the proper location or fails to file it in all the required locations, the filing is ineffective, subject to two exceptions. If the improper filing is made in good faith, it is effective for any collateral for which the filing complied with the requirements of Article 9. An improper filing made in good faith is also effective for collateral covered by the financing statement against any person who has knowledge of the contents of that financing statement.

   c. Subsequent change of Information–A change in the use of collateral does not impair the original filing, nor does a change in location provided the change is intrastate. Interstate changes may necessitate a new filing.

2. Possession–Possession by the secured party perfects a security interest in goods, instruments, negotiable documents, or chattel paper. Subject to the limited exception of the twenty-one day temporary period of perfection, possession is the only way to perfect a security interest in instruments. It is the usual and advisable method to perfect a security interest in both negotiable documents and chattel paper. A pledge or possessory security interest is the delivery of personal property to a creditor, or to a third party acting as an agent for the creditor, as security for the payment of a debt. A field warehouse is a common kind of pledge for financing inventory. It allows the debtor access to the pledged goods and at the same time gives the secured party control over the property. In this type of arrangement, a professional warehouseman establishes a warehouse on the debtor's premises by enclosing a portion of the premises and posting appropriate signs. The secured party legally possesses the goods but allows the debtor access to the inventory.

3. Automatic Perfection–In some situations there is automatic perfection upon attachment. The most important situation to which automatic perfection applies is a purchase money security interest in consumer goods. There is also automatic perfection of a partial or isolated assignment of accounts that does not transfer a significant part of the outstanding accounts of the assignor.

4. Temporary Perfection–A security interest in negotiable documents or instruments is automatically perfected without filing or taking possession for twenty-one days from the time it attaches, to the extent that it arises for new value given under a written security agreement. After that period expires, the security interest becomes unperfected unless it is perfected by other available means of perfection (i.e., filing or possession). Even though the interest is temporarily perfected during the twenty-one days, a holder in due course or a holder to whom the document has been duly negotiated will take priority over the security interest. A security interest in proceeds is automatically perfected for ten days after receipt of the proceeds if the security interest in the original collateral was perfected.

E. Priorities Among Competing Interests–A security interest must be perfected to be effective against other creditors of the debtor, the debtor's trustee in bankruptcy, and transferees of the debtor. However, perfection does not mean that the secured party will have priority over all third parties with an interest in the collateral. Article 9 establishes a complex set of rules that determine relative priorities among parties.

  1. Against Unsecured Creditors–When a security interest attaches, it has priority over claims of other creditors without a security interest or lien. This priority does not depend upon perfection. Without attachment, the creditor is an unsecured or general creditor.

2. Against Other Secured Creditors–The rights of a secured creditor against other secured creditors depends upon which security interests are perfected, when they are perfected, and the type of collateral.

    a. Perfected versus Unperfected–A creditor with a perfected security interest has greater rights in the collateral than a creditor with an unperfected security interest.

    b. Perfected versus Perfected–If two parties each have perfected security interests, they rank according to priority in time of filing or perfection. The first party to file or perfect has priority, provided that there is no subsequent period when there is neither filing nor perfection. This rule gives special treatment to filing, because it can occur prior to attachment and thus grants priority from a time that may precede perfection. Where there is a purchase money security interest in the collateral, the rules vary depending upon whether the collateral is noninventory or inventory. A purchase money security interest in noninventory collateral takes priority over a conflicting security interest if the purchase money security interest is perfected at the time the debtor receives possession of the collateral or within ten days of receipt. Thus, the secured party has a ten-day grace period although most states have extended this grace period. A purchase money security interest in inventory has priority over conflicting security interests if the following requirements are met. The holder must perfect his interest in the inventory at the time the debtor receives it. He must also notify, in writing, all holders of conflicting security interests who have filed a financing statement covering the same type of inventory of his acquisition of a purchase money security interest and must give a description of the secured inventory.

    c. Unperfected versus Unperfected–If neither security interest is perfected, then the first to attach has priority. If neither attaches, both creditors are general, unsecured creditors.

3. Against Buyers–A security interest continues in collateral even though it is sold, unless the secured party authorizes the sale. The security interest also continues in any identifiable proceeds from the sale of the collateral.

    a. Buyers in the Ordinary Course of Business–A buyer in the ordinary course of business takes collateral free of any security interest created by the seller, even if the security interest is perfected and the buyer knows of its existence. A buyer in the ordinary course of business is a person who buys from a merchant in good faith, without knowledge that the sale violates a security interest. This rule applies primarily to purchasers of inventory.

    b. Buyers of Farm Products–Buyers in the ordinary course of business of farm products, although not protected by Article 9, are protected by the Federal Food Security Act. This act defines a buyer in the ordinary course of business as "a person who, in the ordinary course of business, buys farm products from a person engaged in farming operations who is in the business of selling farm products." The act provides that such a buyer shall take free of most security interests created by the seller, even if it is perfected and the buyer knows of the existence of the interest.

    c. Buyers of Consumer Goods–A buyer who buys consumer goods without knowledge of a security interest, for value, and for his own personal, family or household use, takes the goods free of any purchase money security interest automatically perfected, but takes the goods subject to a security interest perfected by filing.

d. Other Buyers–An unperfected security interest is subordinate to the following rights: (1) a purchaser who gives value for collateral consisting of goods, instruments, documents, and chattel paper, who takes the collateral without knowledge of the existing security interest and before it is perfected; and (2) a purchaser who takes collateral consisting of accounts and general intangibles who takes the collateral for value, without knowledge of the security interest, and before perfection. In both of these cases, a purchaser with knowledge of the unperfected security interest takes the collateral subject to that interest. A purchaser of chattel paper or of an instrument who gives new value and takes possession of it in the ordinary course of his business has priority over a perfected security interest in the chattel paper or instrument if he acts without knowledge of such an interest. A holder in due course of a negotiable instrument, a holder to whom a negotiable document of title has been duly negotiated, and a *bona fide* purchaser of an investment security take priority over an earlier security interest even though perfected.

4. Against Lien Creditors–A lien creditor is a creditor who has acquired a lien on the property by judicial decree and includes a trustee in bankruptcy. A trustee in bankruptcy is a representative of the estate in bankruptcy who is responsible for collecting, liquidating, and distributing the debtor's assets. A perfected security interest has priority over lien creditors who acquire their lien after perfection. An unperfected security interest is subordinate to the rights of a person who becomes a lien creditor before the security interest is perfected.

5. Against Trustee in Bankruptcy–The Bankruptcy Code empowers a trustee in bankruptcy to (a) take priority over an unperfected security interest, and (b) avoid preferential transfers.

a. Priority over Unperfected Security Interest–A trustee in bankruptcy may invalidate any security interest that is voidable by a creditor who obtained a judicial lien on the date of the filing of the bankruptcy petition. Under the UCC and the Bankruptcy Code, the trustee has priority over a creditor with a security interest that was not perfected when the bankruptcy petition was filed. A creditor with a purchase money security interest who files within the statutory grace period after the debtor receives the collateral will defeat the trustee, even if the petition is filed before the creditor perfects and after the creation of the security interest.

b. Avoidance of Preferential Transfers–The Bankruptcy Code provides that a trustee in bankruptcy may invalidate any transfer of property–including the granting of a security interest–from the debtor, provided that the transfer (1) was to or for a benefit of a creditor; (2) was made on account of an antecedent debt; (3) was made at a time the debtor was insolvent; (4) was made on or within ninety days before the filing of the bankruptcy petition, or if made to an insider, was made within one year before the date of filing; and (5) enabled the transferee to receive more than he would have received in bankruptcy. An insider includes a relative or general partner of a debtor as well as some others. If a security interest is invalidated as a preferential transfer, the creditor may still make a claim for the unpaid debt, but the creditor's claim is unsecured.

F. Default–After default, the secured party may ask for a judgment or foreclosure or otherwise enforce the security interest by available judicial procedure. Unless the debtor has waived his rights in the collateral, he has a right of redemption, which is the freeing of the collateral of the security interest by paying off the loan.

1. Repossession–Unless the parties have agreed otherwise, the secured party may take possession of the collateral on default without judicial process if it can be done without a breach of the peace. After default, the secured party may leave it on the debtor's premises and render it unusable until disposing of it.

2. Sale of Collateral–The secured party may sell, lease or otherwise dispose of any collateral in its existing condition at the time of default or following any commercially reasonable preparation or processing. The debtor is entitled to any surplus and is liable for any deficiency, except that in the case of a sale of accounts or chattel paper, he is not entitled to any surplus or liable for a deficiency unless the security agreement so provides. The collateral may be disposed of at public or private sale, so long as all aspects of its disposition, including its method, time, place, and terms, are "commercially reasonable."

3. Retention of Collateral–After default and repossession, the secured party may send written notice to the debtor that he proposes to retain the collateral in satisfaction of the obligation. If no objection is received within twenty-one days, the secured party may retain the collateral. If there is objection within the period, the collateral must be disposed of as provided in the Code. In the case of consumer goods, if the debtor has paid 60 percent of the obligation and has not signed a statement after default renouncing his rights, the secured party must dispose of the property by sale within ninety days after repossession or be liable for not less than the service charge plus 10% of the principal.

KEY TERMS

1. Secured transaction

2. Debtor

3. Secured party

4. Collateral

5. Security agreement

6. Security interest

7. Purchase money security interest

8. Consumer goods

9. Farm products

10. Inventory

11. Equipment

12. Fixtures

13. Indispensable paper

14. Chattel paper

15. Instruments

16. Documents

17. Intangibles

18. Accounts

19. General intangibles

20. Attachment

21. Value

22. Rights in collateral

23. Pledge

24. After-acquired property

25. Proceeds

26. Perfection

27. Financing statement

28. Certificate of title

29. Field warehouse

30. Automatic perfection

31. Buyer in the ordinary course of business

32. Lien creditor

33. Trustee in bankruptcy

34. Redemption

TRUE/FALSE

_____ 1. Article 9 of the UCC governs financing transactions involving security in real property.

_____ 2. A security interest in property may continue even after the underlying debt is discharged.

_____ 3. A security interest can be perfected without attachment.

_____ 4. A security interest will be perfected if the interest has attached and the secured party files a financing statement signed by the creditor.

_____ 5. Under the Code, a security agreement does not have to be in writing when the collateral is pledged or is in the possession of the secured party pursuant to an agreement.

_____ 6. A financing statement is generally effective for five years from the date of filing.

_____ 7. Unless the parties agree otherwise, a security agreement covering the debtor's inventory does not give the secured party rights to the proceeds from the sale of that inventory.

_____ 8. Goods bought primarily for personal, family or household purposes are classified as equipment.

_____ 9. A security interest in goods represented by a negotiable document is perfected by negotiation of the document.

_____ 10. If two parties have unperfected security interests in the same collateral, the first to attach has priority.

_____ 11. A buyer in the ordinary course of business takes collateral free of any security interest created by any previous seller of the collateral.

_____ 12. Unless the parties have otherwise agreed, after default the secured party may take possession of the collateral without judicial process if it can be done without a breach of the peace.

_____ 13. Unless the debtor waived his rights in the collateral after default, he has a right of redemption at any time before the secured party disposes of the collateral or enters into a contract to dispose of it.

_____ 14. In a PMSI in noninventory, the secured party has a ten day grace period in which to perfect.

_____ 15. Filing a financing statement is the general method of perfecting a security interest in instruments.

MULTIPLE CHOICE

_____ 1. A secured transaction includes which of the following?
   a. A debt or obligation to pay money.
   b. An interest of the creditor in property of the debtor.
   c. Both a and b.
   d. Neither a nor b.

_____ 2. Every consensual secured transaction involves which of the following?
   a. A debtor.
   b. A security agreement.
   c. A security interest.
   d. All of the above.

_____ 3. In general, a security interest in an instrument can be perfected by:
   a. the secured party's taking or retaining possession of the instrument.
   b. the secured party's filing a financing statement.
   c. either (a) or (b).
   d. both (a) and (b).

_____ 4. In order for a security interest to attach, an agreement between the debtor and creditor must:
   a. be signed by the debtor.
   b. be notarized.
   c. describe the collateral.
   d. (a) and (c) but not (b).

_____ 5. A tractor used by a farmer to plow his land, if collateral in which a security interest is granted, is classified as:
   a. farm products.
   b. equipment.
   c. either (a) or (b).
   d. both (a) and (b).

_____ 6. Under the Code, collateral is classified according to its nature. Which of the following are proper classifications?
   a. Goods.
   b. Indispensable paper.
   c. Both (a) and (b).
   d. Neither (a) nor (b).

_____ 7. A creditor with an unperfected, but attached security interest has greater rights in the collateral than:
  a. the debtor's trustee in bankruptcy.
  b. the debtor's secured creditors.
  c. the debtor.
  d. none of the above.

_____ 8. As between two parties with continuously perfected security interests in the same collateral, the party with the superior interest is the one who:
  a. first filed a financing statement covering the collateral.
  b. first perfected his security interest.
  c. first did (a) or (b), whichever first occurred.
  d. first did (a) and (b), whichever first occurred.

_____ 9. A perfected security interest has priority over claims of:
  a. lien creditors of the debtor.
  b. unsecured creditors of the debtor.
  c. the debtor himself.
  d. all of the above.

_____ 10. On the debtor's default, the secured party may do all of the following except:
  a. foreclose on his claim.
  b. take possession of the collateral even if it requires a breach of the peace.
  c. reduce his claim to judgment.
  d. render the collateral unusable on the debtor's premises.

_____ 11. Donald Debtor takes out a $2,000 loan from Consumer Credit Corporation on May 15 to buy a new video camcorder to record his brother's wedding. He buys the camcorder immediately and signs a financing agreement. On May 20, before Consumer Credit has had an opportunity to file the financing statement, Donald files for bankruptcy. Consumer Credit files the financing statement on May 22. It is now July and the trustee in bankruptcy claims that he is entitled to the camcorder to sell and use the proceeds to pay the expenses of administration and the general creditors of the estate. As between the trustee in bankruptcy and Consumer Credit, who is entitled to the video camcorder?
  a. Consumer Credit, because its security interest is a purchase money security interest in consumer goods that is thus automatically perfected.
  b. Consumer Credit, because it has a perfected security interest that it filed within ten days of the debtor's receipt of collateral.
  c. The trustee, because this was a preferential transfer.
  d. The trustee, because the trustee always has the power to invalidate a perfected security interest.

_____ 12. David loaned Elvis $1,000 to buy a big screen television for his business. Elvis signed a security agreement, which David filed in his personal files, but not with the County Recorder. A week later, Elvis used the big screen television as collateral on a loan from Consumer Credit, which filed its security interest with the County Recorder on the same day. A month later, David notices the financing agreement in his personal files and files it with the County Recorder. Who has priority?
   a. David, because his security interest was the first to attach.
   b. David, because he has a purchase money security interest.
   c. Consumer Credit, because it was the first to file.
   d. Consumer Credit, because it has the most recent security interest.

_____ 13. David loaned Elvis $1,000 to buy a big screen television for his business. Elvis signed a financing statement, which David filed in his personal files, but not with the County Recorder. A week later, Elvis used the big screen television as collateral on a loan from Consumer Credit. Elvis signed a financing statement, but the new manager had forgotten to study business law and didn't know that he was supposed to file it with the County Recorder. Who has priority?
   a. David, because his security interest was the first to attach.
   b. David, because he has a purchase money security interest.
   c. Consumer Credit, because it has the most recent security interest.
   d. Neither party, because neither has a perfected security interest.

_____ 14. A common arrangement for financing inventory which allows the debtor access to the pledged goods but gives the secured party control over the property is referred to as a:
   a. field warehouse.
   b. purchase money security interest.
   c. fixture.
   d. none of the above.

_____ 15. If a debtor transfers a security interest and within ninety days files bankruptcy, a trustee in bankruptcy may invalidate that transfer if:
   a. the transfer was to or for the benefit of a creditor.
   b. the transfer was made on account of an antecedent debt.
   c. the transfer was made at the time the debtor was insolvent and allowed the transferee to receive more than he would in bankruptcy.
   d. all of the above are required.

SHORT ESSAY

1. Define "secured transaction" and describe its purpose.

_____

_____

_____

_____

2. Outline briefly the steps that a lender must go through to attain a perfected security interest in a boat as collateral for a loan.

_____

_____

_____

_____

3. List the classifications of collateral according to the nature of the collateral and give examples of each.

_____

_____

_____

_____

4. Equity Credit loaned $30,000 to Gamble's Store to purchase televisions for its inventory. Gamble signed a financing agreement which Equity Credit filed in the appropriate office. Fred purchased a television that was subject to the security interest held by Equity Credit. Whose interest in the television has priority?

_____

_____

_____

_____

5. What are the rights of the secured party after default of the debtor?

_____

_____

_____

_____

Chapter 40
Suretyship

PURPOSE

In this chapter you study the law of suretyship. A surety is one who promises to pay the debt of another if the other party fails to perform. A surety is often used in addition to or instead of a security interest in order to further reduce the risk of the creditor in extending credit. Sureties are also used by employers to protect against losses caused by employees who embezzle the employer's fund. They are frequently required in construction contracts to bond the performance of the contract, and they are commonly used in contracts involving minors so that a party with full contractual capacity is responsible for the obligations arising from the contracts.

CHAPTER CHECKPOINTS

After reading and studying this chapter, you should be able to:

1. Identify five types of sureties.

2. Explain the requirements for the formation of a suretyship relationship.

3. List and discuss the rights of a surety and of a cosurety.

4. Discuss the rights of a creditor against a surety.

5. Identify the personal defenses of the principal debtor, the personal defenses of the surety, and the defenses of both the surety and the principal debtor.

CHAPTER OUTLINE

A. Nature and Formation–A surety promises to answer for the payment of a debt or the performance of a duty owed to one person (the creditor) by another (the principal debtor) on the failure of the principal debtor to make payment or otherwise perform the obligation. The surety relationship involves three parties–the principal debtor, the creditor, and the surety–and three contractual obligations. When there is more than one person bound for the same debt of the principal debtor, they are cosureties. The creditors' rights against the principal debtor are determined by the contract between them. If the surety is an absolute surety, then the creditor may hold the surety liable as soon as the principal debtor defaults. If the surety is a conditional guarantor of collection, he is liable only when the creditor exhausts his legal remedies against the principal debtor. The conditional guarantor is liable if the creditor obtains a judgment against the principal debtor and is unable to collect under the judgment. Surety and guarantor are used almost synonymously in common usage; however, strictly speaking, a surety is bound with the principal debtor as a primary obligor and usually on the same instrument, whereas the guarantor is separately or collaterally bound to pay if the principal debtor does not.

   1. Types of Sureties–A suretyship arrangement is frequently used by creditors seeking to reduce the risk of default by their debtors. The effect of the surety's promise is to give the creditor recourse for payment against two persons instead of one. A suretyship relation also arises when an owner of property subject to a mortgage sells the property to a purchaser who assumes the mortgage. By assuming the obligation, the purchaser becomes the principal debtor and is personally obligated to pay the seller's debt to the lender. The seller remains liable to the lender and is a surety on the obligation. If the purchaser takes the property subject to the mortgage, the purchaser is not a surety. There are numerous specialized kinds of suretyship including (1) fidelity, (2) performance, (3) official, and (4) judicial. Fidelity bonds are undertakings by a surety to protect an employer against the dishonesty of an employee. Performance bonds guarantee the performance of the terms and conditions of a contract. Statutes commonly require official bonds of a public officer for the faithful performance of duties; they obligate the surety for all losses caused by the officer's negligence or nonperformance of duties. Judicial bonds are provided on behalf of a party to a judicial proceeding to cover losses caused by delay or deprivation of property resulting from the institution of the action. In a criminal proceeding, the judicial bond is called a bail bond and is to assure the appearance of the defendant at court proceedings.

   2. Formation–The suretyship relationship is contractual and must satisfy the usual elements of a contract. Under the statute of frauds, the contractual promise of a surety to the creditor must be in writing to be enforceable. The writing requirement applies only to collateral promises. Under the main purpose doctrine, if the main purpose of the promisor (surety) is to obtain an economic benefit that he did not previously enjoy, then the promise is not within the statute of frauds. The promise of a surety is not binding without consideration. The surety's promise is usually supported by the same consideration that supports the principal debtor's promise, because the

surety's promise is made to induce the creditor to confer a benefit on the principal debtor. However, if the surety's promise is made after the principal debtor's receipt of the creditor's consideration, then the surety's promise must be supported by new consideration.

B. Rights of Surety–If the principal debtor defaults, the surety has a number of rights against the principal debtor, third parties and cosureties. These are: (1) exoneration, (2) reimbursement, (3) subrogation, and (4) contribution. A surety has no right to compel the creditor to collect from the principal debtor or to take action against collateral. Unless the suretyship contract so provides, the creditor is not required to give notice to the surety of the principal debtor's default.

1. Exoneration–The surety has the right to require that the principal debtor pay the creditor when the obligation is due. This right is called the right of exoneration and is enforceable at equity. The surety's remedy of exoneration does not affect the creditor's right to proceed against the surety. A surety also has a right of exoneration against his cosureties.

2. Reimbursement–When a surety pays the creditor on the default of the principal debtor, the surety has the right of reimbursement against the principal debtor. However, the surety has no right to reimbursement until he has actually made payment, and then only to the extent of payment.

3. Subrogation–Once the surety has paid the principal debtor's entire obligation, he "steps into the shoes" of the creditor. This is called subrogation and includes the creditor's rights: (1) against the principal debtor, including the creditor's priorities in a bankruptcy proceeding; (2) in security of the principal debtor; (3) against third parties, such as co-makers, who are also obligated on the principal debtor's obligation; and (4) against cosureties.

4. Contribution–When there is more than one surety, the cosureties are jointly and severally liable for the principal debtor's default up to the amount of each surety's undertaking. The creditor may proceed against any or all of the cosureties and collect the entire amount of the default from any of them, limited to the amount that surety has agreed to guarantee. When a surety pays the obligation of the principal debtor, she is entitled to have any cosureties pay to her their proportionate share of the obligation. This payment from cosureties of their proportionate share is known as contribution. The right and extent of contribution is determined by the contractual agreement among the cosureties. If there is no such agreement, sureties who are obligated for equal amounts, share equally. If X, Y and Z are cosureties for PD to C in the amounts of $5,000, $10,000 and $15,000 respectively (a total of $30,000), then X's share of the total is one-sixth ($5,000/$30,000), Y's share of the total is one-third ($10,000/$30,000), and Z's share is one-half ($15,000/$30,000).

C. Defenses of Surety–The usual contractual defenses are applicable. These could result from (1) the nonexistence of the principal debtor's obligation, (2) a discharge of the principal debtor's obligation, (3) a modification of the principal debtor's contract, or (4) a variation of the surety's risk.

1. Personal Defenses of Principal Debtor–Defenses that a principal debtor may assert against the creditor that are available only to him are called personal defenses of the principal debtor. The principal debtor's incapacity due to infancy or mental incompetence is a defense for the principal debtor but may not be used by the surety. A discharge of the principal debtor's obligation in bankruptcy does not discharge the surety's liability to the creditor on the obligation. The surety may not use as a set-off any claim that the principal debtor has against the creditor.

2. Personal Defenses of Surety–Defenses that only the surety may assert are called personal defenses of the surety. The surety may use as a defense his own incapacity, noncompliance with the statute of frauds, the absence of mutual assent or consideration to support his obligation. Fraud or duress practiced by the creditor is a defense for the surety. If the surety requests information before agreeing to become a surety, the creditor must disclose it. The concealment of material facts constitutes fraud. If the creditor knows, or should know, that the surety is being deceived, then the creditor is under a duty to disclose the information. Nondisclosure is considered fraud. Fraud by the principal debtor may not be asserted against the creditor if the creditor is not aware of it. Similarly, duress by the principal debtor on the surety is not a defense against the creditor. If an intended cosurety does not sign, then the surety is not liable. Claims that the surety has against the creditor may be set off against the creditor, unless the creditor is insolvent in which case the surety may only do so if the principal debtor is also insolvent. If the principal debtor and the creditor modify the contract without the surety's assent, then the surety is discharged. If the creditor releases or impairs the value of the security, the surety is discharged to the extent of the value of the security that has been released or impaired. Similarly, if the creditor releases a cosurety, the other cosureties are discharged to the extent of the contributive share of the surety released.

3. Defenses of Both Surety and Principal Debtor–Some defenses are available to both the surety and the principal debtor. These include forgery of the debtor's signature on an instrument, fraud or duress by the creditor on the principal debtor, the fraudulent material alteration of the contract by the creditor, the absence of mutual assent or consideration to support the obligation of the principal debtor, illegality and impossibility of performance of the principal debtor's contract, the creditor's release of the principal debtor, and the creditor's refusal to accept the tender of payment or performance by either the principal debtor or the surety.

KEY TERMS

1. Surety

2. Cosureties

3. Absolute surety

4. Conditional guarantor of collection

5. Fidelity bond

6. Performance bond

7. Official bond

8. Judicial bond

9. Bail bond

10. Exoneration

11. Reimbursement

12. Subrogation

13. Contribution

TRUE/FALSE

_____ 1. A fidelity bond guarantees the performance of the terms and conditions of the contract.

_____ 2. As the obligations a surety owes to the creditor arise from law, the usual legal defenses apply.

_____ 3. A surety who is liable to a creditor immediately upon the default of the principal debtor is an absolute surety.

_____ 4. A surety who is required to pay the creditor has fulfilled his contractual obligation and has no recourse against the principal debtor.

_____ 5. If there is no agreement otherwise, sureties obligated for equal amounts share equal liability.

_____ 6. Carl Contractor signs a suretyship agreement that contains both his name and that of Bill Businessman as sureties. Carl is under the impression at the time of signing that both he and Bill will be cosureties on the agreement. However, Bill changes his mind and never signs it. Carl is not liable even though he has signed the instrument.

_____ 7. Belinda Businesswoman is a conditional guarantor of collection on a note to First Bank on which Donald Debtor is the principal debtor. Belinda will only be liable when First Bank obtains a judgment against Donald and is unable to collect that judgment.

_____ 8. Bill Businessman is an absolute surety on a note to First Bank on which Donald Debtor is the principal debtor. If Donald defaults on the note because he doesn't feel like paying it, then Bill can sue in equity to obtain a court decree ordering Bill to pay First Bank. However, even if Bill obtains the court decree, he may still have to pay First Bank on Donald's behalf.

_____ 9. If a purchaser takes property subject to a mortgage, he becomes a surety for the mortgage obligation.

_____ 10. The creditor may proceed against any or all cosureties and collect the entire amount from any of them, because they are jointly and severally liable for the principal debtor's default limited only by the amount each has agreed to guarantee.

_____ 11. A suretyship agreement need not be in writing to be enforceable.

_____ 12. An official bond is to assure the appearance of the defendant in court.

_____ 13. A suretyship arrangement is frequently used by creditors to reduce the risk of default by their debtors.

_____ 14. The promise of a surety is binding without consideration.

_____ 15. If the principal debtor owes several debts to the creditor and makes a payment without specifying the debt to which it should apply, the creditor _must_ apply the payment to the most recent obligation.

MULTIPLE CHOICE

_____ 1. Upon the surety's payment of the principal debtor's entire obligation, the surety obtains all of the rights the creditor has against or through the principal debtor. The term for the surety's "stepping into the shoes" of the creditor is known as:
a. exoneration.
b. reimbursement.
c. subrogation.
d. contribution.

_____ 2. Which of the following would be considered to be types of sureties?
a. Fidelity bond.
b. Performance bond.
c. Judicial bond.
d. All of the above.

_____ 3. David agreed to loan Elvis $5,000 for his construction business for which Elvis signed a promissory note. One week later, David heard that Elvis's business was in trouble and that he might have problems repaying the loan. As a result of having heard this information, David asked Fred to guarantee the loan. Fred gave a glowing oral endorsement of Elvis and of Elvis's business and then orally promised to pay the $5,000 if Elvis did not. Fred added that he has done business with Elvis for five years and that Elvis buys all of his supplies from Fred's lumberyard. Is Fred's agreement to pay the $5,000 if Elvis does not enforceable?
a. Yes, because it was made freely and without coercion.
b. No, because the statute of frauds requires that the suretyship agreement be in writing.
c. Yes, because even though the statute of frauds applies, the main purpose rule exception will probably make the agreement enforceable.
d. No, because there is no consideration for Fred's promise.

_____ 4. Harold, Ike and John are cosureties for Keith to Lyle in the amounts of $10,000, $15,000 and $25,000 respectively. What proportion of the remaining debt must Harold contribute in the event that Keith defaults on the obligation owed to Lyle?
  a. One-tenth.
  b. One-fifth.
  c. One-fourth.
  d. One-third.

_____ 5. Alfred approached Bradley to borrow $15,000. Bradley demanded that Alfred obtain a surety and Clarence agreed to act as one. If Alfred defaults, which of the following defenses could Clarence raise?
  a. Alfred's fraud in securing Clarence as a surety.
  b. Alfred's having tendered payment to Bradley which Bradley refused to accept.
  c. Alfred's insolvency at the time the loan was made.
  d. The fact that Alfred furnished no consideration to Clarence for agreeing to act as a surety.

_____ 6. Which of the following is correct with regard to subrogation?
  a. A surety cannot use it to assert the creditor's rights against cosureties.
  b. A surety cannot use it against the principal debtor to assert the creditor's priorities in bankruptcy.
  c. It arises only if it is given to a surety in a written suretyship agreement.
  d. It permits the surety to assert rights that he would not otherwise be able to raise.

_____ 7. Which of the following is not a personal defense of the principal debtor?
  a. His incapacity due to infancy or mental incompetence.
  b. Noncompliance with the statute of frauds.
  c. His discharge in bankruptcy.
  d. Any set-off claim that he may have against the creditor.

_____ 8. First Bank induces Carl Contractor to act as a surety for Donald Debtor based upon false representations of material fact made to Carl that First Bank knew were false and that Carl justifiably relied upon.
  a. Donald may use the false representations as a defense.
  b. Carl may use the false representations as a defense.
  c. Both Donald and Carl may use the false representations as a defense.
  d. Neither Donald nor Carl may use the false representations as a defense.

_____ 9. The right of a surety to be relieved of her obligation by having the principal perform the obligation is known as:
   a. exoneration.
   b. reimbursement.
   c. subrogation.
   d. contribution.

_____ 10. Steven is the surety on a loan that Thomas made to Vincent. Which of the following is correct with regard to Steven's legal relationship to Thomas and Vincent?
   a. If Vincent defaults and Steven pays, Steven is entitled to be subrogated to the rights of Thomas but does not have the right to reimbursement from Vincent.
   b. Steven is a fiduciary to Thomas.
   c. Steven has the right of exoneration against Thomas.
   d. Steven has the right of contribution from Thomas.

_____ 11. The _____ is liable to a creditor immediately upon the default of the principal debtor.
   a. conditional guarantor of collection
   b. absolute surety
   c. cosurety
   d. none of the above

_____ 12. The suretyship relationship:
   a. requires consideration.
   b. is contractual.
   c. must be in writing to be enforceable.
   d. all of the above.

_____ 13. Caldwell Corporation applies to First Bank for a loan. The bank refuses to extend credit unless Samuels, the sole shareholder, promises to repay the loan if Caldwell does not. Samuels is a:
   a. surety.
   b. principal debtor.
   c. creditor.
   d. none of the above.

_____ 14. Which of the following defenses would be available to a surety?
   a. The nonexistence of the principal debtor's obligation.
   b. A discharge of the principal debtor's obligation.
   c. A variation of the surety's risk.
   d. All of the above.

_____ 15. Which of the following would be a defense available to a surety?
   a.   The principal debtor's obligation has been discharged.
   b.   The principal debtor's contract has been modified.
   c.   The surety's risk has been materially altered.
   d.   All of the above.

SHORT ESSAY

1. Anita, Barbara and Clara are cosureties for Diane to Edward in the amounts of $10,000, $20,000 and $30,000 respectively. What is the contributive share of each in the event of Diane's default on the debt owed to Edward? Explain.

_____

_____

_____

_____

2. Harold was a surety for Ike to John in the amount of $20,000. On the due date for the repayment of the debt, Ike was unable to pay the $20,000. John then gave Ike a 60-day extension, but he failed to notify Harold of the extension, even though John knew where to reach him. At the end of the 60-day period, Ike was still unable to pay John. At that point, John sought payment from Harold. Discuss the effect of the extension on Harold as surety.

_____

_____

_____

_____

3. Harold was a surety for Ike to John in the amount of $20,000. On the due date for the repayment of the debt, Ike was unable to pay the $20,000. Harold was out of town on business at the time and did not return for six months. John now seeks payment from Harold, but Harold claims he has been discharged due to John's failure to notify him of the default in a timely manner. Is this a valid defense? Explain.

_____

_____

_____

_____

4. Identify the following types of sureties.
   a. Carl Contractor posts a bond to protect the state of Wisconsin from any losses that may result from his failure to complete the construction of a state highway in a timely fashion and according to the contract specifications.
   b. An accused burglar pays an insurance company $1,000 whereupon the insurance company posts $10,000 with the clerk of courts to assure the accused burglar will appear for his trial.
   c. Theresa is a teller at First Bank and handles large amounts of money for the bank on a daily basis. The bank pays a bonding company to protect it against any possible dishonesty on the part of Theresa and the other tellers.
   d. Paul is a paralegal for the law office of Swift and Swift. He is also a notary public. On becoming a notary, Paul paid an insurance company to furnish a bond to the secretary of state assuring his proper performance of his duties in the office of notary.

   _____
   _____
   _____
   _____

5. List and briefly describe the defenses of a surety.

   _____
   _____
   _____
   _____

Chapter 41
Bankruptcy

PURPOSE

Various solutions to the conflict between creditor rights and relief for the overburdened debtor have developed. These include voluntary adjustments and compromises requiring payment in installments over time. Other voluntary methods include compositions and assignments of assets by a debtor to a trustee or assignee for the benefit of creditors. However, the most adaptable and frequently employed method of debtor relief and the one that also affords some protection to creditors is a proceeding in a federal court under the federal bankruptcy laws. In this chapter, you study the various chapters of the U.S. Bankruptcy Code, as well as several forms of nonbankruptcy compromises to resolve conflicts among debtors and creditors.

CHAPTER CHECKPOINTS

After reading and studying this chapter, you should be able to:

1. Distinguish between Chapters 7, 11, 12, and 13 bankruptcy proceedings.

2. Discuss the administration of a bankruptcy case including the filing of a voluntary or involuntary petition, automatic stay, duties and powers of the trustee, and meetings of creditors.

3. Outline the steps involved in a Chapter 7 bankruptcy and identify property of the estate, assets which are exempt, the priority in which the debtor's debts will be paid from the estate, nondischargeable debts, and events that result in denial of the discharge.

4. Distinguish between a fraudulent transfer and a voidable preference.

5. List the various forms of nonbankruptcy compromises and distinguish them from the relief available under the Bankruptcy Code.

CHAPTER OUTLINE

I. Federal Bankruptcy Law–Bankruptcy legislation serves a dual purpose: (1) to bring about an equitable distribution of the debtor's property among creditors, and (2) to discharge the debtor from her debts and enable her to start afresh. The legislation also provides uniform treatment of similarly situated creditors, preserves existing business relations, stabilizes commercial usages, and brings about a speedy equitable distribution of the debtor's assets.

   A. Case Administration–Chapter 3–Chapter 3 of the Bankruptcy Code contains provisions dealing with the commencement of the case, the officers who administer the case, the meetings of creditors, and the administrative powers of the various officers.
      1. Commencement of the Case–The filing of a voluntary or involuntary petition begins the jurisdiction of the bankruptcy court and the operation of the bankruptcy laws.
         a. Voluntary Petitions–Any person eligible to be a debtor under a given bankruptcy proceeding may file a voluntary petition under that chapter. The debtor need not be insolvent to file the petition. Commencement of a voluntary case constitutes an automatic order for relief. The petition must include a list of all creditors (secured and unsecured), a list of all property owned by the debtor, a list of property claimed to be exempt, and a statement of the debtor's affairs.
         b. Involuntary Petitions–An involuntary petition in bankruptcy may be filed only under Chapter 7 for liquidation or Chapter 11 for reorganization. It may be filed: (1) by 3 or more creditors who have unsecured claims that total $10,000 or more, or (2) if there are fewer than 12 creditors of the debtor, by one or more creditors whose total claims equal $10,000 or more. If the debtor does not contest the petition, the court will enter an order for relief against the debtor. If the debtor opposes the petition, the court may enter an order of relief only if (1) the debtor is not paying his debts as they become due, or (2) within 120 days before the filing of the petition a custodian or receiver took possession of substantially all of the debtor's property to enforce a lien against it.
      2. Automatic Stays–The filing of a voluntary or involuntary petition operates as a stay against (prevents) attempts by creditors to begin or continue to recover claims against the debtor, to enforce judgments against the debtor, or to create or enforce liens against the debtor. The stay applies to both secured and unsecured creditors.
      3. Trustees–The trustee is the representative of the estate and has the capacity to sue and be sued.

Under Chapter 7, trustees are selected by a vote of the creditors; in chapter 11 proceedings the creditors may elect a trustee if the court orders the appointment of a trustee for cause; in chapters 12 and 13, the trustee is appointed. The trustee collects, liquidates, and distributes the debtor's estate under Chapter 7. The trustee may (1) use, sell, or lease property of the estate; (2) deposit or invest money of the estate; (3) employ attorneys, accountants, appraisers, or auctioneers; and (4) assume or reject any executory contract or unexpired lease of the debtor. Trustees under Chapters 11, 12, and 13 perform some but not all of the duties of a Chapter 7 trustee.

4. Meetings of Creditors–Within a reasonable time after relief is ordered, a meeting of creditors must be held. The debtor must appear and submit to examination by creditors and the trustee regarding his financial situation.

B. Creditors, the Debtor and the Estate–Chapter 5
1. Creditors–A creditor is any entity having a claim against the debtor. A claim is a right to payment.
   a. Proofs of Claim–If a creditor does not file a proof of claim in a timely manner, the debtor or trustee may file a proof of such claim. Filed claims are allowed unless an interested party objects. The court will not allow a claim that (1) is unenforceable against the debtor, (2) is unmatured, (3) may be offset against a debt, or (4) is for services of an insider or attorney in excess of the reasonable value of such services. An insider includes a relative or general partner of the debtor, a partnership in which the debtor is a partner, or a corporation in which the debtor is an officer, director, or person in control.
   b. Secured Claims–A secured claim is one with a lien on property of the estate of the debtor. It is unsecured to the extent that the value of the interest is less than the allowed amount of the claim.
   c. Priority of Claims–After secured claims have been satisfied, the remaining assets are distributed among creditors with unsecured claims. Certain classes of unsecured claims have priority, which means that they have the right to be paid in full before any distribution is made to claims of lesser rank. Each claimant within a priority class shares pro rata if the assets are not sufficient to satisfy all claims within that class. The following claims have priority in the following order: (1) expenses of administration of the debtor's estate; (2) unsecured claims of "gap" creditors, in an involuntary case; (3) unsecured claims of up to $4,000 for wages, salaries, or commissions earned within ninety days before the filing of the petition; (4) unsecured claims for contributions to employee benefit plans; (5) unsecured claims up to $4,000 for grain or fish producers against a storage facility; (6) unsecured claims up to $1,800 for consumer deposits; (7) alimony and support of a spouse or child; and (8) income, property, employment or excise taxes owed to governmental units.
   d. Subordination of Claims–In proper cases, the bankruptcy court can in its discretion apply equitable priorities. By applying the doctrine of subordination of claims, when the bankruptcy court has two claims of equal priority, it may pay one in full before paying anything on the other claim. Subordination is applied when allowing a claim in full would be unfair and inequitable to other creditors.
2. Debtors–The Bankruptcy Code explicitly subjects the debtor to specified duties while exempting some of his property and discharging most of his debts.

a. Debtor's Duties–The debtor must file a list of creditors, a schedule of assets and liabilities, and a statement of financial affairs. The debtor must cooperate with the trustee and surrender to her all property of the estate and all records relating to property of the estate.

b. Debtor's Exemptions–The Code specifically exempts certain property of the debtor from the bankruptcy proceedings, including: (1) up to $15,000 in equity in a residence or burial plot; (2) up to $2,400 in equity in one motor vehicle; (3) up to $400 for any particular item of household furnishings, goods or apparel; (4) up to $1,000 in jewelry; (5) property up to $800 plus any unused amount of the first exemption; (6) up to $1,500 in implements, professional books, or tools of the debtor's trade; (7) unmatured life insurance contracts owned by the debtor; (8) professionally prescribed health aids; (9) social security, veteran's, and disability benefits; (10) unemployment compensation; (11) alimony and support payments; (12) payments from pension, profit-sharing, and annuity plans; and (13) payments from a crime victim's reparation law, and up to $15,000, not including pain and suffering, from a personal injury award. The debtor has the option of using either the above exemptions from the Bankruptcy Code or the exemptions available under state law, but states may limit them to the exemptions provided by state law.

c. Discharge–Discharge relieves the debtor from liability for all dischargeable debts. However, certain debts are nondischargeable. A discharge voids any judgment obtained concerning that debt and operates as an injunction against the commencement or continuation of any action to recover that debt. The following debts of an individual are not dischargeable in bankruptcy: (1) certain taxes; (2) legal liabilities for money or property obtained by false pretenses; (3) legal liability for willful and malicious injuries to the person or property of another; (4) alimony and child support; (5) debts not scheduled, unless the creditor knew of the bankruptcy; (6) debts created by fraud or embezzlement while acting as a fiduciary; (7) student loans that first became due less than five years before the filing of the petition, unless the debt would impose undue hardship; (8) debts that could have been listed in a previous bankruptcy in which no discharge was issued; (9) consumer debts for luxury goods or services in excess of $1,000 per creditor if incurred within 60 days of the order for relief; (10) cash advances aggregating more than $1,000 obtained under an open-ended credit plan within 60 days before the order for relief; (11) liability for a judgment based upon operation of a motor vehicle while legally intoxicated; and (12) fines, penalties, or forfeitures owed to a governmental entity.

3. The Estate–The commencement of a bankruptcy case creates an estate consisting of all legal and equitable interests of the debtor in nonexempt property at that time. The estate also includes property acquired within 180 days after the filing of the petition, by inheritance, property settlement, divorce decree or from insurance. It includes property that the trustee recovers under powers (1) as a lien creditor, (2) to avoid voidable preferences, (3) to avoid fraudulent transfers, and (4) to avoid statutory liens.

a. Trustee as Lien Creditor–When the case commences, the trustee gains the rights and powers of any creditor with a judicial lien against the debtor that is returned unsatisfied, whether or not such a creditor exists. A judicial lien is a charge or interest in property to secure payment of a debt or performance of an obligation that is obtained by a judgment, levy or some other legal or equitable process. The trustee is an ideal creditor possessing every right and power conferred by the law of the state on its most favored creditor who has acquired a lien by legal or equitable proceedings. Thus, the trustee, as a hypothetical lien creditor, has priority over a creditor with a security interest that was not perfected when the bankruptcy petition was filed. A creditor with a purchase money security interest who files within the allowed grace period of the debtor's receiving the collateral will defeat the trustee.

  b. Voidable Preferences–The Bankruptcy Code invalidates certain preferential transfers. The trustee may recover any transfer of property of the debtor (1) to or for the benefit of a creditor; (2) for or on account of an antecedent debt owed by the debtor before the transfer was made; (3) made while the debtor was insolvent; (4) made on or within ninety days before the date of the filing of the petition; or, if the creditor was an "insider" within one year of the date of the filing of the petition; and (5) that enables such creditor to receive more than he would have received under Chapter 7. A transfer is any means, whether direct or indirect, voluntary or involuntary, of disposing of property or an interest in property, including the retention of title as a security interest. It is presumed the debtor has been insolvent on and during the ninety days immediately preceding the date of the filing of the petition. Insolvency is a financial condition where the sum of debts exceed the fair value of assets. Not all transfers made within ninety days of bankruptcy are voidable. Exception for pre-bankruptcy transfers include: (1) exchanges for new value, (2) enabling security interests, (3) payments in ordinary course, (4) consumer debts, and (5) alimony and support.

  c. Fraudulent Transfers–The trustee may avoid fraudulent transfers made on or within one year before the date of the filing of the petition. One type of fraudulent transfer consists of the debtor's transferring property with the actual intent to hinder, delay, or defraud any of her creditors. Another type is the transfer by the debtor of property for less than a reasonably equivalent consideration while she is insolvent or would become insolvent because of the transfer.

  d. Statutory Liens–A statutory lien is one that arises solely by statute and does not include a security interest or judicial lien. The trustee may avoid a statutory lien on property of the debtor if the lien (1) first becomes effective when the debtor becomes insolvent, (2) is not perfected or enforceable on the date of the filing of the petition against a *bona fide* purchaser, or (3) is for rent.

C. Liquidation–Chapter 7–The Bankruptcy Code has established two approaches to accomplishing its goals: liquidation and adjustment of debts. Chapter 7 uses liquidation, whereas Chapters 11, 12 and 13 use the adjustment of debts.

1. Proceedings–Chapter 7 proceedings apply to all debtors except railroads, insurance companies, banks, savings and loan associations, homestead associations and credit unions. Once a voluntary or involuntary petition has been filed, the court enters an order for relief and appoints an interim trustee who serves until a permanent trustee is selected by the creditors. Under Chapter 7, the trustee collects and reduces to money the property of the estate; accounts for all property received; investigates the financial affairs of the debtor; examines, and if appropriate, challenges proofs of claim; may oppose the discharge of the debtor; and makes a final report of the administration.

2. Dismissal–The court on its own motion, after notice and a hearing, may dismiss a case filed by an individual debtor whose debts are primarily consumer debts.

3. Distribution of the Estate–After the assets have been collected, the trustee distributes them to the creditors. If any remain, they are distributed to the debtor. The order of distribution is as follows: (1) secured creditors on their security interests; (2) creditors with priority in the order provided in the statute; (3) unsecured creditors who filed claims on time, or tardily if they did not have notice or actual knowledge of the bankruptcy; (4) unsecured creditors who filed claims late; (5) claims for fines, multiple, exemplary, or punitive damages; (6) interest at the legal rate from the date of the filing of the petition to all of the above claimants; and (7) the remainder, if any, to the debtor.

4. Discharge–A discharge under Chapter 7 relieves the debtor of all debts that arose before the date of the order for relief, except for those debts that are not dischargeable. After distribution of the estate, the court will grant the debtor a discharge unless the debtor (1) is not an individual, (2) has destroyed or falsified records, (3) has committed fraud, (4) has transferred property defrauding his creditors, (5) under Chapter 7 or 11 has been granted a discharge within 6 years, (6) has refused to obey a court order, (7) has failed to explain any losses of assets, or (8) has executed a waiver of discharge.

   A debtor will also be denied a discharge under Chapter 7 if she received a Chapter 12 or 13 discharge within the past six years unless payments under that Chapter's plan totaled at least (1) 100 percent of the allowed unsecured claims or (2) 70 percent of such claims and the plan was the debtor's best effort.

D. Reorganization–Chapter 11–Reorganization is the means by which a distressed business enterprise and its value as a going concern are preserved through the correction or elimination of factors causing the distress. Chapter 11 governs reorganization of eligible debtors, including partnerships, corporations, and individuals.

1. Proceedings–Any person who may be a debtor under Chapter 7 (except stockbrokers and commodity brokers) and railroads may be debtors under Chapter 11. Petitions may be voluntary or involuntary. Under the 1994 Reform Act qualifying small businesses may elect streamlined procedures designed to expedite the administration of Chapter 11. After the order for relief, a committee of unsecured creditors is appointed, consisting of persons who hold the seven largest unsecured claims against the debtor. The court may order the appointment of additional committees. The committee may with court approval employ attorneys, accountants, and other agents to perform services. The debtor remains in possession and management of the property of the estate unless the court orders the appointment of a trustee to operate the debtor's business. One important duty of a trustee is to file a plan or a report on why there will be no plan or to recommend conversion of the case to Chapter 7.

2. Plan of Reorganization–The debtor may file a plan at any time and has the exclusive right to file a plan during the 120 days after the order for relief, unless a trustee has been appointed. Then other parties in interest, including the trustee, or a creditors' committee may file a plan. A plan of reorganization must divide creditors' claims and shareholders' interests into classes, specify how each class will be treated, deal with each class equally, and provide adequate means for

implementing the plan. Information on the plan must be sent to each claim holder before the plan is accepted or rejected.

3. Acceptance of Plan–Each class of claims has the opportunity to accept or reject the proposed plan. A class of claims has accepted a plan if it has been accepted by creditors that hold at least two-thirds in amount and more than one-half in number of the allowed claims of such class. Acceptance of a plan by a class of interests requires acceptance by holders of at least two-thirds in amount of the allowed interests of such class.

4. Confirmation of Plan–A plan must be confirmed by the court before it is binding on any parties. The plan must meet the requirements of good faith, feasibility, cash payments to certain classes of creditors, and acceptance by at least one class of claims.

5. Effect of Reorganization–After confirmation, the plan binds the debtor and any creditor, equity security holder, or general partner of the debtor. After the entry of a final decree closing the proceedings, the debtor is discharged from all of its debts and liabilities that arose before the date of confirmation of the plan except as otherwise provided in the plan, order of confirmation, or the Bankruptcy Code.

E. Adjustment of Debts of a Family Farmer–Chapter 12–The purpose of Chapter 12 is to provide a proceeding for family farmers who do not qualify for Chapter 13 and find Chapter 11 overly burdensome. Family farmers are defined as individuals, or individuals and their spouses, who are engaged in farming and who receive 50 percent of their gross income from farming. A corporation or partnership may also qualify if additionally one family holds 50 percent of the stock or equity, and more than 80 percent of the assets of the corporation or partnership are related to the farming operation. By a "sunset" provision Chapter 12 will expire in 1998 unless Congress reenacts it. The provisions of Chapter 12 are based on and are substantially the same as those of Chapter 13.

F. Adjustment of Debts of Individuals–Chapter 13–This chapter permits an individual debtor to file a repayment plan that will discharge him from almost all of his debts when he completes his payments under the plan.

1. Proceedings–Chapter 13 provides for the adjustment of debts of an individual with regular income who owes liquidated, unsecured debts of less than $250,000 and secured debts of less than $750,000. Sole proprietorships are eligible, however partnerships and corporations are not. A Chapter 13 case may only be initiated by a voluntary petition. A trustee is appointed in every case.

2. The Plan–The debtor files the plan and may modify it at any time before confirmation. It must meet three requirements. It must (1) require the debtor to submit all or any portion of future earnings or income of the debtor, as is necessary for the execution of the plan, to the supervision and control of the trustee; (2) provide for full payment on a deferred basis of all claims entitled to a priority unless a holder of a claim agrees to a different treatment of such claim; and (3) if the plan classifies claims, it must provide the same treatment for each claim in the same class. The plan may not provide for payments over a period longer than three years, unless the court approves a longer period, not to exceed five years.

3. Confirmation–The plan will be confirmed by the court if the plan meets the following requirements: (1) the plan must comply with applicable law and be proposed in good faith; (2) the

value of the property to be distributed to unsecured creditors must be not less than would be paid them under Chapter 7; (3) either the secured creditors must accept the plan, or the plan must provide that the debtor will surrender to the secured creditors the collateral, or the plan must permit the secured creditors to retain their security interest and the value of the property to be distributed to them is not less than the allowed amount of their claim; (4) the debtor must be able to make all payments and comply with the plan; and (5) if the trustee or holder of an unsecured claim objects to the confirmation of the plan, then the plan must either provide for payment in full of that claim or provide that all the debtor's disposable income for three years apply to the payments under the plan.

4. Effect of Confirmation–The provisions of a confirmed plan, which vest in the debtor all property of the estate free and clear of any creditor's claim or interest for which the plan provides, bind the debtor and all other creditors. A play may be modified after confirmation at the request of the debtor, the trustee, or a holder of an unsecured claim.

5. Discharge–After a debtor completes all payments under the plan, the court will grant him a discharge of all debts except the nondischargeable debts for alimony, maintenance, and support and certain long-term obligations on which payments extend beyond the term of the plan. A debtor discharged under Chapter 13 is not subject to the limitation under Chapter 7 that prohibits a debtor from obtaining a discharge again under that chapter for six years. Even if all payments have not been made, the court may grant a "hardship discharge" if the debtor's failure to complete payments is due to circumstances for which the debtor should not justly be held accountable.

II. Creditors' Rights and Debtor Relief Outside of Bankruptcy–The rights and remedies of debtors and creditors outside of bankruptcy are principally governed by state law. Bankruptcy is often viewed as a last resort, and it is often in the best interests of both debtor and creditors to resolve their claims outside of bankruptcy.

A. Creditor's Rights–When a debtor fails to pay a debt, the creditor may file suit to collect the debt. The objective of a lawsuit is to obtain a judgment and to collect that judgment.

1. Prejudgment Remedies–Because litigation takes time, the creditor may use certain prejudgment remedies such as attachment to protect against the debtor's disposing of his assets. Attachment is the seizure of property to bring it under the custody of the court. Similar in purpose is the remedy of prejudgment garnishment, which is a proceeding by a creditor against a third person who owes money to the debtor.

2. Postjudgment Remedies–If the debtor still has not paid the claim, the creditor may proceed to trial and try to obtain a court judgment against the debtor. If the debtor does not voluntarily pay the judgment, the creditor can use postjudgment remedies to collect. A writ of execution is an order served by the sheriff upon the debtor demanding payment of a court judgment against the debtor. Nonexempt property seized by the sheriff may be advertised for sale and sold at a public sale under the writ of execution. If the proceeds of the sale do not produce sufficient funds to pay the judgment, the creditor may institute a supplementary proceeding to locate money or other property belonging to the defendant. The creditor may also proceed by garnishment against the debtor's employer or a bank in which the debtor has an account.

B. Debtor's Relief–There are inherent conflicts between creditors' rights and debtor relief, which include: (1) the right of diligent creditors to pursue their claims to judgment and to satisfy their judgments by sale of property to the debtor; (2) the right of unsecured creditors who have refrained from suing the debtor; and (3) the social policy of giving relief to a debtor who has contracted debts beyond his ability to pay and who may be confronted by a lifetime burden. Various forms of non-bankruptcy compromises have been developed to resolve these conflicts.

1. Compositions–A common law or nonstatutory composition is an ordinary contract or agreement between the debtor and her creditors under which the creditors receive a proportional part of their claims and the debtor is discharged from the balance of the claims. It requires the formalities of a contract.

2. Assignments for Benefit of Creditors–A common law or nonstatutory assignment for the benefit of creditors is a voluntary transfer by the debtor of some of his property to a trustee, who applies the property to the payment of all of the debtor's debts. The advantage of the assignment over the composition is that it prevents the debtor's assets from being attached or executed and halts the race of diligent creditors to attach. It does not require the consent of the creditors, and payment by the trustee of part of the claims does not discharge the debtor from the balance of them.

3. Statutory Assignments–Because assignments benefit creditors by protecting the debtor's assets from attachment, there have been statutory attempts to combine the idea of the assignment with a corresponding benefit to the debtor by discharging him from the balance of his debts. Since the United States Constitution prohibits a state from impairing the obligation of a contract between private citizens, it is impossible for a state to force all creditors to discharge a debtor on a *pro rata* distribution of assets, although the federal government does have such power and exercises it in the Bankruptcy Code.

4. Equity Receiverships–The receiver is a disinterested person appointed by the court who collects and preserves the debtor's assets and income and disposes of them at the direction of the court. The court may instruct her to (1) liquidate the assets by public or private sale; (2) operate the business as a going concern temporarily; or (3) conserve the assets until final disposition of the matter before the court. Petitions for appointment of a receiver will be granted when made by (1) a secured creditor seeking foreclosure of his security; (2) a judgment creditor after exhausting legal remedies to satisfy the judgment; or (3) a shareholder of a corporate debtor where it appears that the assets of the corporation will be dissipated by fraud or mismanagement. Insolvency is one of the factors considered by the court in appointing a receiver.

KEY TERMS

1. Voluntary petition

2. Involuntary petition

3. Automatic stay

4. Trustee

5. Claim

6. Insider

7. Secured claim

8. Priority

9. Subordination of claims

10. Discharge

11. Estate

12. Judicial lien

13. Voidable preference

14. Insolvency

15. Fraudulent transfer

16. Statutory lien

17. Liquidation

18. Reorganization

19. Adjustment of debts of a family farmer

20. Adjustment of debts of individuals

21. Attachment

22. Garnishment

23. Writ of execution

24. Composition

25. Assignment for benefit of creditors

26. Receivership

TRUE/FALSE

_____ 1. Federal bankruptcy law is generally superseded by state insolvency laws.

_____ 2. Chapter 13 of the Bankruptcy Code applies to individuals with regular income who owe liquidated, unsecured debts of less than $250,000 and secured debts of less than $750,000.

_____ 3. The jurisdiction of the bankruptcy court and the operation of the bankruptcy laws are commenced by the filing of a voluntary or involuntary petition.

_____ 4. The filing of a voluntarily or involuntary petition prevents creditors from enforcing judgments against the debtor.

_____ 5. As the representative of the estate, the trustee in bankruptcy has the capacity to sue or to be sued.

_____ 6. A secured creditor's claim is secured to the extent of the allowed amount of his claim, even if that amount exceeds the value of his interest in the debtor's property.

_____ 7. After creditors with secured claims and creditors with claims having a priority have been satisfied, creditors with allowed, unsecured claims share proportionately in any remaining assets.

_____ 8. The debtor's estate in bankruptcy includes any property received by the debtor by inheritance or as a beneficiary of a life insurance policy within one year after commencement of the case.

_____ 9. All transfers made by the debtor within ninety days of bankruptcy are voidable.

_____ 10. Any person who may be a debtor under Chapter 7 (except stockbrokers and commodity brokers), and railroads may be a debtor under Chapter 11.

_____ 11. Under Chapter 11, the debtor will remain in possession of and management of the property of the estate unless the court appoints a trustee, who then may operate the debtor's business.

_____ 12. A plan of reorganization under Chapter 11 need not be confirmed by the court to be binding on the parties.

_____ 13. Most bankruptcy petitions are filed involuntarily.

_____ 14. A plan under Chapter 13 will not be confirmed by the bankruptcy court if the value of the property to be distributed to unsecured creditors under the plan is less than they would receive under Chapter 7.

_____ 15. The trustee may avoid fraudulent transfers made within one year before the date of the filing of the petition.

MULTIPLE CHOICE

_____ 1. The Chapter of the Bankruptcy Code containing the provisions dealing with case administration is:
   a. Chapter 1.
   b. Chapter 3.
   c. Chapter 4.
   d. Chapter 5.

_____ 2. Chapter 7 of the Bankruptcy Code applies to which of the following debtors?
   a. Railroads.
   b. Insurance companies.
   c. Credit unions.
   d. None of the above.

_____ 3. Which of the following individual debts may be discharged in bankruptcy?
   a. Customs duties.
   b. Alimony and child support.
   c. Unsecured consumer loans.
   d. None of the above.

_____ 4. Which of the following is not a duty or power of a trustee under the Bankruptcy Code?
   a. To use, sell or lease property of the estate.
   b. To deposit or invest money of the estate.
   c. To conduct the affairs of the debtor's estate for the trustee's own benefit.
   d. To assume or reject any executory contract or unexpired lease of the debtor.

_____ 5. Under Chapter 3 of the Bankruptcy Code the filing of an involuntary petition operates as a stay against which of the following?
   a. Attempts by creditors to begin to recover claims against the debtor.
   b. Attempts by creditors to continue to recover claims against the debtor.
   c. The enforcement of judgments against the debtor.
   d. All of the above.

_____ 6. A creditor's claim will be denied by the bankruptcy court as that of an insider if the creditor is any of the following except:
   a. a general partner of the debtor.
   b. a partnership in which the debtor is a limited partner.
   c. a relative of the debtor.
   d. a corporation of which the debtor is a director.

_____ 7. Which of the following items of the debtor's property is exempted from the bankruptcy proceedings by the Bankruptcy Code?
   a. Social security benefits.
   b. Alimony.
   c. Unemployment compensation.
   d. All of the above.

_____ 8. Under the bankruptcy code, a trustee may recover property of the debtor which has been transferred in which of the following situations?
   a. Debtor purchases an automobile for $9000.
   b. Debtor makes a payment in the ordinary course of business.
   c. Debtor makes a payment on a $1000 obligation past due.
   d. Debtor purchases a refrigerator and grants seller a security interest which the seller perfects within one week.

_____ 9. The estate in bankruptcy includes property that the trustee recovers under his powers:
   a. as a lien creditor.
   b. to avoid a voidable preference.
   c. to avoid a fraudulent transfer.
   d. all of the above.

_____ 10. The trustee may avoid a fraudulent transfer made by the debtor on or within _____ before the date of the filing of the petition.
   a. 60 days
   b. 90 days
   c. 180 days
   d. one year

_____ 11. After distribution of the estate, the court will grant the debtor a discharge unless the debtor:
   a. is not an individual.
   b. has within 6 years before the bankruptcy been granted a discharge.
   c. has destroyed or falsified records.
   d. all of the above.

_____ 12. A court will confirm a plan of reorganization under Chapter 11 of the Bankruptcy Code only if it meets the requirements of the Code, including all of the following except:
   a. the plan must be accepted by all of the creditors.
   b. certain classes of creditors must have their allowed claims paid in full in cash immediately, or in some instances, upon a deferred basis.
   c. the court must find that the plan is feasible.
   d. the plan must have been proposed in good faith.

_____ 13. Under the exemptions found in the Bankruptcy Code, which of the following items may be kept by the debtor?
   a. $7,500 equity in property used as a residence.
   b. A $500 diamond ring.
   c. A $400 VCR.
   d. All of the above can be exempt from the bankruptcy proceeding and may be kept by the debtor.

_____ 14. Which of the following is a correct statement regarding the automatic stay?
   a. It permanently discharges the debtor's obligation to pay.
   b. It is discretionary with the court.
   c. It automatically comes into existence when the debtor's petition is filed.
   d. It applies only to unsecured creditors.

_____ 15. An agreement between the debtor and two or more of her creditors that each will take a portion of the claim as payment in full is a:
   a. composition.
   b. assignment for benefit of creditors.
   c. statutory assignment.
   d. None of the above.

SHORT ESSAY

1. Discuss the difference between voluntary and involuntary petitions in bankruptcy.

   _____
   _____
   _____
   _____

2. What is the effect of filing a petition in bankruptcy?

   _____
   _____
   _____
   _____

3. Distinguish between Chapters 7, 11, 12 and 13 bankruptcy.

   _____
   _____
   _____
   _____

4. Big Bucks, Inc. filed for bankruptcy. It has the following outstanding debts:

    Fees earned by the trustee in bankruptcy $6,000
    Fees earned by attorneys of the bankruptcy estate $3,000
    Unsecured claim for income tax $25,000
    Claim for $50,000 secured by inventory worth $10,000 $50,000
    Claim for wages of an employee earned within one
         month of filing the petition $1,500

    In what order will these claims be paid?

    _____
    _____
    _____
    _____

5. Identify and discuss briefly three nonbankruptcy forms of compromises that have been developed to provide relief to debtors.

    _____
    _____
    _____
    _____

Part VIII
Sample Examination

MULTIPLE CHOICE

_____ 1. Which of the following is NOT covered by Article 9 of the UCC?
   a. A mortgage on an office building.
   b. A mechanic's lien on a house.
   c. The cash purchase of a TV.
   d. None of the above are covered.

_____ 2. Andrew Attorney buys a set of tax books to include in his office library. He gives First Bank a security interest in the books in return for a $1,500 loan which he uses to purchase the books. Under Article 9 of the Code, the books would be classified as:
   a. consumer goods.
   b. equipment.
   c. inventory.
   d. fixtures.

_____ 3. Andrew Attorney buys a set of encyclopedias to include in his home library. He gives First Bank a security interest in the books in return for a $1,500 loan which he uses to purchase the books. Under Article 9 of the Code, the books would be classified as:
   a. consumer goods.
   b. equipment.
   c. inventory.
   d. fixtures.

_____ 4. Which of the following must be done in order for a security interest in goods to attach?
   a. The secured party must give value.
   b. The debtor must sign a security agreement which describes the goods.
   c. The debtor must retain possession of the goods.
   d. The secured party must properly file a financing statement.

_____ 5. Which of the following is/are necessary in a security agreement to create a security interest?
   a. Agreement must be in writing.
   b. Agreement must be signed by the debtor.
   c. Agreement must contain a reasonable description of collateral.
   d. All of the above.

_____ 6. In which of the following situations is a security interest automatically perfected?
   a. First Bank loans $1,000 to Harold Homemaker so that Harold may purchase a gold necklace for his wife which Harold then gives to her on their anniversary.
   b. . First Bank loans $1,000 to Harold Homemaker so that Harold may purchase a computer for his office which Harold then purchases and allows his secretary to use.
   c. First Bank files a financing statement covering the computer which Harold Homemaker purchased for his office.
   d. Harold Homemaker purchases a refrigerator and uses his bank credit card to finance it.

_____ 7. Bill Businessman grants a security interest in a Picasso painting to First Bank. In accordance with the loan agreement, the bank advances $5,000 to Bill. First Bank then files a financing statement. Six months later, Bill needs more money and goes to his friend David who owns an art gallery and deals in art. David advances $2,000 to Bill based on Bill's pledge of the painting.
   a. Both First Bank and David have a perfected security interest in the painting.
   b. First Bank has a perfected security interest, but David does not, because he has not filed a financing statement.
   c. The interest of First Bank has priority over that of David, because First Bank was the first to file or perfect its security interest.
   d. Two of the above are correct, (a) and (c).

_____ 8. First Bank loans Bill Businessman $1,500 so that Bill may purchase a personal computer and printer for his son Junior to use in writing term papers for school. Bill signs a financing statement which First Bank duly files. Junior never uses the computer so Bill puts an ad in the paper and sells it to Carol Consumer. If Bill defaults on the loan, which of the following is correct?
   a. The bank has a perfected security interest, because it has filed a financing statement.
   b. The bank has a perfected security interest, because it gave Bill the money to purchase an item of consumer goods, as a result of which its security interest is automatically perfected.
   c. As between the bank and Carol, Carol will prevail, because she is a buyer in the ordinary course of business.
   d. Two of the above are correct, (a) and (c).

_____ 9. First Bank loans Bill Businessman, $1,500 so that Bill may purchase a personal computer for his office secretary. Bill signs a financing statement which First Bank duly files. His secretary never uses the computer, so Bill puts an ad in the paper and sells it to Carol Consumer. If Bill defaults on the loan, which of the following is correct?
   a. The bank has a perfected security interest, because it has filed a financing statement.
   b. The bank has a perfected security interest, because it gave Bill the money to purchase the item.
   c. As between the bank and Carol, the bank will prevail and be able to repossess the computer, because it has a perfected security interest which it has filed, if it has not authorized the sale.
   d. Two of the above are correct, (a) and (c).

_____ 10. First Bank loans Bill Businessman $1,500 so that Bill may purchase a personal computer for his office secretary. Bill signs a financing statement which First Bank duly files within ten days. After Bill purchases the computer, he takes out a loan at Valley Bank, gives the computer as collateral and signs a financing statement, which Valley Bank then duly files. His secretary never uses the computer, so Bill puts an ad in the paper and sells it to Carol Consumer. If Bill defaults on the loans, which of the following is correct?
   a. Both First Bank and Valley Bank have perfected security interests in the computer, which is classified as noninventory collateral.
   b. First Bank has a perfected purchase money security interest while Valley Bank has only a perfected security interest.
   c. Both First Bank and Valley Bank have rights in the computer that are superior to those of Carol Consumer even if she had no knowledge of the two security interests.
   d. All of the above are correct.

_____ 11. First Bank loans Marlin, who is the owner of Marlin's Department Store, $15,000 so that he may purchase personal computers for the store's inventory. Marlin signs a financing statement which First Bank duly files before Marlin takes possession. After Marlin purchases the computers, he then goes to Valley Bank and takes out a loan for which he gives the computers as collateral. Marlin signs a financing agreement which Valley Bank then duly files. Later Carol Consumer comes into the store and purchases one of the computers. If Marlin defaults on the loans, which of the following is correct?
   a. First Bank and Valley Bank both have perfected security interests in the computers.
   b. First Bank has a purchase money security interest in inventory, which has priority over conflicting security interests if certain requirements have been met.
   c. Carol is a buyer in the ordinary course of business whose interest in the computer she purchased is superior to that of both First Bank and Valley Bank.
   d. All of the above are correct.

_____ 12. The right of a surety who has paid the creditor to be repaid by the debtor is:
   a. exoneration.
   b. reimbursement.
   c. subrogation.
   d. contribution.

_____ 13. Which Chapter of the Bankruptcy Code is available for adjustment of debts of a family farmer?
   a. Chapter 7.
   b. Chapter 9.
   c. Chapter 11.
   d. Chapter 12.

_____ 14. A trustee in bankruptcy may avoid a statutory lien on property of the debtor if which of the following is true with respect to the lien?
   a. It first becomes effective when the debtor becomes insolvent.
   b. It is for rent.
   c. Both (a) and (b).
   d. Neither (a) nor (b).

_____ 15. If the only nonexempt asset in a bankruptcy estate is a piece of equipment valued at $25,000, which of the following claims will be paid first by the trustee in bankruptcy?
   a. The wages, salaries and commissions earned by employees within ninety days before the filing of the petition and the cessation of a business.
   b. The necessary expenses of the trustee in administering the estate.
   c. Unsecured claims in the amount of $15,000.
   d. A claim of $15,000 by a bank and secured by the piece of equipment where the bank has duly filed a financing statement.

_____ 16. If the only nonexempt asset in a bankruptcy estate is a piece of equipment valued at $25,000, which of the following claims will be paid second by the trustee in bankruptcy?
   a. The wages, salaries and commissions earned by employees within ninety days before the filing of the petition and the cessation of the business.
   b. The necessary expenses of the trustee in the administration of the estate.
   c. Unsecured claims in the amount of $15,000.
   d. A claim of $15,000 by a bank and secured by the piece of equipment where the bank has duly filed a financing statement.

_____ 17. A company files for bankruptcy. Its only nonexempt asset is a piece of equipment valued at $25,000. The claims that have been approved by the trustee for payment are as follows:
   (1) $10,000 in wages, salaries and commissions earned by employees within ninety days before the filing of the petition and the cessation of the business.
   (2) $3,000 in expenses of the trustee in the administration of the estate.
   (3) Unsecured claims in the amount of $15,000.
   (4) A claim of $15,000 by a bank and secured by the piece of equipment where the bank has duly filed a financing statement.
   How much money will be available to pay the $10,000 claim of the employees?
   a. $15,000.
   b. $10,000.
   c. $7,000.
   d. No money will be left to pay the employees.

_____ 18. A company files for bankruptcy. Its only nonexempt asset is a piece of equipment valued at $25,000. The claims that have been approved by the trustee are as follows:

(1) $10,000 in wages, salaries and commissions earned by employees within ninety days before the filing of the petition and the cessation of the business.

(2) $3,000 in expenses of the trustee in the administration of the estate.

(3) Unsecured claims in the amount of $15,000.

(4) A claim of $15,000 by a bank and secured by the piece of equipment where the bank has duly filed a financing statement.

How much money will be available to pay the unsecured creditors?

a. $25,000.

b. $10,000.

c. $7,000.

d. No money will be available to pay the unsecured creditors.

_____ 19. Which of the following is/are required for the confirmation of a Chapter 11 plan?

a. Feasibility.

b. Cash payments to certain creditors.

c. Good faith.

d. All of the above.

_____ 20. Bill Businessman has an allowed claim of $5,000 against the bankruptcy estate of Donald Debtor. He has a valid security interest in a painting owned by Donald, which security interest is in the amount of $3,000 and which painting is valued by the trustee at $5,000.

a. Bill will probably receive nothing from the bankruptcy estate, because the priorities stated in the Bankruptcy Code will be paid before his claim.

b. Bill will probably receive the full $5,000 from the bankruptcy estate.

c. Bill will receive the $3,000 which is secured by the painting, but is a general creditor in the amount of $2,000 and may or may not receive that money from the estate.

d. Bill will probably receive nothing from the bankruptcy estate, because his claim is a voidable preference.

Chapter 42
Protection of Intellectual Property

PURPOSE

In this chapter, you study the law that has been developed to prevent businesses from taking unfair advantage of their competitors. An important part of this area of law involves the protection of intellectual property. Intellectual property includes trade secrets, trade symbols, copyrights, and patents. Businesses would be less willing to invest their resources in research and development unless the resulting discoveries, inventions, and processes were protected by patents and trade secrets. Similarly, business would not be secure in devoting time and money to the marketing of its products and services if its trade symbols and trade names were not protected. Without copyright protection, the publishing, entertainment, and computer software industries would be vulnerable. In this chapter, you study the law protecting (1) trade secrets; (2) trade symbols, which include trademarks, service marks, certification marks, collective marks, and trade names; (3) copyrights; and (4) patents.

CHAPTER CHECKPOINTS

After reading and studying this chapter, you should be able to:

1. Explain what is protected by trade secrets and how they may be infringed.

2. Distinguish among trademarks, service marks, certification marks, collective marks and trade names.

3. Discuss the extent to which trade names are protected.

4. Distinguish between a patent and a copyright and compare the protection given to each.

450

5. List and discuss the remedies for copyright infringement and those for patent infringement.

CHAPTER OUTLINE

A. Trade Secrets–Every business has secret information. This commercially valuable, secret information is considered a trade secret. Trade secrets include customer lists, contracts with suppliers and customers, secret formulas, processes, and methods used in the production of goods. Trade secrets are disclosed in confidence to employees with the understanding that the employee will not disclose the information. If a person misappropriates (wrongfully uses) a trade secret, the owner of the information may obtain damages, and where appropriate injunctive relief. Trade secrets are misappropriated in two ways: (1) an employee wrongfully uses or discloses it; or (2) a competitor wrongfully obtains it. An employee is under a duty of loyalty to his employer which includes the nondisclosure of trade secrets to competitors. In the absence of a contract restriction, after termination of employment, the employee may compete with his former employer, but he may not use trade secrets or disclose them to third persons. He is entitled to use skill, knowledge and general information acquired during the employment relationship. Industrial espionage by means of electronic surveillance, spies or discovery of trade secrets by means other than one's own independent research efforts or inspection of the finished product is improper unless the other party voluntarily discloses the secret or fails to take reasonable precautions to protect its secrecy.

B. Trade Symbols–One of the earliest forms of unfair competition was the fraudulent marketing of one person's goods as those of another referred to as "passing off" or "palming off." The Federal Trademark Act (the Lanham Act) provides protection against palming off, a practice which results in deception of the public and loss of trade by honest businesses by cashing in on the good name, goodwill and reputation of a competitor. This section also prohibits the false description or representation of a person's own goods or services. In 1988, the section was amended to prohibit misrepresentations of another's goods, services or commercial activities. The Lanham Act established a registration of trade symbols and protection against misuse or infringement by injunctive relief and the right of action for damages against an infringer.

1. Types of Trade Symbols–The Lanham Act recognizes four types of trade symbols or marks. A trademark is a distinctive mark, word, letter, number, design, picture, or combination in any form or arrangement that is adopted or used by a person to identify goods he manufactures or sells. A service mark is used to identify and distinguish the services of one person from those of another. The titles, character names, and other distinctive features of radio and television shows may be registered as service marks. A certification mark is a distinctive symbol, work, or design used with goods or services to certify specific characteristics. These characteristics include regional or other origin, material, mode of manufacture, quality, accuracy, or other characteristics. The owner of the certification mark need not be the producer or provider of the goods or services. A collective mark is a distinctive mark or symbol used to indicate either membership in a trade union, trade association, fraternal society, or other organization, or that the goods or services are produced by members of a collective group. The owner of a collective mark is the group to which the producer or provider belongs.

2. Registration–To be protected by the Lanham Act, a mark must be distinctive so that it identifies the origin of the goods or services. Marks that are fanciful or arbitrary satisfy the distinctiveness requirement. A word describing the ingredients, quality, purpose, function or uses of a product may not be monopolized as a mark. The word "Plow" cannot be a trademark for plows, but it may be one for shoes. To obtain federal protection, the mark must be registered with the Patent and Trademark Office. Registration gives nationwide constructive notice of the mark to all users, and it permits the registrant to use the federal courts to enforce it. The mark is *prima facie* evidence of the registrant's exclusive right to use it. To retain trademark protection an owner must not abandon the mark by failing to make bona fide use of it in the ordinary course of trade.

3. Infringement–Infringement occurs when a person without authorization uses an identical or substantially indistinguishable mark that is likely to cause confusion or mistake, or to deceive. Neither intent to cause confusion nor proof of actual confusion are required. If an appreciable number of ordinarily prudent purchasers are likely to be confused or misled, then infringement occurs. Courts consider the following factors in deciding whether infringement has occurred: the strength of the mark, the intent of the unauthorized user, the degree of similarity between the two marks, the relation between the two marks, the relation between the two products or services identified by the marks, and the marketing channels through which the goods or services are purchased.

4. Remedies– Remedies under the Lanham Act include: (1) injunctive relief, (2) an accounting for profits, (3) damages, (4) destruction of infringing articles; (5) attorney's fees in exceptional cases, and (6) costs. In assessing profits, the plaintiff need only prove the gross sales made by the defendant; the defendant must prove any costs to be deducted. The court may award an amount it determines to be just, and it may award up to three times the actual damages. When an infringement is knowing and intentional, the court shall award attorney's fees plus the greater of treble profits or treble damages, unless there are extenuating circumstances. Where a counterfeit mark is intentionally and knowingly used, criminal sanctions may be imposed which include a fine of up to $250,000 and/or imprisonment up to five years. The counterfeit goods may be destroyed. If the infringer is a corporation, the fine may be up to $1 million for the first offense and up to $5 million for a repeat offense.

C. Trade Names–A trade name is any name used to identify a business, vocation, or occupation. Descriptive and generic words, and personal and generic names may become protected as trade names upon acquiring a special significance in the trade. This special significance is referred to as "secondary meaning." Although trade names may not be federally registered under the Lanham Act, they are protected, and a person who palms off his goods or services is liable in damages and may be enjoined from doing so.

D. Copyrights–A copyright is the exclusive right to original works of authorship. Under the Federal Copyright Act, original works which can be protected include literary works, musical works, dramatic works, pantomimes, choreographic works, pictorial, graphic and sculptural works, motion pictures and other audiovisual works, sound recordings and architectural works. This list is not exhaustive, as under the act copyright protection is available for "original works of authorship in any tangible medium of expression, now known or later developed." In 1980, the Copyright Act extended protection to computer programs. Copyright protection cannot be obtained for any idea, procedure, process, system, method of operation, concept, principle, or discovery. Copyright protection extends only to an original expression of an idea.

1. Procedure–Registration of the copyright is not required as copyright protection begins as soon as a work is fixed in a tangible medium. Registration is advisable, because it is a condition of certain remedies for copyright infringement. Applications are filed with the Register of Copyrights, Copyright Office, Library of Congress, Washington, D.C. When a work is published, a notice of copyright should be placed on all publicly distributed copies to give reasonable notice of the claim.

2. Rights–In most instances, copyright protection continues for the period of the author's life plus an additional fifty years. The Copyright Act gives the owner of the copyright the exclusive right, and to authorize others, to reproduce the work, prepare derivative works, distribute copies or recordings, perform the work publicly, and display the work publicly. These broad rights are subject to "compulsory licenses" and "fair use." Compulsory licenses permit certain limited uses of copyrighted materials upon the payment of specified royalties and compliance with statutory conditions. Under the act, the fair use of a copyrighted work for purposes such as criticism, comment, news reporting, teaching, scholarship, or research is not an infringement of the copyright. The following factors are used in determining whether a particular case is a fair use: (1) the purpose and character of the use including whether such use is of a commercial nature or is for nonprofit educational purposes; (2) the nature of the copyrighted work; (3) the amount and substantiality of the portion used in relation to the work as a whole; and (4) the effect of the use upon the potential market for or value of the work.

3. Ownership–The ownership of a copyright may be transferred in whole or in part by conveyance, will, or intestate succession. A transfer of copyright ownership is not valid unless there is a note or memorandum of the transfer in writing and signed by the owner of the rights or by the owner's authorized agent. An author may terminate any transfer of copyright ownership, other than a work for hire, if timely done. Ownership of a copyright or of the exclusive rights under a copyright is distinct from ownership of a material object in which the work is embodied. The purchase of a textbook does not affect the publisher's copyright, nor does it authorize the purchaser to make and sell copies of the book.

4. Infringement and Remedies–Infringement occurs when someone without authorization exercises the rights exclusively reserved for the owner. To prove infringement, the plaintiff must establish that he owns the copyright and that the defendant violated one or more of his exclusive rights under the copyright. The copyright must be registered in order to sue for infringement unless the work is a Berne Convention work and the country of origin is not the United States. If an infringement occurs after registration, the following remedies are available: (1) injunction, (2) impoundment and possible destruction of the infringing articles, (3) actual damages plus profits made by the infringer in addition to the statutory damages of at least $500, but no more than $20,000 and up to $100,000 if the infringement is willful, (4) costs and, in the court's discretion, reasonable attorney's fees to the prevailing party, or (5) criminal penalties for willful infringement for purposes of commercial advantage or private gain of up to $10,000 or up to one year in prison. For large-scale piracy, the Piracy and Counterfeiting Amendments Act of 1982 imposes

harsher punishments of up to $250,000 in fines and five years in prison for pirating 1,000 recordings or 65 films within 180 days.

E. Patents–A patent is a grant to the inventor by the federal government of the exclusive right to make, use, or sell the invention for the period of the patent, which is currently fourteen years for design patents and seventeen years for all others. The owner may license others to use the patent on a royalty basis. However, the patent may not be renewed. Upon its expiration, the invention enters the "public domain" and anyone may use it.

1. Patentability–Under the Patent Act, any new and useful process, machine, manufacture, or composition of matter, or any new and useful improvement thereof may be patented. Naturally occurring substances, laws of nature, principles, systems of bookkeeping, fundamental truths, methods of calculation, and ideas are not patentable. Computer programs are not patentable, but may be copyrighted. To be patentable, the process, machine, manufacture, or composition of matter must have three criteria: (1) novelty, (2) utility, and (3) nonobviousness.

2. Procedure–A patent is issued by the United States Patent and Trademark Office based on a patent application that contains a "specification" describing how the invention works, and "claims" describing the features of the invention that make it patentable. The applicant must be the inventor. The Patent Office then makes an examination and determines whether the submitted invention has novelty (does not conflict with a prior pending application or issued patent), utility, and is nonobvious. A patent application is confidential, but the confidentiality ends upon the granting of the patent. The applicant may apply for reexamination if the application is rejected, and if the application is rejected again, the applicant may appeal to the Patent and Trademark Office's Board of Appeals. From there, appeal is to the federal courts.

3. Infringement–A direct infringer is anyone who makes, uses or sells a patented invention without permission. Good faith or ignorance is not a defense to direct infringement. An indirect infringer is a person who actively encourages another to make, use or sell a patented invention without permission. A person is a contributory infringer if he knowingly sells or supplies a part or component of a patented invention, unless the item supplied is a staple or commodity or it is suitable for noninfringing use. Good faith and ignorance are defenses to contributory infringement.

4. Remedies–Under the Patent Act, remedies include: (1) injunctive relief, (2) damages adequate to compensate the plaintiff but "in no event less than a reasonable royalty for the use made of the invention by the infringer", (3) treble damages when appropriate, (4) attorney's fees in exceptional cases such as knowing infringement, and (5) costs.

KEY TERMS

1. Infringement

2. Trade secret

3. Misappropriate

4. Mark

5. Trademark

6. Service mark

7. Certification mark

8. Collective mark

9. Secondary meaning

10. Trade name

11. Copyright

12. Compulsory license

13. Fair use

14. Patent

15. Direct infringer

16. Indirect infringer

17. Contributory infringer

TRUE/FALSE

_____ 1. The granting of a patent guarantees the patentee the exclusive right to make, use, or sell his invention for the period of the patent.

_____ 2. The owner of a certification mark must be the producer or provider of the mark.

_____ 3. Copyright protection may be used to protect an original idea or concept.

_____ 4. Under the "fair use" doctrine, use of a copyrighted work for teaching is an infringement.

_____ 5. Tel-Ko Computer Company has been having problems with competitors copying and selling its computer software. Computer software may be copyrighted.

_____ 6. Tel-Ko Computer Company has invented a new and innovative personal computer. A computer may be copyrighted.

_____ 7. In order to recover statutory damages and attorney's fees for copyright infringement, the work must be registered.

_____ 8. The "Underwriter's Laboratory" symbol is an example of a collective mark.

_____ 9. The Lanham Act provides protection against the palming off of another's goods as one's own.

_____ 10. Edward has worked as an engineer in the product development department of Tel-Ko Computer Company. Edward may quit the Tel-Ko job and then sell to Tel-Ko's competitors the secret information he has learned in his job.

_____ 11. The fraudulent marketing of one person's goods as those of another is known as "palming off."

_____ 12. Infringement of a mark may occur even in the absence of intent to cause confusion among purchasers.

_____ 13. If a person misappropriates a trade secret, the owner of the information may obtain damages.

_____ 14. Copyright protection lasts for a period of the author's life plus seventy years.

_____ 15. Compulsory licenses permit certain limited uses of copyrighted material upon payment of specified royalties and compliance with statutory conditions.

MULTIPLE CHOICE

_____ 1. A _____ is often used to identify a provider's services.
   a. trademark
   b. service mark
   c. collective mark
   d. certification mark

_____ 2. To obtain federal protection, a mark must be registered and the registrant must:
   a. have actually used the mark.
   b. have demonstrated a bona fide intent to use the mark in commerce and actually use it within six months.
   c. either (a) or (b).
   d. neither (a) nor (b).

_____ 3. "Kodak," "Nylon," and "Coke" are examples of:
   a. trade names.
   b. service marks.
   c. trademarks.
   d. copyrights.

_____ 4. Which of the following items would not be patentable?
   a. A computer.
   b. A genetically engineered bacterium.
   c. An idea such as Einstein's formula $E = MC^2$.
   d. A process by which to manufacture a new product.

_____ 5. The Lanham Act provides criminal sanctions for intentionally and knowingly using a counterfeit mark of up to five years in prison and up to:
   a. $25,000.
   b. $150,000.
   c. $200,000.
   d. $250,000.

_____ 6. Who grants a patent?
   a. The United States Patent and Trademark Office.
   b. The Secretary of State of the state where the inventor resides.
   c. The Federal Trade Commission.
   d. The Library of Congress.

_____ 7. The big "G" on a box of General Mills breakfast cereal is an example of a:
   a. service mark.
   b. copyright.
   c. collective mark.
   d. trademark.

_____ 8. Belinda Businesswoman photocopies ten copies of an article from the _Wall Street Journal_ and distributes them at the weekly management meeting of the Tel-Ko Computer Company management team. Which of the following is correct with regard to the copyright on the article which is held by the _Wall Street Journal?_
   a. Belinda has probably infringed the copyright if she neglected to obtain the permission of the _Wall Street Journal._
   b. Copyright protection does not extend to newspaper articles.
   c. This is probably the fair use of the copyrighted article which is not an infringement.
   d. Belinda appears to have violated the Piracy and Counterfeiting Amendments Act of 1982.

_____ 9. The "REAL" symbol used to identify genuine dairy products is an example of a:
   a. trademark.
   b. service mark.
   c. collective mark.
   d. certification mark.

_____ 10. To register a mark with the Patent and Trademark Office an applicant must:
   a. have actually used the mark in commerce.
   b. demonstrate a bona fide intent to use the mark in commerce and actually use it within six months.
   c. both (a) and (b).
   d. either (a) or (b).

_____ 11. If Jons, a famous musician, wants to protect one of his original works, he should use a:
   a. patent.
   b. copyright.
   c. trade name.
   d. trademark.

_____ 12. Marriott has a distinctive mark which is used to identify its hotels. This is an example of a:
   a. copyright.
   b. collective mark.
   c. service mark.
   d. certification mark.

_____ 13. Trade secrets are misappropriated by:
   a. an employee wrongfully using or disclosing it.
   b. a competitor wrongfully obtaining it.
   c. a competitor obtaining it by independent research efforts.
   d. two of the above are correct, (a) and (b).

_____ 14. Which of the following remedies are provided by the Lanham Act for infringement of a mark?
   a. Destruction of infringing articles.
   b. An accounting for profits.
   c. Both a and b.
   d. Neither a nor b.

_____ 15. If Bobby actively encourages Tel-Ko Company to make a machine and he knows it is a patented item and they do not have permission, Bobby is:
   a. an indirect infringer.
   b. a direct infringer.
   c. a contributory infringer.
   d. none of the above.

SHORT ESSAY

1. If registration of a copyright is not necessary and copyright protection begins as soon as the work is fixed in a tangible medium, what is the advantage in registering it?

_____

_____

_____

_____

2. Define the four types of trade symbols recognized by the Lanham Act.

_____

_____

_____

_____

3. What factors are considered in determining whether use made of a work is a "fair use"?

_____

_____

_____

_____

4. Mark, a salesman for Tel-Ko Computer Company, resigns from his job. He then accepts employment with CompCo, a competitor of Tel-Ko. Mark provides a list of Tel-Ko's customers to CompCo which he had obtained as an employee of Tel-Ko. What is the result?

_____

_____

_____

_____

5. What remedies are available for infringement of trade symbols?

_____

_____

_____

_____

Chapter 43
Antitrust

PURPOSE

Free and fair competition in industry and trade have historically been the backbone of our free enterprise system. However, with the concentrations of economic power created by the combining of forces within the business world, the need for government regulation has become increasingly apparent. With the growth of big business in the last half of the nineteenth century, the federal government came to the aid of state lawmakers in controlling business operations to assure free and fair competition. The Sherman Antitrust Act, enacted in 1890, was the first such legislative action taken by Congress. This act sought to control unfair competition by prohibiting contracts, combinations, and conspiracies that restrain trade as well as monopolies, attempts to monopolize, and conspiracies to monopolize. Other statutes in the field followed, including the Clayton Act, the Robinson-Patman Act, and the Federal Trade Commission Act. These statutes further regulated anticompetitive practices. This chapter discusses these acts and their implications regarding business practices. You will examine the various rights protected by federal legislation and the remedies provided upon infringement of fair competition.

CHAPTER CHECKPOINTS

After reading and studying this chapter, you should be able to:

1. Discuss the Sherman Antitrust Act and its rules governing trade restraints and monopolization.

2. Discuss the Clayton Act and its rules governing (a) tying contracts, (b) exclusive dealing, and (c) mergers.

3. Discuss the Robinson-Patman Act and the various defenses to it.

4. Distinguish between horizontal and vertical restraints and discuss when they are legal and when they are illegal.

5. Discuss the role of the FTC and Justice Department in antitrust enforcement.

CHAPTER OUTLINE

A. Sherman Antitrust Act–Section 1 of the Sherman Act prohibits contracts, combinations, and conspiracies that restrain trade. Section 2 outlaws monopolies and attempts to monopolize. Failure to comply with either section is a crime. Individual offenders are subject to three years in prison and/or fines of up to $350,000. Corporate offenders are subject to fines of up to $10,000,000. Federal courts have the power to issue injunctions to restrain violations. A person injured by a violation may sue in a civil suit for treble damages, which are three times the actual loss sustained. The United States Department of Justice and the Federal Trade Commission have the duty to institute appropriate enforcement proceedings. Since 1992 the Justice Department also considers conduct by foreign companies that harm U.S. exports.

   1. Restraint of Trade–Section 1 of the Sherman Act provides that "every contract, combination in the form of trust or otherwise, or conspiracy, in restraint of trade or commerce among the several states, or with foreign nations is hereby declared to be illegal."

      a. Standards–The courts have interpreted Section 1 to invalidate only unreasonable restraints of trade. This standard is known as the rule of reason test; it requires that a court balance the anticompetitive effects of an agreement against the procompetitive effects of the restraint. Because this standard places a substantial burden upon the judicial system, the U.S. Supreme Court declared that certain categories of restraints are unreasonable and thus illegal *per se*. In such a case, the plaintiff is required to show only that the type of restraint occurred and does not need to prove that it limited competition.

      b. Horizontal and Vertical Restraints–Restraints may be classified as either horizontal or vertical. A horizontal restraint involves collaboration among competitors at the same level in the chain of distribution. An agreement among manufacturers would be horizontal as would an agreement among retailers. A vertical restraint is one that is made by parties that are not in direct competition at the same level of distribution. An agreement between a manufacturer and a wholesaler would be vertical. Horizontal market allocations are illegal *per se*, whereas vertical market allocations are subject to the rule of reason.

      c. Concerted Action–Section 1 does not prohibit unilateral conduct, only concerted action. Concerted action by express agreement or by circumstantial evidence may be established. Conscious parallelism in the form of similar patterns of conduct among competitors is not sufficient in itself to infer a conspiracy in violation of Section 1 without an additional factor.

      d. Price Fixing–Price fixing is an agreement with the purpose or effect of inhibiting price competition; it can involve raising, depressing, fixing, pegging, or stabilizing prices. It is the primary and most serious *per se* violation under the Sherman Act. All horizontal price-fixing agreements are illegal *per se*. Retail price maintenance is a vertical form of price fixing in which the wholesaler fixes the prices at which its purchasers must resell the product; it is a *per se* violation of Section 1. The prohibition against price fixing covers any agreement between sellers to establish maximum as well as minimum prices.

e. Market Allocations–In market allocation, competitors agree not to compete with each other in specified markets. These markets may be defined by geographic area, type of customer, or class of product. All horizontal agreements to divide markets are illegal *per se*, because their effects give monopoly power in that market to the remaining firm which can control price. Vertical territorial and customer restrictions are no longer illegal *per se* but are judged by the rule of reason. In 1985, the U.S. Department of Justice issued a "market structure screen" which it uses in determining whether vertical territorial restrictions are in compliance with the rule of reason.

f. Boycotts–The refusal of a seller to deal with any particular buyer does not violate the act, because the Sherman Act does not apply to unilateral action. Thus, a manufacturer can refuse to sell to a retailer who persists in selling below the manufacturer's suggested retail price. On the other hand, group boycotts are prohibited, because they are a concerted refusal to deal. A boycott is an agreement among parties not to deal with a third party. Some group boycotts are illegal *per se*, while others are subject to the rule of reason.

g. Tying Arrangements–A tying arrangement is one in which the sale of a desired product (the tying product) is conditioned upon the buyer's purchasing of a second product (the tied product). An example would be if the manufacturer of photocopying equipment required that all purchasers of its photocopiers also purchase from it all of the paper they will use with the copier. Because these arrangements limit the freedom of choice of buyers and may exclude competitors, the law closely scrutinizes tying arrangements. A tying arrangement exists where a seller exploits its economic power in one market to expand its empire to another market. When the seller has considerable economic power in the tying product or when a substantial amount of interstate commerce in the tied product is affected, the tying arrangement is *per se* illegal. If the seller lacks economic power, the tying arrangement is judged by the rule of reason.

2. Monopolies–According to economic analysis, a monopolist uses its power to limit production and increase prices. A monopolistic market produces fewer goods at a higher price than a competitive market. Section 2 prohibits monopolies, attempts to monopolize, and conspiracies to monopolize. Unlike Section 1, it also prohibits unilateral action by one firm.

a. Monopolization–Although the language of Section 2 appears to prohibit all monopolies, the courts have required either the unfair attainment of the monopoly power or the abusive use of that power once attained in addition to the mere possession of market power. Monopoly power is the ability to control price or exclude competitors from the marketplace; the issue of monopoly power involves defining what degree of market dominance constitutes monopoly power. Market share, which is the fractional share of the total relevant product and geographic markets possessed by a firm, is the most common test of monopoly power. The relevant product market includes products that are substitutable for the firm's product on the basis of price, quality and adaptability for other purposes. The relevant geographic market is the territory in which the firm sells its products or services; it may be local, regional or national depending upon the product. Both monopoly power and unfair conduct must be shown for a firm to violate Section 2. Three different approaches have been used by the courts to determine what constitutes unfair conduct. There is no definitive answer to the basic question of what conduct, beyond the mere possession of monopoly power, violates Section 2.

    b. Attempts to Monopolize–Section 2 also prohibits attempts to monopolize. The standard test requires proof of a specific intent to monopolize plus a dangerous probability of success, but this standard leaves unanswered such questions as what constitutes an attempt to monopolize and how much power must be achieved.

    c. Conspiracies to Monopolize–Conspiracies to monopolize which generally constitute a combination in restraint of trade are a violation of Section 2 as well as Section 1.

B. Clayton Act–Congress strengthened the Sherman Act by adopting the Clayton Act in 1914. It was expressly designed "to supplement existing laws against unlawful restraints and monopolies." The Act only provides for civil actions which may be brought either by private parties in federal court for treble damages and attorneys' fees or by the Justice Department and the Federal Trade Commission to prevent and restrict violations of the act. The major provisions of the Clayton Act deal with price discrimination, tying contracts, exclusive dealing and mergers.

    1. Tying Contracts and Exclusive Dealing–Section 3 of the Clayton Act prohibits tying arrangements and exclusive dealing, selling, or leasing arrangements that prevent purchasers from dealing with the seller's competitors where the effect may be to substantially lessen competition or tend to create a monopoly. It is intended to attack practices before they ripen into violations of Section 1 or 2 of the Sherman Act. Section 3 applies only to practices involving commodities. Exclusive dealing arrangements are agreements by which the seller or lessor of a product conditions the agreement upon the buyer's or lessee's promise not to deal in goods of a competitor. For example, a manufacturer of razors might require that retailers who wish to sell its line not carry competing merchandise.

    2. Mergers–Mergers may be classified as horizontal, vertical, or conglomerate. A horizontal merger involves the acquisition by one company of all or part of the stock or assets of a competing company. A vertical merger is the acquisition by a company of one of its customers or suppliers. It is a forward merger if the acquiring company purchases a customer; it is a backward merger if the acquiring company purchases a supplier. A conglomerate merger is an acquisition that does not involve a competitor, customer, or supplier. Section 7 of the Clayton Act prohibits the merger or acquisition by a corporation of stock or assets of another corporation where the effect may be to substantially lessen competition or tend to create a monopoly. The principal objective of antitrust law governing mergers is to maintain competition. Horizontal mergers are scrutinized most carefully. The courts consider various factors in reviewing the legality of each type of merger.

    3. Interlocking Directorates–Section 8 of the Clayton Act prohibits interlocking directorates in competing corporations engaged in interstate commerce where the combined capital of the corporations exceeds a stated amount ($10,000,000 in 1990). Since the prohibition is only in competing corporations, it does not apply to directors serving on vertically associated boards.

C. Robinson-Patman Act–The Robinson-Patman Act amended the Clayton Act to prohibit buyers from inducing and sellers from granting price discrimination in interstate commerce of commodities of similar grade and quality. The price discrimination must substantially lessen competition or tend to create a monopoly to be a violation. Under this act, sellers are prevented from granting discounts to buyers, unless the same discounts are offered to all other purchasers on proportionately equal terms. The act imposes liability on the buyer as well as the seller by making it unlawful for a person to knowingly "induce or receive" an illegal discrimination in price. Violations are civil rather than criminal wrongs. Price differentials are permitted when justified by proof of either a cost savings to the seller or a good faith price reduction to meet the lawful price of a competitor.

1. Primary-Line Injury–Injuries accruing to sellers' competitors are called "primary-line" injuries. The Act forbids price discrimination only where the effect is to lessen competition or create a monopoly. Thus the plaintiff must show that the defendant, with intent to harm competition, engaged in predatory pricing or present a detailed market analysis that demonstrates how the defendant's price discrimination actually harmed competition.

2. Secondary-Line Injury–Involves discounts granted to large buyers. To prove the required harm to competition, a plaintiff must either show substantial and sustained intra-market price differentials or offer a detailed market analysis that demonstrates actual harm to competition.

3. Cost Justification–If a seller can show that it costs less to sell a product to a particular buyer, the cost savings may be lawfully passed along. Calculating and proving such savings is difficult.

4. Meeting Competition–A seller may lower his price in a good faith attempt to meet competition. This defense may be used if a seller does not know the competitor's price, cannot reasonably determine it, and acts reasonably in setting its own price.

D. Federal Trade Commission Act–In 1914, Congress enacted the Federal Trade Commission Act, creating the Federal Trade Commission (FTC), which is charged with the duty of preventing unfair methods of competition and unfair or deceptive acts or practices in commerce. The five-member commission is empowered to conduct appropriate investigations and hearings. It may issue cease and desist orders which have the effect of injunctions and which are enforceable in the federal courts against violators. It may also order other relief, such as affirmative disclosure, corrective advertising, and the granting of licenses to patents on a reasonable royalty basis. The FTC investigates possible violations of the antitrust laws and also unfair methods of competition.

KEY TERMS

1. Treble damages

2. Rule of reason

3. Illegal *per se*

4. Horizontal restraints

5. Vertical restraints

6. Conscious parallelism

7. Price fixing

8. Retail price maintenance

9. Market allocation

10. Boycott

11. Tying arrangement

12. Monopoly power

13. Market share

14. Exclusive dealing arrangement

15. Horizontal merger

16. Vertical merger

17. Forward merger

18. Backward merger

19. Conglomerate merger

20. Price discrimination

21. Cease and desist order

TRUE/FALSE

_____ 1. Agreements between parties at the same level in the chain of distribution are horizontal restraints of trade.

_____ 2. Section 1 violations of the Sherman Act require at least two parties.

_____ 3. Justice Department enforcement efforts under the Sherman Act extend to foreign companies that harm U.S. exports.

_____ 4. While the Sherman Act prohibits sellers' agreements to establish minimum prices, sellers are free to agree to establish maximum prices.

_____ 5. All vertical price-fixing agreements are illegal _per se_.

_____ 6. Because of their tendency to exclude competitors from the market, all tying arrangements have been declared illegal _per se_.

_____ 7. Under the Robinson-Patman Act, liability may be imposed upon buyers as well as sellers.

_____ 8. Exclusive dealing arrangements are agreements by which the seller or lessor of a product conditions the agreement upon the buyer's or lessor's promise not to deal in the goods of a competitor.

_____ 9. A good faith price reduction to meet the price of a competitor is a defense to a charge of price discrimination under the Robinson-Patman Act.

_____ 10. A vertical merger occurs when a wholesale manufacturer acquires a retail outlet for its products by way of merger.

_____ 11. The Federal Trade Commission was established to prevent unfair methods of competition in commerce.

_____ 12. The Clayton Act prohibits every contract, combination, or conspiracy in restraint of trade.

_____ 13. Retail price maintenance is a horizontal form of price fixing.

_____ 14. A manufacturer who refuses to sell to a retailer who persists in selling below the manufacturer's suggested retail price is a boycott and violates the Sherman Act.

_____ 15. The possession of monopoly power is a violation of Section 2 of the Sherman Act.

MULTIPLE CHOICE

_____ 1. Sherman Act corporate offenders are subject to fines up to:
   a. $350,000.
   b. $500,000.
   c. $1,000,000.
   d. $10,000,000.

_____ 2. The rule of reason test is used to determine the legality of:
   a. horizontal price-fixing agreements.
   b. vertical territorial and customer restrictions.
   c. horizontal market allocation agreements.
   d. retail price maintenance agreements.

_____ 3. A company is not in possession of monopoly power if its share of the market is:
   a. 100%.
   b. 85%.
   c. 75%.
   d. 50%.

_____ 4. Labor unions are exempted from the antitrust laws by:
  a. the Sherman Act.
  b. the Clayton Act.
  c. the Robinson-Patman Act.
  d. the FTC Act.

_____ 5. If a seller fixes the price at which its purchasers must resell its product this would be:
  a. horizontal price fixing.
  b. vertical price fixing.
  c. conscious parallelism.
  d. none of the above.

_____ 6. A person who knowingly induces or receives an illegal discrimination in price has violated:
  a. the Sherman Act.
  b. the Clayton Act.
  c. the Robinson-Patman Act.
  d. none of the above.

_____ 7. A corporation which acquires the stock of another corporation where the effect may be substantially to lessen competition between the two corporations has violated:
  a. the Sherman Act.
  b. the Clayton Act.
  c. the Robinson-Patman Act.
  d. the FTC Act.

_____ 8. A company which engages in unfair methods of competition has violated:
  a. the Sherman Act.
  b. the Clayton Act.
  c. the Robinson-Patman Act.
  d. the FTC Act.

_____ 9. Which one of the following is not a _per se_ violation of the Sherman Act?
  a. Price fixing.
  b. Horizontal market allocation.
  c. Vertical market allocation.
  d. Group boycotts.

_____ 10. A _____ merger involves the acquisition by a company of all or substantially all or part of the stock or assets of a competing company.
  a. horizontal
  b. vertical
  c. conglomerate
  d. monopolistic

_____ 11. If RAC and Sonny, both manufacturers of color televisions, agree that RAC shall have the exclusive right to sell color televisions in Illinois and Iowa and that Sonny shall have the exclusive right in Minnesota and Wisconsin, they have committed a violation of:
   a.   the Clayton Act.
   b.   the Sherman Act.
   c.   the FTC Act.
   d.   none of the above.

_____ 12. Which of the following demonstrates economic power in determining whether a tying arrangement exists?
   a.   A dominant position in the tying market.
   b.   An advantage not shared by competitors in the tying market.
   c.   A substantial number of customers have accepted the tying arrangement.
   d.   Any of the above.

_____ 13. If IBM purchased a manufacturer of microchips, this would be:
   a.   a vertical merger.
   b.   a horizontal merger.
   c.   a conglomerate merger.
   d.   none of the above.

_____ 14. The Federal Trade Commission can:
   a.   issue cease and desist orders.
   b.   conduct investigations.
   c.   order corrective advertising.
   d.   all of the above.

_____ 15. Sellers of goods are prevented from granting discounts to buyers unless the same discounts are offered to all other purchasers on proportionately equal terms under the:
   a.   Sherman Act.
   b.   Clayton Act.
   c.   Robinson-Patman Act.
   d.   FTC Act.

SHORT ESSAY

1.   What is the purpose of the federal antitrust statutes?

_____

_____

_____

_____

2. According to economic theory, how does a monopolistic market differ from a competitive market?

_____

_____

_____

_____

3. Discuss the Robinson-Patman Act and defenses to it.

_____

_____

_____

_____

4. Discuss the Clayton Act.

_____

_____

_____

_____

5. Disco is a discount chain store that sells goods below the manufacturers' suggested retail prices. X, Y, and Z, three large manufacturers, agree that they will not sell to Disco unless Disco stops its discount pricing. If Disco refuses and sues X, Y, and Z because they will not sell to Disco, what is the result?

_____

_____

_____

_____

Chapter 44
Consumer Protection

PURPOSE

Historically, consumers were subject to the rule of *caveat emptor* or "let the buyer beware." However, in recent years, the law has abandoned this principle in consumer transactions and today gives greater protection to consumers in the form of federal and state statutes. A consumer transaction is one involving goods, credit, services, or land acquired for personal, household, or family purposes. In this chapter, you study the most important consumer protection statutes and the governmental agencies charged with enforcement of these statutes.

CHAPTER CHECKPOINTS

After reading and studying this chapter, you should be able to:

1. Discuss the role of the Federal Trade Commission (FTC) in consumer protection and list the remedies used by this agency.

2. Discuss the purpose and authority of the Consumer Product Safety Commission.

3. List the principle provisions of the Magnuson-Moss Warranty Act and distinguish between a full and limited warranty.

4. Summarize the major provisions of the Equal Credit Opportunity Act, the Federal Consumer Credit Protection Act, the Truth-in-Lending Act, the Fair Credit Billing Act, the Credit Card Fraud Act, the

Real Estate Settlement Procedures Act, the Fair Credit Reporting Act, and the Fair Debt Collection Practices Act.

5. Distinguish between an open-ended credit account and a closed-ended credit account.

CHAPTER OUTLINE

A. State and Federal Consumer Protection Agencies–Legislatures and administrative bodies at the federal, state, and local levels actively seek to protect consumers through the enactment of laws and regulations.

    1. State and Local Consumer Protection Agencies–These agencies deal with fraudulent and deceptive trade practices and fraudulent sales practices and help consumers resolve complaints about defective goods or poor service.

    2. The Federal Trade Commission–In 1914, Congress established the Federal Trade Commission (FTC) and charged it with the duty to prevent unfair methods of competition in commerce and unfair or deceptive trade practices in commerce. It has the power to issue substantive rules, to conduct appropriate investigations and hearings, and to issue cease and desist orders.

        a. Standards–The FTC has issued three policy statements. The first one dealt with the meaning of unfairness and applies a cost-benefit analysis. The second statement dealt with the meaning of deception and provides that it is a misrepresentation, omission or practice that is likely to mislead the consumer acting reasonably in the circumstances, to the consumer's detriment. The third statement involved ad substantiation and requires that advertisers have a reasonable basis for their claims at the time their claims are made.

        b. Remedies–The FTC has three additional remedies. Affirmative disclosure is frequently employed by the FTC and requires the offender to provide certain information in its advertisement so that it is not deceptive. Corrective advertising requires disclosure in an advertisement that previous ads were deceptive. Multiple product orders require the deceptive advertiser to cease and desist from deceptive statements on all products it sells.

    3. The Consumer Product Safety Commission–The Consumer Product Safety Act (CPSA) established a federal agency, the Consumer Product Safety Commission (CPSC). The CPSC can set safety standards for consumer products; ban unsafe products; issue administrative "recall" orders to compel repair, replacement, or refunds for products that present hazards; and seek court orders to require recall of "imminently hazardous" products.

    4. Other Federal Consumer Protection Agencies–Other federal agencies that play a major consumer protection role are the National Highway Traffic Safety Administration (NHTSA), which sets safety standards for motor vehicles to address crash prevention and crashworthiness, and the Food and Drug Administration (FDA), which sets standards for products or requires premarket approval of products to regulate adulterated and misbranded products.

B. Consumer Purchases–A number of laws protect consumers in their purchases. The UCC is the basic building block of laws that protect consumers, but there is also common law and federal and state statutes.

1. Federal Warranty Protection–In 1974 Congress enacted the Magnuson-Moss Warranty Act, which requires that sellers of consumer products give adequate information about warranties. The FTC administers and enforces the act. The act applies to consumer products with written warranties. A consumer product is any item of tangible personal property that is normally used for family, household, or personal use and that is distributed in commerce.

    a. Presale Disclosures–The act contains presale disclosure provisions intended to prevent confusion and deception and to enable purchasers to make educated personal comparisons. A person making a warranty must fully and conspicuously disclose in simple language the terms and conditions of such warranty.

    b. Labeling Requirements–The second major part of the act contains labeling requirements in which written warranties are divided into two categories–limited and full. A full warranty is one under which the warrantor will repair the product and, if unsuccessful, will replace or refund. No limitation may be placed on the duration of any implied warranty by a full warranty. A limited warranty is any warranty not designated as full.

    c. Limitations on Disclaimers–The act provides that a written warranty may not disclaim any implied warranty. A full warranty must not disclaim, modify, or limit any implied warranty, and a limited warranty may not disclaim or modify any implied warranty but may limit its duration to that of the written warranty.

2. State "Lemon Laws"–State legislatures have enacted lemon laws that attempt to provide rights to new car purchasers that are similar to full warranties under the Magnuson-Moss Warranty Act. A lemon is a car that continues to have a defect substantially impairing the use, value, or safety of a car after a reasonable number of attempts by the manufacturer to repair the defect. These laws require the manufacturer to repair the defect. These laws require the manufacturer to replace the car or refund the retail price, less an allowance for the use of the car.

3. Consumer Right of Rescission–Rescission is the right to cancel a contract. In most cases, a consumer is legally obligated once he has signed a contract. However, in many states, statutes allow a consumer a brief period (usually two or three days) in which to rescind an otherwise binding credit obligation if the solicitation occurred in his home. The FTC also has a trade regulation that applies to door-to-door sales of goods and services for more than $25 and that allows a consumer to rescind the contract within three days of signing regardless of whether the sale is for cash or on credit. The Federal Consumer Credit Protection Act (FCCPA) allows a consumer three days to withdraw from any credit obligation secured by a mortgage on his home, unless the credit was used to acquire the dwelling. The Interstate Land Sales Full Disclosure Act requires the developer of unimproved land to file a detailed statement of record with information about subdivisions with the Department of Housing and Urban Development before offering the lots for sale or lease and to provide a property report to each prospective purchaser or lessee. The contract may be revoked at the option of the purchaser within seven days. If the property report is not given to the purchaser before signing the contract, the purchaser has two years to revoke.

C. Consumer Credit Transactions–In the absence of special regulation, consumer credit transactions are governed by laws regulating commercial transactions generally. A consumer credit transaction is any credit transaction involving goods, services, or land acquired for personal, household, or family purposes. Regulation of consumer credit has increased due to the dramatic expansion and the numerous abuses in credit transactions. In response, Congress passed the Federal Consumer Credit Protection Act (FCCPA) in 1968 which requires disclosure of finance charges, credit extension charges, and sets limits on garnishment proceedings. Also in 1968, the National Conference of Commissioners on Uniform State Laws promulgated the Uniform Consumer Credit Code (UCCC) which integrated into one law the regulation of all consumer credit transactions.

1. Access to the Market–The Equal Credit Opportunity Act prohibits all businesses that regularly extend credit from discriminating in extending credit on the basis of sex, marital status, race, color, religion, national origin, or age. The FTC has overall enforcement authority.

2. Disclosure Requirements–Title One of the FCCPA is known as the Truth-in-Lending Act. It has superseded state disclosure requirements relating to credit terms for consumer loans and credit sales under $25,000. An important requirement in the act is that sales finance and interest rates must be quoted in terms of an APR (annual percentage rate) and must be calculated on a uniform basis. The Federal Reserve Board issued Regulation Z to carry out its enforcement and interpretation of the act. Congress passed the Fair Credit and Charge Card Disclosure Act of 1988 which adds to the Truth-in-Lending Act requiring all credit and charge card applications and solicitations to include extensive disclosures.

    a. Credit Accounts–Under the Truth-in-Lending Act, a creditor must inform consumers who open revolving or open-ended credit about how the finance charge is computed, when it is charged, what other charges may be imposed, and whether a security interest is retained. An open-end credit account is one that permits the debtor to enter into a series of credit transactions that he may pay off in installments or in a lump sum, such as store credit cards, Visa and MasterCard. Closed-ended credit is credit extended for a specified period of time during which periodic payments are generally made in an amount and at a time agreed on in advance.

    b. ARMs–The ARM disclosure rule applies to any loan that is (1) a closed-end consumer transaction, (2) secured by the consumer's principal residence, (3) longer than one year in duration, and (4) subject to interest rate variation. Disclosures required must be made when a creditor furnishes an application to a prospective borrower or before the creditor receives payment of a nonrefundable fee, whichever occurs first.

    c. Home Equity Loans–The 1988 Home Equity Loan Consumer Protection Act (HELCPA) requires lenders to provide a disclosure statement and consumer pamphlet to a prospective consumer borrower. The Act applies to all open-end credit plans to be secured by the consumer's principal dwelling. The disclosure statement must include a statement that (1) a default on the loan may result in the consumer's loss of the dwelling, (2) some conditions must be met, and (3) the creditor may, under certain circumstances terminate the plan and accelerate the outstanding balance, prohibit further extension of credit, reduce the plan's credit limit, or impose fees upon the termination of the account. Regulation Z provides the consumer with the right to rescind such a plan until midnight on the third day following the opening of the plan, until delivery of a notice of the right to rescind, or until delivery of all material disclosures, whichever comes last.

  d. Billing Errors–The 1975 Fair Credit Billing Act sets forth procedures for the consumer to follow in making complaints about specified errors in billing. The Real Estate Settlement Procedures Act (RESPA) provides consumers who purchase a home with greater and more timely information on the nature and cost of the settlement process and protects them from unnecessarily high settlement charges. The act prohibits kickbacks and referral fees. It is administered by the Secretary of Housing and Urban Development.

3. Contract Terms–Contract documents are frequently printed forms containing blank spaces to be filled in by the creditor at the time of the extension of credit. Standardization facilitates transfer of the rights of the creditor to a third party. Almost all states impose statutory ceilings on the amount that may be charged for the extension of consumer credit. Most statutes require a creditor to permit the debtor to pay the obligation in full at any time before the date of maturity. The FTC has adopted a rule that limits the rights of a holder in due course of an instrument evidencing a debt that arises out of a consumer credit contract. A similar rule applies to credit card issuers under the Fair Credit Billing Act.

4. Consumer Credit Card Fraud–In 1984 Congress enacted the Credit Card Fraud Act which prohibits possessing unauthorized cards, counterfeiting credit cards, using account numbers alone, and using cards obtained from a third party with his consent. The FCCPA provides protection to the credit card holder from loss by limiting the card holder's liability for unauthorized use of a credit card to $50.

5. Fair Reportage–In 1970 Congress enacted the Fair Credit Reporting Act, which applies to consumer reports used for purposes of securing employment, insurance, and credit. The act prohibits inaccurate or specified obsolete information in consumer reports. Agencies must give written advance notice to consumers that a report may be made. The consumer may request information in the agency's files. If the consumer notifies the agency of disagreement with the accuracy and completeness of information in the file, the agency must reinvestigate the latter. The consumer may submit a brief statement to be incorporated into the report.

6. Creditors' Remedies–The creditor may impose a delinquency charge for late payments. If the consumer defaults, the creditor may declare the entire balance immediately due and payable and may sue on the debt.

  a. Wage Assignments and Garnishment–Some states prohibit wage assignments. Under the FCCPA and the laws of most states, a limitation is imposed on the amount that may be deducted per pay period. The FCCPA prohibits discharge of an employee solely because a creditor uses a wage assignment.

  b. Security Interest–In the case of credit sales, the seller may retain a security interest in the goods sold. Where the debt is secured by property as collateral, the creditor, on default of the debtor, may take possession of the property and either retain it in full satisfaction of the debt or sell it. If the proceeds are less than the debt, the creditor can sue for the balance.

  c. Debt Collection Practices–In 1977 Congress enacted the Fair Debt Collection Practices Act to eliminate abusive, deceptive, and unfair practices in collecting consumer debts by debt collection agencies. The act is enforced by the FTC, and consumers may recover damages from the collection agency for violations.

KEY TERMS

1. Cease and desist order

2. Affirmative disclosure

3. Corrective advertising

4. Multiple product order

5. Warranty

6. Consumer product

7. Full warranty

8. Limited warranty

9. Consumer credit transaction

10. APR

11. Open-ended credit

12. Closed-ended credit

TRUE/FALSE

_____ 1. The Food and Drug Administration is the oldest federal consumer protection agency.

_____ 2. Under Federal Trade Commission standards, deception may occur through either false representations or material omissions.

_____ 3. Under the Magnuson-Moss Warranty Act, a written warranty may disclaim or modify any implied warranty.

_____ 4. A contract subject to the Interstate Land Sales Full Disclosure Act must clearly provide that the contract may be revoked at the option of the purchaser within two years of signing the contract.

_____ 5. Violators of the Equal Credit Opportunity Act are subject to civil actions to recover actual and punitive damages.

_____ 6. The Federal Trade Commission has as one of its responsibilities the enforcement of rules to prevent unfair business practices by interstate moving companies.

_____ 7. The Fair Credit Billing Act requires creditors to explain or correct billing errors.

_____ 8. Most states impose statutory ceilings on the amount that may be charged for the extension of' consumer credit.

_____ 9. Under the Fair Credit Reporting Act, a consumer is entitled to read and copy all information pertaining to him in the consumer reporting agency's files.

_____ 10. The Consumer Product Safety Commission has authority to ban unsafe products.

_____ 11. The Fair Debt Collection Practices Act prohibits debt collection conduct by debt collectors other than the creditor that is harassing, oppressive, or abusive.

_____ 12. Corrective advertising is a disclosure in an advertisement that previous ads were deceptive.

_____ 13. Deception may occur by a misrepresentation, but not by a material omission.

_____ 14. The FTC ad substantiation policy requires that advertisers have a reasonable basis for their claims at the time their claims are made.

_____ 15. State legislatures have enacted lemon laws that attempt to provide rights to used car purchasers.

MULTIPLE CHOICE

_____ 1. Today, most consumer protection takes the form of statutory enactments. Which of the following normally initiates complaints?
   a. The FTC.
   b. The injured party.
   c. The attorney general of the state in which the injured party resides.
   d. Any of the above.

_____ 2. To justify a finding of unfairness, the injury must satisfy which of the following standards?
   a. Unfairness.
   b. Deception.
   c. Ad substantiation.
   d. All of the above.

_____ 3. Under the Magnuson-Moss Warranty Act, a seller may disclaim any and all implied warranties if:
   a. he gives no written warranty.
   b. the product is for personal use only.
   c. the product costs $10 or less.
   d. none of the above.

_____ 4. Under the FTC's door-to-door sales rule, a consumer may only revoke a door-to-door sales contract if:
   a. the sale is on credit.
   b. any credit obligation he incurs pursuant to the contract is secured by a mortgage on his home.
   c. the sale is for $25 or more.
   d. it is within 5 days.

_____ 5. Which of the following acts requires a creditor, within thirty days of receiving an application for credit, to notify the applicant of action taken and to provide specific reasons for a denial of credit?
   a. Consumer Credit Protection Act.
   b. Equal Credit Opportunity Act.
   c. Fair Credit Reporting Act.
   d. Fair Credit Billing Act.

_____ 6. The Equal Credit Opportunity Act prohibits businesses that regularly extend credit from discriminating in extending credit on the basis of:
   a. sex.
   b. marital status.
   c. age.
   d. all of the above.

_____ 7. Under the Consumer Credit Protection Act, sales finance charges and interest rates must be quoted in terms of:
   a. add-ons.
   b. discounts.
   c. annual percentage rates.
   d. none of the above.

_____ 8. Which of the following laws prohibits kickbacks and referral fees with respect to federally related mortgage loans?
   a. Interstate Land Sales Full Disclosure Act.
   b. Real Estate Settlement Procedures Act.
   c. Fair Credit Billing Act.
   d. Consumer Credit Protection Act.

_____ 9. Which of the following was the Consumer Product Safety Act enacted to accomplish?
   a. To protect the public against unreasonable risk of injury.
   b. To assist consumers in evaluating the comparative safety of consumer products.
   c. To develop uniform safety standards.
   d. All of the above.

_____ 10. The FTC is charged with which of the following major functions?
    a. To prevent unfair methods of competition.
    b. To prevent unfair and deceptive trade practices.
    c. To prevent mail fraud operations.
    d. (a) and (b) but not (c).

_____ 11. Under the _____, a consumer is allowed three days during which to withdraw from any credit obligation secured by a mortgage on his home, unless the extension of credit was made to acquire the dwelling.
    a. Interstate Land Sales Full Disclosure Act
    b. Federal Consumer Credit Protection Act
    c. Equal Credit Opportunity Act
    d. Uniform Consumer Credit Code

_____ 12. Which of the following has authority to provide grants-in-aid for state highway safety programs?
    a. FTC.
    b. CPSC.
    c. NHTSA.
    d. FDA.

_____ 13. Which of the following would not be prohibited by the Equal Credit Opportunity Act?
    a. First Bank only issues its Visa cards to married women in their husband's name.
    b. First Bank refuses to extend credit to men over the age of 70.
    c. First Bank refuses to extend credit to people having an income of less than $12,000.
    d. First Bank refuses to extend credit to members of the Unification Church.

_____ 14. Which of the following is/are covered by the Fair Credit Reporting Act?
    a. Reports by credit agencies.
    b. A creditor calling the debtor in the middle of the night.
    c. A credit check done by a credit agency.
    d. Two of the above are correct, (a) and (c).

_____ 15. The FTC has issued an order of affirmative disclosure against the Warner-Lambert Company. What does the order require?
    a. It requires that they provide certain information in their advertisement in order for the ad not to be considered deceptive.
    b. It provides affirmative disclosure of the source of the information used in the original ad.
    c. It requires that the company cease and desist from deception with regard to all products that it markets.
    d. All of the above are required by affirmative disclosure.

SHORT ESSAY

1. What is the purpose of the FTC and the CPSA?

_____

_____

_____

_____

2. What are the characteristics of a "full" warranty under the Magnuson-Moss Warranty Act?

_____

_____

_____

_____

3. What information must a creditor give to a consumer who is opening an open-ended credit account?

_____

_____

_____

_____

4. What information must a creditor give to a consumer who is opening a closed-end credit account?

_____

_____

_____

_____

5. Discuss the Truth in Lending Act.

_____

_____

_____

_____

Chapter 45
Employment Law

PURPOSE

The common law governed the relationship between employer and employee in terms of tort and contract duties. This common law has been supplemented by federal and state legislation. In this chapter, you study (1) labor law–the general framework in which management and labor negotiate and bargain over the terms of employment; (2) employment discrimination law–federal legislation to prohibit discrimination in employment based upon race, sex, religion, age, handicap, or national origin; and (3) employee protection law–legislation which mandates that employers provide a safe and healthy work environment for their employees and provide compensation to employees injured during the course of employment.

CHAPTER CHECKPOINTS

After reading and studying this chapter, you should be able to:

1. List and discuss the major federal statutes that govern the relationship between an employer and a union representing employees.

2. List the unfair labor practices of an employer and of a union and distinguish between a closed shop and a union shop.

3. List the major federal statutes that govern the area of employment discrimination and discuss the provisions of each.

4. Discuss how the workers' compensation laws changed the common law with respect to injuries sustained by employees on the job.

5. List the major provisions of the OSHA and Social Security statutes and discuss the purpose and effect of OSHA on employment conditions.

CHAPTER OUTLINE

A. Labor Law–These statutes provide the general framework in which management and labor negotiate and bargain over the terms of employment. They are designed to promote both labor-management harmony and the welfare of society at large.

1. Norris-LaGuardia Act–This act was enacted in 1932 in response to the growing criticism of the use of injunctions in peaceful labor disputes. It withdrew from the federal courts the power to issue injunctions in nonviolent labor disputes. The term labor dispute includes any controversy concerning terms or conditions of employment or union representation. The act declared the policy of the United States to be that labor has full freedom to form labor unions and prohibited "yellow dog" contracts requiring employees to promise not to join a union.

2. National Labor Relations Act–The NLRA or Wagner Act was enacted in 1935 and marked an affirmative effort by the federal government to support collective bargaining and unionization. The act provides that "the right to self-organization, to form, join or assist labor organizations, to bargain collectively through representatives of their own choosing, and to engage in concerted activities for the purpose of collective bargaining or other mutual aid or protection" is a federally protected right. The act gave employees the right to be represented by a union and enforces this right by prohibiting certain conduct known as unfair labor practices by employers and unions. Unfair employer practices prohibited by the act include interference with the right to unionize, discriminating against union members and refusing to bargain in good faith. The act establishes the National Labor Relations Board (NLRB) to remedy unfair labor practices and to supervise elections.

3. Labor-Management Relations Act–The LMRA or Taft-Hartley Act was passed by Congress in 1947 in response to an increase in union membership and labor unrest following passage of the NLRA. The act prohibits certain unfair union practices such as coercing employees to join a union, causing employers to discharge nonunion employees, refusing to bargain in good faith, levying excessive union dues, featherbedding, and engaging in secondary activities, such as boycotts, strikes or picketing an employer with whom there is no labor dispute. The act also fosters employer free speech by declaring that no employer unfair labor practices can be based on a statement of opinion. The LMRA also prohibits the closed shop, which is a contract that requires the employer to hire only union members. A union shop contract permits the employer to hire nonunion members but requires them to join the union within a specified period after being hired. A right-to-work law is a state statute that prohibits union shop contracts. Finally, the act reinstates the civil injunctions in labor disputes if requested by the NLRB to prevent an unfair labor practice and grants the president the power to obtain an injunction for an eighty-day cooling-off period.

4. Labor-Management Reporting and Disclosure Act–This act, also known as the Landrum-Griffin Act, was passed in 1959 to eliminate corruption in labor unions. It established a reporting system and enacted a union "bill of rights" designed to make unions more democratic.

B. Employment Discrimination Law–These federal statutes prohibit discrimination in employment on the basis of race, sex, religion, national origin, age, and handicap. Two recent discrimination laws are: the Civil Rights Act of 1991 and the Americans with Disabilities Act of 1990. Most states have enacted similar laws.

1. Equal Pay Act–This act prohibits an employer from discriminating between employees on the basis of sex by paying unequal wages for the same work. An employer may pay unequal wages for equal work to members of the opposite sex if the pay differential is based on a seniority system, a merit system, a system that measures earnings by quantity or quality of production, or any factor except sex. Remedies include back pay, an award of liquidated damages, and injunctions to prohibit further unlawful conduct. Today, the act is enforced by the Equal Employment Opportunity Commission (EEOC).

2. Civil Rights Act of 1964–Title VII of the Civil Rights Act of 1964 prohibits employment discrimination on the basis of race, color, sex, religion, or national origin in hiring, firing, compensating, promoting, or training and other employment-related processes. In 1978 Title VII benefits were extended to pregnant women. The act applies to employers in any business affecting commerce and having fifteen or more employees. The EEOC is the enforcement agency.

   a. Proving Discrimination–The following types of conduct are prohibited by the act: (1) disparate treatment–a *prima facie* case of discrimination is shown if the plaintiff (a) is within a protected class, (b) applied for an open position, (c) was qualified for the position, (d) was denied the job, and (e) the employer continued to try to fill the position; (2) present effects of past discrimination–conduct by an employer that is "neutral" and nondiscriminatory on its face is illegal if it perpetuates past discriminatory practices; and (3) disparate impact–"neutral" rules are illegal if they have an adverse impact on a protected class and are not necessary to the business.

   Defenses in the act include: (1) a *bona fide* seniority or merit system, (2) a professionally developed ability test, and (3) a *bona fide* occupational qualification (BFOQ). Remedies include injunction, appropriate affirmative action, and reinstatement of employees and award of back pay. Affirmative action is the active recruitment of a designated group of applicants.

   b. Reverse Discrimination–Reverse discrimination refers to affirmative action that directs an employer to remedy the underrepresentation of a given race or sex in a traditionally segregated job by considering an individual's race or gender when hiring or promoting. When a state or local government adopts an affirmative action plan that is challenged as illegal reverse discrimination, the plan is subject to strict scrutiny under the Equal Protection Clause of the 14th Amendment.

   c. Sexual Harassment–In 1980, the EEOC issued a definition of sexual harassment. Sexual harassment may constitute sexual discrimination in violation of Title VII. An employer is liable for sexual harassment committed by an employee if it knew or should have known of the harassment. If the employee is an agent of the employer or is in a supervisory position over the victim, the employer may be liable even without knowledge or reason to know.

   d. Comparable Worth–Because the Equal Pay Act only requires equal pay for equal work, it does not apply to different jobs even if they are comparable. It provides no remedy for women whose traditional jobs have been systematically undervalued and underpaid. The concept of comparable worth provides that the relative values to an employer of different jobs should be measured through a rating system or job evaluation that is free of sex bias. The concept of comparable worth is covered by Title VII but has met with limited success in the courts. Some states have adopted requirements that public and private employers pay equally for comparable worth.

3. Executive Order–In 1965 President Johnson issued an Executive Order that prohibited discrimination by federal contractors on the basis of race, color, sex, religion, or national origin on any work performed by the contractor during the period of the federal contract. It also requires affirmative action by federal contractors. The Secretary of Labor, Office of Federal Contract Compliance Programs (OFCCP) administers enforcement of the program.

4. Age Discrimination in Employment Act of 1967–This act prohibits discrimination in hiring, firing, compensating or otherwise on the basis of age. It applies to private employers having twenty or more employees and to all governmental units. It also prohibits the mandatory retirement of most employees under the age of seventy. Statutory defenses include a *bona fide* occupational qualification, a *bona fide* seniority system, and any other reasonable action. Remedies include back pay, injunction, affirmative action, and liquidated damages.

5. Handicap Discrimination–The Rehabilitation Act of 1973 requires federal contractors and agencies to take affirmative action to hire qualified handicapped persons. It prohibits discrimination on the basis of handicap in federal programs and programs that receive federal financial assistance. A handicapped person is one who (1) has a physical or mental impairment that substantially affects one or more major life activities, (2) has a history of major life activity impairment, or (3) is regarded as having such an impairment. Alcohol and drug abuses are not handicaps under this statute.

C. Employee Protection–Employees are accorded a number of protections relating to their jobs including a limited right not to be unfairly dismissed, a right to a safe and healthy workplace, compensation for injuries sustained in the workplace, and some financial security upon retirement or loss of employment.

1. Employee Termination at Will–Under the common law, a contract of employment for other than a definite term is terminable at will by either party. Under this rule an employer may dismiss an employee at will "for good cause, for no cause, or even for cause morally wrong, without being thereby guilty of legal wrong." In recent years, judicial exceptions have developed, federal and state statutes have been enacted, and contractual agreements have been used to limit the rule.

a. Statutory Limitations–Federal legislation that limits an employer's right to discharge include (1) those that protect certain employees from discriminatory discharge, (2) those that protect certain employees in the exercise of statutory rights, and (3) those that protect certain employees from discharge without cause. There are also state statutes that protect workers from discriminatory discharge for filing worker's compensation claims as well as many state statutes that parallel federal legislation.

b. Judicial Limitations–Judicial limitations on the employment-at-will doctrine have been based on contract law, tort law, or a public policy. Cases founded in contract theory have relied on arguments that include the employer's promise of work for a reasonable period, the breaking of implied-in-fact promises of employment for a specific duration, the existence of express or implied provisions of continued employment conditioned upon satisfactory work performance, the assurance of nondismissal except for cause, and the giving of additional consideration beyond the performance of services to support job security. Tort obligations imposed on employers are frequently based upon the torts of intentional infliction of emotional distress and interference with employment relations. Public policy cases generally involve dismissal for refusing to violate a statute, exercising a statutory right, performing a statutory obligation, or reporting an alleged violation of a statute in the public interest.

2. Occupational Safety and Health Act–In 1970 Congress enacted this act, which established the Occupational Safety and Health Administration (OSHA) to develop standards, conduct inspections, monitor compliance, and institute enforcement actions against those who are not in compliance. The act requires each employer to meet the general duty to provide a work environment "free from recognized hazards that are causing or likely to cause death or serious physical harm to his employees." Employers and employees must comply with OSHA rules and regulations. Employers may not discharge or discriminate against employees who exercise rights under the act. OSHA inspects workplaces and issues citations for which an employer may be both civilly and criminally liable. Most states have some form of state regulation of health and safety in the workplace.

3. Employee Privacy–The fundamental right to privacy, a product of common law, protects employees from unwanted searches, electronic monitoring and other forms of surveillance, and disclosure of confidential records by the tort of invasion of privacy. This actually consists of four different torts: (1) unreasonable intrusion into the seclusion of another; (2) unreasonable public disclosure of private facts; (3) unreasonable publicity that places another in a false light; and (4) appropriation of a person's name or likeness. Additionally, employees receive protection from Federal and some state legislation. By U.S. Supreme Court decision it would appear that a government employer may use (1) random or universal testing where public health or safety or national security is involved and (2) selective drug testing where there is a sufficient cause to believe an employee has a drug problem. In the absence of a state statute, private sector employees have little or no protection from drug or alcohol tests. In a union setting such tests would be subject to collective bargaining. The Federal Employee Polygraph Protection Act of 1988 prohibits private employers from requiring employees or prospective employees to undergo a lie detector test, inquiring about the results of such a test, or using the results of such a test or the refusal to be thus tested as grounds for an adverse employment decision. The Act provides for certain exemptions with regard to government employers, security firms and manufacturers of controlled substances. Manufacturers investigating an economic loss or injury to its business may test; however, the use of the test must meet certain requirements: (1) it must be designed to investigate a specific incident or activity, not a chronic problem; (2) the employee must have had access to the property that is the subject of the investigation.

4. Workers' Compensation–In order to provide speedier and more certain relief to injured employees, all states have adopted statutes which provide workers' compensation. These statutes create boards to determine whether an injured employee is entitled to receive

compensation and, if so, the amount. The common law defenses have been abolished. Employees are entitled to compensation if the employee is injured and if that injury arose out of and in the course of employment. Actions at law against the employer by the employee are not permitted, because the courts have no jurisdiction except to review decisions of the workers' compensation board or commission.

5. Social Security and Unemployment Insurance–Social Security was enacted in 1935 to provide limited retirement and death benefits to certain employees. The system now covers almost all employees and contains four major benefit programs: (1) Old-Age and Survivors Insurance (OASI), (2) Disability Insurance (DI), (3) Hospitalization Insurance (Medicare), and (4) Supplemental Security Income (SSI). The system is financed by contributions (taxes) paid by employers, employees, and self-employed individuals. Benefits vary depending on the particular program and whether the beneficiary is "fully" insured. Dependents (spouses and children) are also eligible for certain Social Security benefits. The federal unemployment insurance system was initially created by Title IX of the Social Security Act of 1935. It has been supplemented by the Federal Unemployment Tax Act and numerous other federal statutes. Employees do not pay the tax. The purpose of the tax is to provide unemployment compensation, the exact amount of which is based on each state's formula to workers who have lost their jobs and cannot find other employment.

6. Fair Labor Standards Act–The Fair Labor Standards Act (FLSA) regulates the employment of child labor outside of agriculture. The act prohibits the employment of anyone under fourteen years in nonfarm work except for newspaper deliverers and child actors. Fourteen and fifteen-year-olds may work a limited number of hours in nonhazardous occupations. Sixteen and seventeen-year-olds may work in any nonhazardous job, while eighteen-year-olds may work in any job. The FLSA imposes wage and hour requirements upon covered employers and provides for a minimum wage and overtime pay of time-and-a-half for hours worked in excess of forty hours per week.

7. Worker Adjustment and Retraining Notification Act–WARN requires an employer to provide sixty days' advance notice of a plant closing or mass layoff. A "plant closing" is a permanent or temporary shutting down of a single site or units within a site if the shutdown results in fifty or more employees losing employment during any thirty-day period. A "mass layoff" is a loss of employment during a thirty-day period either for 500 employees or for at least one-third of the employees at a given site, if that one-third equals or exceeds fifty employees.

8. Family and Medical Leave Act of 1993–Employees must be given up to twelve weeks of leave during any twelve-month period for the birth of a child; adopting or gaining foster care of a child; or the care of a spouse, child, or parent who suffers from a serious health condition. Eligibility is based upon an employee having worked for the employer at least twelve months and having worked at least 1250 hours during the twelve months preceding the leave request. The Act applies to employers with fifty or more employees as well as governments at the Federal, State, and local levels. The requested leave may be paid, unpaid, or a combination of both.

KEY TERMS

1. Labor dispute

2. Unfair labor practice

3. Unfair employer practice

4. Unfair union practice

5. Closed shop

6. Union shop

7. Right-to-work law

8. Equal pay

9. Employment discrimination

10. Affirmative action

11. Reverse discrimination

12. Sexual harassment

13. Comparable worth

14. Fellow servant rule

15. Workers' compensation

16. Social security

17. Unemployment compensation

TRUE/FALSE

_____ 1. The National Labor Relations Act guarantees the right of employees to bargain collectively.

_____ 2. The Fair Labor Standards Act regulates the employment of child labor.

_____ 3. The Equal Pay Act prohibits an employer from discriminating between employees on the basis of race, color, sex, religion or national origin by paying unequal wages for equal work.

_____ 4. The Civil Rights Act of 1964 applies to employers engaged in an industry affecting commerce and having fifteen or more employees.

_____ 5. By presidential executive order federal contractors are exempt from affirmative action in recruiting..

_____ 6. Title VII does not prohibit discrimination based on age.

_____ 7. The customers at Chez Chic Restaurant prefer to be served by male waiters. The restaurant owner can refuse to hire women based upon sex being a *bona fide* occupational qualification.

_____ 8. Sexual harassment is not covered by the federal discrimination laws.

_____ 9. If a state government's affirmative action plan is challenged, it is subject to strict scrutiny under the Equal Protection Clause.

_____ 10. The National Labor Relations Act is also known as the Wagner Act.

_____ 11. The Social Security system is financed by taxes paid by employers, employees, and self-employed individuals.

_____ 12. Common law employer defenses such as the fellow-servant rule, contributory negligence and voluntary assumption of the risk are eliminated by workers' compensation statutes.

_____ 13. Under the Family and Medical Leave Act of 1993 requested leave must be paid leave.

_____ 14. The Equal Pay Act applies to different jobs that are comparable as well as to jobs that are equal jobs.

_____ 15. The Pregnancy Discrimination Act extends the benefits of the Civil Rights Act to pregnant women.

MULTIPLE CHOICE

_____ 1. An employer who refuses to bargain in good faith with the duly established representatives of his employees has violated the:
   a. Norris-LaGuardia Act.
   b. National Labor Relations Act.
   c. Labor-Management Relations Act.
   d. Labor-Management Reporting and Disclosure Act.

_____ 2. A union which goes on strike to force an employer to fire a nonunion employee has violated the:
   a. Norris-LaGuardia Act.
   b. National Labor Relations Act.
   c. Labor-Management Relations Act.
   d. Labor-Management Reporting and Disclosure Act.

3. Under the NLRA, which of the following is/are unfair labor practices?
   a. To dominate a union.
   b. To discriminate against union members.
   c. To refuse to bargain in good faith.
   d. All of the above.

4. The federal statute that prohibits the mandatory retirement of most employees:
   a. Rehabilitation Act of 1973.
   b. Civil Rights Act of 1964.
   c. Age Discrimination in Employment Act of 1967.
   d. Executive Order of 1965.

5. An employee who sues his employer under a workers' compensation statute for injuries arising out of and in the course of his employment is subject to the defense of:
   a. contributory negligence.
   b. assumption of the risk.
   c. the fellow servant rule.
   d. none of the above.

6. The _____ is responsible for enforcing federal anti-discrimination laws.
   a. NLRB
   b. OSHA
   c. EEOC
   d. Social Security Administration

7. Which of the following is a protection accorded an employee relating to her job?
   a. Right to a safe and healthy workplace.
   b. Compensation for injuries sustained in the workplace.
   c. Some financial security upon retirement.
   d. All of the above.

8. Under the common law, employers may dismiss their employees at will:
   a. for good cause.
   b. for no cause.
   c. both of the above.
   d. none of the above.

9. Which of the following employees would not be covered by the Rehabilitation Act of 1973?
   a. An alcoholic.
   b. A victim of AIDS.
   c. A victim of tuberculosis.
   d. A polio victim in a wheelchair.

_____ 10. The Americans with Disabilities Act provides assistance to the handicapped in which of the following?
  a. Rehabilitation training.
  b. Access to public facilities.
  c. Employment.
  d. All of the above.

_____ 11. Which of the following is a valid discrimination allegation defense under the Civil Rights Act of 1964?
  a. A *bona fide* seniority or merit system.
  b. A professionally developed ability test.
  c. A bona fide occupational qualification.
  d. All of the above.

_____ 12. Which one of the following defenses may be used by an employer to avoid responsibility for paying an employee's claim for workers' compensation?
  a. The employee assumed the risk of the injury.
  b. The employee was contributorily negligent.
  c. A co-worker actually caused the injury.
  d. The injury did not occur on the job.

_____ 13. Under the Labor-Management Relations Act which of the following union activities would be considered an unfair labor practice?
  a. Causing an employer to discriminate against a nonunion employee.
  b. Coercing an employee to join a union.
  c. Levying excessive dues.
  d. All of the above are unfair labor practices.

_____ 14. Which of the following is an unfair employer practice?
  a. Refusal to bargain in good faith.
  b. Discrimination against union members.
  c. Interference with the right of employees to unionize and bargain collectively.
  d. All of the above are unfair employer practices.

_____ 15. In which of the following situations would the employer have liability for sexual harassment?
  a. An employee sexually harasses another employee and the employer does not take immediate action when he knows about the harassment.
  b. An employee sexually harasses another employee and the employer does not take immediate action when he should have known about the harassment regardless of whether the employer does in fact know of it.
  c. An employer would be liable in both of the above situations.
  d. An employer can never be held responsible for sexual harassment by one employee against another employee.

SHORT ESSAY

1. What are the basic defenses available to an employer who has been charged with employment discrimination?

    _____

    _____

    _____

    _____

2. What are the remedies available to an employee who brings a successful employment discrimination action?

    _____

    _____

    _____

    _____

3. What is the doctrine of comparable worth? Explain.

    _____

    _____

    _____

    _____

4. Ed, an employee of Ace Delivery, was injured in a car accident while making a delivery. The wreck was due to the negligence of Wes, the other driver. If Ace Delivery is covered by workers' compensation, what is the result?

    _____

    _____

    _____

    _____

5. Darla, an employee of First Bank, has brought an action against the bank based upon the alleged sexual harassment of Doug, her co-worker. What must she establish in order to prevail in this action?

    _____

    _____

    _____

    _____

Chapter 46
Securities Regulation

PURPOSE

The primary purpose of federal securities regulation is to prevent fraudulent practices in the sale of securities and thereby foster public confidence in the securities market. Federal securities law consists principally of two statutes: the Securities Act of 1933, which focuses on the issuance of securities, and the Securities Exchange Act of 1934, which deals mainly with trading in issued securities. Both statutes are administered by the Securities and Exchange Commission (SEC), an independent, quasi-judicial agency. In addition to the federal laws regulating the sale of securities, there are also state laws, commonly known as Blue Sky laws, which prohibit fraud in the sale of securities and sometimes require state registration. In this chapter, you study the 1933 Act and the 1934 Act.

CHAPTER CHECKPOINTS

After reading and studying this chapter, you should be able to:

1. Identify the scope and purpose of the Securities Act of 1933 and Securities Exchange Act of 1934.

2. Define a security and recognize exempt securities and exempt transactions..

3. Summarize the requirements and applications of Rule 10b-5.

4. Summarize the federal securities provisions dealing with proxy solicitations and tender offers.

5. Discuss the sanctions for noncompliance with the disclosure and antifraud requirements of the 1934 Act.

CHAPTER OUTLINE

I. The Securities Act of 1933–This act, also called the "Truth in Securities Act," requires that a registration statement be filed with the SEC and become effective before any securities may be offered for sale to the public unless either the securities or the transaction in which they are offered are exempt from registration. The purpose of registration is to disclose financial and other information to potential investors. They must be furnished with a prospectus containing the important data set forth in the registration statement. The antifraud provisions of the act apply regardless of whether registration is required. Civil and criminal liability may be imposed for violations of the act.

A. Definition of a Security–The 1933 Act defines the term security to include any note, stock, bond, debenture, evidence of indebtedness, preorganization certificate or subscription, investment contract, voting-trust certificate, fractional undivided interest in oil, gas, or other mineral rights, or in general, any interest or instrument commonly known as a security. Under the Howey test, a financial instrument or transaction that involves (1) an investment in a common venture (2) premised on a reasonable expectation of profit (3) to be derived from the efforts of others, constitutes an investment contract. Courts have generally interpreted this statutory definition to include limited partnership interests, citrus groves, whiskey warehouse receipts, real estate condominiums, cattle, franchises and pyramid schemes.

B. Registration of Securities–The 1933 Act prohibits the offer or sale through the use of the mails or any means of interstate commerce of any security unless a registration statement for that security is in effect or an exemption from registration is secured. The purpose of registration is to provide adequate and accurate disclosure of financial and other information.

1. Disclosure Requirements–In general, registration requires disclosure of the following information: (1) a description of the registrant's properties and business, (2) a description of the significant provisions of the security and its relationship to the registrant's other capital securities, (3) information about the management of the registrant, and (4) financial statements certified by independent public accountants. In 1992 new disclosure requirements regarding compensation paid to senior executives and directors were added. The registration statement must be signed by the issuer, its chief executive, financial and accounting officers, and a majority of the board of directors. The information becomes public immediately upon filing. It is unlawful to sell the securities until the effective date, although after the filing of the registration statement, the securities may be offered (1) orally; (2) by certain summaries of the information in the registration statement; (3) by a "tombstone advertisement" that identifies the security; or (4) by a preliminary prospectus, called a "red herring".

2. Integrated Disclosure–The disclosure system under the 1933 Act developed independently of that required under the 1934 Act. As a result, issuers were compelled to provide duplicative or overlapping disclosure. In 1982 the SEC adopted an integrated disclosure system to reduce or eliminate unnecessary duplication. Under this system, there are three levels of disclosure. All issuers may use the detailed form. Corporations that have continuously reported under the 1934 Act for at least three years are permitted to disclose less detailed information in the 1933 Act registration statement and to incorporate by reference information in reports filed under the 1934

Act. Those corporations that have filed under the 1934 Act and also have a minimum market value of voting stock of $75 million are permitted to disclose even less detail in the 1933 Act registration and to incorporate even more information by reference to 1934 Act reports.

3. Shelf Registrations–Shelf registrations permit certain qualified issuers to register securities that are to be offered and sold "off the shelf" on a delayed or continuous basis. The information in the original registration must be kept accurate and current. Only companies eligible to use the shorter forms of registration qualify for shelf registration.

C. Exempt Securities–The 1933 Act exempts specific securities from its registration requirements.

1. Short-Term Commercial Paper–Notes, drafts, bankers' acceptances (drafts accepted by banks) issued for working capital that have a maturity of not more than nine months when issued are exempt under the Act. The exemption is not available if the proceeds are used for permanent purposes such as the acquisition of a plant or if the paper is not ordinarily of the type purchased by the general public.

2. Other Exempt Securities–The following kinds of securities are also exempt from registration: (1) securities of domestic governments; (2) securities of domestic banks and savings and loan associations; (3) securities of nonprofit charitable organizations; (4) securities issued by federally regulated common carriers; and (5) insurance policies and annuity contracts issued by state regulated insurance companies. The Bankruptcy Code exempts securities issued by a debtor if they are offered under a reorganization plan.

D. Exempt Transactions for Issuers–An exempt transaction is the issuance of securities not subject to the registration requirements of the 1933 Act. Exempt transactions include: (1) private placements, (2) limited offers not exceeding $5 million, (3) limited offers not exceeding $1 million, and (4) limited offers solely to accredited investors. Except for Rule 504, these registration exemptions apply to transactions only in which the securities are issued; therefore any resale must be made by registration unless the resale qualifies as an exempt transaction. The 1933 Act also identifies other exemptions which are in effect transaction exemptions including intrastate issues, exchanges between an issuer and its security holders, reorganization securities issued with court or government approval, and Regulation A which permits an issuer to sell a limited amount of securities in an unregistered public offering under certain conditions.

1. Limited Offers–Regulation D contains three separate exemptions (Rules 504, 505, and 506) each involving limited offers. Section 4(6) also provides for small issues. Securities sold under these exemptions are restricted securities and may be resold only by registration or in another transaction exempt from registration. An issuer who uses these exemptions must take reasonable care to assure against nonexempt, unregistered resales of the restricted securities. Reasonable care includes the following: (a) making a reasonable inquiry to determine if the purchaser is acquiring the securities for herself or for other persons; (b) providing written disclosure to each purchaser prior to the sale stating that the securities have not been registered and therefore cannot be resold unless they are registered or an exemption is available; and (c) placing a legend on the certificate stating that the securities have not been registered and that they are restricted securities.

a. Private Placements–The private placement provision exempts "transactions by an issuer not involving any public offering." Rule 506 of the SEC establishes a nonexclusive safe harbor for limited offers and sales without regard to the dollar amount of the offering. General advertising or solicitation is not permitted. The issue may be purchased by an unlimited number of "accredited investors" and by no more than thirty-five other purchasers. Accredited investors include banks, insurance companies, investment companies, executive officers or directors of the issuer, savings and loan associations, registered broker-dealers, business entities with total assets in excess of $5 million, any person whose net worth exceeds $1 million, and any person with an annual income over $200,000. Nonaccredited investors must be given specified material information before the sale about the issuer, its business, and the securities being offered. The issuer must take precautions against nonexempt, unregistered resales and must notify the SEC of sales made under the exemption.

b. Limited Offers Not Exceeding $5 Million–Rule 505 exempts from registration offerings by noninvestment company issuers that do not exceed $5 million over twelve months. General advertising or solicitation is not permitted. The issue may be purchased by an unlimited number of accredited investors and by no more than thirty-five other purchasers. Nonaccredited investors must be given specified material information before the sale about the issuer, its business, and the securities being offered. Unlike Rule 506, the issuer is not required to believe reasonably that each nonaccredited investor, either alone or with his representative, has sufficient knowledge and experience in financial matters to be capable of evaluating the merits and risks of the investment. The issuer must take precautions against nonexempt, unregistered resales and must notify the SEC of sales made under the exemption.

c. Limited Offers Not Exceeding $1 Million–Rule 504 provides private, noninvestment company issuers with an unconditional exemption from registration for small issues not exceeding $1 million within twelve months. The SEC must be notified. The rule permits sales to an unlimited number of investors and does not require any information to be furnished to them.

d. Limited Offers Solely to Accredited Investors–Section 4(6) provides an exemption for offers and sales by an issuer made solely to accredited investors if not in excess of $5 million. General advertising or public solicitation is not permitted. As with Rules 505 and 506, an unlimited number of accredited investors may purchase the issue; however, no unaccredited investors may purchase. The issuer must take precautions against nonexempt, unregistered resales and must notify the SEC of sales made under the exemption.

2. Regulation A–This regulation permits an issuer to offer up to $5 million of securities in any twelve-month period without registering them provided that the issuer files an offering statement with the SEC's regional office prior to the sale of the securities. An offering circular must be provided to offerees and purchasers. Filings are less detailed and time-consuming than full registration statements. Because each purchaser must be supplied with an offering circular, securities sold under Regulation A may be freely resold after issuance.

3. Intrastate Issues–An issue offered and sold only to persons who live in a single state where the issuer is resident and doing business is also exempt under the 1933 Act. The exemption is intended to apply to local issues that represent local financing by local persons to be carried out through local investments. Rule 147 provides a "nonexclusive safe harbor" for securing the

intrastate exemption. Rule 147 requires that: (1) the issuer be incorporated in the state in which the issuance occurs; (2) the issuer be principally doing business in that state; (3) all offerees and purchasers be residents of that state; (4) no resales be made to nonresidents during the period of sale and for nine months thereafter; and (5) precautions be taken against interstate distributions.

E. Exempt Transactions for Non-Issuers–The 1933 Act requires registration for any sale by any person (including non-issuers) of any nonexempt security unless there is a statutory exemption. However, the Act provides a transaction exemption for any person other than an issuer, underwriter, or dealer, as well as most transactions by dealers and brokers. These exemptions do not extend to some situations involving resales by non-issuers which must be made pursuant to registration, Rule 144, or Regulation A.

   1. Rule 144–Rule 144 of the SEC sets forth conditions that, if met by an affiliate or any person selling restricted securities, exempt her from registering them. There must be adequate current public information about the issuer, the person selling the securities must have owned them for at least two years, must sell them only in limited amounts in unsolicited brokers' transactions, and must give notice of the sale to the SEC. An affiliate is a person who controls, is controlled by, or is under common control with the issuer.

   2. Rule 144A–Rule 144A provides an additional nonexclusive safe harbor from registration for re-sales of restricted securities. Only securities that at the time of issue are not of the same class as securities listed on a national securities exchange or nonfungible securities may be sold under Rule 144A. Additionally, the seller under this rule must take steps to ensure that the buyer knows the seller is relying on Rule 144A in this transaction.

   3. Regulation A–Regulation A, in addition to providing an exemption for issuers from registration for securities up to $5 million, also provides an exemption for non-issuers. A $1.5 million limit is placed on the total amount of securities sold in any twelve-month period by all non-affiliates. All conditions imposed on issuers by Regulation A must be met.

F. Liability–Sanctions for noncompliance with the 1933 Act include administrative remedies by the SEC, civil liability to injured investors, and criminal penalties.

   1. Unregistered Sales–Section 12(1) of the act imposes civil liability for the sale of an unregistered security that is required to be registered, the sale of a registered security without delivery of a prospectus, the sale of a security by use of a prospectus that is not current, or the offer of a sale before filing of the registration statement. There are no defenses. The person who purchases a security in violation of the act has the right to tender it back to the seller and recover the purchase price, or if he no longer owns it, to recover monetary damages from the seller.

   2. False Registration Statements–Section 11 of the act imposes liability for the inclusion in the registration statement of any untrue statement or omission of a material fact. A matter is material if a reasonable investor would attach importance to it in deciding whether to purchase a security. Liability is imposed on: (1) the issuer; (2) all persons who signed the registration statement, including the principal executive officer, the principal financial officer, and the principal accounting officer; (3) every person who was a director or partner; (4) every accountant, engineer, appraiser, or expert who prepared or certified any part of the registration statement; and (5) all underwriters. Liability is joint and several and extends to any person who acquires

the security without knowledge of the untruth or omission for the amount paid for the security less either its value at the time of suit or the price for which it was sold. An expert is liable only for the portion of the registration that he prepared or certified. Defendants other than the issuer may assert the defense of due diligence. This defense requires that the defendant had a reasonable belief that there were no untrue statements or material omissions.

3. Antifraud Provision–The 1933 Act contains two broad antifraud provision that applies to all securities. Section 12(2) imposes liability on any person who offers or sells a security by means of a prospectus or oral communication that contains an untrue statement of material fact or an omission of a material fact. Liability extends only to the immediate purchaser, provided she did not know of the untruth. The seller may avoid liability by proving that he did not know and could not have known of the untrue statement or omission. The seller is liable for the amount paid. Section 17(a) makes it unlawful to (a) employ any device, scheme or artifice to defraud; (b) obtain money or property by means of any untrue statement of a material fact or omission of a material fact; and (c) engage in any transaction, practice, or course of business that would constitute a fraud or deceit upon the purchaser.

4. Criminal Sanctions–The 1933 Act imposes criminal sanctions on any person who willfully violates any of the provisions of the act or the rules and regulations promulgated by the SEC. A fine of not more than $10,000 or imprisonment for not more than five years or both may be imposed for criminal violations.

II. The Securities Exchange Act of 1934–This Act deals mainly with the secondary distribution (resale) of securities. It seeks to ensure fair and orderly securities markets by establishing rules for the operation of the markets and by prohibiting fraudulent and manipulative practices. The Act provides protection for holders of securities listed on national exchanges and holders of equity securities of companies traded over the counter if their assets exceed $5 million and they have a class of equity securities with 500 or more shareholders.

A. Disclosure–The 1934 Act imposes significant disclosure requirements upon reporting companies including filing registrations of securities, periodic reports, disclosure statements for proxy solicitations, and disclosure statements for tender offers, as well as compliance with the Foreign Corrupt Practices Act. A 1992 requirement imposes disclosure regarding compensation paid to senior executives and directors.

1. Registration Requirements for Securities–The 1934 Act requires all regulated publicly held companies to register with the SEC. These registrations are one-time registrations that apply to the entire class of securities. Registration requires disclosure of the organization, financial structure, and nature of the business; the terms, positions, rights, and privileges of the different classes of outstanding securities; the names of the directors, officers, and underwriters and each holder who owns more than 10% of any class of nonexempt equity security; bonus and profit-sharing arrangements; and balance sheets and profit and loss statements for the three preceding fiscal years.

2. Periodic Reporting Requirements–Annual and periodic updates must be filed by the issuer. Directors, officers, and any person who owns more than 10% of a registered equity security must file reports for any month that there has been any changes in his ownership.

3. Proxy Solicitations–A proxy is a writing signed by a shareholder of a corporation authorizing a named person to vote his shares of stock at a specified meeting of the shareholders. The 1934 Act regulates the proxy solicitation process. It makes it unlawful for any person to solicit any proxy concerning any registered security "in contravention of such rules and regulations as the Commission may prescribe." Solicitation includes any request for a proxy, any request not to execute a proxy, or any request to revoke a proxy.

   a. Proxy Statements–Solicitation is prohibited unless each person has been furnished with a written proxy statement containing specified information. A soliciting issuer must furnish security holders with a proxy statement, a proxy form, and in the case of the election of directors an annual report along with the proxy statement.

   b. Shareholder Proposals–Where management makes a solicitation, the corporation must, on written request, mail the communication of any security holder entitled to vote at his expense or, furnish to the security holder a current list of other holders. Similarly, management must include any timely proposals for action at a forthcoming meeting in its proxy statement and provide security holders with an opportunity to vote for or against it. If management opposes the proposal, it must include a statement by the security holder. Management may omit a proposal if (1) under state law it is not a proper subject for shareholder action, (2) it is not significantly related to the business of the issuer, (3) it is beyond the issuer's power to accomplish, or (4) it relates to the conduct of the ordinary business operations of the issuer.

4. Tender Offers–A tender offer is a general invitation to the shareholders of a company to purchase their shares at a specified price. The 1968 Williams Act amended the 1934 Act to extend reporting and disclosure requirements to tender offers and other block acquisitions. The purpose of the act is to provide public shareholders with full disclosure so that they may make informed decisions.

   a. Disclosure Requirements–The 1934 Act imposes disclosure requirements in three situations: (1) a person or group acquires more than 5% of a class of voting securities registered under the act, (2) a person makes a tender offer for more than 5% of a class of registered equity securities, or (3) the issuer makes an offer to repurchase its own shares. The disclosure requirements for each is substantially the same. A statement must be filed with the SEC containing (1) the person's background, (2) the source of the funds used to acquire the securities, (3) the purpose of the acquisition, (4) the number of shares owned, and (5) any relevant contracts, arrangements, or understandings. Anyone soliciting shareholders to accept or reject a tender offer is also subject to disclosure. The target company has ten days in which to respond to the bidder's tender offer by (1) recommending acceptance or rejection, (2) expressing no opinion and remaining neutral, or (3) stating that it is unable to take a position.

   b. Required Practices–A tender offer must be kept open for at least twenty business days. Shareholders who tender their shares may withdraw them at any time during the period. All shares tendered must be purchased for the same price. A tender offeror who offers to purchase less than all the outstanding securities of the target must accept, on a *pro rata* basis, securities tendered during the offer.

    c. Defensive Tactics–When confronted by an uninvited takeover bid, or by a potential, uninvited bid, management of the target company may decide either to oppose the bid or to seek to prevent it. The tactics continue to evolve.

    d. State Regulation–More than two-thirds of the states have enacted statutes regulating tender offers. Most tend to protect the target company from an unwanted tender offer. Some give the state the power to review the merits of the offer or the adequacy of disclosure or impose waiting periods before the tender offer is effective. They generally have more detailed disclosure requirements than are found in the Williams Act.

  5. Foreign Corrupt Practices Act–In 1977 Congress enacted the Foreign Corrupt Practices Act. The act imposes internal control requirements on companies with registered securities and prohibits all domestic concerns from bribing foreign governmental officials. The accounting requirements of the FCPA were enacted (1) to assure that an issuer's books accurately reflect financial transactions, (2) to protect the integrity of independent audits of financial statements, and (3) to promote the reliability of financial information required by the 1934 Act.

B. Liability–The 1934 Act imposes sanctions for noncompliance with its disclosure and antifraud requirements including civil liability to injured investors and issuers, civil penalties, and criminal penalties.

  1. Misleading Statements in Reports–Section 18 imposes civil liability upon any person who makes or causes to be made any false or misleading statement with respect to any material fact in any application, report, document, or registration filed with the SEC under the 1934 Act. A person is not liable if she proves that she acted in good faith and had no knowledge that such statement was false or misleading.

  2. Short-Swing Profits–Section 16(b) imposes liability upon insiders–directors, officers, and any person owning more than 10% of the stock of a corporation listed on a national stock exchange or registered with the SEC–for all profits resulting from their short-swing trading in such stock. The corporation is entitled to recover any and all profit realized by an insider who sells such stock within six months from the date of its purchase or who purchases such stock within six months from the date of a sale of the stock. "Profit" is calculated by matching the highest sale price against the lowest purchase price within six months of each other, and losses cannot be used to offset profits.

  3. Antifraud Provisions–Section 10(b) of the 1934 Act and SEC Rule 10b-5 make it unlawful for any person to do any of the following when using the mails or any other facilities of interstate commerce in connection with the purchase or sale of any security: (1) employ any device, scheme, or artifice to defraud; (2) make any untrue statement of a material fact; (3) omit to state a material fact without which the information is misleading; or (4) engage in any act, practice, or course of business that operates or would operate as a fraud or deceit on any person. The rule applies to the purchase and sale of any security regardless of whether it is registered, how it is traded, or whether it is part of an initial issuance or a secondary distribution.

    a. Requisites of Rule 10b-5–Elements that must be proved to recover damages include: (1) a misstatement or omission, (2) that is material, (3) made with scienter, and (4) relied upon (5) in connection with the purchase or sale of a security. Scienter is intentional and knowing conduct.

b. Insider Trading–Rule 10b-5 applies to sales or purchases of securities made by an "insider" who possesses material information that is not available to the public. Insiders include directors, officers, employees, and agents of the issuer as well as those with whom the issuer has entrusted information solely for corporate purposes, such as underwriters, accountants, lawyers, and consultants. In some instances tippees, who are persons who receive material, nonpublic information from insiders, are also precluded from trading on that information.

4. Express Insider Trading Liability–Section 20A imposes civil liability upon any person who violates the act by purchasing or selling a security while in possession of material, nonpublic information. The total amount of damages may not exceed the profit gained or loss avoided by the violation less any amount disgorged to the SEC pursuant to a court order.

5. Civil Penalties for Insider Trading–The SEC is authorized to bring an action in a U.S. district court to have a civil penalty imposed upon any person who purchases or sells a security while in possession of material, nonpublic information. Any person who controlled the violator is also liable if the controlling person knew or recklessly disregarded the fact that the controlled person was likely to commit a violation. The transaction must be on or through a national securities exchange or through a broker or dealer. The penalty may not exceed three times the profit gained or the loss avoided as a result of the unlawful purchase or sale. "Profit gained" or "loss avoided" is "the difference between the purchase or sale price of the security as measured by the trading price of the security a reasonable period after public dissemination of the nonpublic information."

6. Misleading Proxy Statements–Any person who distributes a materially false or misleading proxy statement may be liable to a shareholder who suffers a loss caused by purchasing or selling a security in reliance upon the statement. A misstatement or omission is material if there is a substantial likelihood that a reasonable shareholder would consider it important in deciding how to vote. Remedies include injunction, rescission, damages, and attorney's fees.

7. Fraudulent Tender Offers–Section 14(e) makes it unlawful for any person to make any untrue statement of material fact or omit to state any material fact or to engage in any fraudulent, deceptive, or manipulative practices in connection with any tender offer. Some courts have implied civil liability.

8. Antibribery Provision of FCPA–The FCPA makes it unlawful for any domestic concern or any of its officers, directors, employees, or agents to offer or give anything of value directly or indirectly to any foreign official, political party, or political official for the purpose of (1) influencing any act or decision of that person or party in his or its official capacity, (2) inducing an act or omission in violation of his or its lawful duty, or (3) inducing such person or party to use his or its influence to affect a decision of a foreign government in order to assist the domestic concern in obtaining or retaining business. Violations can result in fines of up to $2 million for companies; individuals may be fined a maximum of $100,000 and imprisoned up to five years or both. A civil penalty of up to $10,000 may be imposed.

9. Criminal Sanctions–Section 32 of the 1934 Act imposes criminal sanctions on any person who willfully violates any of the provisions of the act or the rules and regulations promulgated by the SEC pursuant to the act. Conviction may carry a fine of not more than $1 million or imprisonment of not more than ten years or both for individuals.

KEY TERMS

1. Blue Sky Laws

2. Prospectus

3. Security

4. Shelf registration

5. Restricted securities

6. Private placement

7. Accredited investors

8. Offering circular

9. Affiliate

10. Control

11. Due diligence defense

12. Proxy

13. Proxy statement

14. Tender offer

15. Short-swing profits

16. Insider

17. Tippee

TRUE/FALSE

_____ 1. A primary purpose in requiring a registration statement be filed with the SEC is to allow the SEC to verify the information contained therein and guarantee its accuracy.

_____ 2. Exempt securities may be resold without registration.

_____ 3. Under the Securities Enforcement Remedies and Penny Stock Reform Act, the SEC may impose administrative, civil penalties up to $500,000.

_____ 4. Securities sold in an exempt transaction may be resold only by registration.

_____ 5. Securities sold under the private placement exemption may be purchased by an unlimited number of purchasers.

_____ 6. Computer bulletin boards are defined by the SEC as electronic media and must therefore meet SEC requirements.

_____ 7. A registration statement becomes public immediately on filing with the SEC.

_____ 8. The Securities Exchange Act of 1934 applies only to companies whose assets exceed $3 million and who have a class of equity securities with 500 or more shareholders.

_____ 9. Under the integrated reporting system with respect to registration of securities, the SEC defines a small business issuer as a non-investment company whose annual revenues total less than $25 million and whose voting stock has a market value of less than $25 million.

_____ 10. Under Rule 10b-5, liability may be imposed upon buyers as well as sellers.

_____ 11. Fines imposed upon individuals for violations of the Foreign Corrupt Practices Act may not be paid by the issuing corporation.

_____ 12. Scienter is required for an individual to violate the provisions of Rule 10b-5.

_____ 13. The 1934 Act imposes disclosure requirements for a person who makes a tender offer for more than 5 percent of a class of registered equity securities.

_____ 14. Limited partnership interests are not considered securities as defined by the 1933 Act.

_____ 15. The Reform Act provides "forward-looking" statements a "safe harbor" from civil liability.

MULTIPLE CHOICE

_____ 1. The effective date of a registration statement is:
   a. the day it is filed with the SEC.
   b. the tenth day after it is filed with the SEC.
   c. the twentieth day after it is filed with the SEC.
   d. none of the above.

_____ 2. The "forward-looking" safe harbor provision eliminates civil liability if the statement is:
   a. immaterial.
   b. made without knowledge of its falsity.
   c. either (a) or (b).
   d. neither (a) nor (b).

_____ 3. "Forward-looking" statements include which of the following?
  a. Projections of revenues.
  b. Earnings per share.
  c. Capital expenditures.
  d. All of the above.

_____ 4. Under the Howey test an investment contract must:
  a. involve an investment in a common venture.
  b. be premised on a reasonable expectation of profit.
  c. be derived from the efforts of others.
  d. all of the above.

_____ 5. Under Rule 506 of the SEC, an issuer may make a private placement of unregistered securities of up to:
  a. $500,000.
  b. $1,500,000.
  c. $5,000,000.
  d. none of the above.

_____ 6. Violators of the 1933 Act are subject to:
  a. administrative remedies by the SEC.
  b. civil liability to injured investors.
  c. criminal penalties.
  d. all of the above.

_____ 7. There are no defenses to:
  a. selling an unregistered security which is required to be registered.
  b. including in a registration statement any untrue statement or omission of material fact.
  c. selling a security by means of a prospectus which includes an untrue statement of material fact or an omission of a material fact.
  d. (b) and (c) but not (a).

_____ 8. Corporate insiders who buy the stock of the corporation will be liable to the corporation for any profits made pursuant to a sale of that stock within:
  a. 20 days.
  b. 90 days.
  c. 6 months.
  d. 12 months.

_____ 9. Assume Alice, an officer of the Tel-Ko Computer Corporation, buys 700 shares of Tel-Ko stock on January 1 for $10 per share and 800 shares of Tel-Ko stock on March 15 for $8 per share. If Alice then sells 600 of these shares on June 30 for $12 per share and the remaining 900 shares on October 15 for $14 per share, Alice will be liable to Tel-Ko for:
   a. $12,000.
   b. $2,000.
   c. $2,400.
   d. $4,000.

_____ 10. Under the 1933 Act which of the following transactions would be exempt from registration?
   a. Private placements.
   b. Limited offers solely to accredited investors.
   c. Limited offers not exceeding $1 million.
   d. All of the above.

_____ 11. Sanctions under the 1934 Act for noncompliance with the act include which of the following?
   a. Civil liability to injured investors.
   b. Civil penalties.
   c. Criminal penalties.
   d. All of the above.

_____ 12. Which of the following is correct with respect to Section 16(b)?
   a. It applies only to transactions involving registered securities.
   b. It uses the same definition of "insider" as does Rule 10b-5.
   c. It requires that an insider possess material nonpublic information.
   d. All of the above are correct with respect to 16(b).

_____ 13. Which of the following are included within the definition of insiders for the purposes of Rule 10b-5?
   a. Directors.
   b. Officers.
   c. Employees.
   d. Directors, officers and employees are all insiders under Rule 10b-5.

_____ 14. Which rule exempts from registration offerings by noninvestment company issuers that do not exceed $5 million over twelve months?
   a. Rule 10b-5.
   b. Rule 14a-3.
   c. Rule 504.
   d. Rule 505.

_____ 15. Which of the following would ordinarily not be considered a security under the federal securities law?
   a.   A limited partnership interest.
   b.   An insurance policy.
   c.   Bonds of a corporation.
   d.   An interest in a citrus grove.

SHORT ESSAY

1.   What is the primary purpose of federal securities regulation?

   _____
   _____
   _____
   _____

2.   What information must typically be disclosed in a registration statement?

   _____
   _____
   _____
   _____

3.   Define a security.

   _____
   _____
   _____
   _____

4.   Explain who would be considered an "insider" under Rule 10b-5.

   _____
   _____
   _____
   _____

5.   Big Bucks Corporation has assets of $3,000,000 and 300 shareholders owning common stock. The board of directors plans to issue $500,000 of common stock to raise additional capital. If Big Bucks plans to trade the stock over the counter, does it need to register with the SEC?

   _____
   _____
   _____
   _____

Chapter 47
Accountants' Legal Liability

PURPOSE

An accountant is subject to potential civil liability arising from the professional services he provides to his clients and third parties. This legal liability is imposed by both the common law at the state level as well as federal securities laws. In addition, an accountant may violate criminal laws in connection with his work. In this chapter you study accountants' legal liability under both state and federal law.

CHAPTER CHECKPOINTS

After reading and studying this chapter, you should be able to:

1. Identify situations in which an accountant may have contract liability based upon implicit and explicit contract terms.

2. Identify situations in which an accountant may have tort liability based upon negligence or fraud.

3. Summarize the rights and privileges given to accountants under state law regarding the ownership of working papers and the existence of an accountant-client privilege.

4. Summarize the potential civil and criminal liability of an accountant under the Securities Act of 1933.

5. Summarize the potential civil and criminal liability of an accountant under the Securities Exchange Act of 1934.

CHAPTER OUTLINE

A. **Common Law**–An accountant's legal responsibility under state law may be based on (1) contract law, (2) tort law, or (3) criminal law. Common law also gives accountants rights and privileges such as the ownership of working papers and in some states a limited accountant-client privilege.

　1. **Contract Liability**–The employment contract between accountant and client is subject to the general principles of contract law. On entering into a binding contract (an engagement), the accountant is bound to perform all of the duties explicitly agreed to under the contract. An accountant also implicitly agrees to perform the contract in a competent and professional manner. An accountant is held to those standards that are generally accepted by the accounting profession, such as Generally Accepted Accounting Standards (GAAS) and Generally Accepted Accounting Principles (GAAP). He may by agreement explicitly agree to standards beyond GAAS. If an accountant breaches his contract, he will incur liability not only to his client but also to third-party beneficiaries who were not parties to the contract but whom the contracting parties intended to benefit under the contract. An accountant will not be entitled to any compensation if he materially breaches a contract. If the accountant substantially performs his duties, he is generally entitled to be compensated the agreed fee less any damages caused by the nonmaterial breach.

　2. **Tort Liability**–An accountant may incur tort liability to his client or third parties for negligence or fraud. A tort is a private or civil wrong, other than a breach of contract, for which the courts will provide a remedy in the form of an action for damages.

　　a. **Negligence**–An accountant is negligent who does not exercise the degree of care a reasonably competent accountant would exercise under the circumstances. An accountant is not liable for honest inaccuracies or errors of judgment so long as she exercises reasonable care in performing her duties. An accountant is not an insurer of the accuracy of her reports provided she acts in a reasonably competent and professional manner. Historically, an accountant's liability for negligence extended only to the client and to third-party beneficiaries. Privity of contract was required to pursue a cause of action based on negligence according to the landmark case of *Ultramares Corp. v. Touche*. However, in recent years the majority of the states and the Restatement of Torts adopts a foreseen users' test which expands the class of protected individuals to those who the accountant knew would use the work product or those who use the accountant's work for a purpose for which the accountant knew the work would be used. The class does not include potential investors and the general public, although some courts have extended liability to reasonably foreseeable plaintiffs who are neither known nor members of a class of intended recipients.

　　b. **Fraud**–An accountant who commits a fraudulent act is liable to any person who the accountant should have reasonably foreseen would be injured by the misrepresentation and who justifiably relied upon it. The required elements of fraud are: (1) a false representation (2) of fact (3) that is material (4) made with knowledge of its falsity and intention to deceive (5) justifiably relied on, and (6) causes injury to the plaintiff. An accountant who commits fraud is liable for both compensatory and punitive damages.

3. Criminal Liability–An accountant's criminal liability in rendering professional services is based primarily on the federal law of securities regulation and taxation. An accountant who knowingly and willfully certifies false documents, alters or tampers with accounting records, uses false financial reports, gives false testimony under oath, or commits forgery violates state criminal law. Criminal liability exists under the Internal Revenue Code for knowingly preparing false or fraudulent tax returns and for willfully assisting or advising a client to prepare a false return. Violators are subject to a fine not to exceed $100,000 ($500,000 for a corporation) or three years imprisonment or both.

4. Client Information–Two legal issues arise concerning client information obtained while providing services: (1) who owns the working papers generated by the accountant and (2) whether the client information is privileged.

   a. Working Papers–An accountant is held to be the owner of his working papers and thus need not surrender them to his client. Nevertheless, the accountant may not disclose the contents of these papers unless (1) the client consents or (2) a court orders the disclosure.

   b. Accountant-Client Privilege–The question of a possible accountant-client privilege frequently arises in tax disputes, criminal prosecution, and civil litigation. If information is considered to be privileged, it may not be admitted into evidence over the objection of the person possessing the privilege. Neither common law nor federal law recognizes a privilege. However, some states have adopted statutes granting some form of privilege, usually to the client, although a few extend the privilege to the accountant. It is generally considered to be professionally unethical for an accountant to disclose confidential communications from his client, unless the disclosure is in accordance with (1) the AICPA or GAAS requirements, (2) a court order, or (3) the client's request.

B. Federal Securities Law–Accountants may be both civilly and criminally liable under provisions of the 1933 and 1934 Acts.

1. Securities Act of 1933–Accountants are subject to civil liability under Section 11 of the 1933 Act if the financial statements they prepare or certify for inclusion in a registration statement contain any untrue statement or omission of material fact. Liability extends to anyone who acquires the security without knowledge of the untruth or omission. There is no requirement of privity nor proof of reliance on the financial statements under Section 11. An accountant may raise the defense of due diligence, which requires that she had, after reasonable investigation, reasonable grounds to believe and did believe that the financial statements were true, complete and accurate. The standard of reasonableness is that required of a prudent man in the management of his own property. Section 11 imposes liability for negligence in the conduct of the audit or the presentation of information in the financial statements. An accountant who willfully violates this section may be held criminally liable for a fine of not more than $10,000 or imprisonment of not more than five years or both.

2. Securities Exchange Act of 1934–Section 18 of the 1934 Act imposes civil liability on an accountant who makes or causes to be made any false or misleading statement about any material fact in any application, report, document or registration filed with the SEC under the

1934 Act. Liability extends to any person who purchased or sold a security in reliance on that false or misleading statement. An accountant is not liable who acted in good faith and had no knowledge the statement was false or misleading. Accountants may also be civilly liable for violations of Rule 10b-5, which may be for either direct participation or for indirect participation resulting from aiding and abetting others to violate the rule. Rule 10b-5 applies to both oral and written misstatements or omissions of material facts and to all securities. Liability extends to purchasers and sellers who rely on the misstatement or omission of material fact in connection with the purchase or sale of a security. Liability is imposed only if the accountant acted with scienter, which includes intentional or knowing conduct, as well as a reckless disregard of the truth. Accountants are subject to criminal liability for any willful violation of either Section 18 or Rule 10b-5. Violators are subject to a fine of not more than $1 million or imprisonment for not more than ten years or both. An accounting firm may be fined up to $2.5 million.

KEY TERMS

1. Engagement

2. Third-party beneficiary

3. Negligence

4. Privity

5. Foreseen users

6. Fraud

7. Working papers

8. Accountant-client privilege

9. Due diligence

10. Scienter

TRUE/FALSE

_____   1. An accountant is not permitted to disclose confidential information from his client even if a court orders the disclosure.

_____   2. An accountant who does not perform an audit on time when time is of the essence is entitled to be compensated for the contractually agreed-upon fee less damages.

_____ 3. Scienter is required for an accountant to violate 10b-5 of the Securities Exchange Act of 1934.

_____ 4. An accountant is negligent if she does not exercise the degree of care a reasonably competent accountant would exercise under the same circumstances.

_____ 5. An accountant who commits fraud is liable only to the party with whom the accountant has contracted.

_____ 6. Contributory negligence is a common defense raised by accountants in professional liability cases.

_____ 7. The client is held to be the owner of working papers prepared by an accountant.

_____ 8. Both common law and federal law recognize the existence of an accountant-client privilege.

_____ 9. No criminal liability exists under the Securities Exchange Act of 1934.

_____ 10. By agreeing to render services, an accountant is held to those standards generally accepted by the accounting profession such as GAAS.

_____ 11. If an accountant breaches her contract, she will be liable not only to her client but also to third-party beneficiaries.

_____ 12. Due diligence is not a defense to an action brought under the Securities Act of 1933.

_____ 13. All communication between an accountant and client is privileged and may not be admitted into evidence in a court proceeding.

_____ 14. Accountants may be both civilly and criminally liable under the provisions of the federal securities laws.

_____ 15. Criminal sanctions may be imposed on accountants under the Internal Revenue Code for knowingly preparing false or fraudulent tax returns.

MULTIPLE CHOICE

_____ 1. Which of the following is a defense under Section 11 of the 1933 Act?
   a. Lack of scienter.
   b. Due diligence.
   c. Lack of privity.
   d. All of the above are defenses under Section 11.

_____   2. Historically, an accountant's liability for negligence extended to which of the following?
    a. The client.
    b. Third-party beneficiaries.
    c. The client and third-party beneficiaries.
    d. The client, third-party beneficiaries and foreseen users.

_____   3. An accountant's legal responsibility under State law may be based upon:
    a. Contract law.
    b. Tort law.
    c. Criminal law.
    d. Any of the above.

_____   4. In which of the following situations may an accountant disclose the contents of working papers?
    a. When the client consents.
    b. When a court orders the disclosure.
    c. When the IRS summons them as part of criminal investigation.
    d. An accountant may disclose working papers in all of the above situations.

_____   5. The legal basis for the accountant-client privilege is:
    a. state common law.
    b. state statute.
    c. federal statute.
    d. state common law as well as both state and federal statute.

_____   6. Arthur, who is a CPA, was hired to audit the books of Tel-Ko Computers. During the audit, Oscar, an officer of the corporation, notified Arthur that he suspected the company's treasurer was engaged in a scheme to embezzle money from the corporation. Arthur did not pursue the matter, because he was anxious to complete the job in time for his scheduled summer vacation. If it later becomes known that the treasurer was in fact embezzling corporation money, which of the following is correct?
    a. Arthur has no liability if he followed Generally Accepted Auditing Standards.
    b. Arthur is guilty of negligence.
    c. If the financial statement Arthur prepared is included in a securities registration statement, Arthur is probably liable under Section 11 of the 1933 Act.
    d. Both (b) and (c) are correct.

_____   7. Which of the following can give rise to an accountant's criminal liability?
    a. Knowingly preparing a fraudulent tax return.
    b. Falsely certifying a document.
    c. Willfully violating Section 18 of the 1934 Act or Rule 10b-5.
    d. All of the above can give rise to criminal liability.

8. Penalties for the fraudulent preparation of a tax return may be three years in prison and a fine of:
   a. $5,000.
   b. $10,000.
   c. $50,000.
   d. $100,000.

9. Which of the following is necessary for an accountant to have liability under Rule 10b-5?
   a. Scienter.
   b. Mere negligence.
   c. Reckless disregard of the truth.
   d. Two of the above are correct, (a) or (c).

10. Who owns an accountant's working papers?
    a. The client.
    b. The accountant.
    c. The IRS.
    d. The SEC.

11. The Restatement of Torts has adopted the rule that accountants are liable for negligence to:
    a. reasonably foreseeable plaintiffs.
    b. clients and third-party beneficiaries.
    c. those the accountant knew would use the work.
    d. two of the above are correct, (b) and (c).

12. Under the Securities Exchange Act of 1934, an accountant can be held criminally liable if he makes any false or misleading statement about any material fact in any report filed with the SEC and he acted:
    a. willfully.
    b. negligently.
    c. in violation of GAAS.
    d. none of the above.

13. Under Section 11 of the Securities Act of 1933, an accountant may be civilly liable to:
    a. only those in privity with the accountant.
    b. only those who rely on the financial statements containing the untrue statement or omission.
    c. only those in privity and who rely on the financial statement.
    d. anyone who acquires the security without knowledge of the untrue statement or omission.

14. Audit requirements include which of the following?
    a. Establish procedures to detect material illegal acts.
    b. Identify material related party transactions.
    c. Evaluate the ability to continue as a going concern.
    d. All of the above.

_____ 15. To recover money damages from an accountant for fraud, a person must prove:

    a. that the accountant made a negligent misrepresentation.

    b. that the accountant made a false misrepresentation with the intent to deceive which was relied upon and caused injury.

    c. that the accountant did not comply with GAAS.

    d. all of the above.

SHORT ESSAY

1. Kind and Kind, CPA's, has audited the Consumer Credit Corporation for the past ten years. The SEC has recently commenced an investigation against CCC for possible violations of the federal securities laws. As part of its investigation, the SEC has subpoenaed all of Kind and Kind's working papers pertaining to the audit of CCC. Does Kind have to produce its working papers? Explain.

    _____

    _____

    _____

    _____

2. Arthur and Arthur Company, CPA's, audited the financial statements included in the annual report submitted by Tel-Ko Computer Company to the SEC. The audit failed to detect numerous false and misleading statements in the financial statements. If the SEC initiates criminal proceedings against Arthur and Arthur Company under the 1934 Act, what must the SEC prove for Arthur and Arthur to be held criminally liable?

    _____

    _____

    _____

    _____

3. Explain the difference in explicit and implicit contract terms which may lead to liability for an accountant.

    _____

    _____

    _____

    _____

4. Kind and Kind, CPA's, prepare an audit report for Tel-Ko Computer Company. Tel-Ko uses the audit report to obtain a loan from First Bank. If the audit report is not accurate and Tel-Ko defaults on the loan because of insolvency, what is the result?

    _____

    _____

    _____

    _____

5. Briefly identify the sources of accountant liability.

_____

_____

_____

_____

Chapter 48
Environmental Law

PURPOSE

With the advancement of urbanization the effect on the environment became a matter of greater concern. Air became dirtier and water more polluted. Individuals and environmental groups brought private actions against polluters, but the common law proved unable to control environmental damage. In response the federal and state governments enacted a variety of statutes designed to promote environmental concerns and prevent environmental harm. In this chapter, you study both common law cause of action for environmental damage and federal regulation of the environment.

CHAPTER CHECKPOINTS

After reading and studying this chapter, you should be able to:

1. Identify and discuss the various common law theories supporting actions for environmental damage.

2. Distinguish between a public nuisance and a private nuisance and explain the difficulties involved in prevailing in an attempt to recover or abate either.

3. Identify important legislative acts regulating the environment.

4. Discuss the procedure for an environmental impact statement and explain its scope.

5. Explain the purpose and scope of the Comprehensive Environmental Response, Compensation and Liability Act (CERCLA).

CHAPTER OUTLINE

A. Common Law Actions for Environmental Damage–Private tort actions may be used to recover for harm to the environment. Such suits rely on the theories of nuisance, trespass, and strict liability.

   1. Nuisance–Nuisance encompasses two distinct types of wrong: private nuisance and public nuisance. A private nuisance involves an interference with the use and enjoyment of a person's land, while a public nuisance is an act which interferes with a public right.

      a. Private nuisance–Private nuisance is a substantial and unreasonable interference with the use and enjoyment of another's land. In an action for damages a plaintiff need not prove that the defendant's conduct is unreasonable. However, in an action seeking an injunction, the reasonableness of the defendant's conduct is an issue.

      b. Public nuisance–A public nuisance is an interference with the health, safety, or comfort of the public. Suits to stop a public nuisance are brought by a public representative, such as the attorney general. Because public representatives often will not, and private parties may not, sue, relatively few public nuisance actions have been brought against polluters.

   2. Trespass to Land–Trespass to land involves action by one party which directly results in an invasion which interferes with the right of exclusive possession of the property of another. Trespass differs from private nuisance in that nuisance does not require an interference with the plaintiff's possession of the land.

   3. Strict Liability for Abnormally Dangerous Activities–To establish strict liability, a plaintiff must show that the defendant is carrying on an unduly dangerous (ultrahazardous) activity in an inappropriate location and that the plaintiff has suffered damage because of this activity.

   4. Problems Common to Private Causes of Action–Problems associated with the bringing of a private cause of action include: (1) high costs associated with private litigation (including the payments of one's own legal fees); (2) injunctive relief is often denied because of successful equity defenses; (3) public representatives are unwilling to bring actions because of concern over the economic impact; (4) relief for aesthetic injury is generally not available; (5) there may be a question of causation if more than one defendant is polluting; and (6) recovery is often limited to monetary damages and the defendant remains free to continue to pollute.

B. Federal Regulation of the Environment–Because private causes of action proved inadequate, federal, state, and some local governments have enacted statutes designed to protect the environment.

   1. National Environmental Policy Act–In 1969 Congress enacted the National Environmental Policy Act (NEPA) to establish environmental protection as a goal of federal policy. NEPA has two major substantive sections, one of which created the Council on Environmental Quality (CEQ), and the other established the requirement for an environmental impact statement (EIS) in those cases where legislation or federal action would have a significant environmental effect.

      a. Council on Environmental Quality–CEQ, as part of the Executive Office of the President, makes recommendations on environmental matters and prepares annual reports on the condition of the environment.

      b. Environmental Impact Statements–NEPA focuses on the government's continuing concern with protection of the environment. NEPA's promotion of environmental considerations is effected through EIS requirement.

(1) Procedure for Preparing EIS–When proposing legislation or considering a major federal action the federal agency initially makes an "environmental assessment," which is a short analysis of the need for an EIS. If the agency decides no EIS is required, the public is informed of this decision. If an EIS is required, a determination is made of the "scope" of the EIS. A draft EIS is made available for comments, followed by a final EIS.

(2) Scope of EIS Requirement–The EIS requirement of NEPA applied to a broad range of projects. "Federal action" occurs when an agency proposes to build a facility itself, and also whenever an agency makes a decision which permits action by other parties which will affect the quality of the environment. The EIS requirement also applies to a broad range of types of effects.

(3) Content of EIS–The EIS must contain a statement of any adverse environmental effects which cannot be avoided, reasonable alternatives, the relationship between local short-term uses of the environment and the maintenance and enhancement of long-term productivity, as well as any irreversible and irretrievable commitments of resources involved in the proposed action.

(4) Nature of EIS Requirement–NEPA requirements are primarily procedural and impose no requirement that the relevant federal agency take steps to mitigate the adverse effects of the proposed federal action.

2. Clean Air Act–The Act establishes two regulatory schemes. While the states retain primary responsibility for regulating existing stationary sources and motor vehicles then in use, the federal government regulates new sources, new vehicles, and hazardous air pollutants.

a. Existing Stationary Sources and Motor Vehicles then in Use–The 1970 Amendments provided that, in respect of existing stationary sources and motor vehicles then in use, the federal government would set national air quality standards that the states would be primarily responsible for achieving.

(1) National Ambient Air Quality Standards–The EPA Administrator establishes "primary" standards to protect the health and "secondary" standards to protect the public welfare with respect to five major classes of pollutants.

(2) State Implementation Plans–Each state must submit to the EPA a state implementation plan (SIP) which, if it meets certain statutory conditions and if the state adopts the SIP after public hearings, must be approved by the EPA.

(3) Prevention of Significant Deterioration Areas–Congress, in 1977 Amendments, established a policy of preventing deterioration of the quality of air which exceeded the NAAQS levels. In PSD areas, only limited increases in air pollution are allowed.

(4) Nonattainment Areas–The 1977 and 1990 Amendments also established special rules for areas that did not meet the applicable NAAQS. In these nonattainment areas, total emissions from existing stationary sources and the proposed new or modified source together must be less than the total emissions allowed from existing sources at the time the permit is sought. To obtain a permit in such an area the owner/operator must reduce total emissions from all sources.

b. New Source Standards–The Clean Air Act authorizes the federal government to establish national emission standards for new stationary sources, hazardous air pollutants, and new vehicles.

    (1) New Stationary Sources–The Administrator must establish standards of performance for stationary sources that are constructed or modified after the publication of applicable regulations. The standard governing new sources is more stringent than the standard governing existing sources.

    (2) New Vehicles–The Act requires the Administrator to establish emission standards for new motor vehicles and new motor vehicle engines. The 1990 Amendments require reformulated fuels to be employed in order to reduce ozone and carbon monoxide pollution.

    (3) Hazardous Air Pollutants–The Act authorizes the Administrator to establish national emission standards for hazardous or toxic air pollutants which may result in an increase in mortality or an increase in serious irreversible, or incapacitating reversible illness. The standard must be set at a level which "provides an ample margin of safety to protect the public health."

    (4) Acid Rain–The 1990 Amendments attempt to halt the destruction of the environment due to precipitation that contains high levels of sulfuric or nitric acid. A schedule of allowances is established that will significantly reduce the emissions of sulfur dioxide and nitrous oxides by the year 2000.

3. Clean Water Act–The Act, which applies to all navigable waters in the United States and to tributaries of navigable waters, interstate waters and their tributaries, nonnavigable intrastate waters if misuse could affect interstate commerce, and freshwater wetlands, attempts to comprehensively restore and maintain the chemical, physical, and biological integrity of the nation's waters and establishes different schemes for existing sources and new sources. The Act also provides different programs for point sources of pollution and non-point sources.

    a. Point Sources–A point source is "any discernible, confined and discrete conveyance * * * from which pollutants are or may be discharged." The Act requires that the EPA Administrator establish effluent limitations for categories of existing point sources.

        (1) Effluent Limitations–Effluent limitations require application of the best practicable control technology currently available by 1977 and application of the best available technology economically achievable by 1983. Somewhat different standards apply to publicly owned treatment works.

        (2) National Pollutant Discharge Elimination System–NPDES requires any person responsible for the discharge from a point source of a pollutant into the waters of the United States to obtain a discharge permit from EPA, the Army Corps of Engineers, or the relevant state.

        (3) The 1977 Amendments–Recognizing that the deadlines set in 1972 would not be met, Congress extended and modified the deadlines in the 1977 Amendments which divided pollutants into three categories–toxic, conventional, and nonconventional–and established different deadlines and standards for each.

    b. Nonpoint Source Pollution–Because of the difficulty in controlling nonpoint source pollution, Congress amended the Act in 1987. These amendments require states to identify state waters that will not meet the Act's requirements without management of non-pollution sources and to institute "best management practices" to control nonpoint sources of pollution. The EPA must approve each state's management plan.

   c. New Source Performance Standards–The Administrator is required to establish federal standards of performance for new sources. Requiring the best available demonstrated control technology standard, permitting no discharge of pollutants is the preferred standard for new sources.

4. Hazardous Substances–Advances in technology allow for the production of numerous new substances, some of which have proven extremely hazardous to health. In response to this, Congress enacted various statutes to deal with different aspects of the harm.

   a. Federal Insecticide, Fungicide and Rodenticide Act–FIFRA requires that a pesticide be registered with the EPA before any person may distribute it. Registration is legal only if the pesticide's composition warrants the proposed claims for it, the pesticide will perform its intended function without "unreasonable adverse effects on the environment," the pesticide will not generally cause unreasonable adverse effects on the environment when used in accordance with widespread and commonly recognized practice, and the pesticide complies with FIFRA labeling requirements. In 1988 Congress amended FIFRA to require the re-registration of pesticides registered before 1984 which had been registered under less strict standards.

   b. Toxic Substance Control Act–The TSCA requires a manufacturer to notify the EPA before it manufactures a new chemical or makes a significant new use of an existing chemical. The EPA may require testing of any substance, whether existing or new, if (1) the manufacture or distribution of the substance may present an unreasonable risk of injury to health or the environment, (2) there is insufficient data on the effects of the substance on health and the environment, and (3) testing is necessary to develop such data. If a substance "presents or will present an unreasonable risk of injury to health or the environment," the EPA may restrict or prohibit use of the substance.

   c. Resource Conservation and Recovery Act–RCRA provides a comprehensive scheme for treatment of solid waste, particularly hazardous waste. Responsibility is divided such that the states have primary responsibility for nonhazardous waste and the EPA regulates all phases of hazardous waste. The statute requires the EPA to establish a manifest system, providing a form on which the generator (an entity that produces hazardous waste) must specify the quantity, composition, origin, routing, and destination of a hazardous waste. Owner/operators of hazardous waste treatment, storage, and disposal sites must maintain records and comply with the manifest.

   d. The Superfund–The Comprehensive Environmental Response, Compensation and Liability Act was passed for the cleanup of abandoned or inactive hazardous waste sites. CIRCLA as amended by the Superfund Amendments and Reauthorization Act of 1986 (SARA) requires the federal government to establish a National Contingency Plan (NCP) to prescribe procedures and standards for responding to hazardous substance releases. The Act provides the authority for the federal government to take either removal or remedial actions in response to a release or threatened release of hazardous substances. States and private parties may also engage in response actions.

5. International Protection of the Ozone Layer–In 1987 a treaty entitled the Montreal Protocol on

Substances that Deplete the Ozone Layer was signed by the United States and twenty-three other countries. Under the Montreal Protocol all signatories are obligated to reduce their production and consumption of all chemicals that deplete the ozone layer. An additional treaty was signed which called for the elimination of chlorofluorocarbons (CFCs) and halon by the year 2000. By executive order these chemicals are scheduled to be eliminated in the United States by 1996.

KEY TERMS

1. Private nuisance

2. Public nuisance

3. Trespass to land

4. Strict liability

5. Environmental impact statement

6. Environmental assessment

7. Scoping

8. National ambient air quality standard

9. State implementation plan

10. Prevention of significant deterioration areas

11. Nonattainment areas

12. Bubble concept

13. Acid rain

14. Point source

15. Non-point source

16. Effluent limitation

17. BPT

18. BAT

19. BCT

TRUE/FALSE

_____ 1. Private tort actions may be used to recover for harm to the environment.

_____ 2. Trespass differs from private nuisance in that nuisance does not require an interference with plaintiff's possession of the land.

_____ 3. To be treated as a public nuisance, an activity must interfere with the health, safety, or comfort of the public.

_____ 4. Comparable to other federal environmental statutes, the National Environmental Policy Act focuses on particular environmental damage and specific harmful substances.

_____ 5. "Federal action" within the meaning of NEPA is broadly construed and applies to an unlimited number of situations.

_____ 6. Environmental impact statements provide a basis for evaluating the benefits of a proposed project in light of its environmental risks.

_____ 7. NEPA's requirements are primarily procedural and do not require the relevant federal agency to take steps to mitigate the adverse effects of the proposed federal action.

_____ 8. Under the Clean Air Act the states' primary responsibility is to regulate new sources within the state, new vehicles, and hazardous air pollutants.

_____ 9. Once the EPA promulgates a new ambient air quality standard, every state must submit a state implementation plan detailing how they will maintain the new standard.

_____ 10. In prevention of significant deterioration areas, the EPA will allow increases in air pollution equal to the difference between the current level and the established standard.

_____ 11. Under the "bubble concept" an entire plant is viewed as one source, so that a permit process applies only if total emissions from the plant increase.

_____ 12. Air quality emission standards governing existing sources are more stringent than the standard governing new sources.

_____ 13. Under the Clean Water Act a point source is considered to be any land use that causes pollution, such as runoff from agricultural land use.

_____ 14. An effluent limitation is a technology-based standard that limits the amount of pollutant that may be discharged by a nonpoint source into the water.

_____ 15. Under the Toxic Substances Control Act a manufacturer must notify the EPA before it makes a significant new use of an existing chemical.

MULTIPLE CHOICE

_____ 1. An invasion of land which interferes with the right of exclusive possession of the property would be a:
   a. private nuisance.
   b. public nuisance.
   c. trespass.
   d. none of the above.

_____ 2. While tort liability is generally based on fault, a person may be held strictly liable if the plaintiff can show that the defendant was engaged in an activity that was:
   a. ultrahazardous.
   b. inappropriate for its locale.
   c. either (a) or (b).
   d. both (a) and (b).

_____ 3. In a private nuisance action, which of the following will a court consider before issuing an injunction?
   a. Gravity of harm to the plaintiff.
   b. Social value of defendant's activity.
   c. Public interest.
   d. All of the above.

_____ 4. When the EPA proposes a major federal action and concludes that an EIS is required, the next step in the procedure is:
   a. an environmental assessment.
   b. a comment period.
   c. scoping.
   d. a draft EIS.

_____ 5. NEPA's EIS requirement applies to a broad range of types of effects within the urban environment. To which one of the following would the EIS requirement not apply?
   a. Noise.
   b. Overburdened mass transportation systems.
   c. Crime.
   d. It would apply to all the above as they all affect the urban environment.

_____ 6. Under the Clean Air Act the EPA may impose civil penalties of up to:
   a. $25,000 per violation.
   b. $25,000 per day of violation.
   c. $50,000 per violation.
   d. $50,000 per day of violation.

_____ 7. In a PSD area an owner or operator, in order to receive a permit, must demonstrate that the source:
   a. will not add to pollution beyond the permitted increase.
   b. will utilize the best available control technology.
   c. either (a) or (b).
   d. both (a) and (b).

_____ 8. The Clean Air Act places responsibility on the federal government to establish national emission standards for all of the following except:
   a. existing stationary sources.
   b. new stationary sources.
   c. hazardous air pollutants.
   d. new vehicles.

_____ 9. Under the Clean Water Act, the maximum criminal penalties for knowing violations are 3 years imprisonment and:
   a. $25,000 per violation.
   b. $25,000 per day of violation.
   c. $50,000 per violation.
   d. $50,000 per day of violation.

_____ 10. Under the Clean Water Act "any discernible, confined and discrete conveyance * * * from which pollutants are or may be discharged" is known as:
   a. a point source.
   b. a non-point source.
   c. a nonattainment area.
   d. none of the above.

_____ 11. To which of the following would the Clean Water Act not apply?
   a. Navigable waters in the United States.
   b. Interstate waters and their tributaries.
   c. Freshwater wetlands.
   d. The Clean Water Act would apply to all of the above.

_____ 12. Under the Clean Water Act's 1977 amendments, a new standard was applied to conventional pollutants and was to be achieved by 1984. That standard was:
   a. BAT.
   b. BPT.
   c. BCT.
   d. none of the above.

_____ 13. Under the Federal Insecticide, Fungicide and Rodenticide Act the EPA may impose civil penalties of up to:
   a. $5,000 per offense.
   b. $5,000 per day of offense.
   c. $25,000 per offense.
   d. $25,000 per day of offense.

_____ 14. Which of the following would be grounds for the EPA to require testing of a substance?
   a. The manufacture or distribution of the substance may present an unreasonable risk of injury to health or the environment.
   b. There is insufficient data on the effects of the substance on health and the environment and testing is necessary to develop such data.
   c. Both (a) and (b).
   d. Either (a) or (b).

_____ 15. The Resource Conservation and Recovery Act regulates:
   a. Current and future generation of hazardous waste.
   b. Transportation of hazardous waste.
   c. Disposal of hazardous waste.
   d. All of the above.

SHORT ESSAY

1. Identify and discuss the common law actions for environmental damage.

_____
_____
_____
_____

2. What is the major difference between a private nuisance and a public nuisance and what are some of the problems associated with these causes of action?

_____
_____
_____
_____

3. List and briefly describe the two major substantive sections of the National Environmental Policy Act.

_____
_____
_____
_____

4. Explain the "bubble concept."

_____

_____

_____

_____

5. What is the "Superfund?"

_____

_____

_____

_____

Chapter 49
International Business Law

PURPOSE

Today business requires some understanding of international business practices, because the entire global economy has become increasingly interconnected. Laws vary greatly from country to country and there is no single authority in international law. When the laws of two or more nations conflict, or when one party has violated an agreement that the other party wishes to enforce or to recover damages, it is often difficult to establish who will adjudicate the matter, which laws will be applied, what remedies are available, or where the matter should be decided. In this chapter, you study some of the basic international organizations, agreements and principles that affect international business.

CHAPTER CHECKPOINTS

After reading and studying this chapter, you should be able to:

1. List and discuss the sources and institutions of international law.

2. Discuss the purpose and major provisions of GATT.

3. Compare the doctrines of sovereign immunity and act of state, and distinguish between expropriation and confiscation.

4. Discuss the legal controls imposed on the flow of trade, labor, and capital across national borders.

5. List and briefly describe the forms that a multinational enterprise may choose when conducting its business in a foreign country.

CHAPTER OUTLINE

A. The International Environment–International law includes law that deals with the conduct and relations of nation-states and international organizations as well as some of their relations with persons. As a general rule, international law cannot be enforced, because international courts do not have compulsory jurisdiction to resolve disputes. The courts of a sovereign nation may enforce international law to the same extent as its domestic law if the nation has adopted the international law as the law of the nation.

    1. International Court of Justice–The United Nations has a judicial branch called the International Court of Justice. The ICJ consists of fifteen judges, no two of whom may be from the same sovereign state. Only nations and not private parties may be parties to an action before the court. It has jurisdiction only when nations agree to be bound by its decision, and when countries do not like its decision, they may ignore it.

    2. Regional Trade Communities–International organizations, conferences, and treaties that focus on business and trade regulation are of much greater significance than the ICJ. The European Economic Community (EEC), which is better known as the Common Market, was formed in 1957 by the Treaty of Rome in order to remove trade barriers between member nations and to unify their economic policies. Fifteen nations are members of the EEC. Other important regional trade communities are the Central American Common Market (CACM), the Caribbean Common Market (CARICOM), the Association of South East Asian Nations (ASEAN), the Andean Common Market (ANDEAN), and the Economic Community of West African States (ECOWAS).

    3. International Treaties–A treaty is an agreement between or among independent nations. The U.S. Constitution authorizes the president to enter into treaties with the advice and consent of the Senate "providing two-thirds of the Senators present concur." The Constitution also provides that all valid treaties are the "law of the land," having the legal force of a federal statute. Probably the most important multilateral trade treaty is the General Agreement on Tariffs and Trade (GATT). The GATT, now called the World Trade Organization, has as its basic purpose to facilitate the flow of trade by establishing agreements on potential trade barriers such as import quotas, customs, export regulations, subsidies, and import fees. GATT's most favored nation provision states that all signatories must treat each other as favorably as they treat any other country. Nevertheless, nations may also enter into free trade areas with one or more other nations.

    The North Atlantic Free Trade Agreement (NAFTA) took effect in 1994 and established a free trade area among the United States, Canada, and Mexico. Over fifteen years, the treaty will gradually eliminate all tariffs between these three countries.

B. Jurisdiction Over Actions of Foreign Governments–This section focuses on the power, and the limits upon the power, of a sovereign nation to exercise jurisdiction over a foreign nation or to take property owned by foreign citizens.

    1. Sovereign Immunity–Every nation has absolute and total authority over what goes on within its own territory. This principle of absolute immunity of a foreign sovereign from the courts of the host country is known as sovereign immunity. Congress has enacted the Foreign Sovereign

Immunities Act in order to establish legislatively when immunity would be extended to foreign nations. The act specifically provides that a foreign state shall not be immune from the jurisdiction of courts of the U.S. or of the states if the suit is based upon (1) a commercial activity carried on in the U.S. by the foreign state, (2) an act performed in the U.S. in connection with a commercial activity of the foreign state carried on elsewhere, or (3) a commercial activity of a foreign state carried on outside the U.S. that causes a direct effect in the U.S.

2. Act of State Doctrine–The act of state doctrine provides that the judicial branch of a nation should not question the validity of actions taken by a foreign government within that foreign sovereign's own borders. The U.S. Supreme Court said in 1987 that "Every sovereign State is bound to respect the independence of every other sovereign State, and the courts of one country will not sit in judgment on the acts of the government of another done within its own territory." Exceptions to the act of state doctrine include the following: (a) a sovereign may waive its right to raise the act of state defense and (b) the doctrine may be inapplicable to commercial activities of a foreign sovereign.

3. Taking of Foreign Investment Property–An expropriation or nationalization occurs when a government seizes foreign-owned property or assets for a public purpose and pays the owner just compensation for what is taken. Confiscation is the term used when no payment (or an inadequate payment) is given in exchange for the seized property, or it is seized for a nonpublic purpose. U.S. firms should obtain insurance from a private insurer or the Overseas Private Investment Corporation (OPIC).

C. Transacting Business Abroad–Business abroad may involve selling goods, information, or services or investing capital or arranging for the movement of labor. This section examines the legal controls imposed on the flow of trade, labor and capital across national borders.

1. Flow of Trade–A device that is frequently applied by nations to protect domestic businesses is the tariff which is a duty or tax imposed on goods moving into or out of a country. Tariffs raise the price of imported goods, causing some consumers to purchase less expensive, domestically produced items. Nontariff barriers include unilateral or bilateral import quotas, import bans, overly restrictive safety or manufacturing standards, complicated customs procedures and subsidies to local industry. Export controls are used to control the flow of goods out of a country. They are usually imposed for policy reasons such as national defense, foreign policy, or protection of scarce national resources.

2. Flow of Labor–Almost all countries require that foreigners obtain valid passports before entering their borders. In addition, they may issue visas to foreign citizens permitting them to enter the country for an identified purpose or specified period of time. The U.S. Immigration and Naturalization Service issues various types of visas depending on the purpose of an individual's visit.

3. Flow of Capital–The International Monetary Fund (IMF) was established to facilitate the expansion and balanced growth of international trade, to assist in the elimination of foreign exchange restrictions, and to shorten the duration and lessen the disequilibrium in the international balance of payments of its members. There are also international and regional banks to facilitate the flow of capital and trade.

4. International Contracts–The legal issues inherent in domestic commercial contracts also arise in international contracts. In addition, there are issues such as differences in language, customs,

legal systems and currency. The contract should specify the official language, acceptable currency, choice of law designating what law will govern, and which nation's court will resolve disputes or whether arbitration will be used. It should also include a *force majeure* clause apportioning the liabilities and responsibilities of the parties in the event of an unforeseeable occurrence.

    a. CISG–The United States, as well as over forty other countries, has ratified the U.N. Convention on Contracts for the International Sale of Goods. The CISG governs all contracts for the international sales of goods between parties located in nations that have ratified the CISG.

    b. Letters of Credit–A letter of credit is a promise by a buyer's bank to pay the seller provided certain conditions are met. The buyer then enters into a second contract with a local bank, called an issuer, calling for the bank to pay the agreed price upon presentation of specified documents. The commitment by the buyer's bank is the irrevocable letter of credit. Typically, a correspondent or paying bank located in the seller's country makes payment to the seller.

5. Antitrust Laws–Section 1 of the Sherman Act provides for a broad, extraterritorial reach of the U.S. antitrust laws. Recent amendments to the Sherman Act and the Federal Trade Commission Act limit their application to unfair methods of competition that have a direct, substantial, and reasonably foreseeable effect on U.S. domestic commerce, import commerce, or export commerce.

6. Securities Regulation–Due to increasingly internationalized securities markets, questions regarding applicable laws governing a particular transaction in securities are not uncommon. The Securities Act of 1933 and the Securities Exchange Act of 1934 apply to those securities issued in the United States unless and exemption is available. The antifraud provisions apply, and courts generally find jurisdiction where there is either *conduct* or *effects* in the United States relating to a violation.

7. Protection of Intellectual Property–U.S. intellectual property protection laws do not apply in foreign countries. The owner of an intellectual property right obtains protection from the country in question, and the laws vary substantially from country to country. The United States belongs to some multinational treaties designed to protect intellectual property.

8. Foreign Corrupt Practices Act–The Foreign Corrupt Practices Act (FCPA) prohibits all domestic concerns from bribing foreign governmental or political officials. Violations can result in fines for individuals of up to $100,000 and/or imprisonment of up to five years. Companies violating this law can be fined up to $2 million.

D. Forms of Multinational Enterprises–A multinational enterprise is a business that engages in transactions involving the movement of goods, information, money, people, or services across national borders. Factors to be considered in determining the form of a multinational business enterprise include financing, tax consequences, legal restrictions imposed by the host country, and the degree of control over the business sought by the multinational enterprise.

    1. Direct Export Sales–The seller contracts directly with the buyer in the other country. This is the simplest and least involved form of multinational enterprise.

    2. Foreign Agents–Agency relationships are often used by companies that want limited involvement in the international market.

3. Distributorships–Unlike an agent, a distributor takes title to merchandise it receives. This commonly used form is susceptible to antitrust violations.

4. Licensing–This involves the sale of an intellectual property right, such as patent, trademark, trade secret, or innovative production technology. The foreign firm pays royalties in exchange for the use of the right. Franchising is a form of licensing in which the owner grants permission to a foreign business to use the intellectual property under carefully specified conditions.

5. Joint Ventures–In a joint venture, two or more independent businesses from different countries agree to coordinate their efforts to achieve a common result. They share profits and liabilities according to a contract. Each company can be assigned responsibility for what it does best.

6. Wholly Owned Subsidiaries–The creation of a foreign wholly owned subsidiary can offer numerous advantages, including the opportunity to retain authority and control over all phases of operation and the ability to safeguard technology.

KEY TERMS

1. International law

2. Treaty

3. Sovereign immunity

4. Act of state doctrine

5. Expropriation

6. Confiscation

7. Tariff

8. Letter of credit

9. Multinational enterprise

TRUE/FALSE

_____ 1. Only nations may be parties to an action before the International Court of Justice.

_____ 2. The European Community has the power to make rules which are binding on member nations and which preempt its members' domestic laws.

_____ 3. Unilateral and bilateral import quotas are examples of nontariff barriers to the flow of trade.

_____ 4. The tariff is a frequently used device designed to protect domestic businesses.

_____ 5. The U.S. Constitution provides that all valid treaties are "the law of the land" having the legal force of a federal statute.

_____ 6. A simple majority of the senators present may ratify a treaty under the U.S. Constitution.

_____ 7. A letter of credit transaction is an effective means of managing the risks of international trade and involves three or four different parties and three underlying contracts.

_____ 8. Under GATT's most favored nation provision, signatories are not required to treat other signatories equally with regard to privileges, immunities and favors.

_____ 9. The U.S. Supreme Court holding, that a court should not question the validity of actions a foreign government takes in its own country, is known as the act of state doctrine.

_____ 10. The simplest and least involved multinational enterprise is a direct export sale.

_____ 11. International courts have authority to resolve a dispute only if the parties to the dispute accept the court's jurisdiction over the matter.

_____ 12. Currently, the International Monetary Fund has more than 140 counties as members.

_____ 13. U.S. laws protecting intellectual property do not apply to transactions in other countries.

_____ 14. The United Nations Convention on Contracts for the International Sales of Goods (CISG) governs all contracts for the international sales of goods between parties located in different nations that have ratified the CISG.

_____ 15. The term "multinational enterprise" refers to any business that engages in transactions involving the movement of goods across national borders.

MULTIPLE CHOICE

_____ 1. The EEC is better known as:
   a. the Warsaw Pact.
   b. the Common Market.
   c. the General Agreement on Tariffs and Trade.
   d. the International Monetary Fund.

_____ 2. What is the purpose of a *force majeure* clause?
a. It determines what law applies to a contract.
b. It determines the method of payment for goods sold between a buyer in one country and a seller in another country.
c. It determines the forum in which a dispute must be decided.
d. It apportions the liabilities and responsibilities of the parties in the event of an unforeseeable occurrence.

_____ 3. Which of the following is NOT a nontariff barrier?
a. Quotas.
b. Taxes.
c. Bans.
d. Subsidies.

_____ 4. One precaution that can be taken by U.S. firms to avoid the economic loss caused by the seizure of investment property by a host nation's government is to obtain insurance from either a private insurer or an agency of the U.S. government, which is known as:
a. OPIC.
b. ASEAN.
c. the Commerce Department.
d. the U.S. State Department.

_____ 5. Examples of noncommercial activities to which the doctrine of _____ would extend include nationalizing a corporation, determining the limitations upon the use of natural resources, and granting licenses to export a natural resource.
a. act of state
b. sovereign immunity
c. confiscation
d. expropriation

_____ 6. Which of the following is the West African States counterpart to the European Common Market?
a. CARICOM.
b. ANCOM.
c. COMECON.
d. ECOWAS.

_____ 7. The basic purpose of _____ is to facilitate the flow of trade by establishing agreements on potential trade barriers such as import quotas, customs, and export regulations.
   a. CISG
   b. GATT
   c. IMF
   d. none of the above

_____ 8. Each country has its own immigration policies and regulations which require:
   a. that foreigners obtain valid passports before entering their borders.
   b. that their citizens have a passport to leave or reenter the country.
   c. that foreign citizens obtain a visa to enter the country for an identified purpose.
   d. all of the above.

_____ 9. Which of the following could be an exception to the act of state doctrine?
   a. The doctrine may be inapplicable to commercial activities of a foreign sovereign.
   b. A sovereign may waive its right to raise the doctrine as a defense.
   c. Either (a) or (b).
   d. Neither (a) nor (b), exceptions are not allowed.

_____ 10. The CISG specifically excludes which of the following?
   a. Sales of goods bought for personal, family, or household use.
   b. Sale of ships or aircraft.
   c. Both (a) and (b).
   d. Neither (a) nor (b).

_____ 11. Which of the following should be used by Americana Computer Corporation, a multinational enterprise, if they want a limited involvement in the international market?
   a. Foreign agents.
   b. Direct export sales.
   c. Joint ventures.
   d. Licensing.

_____ 12. An international contract should specify:
   a. what law will govern any breach or dispute.
   b. the official language of the contract.
   c. which nation's court will resolve disputes.
   d. all of the above.

_____ 13. The International Monetary Fund was established to:
   a. facilitate expansion and balanced growth of international trade.
   b. assist in the elimination of foreign exchange restrictions.
   c. shorten the duration in the international balance of payments of members.
   d. all of the above.

_____ 14. The rule that a court should not question the validity of actions taken by a foreign government in its own country is known as:
   a. Act of State Doctrine.
   b. Doctrine of Sovereign Immunity.
   c. U.S. conflicts of laws.
   d. none of the

_____ 15. Denmark seized all of the property of Chemco, Inc., an American company located in Denmark, and assumed ownership of the property for a public purpose after payment of just compensation. This is known as:
   a. confiscation.
   b. nationalization.
   c. sovereign immunity.
   d. none of the above.

SHORT ESSAY

1. The Widget Corporation of America would like to begin marketing its products in the international sector. What forms of multinational business enterprise should it consider?

_____

_____

_____

_____

2. How do expropriation and confiscation differ? What precautions should a firm which deals in the international sector take in order to protect itself against confiscation?

_____

_____

_____

_____

3. Assume you are the manager of a company that has just begun the direct export of your product. What precautions can you take to assure that you will in fact be paid for your products when you have never dealt with the buyer before and you are new to the international legal environment?

_____

_____

_____

_____

4. What items should be specified in a contract involving the sale of goods between a seller in the United States and a buyer in a foreign country?

    _____

    _____

    _____

    _____

5. What is the purpose of the Foreign Corrupt Practices Act?

    _____

    _____

    _____

    _____

Part IX
Sample Examination

MULTIPLE CHOICE

_____ 1. Which of the following is prohibited by the Sherman Act?
   a. A manufacturer assigns exclusive territories to each of its distributors.
   b. Two manufacturers enter into an agreement allocating exclusive territories to each manufacturer.
   c. A manufacturer suggests retail prices for its products.
   d. A manufacturer grants a franchise to a distributor and requires that the franchisee meet certain standards.

_____ 2. With regard to price-fixing agreements, which of the following is generally correct?
   a. They are legal when the parties to the agreement agree to lower their prices for consumers.
   b. They are legal if they meet the rule of reason test.
   c. They are _per se_ illegal under the Sherman Act.
   d. They are legal if they benefit consumers.

_____ 3. A seller of a product conditions its sale on the buyer's purchase of a second product or service. This is an example of a:
   a. market allocation.
   b. group boycott.
   c. vertical restraint.
   d. tying arrangement.

_____ 4. Which of the following is a valid defense against a discrimination charge under the Civil Rights Act of 1964?
   a. A _bona fide_ seniority or merit system.
   b. A _bona fide_ occupational qualification.
   c. A professionally developed ability test.
   d. All of the above.

_____ 5. Which of the following is exempt from the provisions of the Clayton Act?
   a. Professional organizations such as the ABA and the AMA.
   b. Labor organizations.
   c. Agricultural organizations.
   d. (b) and (c) but not (a).

_____ 6. Which of the following is NOT required under the *Howey* test for an investment transaction?
   a. An investment in a common venture.
   b. Premised on an expectation of profit.
   c. Derived from one's own effort.
   d. All of the above are required.

_____ 7. Title I of the FCCPA, which is also known as the _____, has superseded state disclosure requirements relating to credit terms for both consumer loans and credit sales under $25,000.
   a. Equal Credit Opportunity Act
   b. Truth-in-Lending Act
   c. Magnuson-Moss Warranty Act
   d. Fair Credit Billing Act

_____ 8. Happy Homemaker requests a credit card in her own name at Marlin's Department Store. The store manager tells her the store has a policy of only issuing cards to married women in their husband's name. He says she can have a card issued in Harold's name if he completes the application. In all likelihood, Marlin's Department Store is in violation of:
   a. the Federal Consumer Credit Protection Act.
   b. the Fair Credit Reporting Act.
   c. the Equal Credit Opportunity Act.
   d. no laws, because this is an acceptable practice.

_____ 9. What is a "yellow dog" contract?
   a. It is a contract that allows an employer to terminate an employee at will.
   b. It is a contract that prohibits discrimination against persons of oriental heritage.
   c. It is a contract by which an employer requires his employees to promise they will not join a union.
   d. It is a contract that requires the employer to hire only union members.

_____ 10. Which of the following is prohibited by the Labor-Management Relations Act?
   a. A closed shop.
   b. Right-to-work laws.
   c. Discrimination against union members.
   d. Refusal to bargain in good faith with the duly established representatives of the employees.

_____ 11. Sexual harassment is prohibited by which of the following?
   a. The Equal Pay Act.
   b. Title VII of the Civil Rights Act of 1964.
   c. The Rehabilitation Act of 1973.
   d. All of the above.

_____ 12. Which of the following is a correct statement regarding comparable worth?
   a. It is clearly prohibited by the Equal Pay Act.
   b. It is a concept which provides that there should be equal pay for jobs of equal value to the employer.
   c. It has been held by the U.S. Supreme Court to constitute reverse discrimination.
   d. It is an unfair labor practice.

_____ 13. Courts have generally interpreted the statutory definition of the term "security" found in the 1933 Securities Act to include which of the following?
   a. Limited partnership interests.
   b. Citrus groves.
   c. Both (a) and (b).
   d. Neither (a) nor (b).

_____ 14. Which of the following transactions would not be exempt from the registration requirements found in the 1933 Securities Act?
   a. An offering to local resident investors in the city where a corporation is located and in the state in which the corporation is incorporated with $6 million in securities.
   b. An offering of stock in the Valley National Bank of Southern Minnesota.
   c. A private placement to an insurance company.
   d. An offering of limited partnerships in pecan groves to investors in two states where $6 million in the partnerships are offered.

_____ 15. Under which of the federal securities laws is reliance by a third party not required in order to recover against the accountant?
   a. Under Section 11 of the 1933 Act.
   b. Under Section 18 of the 1934 Act.
   c. Under Rule 10b.5 of the 1934 Act.
   d. Reliance is required in all cases.

_____ 16. Which of the following theories could be appropriate in a private tort action to recover for harm to the environment?
   a. Nuisance.
   b. Trespass.
   c. Strict liability.
   d. All of the above.

_____ 17. A defense which an accountant can raise under Section 11 of the 1933 Securities Act is that of:
   a. privity.
   b. negligence.
   c. due diligence.
   d. good faith.

_____ 18. Under the _____, a foreign country would be free from a host country's laws.
   a. sovereign immunity rule
   b. General Agreement on Tariffs and Trade
   c. act of state doctrine
   d. Convention on the International Sale of Goods

_____ 19. The government of Parador seizes an American owned factory for a public purpose and pays the owner compensation for the factory based upon what it considers fair.
   a. If the American owner is not satisfied with the compensation, it could sue in the International Court of Justice.
   b. If the American owner is not satisfied with the compensation, it could sue in an American court under the General Agreement on Tariffs and Trade.
   c. This is an example of a confiscation.
   d. This is an example of an expropriation.

_____ 20. An FTC ruling requiring an advertiser to include in its advertisements information that will insure that the advertisements are not deceptive is called:
   a. affirmative disclosure.
   b. corrective advertising.
   c. multiple product order.
   d. none of the above.

Chapter 50
Introduction to Property and
Property Insurance

PURPOSE

The concept of property is an essential concept in a democratic free enterprise society such as the one in which we live. Property in America occupies a unique status because of the protection expressly granted it by the federal Constitution as well as by most state Constitutions. Two significant aspects of property law concern the transfer of ownership of property and the protection of property through property insurance. Insurance is a contractual undertaking by the insurer to pay a sum of money or give something of value to the insured or a beneficiary on the happening of a contingency or fortuitous event that is beyond the control of the contracting parties. In this chapter you will study two forms of property, real and personal; transfer of title to personal property; and fire and property insurance.

CHAPTER CHECKPOINTS

After reading and studying this chapter, you should be able to:

1. Distinguish between tangible and intangible property, real and personal property, as well as fixtures and give examples of each.

2. Identify and discuss the various methods of transfer of title of personal property.

3. Identify the McCarran-Ferguson Act and explain what the act did with respect to regulation of the insurance industry.

4. Explain what an insurable interest is and why it is required by the law.

5. Distinguish between waiver, estoppel, representations and warranties as they affect forfeiture and avoidance of an insurance policy.

CHAPTER OUTLINE

A. Kinds of Property–Property may be classified as (1) tangible or intangible, and (2) real or personal. These classifications are not mutually exclusive.

    1. Tangible and Intangible–Tangible property consists of physical objects such as a chair, a farm, or a household pet. Intangible property is a protected interest in a thing that is not physical, such as a stock certificate which represents ownership of stock.

    2. Real and Personal–Real property is land and all interests in it (also called realty). Personal property consists of all property that is not real property. The transfer of real property during life can be accomplished only by certain formalities, including the execution of a written instrument known as a deed. On the other hand, personal property can be transferred with relative simplicity and informality. In addition, most states tax both real and personal property. The applicable rate depends on how the property is classified.

    3. Fixtures–A fixture is an article of personal property so firmly attached to real property that an interest in it arises under real property law. In determining whether personal property becomes a fixture, the intention of the parties with conflicting claims to it as expressed in their agreement will control. If there is no agreement, the following factors are relevant in determining whether a particular item is a fixture: (1) the physical relationship of the item to the land or building; (2) the intention of the person who attaches the item to the land or building; (3) the purpose served by the item in relation to the land or building and in relation to the person who brought it there; and (4) the interest of that person in the land or building at the time of the attachment of the item. Although physical attachment is significant, a more important test is whether the item can be removed without material injury to the land or building on the land. A trade fixture is an item used in connection with the tenant's trade. The law of landlord and tenant permits a tenant to remove a trade fixture if the removal can be done without material injury to the structure.

B. Incidents of Property Ownership–Important distinctions exist between real and personal property

    1. Transfer of Property–Transfer of real property requires certain formalities, whereas transfer of personal property is relatively simple and informal.

    2. Taxation–Most states tax both real and personal property, but the applicable rate varies dramatically.

C. Transfer of Title to Personal Property–The acquisition or transfer of title to real property is generally a formal affair. In contrast, title to personal property may be transferred with relative ease and a minimum of formality. The law concerning personal property has been largely codified in the Uniform Commercial Code, especially Article 2 of the UCC, which deals with goods and Articles 3 and 8, which deal with commercial paper and investment securities. However, certain issues involving ownership and transfer of title are not covered by the Code.

1. By Sale–A sale of tangible personal property (goods) is the transfer of title to specified existing goods for a consideration known as the price. Title passes when the parties intend it to pass. Sales of intangible personal property also involve the transfer of title. Some of these sales are governed by the UCC and some, such as copyrights and patents, are governed by specialized federal legislation.

2. By Gift–A gift is the transfer of property from one person to another without consideration. The lack of consideration is the basic distinction between a gift and a sale. To be effective a gift must be completed by delivery. The donor is the person who makes a gift; the donee is the recipient of a gift. A gratuitous promise to make a gift is not binding.

   a. Delivery–Delivery is essential to a valid gift. The term delivery refers to the manual transfer of the item to the donee. Constructive delivery refers to the delivery of something symbolic of control over an item. An irrevocable gift may be effected by constructive delivery when actual delivery of the gift item itself is not possible.

   b. Intent–The law requires that there must be an intent on the part of the donor to make a present gift of the property.

   c. Acceptance–The final requirement of a valid gift is acceptance by the donee.

   d. Classification–Gifts may be either *inter vivos* or *causa mortis*. An *inter vivos* gift is one made by a donor during her lifetime. A gift *causa mortis* is one made by a donor in contemplation of her imminent death.

3. By Will or Descent–Title to personal property is frequently acquired by inheritance from a person who dies, either with or without a will.

4. By Accession–Accession means the right of the owner of property to any increase in it, whether caused by natural or artificial means. The owner of a cow acquires title by accession to any calves born to that cow.

5. By Confusion–Confusion is the intermixing of goods belonging to two or more owners such that the property of all of them can no longer be identified except as part of the mass of like goods. Confusion may result from accident, mistake, willful act, or agreement of the parties. If the goods can be apportioned, each owner who proves his proportion of the whole is entitled to receive his share. If, however, the confusion results from the willful and wrongful act of one of the parties, he will lose his entire interest if he cannot prove his share.

6. By Possession–In some instances, a person may acquire title to movable personal property by taking possession of it. Abandoned property is property intentionally disposed of by the owner. Lost property is property that is unintentionally left by the owner. If the property has been intentionally abandoned, a finder is entitled to the property. Under the general rule, the finder of lost property is entitled to it as against everyone except the true owner. If lost property is in the ground, the owner of the land has a superior claim to that of the finder. Mislaid property is property that is intentionally placed by the owner but unintentionally left. If property is mislaid, most courts hold that the owner of the premises, not the finder, has first claim if the true owner is not discovered. Many states now have statutes that provide a means of vesting title to lost property in the finder when a prescribed search for the owner is fruitless.

D. Concurrent Ownership–Both real and personal property may be owned by a single individual or by two or more persons concurrently. Concurrent ownership or co-tenants each hold an undivided interest in the entire indivisible whole. There are four ways in which personal property may be concurrently owned: (1) joint tenancy, (2) tenancy in common, (3) tenancy by the entireties, and (4) community property.

E. Fire and Property Insurance–Insurance distributes risk among a large number of members (the insured) through an insurance company (insurer). Insurance is a contractual undertaking by the insurer to pay a sum of money or give something of value to the insured upon the happening or a contingency or fortuitous event that is beyond the control of the contracting parties. The McCarran-Ferguson Act places the regulation of insurance on the States.

   1. Fire and Property Insurance–Protects against loss resulting from damages to or destruction of property by fire and related perils such as damage caused by lightning, explosion, earthquake, water, wind, rain, collision, and riot. Coverage is frequently enlarged through an "endorsement" or "rider" to include other perils.

   2. Types of Fire–Policies are generally held to cover damage from "hostile" fires, but not from "friendly" fires.

      a. Friendly fire–Is one that is contained in its intended location, such as a fire in a fireplace, furnace, or stove.

      b. Hostile fire–All fires outside their intended or usual locales are considered to be hostile.

   3. Co-insurance Clauses–Co-insurance is a means of sharing the risk between insurer and insured, in which a person insures property for less than its full or stated value and agrees to share the risk of loss. The formula for recovery is:

Recovery = (Face value of policy) / (Fair market value of property × co-insurance %) × loss

   4. Other Insurance Clauses–Recovery under property insurance policies may be limited by other insurance clauses which require that liability be distributed pro rata among the various insurers.

   5. Types of Policies–Property insurance may be either a valued policy or an open policy. Insurance of property under a marine policy is considered to be valued, whereas non-marine property insurance is presumed to be unvalued or open.

      a. Valued policy–Provides for payment of the full value of the property which is specifically agreed upon by the insured and the insurer at the time the policy is issued.

      b. Open policy–Contains no agreement as to the specific value of the property to be insured. The insurer pays the fair market value of the property calculated immediately prior to its loss.

F. Nature of Insurance Contracts–Basic principles of contract law apply to insurance policies, and insurance policies are generally standardized.

   1. Offer and Acceptance–The applicant is the one who makes the offer, and contract is created when that offer is accepted by the company. A life insurance agent may issue a binding receipt acknowledging payment of the premium and providing for the issuance of a standard policy effective from the date of the medical examination. In fire and casualty insurance, agents use

binders making an agreement legally binding until the completion of the formal contract.

2. Insurable Interest–Is a relationship which a person has with respect to certain property such that the happening of a possible, specific, damage-causing contingency would result in direct loss or injury to her. Its purpose is to protect against the risk of loss, not the realization of gain or profit. It has been developed to eliminate gambling and to lessen the moral hazard.

3. Premiums–Premiums are the amount to be paid, often in installments, for an insurance policy. Regulatory authorities are under a duty to require that companies' rates be reasonable, and not unfairly discriminatory.

4. Defenses of the Insurer–The insurer may assert certain defenses in addition to the ordinary defenses to a contract.

   a. Misrepresentations–For a representation to have legal consequences, it must have been relied on by the insurer as an inducement to enter into the contract, and it must have been substantially false when made, to the insured's knowledge. The principal remedy of the insurer on this is rescission of the contract, and the insurer must return all the premiums that have been paid. Incontestability clause is the prohibition of an insurer to avoid an insurance policy after a specified period of time. It is designed to prevent stale defenses by insurers. An innocent misrepresentation of a material fact is a sufficient ground for avoidance of a policy by the insurer. However, an immaterial misrepresentation is not a ground for avoidance of the policy.

   b. Breach of Warranty–Warranties are conditions that must exist before the contract is effective or before the insurer's promise to pay is enforceable. Failure of the condition to exist relieves the insurer from any obligation to perform its promise. Conditions are either precedent or subsequent.

   c. Concealment–Concealment is the failure of an applicant for insurance to disclose material facts that the insurer does not know. The nondisclosure must normally be fraudulent as well as material to invalidate the policy.

5. Waiver and Estoppel–Waiver is the intentional relinquishment of a known right. Estoppel means that a person is prevented by his own conduct from asserting a position that is inconsistent with acts of his on which another person justifiably relied.

6. Termination–Due performance terminates the insurer's obligation. Normally, the insurer pays the principal sum due and the contract is performed and discharged. Cancellation of an insurance contract by mutual consent is another way of terminating it. To cancel a policy, the insurer must return the unearned portion of the premium. To rescind a policy, the insurer must return all premiums received to the insured.

KEY TERMS

1. Property

2. Tangible property

3. Intangible property

4. Real property

5. Personal property

6. Fixture

7. Sale

8. Gift

9. Donor

10. Donee

11. Constructive delivery

12. Accession

13. Confusion

14. Insurance

15. Fire insurance

16. Co-insurance

17. Title insurance

18. Insurable interest

19. Premiums

20. Warranty

21. Concealment

22. Waiver

23. Estoppel

TRUE/FALSE

_____ 1. All property interests that are not classified as real property or as fixtures are classified as personal property.

_____ 2. The intention of the parties with conflicting claims to the property, as expressed in their agreement, is controlling in determining whether personal property has become a fixture.

_____ 3. A tenant may remove trade fixtures provided he can do so without causing material injury to the real property to which it is affixed.

_____ 4. Land and all interests in land are real property.

_____ 5. As in contract law, in order for a gift to be valid it must be supported by consideration.

_____ 6. The owner of a cow acquires title by accession to any calves born to that cow.

_____ 7. If confusion of goods results by accident and there is not enough left to distribute a full share to each owner, each party will lose his entire interest if he cannot prove his share.

_____ 8. An inter vivos gift is a gift made by a donor in contemplation of the donor's imminent death.

_____ 9. Inter vivos gifts cannot be conditional.

_____ 10. Hereford cattle owned by the Cartright Ranch are accidentally mixed with Hereford cattle owned by the Reagan Ranch. Neither rancher's herd can be specifically identified. If the goods can be apportioned, each ranch is entitled to its proportional share.

_____ 11. Fire insurance policies are standardized in the United States but coverage may be enlarged through an "endorsement."

_____ 12. Property insurance policies are not assignable before loss occurs, but are freely assignable after loss occurs.

_____ 13. The principal remedy of the insurer upon discovery of a misrepresentation by the insured is rescission of the contract.

_____ 14. To invalidate an insurance policy, a nondisclosure must generally be material and fraudulent.

_____ 15. Co-tenants in land each own a specific interest that may be separated from remaining interest.

MULTIPLE CHOICE

_____ 1. A speedboat would be classified as:
   a. tangible property.
   b. intangible property.
   c. personal property.
   d. both (a) and (c).

_____   2. Which of the following would be considered intangible personal property?
a. A stock certificate.
b. A patent.
c. A promissory note.
d. All of the above.

_____   3. In the absence of a binding agreement between the parties, the court, in determining whether an item is a fixture, will consider the following factors:
a. the physical relationship of the item to the land.
b. the intention of the person who attached the item to the land.
c. the interest of the person who attached the item to the land at the time of attachment.
d. all of the above.

_____   4. In determining whether an item is a fixture, the test of "purpose or use" applies only if the item:
a. is affixed to the realty in some way.
b. can be removed without material injury to the realty.
c. either (a) or (b).
d. both (a) and (b).

_____   5. The basic distinction between a gift and a sale is that a gift:
a. requires delivery.
b. lacks any consideration.
c. requires intent on the part of the donor.
d. must be accepted by the donee.

_____   6. Which of the requirements of an effective gift is presumed?
a. Delivery to the donee.
b. Intent on donor's part to make a present gift.
c. Acceptance by the donee.
d. None of the above.

_____   7. If an item is determined to be a fixture, it:
a. can be removed by the seller of the land.
b. is not a part of the realty.
c. will be sold with the land.
d. none of the above.

_____ 8. Under the doctrine of confusion, if James, Kevin and Loren accidentally commingle identical cases of beer, and there is not enough left to distribute a full share to each:
   a. the first owners proving their proportion of the whole are entitled to receive their share.
   b. the loss will be borne by each in proportion to his share.
   c. no party will recover anything unless he can prove his share.
   d. none of the above.

_____ 9. Which of the following are ways by which title to personal property may be obtained?
   a. Possession.
   b. Accession.
   c. Confusion.
   d. All of the above are means by which title to personal property may be obtained.

_____ 10. Which of the following would be considered intangible personal property?
   a. A pen.
   b. A chair.
   c. A stock certificate.
   d. A book.

_____ 11. Which of the following are ways personal property may be concurrently owned?
   a. Joint tenancy.
   b. Tenancy in common.
   c. Community property.
   d. All of the above.

_____ 12. An insurable interest in property must exist at:
   a. the time that the insurance contract is entered into.
   b. the time that the property loss occurs.
   c. either (a) or (b).
   d. both (a) and (b).

_____ 13. A representation by or on behalf of an applicant will have legal consequences if:
   a. it was relied upon by the insurer as an inducement to enter into a contract.
   b. it must have been substantially false when made or it must have become so with the insured's knowledge before the contract was created.
   c. either (a) or (b).
   d. both (a) and (b).

_____ 14. To what does co-insurance refer?

    a. It refers to a policy in which the insured agrees to bear a proportion of the loss.

    b. It refers to the requirement that the insured must maintain more than one policy on the same property in order to ensure complete coverage.

    c. It refers to the fact that a person with property insurance will not be able to recover more than the value of its actual loss.

    d. It refers to the requirement that an insurer must show proof of coverage to a mortgage holder.

_____ 15. Arthur owns a piece of property on which he has an 80% co-insurance policy for fire and property damage. The property is valued at $100,000 and the policy is in the amount of $60,000. If the property is 50% destroyed by fire, how much can Arthur recover from the insurance company?

    a. $30,000.

    b. $37,500.

    c. $40,000

    d. $48,000.

SHORT ESSAY

1. Distinguish between real property, personal property, and fixtures and between tangible and intangible property. Discuss the legal significance, if any, of these distinctions.

_____

_____

_____

_____

2. What is a trade fixture? How does it differ from a fixture?

_____

_____

_____

_____

3. Distinguish between a gift inter vivos and causa mortis.

_____

_____

_____

_____

4. Discuss briefly the concept of insurable interest. What purpose does it serve?

_____

_____

_____

_____

5. Of what significance are warranties in insurance contracts? How do they operate?

_____

_____

_____

_____

Chapter 51
Bailments and Documents of Title

PURPOSE

In this chapter, you study the bailment relationship and documents of title. A bailment is a temporary transfer of personal property without transfer of title, by one person (the bailor) to another person (the bailee) for the accomplishment of a certain purpose, after which the property is to be returned to the bailor or disposed of according to the bailor's directions. Bailments are a common occurrence and are of great commercial importance. Bailments include the transportation, storage, repairing, and renting of goods. Documents of title are frequently used in bailment transactions. A document of title is a warehouse receipt, bill of lading, or other document evidencing a right to receive, hold, and dispose of the document and the goods it covers. To be a document of title, a document must be issued or addressed to a bailee and cover goods in the bailee's possession that are either identified or are fungible portions of an identified mass. Article 7 of the UCC governs documents of title.

CHAPTER CHECKPOINTS

After reading and studying this chapter, you should be able to:

1. Discuss the essential elements of a bailment.

2. List the rights and duties on the part of the bailor and bailee.

3. Discuss the duties of (a) warehouser, (b) carrier, and (c) innkeeper.

4. Define a document of title and discuss the requirements of negotiability for a document of title.

5. Identify and discuss the different types of documents of title and the rights acquired by due negotiation of a negotiable document of title.

CHAPTER OUTLINE

A. Bailments–A bailment is the temporary transfer of possession without title of personal property by one party to another. The bailor is the transferor of the bailed property. The bailee is the recipient of the bailed property. It may be with or without compensation. Bailments are classified as follows: (1) Bailments for the bailor's sole benefit include the gratuitous custody of personal property and the gratuitous services that involve custody of personal property, such as repairs or transportation. (2) Bailments for the bailee's sole benefit are usually limited to the gratuitous loan of personal property for use by the bailee. (3) Bailments for the mutual benefit of both parties include the ordinary commercial bailments, such as when goods are delivered to a repairman or when an automobile is delivered to a parking lot attendant.

1. Essential Elements of a Bailment–The essential elements of a bailment are: (1) delivery of possession by a bailor to a bailee, (2) delivery of personal property and not real property, (3) possession without ownership by the bailee, (4) a determinable period of time, and (5) an absolute duty on the bailee to return the property to the bailor or to dispose of it according to the bailor's directions.

   a. Delivery of Possession–Possession by a bailee in a bailment relationship involves (1) the bailee's power to control, and (2) either an intention to control or an awareness on the part of the bailee that the rightful possessor has given up physical control of the personal property. Parking lot cases, depending on the circumstances may be either a lease arrangement (a right to use the space) or a bailment, where the attendant exercises control over the car.

   b. Personal Property–A bailment can only exist with respect to personal property. Intangible property such as corporate bonds, promissory notes and life insurance policies that are evidenced by written instruments may be the subject matter of bailments.

   c. Possession for a Determinable Time–The person receiving possession must be under a duty to return the personal property and must not obtain title to it. If the identical property transferred is to be returned, the transaction is a bailment; if other property of equal value or the money value may be returned, there is a transfer of title, and the transaction is a sale.

   d. Restoration of Possession to the Bailor–The bailee is legally obligated to restore possession of the property when the period of the bailment ends. Normally, the bailee is required to return the identical goods bailed. Fungible goods are equivalent goods where each unit is the equivalent of every other unit. In the case of fungible goods, such as grain, the bailee is obligated simply to return goods of the same quality and quantity. If the bailee, by mistake or intentionally, misdelivers the property to someone other than the bailor and who has no right to its possession, she is guilty of conversion and is liable to the bailor.

2. Rights and Duties of Bailor and Bailee–The bailee is under a duty to exercise due care for the safety of the property and to return it to the right person. The bailee has the exclusive right to possess the property for the term of the bailment. The bailee may have the right to limit its liability, as well as to receive compensation and reimbursement of expenses.

   a. Bailee's Duty to Exercise Due Care–The bailee must exercise due care not to permit injury to or destruction of the property by him or third parties. The degree of care depends on the nature of the bailment relationship and the character of the property. In the case of a commercial bailment, from which both parties derive a mutual benefit, the law requires the bailee to exercise care that a reasonably prudent person would exercise under the same circumstances. Where the bailment is for the benefit of the bailee alone, the law requires more than reasonable care. Where the bailment is for the benefit of the bailor alone, the law requires a lesser degree of care. Standards will vary according to the character of the property. When property is lost, damaged, or destroyed while in the possession of the bailee, the burden rests on the bailee to prove that he exercised the degree of care required of him.

   b. Bailee's Absolute Liability to Return Property–The bailee is free from liability if she has exercised the degree of care required. This general rule has certain important exceptions that impose an absolute duty on the bailee to return the property undamaged to the proper person. The bailee has liability where he has an obligation by express agreement with the bailor or by custom to insure against certain risks but fails to do so. Where the bailee uses the bailed property in a manner not authorized by the bailor and the property is damaged, the bailee is liable.

   c. Bailee's Right to Limit Liability–The law does not permit certain bailees, including common carriers, public warehousers, and innkeepers, to limit their liability for breach of their duties to the bailor except as provided by statute. Other bailees may vary their duties and liabilities by contract with the bailor. The law requires that any such limitation be properly brought to the attention of the bailor before the property is bailed by her.

   d. Bailee's Right to Compensation–A bailee who by express or implied agreement undertakes to perform work on or render services in connection with the bailed goods is entitled to reasonable compensation for those services or work. Most bailees who are entitled to compensation for work and services performed in connection with bailed goods acquire a possessory lien on the goods to secure the payment of such compensation.

   e. Bailor's Duties–In a bailment for the sole benefit of the bailee, the bailor warrants that she is unaware of any defects in the bailed property. In all other instances, the bailor has a duty to warn the bailee of all defects she knows or should have discovered upon reasonable inspection.

3. Special Types of Bailments–An ordinary bailee is one who must exercise due care. An extraordinary bailee is one who is absolutely liable for the safety of the bailed property without regard to the cause of the loss. Innkeepers and common carriers are extraordinary bailees, where all other bailees are ordinary bailees. An ordinary bailee is liable for such loss or injury only where it resulted from his failure to exercise ordinary or reasonable care. In general, the liability of an extraordinary bailee is absolute; he is liable to the bailor for any loss or injury to the goods regardless of his care or negligence as to their safety.

   a. Pledges–A pledge is a bailment for security in which the owner gives possession of her personal property to another (the secured party) to secure a debt or the performance of some obligation.

   b. Warehousing–A warehouser is a bailee who receives goods to be stored in a warehouse for compensation. At common law his duties were the same as those of an ordinary bailee for compensation. Today they are subject to extensive regulation by state and federal authorities.

   c. Safe Deposit Boxes–A person who rents a safe deposit box enters into a mutual benefit bailment with the bank, which is liable only if negligent.

d. Carriers of Goods–A carrier is anyone who transports goods from one place to another, either gratuitously or for compensation. A common carrier offers its services to the general public. A private or contract carrier limits its services and does not offer them to the general public. The consignor is the person who delivers goods to a carrier for shipment. The consignee is the person to whom the goods are to be delivered by the carrier. The instrument that contains the terms of the contract of transportation is called a bill of lading. A common carrier is under a duty to serve the public to the limits of its capacity and, within those limits, to accept for carriage goods of the kind that it normally transports. A private carrier has no such duty. Both the common and private carriers are under an absolute duty to deliver the goods to the person to whom they are consigned by the shipper. In the absence of special contract terms, a private carrier is liable for the goods it undertakes to carry. On the other hand, a common carrier is under a stricter liability that approaches that of an insurer.

e. Innkeepers–An innkeeper is a hotel or motel operator. At common law, innkeepers were held to the same strict or absolute liability for their guests' belongings as a common carrier. Today, the old common law of strict liability has been substantially modified by case law and statutes.

B. Documents of Title–A document of title is a warehouse receipt, bill of lading, or other document evidencing a right to receive, hold, and dispose of the document and the goods it covers. To be a document of title, a document must be issued by or addressed to a bailee and cover goods in the bailee's possession that are either identified or are fungible portions of an identified mass. A document of title is a symbol of ownership of the goods it describes. Its ownership is equivalent to the ownership or control of the goods it represents. Article 7 of the UCC governs documents of title.

1. Types of Documents of Title

a. Warehouse Receipts–A warehouse receipt is a receipt issued by a person engaged in the business of storing goods for hire. A warehouser is liable for damages for loss or injury to the goods caused by his failure to exercise such care in regard to them as a reasonably careful person would exercise under the circumstances. The warehouser must deliver the goods to the person entitled to receive them under the terms of the warehouse receipt. The liability of a warehouser may be limited by a provision in the warehouse receipt fixing a specific maximum liability per article. A warehouse does not have to keep the goods indefinitely. Depending upon the contract he may notify the person on whose account the goods are held to pay storage and remove the goods. To enforce the payment of his charges and necessary expenses in connection with keeping and handling of goods, a warehouser has a lien on the goods that enables him to sell them at public or private sale after notice and to apply the net proceeds to the amount of his charges. Against a holder of a negotiable warehouse receipt this lien may be limited to the rate specified in the receipt or if no rate is specified then to a reasonable charge for storage subsequent to the date of the receipt.

b. Bills of Lading–A bill of lading is a document issued by a carrier on receipt of goods for transportation. It serves a threefold function: (1) as a receipt for the goods, (2) as evidence of the contract of carriage, and (3) as a document of title. The carrier must deliver the goods to the person entitled to receive them under the terms of the bill of lading. Common carriers are extraordinary bailees and subject to a greater degree of liability, such as a warehouser.

The Code allows a carrier to limit liability by contract. The carrier has a lien on goods in its possession covered by a bill of lading for its charges and expenses necessary for preservation of the goods.

2. Negotiability of Documents of Title–The Code provides that a warehouse receipt, bill of lading, or other document of title is negotiable if, by its terms, the goods are to be delivered to bearer or to the order of a named person or where, in overseas trade, it runs to a named person or assigns. Any other document is nonnegotiable and may be transferred by assignment but may not be negotiated.

   a. Due Negotiation–Due negotiation is a term peculiar to Article 7 and requires not only that the purchaser of the negotiable document must take it in good faith without notice of any adverse claim or defense and pay value, but also that she must take it in the regular course of business or financing and not in settlement or payment of a money obligation. The effect of due negotiation is that it creates new rights in the holder of the document. Defects and defenses available against the transferor are not available against the new holder. The rights of a holder to whom a document has been duly negotiated are that he has: (1) title to the document, (2) title to the goods, (3) all rights accruing under the law of agency or estoppel, and (4) the direct obligation of the issuer to hold or deliver the goods according to the terms of the document.

   b. Rights Acquired in the Absence of Due Negotiation–If a nonnegotiable document or a negotiable document is transferred with due negotiation, the transferee acquires all of the title and rights the transferor had or had actual authority to transfer. The transferee's rights may be defeated (1) by the creditors of the transferor treating the sale as void; (2) by a buyer in possession of the goods who bought the goods from the transferor in the ordinary course of business; or (3) against the bailee through good faith dealings between the bailee and the transferor.

   c. Warranties–The transferor of a document of title for value warrants that the document is genuine, that she had no knowledge of any fact that would impair its validity or worth, and that the negotiation or transfer is rightful.

   d. Ineffective Documents of Title–In order for a person to obtain title to goods by a negotiation to him of a document, the goods must have been delivered to the issuer of the document by the owner of the goods or by one to whom the owner has delivered them with actual or apparent authority to ship, store, or sell them. A thief or finder may not deliver them to a warehouser or carrier in return for a negotiable document of title and thus defeat the rights of the owner.

   e. Lost or Missing Documents of Title–If a document or title has been lost, stolen, or destroyed, a claimant may apply to a court for an order requiring the carrier or warehouser to deliver the goods or issue a substitute document. Delivery of goods under a missing negotiable document without a court order will impose liability on the carrier or warehouser to any person who is thereby injured.

KEY TERMS

1. Bailment

2. Bailor

3. Bailee

4. Bailment for sole benefit of bailor

5. Bailment for sole benefit of bailee

6. Commercial bailment

7. Fungible goods

8. Ordinary bailee

9. Extraordinary bailee

10. Pledge

11. Warehouser

12. Carrier

13. Common carrier

14. Private carrier

15. Consignor

16. Consignee

17. Innkeeper

18. Document of title

19. Warehouse receipt

20. Bill of lading

21. Due negotiation

TRUE/FALSE

_____ 1. Bailed property must be personal but need not be tangible.

_____ 2. In order to establish a bailment relationship, the person receiving possession of the property must be under a duty to return the property.

_____ 3. The bailee has the exclusive right to possess the bailed goods for the term of the bailment.

_____ 4. Except in the case of fungible goods, the bailee is required to return the identical goods bailed.

_____ 5. A private carrier has no duty to accept goods for carriage except where it has agreed to do so by contract.

_____ 6. The extent of a warehouser's liability may be limited by a provision in the warehouse receipt fixing a specific maximum liability.

_____ 7. When a customer rents a safe deposit box, the bailee bank owes the customer the duty to act with ordinary care.

_____ 8. Innkeepers and common carriers are known as ordinary bailees.

_____ 9. After an indorsement in blank or to bearer, a negotiable document of title may be negotiated by delivery alone.

_____ 10. States may by statute prohibit professional bailees from disclaiming liability for their own negligence.

_____ 11. If Julia hangs her coat on a rack at Nick's Restaurant, the restaurant owner is a bailee of the coat.

_____ 12. In a straight bill of lading, the carrier undertakes to deliver the goods at a destination to a named consignee at a specified destination.

_____ 13. A private carrier is liable for the loss of or damage to goods it undertakes to deliver as one who insures the safety of the goods.

_____ 14. No rights are obtained to a document of title in the absence of due negotiation.

_____ 15. Fred, without compensation, loans his textbook to his friend Elmer, so that Elmer may study for a test. This is a bailment for the sole benefit of the bailee.

MULTIPLE CHOICE

_____ 1. Fred parks his car in a parking lot, receives a claim check, locks his car and takes the keys, this is probably a:
   a. bailment for the benefit of the bailor.
   b. bailment for the benefit of the bailee.
   c. mutual benefit bailment.
   d. lease.

_____ 2. Which of the following is not an essential element of a bailment relationship?
   a. Delivery of lawful possession of specific personal property by the bailor to the bailee.
   b. Transfer of title to the property from the bailor to the bailee for a determinable period of time.
   c. An obligation of the bailee to return the property to the bailor or to dispose of it according to the bailor's directions.
   d. All of the above are essential elements of a bailment relationship.

_____ 3. A mutual benefit bailment will terminate on the happening of any of the conditions listed below except:
   a. when the purpose of the bailment is fully accomplished.
   b. when the time for which the bailment was created expires.
   c. when the bailed goods are destroyed.
   d. all of the above.

_____ 4. A bailee is free from liability for casualty to the bailed goods if he exercised the requisite degree of care unless he:
   a. agrees with the bailor to insure the goods against a certain risk, then failed to do so and the casualty to the goods occurred through such a risk.
   b. used the bailed property in a manner not authorized by the bailment and damage results from that use.
   c. delivers the property to the wrong person by mistake.
   d. all of the above.

_____ 5. In order for a carrier to be subject to the rules applicable to common carriers, all of the following conditions must be present except that:
   a. the carriage must be a part of its business.
   b. the majority of the carrier's business must be as a common carrier.
   c. the carriage must be for remuneration.
   d. the carrier must represent to the general public that it is willing to serve the public in the transportation of property.

_____ 6. Which of the following is characteristic of a bill of lading?
    a. It serves as a receipt for the goods.
    b. It serves as evidence of the contract of carriage.
    c. It serves as a document of title.
    d. All of the above.

_____ 7. A document of title is negotiable if it is made payable to any of the following except:
    a. to a named person.
    b. to bearer.
    c. to order.
    d. a document of title is negotiable if made payable to any of the above.

_____ 8. A holder of a negotiable document of title to whom it has been duly negotiated obtains all of the following except:
    a. title to the document.
    b. proof that the document is genuine.
    c. title to the goods.
    d. the holder has all of the above rights.

_____ 9. A person who transfers a document of title for value to other than a collecting bank or other intermediary warrants to his immediate purchaser that:
    a. the document is genuine.
    b. he has no knowledge of any fact that would impair the validity or worth of the document.
    c. his transfer is rightful and fully effective with respect to the document of title and the goods it represents.
    d. all of the above.

_____ 10. A purchaser will obtain title to goods by negotiation to him of a document of title provided the goods have been delivered to the issuer of the document by:
    a. a finder of the goods.
    b. a thief of the goods.
    c. the true owner of the goods.
    d. none of the above.

_____ 11. Arthur rents a car from Ajax Rental. While the car is in his possession, it is stolen.
    a. Arthur is responsible if he did not exercise extreme care.
    b. Arthur is responsible if he did not exercise ordinary care.
    c. Arthur is responsible regardless of how much care he exercised.
    d. Arthur is responsible only if he failed to exercise slight care.

_____ 12. The rights of a holder of a negotiable document of title include:
   a. title to the document.
   b. title to the goods.
   c. both (a) and (b).
   d. neither (a) nor (b).

_____ 13. Arthur brings his car to the garage to have some work done on it. In the trunk of the car is a set of valuable jewels. Is there a bailment relationship between Arthur and the garage?
   a. There is a bailment relationship with respect to both the car and the jewels.
   b. There is a bailment relationship for the car but not the jewels.
   c. There is a bailment relationship for the jewels but not the car.
   d. There is no bailment relationship of either the car or the jewels.

_____ 14. Arthur takes his radio to a repairman who gives Arthur a claim check containing a statement limiting the repairman's liability. This will be effective only if:
   a. the repairman bailee draws Arthur's attention to the writing.
   b. the repairman bailee informs Arthur that it contains a limitation of liability.
   c. the repairman bailee does not coerce Arthur into agreeing with the liability limitation.
   d. all of the above are necessary for the repairman bailee to effectively limit his liability.

_____ 15. A written limitation of liability contained in a claim check will not bind the bailor unless the bailee possesses unequal bargaining power and:
   a. draws the bailor's attention to the writing.
   b. informs the bailor of its contents.
   c. either (a) or (b).
   d. both (a) and (b).

SHORT ESSAY

1. Identify the five essential elements of a bailment.

   _____

   _____

   _____

   _____

2. What are the three basic kinds of bailments and what standard is applied to the bailee's duty to exercise due care under each?

   _____

   _____

   _____

   _____

3. Identify four special types of bailments.

_____

_____

_____

_____

4. Compare and contrast the duties and liabilities of a common carrier with those of a private carrier.

_____

_____

_____

_____

5. Identify and briefly describe the types of documents of title.

_____

_____

_____

_____

Chapter 52
Interests in Real Property

PURPOSE

This chapter discusses the different ways one may hold ownership or claim on real property. Possessory interests in real property are called estates and are classified to indicate quantity, nature, and extent of rights. When the ownership is for an indefinite period of time or for the life of a person, it is known as a freehold estate. This ownership may be with or without condition, depending on the terms by which the property was acquired. Leasehold estates, which include landlord-tenant relationships, are those that exist for a predetermined time. In addition, there are several nonpossessory interests in property, including easements, *profits à prendre*, and licenses. The ownership of interests in property may be held by one individual or concurrently by two or more persons, each of whom is entitled to an undivided interest in the entire property. You will study all of these topics in this chapter.

CHAPTER CHECKPOINTS

After reading and studying this chapter, you should be able to:

1. Define and discuss the various freehold estates.

2. Distinguish between reversion and remainder future interests.

3. Define a leasehold estate and discuss the primary rights and obligations of landlords and tenants.

4. Identify and discuss the various forms of concurrent ownership of real property.

5. Discuss the different forms of nonpossessory interests.

561

CHAPTER OUTLINE

A. Freehold Estates–A freehold estate is a right of ownership of real property for an indefinite time (fee estate) or for the life of a person (life estate).

1. Fee Estates–Fee estate refers to the right to immediate possession for an indefinite period of time with the right to transfer the interest by deed or will. Fee estates include both fee simple and qualified fee estates.

a. Fee Simple Estate–Fee simple means that the property is owned absolutely and can be sold or passed on at will. The absolute rights of transferability and of transmitting by inheritance are basic characteristics of a fee simple estate.

b. Qualified or Base Fee Estate–A qualified fee is an ownership interest subject to its being taken away upon the happening of an event.

2. Life Estates–Life estates are divided into two major classes: (1) conventional life estates or those created by voluntary act, and (2) those established by law such as a wife's dower right in the property of her husband.

a. Conventional Life Estates–A life estate is an ownership right in the property for the life of a designated individual, while the remainder is the ownership estate that takes effect when the prior life estate terminates. A grant or devise "to Alex for life" creates in Alex an estate that terminates on his death. Alex is the life tenant. In a grant "to Alex for life and then to Mario and his heirs" makes Alex the life tenant and Mario the remainderman. Generally, a life tenant may make reasonable use of the property so long as he does not commit "waste," which is any act or omission that does permanent injury to the realty or unreasonably changes its value.

b. Life Estates Established by Law–Under common law, dower is a life estate that a wife who survives her husband has in one-third of all the real property the husband owned during the marriage. Curtesy was the husband's common law estate in the real property of his wife. Unlike dower, curtesy did not exist unless a child was born of the marriage. In most states, the estates of dower and curtesy have been substantially modified or entirely abolished, and in place of them the surviving spouse is given a statutory share in the estate of the deceased spouse.

3. Future Interests–Not all interests in property carry the right to immediate possession, even though the right and title to the interest are absolute. In a grant, "to Adam during his life and then to Barbara and her heirs," Barbara has a definite, existing interest in the property but she is not entitled to immediate possession.

a. Reversions–A reversion is the grantor's right to property upon termination of another estate. A possibility of reverter is a conditional reversionary interest and exists where property may return to the grantor or his successor in interest because of the happening of an event on which a fee simple was to terminate.

b. Remainders–A remainder is an estate in property that, like a reversion, will take effect in possession, if at all, on the termination of a prior estate created by the same instrument. Unlike a reversion, a remainder is held by a person other than the grantor or his successors. A vested remainder is an unconditional remainder that is a fixed, present interest to be enjoyed in the future. A contingent remainder is a remainder interest conditional upon the happening of an event in addition to the termination of the preceding estate. A provision in a will "to David for life and then to his children but if he has no children then to Julie," creates contingent remainders both as to the children and as to Julie.

B. Leasehold Estates–A leasehold estate is the right to possess real property. A lease is a contract in which the landlord grants to the tenant an exclusive right to use and possession of the land for a definite period of time. A tenant has a leasehold interest in real property. The landlord retains an interest in the property called a reversion. The principal characteristics of a leasehold estate are that it continues for a definite term and that it carries with it the obligation on the part of the tenant to pay rent to the landlord.

  1. Creation and Duration–Leaseholds are created by contract and must comply with the usual requirements for formation of a contract. Leases for a specified period of time from one to three years must be in writing.

      a. Definite Term–A lease for a definite term automatically expires at the end of the term. Such a lease is frequently termed an estate for years, even though it may be for one year or shorter. No notice to terminate is required.

      b. Periodic Tenancy–A periodic tenancy is a lease of indefinite duration that continues for successive periods unless terminated by notice to the other party. A periodic tenancy may be terminated by either party at the expiration of any one period but only on adequate notice to the other party.

      c. Tenancy at Will–A tenancy at will is a lease that is terminable at any time.

      d. Tenancy at Sufferance–A tenancy at sufferance is the possession of real property without a valid lease.

  2. Transfer of Interests–Both the tenant's possessory interest in the leasehold and the landlord's reversionary interest in the property may be freely transferred in the absence of contractual or statutory prohibition. One major exception is the tenancy at will.

      a. Transfers by Landlord–After conveying the leasehold interest, a landlord is left with a reversionary interest in the property plus the right to rent and other benefits acquired under the lease. The landlord may transfer either or both of these interests.

      b. Transfers by Tenant–A tenant may dispose of his interest either by (1) assignment, or (2) sublease. Most standard leases, however, require the consent of the landlord to an assignment or sublease of the premises. If a tenant transfers all his interest in the leasehold so that he has no reversionary rights, he has made an assignment. The agreement to pay rent and certain other contractual covenants (express promises) pass to and obligate the assignee of the lease as long as he remains in possession of the leasehold estate. A sublease differs from an assignment in that it involves the transfer by the tenant to another of less than all the tenant's rights in the lease, such that the tenant retains a reversion in the leasehold.

  3. Tenant's Obligations–Although the leasehold estate carries with it an implied obligation on the part of the tenant to pay reasonable rent, the lease contract almost always contains an express promise or covenant by the tenant to pay rent in specified amounts at specified times. Most leases contain a provision to the effect that if the tenant breaches any of the covenants in the lease, the landlord is entitled to declare the lease at an end and may regain possession of the premises. A tenant is under no duty to make any repairs to the leased premises, unless the lease

has specific provisions to the contrary. The tenant is obliged to use the premises so that no substantial injury is caused them.

    a. Destruction of the Premises–Where the tenant leases land together with a building, and the building is destroyed by fire or some other chance event, the common law does not relieve him of his obligation to pay rent or permit him to terminate the lease. The common law rule has been modified by statute in some states.

    b. Eviction–To evict is to remove from the premises. When the tenant breaches one of the covenants in the lease, and the landlord evicts him, the lease is terminated. If the tenant is wrongfully evicted by the landlord, the tenant's obligations under the lease are terminated, and the landlord is liable for breach of the tenant's right of quiet enjoyment.

    c. Abandonment–If the tenant wrongfully abandons the premises before the expiration of the term of the lease and the landlord reenters the premises or relets them to another, a majority of the courts hold that the tenant's obligation to pay rent after reentry terminates.

4. Landlord's Obligations–Under the Fair Housing Act, a landlord cannot discriminate against a tenant with regard to race, color, religion, national origin or familial status. Nevertheless, under the common law, the landlord has few obligations to the tenant. Under the majority rule, at the beginning of the lease, she must give the tenant actual possession.

    a. Quiet Enjoyment–The landlord is bound to provide the tenant with quiet and peaceful enjoyment. Quiet enjoyment is the right of a tenant not to have his physical possession of the premises interfered with by the landlord. Under the doctrine of constructive eviction, a failure by the landlord in any of his undertakings under the lease that causes a substantial and lasting injury to the tenant's enjoyment of the premises is regarded as being an eviction of the tenant. The tenant may abandon the premises and terminate the lease.

    b. Fitness for Use–Under the common law, the landlord has no obligation to maintain the premises in a livable condition or to make them fit for any purpose. However, most courts have abandoned this rule in residential leases by imposing an implied warranty of habitability that the leased premises are fit for ordinary residential purposes. A few states have statutes requiring landlords to keep the residential premises fit for occupation. Zoning and health regulations may also apply.

    c. Repair–Under the common law, unless there is a specific provision in the lease, or a statutory duty to do so, the landlord has no obligation to repair or restore the premises. The landlord does have a duty to maintain, repair and keep in safe condition the common areas of the premises under his control. While at common law the landlord is under no duty to repair, restore, or keep the premises in a livable condition, she may assume those duties in the lease.

    d. Landlord's Liability for Injury Caused by Third Parties–Some States hold landlords liable for injuries suffered by their tenants and others as a result of foreseeable criminal conduct of third parties. While landlords are not insurers of the safety of tenants, they have been held liable for failure "to take minimal precautions to protect members of the public from the reasonably foreseeable criminal acts of third persons."

C. Concurrent Ownership–Two or more persons who hold title concurrently are generally referred to as co-tenants. The two major types of concurrent ownership are joint tenancy and tenancy in common.

1. Tenancy in Common–Tenancy in common is co-ownership whereby each tenant holds an undivided interest with no right of survivorship. The interest of tenants in common may be devised by will or pass by intestate succession. Partition is a physical division of the property, changing undivided interests into smaller parcels owned by each person individually.

2. Joint Tenancy–The most significant feature of joint tenancy is the right of survivorship. On the death of one of the joint tenants, title to the entire property passes by operation of law to the survivor or survivors. To sever means to lose the right of survivorship and to make the tenancy a tenancy in common among the remaining joint tenants and the transferee. A joint tenant may sever the joint tenancy by conveying or mortgaging his interest to a third party. To sustain a joint tenancy, the common law requires the presence of what are known as the four unities of time, title, interest, and possession. A failure of any one of the first three unities will result in a creation of a tenancy in common, because the only unity required of a tenancy in common is the unity of possession.

3. Tenancy by the Entireties–Tenancy by the entireties is created only by a conveyance to a husband and wife. It is co-ownership by spouses in which neither may convey his or her interest during life and thus destroy the right of survivorship.

4. Community Property–In Arizona, California, Idaho, Louisiana, Nevada, New Mexico, Puerto Rico, Texas, Washington, and Wisconsin, under the community property system one-half of any property acquired by the efforts of either the husband or the wife belongs to each spouse. The only property that belongs separately to either spouse is that acquired before the marriage or acquired subsequent to it by gift or inheritance.

5. Condominiums–Condominiums are a form of concurrent ownership that have become commonplace in the United States. The purchaser of a condominium acquires separate ownership to the unit and becomes a tenant in common with respect to the common facilities. The transfer of a condominium conveys both the separate ownership of the unit and the share in the common elements.

6. Cooperatives–A cooperative, usually a corporation, purchases or constructs the dwelling units. It then leases the units to shareholders as tenants, who acquire the right to use and occupy their units.

D. Nonpossessory Interests–A nonpossessory interest in land entitles the holder to use the land or to take something from the land, but the interest does not give him the right to possess the land.

1. Definition of Easements–An easement is a limited right to make use of the land of another in a specific manner that is created by the acts of the parties or by operation of law and that has all the attributes of an estate in the land itself. The dominant parcel of land is the one whose owner has rights in other land. The servient parcel of land is the one that is subject to an easement.

2. Types of Easements–Easements fall into two classes: easements appurtenant and easements in gross. Appurtenant easements are by far the most common. The rights and duties created by such easements pertain to the land itself and not to the particular individuals who may have created them. Therefore, the easement stays with the land when it is sold. The second type of easement is an easement in gross, which is personal to the particular individual who received the right. It does not depend on ownership of the land and amounts to an irrevocable personal right to use.

3. Creation of Easements–The most common way to create an easement is by express grant or reservation. Easements by implication arise whenever an owner of adjacent properties establishes an apparent and permanent use in the nature of an easement, and then conveys one of the properties without mention of any easement. The law implies the grant of an easement by necessity to give a purchaser of land access to his property across the land of the seller. Easements by dedication occur where a landowner dedicates to the public portions of properties such as streets, alleys, parks, etc. Where land is subdivided, both the common law and many state statutes require this. An easement may arise by prescription if certain conditions are met. To obtain an easement by prescription, a person must use a portion of land owned by another in a way (1) that is adverse to the rightful owner's use, (2) that is open and generally known, and (3) that is continuous and uninterrupted for a period of time that varies from state to state.

4. Profits à Prendre–*A profit à prendre* is the right to remove the produce from the land of another. Like an easement, a *profit à prendre* may arise by prescription, but if it comes about by an act of the parties, it must be created with all the formalities of a grant of an estate in real property.

5. Licenses–Permission to make use of one's land generally constitutes a license that creates no interest in the property and is usually exercised only at the will of and subject to revocation by the owner at any time.

KEY TERMS

1. Freehold estate

2. Fee simple estate

3. Fee estate

4. Qualified fee estate

5. Life estate

6. Remainder

7. Waste

8. Dower

9. Curtesy

10. Future interest

11. Reversion

12. Possibility of reverter

13. Vested remainder

14. Contingent remainder

15. Landlord

16. Tenant

17. Leasehold estate

18. Estate for years

19. Periodic tenancy

20. Tenancy at will

21. Tenancy at sufferance

22. Assignment

23. Covenants

24. Sublease

25. Evict

26. Quiet enjoyment

27. Constructive eviction

28. Implied warranty of habitability

29. Co-tenants

30. Tenancy in common

31. Partition

32. Joint tenancy

33. Tenancy by the entireties

34. Community property

35. Condominiums

36. Cooperatives

37. Easement

38. Dominant

`39.   Servient

40.   Appurtenant easement

41.   Easement in gross

42.   *Profit à prendre*

43.   License

TRUE/FALSE

_____   1.   A qualified fee is the largest estate in land.

_____   2.   A fee simple estate is created by any words which indicate an intent to convey absolute ownership.

_____   3.   The holder of a qualified fee interest may transfer that interest, but all transferees will take the property subject to the initial condition imposed by the interest.

_____   4.   A reversion, a life estate, and a remainder are all considered future interests.

_____   5.   A lease is both a contract and a grant of an estate in land.

_____   6.   A lease that does not specify any duration is treated as a tenancy at sufferance.

_____   7.   Unless specifically permitted in the lease, leases are not freely assignable without the landlord's consent.

_____   8.   A tenant is under no duty to make any repairs to the leased premises unless the lease expressly so provides.

_____   9.   Like joint tenants, tenants in common are persons who hold undivided interests in the property, each having the right to possession, but neither claiming any specific portion of the property.

_____   10.   A tenancy by the entireties can only be created in a conveyance to a husband and wife.

_____   11.   The purchaser of a cooperative acquires separate ownership to the unit and becomes a tenant in common in the common facilities.

_____   12.   It is generally the responsibility of the owner of the servient parcel to maintain the easement and keep it in repair.

_____   13.   The interests of the parties holding land as tenants in common may be devised by will as there is no right of survivorship.

_____ 14. Appurtenant easements are easement interests which attach to land and pass with it.

_____ 15. A license is a nonpossessory interest to use the land of another.

MULTIPLE CHOICE

_____ 1. All of the following conveyances will create an unqualified fee simple estate in the transferee except:
   a. "To B."
   b. "To B forever."
   c. "To B so long as she does not remarry."
   d. "To B in fee simple."

_____ 2. A man conveys his house and lot to his widow in "fee simple forever so long as she does not remarry." The widow has:
   a. a fee simple estate.
   b. a fee simple defeasible estate.
   c. a life estate.
   d. an estate for years.

_____ 3. O conveys Greenacre "to A for life, then to B." What interest, if any, does B have in Greenacre?
   a. A reversion.
   b. A vested remainder.
   c. A contingent remainder.
   d. No interest.

_____ 4. A leases a factory to B for 3 years. The written lease provides that rent is to be paid on the first day of each month, and that either party may terminate the lease at any time. The lease can best be described as:
   a. an estate for years.
   b. a periodic tenancy "from year to year."
   c. a periodic tenancy "from month to month."
   d. a tenancy at will.

_____ 5. A freehold estate is a right of ownership of real property for:
   a. an indefinite time.
   b. the life of a person.
   c. either (a) or (b).
   d. neither (a) nor (b).

_____ 6. If a tenant assigns his leasehold interest without the written consent of the landlord as required by the lease, the assignment is:
  a. valid and enforceable.
  b. void and unenforceable by either party.
  c. voidable at the landlord's election.
  d. treated as a sublease.

_____ 7. Which of the following "unities" would be required in joint tenancy?
  a. Time.
  b. Title.
  c. Interest.
  d. All of the above.

_____ 8. A conveys "the back forty" to B. The parcel is bordered on three sides by the remainder of A's farm and on the fourth by a river. At present, B has no access to the highway and the deed from A grants none. Which of the following is correct?
  a. B has an express easement across A's land to the highway.
  b. B has an implied easement across A's land to the highway.
  c. B has an easement by necessity across A's land to the highway.
  d. B has no right to cross A's land to the highway.

_____ 9. If A gives B permission to extract oil from his land, he has given B:
  a. an easement in gross.
  b. a license.
  c. a _profit à prendre_.
  d. none of the above.

_____ 10. A co-ownership of land by spouses in which neither may convey his or her interest during life is a/an:
  a. joint tenancy.
  b. tenancy in common.
  c. tenancy by the entireties.
  d. tenancy at sufferance.

_____ 11. A lease which has specific terms that continue in indefinite succession would be classified as:
  a. tenancy at sufferance.
  b. tenancy at will.
  c. periodic tenancy.
  d. none of the above.

_____ 12. Which of the following is correct with regard to a *profit à prendre?*
   a. Unless it is clearly designated as exclusive, it is subject to similar use by the owner.
   b. It is sometimes difficult to distinguish from a license.
   c. It is the right to remove the produce from another's land.
   d. All of the above are correct.

_____ 13. Catherine tells David that he may cross her land to pick hickory nuts.
   a. This is an easement by prescription.
   b. This is a license.
   c. This is an easement by dedication.
   d. This is an easement by express grant or reservation.

_____ 14. How does a joint tenancy differ from a tenancy in common?
   a. A joint tenancy has the right of survivorship.
   b. Unlike a joint tenancy, the only prerequisite for a tenancy in common is the unity of possession.
   c. The interest of tenants in common may be devised by will.
   d. All of the above are correct.

_____ 15. Sam Student and two of his friends rent an apartment near the campus of Ivory Towers University. When winter comes and the outside temperature is below zero, they discover that the furnace does not work. They notify the landlord, but he says that is not his problem. Does the landlord have any responsibility to maintain the furnace?
   a. Yes, because of his obligation of quiet enjoyment.
   b. Yes, because of the implied warranty of habitability.
   c. Yes, because of his obligation of repair.
   d. Two of the above are correct, (b) and (c).

SHORT ESSAY

1. What are the basic characteristics of a fee simple estate? How do these estates differ from a qualified fee simple estate?

_____
_____
_____
_____

2. Distinguish among a reversion, a possibility of reverter, and a remainder.

_____
_____
_____
_____

3. Distinguish between tenancy in common, joint tenancy, and tenancy by the entireties.

_____

_____

_____

_____

4. What obligations does a landlord owe to her tenant?

_____

_____

_____

_____

5. Distinguish between an estate for years and a periodic tenancy.

_____

_____

_____

_____

Chapter 53
Transfer and Control of Real Property

PURPOSE

The law has always been extremely cautious about the transfer of real property. Title to land may be transferred in three principal ways: (1) by deed, (2) by will or by the law of descent on the death of the owner, and (3) by open, continuous, and adverse possession for a statutorily prescribed period of time. In this chapter, you study the transfer of possession of real property by deed and adverse possession, and you study the public and private controls which affect the acquisition of real property.

CHAPTER CHECKPOINTS

After reading and studying this chapter, you should be able to:

1. List the essential elements in the formation of a contract of sale and a valid deed.

2. Distinguish among the following types of deeds: (a) warranty, (b) special warranty, and (c) quitclaim.

3. Explain what is meant by a secured transaction and distinguish between "assumption of a mortgage" and "subject to the mortgage."

4. Explain how title to land is acquired by adverse possession.

5. Describe the public and private controls placed on land including zoning, eminent domain, and restrictive covenants.

CHAPTER OUTLINE

I.   Transfer of Real Property–The most common way in which real property is transferred is by contract for sale of the land and delivery of the deed upon payment of the agreed-upon consideration. A far less common method of transfer is by adverse possession.

   A.   Contract of Sale–General contract law as modified by the Fair Housing Act (Title VIII of the Civil Rights Act), governs the sale of real property.

      1.   Formation–The buyer and seller must put their agreement in writing in order to meet the requirements of the statute of frauds. Neither party can enforce the agreement unless it is signed by the other party.

      2.   Marketable Title–The law of conveyancing provides that a contract for the sale of land carries with it an implied obligation on the part of the seller to transfer marketable title. Marketable title means that the title is free from (1) encumbrances, (2) defects in the chain of title appearing in the land records, and (3) events depriving the seller of title such as adverse possession or eminent domain. The title search should reveal any defect that has not been specifically excepted in the contract.

      3.   Implied Warranty of Habitability–The obligation of marketable title has nothing to do with the quality of any improvements to the land. The traditional common law rule is *caveat emptor*–let the buyer beware. The buyer has to inspect the property before the sale is completed. The seller is liable only for any misrepresentations or express warranties. A majority of states have relaxed the harshness of this rule in sales by the builder of residential dwellings. In such a sale, the builder-seller impliedly warrants that a newly constructed house is free of latent defects.

   B.   Deeds–A deed is a formal document transferring any type of interest in land.

      1. Types of Deeds–There are three basic types of deeds: warranty, special warranty, and quitclaim.

         a.   Warranty Deed–In a warranty deed, the grantor (seller) promises the grantee (buyer) that she has a valid title to the property. In addition, the grantor obliges herself to make the grantee whole if the grantee suffers any damage because the grantor's title was defective. The promises or covenants in a warranty deed include title, against encumbrances, quiet enjoyment, and warranty.

         b.   Special Warranty Deed–A special warranty deed warrants only that the title has not been impaired, encumbered, or made defective because of any act or omission of the grantor. It does not warrant title as to acts or omissions of others.

         c.   Quitclaim Deed–In a quitclaim deed the grantor transfers whatever interest he has in the property. They are used most frequently when it is desired that persons who have an interest in land release their interest.

      2.   Formal Requirements–Any transfer of an interest in land is within the statute of frauds if it is an interest of more than a limited duration. The description must be sufficiently clear and certain to permit identification of the property conveyed. After describing the property, the deed generally describes the quantity of the estate conveyed to the grantee. Customarily, certain promises called covenants will be included in the deed. The most common of these would be (a) title, (b) against incumbrances, (c) quiet enjoyment, and (d) warranty. Deeds generally end with the

signature of the grantor, a seal, and an acknowledgment before a notary public or other official authorized to verify the authenticity of documents.

3. Delivery of Deeds–A deed does not transfer title to land until it is delivered. Delivery means an intent that the deed is to take effect and is evidenced by the acts or statements of the grantor. Manual or physical transfer of the deed is usually the best evidence of intent, but it is not necessary. A deed is frequently turned over to a third party, called an escrow agent. Escrow is the holding by a third party of a document or funds until all of the conditions in the contract are fulfilled.

4. Recordation–In almost all states, it is not necessary to record a deed in order to pass title from grantor to grantee. However, unless the grantee has the deed recorded, a subsequent good faith purchaser of the property will acquire superior title to the grantee. Recordation consists of delivery of a duly executed and acknowledged deed to the recorder's office in the county where the property is located. In notice states, unrecorded instruments are invalid against any subsequent purchaser without notice. In notice-race states, an unrecorded deed is invalid against any subsequent purchaser without notice of who records first. In race states, an unrecorded deed is invalid against any deed recorded before it.

C. Secured Transactions–A secured transaction includes two elements: (1) a debt or obligation to pay money, and (2) an interest of the creditor in specific property that secures performance of the obligation. Transactions involving the use of real estate as security for a debt are subject to real estate law, which consists of statutes and rules developed by the common laws regarding mortgages and trust deeds. In these cases, the real estate itself is used to secure the obligation, which is evidenced by either a mortgage or a deed of trust. A mortgagor is a debtor who uses real estate to secure an obligation. A mortgagee is a creditor of a secured transaction involving real estate.

1. Form of Mortgages–A mortgage is an interest in land created by a written document that provides security for payment of a debt. The instrument creating a mortgage must meet all the requirements for such documents–it must be in writing, contain an adequate description of the property, and be executed and delivered. A deed of trust is nearly identical to a mortgage, except that under a deed of trust, the property is conveyed not to the creditor as security, but to a third person as trustee for the benefit of a creditor.

2. Rights and Duties–The rights and duties of the parties to a mortgage may depend on whether it is viewed as creating a lien or as transferring legal title to the mortgagee. Most states have adopted the lien theory, which states that the mortgagor retains title, and is entitled to possession of the premises to the exclusion of the mortgagee even in the event of default by the mortgagor. Redemption is the right of the debtor to remove the mortgage by payment of the debt.

3. Transfer of Interests Under the Mortgage–The interests of the original mortgagor and mortgagee can be transferred, and the rights and obligations of the assignees will depend primarily on (1) the agreement of the parties to the assignment, and (2) the legal rules protecting the interest of the one who is party to the mortgage but not to the transfer. A purchaser who assumes the mortgage is personally obligated to pay the mortgagor's debt owing to the mortgagee. The mortgagee can also hold the mortgagor on his promise to pay. A purchaser who purchases the property subject to the mortgage is not personally obligated to pay the debt. In such a case, the transferee's loss is limited to the property. A mortgagee has the right to assign the mortgage to

another person without the consent of the mortgagor. However, an assignee of a mortgage is well advised to obtain the assignment in writing duly executed by the mortgagee and to record it promptly in order to protect his rights against any subsequent persons who acquire an interest in the property without knowledge of the assignment.

4. Foreclosure–Foreclosure is the sale of the mortgaged property upon default to satisfy the debt. The mortgagee will obtain a deficiency judgment for any unsatisfied balance of the debt and may proceed to enforce payment out of other assets of the mortgagor.

D. Adverse Possession–Adverse possession is the acquisition of title to land by open, continuous, and adverse occupancy for a statutorily prescribed period. Any act of dominion by the true owner will stop the period from running, and the period would have to begin from that time.

II. Public and Private Controls–In the exercise of its police power, the state can place controls on the use of privately owned land for the benefit of the community. The state does not pay the owner any compensation for loss or damage sustained by the owner because of legitimate controls. The enforcement of zoning laws is not a taking of property but a regulation of its use. However, the taking of private property for a public purpose or use under eminent domain is not the exercise of police power. The owners of the property so taken are entitled to be paid its fair and reasonable value. Private controls of the use of privately owned property are possible by means of restrictive covenants.

A. Zoning–Zoning is public control over private land use. The validity of zoning is based on the police power of the state. The police power to provide for the public health, safety, morals and welfare is an inherent power of government.

1. Enabling Acts and Zoning Ordinances–The power to zone is generally delegated to local city and village authorities by statutes known as enabling statutes. A typical enabling statute grants the following powers to municipalities: (1) to regulate and limit the height and bulk of buildings; (2) to establish, regulate and limit setback lines; (3) to regulate and determine the area of open spaces; (4) to classify, regulate, and restrict the location of businesses; (5) to divide the municipality into districts; and (6) to set standards to which buildings or structures must conform.

2. Variance–A variance is a use differing from that provided in the zoning ordinance in order to avoid undue hardship.

3. Nonconforming Uses–A zoning ordinance may not immediately terminate a lawful use that existed before it was enacted. The use must be permitted to continue as a nonconforming use for at least a reasonable time.

4. Judicial Review of Zoning–The zoning process is traditionally viewed as legislative. However, it is subject to judicial review on grounds (1) that the zoning ordinance is invalid, (2) that the zoning ordinance has been applied unreasonably, and (3) that the zoning ordinance amounts to a confiscation or taking of property.

5. Subdivision Master Plans–Most states have legislation enabling local authorities to require municipality approval of every land subdivision plat. These enabling statutes provide penalties for failure to secure approval where required by local ordinance.

B. Eminent Domain–Eminent domain is the power to take (buy) private property for public use. The power is carefully circumscribed and controlled. The Fifth Amendment to the federal Constitution provides, "Nor shall private property be taken for public use without just compensation." Similar provisions are found in the constitutions of the states.

1. Public Use–Most states interpret public use to mean "public advantage." Under this definition the power of eminent domain may be delegated to railroad and public utility companies. As society becomes more complex, other public purposes are accepted as legitimate grounds for exercise of the power of eminent domain.

2. Just Compensation–The owners of the property taken must receive just compensation as measured by the fair market value of the property as of the time of taking.

C. Private Restrictions on Land Use–Owners of real property may impose restrictive covenants on the use of land. A restrictive covenant is a private restriction on property contained in a conveyance.

1. Requirements for Running Covenants–If certain conditions are satisfied, then a restrictive covenant will bind not only the original parties to it but also remote parties who subsequently acquire the property. Such a restrictive covenant is said to "run with the land."

2. Restrictive Covenants in Subdivisions–If the entire subdivision has been subjected to a general building plan designed to benefit all the lots, any lot owner in the subdivision has the right to enforce the restriction against a purchaser whose title descends from a common grantor. Many types of restrictive covenants are used in subdivisions. The more common ones limit the use of property to residential purposes, restrict the area of the lot on which a structure can be built, or provide for a special type of architecture. Restrictive covenants are strictly construed against the party asserting their applicability.

3. Termination of Restrictive Covenants–A restrictive covenant may end by the terms of the original agreement. A court will not enforce a restrictive covenant if changed circumstances make enforcement inequitable and oppressive.

4. Validity of Restrictive Covenants–If it appears that the restriction will operate to the general benefit of the owners of all the land intended to be affected, the restriction will be enforced. The usual method of enforcing such agreements is by injunction to restrain violation.

KEY TERMS

1. Marketable title

2. Deed

3. Warranty deed

4. Special warranty deed

5. Quitclaim deed

6. Delivery

7. Escrow

8. Mortgagor

9. Mortgagee

10. Mortgage

11. Deed of trust

12. Redemption

13. Foreclosure

14. Adverse possession

15. Zoning

16. Variance

17. Nonconforming use

18. Eminent domain

19. Restrictive covenant

TRUE/FALSE

_____ 1. The transfer of real estate by deed must be supported by consideration to be valid.

_____ 2. To be enforceable, a contract for the sale of an interest in land must be in writing and signed by the party against whom enforcement is sought.

_____ 3. An agreement for the sale of an interest in land need not contain the price or manner of payment.

_____ 4. In most jurisdictions, consideration must pass between the parties for a deed to be valid.

_____ 5. A deed is not effective to pass title unless and until it is both delivered and recorded.

_____ 6. The provisions of Article 9 of the UCC govern real estate mortgages and deeds of trust.

_____ 7. A mortgagee has the right to assign the mortgage to a third person without the consent of the mortgagor.

_____ 8. When the power of eminent domain is exercised, the award of compensation is given to the holders of all vested and contingent interests in the condemned property.

_____ 9. In a notice-race state, an unrecorded deed is invalid against any subsequent purchaser without notice who records first.

_____ 10. A special warranty deed warrants only that the title has not been impaired, encumbered, or made defective because of anything the grantor has done.

_____ 11. The enforcement of zoning laws constitutes a taking for which the owner of the property must be compensated.

_____ 12. Transfer of title by a quitclaim deed provides the buyer with the greatest assurance.

_____ 13. A court will enforce a restrictive covenant regardless of whether circumstances have changed to make the covenant inequitable and oppressive.

_____ 14. A restrictive covenant prohibiting the owner of property from selling to someone of a particular race or ethnic background will be upheld by the courts.

_____ 15. A builder-seller of residential dwellings impliedly warrants that a newly constructed house is free of latent defects.

MULTIPLE CHOICE

_____ 1. Zoning ordinances are subject to judicial review on the grounds that:
   a. the ordinance amounts to a confiscation or taking of property.
   b. the ordinance bears no reasonable relation to public health.
   c. the ordinance has been applied unreasonably.
   d. any of the above.

_____ 2. Which of the following would render title to be unmarketable?
   a. Defects in the chain of title appearing in the land records.
   b. Events depriving the seller of title such as adverse possession.
   c. Existing zoning restrictions that are not noted on the deed.
   d. All of the above.

_____ 3. By a _____ deed, the grantor obliges herself to make the grantee whole if the grantee suffers any damage because the grantor's title was defective.
   a. warranty
   b. special warranty
   c. quitclaim
   d. none of the above

_____ 4. Which of the following are requirements for an effective deed?
    a. Be written.
    b. Be delivered.
    c. Both (a) and (b).
    d. Neither (a) nor (b).

_____ 5. Title to land may be acquired in which of the following ways?
    a. By gift.
    b. By will.
    c. By adverse possession.
    d. Title may be transferred by any of the above ways.

_____ 6. Which of the following are elements of a secured transaction?
    a. A debt or obligation to pay money.
    b. An interest of the creditor in specific property which secures performance of the obligation.
    c. Neither (a) nor (b).
    d. Both (a) and (b).

_____ 7. The mortgagor retains title to the property in:
    a. a "lien" theory state.
    b. a "title" theory state.
    c. neither (a) nor (b).
    d. both (a) and (b).

_____ 8. Which of the following would be grounds for judicial review of a zoning ordinance?
    a. The zoning ordinance is invalid.
    b. The ordinance has been unreasonably applied.
    c. The ordinance amounts to a confiscation.
    d. All of the above would be grounds.

_____ 9. In many states, if a person openly and continuously occupies the land of another for a statutorily prescribed period, that person will gain title to the land by:
    a. foreclosure.
    b. redemption.
    c. eminent domain.
    d. adverse possession.

_____ 10. Under which of the following circumstances would a nonconforming use be eliminated?
    a. when the use is discontinued.
    b. when a nonconforming structure is destroyed or is substantially damaged.
    c. when a nonconforming structure has been permitted to exist for the period of its useful life.
    d. all of the above.

_____ 11. A restrictive covenant is enforceable only if:
  a. the restriction was intended to benefit the seller of any lot in the tract.
  b. the restriction appears somewhere in the chain of title to which the land of the person seeking to enforce the covenant is subject.
  c. neither (a) nor (b).
  d. both (a) and (b).

_____ 12. Which of the following is/are typically found in the enabling statutes which delegate zoning power to local authorities?
  a. The power to regulate and limit the height and bulk of buildings.
  b. The power to set standards to which buildings must conform.
  c. The power to restrict the location of trades and industries.
  d. All of the above are typically found in enabling statutes.

_____ 13. Andrew Attorney does a title search on property that Ron Realtor wishes to purchase. The search indicates a title defect, because the abstract shows that Carl Contractor could possibly have an interest in the land even though he is not the seller. What type of deed should Ron ask Carl to give him in order to clear up the title defect?
  a. A warranty deed.
  b. A special warranty deed.
  c. A quitclaim deed.
  d. A contract for deed.

_____ 14. Which of the following is generally not required in order to get title to property by adverse possession?
  a. Actual possession of the property in question.
  b. Continuous possession of the property in question for a prescribed period of years.
  c. Hostile or adverse possession of the property in question.
  d. A written deed.

_____ 15. Alicia purchases Brad's house and in so doing assumes the mortgage. Which of the following is correct regarding the assumption of the mortgage?
  a. Alicia is personally liable to pay the mortgage.
  b. Brad is personally liable to pay the mortgage.
  c. Brad is relieved of his obligation to pay the mortgage.
  d. Both Alicia and Brad are personally liable to pay the mortgage.

SHORT ESSAY

1. What are the two essential documents involved in the transfer of real estate? What must or should each document contain?

   _____

   _____

   _____

   _____

2. What are the three types of deeds? How do they differ in effect?

   _____

   _____

   _____

   _____

3. Discuss what is meant by marketable title.

   _____

   _____

   _____

   _____

4. Discuss eminent domain.

   _____

   _____

   _____

   _____

5. Laura buys Blackacre from Steve subject to a $200,000 mortgage granted by Steve to First Bank. If Steve defaults on the mortgage, what is the result?

   _____

   _____

   _____

   _____

Chapter 54
Trusts and Wills

PURPOSE

In addition to the transfer of property by sale and gift, another important way in which a person may convey property is through trusts and wills. Trusts may be either inter vivos (taking effect during the transferor's lifetime) or testamentary (taking effect upon the transferor's death). Wills enable individuals to control the transfer of their property at their death. However, if a person dies intestate (without a will), state law prescribes who shall receive the property. In this chapter, you study both trusts and wills, as well as the manner in which property descends when a person dies intestate.

CHAPTER CHECKPOINTS

After reading and studying this chapter, you should be able to:

1. Describe the differences between an express trust and an implied trust.

2. List the essential elements of a trust.

3. Discuss the formal requirements of making a valid will and how a will may be revoked.

4. Discuss the general rules of intestate succession.

5. Discuss the process involved in the administration of an estate.

CHAPTER OUTLINE

I. Trusts–A trust is the transfer of property to one party for the benefit of another. It may be created by agreement of the parties, by a grant in a will, or by a court decree for any purpose that is not against the law or public policy. The settlor is the creator of the trust. The trustee is the holder of legal title to property for the benefit of another. The beneficiary is the equitable owner of the trust property.

A. Types of Trusts–All trusts may be divided into two major groups: express and implied. Implied trusts are known as either "constructive" or "resulting" trusts.

1. Express Trusts–An express trust is established by voluntary action and is represented by a written document or, in some circumstances, an oral statement or by conduct of the settlor. An express trust of real property must be in writing to meet the requirements of the statute of frauds. No particular words are necessary to create a trust, provided the intent of the settlor is unmistakable. A precatory expression is one that expresses a wish. It must be definite and certain in order to impose a trust upon the property.

a. Charitable Trusts–A charitable trust is designed to benefit humankind.

b. Spendthrift Trusts–A spendthrift trust is one designed to remove the trust estate from the beneficiary's control.

c. Totten Trusts–A totten trust is a tentative trust consisting of a joint bank account opened by the settlor. The trust may be revoked by withdrawing the funds or changing the form of the account. The transfer of ownership becomes complete only upon the depositor's death.

2. Implied Trusts–In some cases, the courts will impose a trust on property because the acts of the parties appear to call for such a construction.

a. Constructive Trusts–A constructive trust is a trust that arises by operation of law to prevent unjust enrichment. A constructive trust will be established where there has been abuse of a confidential relationship or where actual fraud or duress is considered an equitable ground for creating the trust.

b. Resulting Trusts–A resulting trust arises to fulfill the presumed intent of the settlor. It serves to carry out the inferred or presumed intent of the parties in those cases where the intent was inadequately expressed. A resulting trust does not depend on contract or agreement.

B. Creation of Trusts–Each trust has (1) a creator or settlor, (2) a "corpus" or trust property, (3) a trustee, and (4) a beneficiary. No particular words are necessary to create a trust, provided that the intent of the settlor to establish a trust is unmistakable. Consideration is not essential to an enforceable trust.

1. Settlor–Any person legally capable of making a contract may create a trust.

2. Subject Matter–A trust corpus or *res* must be property that is definite and specific.

3. Trustee–Anyone legally capable of holding title to and dealing with property may be a trustee. The lack of a trustee will not destroy the trust. The court will appoint someone to act as trustee if the settlor neglects to appoint one.

a. Duties of the Trustee–A trustee has three primary duties: (1) to carry out the purposes of the trust, (2) to act with prudence and care in the administration of the trust, and (3) to exercise a high degree of loyalty toward the beneficiary. The trustee is required to act with the same degree of care that a prudent person would use to carry out his personal affairs. The trustee is a fiduciary who has a duty of loyalty.

    b. Powers of the Trustee–The powers of the trustee are determined by: (1) the authority granted him by the settlor in the instrument creating the trust, and (2) the rules of law in the jurisdiction in which the trust is established. State laws determine the investments a trustee may make with trust funds. Most states prescribe a prudent investor rule.

    c. Allocation of Principal and Income–Trusts often settle a life estate in the corpus on one beneficiary and a remainder interest on another beneficiary. In these instances, the trustee must distribute the principal to one party (the remainderman) and the income to another (the life tenant or income beneficiary). The trustee must also allocate receipts and charge expenses between the income beneficiary and the remainderman. The general rule in allocating benefits and burdens is that ordinary or current receipts and expenses are chargeable to the income beneficiary, whereas extraordinary receipts and expense are allocated to the remainderman.

  4. Beneficiary–There are very few restrictions on who (or what) may be a beneficiary. In the absence of restrictive provisions, a beneficiary's interest may be reached by creditors, or the beneficiary may sell or dispose of his interest.

C. Termination of a Trust–Unless a power of revocation is reserved by the settlor, the general rule is that a trust, once validly created, is irrevocable. If so reserved, the trust may be terminated at the discretion of the settlor. Normally, the instrument creating a trust establishes a termination date. If both the equitable and legal title are held by the same beneficiary, the merger doctrine applies and the beneficiary holds the property outright.

II. Decedent's Estates–The assets (estate) of a person who dies leaving a valid will are to be distributed according to the directions contained in the will. A will is also called a testament; the maker of a will is called a testator; and gifts made in the will are called devises or bequests. If a person dies without leaving a will (intestate), her property will pass to her heirs and next of kin as provided by state statute. This is known as intestate succession. If a person dies without a will and leaves no heirs or next of kin, her property escheats (reverts) to the state.

A. Wills–A will is a written instrument executed with the formalities required by statutes, whereby a person makes a disposition of his property to take effect after his death. A will is revocable at any time during life. A will takes effect only on the death of the testator.

  1. Mental Capacity–In order to make a valid will, the testator must have both the "power" and the "capacity" to do so.

    a. Testamentary Capacity and Power–The power to make a will is granted by the state to persons who are of a class believed generally able to handle their affairs without regard to personal limitations. In most states, a child under a certain age cannot make a valid will. The capacity to make a will refers to the limits placed on particular persons in the class generally granted the power to make wills because of personal mental deficiencies. A person has sufficient mental capacity to make a will if she is capable of understanding the nature and extent of her property, appreciating the natural objects of her bounty, and formulating a plan of disposition.

b. Conduct Invalidating a Will–A will that transmits property as a result of duress, undue influence, or fraud is no will at all, because it reflects an intent other than the testator's.

2. Formal Requirements of a Will–To be valid, a will must comply with certain formalities. These are necessary to indicate that the testator understood what she was doing and to help prevent fraud.

   a. Writing–A basic requirement to a valid will is that it be in writing. The writing may be informal, as long as it meets the basic requirements of the statute. Pencil, ink, and mimeograph are all valid methods.

   b. Signature–A will must be signed by the testator. The signature verifies that the will has been executed. Most statutes require the signature to be at the end of the will.

   c. Attestation–With a few isolated exceptions, a written will must be attested or certified by witnesses. Usually two or three witnesses are required. The most common restriction is that a witness must not have any interest under the will.

3. Revocation of a Will–A will is revocable by the testator. Under certain circumstances, a will may be revoked by operation of law.

   a. Destruction or Alteration–Tearing, burning, or otherwise destroying a will is a strong sign that the testator intended to revoke it. Unless it can be shown that the destruction was inadvertent, it is an effective way of revoking a will. In some states the testator may partially revoke a will by erasure or obliteration of a part of a will. Substituted or additional bequests made by insertions between the written or printed lines are not effective without reexecution and reattestation.

   b. Subsequent Will–The execution of a second will does not in itself constitute a revocation of an earlier will. The first will is revoked only to the extent it is inconsistent with the second. The most certain manner of revocation is the execution of a later will containing declaration that all former wills are revoked.

   c. Operation of Law–A marriage generally revokes a will executed before the marriage. Divorce, however, does not revoke a will for the benefit of the other party. Many statutes provide that a subsequent marriage does not affect an existing will but a divorce revokes gifts to a former spouse. The birth of a child after execution of a will may revoke a will at least as far as that child is concerned, but this is not true in all states.

4. Effectiveness of Testamentary Provisions

   a. Renunciation by the Surviving Spouse–Statutes generally provide for a right of renunciation by a surviving spouse and set forth the method of accomplishing it.

   b. Abatement and Ademption of a Bequest–The reduction or elimination of gifts can occur upon the reduction in the value of the estate after the execution of the will. This is called abatement. Ademption occurs when a testator removes the subject of a gift or it is no longer available for transfer.

5. Special Types of Wills–There are many special types of wills.

   a. Nuncupative Wills–A nuncupative will is an oral declaration made before witnesses without any writing. They are authorized in only a few jurisdictions.

   b. Holographic Wills–A holographic will is one entirely in the handwriting of the testator. In some jurisdictions it is valid without witnesses. It must strictly comply with statutory requirements for such wills.

    c. Soldiers' and Sailors' Wills–Most statutes relax the formal will requirements for soldiers on active duty and sailors while at sea.

    d. Conditional Wills–One that takes effect only on the happening of a specified contingency.

    e. Joint and Mutual or Reciprocal Wills–A single instrument made the will of two or more persons is a joint will. Mutual or reciprocal wills are separate instruments with reciprocal terms in favor of each other.

    f. Living Wills–Almost all states have adopted statutes permitting living wills. A living will is a document that complies with the statutory requirements by which an individual declares that she does not wish to receive extraordinary medical treatment to preserve her life.

  6. Codicils–A codicil is an addition to or a revision of a will generally by a separate instrument in which the will is expressly referred to and, is incorporated into the codicil by reference. A codicil must meet all of the requirements of a will.

B. Intestate Succession–Property not effectively disposed of before death or by will passes in accordance with the law of intestate succession. The rules set forth in statutes for determining to whom the decedent's property shall be distributed assure an orderly transfer of title to property and purport to carry out what would probably be the wishes of the decedent. The rules of descent vary widely from state to state. Except for the statutory rights of the widow, the intestate property passes in equal shares to each child of the decedent living at the time of his death. The share of any child who dies before the decedent is equally divided among that child's children. Per stirpes is a class or group of distributees that take the share their deceased ancestor would have been entitled to, taking thus by their right of representing such ancestor and not as so many individuals. Per capita is an equal share given to each of a number of persons, all of whom stand in equal degree to the decedent without reference to the right of representation.

C. Administration of Estates–The procedure of managing the distribution of decedents' estates is referred to as probate. The first legal step after death is to determine whether the deceased left a will. If there is a will, most likely the testator named her executor. If there is no will or no one named as executor in the will, the court will on petition appoint an administrator. Soon after the admission of the will to probate, the personal representative, who is a fiduciary, must file an inventory. The executor or administrator will then begin her duties of collecting the assets, paying the debts, and disbursing the remainder according to the will or intestate succession. An executor is the person named in the will and appointed by the court to administer the will. An administrator is a person appointed by the court to administer the estate when there is no will or the person named in the will fails to qualify. In the administration of every estate, there are probate expenses as well as fees to be paid to the executor or administrator, attorneys' fees, and taxes imposed by both the federal and state governments.

KEY TERMS

1. Trust

2. Settlor

3. Trustee

4. Beneficiary

5. Express trust

6. Testamentary trust

7. *Inter vivos* trust

8. Charitable trust

9. Spendthrift trust

10. Totten trust

11. Implied trust

12. Constructive trust

13. Resulting trust

14. Trust corpus

15. Intestate

16. Will

17. Codicil

18. Nuncupative will

19. Holographic will

20. Intestate succession

21. *Per stirpes*

22. *Per capita*

23. Probate

24. Executor

25. Administrator

TRUE/FALSE

_____ 1. Legal title to property may be held by one or more persons while at the same time its use, enjoyment and benefit belong to one or more others.

_____ 2. An express trust is established by voluntary action.

_____ 3. A constructive trust is created by express language of the settlor, written or oral, by which specific property is transferred to a trustee for the use and benefit of one or more beneficiaries.

_____ 4. A trust established during the lifetime of the settlor is called a testamentary trust.

_____ 5. In a spendthrift trust the beneficiary's interest may be reached by his creditors.

_____ 6. Anyone legally capable of holding title to and dealing with property may be a trustee.

_____ 7. The death of a trustee destroys the trust.

_____ 8. In general, unless the settlor reserves a power of revocation, a trust once validly created is irrevocable.

_____ 9. A will is generally revocable by the testator at any time during his lifetime.

_____ 10. A bequest is a gift by will of real property.

_____ 11. A witness to a will must not have any interest under the will.

_____ 12. A codicil must be executed with all of the formal requirements of a will.

_____ 13. Legally adopted children are generally recognized as lawful heirs of their adopting parents.

_____ 14. The rules of descent are uniform throughout the United States.

_____ 15. Many states hold that a divorce will revoke all gifts made to a former spouse under a preexisting will.

MULTIPLE CHOICE

_____ 1. Implied trusts imposed upon property by court order are:
   a. constructive trusts.
   b. resulting trusts.
   c. either (a) or (b).
   d. neither (a) nor (b).

_____ 2. If a director of a corporation is found to have taken advantage of a "corporate opportunity," the court will impose:
   a. an express trust.
   b. a constructive trust.
   c. a resulting trust.
   d. a charitable trust.

_____ 3. In order to create a valid trust you must have all of the following except:
   a. settlor.
   b. codicil.
   c. trustee.
   d. beneficiary.

_____ 4. A spendthrift clause in a trust instrument will insulate income already received from the trust by the beneficiary from:
   a. the claims of the beneficiary's creditors.
   b. the beneficiary's control.
   c. neither (a) nor (b).
   d. both (a) and (b).

_____ 5. Sally deposits money into a joint bank account in the name of "Sally, in trust for Roger." This is known as:
   a. a charitable trust.
   b. a totten trust.
   c. a resulting trust.
   d. an *inter vivos* trust.

_____ 6. Which of the following is not a duty of a trustee?
   a. To carry out the purposes of the trust.
   b. To act with prudence and care in the administration of the trust.
   c. To exercise a high degree of loyalty toward the beneficiary.
   d. To act as a guarantor for the liabilities of the trust.

_____ 7. In order to make a valid will, the testator must have:
   a. the "power" to make a valid will, as defined by state law.
   b. the "capacity" to make a valid will.
   c. either (a) or (b).
   d. both (a) and (b).

8. To incorporate by reference a memorandum into a will, all of the following conditions must exist except:
   a. it must be in writing.
   b. it must be in existence when the will is executed.
   c. it must be physically attached to the will.
   d. it must be adequately described in the will.

9. Which of the following will result in the revocation of a will?
   a. The testator is divorced after having executed the will.
   b. The testator executes a codicil.
   c. The testator marries after having executed the will.
   d. The testator tears the will in half thinking that it is a void "I.O.U."

10. If A executes a will leaving Blackacre to B, but then sells the land for $20,000 before he dies, on A's death, B will receive:
    a. Blackacre.
    b. $20,000.
    c. $20,000 and Blackacre.
    d. nothing.

11. In which of the following situations will a will be declared invalid?
    a. The testator was incompetent most of the time, but executed the will during one of his periods of lucidity.
    b. The will was executed under fraudulent circumstances.
    c. A will is invalid in both of the above circumstances.
    d. A will is not invalid under either of the above circumstances.

12. A _____ is an addition to or a revision of a will by a separate instrument.
    a. devise
    b. hologram
    c. codicil
    d. settlor

13. Which of the following is generally correct regarding the course of descent?
    a. At common law, property could not lineally ascend to one's parents.
    b. At common law, a stepchild was considered an heir.
    c. All states distribute property on a per capita basis.
    d. None of the above is correct.

_____   14. A _____ will is used to reject the use of life-prolonging medical procedures.
   a.   Nuncupative will.
   b.   Holographic will.
   c.   Soldiers' and sailors' will.
   d.   Living will.

_____   15. Which of the following will automatically revoke a will?
   a.   The execution of a second will.
   b.   The tearing, burning or otherwise destroying of a will.
   c.   The divorce of a spouse.
   d.   In each of the above situations, evidence of intent to revoke would need to be shown before the act would revoke the will.

SHORT ESSAY

1.   What are the four essential elements of a trust?

_____

_____

_____

_____

2.   What is the difference between an express trust and an implied trust?

_____

_____

_____

_____

3.   List and define five special types of wills.

_____

_____

_____

_____

4.   What are the requirements of a valid will? When does it become effective?

_____

_____

_____

_____

5. Outline briefly the steps involved in the administration of an estate.

_____

_____

_____

_____

Part X
Sample Examination

MULTIPLE CHOICE

_____ 1. Which of the following would be considered intangible personal property?
a. A book.
b. An apartment lease.
c. A copyright.
d. A pet dog.

_____ 2. Which of the following would not be considered in determining whether property had become a fixture?
a. The physical relationship of the item to the land.
b. The intent of the owner of the land to which the item is attached.
c. The purpose the item serves with respect to the land.
d. The intent of the person who attached the item to the land.

_____ 3. A _____ is a transfer of property from one person to another for consideration.
a. sale
b. gift
c. bailment
d. trust

_____ 4. The individual designated to manage a trust is known as the:
a. trustee.
b. beneficiary.
c. settlor.
d. executor.

_____ 5. When Arthur dies and his will is probated, Brad receives a life estate in Arthur's house. What happens to the house when Brad dies, if no one else is mentioned in the will as receiving an interest in the house?
a. It goes to Brad's heirs.
b. It reverts to Arthur's heirs.
c. It goes to the state.
d. It is shared by Brad's heirs and Arthur's heirs.

_____ 6. When Arthur dies and his will is probated, Brad receives a life estate in Arthur's house. The will also states that on Brad's death, the house will go to Clark. Clark's interest in the house is known as a:
   a. possibility of reverter.
   b. vested remainder.
   c. contingent remainder.
   d. periodic tenancy.

_____ 7. Albert conveys part of his land to Barbara. The part conveyed to Barbara is so situated that Barbara would have no access to it except across Albert's remaining land. Under these facts, Barbara has an easement by:
   a. express grant or reservation.
   b. implied grant or reservation.
   c. necessity.
   d. prescription.

_____ 8. Albert grants to Brian, an adjoining landowner, the right to cross his land and to gather black walnuts from the trees located there. Brian has a/an:
   a. easement by prescription.
   b. *profit à prendre*.
   c. license.
   d. either a *profit à prendre* or a license.

_____ 9. Bill Businessman rents a car from Ajax Car Rental while on a business trip to Los Angeles. This is an example of a/an:
   a. extraordinary bailment.
   b. constructive bailment.
   c. gratuitous bailment.
   d. bailment for mutual benefit.

_____ 10. A distinctive symbol used to identify goods or products is called a:
   a. service mark.
   b. certification mark.
   c. collective mark.
   d. trademark.

_____ 11. Neil Neighbor borrows Harold Homemaker's snowblower to clear his own driveway of snow. This is an example of a:
   a. bailment for mutual benefit.
   b. bailment for the benefit of the bailor.
   c. bailment for the benefit of the bailee.
   d. gift.

_____ 12. Which of the following is correct regarding a trade fixture?
    a. It is considered to be personal property belonging to the tenant.
    b. It belongs to the landlord upon termination of the lease agreement.
    c. It becomes so attached as to be considered part of the real property.
    d. Two of the above are correct, (b) and (c).

_____ 13. A grant by the federal government of a limited monopoly right of an author to control the copying, publication, or other use of works of authorship fixed in any tangible medium of expression is a:
    a. patent.
    b. copyright.
    c. trade secret.
    d. trademark.

_____ 14. Sam Student rents an apartment from Ron Realtor. The lease is for a six month period with rent due on the first of each month. The rental agreement is for a:
    a. periodic tenancy.
    b. tenancy from month to month.
    c. tenancy at will.
    d. tenancy at sufferance.

_____ 15. Sam Student rents an apartment from Ron Realtor. The lease is for a six month period with rent due on the first of each month. At the end of six months, Sam continues in possession of the apartment, but no new lease is drafted and signed by either party. The rental agreement is for a:
    a. periodic tenancy.
    b. tenancy from month to month.
    c. tenancy at will.
    d. tenancy at sufferance.

_____ 16. A lease of indefinite duration which continues for successive periods and requires notice to terminate is a:
    a. periodic tenancy.
    b. tenancy for years.
    c. tenancy at will.
    d. tenancy by sufferance.

_____ 17. Lyle Landowner has a building valued at $100,000. He has an 80% co-insurance policy on the property in the face amount of $65,000. If the building is totally destroyed in an earthquake, Lyle will be able to recover what amount of money?
   a. $64,000.
   b. $65,000.
   c. $81,250.
   d. $100,000.

_____ 18. Which of the following is required to incorporate by reference a memorandum into a will?
   a. The memorandum must be in writing.
   b. The memorandum must be in existence when the will is executed.
   c. Both (a) and (b).
   d. Neither (a) nor (b).

_____ 19. The Individual Indemnity Insurance Company wishes to deny a claim and pay nothing at all. In which of the following situations would it be likely to successfully avoid all liability on a claim involving life insurance?
   a. The applicant lied about her age in order to obtain the policy.
   b. The applicant knew he had AIDS at the time he applied for the policy, but lied about it to the agent.
   c. The policy has an incontestability clause.
   d. The applicant had another policy with a different insurance company.

_____ 20. Sarah Salesclerk and her boyfriend go to a restaurant for dinner. While washing her hands in the restroom, Sarah removes her watch and accidentally leaves it there. Later in the evening, a waitress finds it and turns it over to the restaurant owner. The owner puts it in the restaurant safe and then forgets about it until six months later when the cleaning lady finds it there and shows it to the restaurant manager. Assuming that Sarah never returned to the restaurant to look for the watch, who has first claim to it?
   a. The waitress.
   b. The restaurant owner.
   c. The cleaning lady.
   d. None of the above, because Sarah is the true owner and has only mislaid the property.

CPA Exam
Business Law Section[1]

The Business Law section tests the candidates' knowledge of the legal implications of business transactions, particularly as they relate to accounting and auditing. The section includes the CPA and the law, business organizations, contracts, debtor-creditor relationships, government regulation of business, Uniform Commercial Code, and property. The subjects on the examination normally are covered in standard textbooks on business law, auditing, taxation, and accounting. Candidates are expected to recognize the existence of legal implications and applicable basic legal principles, and they are usually asked to indicate the probable result of the application of such basic principles.

The Business Law section is chiefly conceptual in nature and is broad in scope. It is not intended to test competence to practice law or expertise in legal matters, but to determine that the candidates' knowledge is sufficient (1) to recognize relevant legal issues, (2) to recognize the legal implications of business situations, (3) to apply the underlying principles of law to accounting and auditing situations, and (4) to seek legal counsel or recommend that it be sought.

This section deals with federal and widely adopted uniform laws. Where there is no federal or appropriate uniform law on a subject, the questions are intended to test knowledge of the majority rules. Federal tax elements may be covered where appropriate in the overall context of a question.

---

[1]Reprinted with permission from *Information for the CPA Candidate*, Copyright 1991 by American Institute of Certified Public Accountants, Inc.

Business Law–Content Specification Outline

I. The CPA and the Law (10 percent)
    A. Common Law Liability to Clients and Third Persons
    B. Federal Statutory Liability
        1. Securities Act
        2. Internal Revenue Code
    C. Workpapers, Privileged Communication, and Confidentiality

II. Business Organizations (20 percent)
    A. Agency
        1. Formation and Termination
        2. Liabilities of Principal
        3. Disclosed and Undisclosed Principals
        4. Agent's Authority and Liability
    B. Partnerships and Joint Ventures
        1. Formation and Existence
        2. Liabilities and Authority of Partners and Joint Owners
        3. Allocation of Profit or Loss
        4. Transfer of Interest
        5. Termination, Winding Up, and Dissolution
    C. Corporations
        1. Formation, Purposes, and Powers
        2. Stockholders, Directors, and Officers
        3. Financial Structure, Capital, and Dividends
        4. Merger, Consolidation, and Dissolution
    D. Estates and Trusts
        1. Formation and Purposes
        2. Allocation Between Principal and Income
        3. Fiduciary Responsibilities
        4. Distributions and Termination

III. Contracts (15 percent)
    A. Offer and Acceptance
    B. Consideration
    C. Capacity, Legality, and Public Policy
    D. Statute of Frauds
    E. Statute of Limitations
    F. Fraud, Duress, and Undue Influence
    G. Mistake and Misrepresentation
    H. Parol Evidence Rule
    I. Third Party Rights

J. Assignments

K. Discharge, Breach, and Remedies

IV. Debtor-Creditor Relationships (10 percent)
  A. Suretyship
    1. Liabilities and Defenses
    2. Release of Parties
    3. Remedies of Parties
  B. Bankruptcy
    1. Voluntary and Involuntary Bankruptcy
    2. Effects of Bankruptcy on Debtor and Creditors
    3. Reorganizations

V. Government Regulation of Business (10 percent)
  A. Regulation of Employment
    1. Federal Insurance Contributions Act
    2. Federal Unemployment Tax Act
    3. Workers' Compensation Acts
  B. Federal Securities Acts
    1. Securities Regulation
    2. Reporting Requirements
    3. Exempt Securities and Transactions

VI. Uniform Commercial Code (25 percent)
  A. Commercial Paper
    1. Types of Negotiable Instruments
    2. Requisites for Negotiability
    3. Transfer and Negotiation
    4. Holders and Holders in Due Course
    5. Liabilities, Defenses, and Rights
    6. Discharge
  B. Documents of Title and Investment Securities
    1. Warehouse Receipts
    2. Bills of Lading
    3. Issuance, Transfer, and Registration of Securities
  C. Sales
    1. Contracts Covering Goods
    2. Warranties
    3. Product Liability
    4. Risk of Loss
    5. Performance and Obligations
    6. Remedies and Defenses

Answers to Chapter Tests and Sample Examinations

Chapter 1

True/False:

1. T	6. T	11. F
2. F	7. F	12. T
3. F	8. T	13. F
4. T	9. F	14. F
5. F	10. T	15. T

Multiple Choice:

1. d	6. d	11. c
2. c	7. b	12. a
3. c	8. d	13. c
4. d	9. d	14. d
5. c	10. a	15. c

Short Essay:

1. In civil law systems, the legislatures create the laws and the judges initiate and conduct the litigation through the inquisitorial method of adjudication. In common law systems, the legislatures, administrative agencies and the judges create the laws, the parties initiate and conduct the litigation through the adversary system, and the judges act as referees to insure that the parties follow the procedural rules.

2. A right is the capacity of a person, aided by the law to require another person or persons to perform or refrain from performing a certain act. A duty is the obligation the law imposes upon a person to perform a certain act or to refrain from performing a certain act. Duty and right are correlatives.

3. While moral and ethical concepts greatly influence the law, they are not the same. In many areas they will overlap, such as stealing from one another. Stealing would be both morally and legally wrong.

There are areas of law which do not relate to morals (drive on the right side of the road) and areas of moral conduct which do not relate to the law (watching a blind man walk off a cliff).

4. They are similar in that they were both drafted by legal scholars who were concerned that legal rules be good rules that have wide applicability nationwide. They are different in that the Restatements of Law are not law in and of themselves, but are statements of what legal scholars believe the common law to be; where there is more than one rule in existence in the common law, the Restatements reflect what they believe the law should be. In contrast, the UCC is statutory law in all fifty states, because the UCC has been adopted by the state legislatures.

5. A civil action in tort could be brought by Alice against George, and also a criminal action could be brought against George by the state. In a civil action, the plaintiff brings the action against the defendant, the burden of proof is preponderance of the evidence, and the action in this case would result in money damages. In a criminal action, the government brings the action against the defendant, the burden of proof is beyond a reasonable doubt, and the action results in a fine and/or imprisonment.

Chapter 2

True/False:

1. T	6. F	11. F
2. F	7. T	12. T
3. T	8. T	13. F
4. T	9. T	14. T
5. T	10. F	15. T

Multiple Choice:

1. d	6. b	11. d
2. a	7. c	12. d
3. d	8. d	13. c
4. c	9. a	14. a
5. a	10. b	15. d

Short Essay:

1. Utilitarians believe that moral actions are those that produce the greatest net pleasure compared to the net pain. They assess good and evil in terms of consequences of actions. Deontologists believe that actions must be judged by their motives and means as well as their results. They address the practical problems of utilitarianism by holding that certain underlying principles are right or wrong irrespective of any pleasure or pain calculations.

2. Kant asserted that conduct should be such that the actor can, at the same time, will that the conduct should become a universal law of conduct. Additionally, one should acts as never to treat another human being merely as a means to an end.

3. The arguments for corporate social responsibility include: (1) corporations have limited liability and other rights which carry a responsibility to contribute to the betterment of society; (2) the more socially responsible that companies act, the less the government must regulate; and (3) enhanced goodwill created by involvement in social causes means stronger profits in the long run. The arguments against corporate social responsibility include: (1) businesses are established to permit people to engage in profit-making, not social activities; (2) whenever companies stray from their designated role of profit-maker, they take unfair advantage of company employees and shareholders; (3) corporations are private institutions that are subject to a lower standard of accountability than public bodies; and (4) corporations may not possess the ability to recognize and manage socially useful activities.

4. Lawrence Kohlberg has observed that people progress through stages of moral development according to two major variables: age and education. During the first level–the preconventional level–a child's conduct is a reaction to the fear of punishment and to the pleasure of reward. During adolescence–the conventional level–people conform their behavior to meet the expectations of family, peers, and society. Most adults operate at this level. The third level–the postconventional level–is where they accept and conform to moral principles because they understand why the principles are right and binding.

5. While corporations should be socially responsible, some feel that their greatest social obligation is to return as much money as possible to their stakeholders from their profit-making activities. The argument has been made that when companies such as Big Bucks provide funding for social causes that they are taking unfair advantage of company employees and shareholders. They argue that these funds rightfully belong to the shareholders or employees, so a decision by the board of directors to support social concerns with the money is unfair. They feel that shareholders and employees can decide independently if they wish to make charitable contributions. On the other hand, some feel that corporations carry a responsibility to society to contribute to its overall well-being. The proponents of this view feel that corporate America cannot ignore the multitude of pressing needs that remain, despite the efforts of government and private charities.

Chapter 3

True/False:

1. T	6. T	11. T
2. F	7. T	12. T
3. T	8. F	13. T
4. F	9. F	14. F
5. T	10. F	15. T

Multiple Choice:

1. c	6. b	11. a
2. b	7. a	12. d
3. c	8. d	13. c
4. d	9. b	14. b
5. c	10. c	15. b

Short Essay:

1. Jurisdiction is the power or authority of a court to hear a case. Venue is the geographical location where the case should be heard when there are several courts of the same jurisdiction.

2. The judge assumes that all the evidence introduced by the non-moving party is true. He then asks himself whether this evidence, if true, would be sufficient for the jury to find in favor of the non-moving party. If the evidence of the non-moving party, assumed to be true, is not sufficient for the jury to find in favor of the non-moving party, then there is no point in requiring the moving party to try to disprove that evidence. Thus, the moving party will be entitled to a directed verdict.

3. The major advantages of court adjudication are that it is binding, and it is based upon public norms and precedents; the major disadvantages include that it is expensive, it is time-consuming, it has limited remedies, and judges may lack special expertise. The major advantages of arbitration are that it is binding, the parties control the process, there is privacy, arbitrators have special expertise, and you can get a speedy resolution of your dispute; the major disadvantages include that there are no public norms, no precedents, and no uniformity. The major advantages of mediation are that it preserves relations, the parties control the process, and there is privacy; the major disadvantages include that it is not binding, it lacks finality, and there is no precedent nor uniformity.

4. The federal court system includes: (a) U.S. district courts, which are trial courts; (b) appeals courts for each circuit in the U.S.; and (c) the U.S. Supreme Court, which for the most part hears cases by writ of *certiorari* on appeal from the various courts of appeal. It can also hear some cases on appeal from a state supreme court. A typical state court system includes: (a) municipal courts or some other type of special local court; (b) district courts, which are trial courts of general jurisdiction (this court is usually the equity court; in California, it is called the Superior Court and in New York, it is called the Supreme Court); (c) an intermediate appellate court exists in most states (in some states, the court listed in (b) has some appellate jurisdiction); and (d) a state supreme court (in New York, this court is known as the Court of Appeals.)

5. (a) Pleadings–filing of a complaint, service of a summons and filing of an answer, reply and/or counterclaim; (b) Possible demurrer or motion to dismiss for failure to state a claim; (c) Discovery in the form of depositions, interrogatories, requests for admission, and examinations of various sorts; (d) Pretrial conference to clarify issues and set a date for a trial; (e) Trial–consists of jury selection or *voir dire*, opening statements, examination and cross-examination of witnesses, closing statements, jury instructions and verdict; (f) Motion for a new trial or executing of judgment if no appeal; and (g) Appeal.

Chapter 4

True/False:

1. T	6. T	11. F
2. T	7. T	12. F
3. T	8. T	13. T
4. T	9. T	14. T
5. F	10. T	15. F

Multiple Choice:

1. d	6. c	11. a
2. d	7. a	12. c
3. b	8. c	13. b
4. c	9. b	14. b
5. d	10. d	15. a

Short Essay:

1. The U.S. Constitution enumerates the powers of the Federal government. All powers not so enumerated are specifically reserved to the States. While the States retain considerable powers, the U.S. Constitution provides, under the supremacy clause, that within its own sphere, Federal law is supreme and State law must, where there may be some conflict between the two, yield.

2. The rational relationship test is applied to economic legislation. It must be conceivable that the legislation bears a rational relationship to a bona fide governmental interest. The strict scrutiny test is more stringent and is applied to legislation affecting fundamental rights, e.g., right to vote, right to privacy, and free speech.

3. The court would be concerned with (1) the necessity and importance of the state regulation, (2) the burden it imposes on interstate commerce, and (3) the extent to which it discriminates against interstate commerce in favor of local concerns.

4. A state may not regulate activities if it would produce an undue burden on interstate commerce. The Supreme Court considers whether the regulation is necessary as well as the burden it would impose on interstate commerce. Note that states may not tax goods that continue to remain in the stream of commerce. Taxes may only be imposed after the movement of the goods has ceased.

5. The First Amendment's guarantee of free speech applies to corporations. Accordingly, corporations may not be prohibited from speaking out on political issues. Commercial speech is also protected under the First Amendment but to a lesser degree than private speech. Government regulation of false and misleading advertising is permissible under the First Amendment. Because defamation involves a communication, the protection extended to speech by the First Amendment applies. However, the Supreme Court has ruled that a public official who is defamed may not recover in an action of defamation unless the statement was made with actual malice.

Chapter 5

True/False:

1. F	6. F	11. T
2. F	7. T	12. T
3. T	8. T	13. T
4. F	9. F	14. F
5. F	10. T	15. F

Multiple Choice:

1. d	6. d	11. d
2. d	7. a	12. a
3. d	8. d	13. b
4. c	9. c	14. d
5. c	10. b	15. d

Short Essay:

1. Administrative agencies exercise powers that have been allocated by the Constitution to the three separate branches of government. Agencies exercise legislative power when they make rules, executive power when they enforce the law, and judicial power when they adjudicate disputes.

2. In informal rulemaking, the agency must provide prior notice of a proposed rule usually by publication in the Federal Register, an opportunity for interested parties to participate, and publication of a final draft containing a concise general statement of its basis and purpose at least thirty days before the rule's effective date. In formal rulemaking, the agency must base its rules upon consideration of the record of the trial-like agency hearing and include a statement of "findings and conclusions, and the reasons or basis therefore, on all the material issues of fact, law, or discretion presented on the record." Hybrid rulemaking results from combining the informal procedures of the APA with the additional procedures specified by the enabling statute.

3. In exercising judicial review of agency action, the court may either compel agency action unlawfully withheld or set aside impermissible agency action. In making these determinations the court must review the whole record and may set aside agency action only if the error is prejudicial. The court decides all relevant questions of law, interprets constitutional and statutory provisions, and determines the meaning of the terms of an agency action.

4. In order to provide for accountability to the public, Congress enacted the Freedom of Information Act and the Government in the Sunshine Act. The Government in the Sunshine Act applies to all multi-member bodies whose members are appointed by the President with the advice and consent of the Senate. Executive agencies such as the Environmental Protection Agency, the Food and Drug Administration, and the National Highway Safety Administration are exempt. Agencies covered by the act may generally close meetings for specified reasons.

5. The three types of rules promulgated by administrative agencies include: legislative rules, interpretative rules, and procedural rules. Legislative rules are substantive rules issued by an administrative agency under the authority delegated to it by the legislature. Interpretative rules are statements issued by an administrative agency indicating its construction of its governing statute. Procedural rules are rules issued by an administrative agency establishing its organization, methods of operation and rules of conduct for practice before it.

Chapter 6

True/False:

1. F	6. F	11. F
2. F	7. F	12. F
3. F	8. T	13. T
4. T	9. T	14. F
5. T	10. T	15. F

Multiple Choice:

1. d	6. d	11. d
2. c	7. a	12. c
3. a	8. a	13. d
4. d	9. a	14. c
5. b	10. d	15. c

Short Essay:

1. The mental element required for conviction of criminal conduct has undergone change in recent times. Courts now recognize three degrees of mental fault. First, subjective fault where there is a purposeful or knowing act such as would occur in embezzlement or larceny. Second, objective fault where one might be negligent or careless and thirdly, liability without fault where no evil intent is required. An example of the latter would be statutory wrongs involving the sale of alcohol to a minor or the sale of adulterated food.

2. The four defenses most relevant to white-collar crimes and crimes against business include: (1) defense of person or property which allows individuals to use reasonable force to protect themselves, others, and their property, and deadly force to protect themselves and others if they are threatened with death or serious bodily harm; (2) duress which is coercion by threat of serious bodily injury; (3) mistake of fact which occurs if a person reasonably believes the facts to be such that his conduct would not constitute a crime; and (4) entrapment which arises when a person is induced into committing a crime by a government official.

3. The Racketeering Influenced and Corrupt Organizations Act (RICO) was enacted to terminate the infiltration of organized crime into legitimate business. The act subjects enterprises that engage in a pattern of racketeering to severe civil and criminal penalties.

4. A search warrant is not required in the following situations: (a) hot pursuit of a fugitive, (b) voluntary consent is given, (c) an emergency, (d) search incident to a lawful arrest, (e) evidence of a crime in plain view of a law enforcement officer, or (f) a delay which would hinder an investigation.

5. The fourth, fifth, and sixth amendments of the U.S. Constitution provide important protections for those accused of criminal conduct. The fourth protects all persons against unreasonable searches and seizures, thereby protecting privacy and safeguarding against arbitrary invasions by governmental officials. The fifth amendment protects persons against self-discrimination, double jeopardy, and being charged with a capital or infamous crime except by grand jury indictment. The sixth amendment ensures that the accused shall receive a speedy and public trial by an impartial jury. All of these protections are extended to state actions by the fourteenth amendment.

Chapter 7

True/False:

1. F	6. T	11. T
2. F	7. T	12. T
3. T	8. T	13. T
4. F	9. T	14. T
5. F	10. T	15. T

Multiple Choice:

1. d	6. d	11. c
2. a	7. a	12. b
3. c	8. d	13. b
4. b	9. b	14. d
5. d	10. d	15. b

Short Essay:

1. Trespass is an interference with a person's right to the exclusive possession of his property, while nuisance is an interference with a person's right to use and enjoy his property. Trespass usually occurs when the wrongdoer attempts to exercise possession of the land by actually coming onto the land. Nuisance, on the other hand, usually occurs when the wrongdoer makes it difficult or impossible for the property owner to use or enjoy his land by subjecting it to such irritants as dirt, smoke, noise, or unpleasant odors.

2. For purposes of tort law, a wrongdoer intends to commit a particular tort if he acts with the purpose or motive of achieving the tortious result or with the knowledge that such tortious result is substantially certain to occur as a natural consequence of his actions. For example, if A throws a rock at B, hoping to hit her, he has acted with the purpose of battering her and so he has the requisite intent. If however, A throws a rock into a large crowd at a rock concert, not hoping to hit anyone at all, he can hardly be surprised when someone is in fact hit. Thus, he will have acted with the knowledge that a battery was

substantially certain to occur as a natural consequence of his action and so he would have the requisite intent.

3. Economic or pecuniary interests include a person's existing and prospective contractual relations, a person's business reputation, a person's name and likeness, and a person's freedom from deception.

4. (a) Arnold has probably committed assault, battery and conversion, because he put Benjamin in fear for his life or safety, inflicted offensive bodily harm and permanently deprived him of his property in the form of the wallet. (b) Arnold has committed the crimes of assault, theft, and robbery. (c) In a tort action, Benjamin sues to recover compensation for the injury he sustained as a result of Arnold's wrongful conduct. For the commission of the crimes, the state may bring appropriate action against Arnold resulting in payment of a fine and/or imprisonment.

5. While tort law gives persons redress from civil wrongs or injuries to their person, property, and economic interests, defendants may not be liable if their conduct was privileged. There are societal interests which are deemed of such importance that the law confers immunity from tort liability for the damage caused by the actor. Such defenses would be: (1) consent to the conduct by the plaintiff, (2) self-defense (to one-self, to others, or to property) under appropriate circumstances, and (3) conditional or absolute privilege.

Chapter 8

True/False:

1. T	6. T	11. T
2. F	7. T	12. T
3. F	8. T	13. T
4. T	9. F	14. F
5. T	10. T	15. T

Multiple Choice:

1. d	6. a	11. c
2. c	7. d	12. b
3. b	8. c	13. c
4. b	9. c	14. b
5. a	10. a	15. d

Short Essay:

1. The reasonable person standard is ordinarily used to determine a defendant's negligence by comparing what the defendant did to what a reasonable person acting prudently and with due care under the circumstances would have done. Some statutes impose a specific standard of care upon certain classes of defendants for the protection of certain classes of plaintiffs. Thus, the courts may take the requirements of a statute as the applicable standard of care in determining the negligence of a particular defendant if

the defendant violated a statute which is intended to protect a particular class of persons of which the plaintiff is a member against the particular hazard and kind of harm which resulted.

2. The elements are: (1) breach of duty of care, (2) proximate cause, and (3) injury.

3. The doctrine of strict liability or liability without fault is not based upon any particular fault of the defendant. Rather, it is based upon the nature of the activity in which the defendant is engaged. Certain types of activities are socially desirable but pose significant risks of harm regardless of how carefully they are conducted. Thus where the activities are in themselves abnormally dangerous, or where one keeps animals, or where one sells defective, unreasonably dangerous products, liability may be imposed even though the actor neither intended any harm nor acted in a negligent manner.

4. A few states have abandoned any distinction between these three classifications of persons. For those states which still recognize a difference however, the courts generally recognize a reasonable care standard with respect to trespassers, a duty to warn to licensees and, a duty to exercise reasonable care to protect against dangerous conditions about which the possessor should know and which the invitee is unlikely to discover.

5. Contributory negligence is defined as failure of a plaintiff to exercise reasonable care that legally causes the plaintiff's harm. If negligence of the plaintiff together with negligence of the defendant proximately caused the injury sustained by the plaintiff, he cannot recover any damages from the defendant in those few states where contributory negligence is still recognized. Comparative negligence divides damages between the plaintiff and defendant where the negligence of each has caused the harm.

Part I: Sample Examination

1. c	8. c	15. b
2. c	9. d	16. d
3. a	10. b	17. a
4. c	11. d	18. c
5. a	12. c	19. b
6. d	13. d	20. b
7. b	14. c	

Chapter 9

True/False:

1. T	6. T	11. T
2. T	7. F	12. F
3. F	8. F	13. T
4. F	9. F	14. T
5. T	10. T	15. T

Multiple Choice:

1. a	6. d	11. d
2. b	7. c	12. d
3. d	8. a	13. d
4. d	9. c	14. d
5. a	10. c	15. a

Short Essay:

1. The law of contracts is governed primarily by state common law. An often-cited source of this law is found in the Restatements of the Law of Contracts promulgated by the American Law Institute. In all states except Louisiana, however, Article 2 of the UCC governs sales. A sale is a contract involving the transfer of title to goods from seller to buyer for a price. In all transactions to which Article 2 does not apply, and in all those governed by Article 2 but where general contract law has not been specifically modified by the Code, contract common law continues to apply.

2. The contract to provide accounting services to Clem for $15,000 does not depend upon formality for its legal validity, and therefore is classified as an informal contract. Moreover, the contract involves an oral manifestation of willingness by both parties to enter into a contract, and therefore it is express, even though not in writing. The contract also involves an exchange of promises–Arthur's promise to provide accounting services for 1 year in exchange for Clem's promise to pay $15,000 to Arthur–and therefore is bilateral. There is no evidence that the contract is void, voidable, or otherwise unenforceable, therefore it is valid. Finally, since, at its inception, neither party has performed any of its duties, the contract is executory.

3. Under the doctrine of Promissory Estoppel and the theory of quasi-contract promises are sometimes enforced even though they do not meet contractual requirement. Under Promissory Estoppel a noncontractual promise will be enforced where there has been justifiable reliance on the promise and justice requires enforcement. A quasi-contract is not actually a contract at all because it is based neither on an express nor an implied promise but rather is an obligation imposed by law to avoid injustice.

4. A contract has the element of consideration associated with it. The obligations associated with a contract have been bargained for, whereas the giving of a gift is a gratuitous situation and therefore not enforceable.

5. A quasi contract is another form of implied contract, but rather than being implied in fact it is implied in law. Actually it is not a contract at all because it is not based on either an express or implied promise. It is an obligation imposed by law to avoid an injustice.

Chapter 10

True/False:
1. T	6. F	11. T
2. T	7. T	12. T
3. T	8. F	13. F
4. T	9. F	14. T
5. T	10. T	15. F

Multiple Choice:
1. d	6. c	11. b
2. d	7. d	12. d
3. c	8. d	13. c
4. c	9. c	14. d
5. c	10. b	15. b

Short Essay:

1. An offer need not take any particular form to have legal effect but it must (1) be communicated to the offeree; (2) manifest an intent to enter into a contract; and (3) be sufficiently definite and certain. Those being present, if a communication creates in the mind of a reasonable person in the position of the offeree an expectation that his acceptance will conclude a contract, then the communication is an offer.

2. An offer may lapse either upon the running of the period of time specified in the offer itself, or if no such time is stated, upon the expiration of a reasonable period of time. The offeror may also revoke his offer at any time prior to acceptance unless the offer is held open by an option contract, is a merchant's firm offer under the Code, is statutorily irrevocable, or is for a unilateral contract and the offeree has begun the requested performance. An offeree's power of acceptance may also be terminated by the offeree's communicated rejection. The rejection is effective from the moment that it is received by the offeror. A counteroffer or a conditional acceptance both indicate an unwillingness to agree to the terms of the offer and, therefore, operate as a rejection. They are to be distinguished, however, from mere inquiries about the possibility of obtaining new or different terms for the contract, as these do not terminate the offer. Finally, an offer will be terminated by the death or incompetency of the offeror or of the offeree, by the destruction of the specific subject matter of the contract, or if performance of the previously valid offer is subsequently made illegal.

3. Under the common law "mirror image rule," an acceptance must be positive and unequivocal. It may not change any of the terms of the offer, nor add to, subtract from, or otherwise qualify the terms of the offer in any way. Any communication that attempts to do so is not acceptance but rather is a mere counteroffer. In contrast, the Code modifies this rule to account for the realities of modern business practices, the most notable being the extensive use of the standardized business form. The Code focuses on the intent of the parties; if the offeree definitely and seasonably expresses his acceptance of the offer

and does not expressly make his acceptance conditional on the buyer's assent to the different or additional terms, then a contract is formed. Here the issue becomes whether the seller's different or additional terms become part of the contract. The Code provides rules to resolve these disputes depending on whether the parties are merchants and on whether the terms are additional or different terms.

4. The formation of a contract depends upon the acceptance of the offer. In a bilateral contract this is some overt act by the offeree that manifests her intent to the terms of the offer. Generally, if the offeror and offeree are not speaking face to face this would occur upon the dispatch of the acceptance. In a unilateral contract it is the performance of the requested act with the intention of accepting.

5. (a) The common law follows the "mirror image rule" which states that offers and acceptances must be mirror images of each other. In 2-207 (the battle of the forms section), the Code allows for the acceptance of an offer where the terms of the acceptance vary from those of the offer. (b) The common law required definiteness and certainty in the terms of an offer. The UCC has "gap filler" provisions in 2-305, 2-308 and 2-309 that allow a contract to exist when certain terms are left open. (c) At common law, an offer which says it will be kept open for a specified period of time can be terminated at any time in the absence of consideration. Under UCC 2-205, a firm offer in writing by a merchant is binding even without consideration. (d) At common law, an offer must be accepted in the manner specified. Under the UCC, an offer may be accepted in any manner and by any medium reasonable under the circumstances. In general, the Code looks at whether the parties intended to form a contract rather than at technical rules regarding the exact moment of acceptance of an offer.

Chapter 11

True/False:

1. F	6. F	11. F
2. F	7. F	12. T
3. F	8. F	13. T
4. T	9. T	14. F
5. T	10. F	15. F

Multiple Choice:

1. a	6. d	11. c
2. c	7. a	12. c
3. d	8. b	13. d
4. d	9. a	14. d
5. d	10. c	15. b

Short Essay:

1. There are two basic types of duress. The first occurs when a party is compelled to assent to a contract through physical force. This form of duress renders the purported agreement void. The second type of duress involves the use of improper threats to compel a person to enter into a contract. The threat may be explicit or inferred from words or conduct. A subjective test is used to determine whether the threat

actually induced assent on the part of the person claiming to be the victim of duress. Duress of this kind renders the resulting contract voidable at the option of the coerced.

2. (a) The elements necessary to establish fraud in the inducement include: false representation, of fact, that is material, made with knowledge of its falsity and the intention to deceive, and that is justifiably relied on. (b) In general, a statement of opinion cannot constitute fraud in the inducement. However, a statement of opinion by an expert is treated as being a statement of fact. (c) Puffing is rather general and is considered to be "sales talk." A statement such as "This is the best car in town" is puffing. A statement such as *Consumer Reports* rates this the best car of the year" is a statement of the fact that it has in fact been so rated by *Consumer Reports*.

3. The contract is voidable due to mutual mistake of fact. The contract was here entered into based upon a mutual mistake of material fact.

4. Where there is made a material false statement that induces another to rely justifiably to their injury, but that statement is made without scienter, there has been a non-fraudulent misrepresentation. In order to recover under these circumstances, all other elements of fraud must be present and the misrepresentation must be material. Rescission and damages are available.

5. Undue influence is the unfair persuasion of a person by a party in a dominant position based on a relationship of trust and confidence. It generally occurs where there is a confidential relationship such as a guardian and ward or physician and patient where the dominant party takes unfair advantage of the other.

Chapter 12

True/False:

1. F	6. F	11. T
2. T	7. F	12. F
3. F	8. F	13. T
4. F	9. F	14. T
5. T	10. T	15. F

Multiple Choice:

1. d	6. b	11. b
2. c	7. d	12. c
3. a	8. d	13. c
4. c	9. b	14. c
5. d	10. a	15. b

Short Essay:

1. Mutuality of consideration means that the promises or performance of both parties to a contract must be legally sufficient for the contract to be enforceable by either. To be legally sufficient, a promise or performance must be either a legal benefit to the promisor or a legal detriment to the promisee. In this

regard, legal benefit means the obtaining by the promisor of that which he had no legal right to obtain. A legal detriment means the doing of that which the promisee was under no prior legal obligation to do, or the refraining from doing that which he was previously under no legal obligation to refrain from doing.

2. The two essential elements of consideration are (1) legal sufficiency (value) and (2) bargained-for exchange. In short, consideration is a bargained-for exchange of value. The adequacy of consideration, however, is irrelevant and the subject matter that the parties respectively have exchanged need not have approximate value. Rather, the law will treat the parties as having considered the subject of the exchange adequate by reason of their having freely agreed to the exchange.

3. Where a promise made is entirely optional with regard to performance, the law considers this to be no promise at all. Thus where a statement that is in the form of a promise but imposes no obligation upon the maker is an illusory promise and not considered to be consideration for a return promise, no contract exists. However, many courts are beginning to transform otherwise illusory promises into actual promises by implying an obligation of good faith..

4. Sam has detrimentally relied upon Big Bucks' promise of a job. He can sue to enforce the contract based upon his detrimental reliance.

5. There are several situations governed by Article 2 of the UCC in which no consideration is required for enforceability. Modification of a preexisting contract, firm offers by merchants, a written waiver or renunciation to settle a dispute, as well as output and requirements contracts, are all enforceable without consideration.

Chapter 13

True/False:

1. T	6. F	11. F
2. F	7. F	12. T
3. T	8. F	13. T
4. F	9. T	14. T
5. F	10. F	15. T

Multiple Choice:

1. d	6. d	11. d
2. b	7. d	12. a
3. d	8. c	13. d
4. c	9. d	14. c
5. b	10. d	15. b

Short Essay:
1. The Restatement does not define "illegal bargain" but rather focuses upon public policy and whether by that policy the bargain should be enforced. This allows the court to be more flexible in determining the enforceability of questioned agreements by weighing the policy against the effect upon the contracting parties.

2. The two types of licensing statutes are those which are regulatory in nature and those enacted in order to raise revenue. A regulatory licensing statute is one designed to protect the public against services provided by unqualified individuals. If violated, there can be no recovery for professional services rendered by a person not having the required license. A revenue-raising licensing statute is one designed solely to raise revenue, and does not seek to protect the public from services provided by incompetents. Accordingly, agreements by persons not having the license required by such a statute are enforceable.

3. The doctrine of unconscionability permits the courts to resolve issues of unfairness with regard to either procedural unfairness or substantive unfairness. The doctrine with regard to contracts of adhesion is related to the doctrine of unconscionability in that it allows the courts to revise standard form contracts offered on a "take-it-or-leave-it" basis.

4. With few exceptions, illegal agreements are unenforceable. As a general rule, where the parties to an illegal agreement are in *pari delicto* the courts will aid neither party. However, where one party withdraws prior to performance or is protected by statute, or where one party is not equally at fault or can make a claim of excusable ignorance, the courts may allow certain actions with regard to the agreement.

5. Any attempt to eliminate competition or otherwise obstruct trade or commerce is met with resistance. Thus contracts which somehow restrain trade, etc., will be allowed to stand only if they are reasonable. Thus, if the restraint protects a property interest of the promisee or if the restraint is no more extensive than is reasonably necessary to protect that interest, the agreement will likely be enforceable.

Chapter 14

True/False:

1. T	6. T	11. T
2. T	7. T	12. F
3. F	8. F	13. F
4. T	9. F	14. T
5. F	10. T	15. T

Multiple Choice:

1. b	6. d	11. b
2. d	7. d	12. c
3. a	8. b	13. d
4. c	9. d	14. c
5. b	10. d	15. a

Short Essay:

1. Generally, all persons are regarded as having capacity to contract unless specifically designated otherwise. Minors, incompetent persons, and intoxicated persons are limited to some extent. Minor's contracts are voidable at the option of the minor. If one has been adjudicated incompetent and a guardian appointed, contracts entered into by the incompetent are void. One not so adjudicated but who is nevertheless unable to understand the nature and consequence of his acts or one who cannot understand the nature and consequence of her actions due to intoxication, entered into voidable contracts.

2. Not all contracts entered into by minors are voidable. Where a minor contracts for a necessary, they will be held liable for the reasonable value of the item contracted for. Today the courts generally define "necessaries" as those things that the minor needs to maintain himself in his particular station in life.

3. The act of ratification makes the contract binding, and if properly ratified a contract may not thereafter be disaffirmed. Ratification may occur in three ways: (1) through express language, (2) as implied from conduct, and (3) through failure to make a timely disaffirmance.

4. States do not agree whether a minor who misrepresents his age has the power to disaffirm a contract. Under the prevailing view, Tim may disaffirm the contract. However, some states would not allow Tim to disaffirm if the bank officer in good faith relied upon the misrepresentation.

5. The contract between Don and Lucy is voidable at the option of Don if he is unable to comprehend the subject of the contract, its nature, and its probable consequences. If Don has been adjudicated incompetent by a court, the contract is void and has no legal effect.

Chapter 15

True/False:

1. F	6. T	11. F
2. T	7. F	12. F
3. T	8. T	13. F
4. T	9. F	14. T
5. F	10. F	15. T

Multiple Choice:

1. c	6. d	11. c
2. d	7. c	12. c
3. d	8. d	13. a
4. b	9. b	14. d
5. b	10. c	15. d

Short Essay:

1. The following five kinds of contracts are within most state statutes: (1) promises to answer for the duty of another, (2) promises of an executor or administrator to answer personally for a duty of the decedent whose funds he is administering, (3) agreements upon consideration of marriage, (4) agreements for the sale of an interest in land and, (5) agreements not to be performed within one year.

2. As a general rule, a promise to transfer an interest in land is within the statute of frauds and therefore must comply with its requirements. There are two exceptions to that rule, however. The first involves a promise to make a short-term lease. In most states, this is defined by statute to include leases that are for one year or less in duration. The second involves an oral contract that may be enforced if the party seeking enforcement has so changed his position in reasonable reliance upon the contract that injustice can only be prevented by enforcing the contract.

3. The general statute of frauds requires that an agreement be in writing to be enforceable. The writing has to be signed by the party to be charged or his agent, specify the parties to the contract, and specify with reasonable certainty the subject matter and the essential terms of the unperformed promises. The statute of frauds provision under the UCC is more liberal. The Code requires only a writing that is sufficient to indicate that a contract has been made between the parties, signed by the party against whom enforcement is sought or by his authorized agent, and specify the quantity of goods to be sold. An oral contract for the sale of goods may comply with the requirements of the Code in the following three instances: (1) where the party defending against the contract admits it by pleading, testimony, or otherwise in court; (2) under certain circumstances, where the goods are to be specially manufactured; and (3) where there has been payment or delivery and acceptance.

4. The parol evidence rule does not apply in the following six situations: (1) where the contract is partly written and partly oral; (2) where there is a clerical or typographical error which obviously does not represent the agreement of the parties; (3) where there is a lack of contractual capacity on the part of one of the parties; (4) where there is a defense asserted of fraud, duress, undue influence, mistake or illegality; (5) a condition precedent agreed upon and to which the entire agreement was made subject; and (6) a subsequent mutual rescission or modification of the written contract.

5. Oral contracts modifying previously existing contracts are unenforceable if the resulting contract is within the statute of frauds. The contract between Betty and Big Bucks is within the statute of frauds because it cannot be performed in one year. Therefore, the oral contract modifying the existing contract is unenforceable.

Chapter 16

True/False:

1. F	6. T	11. T
2. F	7. T	12. T
3. T	8. F	13. F
4. F	9. T	14. T
5. T	10. F	15. T

Multiple Choice:

1. a	6. b	11. c
2. d	7. a	12. c
3. d	8. c	13. a
4. a	9. a	14. b
5. c	10. c	15. d

Short Essay:

1. An assignment of rights is the voluntary transfer to a third party (the assignee) of the rights arising from a contract. A delegation of duties, on the other hand, is a transfer to a third party (the delegatee) of the contractual duty to perform. An effective assignment extinguishes the assignor's right of performance by the obligor. Therefore, only the assignee has a right to the obligor's performance. A delegation of duty, however, does not extinguish the delegator's duty to perform, but only results in an additional party, the delegatee, also being obligated.

2. Parties involved might be the assignor, the assignee, the delegator, the delegatee, the obligor and the obligee. The assignor would be the party transferring her rights under a contract to some third party known as the assignee. Duties may sometimes be delegated and the delegator would be the person transferring her duty to perform to some third party known as the delegatee. The person who then must perform the obligations imposed by the contract would be the obligor and the person to whom that performance is owed would be the obligee.

3. Non-assignable rights include those which (1) materially change the obligor's duty or increase the risk or burden upon the obligor, (2) transfer highly personal contract rights, (3) are validly prohibited by the contract, or (4) are prohibited by statute or public policy.

4. Rocky's duty to perform at the university is a nondelegable duty because it is personal in nature, therefore his duty may not be delegated. However, his right to payment of money may be assigned.

5. Where contracts are made which benefit a third party, i.e. not a party to the contract, the third party may be classified as either an intended beneficiary or an incidental beneficiary. The intended beneficiary may be either a donee or creditor beneficiary and in either case the beneficiary may enforce the agreement against the obligor. The incidental beneficiary, however, does not have the right of enforcement.

Chapter 17

True/False:

1. T	6. T	11. T
2. F	7. T	12. T
3. T	8. F	13. F
4. T	9. T	14. F
5. F	10. T	15. T

Multiple Choice:

1. b	6. b	11. b
2. d	7. d	12. c
3. d	8. d	13. d
4. d	9. c	14. c
5. a	10. c	15. b

Short Essay:

1. A condition in a contract is an event whose happening or non-happening affects a duty of performance. Many times express conditions are explicitly set forth in the contractual language and call for a personal satisfaction of one party as approval of the other's performance. The courts, depending upon the circumstances, recognize both a subjective satisfaction based upon a party's honestly held opinion, or an objective satisfaction based upon whether a reasonable person would be satisfied.

2. At common law, a party was discharged from his duty to perform under the contract on grounds of impossibility only if it was objectively impossible for anyone to perform. The courts also generally regarded frustration of purpose as a discharge where the purpose of the contract was frustrated by fortuitous circumstances that deprived the performance of the value attached to it by the parties. The Restatement and the Code positions, however, are that literal impossibility is not required, and that commercial impracticability resulting from a supervening event will excuse nonperformance. The supervening event, however, must have been a "basic assumption" that both parties made when they entered into the contract.

3. The Code requires that a seller tender goods that conform exactly to the contract. Common law requires a material breach before a party could sue.

4. Contracts may be discharged by operation of law under the following circumstances: (1) Impossibility will excuse performance if no one could, under the circumstances, perform. Destruction of the subject matter or subsequent illegality would be examples. (2) Frustration of purpose or (3) commercial impracticability are also conditions which might cause the contract to be discharged by operation of law.

5. If Carol promises to buy Jim's land for $100,000, provided she can obtain financing in the amount of $75,000 at 10 percent or less, Carol's obtaining the financing is a condition precedent to her duty. If Carol promises to work for Big Bucks, Inc. for one year unless she is admitted to graduate school at Ivory Towers University, her admission to graduate school is a condition subsequent. If she is admitted

to graduate school, then her duty to work is terminated. If the contract for the sale of Jim's land to Carol provides that Jim is to deliver the deed on payment of the purchase price, then Jim has no duty to deliver the deed until Carol pays the purchase price and Carol has no duty to pay until Jim delivers the deed. These are concurrent conditions and each party's duty is conditioned on performance by the other.

Chapter 18

True/False:

1. T	6. F	11. T
2. F	7. T	12. F
3. F	8. F	13. T
4. T	9. T	14. F
5. T	10. F	15. T

Multiple Choice:

1. d	6. a	11. c
2. c	7. d	12. b
3. b	8. d	13. c
4. c	9. c	14. d
5. c	10. a	15. d

Short Essay:

1. The most frequent award in breach of contract actions is monetary damages. Where the amount of the damages can be determined as being foreseeable and capable of being established with reasonable certainty, and where these damages could not be avoided the award thereof is appropriate. In determining the damages the court will consider: (1) compensatory damages, (2) incidental damages, (3) consequential damages, and (4) reliance damages. Under certain circumstances, where the plaintiff has not sustained damages nominal damages may be awarded.

2. Under the doctrine of mitigation of damages, the party injured by a breach of contract must take such steps as may be reasonably calculated to lessen the damages that he may sustain. Damages are not recoverable for losses that the injured party could have avoided without undue risk, burden or humiliation.

3. The two major equitable remedies applicable to a breach of contract are the decree of specific performance and the injunction. A decree of specific performance orders a breaching party to render the performance promised under the contract. In contrast, an injunction is an order issued by a court of equity commanding a person to refrain from doing a specific act or engaging in specified conduct. Generally, both are available only where damages for a breach would be inadequate. However, a court will not decree specific performance of a contract for personal services. Nor will it issue an injunction to enforce an exclusive personal service contract if the probable result would be to leave the employee without other reasonable means of making a living.

4. Restitution is the act of returning to the aggrieved party the consideration, or the value thereof if the actual consideration cannot be returned, which was given to the other party. Such an award would be available in several situations: (1) as an alternative remedy for a party injured by breach; (2) for a party in default; (3) for a party who may not enforce a contract because of a limitation; or (4) for a party wishing to rescind a voidable contract.

5. The right to recover compensatory damages for breach of contract is always available to the injured party. Therefore, Jill may recover $2,000 to compensate her for her loss due to Big Bucks' failure to perform. She may also recover $300 in incidental damages which are damages arising directly out of a breach of contract.

Part II: Sample Examination

1. c	8. d	15. b
2. a	9. a	16. b
3. b	10. d	17. d
4. a	11. d	18. d
5. b	12. d	19. d
6. a	13. b	20. d
7. c	14. a	

Chapter 19

True/False:

1. T	6. F	11. T
2. F	7. T	12. T
3. T	8. T	13. T
4. T	9. F	14. F
5. T	10. F	15. T

Multiple Choice:

1. c	6. d	11. b
2. b	7. d	12. b
3. d	8. d	13. d
4. d	9. d	14. d
5. d	10. d	15. a

Short Essay:

1. The principal/agent relationship may be terminated by operation of law or by acts of the parties themselves. Termination by operation of law occurs in those situations where the principal has become bankrupt or where either party has died or become incapacitated. Also where the circumstances have changed, the subject matter has been destroyed or the law itself has changed, the relationship will be

terminated.   The parties may terminate the relationship themselves by agreement, fulfillment of the purpose, lapse of time or by either party withdrawing subject to irrevocable agencies where the agency is coupled with an interest and the agent has a security interest in the subject matter of the agency.

2. An agent may not (a) represent his principal in any transaction in which he has a personal interest; (b) take a position in conflict with the interests of his principal; (c) compete with his principal; (d) act on behalf of a competitor or for persons whose interests conflict with those of the principal; (e) use for his own benefit, and contrary to the interests of his principal, information obtained in the course of the agency; or (f) make a secret profit out of any transaction subject to the agency.

3. Should an agent violate any fiduciary duty, she would be liable to her principal for breach of contract. Additionally, she would be liable in tort for any losses caused by her conduct as well as restitution for profits made or property received. Of course, the relationship may be terminated.

4. From time to time an agent will contribute her own funds or property to the agency. Where the agency is thus coupled with an interest of the agent in the subject matter, the authority of the agent may not be revoked by the principal. Additionally, neither the incapacity nor the bankruptcy of the principal will terminate the authority of the agent. Normally not even the death of the principal will terminate the agency, unless the duty for which the security was given terminates with her death.

5. An agent must act with reasonable care and skill in performing the work for which he is employed. Therefore, A would be liable to P for breach of the duty of diligence.

Chapter 20

True/False:

1. T	6. F	11. F
2. T	7. T	12. T
3. T	8. T	13. T
4. T	9. F	14. F
5. F	10. F	15. T

Multiple Choice:

1. d	6. b	11. d
2. c	7. d	12. b
3. c	8. a	13. b
4. a	9. a	14. a
5. d	10. c	15. c

Short Essay:
1. Actual authority is based upon words or conduct of the principal manifested to the agent. Apparent authority is based upon words or conduct of the principal which manifests to a third person that the agent has actual authority. Actual authority gives an agent both the power and the right to bind his principal in legal relations with third persons, while apparent authority gives the agent the power but not necessarily the right to bind his principal.

2. An agent has the power to bind her principal when the principal is legally bound by the act of the agent. An agent has the right to bind her principal whenever she may do so without violating her duty of obedience by exceeding her actual authority. For example, when an agent has apparent authority but not actual authority, she has the power but not the right to bind her principal. Thus, the principal is legally bound by the act of the agent, but by exceeding her actual authority, the agent has violated her duty of obedience and is liable to the principal for any resulting loss.

3. One of the ways liability to third parties may be imposed upon the principal would be in a situation where the principal was not careful in the hiring process. Called negligent hiring doctrine, this arises when the principal does not exercise proper care in selecting an agent for the job to be performed. This doctrine has also been used to impose liability on a principal for intentional torts committed by an agent against customers of the principal.

4. Once authority terminates, by either operation of law or acts of the parties, actual authority ends. If the termination is by operation of law apparent authority also ends and no notice to third parties is required. If termination is by acts of the parties apparent authority continues until notice is given to third parties. Actual notice must be given to third parties with whom business dealings have occurred or begun; constructive notice only need be given to all other third parties.

5. To avoid personal liability, an agent must disclose both that he is acting as an agent and the identity of his principal. Therefore, because Rob is acting on behalf of an undisclosed principal, he would be personally liable on the contract with Dan.

Part III: Sample Examination

1. T
2. T
3. T
4. T
5. T
6. F
7. T
8. F
9. F
10. F
11. d
12. d
13. b
14. b
15. c
16. c
17. c
18. b
19. b
20. c

Chapter 21

True/False:

1. T	6. T	11. T
2. T	7. F	12. F
3. T	8. F	13. T
4. T	9. F	14. T
5. F	10. F	15. F

Multiple Choice:

1. b	6. b	11. b
2. c	7. b	12. d
3. d	8. b	13. c
4. d	9. d	14. d
5. b	10. a	15. d

Short Essay:

1. Article 2 of the Uniform Commercial Code is expressly applicable to contracts for the sale of goods, as it defines those terms. General contract law, however, continues to govern aspects of the sale of goods not specifically modified by the Code as well as contracts outside the scope of the Code. These include transactions other than sales, such as bailments, leases and gifts, as well as sales of things other than goods, such as services, real property, and intangibles. Nevertheless, the Code is often applied by analogy to nonsales transactions, thereby expanding the scope of its principles and policies.

2. A "sale" is the transfer of title to goods from a seller to a buyer for a price which may be either money, other goods, real property or services. "Goods" are defined as personal property which is tangible and movable.

3. As long as the parties to a contract do not disclaim the obligations of good faith, diligence, reasonableness, and care they are free to alter or modify most of the provisions of the Code. Many provisions may even be eliminated if the parties so desire. The parties may even by agreement determine what standards are to be used to measure the performance with regard to the fundamental principles of Article 2.

4. A firm offer is a signed writing by a merchant to hold open an offer for the sale or purchase of goods for a period of time of up to three months. Under the Code, such offers are binding on the merchant even though no consideration is given and cannot be revoked for the time stated or if no time is stated, for a reasonable period of time.

5. An agreement modifying a contract for the sale of goods must be in writing if the resulting contract is within the statute of frauds. Even though the original contract for the sale of the wheat was not required to be in writing, the subsequent modification resulted in a contract that was within the statute of frauds. Therefore, the modified contract is unenforceable.

Chapter 22

True/False:
1. T	6. F	11. T
2. T	7. T	12. T
3. T	8. T	13. T
4. T	9. T	14. F
5. F	10. T	15. T

Multiple Choice:
1. c	6. d	11. a
2. c	7. a	12. b
3. c	8. b	13. c
4. d	9. d	14. d
5. d	10. d	15. d

Short Essay:
1. Once a seller tenders conforming goods to the buyer, the seller is then entitled to have the goods accepted and to be paid the contract price. Tender requires the seller to make available goods that conform to the contract at the buyer's disposition and give the buyer reasonable notification to enable her to take delivery.

2. Unless the parties otherwise agree, the place for delivery of goods is the seller's place of business. Under a shipment contract, however, the seller is obligated to send the goods to the buyer (although he is not required to deliver them to a particular place as in a destination contract). Discharge of his duty of performance under a shipment contract requires the seller to: (1) deliver the goods to a carrier, (2) make a reasonable contract for their shipment, (3) obtain and promptly deliver or tender to the buyer any documents necessary to allow the buyer to obtain possession of the goods from the carrier, and (4) promptly notify the buyer of the shipment.

3. Under the perfect tender rule, the seller's tender of performance must conform exactly to the contract. There are three qualifications to this rule: (1) agreement of the parties may limit the operation of this rule; (2) if the time for performance has not expired the seller may cure or correct the nonconforming tender; and (3) in installment contracts the buyer may reject a nonconforming installment if it substantially impairs the value of that installment and cannot be cured.

4. A rejection is a manifestation by the buyer of his unwillingness to become owner of the goods. To be effective, it must be made within a reasonable time after the goods have been tendered or delivered and the seller must be reasonably notified. A buyer may rightfully reject goods that do not conform to the contract, but any exercise of ownership of the goods by the buyer after rejection is wrongful as against the seller. Finally, a buyer's duty after rejection varies depending on whether or not he is a merchant. A revocation of acceptance is a manifestation of unwillingness to remain the owner of the goods after the buyer has already accepted them. A buyer may revoke his acceptance of nonconforming goods only if the nonconformity substantially impairs the value of the goods and the acceptance was (a) based on the

reasonable assumption that the seller would cure the nonconformity and did not, or (b) without discovery of the nonconformity and such acceptance was reasonably induced by the difficulty of discovery before acceptance or by assurances of the seller. Upon revocation of acceptance, the buyer is in the same position with respect to the goods and has the same rights and duties with regard to them as if he had rejected them.

5. The parties to a contract can be relieved of their obligations of full performance in three instances. The first is if there has been a loss of goods that were identified when the contract was made, and the loss occurred without the fault of either party and before risk of loss passed to the buyer. If the loss was total, the contract is avoided; if partial, it is voidable at the election of the buyer. The second instance is upon the nonhappening of a presupposed condition that was a basic assumption of the contract. The parties are relieved from their obligation of performance, however, only to the extent of the nonhappening of the condition. Finally, where neither party is at fault and the agreed manner of delivery of the goods becomes commercially impracticable, a substituted manner of performance must be tendered by the seller and accepted by the buyer.

Chapter 23

True/False:

1. T	6. F	11. F
2. T	7. F	12. T
3. F	8. T	13. T
4. T	9. F	14. F
5. T	10. F	15. T

Multiple Choice:

1. b	6. b	11. c
2. d	7. d	12. a
3. c	8. c	13. c
4. b	9. b	14. d
5. b	10. c	15. d

Short Essay:

1. At common law, risk of loss was placed upon the party that had title to the goods at the time in question. The Code, however, employs a transactional approach that diminishes the importance of the concept of title. Accordingly, the Code sets forth a detailed set of rules for allocating risk of loss depending on whether there has been a breach of the sales contract. In the absence of a breach, the Code attempts to place the risk of loss upon the party who is more likely to have greater control over the goods or is better able to prevent the loss.

2. Two types of trial sales, where the buyer is permitted to try the goods for a period of time to determine satisfaction, are recognized by the Code. First, in a sale on approval possession, but not title, is transferred to the buyer for a designated or reasonable time. Both title and risk of loss remain with the seller.

Second, in a sale or return the goods are sold and delivered to the buyer who also accepts the risk of loss. Return of the goods is at the buyer's risk and expense. In the absence of agreement, if the goods are delivered primarily for the buyer's use, the transaction is a sale of approval but if the goods are delivered primarily for resale by the buyer, it is a sale or return.

3. Where the owner of goods entrusts those goods to a merchant who deals in goods of that kind, the merchant has the power to transfer title to those goods to a buyer in the ordinary course of business. A buyer in the ordinary course of business is one who in good faith and without knowledge that the sale to him is in violation of the ownership rights or security interest of another buys those goods. In such a case the "true" owner has a right of recourse against the merchant bailee for value of the goods but the Code protects buyers of such and the buyer in the ordinary course of business acquires good title.

4. Where the buyer has accepted nonconforming goods, and thereafter by timely notice to the seller rightfully revokes her acceptance, she may treat the risk of loss, to the extent of any deficiency in insurance coverage, as resting from the beginning on the seller.

5. Goods should be protected against loss whenever possible, but for a policy of insurance to be valid, the insured must have an insurable interest. The common law allowed only one with title or a lien to purchase such protection. The code, however, extends this right to a buyer who has an interest in goods that have been identified to the contract. Referred to as a special property interest, this allows both the seller and the buyer to protect themselves against loss.

Chapter 24

True/False:

1. T	6. F	11. T
2. F	7. T	12. T
3. F	8. F	13. F
4. T	9. F	14. T
5. F	10. F	15. F

Multiple Choice:

1. b	6. d	11. b
2. d	7. a	12. d
3. d	8. c	13. a
4. b	9. c	14. d
5. d	10. a	15. d

Short Essay:

1. Generally a warranty is considered to be an obligation of the seller to the buyer concerning the title, quality, characteristics, or condition of goods sold. The seller will warrant, unless properly disclaimed, that she has and can transfer title to the goods without any lien that the buyer is not aware of. The seller may also make either an express warranty or an implied warranty. Express warranties may arise by the

seller making an affirmation of fact about the goods, or by describing the goods, or through the use of a sample or model of the goods. Implied warranties arise out of the circumstances of the sale.

2. Under the implied warranty of merchantability, a merchant seller impliedly warrants that the goods that are of the kind in which he deals are merchantable–i.e., that they are reasonably fit for the ordinary purpose for which they are manufactured and sold, and also that they are fair, average quality. The warranty may be disclaimed, unless barred by the Magnuson-Moss Act, by a conspicuous writing containing language that specifically includes merchantability or a similar oral disclaimer. Under the implied warranty of fitness for a particular purpose, any seller, whether a merchant or a nonmerchant, impliedly warrants that the goods are reasonably fit for the particular purpose of the buyer for which the goods are required, provided at the time of contracting the seller has reason to know such particular purpose and that the buyer is relying upon the seller's skill and judgment to furnish suitable goods. The disclaimer of an implied warranty to fitness for the particular purpose must be in writing and conspicuous.

3. In order to recover under a theory of strict liability in tort, a seller must show that: (1) the defendant was engaged in the business of selling such a product; (2) the defendant sold the product in a defective condition; (3) the defective condition made the product unreasonably dangerous to the user or consumer or to his property; (4) the defect in the product existed at the time it left the hands of the defendant; (5) the defective condition was attributable to the defendant; (6) the plaintiff sustained physical harm or property damage by use or consumption of the product; and (7) the defective condition was the proximate cause of such injury or damage. Many of the traditional obstacles to recovery are not applicable to a claim of strict liability in tort. Liability cannot generally be modified or disclaimed, and there is no requirement of horizontal or vertical privity. Moreover, contributory negligence is, for the most part, not recognized as a valid defense; comparative negligence, however, has on occasion been applied to limit a plaintiff's recovery to account for his degree of fault. Finally, voluntary assumption of risk and misuse or abuse of the product are valid defenses to an action based on strict liability in tort.

4. The kinds of defects which give rise to a defective condition include: (a) manufacturing defects which occur when the product is not properly made and fails to meet its own manufacturing specifications; (b) design defects which occur when a product is produced as specified but is dangerous or hazardous because its design is inadequate; and (c) inadequate warnings or instructions which are considered a defect when as a result of a failure to warn or to provide adequate directions for safe use, the product becomes dangerous.

5. In order to relieve manufacturers from liability concerns years after the product has left their control, many states have enacted statutes of repose which limit the time period–typically to between six and twelve years–for which a manufacturer is liable for injury caused by a defective product.

Chapter 25

True/False:

1. T	6. F	11. T
2. F	7. T	12. T
3. T	8. T	13. F
4. T	9. F	14. T
5. T	10. T	15. T

Multiple Choice:

1. c	6. b	11. c
2. b	7. d	12. c
3. b	8. a	13. a
4. c	9. b	14. b
5. d	10. d	15. c

Short Essay:

1. If a buyer has rightfully rejected the seller's nonconforming tender of goods, the buyer has several nonexclusive remedies for the seller's breach. First, the buyer may cancel the contract. He may also recover any payments already made, and establish a security interest in any of the seller's goods that are already in his possession to the extent of any payment of the price already made. Finally, he may also cover and recover damages or simply seek market price damages for the seller's breach.

2. All of the remedies outlined in question 1 are available to a buyer if the seller repudiates a contract, and several more are also available. First, the buyer may maintain an action for replevin of goods that have been identified to the contract if the buyer after a reasonable effort is unable to effect cover for such goods, or if the goods have been shipped under reservation of a security interest in the seller and satisfaction of this security interest has been made or tendered. In addition, if the goods are unique or if money damages would not be an adequate remedy, the buyer may seek specific performance.

3. Several remedies are available to the seller after buyer has wrongfully rejected a conforming tender of goods. First, the seller may cancel the contract. He may also withhold delivery of additional goods and identify goods to the contract. He may resell and recover damages or just recover market price damages. Finally, if appropriate, a seller may bring an action for price–this is most likely to occur if conforming goods have been lost or damaged after the risk of loss has passed to the buyer, or where goods have been identified to the contract and there is no ready market available for their resale at a reasonable price.

4. Cover is a remedy which allows an aggrieved buyer to purchase needed goods to replace those due under the terms of the contract with the original seller. The buyer must act in good faith, and without unreasonable delay. The buyer may then recover from the original seller the difference between the cost of cover and the contract price, plus any incidental and consequential damages, less expenses saved because of the seller's breach if any.

5. The parties may provide for liquidated damages in their contract by specifying the amount or measure of damages that either party may recover in the event of a breach by the other party. The parties may also expressly limit or exclude consequential damages unless such limitation or exclusion would be unconscionable. The limitation of consequential damages for personal injury from breach of warranty in the sale of consumer goods is always unconscionable, whereas limitations of such damages where the loss is commercial is not.

Part IV: Sample Examination

1. b	8. d	15. a
2. a	9. b	16. c
3. b	10. b	17. d
4. b	11. d	18. c
5. b	12. d	19. b
6. b	13. c	20. d
7. b	14. c	

Chapter 26

True/False:

1. T	6. F	11. T
2. F	7. T	12. F
3. F	8. F	13. F
4. F	9. T	14. T
5. F	10. F	15. T

Multiple Choice:

1. d	6. c	11. b
2. c	7. a	12. d
3. c	8. c	13. b
4. d	9. d	14. d
5. b	10. d	15. d

Short Essay:

1. Negotiability is a concept that makes written instruments a readily accepted form of payment in substitution for money. In time, an instrument which has a promise to pay, rather than payment, came to be accepted as negotiable and the use of commercial paper as a means of extending credit became acceptable. Thus negotiability invests commercial paper with a high degree of marketability and commercial utility. It allows commercial paper to be freely transferable and enforceable.

2. It is nonnegotiable because it is not payable to order or to bearer, and it does not contain an unconditional promise or order to pay.

3. These are words of negotiability which indicate that the maker or drawer intends that the instrument pass into the hands of someone other than the payee. Revised Article 3 provides that a *check* which meets all of the negotiability requirements, except it does not state whether it is an order instrument or a bearer instrument, is nevertheless negotiable. This applies only to checks.

4. The notation does not violate the particular fund doctrine and does not destroy the negotiability of the draft. It is a mere bookkeeping notation.

5. It is nonnegotiable because it is not payable to order or to bearer, and the promise to pay is conditional. Payment of the instrument is conditional upon the helicopter meeting contractual specifications.

Chapter 27

True/False:
1. F
2. T
3. T
4. T
5. T
6. F
7. T
8. F
9. T
10. F
11. F
12. T
13. F
14. T
15. F

Multiple Choice:
1. c
2. d
3. b
4. d
5. c
6. b
7. d
8. c
9. b
10. a
11. d
12. d
13. c
14. b
15. c

Short Essay:
1. Order paper is an instrument that is payable to order and requires both possession and indorsement by the appropriate parties for the transferee to be a holder. Bearer paper is an instrument payable to bearer and is transferred by mere possession. Because bearer paper runs to whoever is in possession of it, a finder or a thief would be a holder even though he did not receive possession by voluntary transfer.

2. A transfer by negotiation is the transfer of a negotiable instrument in such a manner that the transferee becomes a holder. An assignment is the voluntary transfer to some third party of the rights arising from a contract. Whether the transfer is by negotiation or by the assignment the transferee acquires the rights that her transferor had.

3. A restrictive indorsement is an indorsement attempting to limit the rights of the indorsee by: (a) placing a condition in the indorsement, or (b) prohibiting further transfer, or (c) limiting further negotiation to those consistent with the indorsement, or (d) requiring the indorsee to pay or apply all funds in accordance with the indorsement.

4. No, negotiation of a negotiable instrument is separate from the underlying contractual transaction. This rule is followed in order to allow negotiable instruments to move freely in the marketplace. It is this feature of negotiability that gives the holder of an instrument the right to payment and that allows a holder in due course a unique legal position in that the holder in due course has greater rights in the instrument than the transferee from whom he received it.

5. An indorsement "without recourse" is the customary manner of disclaiming an indorser's liability on an instrument. It is a qualified indorsement which disclaims contract liability but does not entirely remove the warranty liability of the indorser.

Chapter 28

True/False:

1. F	6. T	11. T
2. T	7. F	12. F
3. F	8. T	13. F
4. T	9. T	14. F
5. T	10. T	15. T

Multiple Choice:

1. e	6. c	11. d
2. d	7. d	12. d
3. c	8. a	13. d
4. a	9. b	14. c
5. d	10. c	15. b

Short Essay:

1. "Good faith" is defined as "honesty in fact and the observance of reasonable commercial standards of fair dealing." There is both a subjective and objective component. The subjective component measures good faith by what the purchaser knows or believes. The objective component concerns the observance of reasonable commercial standards of fair dealing.

2. A mere holder is nothing more than an assignee. Thus, he takes the rights his transferor had and is subject to the claims and defenses that could be asserted against his transferor. A holder in due course, on the other hand, takes the instrument free from any claims and free from most defenses. Thus, a holder in due course will be entitled to payment in many cases where a mere holder would not be.

3. Under the shelter rule a holder who does not qualify to be a holder in due course may nevertheless acquire all the rights of a holder in due course if some previous holder had been a holder in due course. The rule does not apply to a transferee (1) who has himself been a party to any fraud or illegality affecting the instrument or (2) who as a prior holder had notice of a claim or defense.

4. B is not a holder in due course, since he has taken the instrument when overdue, did not pay value, and has notice of M's defense. However, due to the shelter rule B acquires H's rights as a holder in due

course, and M cannot successfully assert her defense against B because it is only a personal defense. The shelter rule confers on a transferee all the rights of the transferor.

5. Any alteration that changes the contract of any party to the instrument in any way is a material alteration. In keeping with the preferential position accorded a holder in due course, he may enforce any altered instrument according to its original terms. Therefore, because Harry is a holder in due course, he may enforce the note in the amount of $2,000.

Chapter 29

True/False:

1. T	6. F	11. T
2. T	7. F	12. F
3. T	8. T	13. T
4. T	9. T	14. T
5. F	10. T	15. T

Multiple Choice:

1. d	6. c	11. a
2. d	7. b	12. a
3. c	8. c	13. c
4. d	9. c	14. d
5. d	10. a	15. d

Short Essay:

1. Contractual liability is imposed upon those parties who have signed commercial paper whether it be in a primary or secondary status. There are parties to commercial instruments who may never sign those instruments and will therefore not be liable on a contractual basis or theory. Warranty liability is imposed on both parties who do sign and on those who do not sign commercial paper. It would apply to (1) those who transfer an instrument, and (2) those who receive payment or acceptance of an instrument.

2. The drawers and indorsers of an instrument are secondarily liable to pay the instrument, unless they disclaim their liability by adding the notation "without recourse". Their liability is subject to the conditions of presentment, dishonor, and notice of dishonor. Because Cathy indorsed the instrument "without recourse", she has disclaimed her secondary liability. Ben may proceed against you and your roommate on the basis of your secondary liability, but your liability is contingent upon the conditions being met. The check has been presented for payment and has been dishonored. In order for Ben to succeed against you or your roommate, each of you must be given proper notice of the dishonor. Any notice by a bank must be given before midnight on the first banking day after it receives notice of dishonor. Any non-bank must give notice before midnight of the third business day after dishonor or receipt of notice of dishonor.

3. Under primary liability, one is absolutely and unconditionally liable to pay a negotiable instrument, while under secondary liability, one is only liable to pay a negotiable instrument subject to the conditions of presentment, dishonor, and notice of dishonor.

4. Parties may be discharged from liability by performance, tender of payment, cancellation and renunciation, impairment of recourse or collateral, or reacquisition. Fraudulent or material alterations may also discharge parties as does unexcused delay in presentment, notice of dishonor, or protest. No discharge of a party is effective against a subsequent holder in due course however, unless he has knowledge of the discharge when he acquires the instrument.

5. The unnamed principal is not liable on the note, but you would be liable. Parol evidence is admissible to prove the agency relationship and to establish liability of the unnamed principal.

Chapter 30

True/False:

1. F	6. T	11. T
2. F	7. F	12. F
3. T	8. T	13. T
4. F	9. F	14. T
5. F	10. T	15. T

Multiple Choice:

1. c	6. c	11. d
2. d	7. c	12. b
3. b	8. d	13. d
4. a	9. c	14. b
5. c	10. a	15. c

Short Essay:

1. When an item is restrictively indorsed with words such as "pay any bank," it is locked into the bank collection system, and only a bank may acquire the rights of a holder.

2. Upon the receipt of a deposit from a customer a bank will credit the customer's account by the amount of the deposit. Provisional credit is thereby extended to the customer until such time as the deposit instrument clears. The provisional settlements made in the collection chain are all directed toward final payment of the item by the payor bank. Final payment occurs when the payor bank does any of the following: (1) pays an item in cash; (2) settles and does not reserve the right to revoke the settlement; (3) makes a provisional settlement and does not revoke it at the time and in the manner permitted; or (4) completes the process of posting the item to the account of the drawer. (Note: Revised Article 4 has abandoned posting as a test for determining when final payment is made.)

3. Arthur must examine his bank statement and report the payment of the forged check to the bank. The bank will in all likelihood bear the loss, unless it can find Carl, who will have liability for the forgery

both criminally and based upon several of the civil provisions in the Code. The forged signature is that of Carl even though he signed Brad's name. Carl has also breached both the indorser's warranties and the presenter's warranties and thus has liability based on both the contract of indorsement and the warranty provisions of the Code. The bank has liability to Brad for conversion.

4. David is liable for only $50, because he immediately notified the bank within two days of learning of the loss or theft. If he had not immediately notified the bank, his liability would have been for $500. If he had failed to notify the bank within sixty days, he would bear the entire loss.

5. East Company is the originator which is the sender of the first payment order. East Company is also a sender which is the party who gives an instruction to the receiving bank. FNB is the receiving bank who receives the sender's instructions. FNB is also the originator's bank and the beneficiary's bank. West is the beneficiary who is to be paid by the beneficiary bank.

Part V: Sample Examination

1. a	8. a	15. c
2. b	9. b	16. a
3. c	10. b	17. c
4. c	11. c	18. b
5. b	12. d	19. d
6. d	13. b	20. d
7. c	14. b	

Chapter 31

True/False:

1. T	6. T	11. T
2. T	7. F	12. T
3. F	8. T	13. F
4. F T	9. F	14. F
5. T	10. T	15. F

Multiple Choice:

1. d	6. c	11. b
2. b	7. c	12. d
3. d	8. a	13. a
4. c	9. d	14. b
5. b	10. d	15. a

Short Essay:

1. The court will look for three components to determine whether a partnership exists. Specifically, the court will determine whether there exists: (a) an association–two or more persons who agree to become partners, (b) a business–an intention to acquire profits and a continuous series of commercial activities, and (c) co-ownership–a sharing of profits and the right to manage and control the business.

2. A partnership agreement should include the following: (1) names of each partner and partnership name, (2) nature of business, (3) length of time partnership is to last, (4) capital contribution of each partner, (5) how profits and losses are to be shared, (6) who is to have what authority, (7) how the partners are to be paid, (8) special restrictions on partners, if any, (9) withdrawal rights of partners, and (10) distribution upon termination.

3. At common law, a partnership was regarded as a legal aggregate: i.e. a group of individuals having no legal existence apart from its members. However, under the UPA partnerships may be treated as a legal entity–that is as an organization having a legal existence separate from that of its members. The assets of the firm and title to real estate are but two ways the UPA treats partnerships as a legal entity. Other ways the UPA recognizes the legal entity theory are the fiduciary duty of partners to the partnership and the partners' roles as agents of the partnership. However, a partnership cannot be sued or sue in the firm name unless authorized by statute to do so. This would be considered as a legal aggregate characteristic. The Internal Revenue Service treats partnerships as legal aggregates in that the firm does not pay an income tax separate from its members.

4. Partners may be either general or limited. Beyond that, partners may also be classified as silent, one who elects to take no part in the partnership business; or secret, one whose membership in the firm is not disclosed to the public; or ostensible, one who has consented to be held out as a partner whether he is a real partner or not. Additionally, one may be a dormant partner, which is one who is both a secret and silent partner, as well as a subpartner, which is one who has a contractual arrangement with a partner which entitles him to a share of that partner's profits.

5. Your partnership agreement should include: (1) the firm name and identity of the partners; (2) the nature and scope of the partnership business; (3) the duration of the partnership; (4) the capital contributions of each partner; (5) the division of profits and sharing of losses; (6) the duties of each partner in the management; (7) a provision for salaries; (8) restrictions, if any, on the authority of particular partners to bind the firm; (9) the right of a partner to withdraw from the firm, and the terms, conditions, and required notice for withdrawal; and (10) a provision for continuation of the business by the remaining partners, if desired, in the event of the death of a partner or other dissolution.

Chapter 32

True/False:

1. T	6. T	11. F
2. F	7. F	12. T
3. F	8. F	13. F
4. T	9. T	14. F
5. T	10. T	15. T

Multiple Choice:

1. d	6. c	11. c
2. c	7. b	12. b
3. d	8. b	13. d
4. d	9. a	14. c
5. d	10. b	15. d

Short Essay:

1. Partners are provided, by law, with various rights because of their status as partners. They have rights in specific partnership property, referred to as tenants in partnership, as well as their interest in the partnership itself. Additionally, they have a right to share in distributions, a right to participate in management, a right to choose associates and a right of enforcement.

2. All partners within a partnership have a fiduciary duty to one another and to the partnership. They must operate in a loyal fair manner demonstrating good faith in all partnership business. In addition they have a duty of obedience, to follow partnership agreement and other business decisions, and the duty of care.

3. If a wrongful act or omission of any partner is related to the ordinary course of business within the partnership or with the authority of the partners, the partnership will be liable for loss or injury caused by that act of omission. Such liability is joint and several. Under such liability the creditors may sue the partners jointly as a group or separately as individuals. A partner will not, however, be liable for the crimes of her partners unless she either authorized or participated in them.

4. In the absence of an agreement on the sharing of profits, the UPA provides that profits must be shared equally, regardless of the capital contribution of each of the partners. Each partner would receive $12,000.

5. The UPA provides that a partnership is liable for loss or injury caused by any wrongful act or omission of any partner while acting within the ordinary course of the business of the partnership. If the partnership is liable, then each partner has unlimited personal liability for the obligation. The liability of

partners for a tort committed by any partner or by an employee of the firm in the course of partnership business is joint and several. Therefore, the partnership as well as the individual partners are liable to Sue.

Chapter 33

True/False:

1. T	6. T	11. T
2. T	7. F	12. F
3. T	8. F	13. T
4. F	9. T	14. F
5. T	10. T	15. T

Multiple Choice:

1. b	6. d	11. a
2. c	7. d	12. d
3. d	8. c	13. d
4. c	9. d	14. a
5. c	10. b	15. b

Short Essay:

1. Winding up a partnership involves: (a) completing unfinished business, (b) collecting debts, (c) taking inventory, (d) reducing assets to cash, (e) auditing the partnership books, (f) paying creditors, and (g) distributing the remaining assets to the partners.

2. Should the partnership agreement provide for continuation of the business and a specified settlement to the departing partner, termination need not occur. Also remaining partners may continue to do business following a wrongful dissolution by paying the withdrawing partner the value of his interest less the amount of damages sustained by the breach. Additionally, the business may continue after expulsion. The expelled partner is discharged from liabilities and receives cash due him.

3. During the winding up process, liabilities of a partnership are paid out of partnership assets in the following order: (1) amounts owing to creditors other than partners, (2) amounts owing to partners other than for capital and profits, (3) amounts owing to partners for capital contributions, and (4) amounts owing to partners for profits.

4. The order of distribution of a general partnership's assets is: (a) to creditors other than partners, (b) to partners other than for capital and profits, (c) to partners for capital contributions, and (d) to partners for profits. The $123,000 would be distributed as follows:

123,000
−40,000 to outside creditors
  83,000
  −2,000 expenses of winding up
  81,000
−15,000 loan by Elvis and Fred
  66,000
−45,000 return of partners' capital
  21,000 divided by 3 = $7,000 profit to each of the three partners

5. On dissolution, the actual authority of a partner to act for the partnership terminates, except so far as may be necessary to wind up partnership affairs. Actual authority to wind up includes completing existing contracts, collecting debts, selling assets, and paying obligations. Although actual authority terminates on dissolution, apparent authority persists and binds the partnership for acts within the scope of the partnership business unless notice of the dissolution is given to the third party.

Chapter 34

True/False:

1. T	6. F	11. T
2. F	7. T	12. T
3. T	8. T	13. T
4. F	9. F	14. T
5. T	10. F	15. T

Multiple Choice:

1. d	6. b	11. d
2. a	7. c	12. b
3. d	8. b	13. d
4. c	9. d	14. c
5. d	10. b	15. d

Short Essay:
1. A limited partner may withdraw as provided in the limited partnership certificate or, under the 1985 Act, the written partnership agreement. If the certificate does not specify when a limited partner may withdraw, she may do so upon giving at least six months' prior written notice to each general partner.

2. A limited partner is protected against unlimited personal liability only if the following conditions are met: (a) there is substantial compliance in good faith with the requirement that a certificate of limited partnership be filed, (b) the surname of the limited partner does not appear in the partnership name, and (c) the limited partner does not take part in control of the business.

3. Known as the "safe harbor" provisions of both versions of the RULPA, activities listed may be performed without being deemed to be management activities which endanger liability protection. These provisions are: (1) being a contractor for, or an agent or employee of, the limited partnership or a general partner; (2) consulting with or advising a general partner with respect to the business of the limited partnership; (3) acting as surety for the limited partnership; (4) approving or disapproving an amendment to the partnership agreement; and (5) voting on various fundamental changes in the limited partnership.

4. A limited liability company is another form of unincorporated business association which provides its membership with liability protection, allows all members to participate in management, and if properly structured, provides taxation as a partnership.

5. Recognition of Limited Liability Partnerships dates to 1991. Considered a general partnership but, by making the statutorily required filing, it limits the liability of its partners for some or all of the partnership obligations. Three different approaches have arisen with respect to limiting the partners' liability. Early statutes limited liability only for negligent acts of the partners but retained unlimited liability for all other obligations. Later statutes extended limited liability to any partnership tort or contract obligation. More recent statutes have provided limited liability for all debts and obligations of the partnership.

Part VI: Sample Examination

1. b	8. c	15. c
2. d	9. b	16. d
3. b	10. d	17. b
4. c	11. d	18. c
5. b	12. a	19. a
6. c	13. c	20. d
7. b	14. d	

Chapter 35

True/False:
1. T
2. T
3. T
4. T
5. T
6. T
7. T
8. F
9. F
10. T
11. T
12. T
13. T
14. F
15. F

Multiple Choice:
1. a
2. d
3. c
4. b
5. c
6. d
7. a
8. b
9. d
10. a
11. d
12. a
13. a
14. d
15. d

Short Essay:
1. The principal attributes of a corporation are: (1) it is considered to be a legal entity, (2) it provides the shareholders with limited liability, (3) ownership, represented by shares of stock, is freely transferable, (5) it is designed to have perpetual existence and (5) its management is centralized. Additionally, it is considered for some purposes a citizen and for other purposes a person.

2. An *ultra vires* act is any action that goes beyond a corporation's express or implied powers. This would include contracts that are made in the name of the corporation. Such contracts are not held to be invalid. The RMBCA allows such activities to be redressed in three different ways: (1) a shareholder action to enjoin the act, (2) a corporate action against the incumbent or former director for exceeding their authority, or (3) an action by the attorney general of the state of incorporation to dissolve the corporation or enjoin it from the unauthorized conduct.

3. A court will pierce the corporate veil where the shareholders (a) have not conducted the business on a corporate basis, (b) have not provided an adequate financial basis for the business, or (c) have used the corporation to defraud.

4. The doctrine of *respondeat superior* imposes full liability on a corporation for the torts committed by its agents and employees during the course of their employment. Because Albert was acting within the scope of employment, both Albert and Carryall Corporation are liable to Brenda for her injuries she sustained as a result of Albert's negligence.

5. Corporations derive their powers from three primary sources. State statutes contain a great many powers extended to properly formed corporations, including perpetual existence, the right to hold property in the corporate name, and all powers necessary or convenient to effect the corporation's purpose. The

corporate charter will grant further powers to the corporation as enumerated in the articles of incorporation. Additionally, the corporation may exercise implied powers necessary or convenient to and consistent with the express powers contained in the corporate articles.

Chapter 36

True/False:

1. F	6. F	11. F
2. T	7. F	12. T
3. T	8. F	13. F
4. T	9. F	14. T
5. T	10. T	15. F

Multiple Choice:

1. c	6. c	11. c
2. d	7. d	12. b
3. a	8. c	13. c
4. c	9. d	14. c
5. d	10. b	15. b

Short Essay:

1. A shareholder has the right to: (a) participate in control of the corporation, (b) participate in the earnings of the corporation, and (c) participate in the residual assets of the corporation upon dissolution.

2. A debt security or bond is a source of capital creating no ownership interest and involving the corporation's promise to repay funds lent to it. An equity security is a source of capital creating an ownership interest in the corporation.

3. For cumulative dividends, if the board does not declare regular dividends on the preferred stock, such omitted dividends cumulate, and no dividend may be declared on the common stock until all dividend arrearages on the preferred stock are declared and paid. If noncumulative, regular dividends do not cumulate on failure of the board to declare them. Cumulative to the extent earned shares cumulate unpaid dividends only to the extent funds were legally available to pay such dividends in that fiscal period.

4. The Revised Act imposes personal liability to the corporation upon directors who wrongfully vote for or assent to the declaration of a dividend or other distribution of corporate assets. A shareholder has an obligation to repay an illegally declared dividend under certain circumstances. Good or bad faith, knowledge of the facts, solvency, or insolvency of the corporation are all taken into consideration.

5. If Julie has preemptive rights, a shareholder's right to purchase a pro rata share of new stock offerings, she will be offered one share of the newly issued stock for every two shares she owns. If she accepts the offer and buys the stock, she will have 150 shares out of a total of 1500 outstanding, and her relative interest in the corporation will be unchanged.

Chapter 37

True/False:

1. T	6. T	11. T
2. F	7. F	12. T
3. F	8. T	13. T
4. F	9. T	14. T
5. T	10. F	15. F

Multiple Choice:

1. c	6. c	11. d
2. a	7. c	12. b
3. b	8. b	13. b
4. a	9. b	14. b
5. b	10. c	15. d

Short Essay:

1. A shareholder may only inspect the books and records of the corporation for a proper purpose. Thus, a shareholder may be denied his right if he attempts to obtain the information for such improper purposes as use by a competitor or sale to a third party.

2. Shareholder approval is required to make certain fundamental changes in the corporation. These changes include: (a) amending the articles of incorporation, (b) effecting a merger, (c) effecting a consolidation, (d) selling or leasing all or substantially all of the assets of the corporation other than in the usual and regular course of business, and (e) effecting a compulsory share exchange.

3. The board of directors has general authority to manage the business and affairs of the corporation. This authority invests the board with the power to: (a) select and remove officers, (b) set management compensation, (c) determine the capital structure, (d) declare dividends, and (e) initiate fundamental changes.

4. The law provides shareholders with certain rights in order to protect their interests in the corporation. Among those rights are (1) the right to obtain information, (2) the right to sue the corporation directly, (3) the right to sue on behalf of the corporation, and (4) the right to dissent. Shareholders have the right to obtain information through an inspection of the corporate books for a *proper purpose*. If the shareholder has a claim against the corporation, she may bring a direct action. A derivative suit is a cause of action brought on behalf of the corporation to enforce a right belonging to the corporation. Finally, a shareholder has the right to dissent from certain corporate actions that require shareholder approval.

5. Directors and officers may be liable for their actions under certain circumstances. The "Business Judgment Rule" acts as a protection against personal liability where it can be shown that the mistake in judgment was an honest mistake made in the belief that the decision would benefit the corporation. When the directors or officers act in good faith, and with due care in arriving at their decisions they will not be liable when those decisions go wrong.

Chapter 38

True/False:

1. F	6. T	11. F
2. T	7. F	12. F
3. F	8. T	13. T
4. T	9. T	14. F
5. F	10. T	15. F

Multiple Choice:

1. d	6. d	11. d
2. d	7. d	12. c
3. c	8. a	13. c
4. a	9. b	14. d
5. c	10. c	15. d

Short Essay:

1. Fundamental changes include: (a) charter amendments, (b) mergers, (c) consolidations, (d) dissolution, (e) sale or lease of all or substantially all of the corporation's assets not in the usual and regular course of business, and (f) compulsory share exchange.

2. Under modern statutes, the typical procedure involves: (a) adoption of a resolution by the board setting forth the proposed amendment, (b) approval by a majority vote of the shareholders, (c) execution and filing of articles of amendment with the secretary of state, and (d) issuance of the certificate of amendment by the secretary of state.

3. This may be accomplished by: (a) purchase or lease of the assets, (b) purchase of a controlling stock interest in the other corporation, (c) merger with the other corporation, or (d) consolidation with the other corporation.

4. Most states grant dissenters' rights to dissenting shareholders of (1) a corporation selling or leasing all or substantially all of its property or assets not made in the usual or regular course of business; (2) each corporation that is a party to a merger, except in short-form mergers where only the dissenting shareholders of the subsidiary have dissenters' rights; and (3) each corporation that is a party to a consolidation.

5. When two or more corporations combine their assets into a single surviving corporation, a merger has occurred. In order for this to happen, both the board of directors and the shareholders of each corporation must approve, except where a corporation owns at least 90 percent of the outstanding shares of a subsidiary corporation. In the latter case, the subsidiary may merge into the parent corporation without approval by the shareholders of either corporation. Following such a merger, the surviving corporation receives title to all of the assets of the merged corporation and assumes all of its liabilities.

Part VII: Sample Examination

1. b	8. c	15. a
2. c	9. b	16. c
3. b	10. a	17. d
4. c	11. d	18. a
5. c	12. c	19. b
6. c	13. d	20. a
7. d	14. d	

Chapter 39

True/False:

1. F	6. T	11. F
2. F	7. F	12. T
3. F	8. F	13. T
4. F	9. T	14. F
5. T	10. T	15. F

Multiple Choice:

1. c	6. c	11. b
2. d	7. c	12. c
3. a	8. c	13. a
4. d	9. d	14. a
5. b	10. b	15. d

Short Essay:

1. A secured transaction can be defined as a consensual security interest wherein the debtor grants a creditor the right to reach specified property of the debtor to pay off the debt in the case where the debtor fails to do so. Two elements of a secured transaction are: (1) a debt or obligation to pay money and (2) an interest of the creditor in specific property of the debtor that secures performance of the obligation.

2. There are two steps that a lender must execute in order to obtain a perfected security interest in the boat as collateral for a loan. The first is to create a security interest and have it "attach" to the collateral, the boat. Attachment occurs upon: (1) the giving of value by the secured party (the lender); (2) the debtor acquiring rights in the boat; and (3) the secured party taking possession of the boat or a security agreement is entered into which is in writing and which contains a description of the collateral and is signed by the debtor. The second step is for the secured party to perfect the security interest. In this case, where the collateral is a boat, perfection is most likely to be effected by filing a financing statement, signed by the debtor, in the appropriate offices. However, perfection can also be obtained by possession or by automatic perfection if the lender satisfies the requirements of a PMSI in consumer goods.

3. Collateral is classified according to its nature as being either (1) goods, (2) indispensable paper or, (3) intangibles. Goods are movable, tangible personal property which may be further classified as consumer goods, farm products, inventory, equipment or fixtures. Indispensable paper is further classified as either; chattel paper, which is a writing that evidences both a debt and a security interest; instruments, which are negotiable; and documents, which represent title. Intangibles are generally accounts receivable and other forms of collateral not otherwise covered.

4. Fred is a buyer in the ordinary course of business from a merchant. Under the Code, even though Equity Credit has a perfected security interest in the goods, Fred takes the television free of that interest regardless of whether he had knowledge of the security interest of Equity Credit.

5. After default by the debtor, the secured party may: (1) ask for a judgment or foreclosure or otherwise enforce the security interest by available judicial procedure; (2) take possession of the collateral without judicial process if it can be done without a breach of the peace; (3) sell, lease, or otherwise dispose of any collateral in its existing condition; or (4) send written notice to the debtor and to other secured parties that he proposes to retain the collateral in complete satisfaction of the obligation.

Chapter 40

True/False:

1. F	6. T	11. F
2. F	7. T	12. F
3. T	8. T	13. T
4. F	9. F	14. F
5. T	10. T	15. F

Multiple Choice:

1. c	6. d	11. b
2. d	7. b	12. d
3. c	8. b	13. a
4. b	9. a	14. d
5. b	10. c	15. d

Short Essay:
1. Cosureties must pay their proportionate share of the obligation paid. If there is no agreement, sureties obligated for equal amounts share equally, but where they are obligated for varying amounts, the proportion of the debt that each surety must contribute is determined by proration according to each surety's undertaking. The total amount of the obligation here is $60,000. Under these facts, Anita's contributive share is one-sixth ($10,000/$60,000); Barbara's contributive share is one-third ($20,000/$60,000); and Clara's is one-half ($30,000/$60,000). If one of the sureties pays the entire amount, that surety is entitled to contribution from the cosureties in their proportionate share of the obligation.

2. Any extension of time within which to pay a debt, which is given by the creditor without first obtaining the surety's consent to the extension, automatically discharges the surety. Because Harold was not notified of the 60 day extension, he is automatically discharged from liability.

3. Harold remains liable. Unless the contract of suretyship provides otherwise, the creditor is not required to give the surety notice of the principal debtor's default. If Harold were a conditional guarantor of collection, he would have the right to have John sue Ike and exhaust his legal remedies of collection before resorting to him. However, because Harold appears to be an absolute surety, he is obligated to pay regardless of the fact he was not notified of Ike's default in a timely manner.

4. (a) Carl has furnished a performance bond. (b) This is a judicial bond. Because it is furnished to assure the appearance of the defendant in court, it is a special form of a judicial bond, known as a bail bond. (c) This is a fidelity bond. (d) This is an official bond.

5. A surety has several personal defenses available only to herself which include her own incapacity, the statute of frauds, various contract defenses to her suretyship undertaking, setoff, modification of the contract, and the creditor's release of security or a cosurety. Additionally, there may be other contract defenses to the contract between the creditor and the principal debtor.

Chapter 41

True/False:

1. F	6. F	11. T
2. T	7. T	12. F
3. T	8. F	13. F
4. T	9. F	14. T
5. T	10. T	15. T

Multiple Choice:

1. b	6. b	11. d
2. d	7. d	12. a
3. c	8. c	13. d
4. c	9. d	14. c
5. d	10. d	15. a

Short Essay:

1. Any person who is eligible to be a debtor under a given bankruptcy proceeding may file a voluntary petition. It is not necessary that they be insolvent. Once filed an order for relief is automatic. An involuntary petition may be filed (1) by three or more creditors who have unsecured claims that total $5000 or more, or (2) if the debtor has fewer than twelve creditors, by one or more creditors whose total unsecured claims equal $5000 or more. Involuntary petition may be filed only under Chapter 7 or Chapter 11 and may not be filed against a farmer or a banking, insurance, or nonprofit corporation.

2. Whether the filing of a petition is voluntary or involuntary, it operates as a stay against all creditors. That is, it restrains all creditors from beginning or continuing to recover claims against the debtor, or creating or enforcing liens against property of the debtor. The stay applies to secured as well as unsecured creditors.

3. Chapter 7, Liquidation, applies to most creditors and distributes equitably the debtor's nonexempt assets and thereafter discharges all dischargeable debts. Chapter 11, Reorganization, attempts to preserve the troubled entity and allow a continuation of business. Chapter 12, Adjustment of Debts of a Family Farmer, works to permit a family farmer, or a farmer who receives at least 50 percent of his income from farming, to file a repayment plan which will discharge him from most debts. Finally, Chapter 13, Adjustment of Debts of Individuals, permits an individual debtor to file a repayment plan which when all payments under the plan are paid will discharge the petitioner from most other debts.

4. (a) Claim for $50,000 secured by inventory worth $10,000 (gets $10,000 from the inventory or sale); (b) Fees earned by the trustee in bankruptcy and fees earned by attorneys of the bankruptcy estate; (c) Claim for wages of an employee earned within one month of filing the petition; (d) Unsecured claim for income tax; (e) Balance of claim ($40,000) that was secured by the inventory.

5. At least three nonbankruptcy forms of compromise have been developed to provide relief to debtors. The first is a composition which is a contract or agreement between the debtor and his creditors by which the latter receive a *pro rata* portion of their claims and the debtor in turn is discharged from the balance of the claims. A second is an assignment for the benefit of creditors, which is a voluntary transfer by the debtor of some or all of his property to a trustee who applies the property to pay all of the debtor's debts. Finally, a court of equity can appoint a disinterested person called a receiver to collect and preserve the debtor's assets and income, and then to dispose of them at the direction of the court that appointed him.

Part VIII: Sample Examination

1. c	8. b	15. d
2. b	9. d	16. b
3. a	10. d	17. c
4. a	11. d	18. d
5. d	12. b	19. d
6. a	13. d	20. c
7. d	14. c	

Chapter 42

True/False:

1. T	6. F	11. T
2. F	7. T	12. T
3. F	8. F	13. T
4. T	9. T	14. F
5. T	10. F	15. T

Multiple Choice:

1. b	6. a	11. b
2. c	7. d	12. c
3. a	8. c	13. d
4. c	9. d	14. c
5. d	10. d	15. a

Short Essay:

1. Registration is advisable, because it is a condition of certain remedies for copyright infringement. Some rights can be permanently lost by failure to register soon enough. If an infringement occurs after registration, the following remedies are available: (1) injunction; (2) impoundment and possible destruction of infringing articles; (3) actual damages plus profits made by the infringer that are in addition to those damages or the statutory damages; or (4) criminal penalties. Registration also serves as proof of the time at which the copyrighted item was fixed in tangible form.

2. The four types of trade symbols recognized by the Lanham Act include: (1) a trademark which is a distinctive symbol, word, or design on a good that is used to identify the manufacturer; (2) a service mark which is a distinctive symbol, word, or design that is used to identify the services of a provider; (3) certification mark which is a distinctive symbol, word, or design used with goods or services to certify specific characteristics; and (4) collective mark which is a distinctive symbol used to indicate membership in an organization.

3. In determining whether the use made of a work in any particular case is a fair use, the following factors are considered: (1) the purpose and character of the use including whether such use is for a commercial nature or is for nonprofit educational purposes; (2) the nature of the copyrighted work; (3) the amount and substantiality of the portion used in relation to the copyrighted work as a whole; and (4) the effect of the use upon the potential market for or value of the copyrighted work.

4. In the absence of a contract restriction, an employee is under no duty upon termination of his employment to refrain from competing or working for a competitor of his former employer, but he may not use trade secrets, such as customer lists, or disclose them to third persons. Because Mark has misappropriated a trade secret, Tel-Ko may obtain damages and possibly injunctive relief.

5. Under the Lanham Act, several remedies for infringement are provided. Injunctive relief, an accounting for profits, damages, destruction of infringing articles are all available. Additionally, attorneys' fees in some exceptional cases and costs may also be available.

Chapter 43

True/False:

1. T	6. F	11. T
2. T	7. T	12. F
3. T	8. T	13. F
4. F	9. T	14. F
5. F	10. T	15. F

Multiple Choice:

1. c	6. c	11. b
2. b	7. b	12. d
3. d	8. d	13. a
4. b	9. c	14. d
5. b	10. a	15. c

Short Essay:
1. Federal antitrust statutes are designed to prevent unreasonable concentration of economic power which would weaken or destroy free and open competition in the marketplace.

2. Economic theory predicts that the goal of every monopolist is to utilize its power to limit production and increase prices. Thus, a monopolistic market will produce fewer goods at a higher price than a competitive market.

3. The Robinson-Patman Act deals with price discrimination and prohibits sellers from giving different prices to buyers of commodities of similar grade and quality. It also prohibits buyers from inducing sellers to do the above. Defenses to charges of a violation include (1) cost justification, (2) meeting competition, and (3) functional discounts.

4. The Clayton Act was passed in 1914 with the express purpose of supplementing existing laws against unlawful restraints and monopolies. It provides only civil remedies. The Act primarily deals with price discrimination, tying arrangements, exclusive dealings and mergers. Subsequently price discrimination became the subject of an amendment called the Robinson-Patman Act. Tying arrangements are prohibited if they tend to create a monopoly or substantially lessen competition. Exclusive dealing arrangements are likewise prohibited if they would tend to create a monopoly or substantially lessen competition, as are mergers.

5. The court would rule for Disco, because X, Y, and Z have committed a *per se* violation of Section 1 of the Sherman Act when they jointly refused to deal with Disco. Such agreement not to deal with a third party constitutes a boycott.

Chapter 44

True/False:

1. T	6. F	11. T
2. T	7. T	12. T
3. F	8. T	13. F
4. F	9. F	14. T
5. T	10. T	15. F

Multiple Choice:

1. d	6. d	11. b
2. d	7. c	12. c
3. a	8. b	13. c
4. c	9. d	14. d
5. b	10. d	15. a

Short Essay:

1. These two consumer protection commissions have a broad range of responsibility. The Federal Trade Commission has two major functions: (1) to prevent "unfair methods of competition in commerce" and (2) to prevent "unfair and deceptive" trade practices. To accomplish this end the commission has established standards. The Consumer Product Safety Commission was established to (1) protect the public against unreasonable risks of injury associated with consumer products, (2) to assist consumers in evaluating the comparative safety of consumer products, (3) to develop uniform safety standards for consumer products and to minimize conflicting state and local regulations and (4) to promote research and investigation into the causes and prevention of product-related deaths, illnesses, and injuries.

2. Under a "full" warranty, the warrantor must: (a) agree to repair without charge the product to conform with the warranty; (b) not limit the duration of any implied warranty; (c) give the consumer the option of a refund or replacement if repair is unsuccessful; and (d) not exclude consequential damages unless conspicuously noted.

3. The creditor must disclose: (a) the cost of the credit; (b) when the finance charge is imposed and how it is computed; (c) what other charges may be imposed; and (d) whether a security interest is retained or acquired by the creditor.

4. The creditor must disclose: (a) the total amount financed; (b) the cash price; (c) the number, amount, and due dates of installments; (d) delinquency charges; and (e) a description of the security, if any.

5. Prior to a consumer formally incurring a contractual obligation for credit loans and credit sales under $25,000, a creditor must present to the consumer a written statement containing information about contract terms such as those things amounting to the cost of credit, i.e. interest, sales charges, finder's fees, mortgage guarantee insurance, etc. Finance charges and interest rates must be quoted in terms of an annual percentage rate.

Chapter 45

True/False:

1. T	6. T	11. T
2. T	7. F	12. T
3. F	8. F	13. F
4. T	9. T	14. F
5. F	10. T	15. T

Multiple Choice:

1. b	6. c	11. d
2. c	7. d	12. d
3. d	8. c	13. d
4. c	9. a	14. d
5. d	10. d	15. c

Short Essay:

1. The basic defenses are: (a) a *bona fide* seniority or merit system, (b) a *bona fide* occupational qualification, and (c) a professionally developed ability test.

2. The remedies are: (a) injunctive relief, (b) affirmative action, and (c) reinstatement and award of back pay.

3. The Equal Pay Act only requires equal pay for equal work. Where jobs are different but comparable, the statute provides no remedy for women who have been systematically undervalued and underpaid. The concept of comparable worth provides that employers should compare the relative values of different jobs in such a way that workers in both jobs would receive the same pay if the jobs were in fact comparable.

4. If Ed can establish that he was in fact injured and that the injury arose out of and in the course of his employment, he can recover workers' compensation. Because a third party, Wes, caused the injury, Ed may also bring a tort action against Wes.

5. Darla would need to prove that the conduct of Doug did in fact constitute sexual harassment within the EEOC guidelines and that First Bank did not take immediate action when it knew or should have known of the harassment. The courts have generally held that sexual harassment that creates a hostile or offensive working environment, even if it does not condition employment benefits upon sexual favors, is a violation. Also, when the employee engaging in sexual harassment is an agent of the employer or is in a supervisory position over the victim, the employer may be liable without knowledge or reason to know.

Chapter 46

True/False:

1. F	6. T	11. T
2. T	7. T	12. T
3. T	8. F	13. T
4. F	9. T	14. F
5. F	10. T	15. T

Multiple Choice:

1. c	6. d	11. d
2. c	7. a	12. a
3. d	8. c	13. d
4. d	9. c	14. d
5. d	10. d	15. b

Short Essay:

1. The primary purpose of federal securities regulation is to prevent fraudulent practices in the sale of securities and thereby maintain public confidence in the securities markets.

2. A registration statement usually includes: (a) a description of the registrant's properties and business, (b) a description of the significant provisions of the security to be offered for sale and its relationship to the registrant's other capital securities, (c) information about the management of the registrant, and (d) financial statements certified by independent public accountants.

3. A two-tier analysis has been developed by the court to identify securities. Under this analysis, the court will treat as a security any financial instrument designated as a note, stock, bond, or other instrument specifically named in the act such as a debenture, preorganization certificate or subscription, investment contract, voting-trust, etc. If a financial transaction lacks the traditional characteristics of an instrument the court will apply a three-part test. Under this test a financial instrument or transaction constitutes an investment contract if it involves (1) an investment in common venture, (2) having a reasonable expectation of profit and, (3) that profit to be derived from the efforts of others not a party to the instrument or transaction.

4. An insider, under Rule 10b-5, is one who might trade on information that is material and not available to the general public. Such parties would be officers, directors, employees and agents of a corporation. Additionally, underwriters, accountants, lawyers and consultants might be considered "insiders" based on information they have received. Should any of these pass information on to others, called tippees, who know or should have known that there has been a breach of fiduciary duty in disclosing such information to the tippee, they too might be liable under 10b-5 for insider trading.

5. Big Bucks has assets of less than $5,000,000 and the class of stock involved is less than 500 shareholders, so the issue is exempt from registration under Rule 505 as long as the issue does not

exceed $5,000,000 over twelve months. General advertising or general solicitation is not permitted. The issue may be purchased by an unlimited number of accredited investors and by no more than 35 other purchasers.

Chapter 47

True/False:

1. F	6. F	11. T
2. F	7. F	12. F
3. T	8. F	13. F
4. T	9. F	14. T
5. F	10. T	15. T

Multiple Choice:

1. b	6. d	11. d
2. c	7. d	12. a
3. d	8. d	13. d
4. d	9. d	14. d
5. b	10. b	15. b

Short Essay:

1. Kind and Kind will probably have to produce its working papers. Although many states have statutes that establish an accountant-client privilege, an accountant's workpapers are not subject to the same protection afforded the attorney-client work product. The accountant's duty is owed to the general investing public. Workpapers cannot be shielded from public scrutiny. The U.S. Supreme Court case of *United States v. Arthur Young & Company* may have relevance to this case also, even though that case involved tax accrual workpapers and this one involves securities workpapers.

2. The SEC must prove that Arthur willfully and knowingly caused false and misleading statements to be made with respect to material facts in the annual report filed with the SEC.

3. One of the primary ways an accountant may face liability is through breach of contract. An accountant normally enters into a binding contract to perform work through an engagement letter, the contents of which are the express, or explicit, obligations to be performed. Failure to perform these explicit obligations may result in the accountant's liability. Also the accountant implicitly agrees to perform in a competent and professional manner, and implicitly promises to perform to those standards expected of all accountants as expressed in guidelines such as GAAS and GAAP.

4. First Bank can recover from the accountant for negligence if it can establish that it was a foreseen user which is one the accountant knew would use the work.

5. Accountant's liability may arise from contract, tort, or criminal law. Under contract law, the accountant could be liable based upon explicit or implicit duties to the other contract party. Additionally, liability may extend to third parties as beneficiaries. Tort liability might arise based upon either the negligence

or fraud of the accountant. Criminal liability may be imposed based upon several federal or state statutes.

Chapter 48

True/False:

1. T	6. T	11. T
2. T	7. T	12. F
3. T	8. F	13. F
4. F	9. T	14. F
5. T	10. F	15. T

Multiple Choice:

1. c	6. b	11. d
2. d	7. d	12. c
3. d	8. a	13. a
4. c	9. d	14. c
5. d	10. a	15. d

Short Essay:

1. Three theories of private tort actions include (1) nuisance, (2) trespass, and (3) strict liability. Nuisance encompasses the two distinct types of wrongs: public nuisance which is an act interfering with a public right, and private nuisance, which is interference by another with the use and enjoyment of a person's own land. Trespass to land involves an invasion which interferes with the plaintiff's right of exclusive possession of the property and which is the direct result of an action by the defendant. Strict liability would be available where an individual is engaged in an abnormally dangerous activity which is both ultrahazardous and inappropriate for its locale.

2. A private nuisance occurs when the defendant has substantially and unreasonably interfered with the use and enjoyment of the plaintiff's land. A public nuisance requires some interference with the health, safety, or comfort of the public.

3. The National Environment Policy Act establishes protection of the environment as a goal of federal policy and has two major substantive sections: (1) the creation of the Council of Environmental Quality, which is a Presidential advisory group charged with the task of preparing annual reports on the condition of the environment, and (2) the requirement that each federal agency, when making a recommendation or report on proposals for legislation or other major federal action, prepare an environmental impact statement.

4. Under the EPA's "bubble concept" an entire plant can be viewed as a single source of emission so that the permit process applies only if total emissions from the whole plant increase. Otherwise each unit at a plant would be treated as a separate source and the owner/operator would be required to obtain a permit whenever it made a change to one unit.

5. In 1980 Congress enacted the Comprehensive Environmental Response, Compensation and Liability Act (CERCLA or the Superfund). It is designed to fill the gap left by RCRA with regard to cleanup of abandoned or inactive hazardous waste sites. The federal government may now take either removal or remedial action in response to either a release or threatened release of hazardous substances and, as long as such actions are consistent with the National Contingency Plan, states and private parties may also engage in response actions.

Chapter 49

True/False:

1. T	6. F	11. T
2. T	7. T	12. T
3. T	8. F	13. T
4. F	9. T	14. T
5. T	10. T	15. T

Multiple Choice:

1. b	6. d	11. a
2. d	7. b	12. d
3. a	8. d	13. d
4. a	9. c	14. b
5. b	10. a	15. b

Short Essay:

1. There are many forms of multinational enterprises. They include: (a) direct export sales, (b) the use of foreign agents, (c) the use of foreign distributors, (d) licensing to a foreign firm, (e) joint ventures, and (f) the use of a wholly owned subsidiary. As a company just entering the foreign market, WCA should first look at direct export, the use of a foreign agent or the use of a foreign distributor. If it considers the use of a foreign agent or the use of a foreign distributor, it should carefully study the agent or the distributor before entering into agreements and should consult legal counsel regarding the laws of the particular country in which it wishes to do business with particular reference to any special provisions regarding the termination of an agent or distributor.

2. Expropriation is a governmental taking of foreign-owned property for a public purpose. When property is expropriated by a foreign government, the government must pay for it. Confiscation is a governmental taking of foreign-owned property without payment or with inadequate payment. To protect itself, a company should take out insurance with the Overseas Private Investment Company.

3. The company should have a good working relationship with a bank that deals in the international sector and that has correspondent banks around the world. The company should consider requiring the buyer to furnish a letter of credit, which is a promise by a buyer's bank to pay the seller provided that certain conditions are met. A letter of credit transaction affords the seller protection against the possibility of nonpayment when dealing in the international sector.

4. A contract involving the sale of goods between a seller in the United States and a buyer in a foreign country should consider such items as: (a) the official language of the contract, (b) the law that governs any breach and if the other country is a party to the CISG whether that will govern the transaction, (c) how any disputes will be settled, (d) acceptable currencies and methods of payment, and (e) a *force majeure* clause apportioning liabilities and responsibilities in the event of any unforeseen occurrences.

5. The FCPA prohibits all domestic concerns from bribing foreign governmental or political officials. Domestic concerns, or any officer, director, employee, or agent thereof may not offer or give anything of value for the purpose of (1) influencing any act or decision in an official capacity, (2) inducing an act or omission in violation of a lawful duty, or (3) inducing anyone to use his influence to affect a decision of a foreign government in order to assist the domestic concern in obtaining or retaining business.

Part IX: Sample Examination

1. b	8. c	15. a
2. c	9. c	16. d
3. d	10. a	17. c
4. d	11. b	18. a
5. d	12. b	19. d
6. c	13. c	20. a
7. b	14. d	

Chapter 50

True/False:

1. T	6. T	11. T
2. T	7. F	12. T
3. T	8. F	13. T
4. T	9. T	14. T
5. F	10. T	15. F

Multiple Choice:

1. d	6. c	11. d
2. d	7. c	12. b
3. d	8. b	13. d
4. d	9. d	14. a
5. b	10. c	15. b

Short Essay:
1. Real property consists of all interests in land. Personal property, in contrast, is every other thing or interest identified as property. A fixture is an item of personal property that has been attached to realty so that an interest in it arises under real property law. These classifications are significant in that real

and personal property rights are governed by different principles of law. Tangible property is property that exists in a physical form; all other property is classified as intangible property. Once again, the determination of various property rights can depend on whether property is classified as tangible or intangible.

2. A fixture is an article or piece of personal property that has been attached in some manner to land or a building so that an interest in it arises under real property law. A trade fixture is one which is used in connection with a trade. Whereas a fixture is likely to become part of the realty, and thus may not be removable, a trade fixture may usually be removed by a lessee provided she may remove the item without material injury to the realty.

3. It is possible to classify gifts in two ways. First, a gift *inter vivos* is a gift made during the lifetime of the donor and is distinguishable from a sale in that it requires no consideration to be effective. It must be accepted by the donee but that is normally presumed. Second, a gift *causa mortis* is a gift made in contemplation of one's death. Unlike a gift *inter vivos* a gift *causa mortis* is a conditional gift which becomes effective only if the donor actually dies as was anticipated. Additionally the donor may not have revoked the gift prior to her death and the donee must have survived the donor's death.

4. An insurable interest is a relationship that a person has to another person, or to certain property, such that the happening of a possible specific damage-causing contingency would result in direct loss or injury to him. The purpose of the concept is to ensure that insurance is used as protection against the risk of loss resulting from the happening of an event, not the realization of profit from idle wagering.

5. Warranties operate as conditions that must exist before the contract of insurance is effective or before the insured's obligation to pay is enforceable. Failure of a certain condition to exist or to occur relieves the insurer from any obligations to perform its promise.

Chapter 51

True/False:

1. T	6. T	11. F
2. T	7. T	12. T
3. T	8. F	13. F
4. T	9. T	14. F
5. T	10. T	15. T

Multiple Choice:

1. d	6. d	11. b
2. b	7. a	12. c
3. d	8. b	13. b
4. d	9. d	14. d
5. b	10. c	15. d

Short Essay:

1. The five essential elements of a bailment are: (1) delivery of possession by a bailor to a bailee, (2) delivery of personal property, (3) possession without ownership by the bailee, (4) a determinable period of time, and (5) an absolute duty on the bailee to return the property to the bailor or dispose of it according to the bailor's directions.

2. The three kinds of bailments are those for the benefit of the bailee, those for the benefit of the bailor, and mutual benefit bailments. In a mutual benefit bailment, the bailee must exercise the degree of care that a reasonably prudent person would exercise under the same circumstances. If the bailment is one for the benefit of the bailee only, a higher degree of care is expected, and if for the bailor's benefit only, a lower degree of care.

3. First is a pledge which is simply a security interest by possession. Second is one who stores goods for compensation, called a warehouser. Third is a carrier who transports goods. Carriers may be classified as either a common carrier or a private carrier. Fourth is an operator of a hotel or motel who stores goods for patrons.

4. Common carriers and private carriers are both bailees, but the common law imposes an extraordinary liability upon the common carrier because of the public nature of its services. For example, a common carrier has a duty to serve the public to the limits of its capacity and, within those limits, to accept for carriage goods of the kind that it normally transports. A private carrier, however, has no duty to accept goods for carriage except where it agrees to do so by contract. A private carrier generally is held liable as an ordinary bailee with respect to the goods that it undertakes to carry. The common carrier, on the other hand, is held to a stricter duty that approaches that of an insurer of the safety of the goods. Finally, both common and private carriers are under an absolute duty to deliver the goods to the person to whom they are consigned by the shipper.

5. A document of title symbolizes ownership of the goods described by the document. One type of document of title is a warehouse receipt, which is a receipt issued by a person engaged in the storing of goods for hire. The warehouser must deliver the goods to the person entitled to receive them under the terms of the warehouse receipt. Another type of document of title is a bill of lading, which is a document issued by a carrier on receipt of goods for transportation. It serves a threefold function: (1) as a receipt for the goods, (2) as evidence of the contract of carriage, and (3) as a document of title.

Chapter 52

True/False:

1. F	6. F	11. F
2. T	7. F	12. F
3. T	8. T	13. T
4. F	9. T	14. T
5. T	10. T	15. T

Multiple Choice:

1. c	6. c	11. c
2. b	7. d	12. d
3. b	8. c	13. b
4. d	9. c	14. d
5. c	10. c	15. b

Short Essay:

1. The two basic characteristics of the fee simple estate are the holder's absolute rights of transferability and of transmitting by inheritance. In contrast, a qualified fee is one that it is possible to convey or will to another to enjoy absolutely, subject, however, to the possibility that it will be taken away at a later date if a certain event takes place.

2. A reversion is the general interest that the grantor retains if he conveys away less than his entire estate. It is a present estate to be enjoyed in the future. A possibility of reverter exists when the property conveyed may return to the grantor or his successor in interest because of the happening of an event upon which a fee simple estate was to terminate. A possibility of reverter is just an expectancy and is not a present estate. Finally, a remainder is an estate in property that, like a reversion, will take effect in possession, if at all, upon the termination of a prior estate created by the same instrument. Unlike a reversion, however, a remainder is held by a person other than the grantor or his successors. There are two kinds of remainders–vested and contingent.

3. All three are forms of concurrent ownership with tenancy in common being the most frequently used. Tenancy in common and joint tenancy both provide an undivided interest in the whole, the right of both tenants to possession, and the right of either to sell his interest during life and thus terminate the original relationship. Tenancy in common does not have a right of survivorship, thus the interests may be devised by will or pass by intestate succession. Joint tenancy has a right of survivorship and thus passes by operation of law to the surviving co-owner. Neither the heirs of the deceased nor his general creditors have a claim to the deceased's interest. A joint tenant may not transfer his interest by executing a will. Tenancy by the entireties is not recognized in all states, but where recognized is created only by a conveyance to a husband and wife. Neither spouse may convey separately his or her interest during life. The right of survivorship remains and creditors cannot attach the interests of either spouse.

4. A landlord must provide quiet enjoyment, which is the right of the tenant to physical possession of the property without interference from the landlord. Also, the tenant would receive an implied warranty from the landlord of habitability. However, unless there is a statute or a specific provision in the lease, the landlord has no duty to repair or restore the premises.

5. An estate for years is a leasehold estate which automatically expires at the end of a definite term. The term may be any time period but has a definite beginning and ending date or time. Thus an estate for years may last less than a year and no notice is required to terminate such a lease. A periodic tenancy has specific terms, such as week to week, month to month, year to year, which continue in indefinite succession. They are automatically renewed for a like period at the end of any given period and notice is required to terminate.

Chapter 53

True/False:
1. F	6. F	11. F
2. T	7. T	12. F
3. F	8. F	13. F
4. F	9. T	14. F
5. F	10. T	15. T

Multiple Choice:
1. b	6. d	11. d
2. d	7. a	12. d
3. a	8. d	13. c
4. c	9. d	14. d
5. d	10. d	15. d

Short Essay:

1. The two essential documents involved in the transfer of real estate are the contract of sale and the deed. The contract of sale must be in writing and signed by the party against whom enforcement is sought to satisfy the statute of frauds. A deed must contain a description of the property that is sufficiently clear and certain to permit identification of the property conveyed. It will also usually describe the quantity of the estate conveyed. It will also contain the appropriate covenants of title, if any. Finally, it must be signed by the grantor, and for purposes of recordation, it must be acknowledged before a notary public.

2. The three types of deeds are the warranty deed, the special warranty deed, and the quitclaim deed. By the warranty deed, the seller promises that he has title to the property and that he will do what is necessary to make the grantee whole if the latter suffers any damage because the grantor's title was defective. In contrast, a special warranty deed is one that warrants only that the title has not been impaired, encumbered or rendered defective by any act or omission of the grantor. The grantor does not warrant that the title may not be defective by reason of the acts or omissions of others. Finally, a quitclaim deed is used to convey all of one's interest in certain property, whatever it might be. No warranties of title are made.

3. Marketable title refers to the condition of the title with respect to (1) encumbrances (such as mortgages, easements, liens, leases, and restrictive covenants), (2) defects in the chain of title, and (3) events that deprive the seller of title, such as adverse possession or eminent domain. It assures the buyer that title is free from any of the above not listed in the contract. The buyer's remedies for breach include specific performance with a price reduction, rescission and restitution, or damages for loss of bargain.

4. Eminent domain is the power of a government to take private land for public use. Such a use need only provide a public advantage. When the government "takes" land in this manner, the fair market value of the land must be given to the landowner from whom the land is taken.

5. A transfer of property subject to the mortgage does not personally obligate the transferee to pay the mortgage debt. Therefore, Laura will not have to pay the $200,000. Her risk of loss is limited to the property.

Chapter 54

True/False:

1. T	6. T	11. T
2. T	7. F	12. T
3. F	8. T	13. T
4. F	9. T	14. F
5. F	10. F	15. T

Multiple Choice:

1. c	6. d	11. b
2. b	7. d	12. c
3. b	8. c	13. a
4. c	9. c	14. d
5. b	10. d	15. d

Short Essay:

1. The four essential elements of a trust are as follows: (1) the trust must have a creator, known as the settlor; (2) there must be a subject matter of the trust, or the trust "corpus" that is definite and certain; (3) there must be a trustee, but the trust will not fail for want of a trustee because the court will appoint one; and (4) there must be a beneficiary of the trust.

2. The primary difference between an express and an implied trust is in the origination of the trust. An express trust is created by voluntary action and may be either oral or written. Examples of an express trust would be: charitable trust, spendthrift trust, and totten trust. An implied trust, however, arises by operation of law where a trust would be imposed to rectify a fraud, to prevent unjust enrichment, or to fulfill a presumed intent of the settlor. Examples are constructive and resulting trusts.

3. Five types of special wills are: Nuncupative, Holographic, Conditional, Joint, and Living wills. A nuncupative will is an oral declaration made before witnesses. A holographic will is one entirely in the handwriting of the testatrix. A conditional will takes effect only on the happening of a specified contingency. A joint will is a single instrument used as the will of two or more persons and signed by all. A living will is a statutory procedure permitting an individual to refuse extraordinary medical treatment in order to preserve the life of the one executing the living will.

4. In order to have a valid will, the testator must have both the testamentary capacity and power to do so. Moreover, the will must be in writing, signed by the testator, and attested by the state required number (generally two or three) disinterested witnesses. But even if all these requirements are satisfied, a will is revocable by the testator and does not become effective until his death.

5. The first step involved in administering an estate is to see if the deceased left a will. If so, the named executor will handle the administration. If there is no will, the court will appoint an administrator. If there is a will, it is submitted to probate by the personal representative, who then must file an inventory of the estate. Assets are then collected, debts paid, and the remainder disbursed according to either the terms of the will, or if there is no will, the laws of intestate succession.

Part X: Sample Examination

1. c	8. b	15. d
2. b	9. d	16. a
3. a	10. d	17. b
4. a	11. c	18. c
5. b	12. a	19. b
6. b	13. b	20. b
7. c	14. a	